# Inciting Democracy

# Inciting Democracy

## A Practical Proposal for Creating a Good Society

**Randy Schutt**

**SpringForward Press**

P. O. Box 608867, Cleveland, Ohio 44108

<http://www.vernalproject.org>

**Inciting Democracy: A Practical Proposal for Creating a Good Society**

Printed in the United States of America

Typeset with Microsoft Word, Microsoft Excel, Canvas, and AppleWorks for the Macintosh by Randy Schutt. Printed on 60# Thor Recycled White D03 paper (85% total recovered fiber, 30% post-consumer) by Thomson-Shore, Inc., Dexter, Michigan, an employee-owned company. The paper used in this publication meets the minimum requirements of the American National Standard for Information Sciences — Permanence of Paper for Printed Library Materials, ANSI Z39.48-1992.

Inquiries regarding requests to reprint all or part of this book should be addressed to:

SpringForward Press
P.O. Box 608867
Cleveland, OH 44108
rschutt@vernalproject.org

ISBN USA 0-9703841-1-4 Paperback

Library of Congress Control Number: 2001116963

Permission to reprint *There's a Hole in my Sidewalk* by Portia Nelson © 1993 was obtained from Beyond Words Publishing, Hillsboro, Oregon, USA.

For information about the author, see page xi.

**Publisher's Cataloging-in-Publication**
*(Provided by Quality Books, Inc.)*

Schutt, Randy.
    Inciting democracy : a practical proposal for creating a good society / Randy Schutt. — 1st ed.
    p.    cm.
    Includes bibliographical references and index.
    LCCN: 2001116963
    ISBN: 0-9703841-1-4

    1. Social problems — United States. 2. Social change — United States. 3. Social values — United States.
    4. Political participation — United States. 5. Social action — United States. 6. Democracy. I. Title.
    HN65.S38 2001            303.48'4'0973            QBI01-200372

# Contents

# Figures and Sidebars

**Chapter 9**

**Chapter 10**

**Appendix A**

**Appendix B**

# About the Author

Randy Schutt is a long-time progressive change activist, researcher, writer, and teacher. He first worked for social change in 1977 with the Stanford Committee for a Responsible Investment Policy (SCRIP) which worked to sever Stanford University's connection to South African apartheid. He then worked for eight years with Citizens for Alternatives to Nuclear Energy (CANE), which was a member-group of the Abalone Alliance and Livermore Action Group (LAG). During this time, he co-authored two books for the Center for Economic Conversion (CEC) and researched military industry for CEC and the Pacific Studies Center (PSC). He also helped to teach two classes at Stanford: one on cooperative decision-making, the other on housing cooperatives.

More recently, he has worked with the Peninsula Peace and Justice Center and served on the board of trustees of Agape Foundation. Since 1980, he has facilitated over fifty workshops for a variety of groups on several topics: cooperative decision-making, nonviolent direct action, nonviolent national defense, strategic planning, and personal transformation.

Randy holds B.S. and M.S. degrees in Mechanical Engineering from Stanford University. He earned a living for several years by working part-time as a solar research engineer. Later, he worked part-time for fifteen years at Stanford as a computer support technician. Randy grew up in Tyler, Texas. He lived for seventeen years in various cooperative households, mostly in the Palo Alto, California, area. He has recently moved to Cleveland, Ohio, to be with his partner, Sue.

# *Acknowledgments*

I am solely responsible for this book and any errors, misrepresentation, or folly it contains. However, I must admit that many of the ideas in this book are not original. I have shamelessly stolen from every source I could, especially from my friends, mentors, and activist colleagues.

A list of all these people is too long to enumerate. Still, I must express thanks to my friends/mentors/colleagues in SCRIP, CANE, the Bay Area Nonviolent Trainers group, CEC, PSC, Agape Foundation, and the Ruckus Society. They taught me much of what I know about progressive social change. I also owe thanks to my wise and supportive housemates at Columbae House, Camp Channing, Guinda House, Oxford House, Baba Yaga House, and Mad Ducks House, to my counseling teachers and peers, and to my colleagues in the nonviolent study group. They have helped me see much farther than I would otherwise and inspired me to look beyond the immediate and obvious.

> *Wise people seek out those who know more than they do… and steal their ideas.*

I give special thanks to my friends for offering their political insights and for helping keep me sane over the thirteen years it took to develop and write this book, especially Jim Caruth, Carol Manahan, Ann Samuelson, Stewart Burns, Matt Nicodemus, Annaloy Nickum, Charlie Metzler, Lee Altenberg, Jo-Anne Scott, Fred Colgan, Dave Offen, Tom Atlee, Louise Yost, Lisa Moulthrop, Sue Helper, and members of my counseling support group. I am also especially grateful to my parents who have always been supportive of my endeavors even when they feared for my safety or disagreed with my ideas.

Many people provided specific help in making this book possible. Those who reviewed some or all of the first full draft of December 1990 included Jan Harwood, Charlie Metzler, Dave Kadlecek, Ann Samuelson, Susan Sandler, Jim Caruth, Lin Hendrix, Bob Cooney, Joel Frankel, Michael Closson, Fred Colgan, Stewart Burns, Louise Yost, Paul Baer, Dave Offen, members of the Nuremburg Action Trainers group (Anna Graves, John Lindsay-Poland, Gil Lopez, David Hartsough, Ken Butigan, Bill Moyer, Fred Cook, and Penn Garvin), Dick Taylor, Tom Atlee, Peter Bergel, Matt Nicodemus, Cheryl Freitas-Farone, Jeff Schutt, Lee Altenberg, Carol Manahan, Peter Wright, Alice Ray, Cliff Johnson, and several others whose names I regrettably forgot to record. I especially appreciate Matt Nicodemus and Susan Sandler for their detailed and constructive comments of this early draft. All these reviewers provided helpful comments, and their misunderstandings of and disagreements with the text drove me to make numerous, major, gigantic revisions.

> *If I have seen further, it is by standing on the shoulders of giants.*
> — Isaac Newton

> *If I have seen further, it is by standing on the backs of the downtrodden masses.* — Activist wit

Those who reviewed some or all of the present manuscript include members of my nonviolent study group (Dave Kadlecek, Charlie Metzler, Ray Kidd, and Ann Samuelson), Mora Dewey, Matt Nicodemus, Jeanne Lewis, Irene Hurd, Stewart Burns, Judy Rock, Steve Rock, Billy Boyd, Lisa Moulthrop, Lee Altenberg, Scott Weikart, Susan Helper, and David Levine.

I especially want to thank Charlie Metzler, Dave Kadlecek, Ray Kidd, and Susan Helper who carefully read the entire manuscript and gave me detailed feedback on every section.

Gaverick Matheny of PEN — the People's Education Network — provided essential help with many of the facts and reference citations. Mark Bult and David Stein offered invaluable help with the design of the book. Stewart Burns carefully edited the final draft, offering many improvements. Finally, David Syring copyedited and indexed the entire book.

Thanks again to everyone who helped in so many ways. I could never have finished without all your help!

— Randy Schutt

# Summary

This book describes a practical, eighty-year strategy for creating a good society. It offers a proposal for increasing the skill, strength, and knowledge of hundreds of thousands of goodhearted people so they can democratically and nonviolently transform society. It also provides a long-term vision of success that can encourage people of goodwill, thus making success more likely.

*We have it in our power to begin the world over again.*
— Thomas Paine

The book first defines the term "good society" as one in which no one is oppressed and in which people treat each other the way they would like to be treated — a safe, fair, just, democratic, humane, compassionate, tolerant, and environmentally sustainable society. The book then identifies the five primary obstacles to creating such a good society:

• Adverse power structure, especially the opposition from the power elite
• Destructive cultural norms
• Dysfunctional emotional conditioning
• Widespread ignorance, especially about positive alternatives
• Lack of progressive resources

The book next skeptically evaluates a variety of social change strategies and processes — exploring what has worked and what has not. This analysis suggests that we can create a truly good society only by using democratic and nonviolent methods that prefigure a good society — in particular, through an extensive education process and through broadly based social change movements that are massive in size — with at least a million progressive activists and advocates working for fundamental change for decades.

The book then details a practical strategy for transformation in which goodhearted people would take several steps:

• Form supportive communities with other people of goodwill.
• Educate themselves and others to overcome their ignorance, hopelessness, and personal limitations.
• Learn to work together and practice change skills.
• Teach these skills to others and support and inspire others to work for positive change.
• Build powerful, grassroots social change organizations.
• Challenge the domination of the power elite and destructive cultural norms in all realms of society.
• Create alternative institutions that can meet everyone's true needs.

To implement this strategy, the book outlines a project consisting of an education and support system that could, over time, generate a force of about a million skilled and dedicated people working simultaneously for progressive change in communities all across the United States. The last section details a plan for implementing this project, beginning with a decentralized education program for dedicated activists.

*The problem of democracy is not the problem of getting rid of kings. It is the problem of clothing the whole people with the elements of kingship. To make kings and queens out of a hundred million people! That is the problem of American democracy.*
— F. C. Morehouse

**Feeling hopeless, tired, and burned-out? Upset that the world seems stupid and crazy? Can't take it anymore? — Don't strive to just survive. Come alive and thrive!**

# Build a Just, Humane, and Democratic Society in Just 32,746 Easy Steps

### *It's simple, it's fun, it's revolutionary!*

- Create the humane, loving society you want and deserve
- Eliminate poverty
- End classism, racism, sexism, ageism, and more
- Stop tanks in their tracks
- Put pizzazz back in your daily life
- Virtually eliminate war and oppression
- Eradicate illiteracy
- Put a spring in your step and a twinkle in your eye

- Stop destruction of the environment
- Curb child abuse, rape, and murder
- Improve your diet, restore your health

> **You owe it to yourself — you owe it to your planet to try this extraordinary new and improved method.**

**It's fun, it's easy — simply follow the clear, step-by-step directions. In just eighty years, you will create a good, long-lasting society that you and your friends can really enjoy. Explained in simple, concise language, this single volume tells you everything you need to know to bring about complete positive transformation OR YOUR MONEY BACK!**

**You'll learn:**

- How to interrupt oppressive behavior in yourself, your friends, your opponents, and your nation while thoroughly enjoying yourself
- How to transform your enemies into friends and your tormentors into allies
- How to help others without hurting yourself
- How to obtain the respect of others without becoming nasty or domineering
- How to overcome "crazy" feelings and move beyond callous indifference
- How to empower yourself and others to "take charge" of the world
- How to create a group of loving supporters
- How you and your million closest friends can have a big impact on the world
- How to gently struggle and warmly snuggle with all kinds of people

**Accept no imitations, accept no substitutions — only true, long-lasting fundamental transformation will give you the satisfaction and security you need and deserve!**

# *Preface*

## WHY I WROTE THIS BOOK

Imagine a society where no one lives in poverty. Imagine a society where it is safe to walk city streets at any hour of the day or night. Imagine a society where addiction to cigarettes, alcohol, and other destructive drugs is rare. Imagine a society where corruption in business and government is not tolerated and is quite uncommon. Imagine a society where murder, rape, domestic violence, and sexual abuse of children are extremely rare occurrences. Imagine a society that values the health and welfare of its citizenry more than anything else — more than power and more than money. Imagine a society where racism, sexism, and other irrational hatreds are virtually unknown. Imagine a society where every citizen is encouraged to understand and participate in civic affairs and most actually do. Imagine a society where people laugh freely, openly, and often. Imagine a society where people are glad to be alive.

*If it were your job to create such a genuinely good society, what would you do? What resources would you need? How would you go about it?*

> *As long as I can conceive something better than myself I cannot be easy unless I am striving to bring it into existence or clearing the way for it.*
> — George Bernard Shaw

These are the questions I address and try to answer in this book. As a long-time progressive activist and student of change, I believe it is possible to create a good society.* But I am also frustrated that those who have worked toward this goal over the last several hundred years have not yet succeeded, and I grow discouraged when it seems we will not achieve this objective anytime soon. I am sure many other people share my frustration and discouragement.

I wrote this book to confirm that it is possible to create a good society and to detail a way it could be done. By showing that it is possible, I hope to encourage us all to do the hard work necessary to accomplish it. By showing one practical way to do it, I offer one possible plan of action.

This book does not really detail the 32,746 steps necessary to build a just, humane, and democratic society as the facetious notice on the facing page proclaims. Rather, it explains what I mean by a "good society," lays out the case for creating a good society, details the obstacles that hinder current efforts, and describes the factors necessary for a progressive change effort to overcome these obstacles. The book then describes what a progressive movement that hopes to bring about fundamental and enduring change might look like as it transforms society over eighty years. Finally, the book specifies a way to bring such a movement into existence by means of an education and support program. The last chapter is an annotated bibliography of books, magazines, radio programs, and web pages covering various social change topics.†

> *A journey of a thousand miles must begin with a single step.* — Lao-Tsu

---

* I use the term "progressive change" to mean efforts to create a good society (as defined in Chapter 2). "Progressive activists" are people of goodwill who are actively working to create such a society and behave as described in Figure 4.2.

† I have tried to make this book readable and understandable to both experienced progressive activists and those new to social change work. For those who are less familiar with social change ideas and methods, Chapter 12 lists many of the books and magazines that have most informed and influenced me over the years. These works provide a good introduction to progressive social change.

When you have finished reading this book, I hope you are convinced it is possible to create a good society. Furthermore, I hope you are inspired to work towards this goal.

We can create a good society. Let's do it!

---

# A VISION

As a way to introduce these ideas, let me describe one possible scenario — first the finale, then the steps leading up to it.

## An Educated, Broad-Based Movement

I visualize a time, perhaps forty years in the future, when there are a million people in the United States working earnestly for deep, far-reaching positive change. These progressive proponents are knowledgeable and skilled in the methods of individual empowerment, critical thinking, scientific investigation, liberating education, cooperation, participatory democracy, organization building, coalition building, respectful conflict resolution, emotional therapy, and nonviolent struggle.

As I envision it, these advocates are largely free from dependency on mainstream institutions. Instead, they support each other — and thereby protect themselves from being attacked or manipulated by powerholders or swayed too much by the dominant culture. They develop a wide array of alternative institutions based on progressive values — personal responsibility, freedom, democracy, respect for dissent, cooperation, altruism, and global stewardship.

With skills, values, and alternatives in hand, these million progressive advocates forcefully challenge existing institutions. They work together in strong, cooperative organizations. They pass on their ideas, skills, and methods to other people directly — without the distorting influences of the news media or other intermediaries — and they do so repeatedly over a long enough time to let the ideas sink in.

*There are those, I know, who will reply that the liberation of humanity, the freedom of man and mind, is nothing but a dream. They are right. It is. It is the American Dream.* — Archibald MacLeish

Over time, they influence vast numbers of people, build a variety of successful alternative institutions, and win many significant changes. By consistently and continuously challenging the old order over several decades, their successes in democratizing power compound at an ever-increasing rate. Each successive generation has incrementally less allegiance to the old order and greater understanding of the new. Moreover, elders wedded to the status quo pass away while young people grow up learning alternative skills and expecting progressive change.

With the active cooperation of a large portion of society and the passive acceptance of most of the rest, these million progressive advocates eventually surmount their own dysfunctional cultural and emotional conditioning and overcome the resistance of the power structure. At a time perhaps eighty years from now, they bring about fundamental and enduring changes in every aspect of society — political, economic, social, and cultural.

In this vision, I do not assume that progressive activists are any more intelligent or virtuous than activists today — only that they are more experienced, have more knowledge, and have greater skills than most current activists. I also do not assume they employ new techniques or strategies — although they might. Instead, I see an expansion of the best of what I have already seen — creative problem solving, potent nonviolent action, convincing alternatives, powerful emotional therapy, a supportive activist community, constructive alliance building, and so forth. Our best is very impressive and — multiplied severalfold — I believe it would energize activists and captivate the whole world.

Let me also say here, before I am misunderstood, that the good society I envision is *not* a blissful paradise, completely free of suffering or discord. There will always be pain and conflict in this world since (1) natural resources are limited, (2) severe natural events such as storms, earthquakes, and disease will always batter us, and (3) humans regularly make mistakes, often disagree with one

*Into each life some rain must fall.* — Henry Wadsworth Longfellow

another, have conflicting desires and interests, and always die eventually. However, in the good society I envision, our difficulties and sorrows are greatly reduced. Conflict is constrained and directed so that it does not demean or destroy people. Life is still hard in many of the ways it is now, but unlike now, people's love and joy vastly outshine their woes and disputes.

Could a million dedicated and skilled activists accomplish enough to bring about such changes? Honestly, I do not know. No one can really know what it would take. Still, I assume there is some level of effort that would be sufficient to bring about fundamental societal transformation. One million activists (about 1/2 percent of the U.S. adult population) working steadily for change over many decades seems like the largest

*The difficult is done at once; the impossible takes a little longer.* — Anthony Trollope

effort for which we could reasonably hope. Based on my experience as an activist, my reading of history, and my careful study of this question, I believe it would also be sufficient. As the collapse of the Soviet bloc and the liberation of South Africa showed, dramatic positive change occurs more easily than we usually suppose. Our hopelessness is often much greater than is actually warranted by reality.

## But How Is It Possible?

*How could we get a million dedicated progressive activists to work together for change? Where would they get the experience and develop the skills they need to be effective? How could they get the support they need to live and work together?*

Again, I see a possible scenario:

Every year, six thousand activists — who are wholly dedicated to making the world a better place — attend a yearlong education program where they learn skills and acquire practical experience. In this program, they develop a deep, broad view of how society currently works and how it could be radically better. They learn a variety of change skills as well as methods to avoid most of the pitfalls that now plague movements for progressive change. They also form bonds and develop trust with many other activists, thus establishing a source of deep, ongoing support. This enables each of them to work diligently for many years and ensures that, consistently, more than 25,000 of them continue to work at least twenty hours per week for fundamental change.

As I envision it, each of these skilled and dedicated activists is able to inform, support, and inspire about six other steadfast activists (150,000 total), each of whom is enabled to work at least three hours each week for change. Each of these activists, in turn, informs, supports, and inspires about six progressive advocates (900,000 total) who are able to work an average of one or two hours each week for change. Together, these progressive activists and advocates number more than a million and constitute a force for change that is several times more powerful than current progressive efforts.

## How Does It Begin?

*What would inspire thousands of people to attend this education program and then devote their time for many years to working for change and supporting other activists?*

I see a few thousand people reading a book outlining this scenario. Inspired by the vision and convinced it might work, a few of them decide to make it a reality.

They develop a curriculum that can provide activists with the necessary skills and experience. Then they recruit thirty activists to attend the first education session. Pleased with the program, these early students tell their friends and colleagues. As the program becomes better known, it grows rapidly in size and then is replicated in fifty locations across the country. As more and more people learn of this change scenario and see it being implemented, they become more hopeful about the prospects for fundamental change. They develop an interest in attending one of the programs offered by this education network. Within a decade, thousands are

enrolling, learning skills, supporting each other, and working together for change.

---

*As anyone knows who has been part of a movement, a demonstration, a campaign, or a strike, struggles undertaken for the most limited and prosaic goals have a way of opening the most profound and lyrical sense of possibility in their participants. To experience even briefly a movement's solidarity, equality, reciprocity, morality, collective and individual empowerment, reconciliation of individual and group, is to have a foretaste of the peaceable kingdom. . . . Once we have experienced solidarity, we can never forget it. It may be short-lived, but its heady sensations remain. It may be still largely a dream, but we have experienced that dream. It may seem impossible, but we have looked into the face of its possibilities.* — Ronald Aronson[1]

---

## THE STRUCTURE OF THIS BOOK

**Chapter 1** describes the events and information that led me to believe it is possible to create a good society.

**Chapter 2** clarifies the term "good society" by detailing some of the basic elements of such a society.

**Chapter 3** investigates the obstacles that stand in the way of creating a good society. As I see it, these obstacles fall into five main categories: opposition from the power structure, destructive cultural conditioning, dysfunctional emotional conditioning, widespread ignorance (especially of progressive alternatives), and a scarcity of progressive resources.

**Chapter 4** briefly reviews and evaluates the strengths and limitations of several historical strategies for fundamental transformation. This exploration uncovers eight crucial characteristics of effective fundamental change efforts, particularly that they be powerful, principled, and democratic. This chapter then outlines a strategy for transformation that consists of widespread education carried out by mass change movements.

**Chapter 5** describes a four-stage strategic program for creating a good society that incorporates these characteristics. In the first stage, progressive activists would lay the groundwork by finding other activists, educating themselves, overcoming their destructive and dysfunctional conditioning, and forming supportive communities with other people of goodwill. In the second stage, they would gather support by raising others' awareness about the possibility of creating a good society and the means to achieve it. They would also build powerful political and social organizations. In the third stage, they would use their strength to challenge vigorously both the power structure and dysfunctional cultural norms by using a variety of nonviolent methods. They would also develop attractive alternative institutions based on progressive ideals. In the last stage, they would diffuse change throughout all of society.

This chapter also outlines a democratic, bottom-up structure in which progressive activists would personally persuade and support others. A small number of dedicated activists would inform, support, and inspire a larger number of steadfast activists who would, in turn, inform, support, and inspire a much larger number of progressive advocates. Together, these activists and advocates would inform, challenge, persuade, and inspire everyone in society.

In this model, the most skilled and experienced activists would constitute a stable and reliable core of activists who would support other activists. They would also broaden other activists' understanding of society, suggest innovative and effective ways to tackle difficult problems, and continue doing tedious or grueling work when other activists stray or falter. This would help to ensure that progressive organizations grow and prosper — and do not go off course, stagnate, or erupt in infighting.

The end of this chapter explains the dynamics of nonviolent struggle since this method would play a crucial role in the project and is often misunderstood.

**Chapter 6** outlines a specific project we could undertake to implement this strategic program and especially to launch the first stage (the "Vernal Education Project"). This project would establish a yearlong education program for dedicated progressive activists. Designed to be inexpensive and practical, this education program would include facilitated workshops, self-study groups, internships, and support groups. It would offer activists a chance to experience and learn direct democracy, cooperation, emotional therapy, personal support, and a variety of social change methods while building strong bonds with other local activists. Students in this program would be encouraged to work for fundamental progressive change at least twenty hours per week for seven years after they graduated.

This chapter also describes how this education program could be replicated across the United States in fifty communities so that, eventually, six thousand students could attend a program every year.

**Chapter 7** shows that this education project could greatly bolster and support progressive change organizations. Calculations, based on reasonable assumptions about the growth of the project and the number of activists who might participate, show that after forty years there would be 25,000 graduates of the yearlong education program working at least twenty hours per week for fundamental progressive change, 150,000 other steadfast activists working at least three hours per week, and an additional 900,000 progressive advocates working a few hours per week. This would constitute an unprecedented force of over one million progressive proponents in all.

I estimate this many activists — most of whom would have much greater knowledge and skill than activists today — could generate an effort perhaps three or four times more powerful than current efforts for fundamental change. Dispersed all across the country, they could create an immense and sustainable movement for progressive change.

**Chapter 8** tells a story that illustrates the many ways this education project could actually inform and support activists.

**Chapter 9** first describes the unique dynamics of social change. It then shows how the Vernal Education Project could affect those dynamics and bring about fundamental transformation of society over eighty years.

**Chapter 10** lays out a specific timeline for implementing this education project, especially the tasks required to launch it.

**Chapter 11** summarizes the main points of the book and then responds to questions and concerns raised by critics.

**Chapter 12** is an annotated list of useful books, articles, and other resources on progressive change.

**Appendix A** outlines some near-term policy changes that could move the United States towards becoming a good society.

**Appendices B** and **C** contain additional figures that I used to verify that this project is workable and feasible. Number-oriented people like me will probably find this interesting; most normal people can safely ignore these appendices without any regrets.

Despite the warnings of Voltaire and Euripides and the disapproval of Emerson, I have also chosen to include throughout the text many clever sayings that I believe succinctly and memorably illuminate ideas. I hope they also add some spice to this treatise and make it easier to digest.

In places, I have also added my own side comments, distinguished by double bars above and below.

*A witty saying proves nothing.* — Voltaire

*Cleverness is not wisdom.* — Euripides

*I hate quotation.* — Ralph Waldo Emerson

*The only limit to our realization of tomorrow will be our doubts of today. Let us move forward with strong and active faith.*
— Franklin Delano Roosevelt

## Ways to Read This Book

I have tried to make this book approachable and readable for many different kinds of people. The main proposal for the Vernal Project is presented in chapters 5, 6, 7, 9, and 10. The earlier chapters explain why I developed this particular proposal and not some other. Those readers interested in the objections raised by critics should turn to Chapter 11. Those who want to know what books have informed my thinking should turn to Chapter 12.

Those readers repelled by tables and charts should still be able to understand the thesis from reading the text. Conversely, those readers who are bored by expository text will probably be able to understand the thesis by studying the tables and charts. Those readers who prefer narrative text may choose to read only the vision section of the Preface and Melissa's Story in Chapter 8.

Feel free to read this book in whatever way works best for you.

## THE FOCUS ON THE UNITED STATES

This book focuses exclusively on fundamental progressive transformation of the United States, but not because I am xenophobic or parochial. I am fully aware of the innumerable interconnections between the United States and other countries, especially as the world's economies become globalized. All parts of the world are now interdependent. Fundamental change in the United States is linked to change in the rest of the world.

I focus on the United States for three main reasons:

(1) The United States is the most influential country in the world — militarily, politically, economically, and culturally.

*The United States maintains a military presence in more than 140 countries.*
— U.S. Dept. of Defense, ***Defense Almanac 1999***[2]

• **Militarily**: The United States is the only military superpower and has military bases and warships in every part of the globe. It is responsible for supplying more than half of all arms sold globally.[3]

• **Politically**: The United States dominates the United Nations Security Council, NATO, and other military and political alliances. Furthermore, through covert means, the CIA and other U.S. intelligence agencies regularly manipulate governments and militaries around the world.

• **Economically**: The U.S. financial system comprises about a quarter of the world monetary system. A large percentage of transnational corporations are headquartered in the United States, and economic decisions made here affect other countries much more than the reverse. The United States dominates the World Bank, the International Monetary Fund, the World Trade Organization, and other global economic institutions.

• **Culturally**: U.S.-generated movies, television shows, advertising, business products (like computers), and consumer products (like Barbie dolls) pervade the rest of the world, propagating U.S. business and pop culture everywhere.

Because of this dominant position, positive change in the United States would likely engender positive changes in other countries. Moreover, without fundamental transformation of this country, the United States will probably continue to thwart positive change elsewhere.

(2) I grew up in this country, have lived here all my life, and am tuned into its culture. I feel I have some understanding of how it operates and how to change it in a positive direction. I have no similar comprehension of any other country or culture.

*My country is the world, and to do good is my religion.*
— Thomas Paine

I assume the changes advocated in this book would be positive if applied to most parts of the world. But without a better understanding, it would be arrogant to tell others how their countries or cultures should change. If people of goodwill in other places find this book useful and applicable to their situation, I hope they will adopt it or adapt it in whatever way they believe best.[4]

(3) I feel it is my primary responsibility to help change my own country and culture. Although there may be greater evils in other places, much must be changed here, too. As a responsible citizen of this country, I feel an obligation to make my country as good as it can be. Especially since I know that the United States is responsible for creating or bolstering much of the evil in other places, I feel a particular responsibility to change this country and curtail its support of oppression elsewhere.

*He loves his country best who strives to make it best.*
— Robert Ingersoll

## A NOTE ON USAGE

Like every modern progressive writer trying to write clear English, I am hindered by the lack of any reasonable gender-neutral terminology. Where possible, I use neutral terms like "people" and "humankind" and rely on the universal singular ("one") or the indefinite plural ("they"). However, sometimes I am forced, for clarity's sake, to use a more specific singular. In most of these cases, I use the terms "she" and "her" in an effort to counter the traditional usage that implies that every important human is male. I considered using "person" and "per" — as in Marge Piercy's novel, ***Woman on the Edge of Time*** — but feared this unusual terminology would be confusing or distracting.

I hope readers will understand that, regardless of the wording, I consider women and men equally capable and I desire political, economic, and social equality for all people.

## JOIN THE DIALOG

After you have read this book, I would love to hear what you think. If you have the capability, it is easiest for me to respond to electronic mail. I will do my best to respond promptly.

Randy Schutt
P. O. Box 608867
Cleveland, OH 44108

Email: rschutt@vernalproject.org
<http://www.vernalproject.org>

---

*Answers — 50 cents*
*Answers requiring thought — $1.00*
*Correct answers — $2.00*
*Dumb looks are still free.*
— Office Graffiti

---

The Vernal Project web site also contains a moderated dialog among all those who are interested in helping the project succeed. Please join this dialog.

---

## NOTES FOR THE PREFACE

**Note**: References include a Library of Congress number — when available — to facilitate locating them in a research library.

[1] Ronald Aronson, **After Marxism** (New York: Guilford Press, 1995, HX44.5 .A78 1994), p. 278.

[2] This is Fact 205 gathered by PEN, the People's Education Network. <http://www.penpress.org> The **Defense Almanac** can be found here:
<http://www.defenselink.mil/pubs/almanac/index.html>

[3] From 1995 to 1997, the United States sold more than $77 billion in arms, about 55% of the global total. U.S. Department of State, Bureau of Arms Control, **World Military Expenditures and Arms Transfers 1998**, Table 3, p. 165.
<http://www.state.gov/www/global/arms/bureau_ac/wmeat98/table3.pdf>

See the summary ("Fact Sheet Released by the Bureau of Verification and Compliance, Washington, DC, August 21, 2000") here:
<http://www.state.gov/www/global/arms/bureau_vc/wmeat98fs.html>

See the complete report here:
<http://www.state.gov/www/global/arms/bureau_vc/wmeat98vc.html>

From 1987 to 1997, the United States sold more than $280 billion in arms, about 5.2% of all U.S. exports for the period. The United States was one of only three countries in which arms exports represented more than 5% of its total exports. Israel and North Korea were the other two countries. U.S. Department of State, Bureau of Arms Control, **World Military Expenditures and Arms Transfers 1998**, Table 2, p. 158.
<http://www.state.gov/www/global/arms/bureau_ac/wmeat98/table2.pdf>

[4] Dennis Altman, in **Rehearsals for Change: Politics and Culture in Australia** (Victoria Australia: Fontana/Collins, 1979, JQ4031 .A45) analyzes the prospects for progressive social change in Australia. He discovers many of the same obstacles there as I do in the United States, and advocates a similar kind of transformation that focuses on both cultural and political change. However, he also points out the many differences in culture and politics between the two countries.

# 1

# Background

## THE IMPETUS FOR THIS PROJECT

Like many other people of my generation, I was greatly inspired by the social change movements of the 1960s and disappointed when they fizzled out. My upbringing and temperament have compelled me to learn why these movements arose and what might have enabled them to continue. I am fortunate to have had a variety of experiences that suggest some possible answers to these questions. This book describes what I have found.

## My Early Inspiration

Raised in the conservative Bible-belt city of Tyler, Texas, in the 1950s and 1960s, I was taught I should strive to be a good person. I did my best and assumed other people did too. Yet, when I looked around, I saw that adults did not treat each other very well (and they treated children worse). Moreover, I saw that my neighbors, teachers, and sometimes even my own family did not always promote virtue. Instead, they often accepted and tolerated pretense, servility, cruelty, oppression, exploitation, and violence. It both frightened and angered me when I realized my elders sometimes lied and the world was not as benevolent as I had been led to believe.

One day in elementary school, my teacher brought in a stack of old *Life* magazines. Leafing through these magazines, I came across a picture of an American soldier carrying a rifle in one hand. His other arm was bleeding and part of it had been shot off. As I stared at this savage war image boldly emblazoned in a popular magazine, I realized that something was very wrong with our entire society. I saw that humans sometimes deliberately inflicted horrible suffering on each other. I realized that the cruelty, fear, hatred, indifference, and hypocrisy I sometimes saw around me were not just family eccentricities or local aberrations, but were endemic to our whole society. I wanted to believe that our society condemned brutality and evil, but at that moment, I realized these things were actually accepted, tolerated, and even glorified.

I vowed to find a way to make the world better if I could. But what should I do? At first I accepted the popular idea that there were evil people who caused all our problems (Communists, homosexuals, and drug addicts were usually the designated monsters) and that to improve society required only locking them up or killing them. However, over time, I realized this simplistic notion was mistaken. I saw that other people were very much like me,

> *It is privilege that causes evil in the world, not wickedness, and not men.* — Lincoln Steffens

not innately good or evil but just human, convulsed by positive and negative forces that propel them one way or another. With this more mature understanding, I realized that creating a good society would require changing these forces so they blew in more positive directions for everyone. So I began to search for ways to shift the forceful winds of society.

## The Encouraging Sixties

As I came of age during the late 1960s and early 1970s, I listened to songs of love and struggle on the radio and watched the many mass movements for political change on TV. The anti-Vietnam war movement, a variety of liberation movements, and the movement to develop cooperative alternatives flourished throughout the nation. Millions of people were passionately fighting for justice and equality. Despite the violence and tragedies of this period, it was a time of great optimism. Hope for the future seemed to encompass our entire society.

In high school, I let my hair grow long, attended memorials for alumni of my school who had died in Vietnam, and wore a black armband for the war dead. I spoke out against racism, wrote letters to the editor of my school paper, and tried to create a community of love and support with my friends. Social change and the potential for creating a better society excited me, but I was also confused and appalled by the violence, hatred, and reckless frenzy that seemed to be a part of progressive change efforts. Though much of what I saw disturbed me, I could also see the potential for remarkable positive change.

## The Inspiring Seventies

As the '60s slid into the '70s, militant rhetoric and revolutionary/apocalyptic posturing grew stale and faded away. Across the country, progressive activists instead quietly implemented many of the ideals formulated and tentatively tested in the '60s.

I remained fascinated by progressive change. However, I was wary of the dishonest and coercive tactics I had seen practiced in electoral politics, and I was critical of the often foolish and misdirected attempts at change that I saw elsewhere. I diligently read books about socialism, feminism, pacifism, humanism, environmentalism, radical education, and anything else I could find that might provide insight into how the world functioned and how to make it better. Still, I stayed on the periphery of most political activity and pursued a conventional career as a mechanical engineer. The depression, anorexia, and suicide of a close friend in 1973 further confused and depressed me, even as it intensified my desire for sweeping change. I was poised for action, but leery of getting involved.

It was not until 1976, in my last year attending Stanford University, that I was drawn into working actively for social change. That year, I moved into a cooperative house with forty-two other students, including several experienced progressive activists with inspiring visions of a good society. These activists worked diligently to implement their ideas — both in the world and in our house. For the first time in my life, I directly experienced what a good society might be like — and I was thoroughly impressed. The goals of these activists were noble, and the work they did was admirable. They had a lot of fun too.

Soon I was working with them to end South African apartheid. I felt fortunate to work with experienced, dedicated activists who knew how to design effective and powerful change campaigns and also knew how to maintain a playful, loving attitude towards their friends and adversaries. It was inspiring and empowering to work with them.

After graduating, I worked with the Abalone Alliance to challenge the nuclear power industry and with the Center for Economic Conversion to shift military corporations to socially beneficial production. I lived in several cooperative households and learned to counsel people in emotional distress. These experiences further excited and tantalized me with the prospects for transforming society.

As I worked for change, my vision of a good society grew clearer. I read more books on cooperation, participatory democracy, self-esteem, nonviolence, education, socialism, anarchism, and feminism. I picked up ideas from utopian novels like ***News from Nowhere***, ***Ecotopia***, ***Ecotopia Emerging***, ***The Dispossessed***, and ***The Kin of Ata are Waiting for You***. None of these works presented a complete or entirely realistic vision. Still, combined with my positive living experiences, they sketched the outlines of a desirable and viable society.

## Some Accomplishments

This was a very exciting time. The Abalone Alliance's powerful effort to stop the Diablo Canyon nuclear power plant and other nukes in California — and to promote environmentally benign alternatives — was largely successful. We delayed Diablo for six years, stopped all the other nuclear plants on the drawing board, assisted the passage of legislation to encourage solar energy and conservation, and helped to launch an alternative energy industry. Our organization grew exponentially from just a handful of people to thousands.

Moreover, the Alliance was structured as an egalitarian and supportive community in which we encouraged each other to strive toward our best selves. We developed gentle, yet effective, processes for cooperatively making decisions and working together. We also developed and used powerful nonviolent tools for challenging injustice, inequality, oppression, and domination, both within our ranks and in the wider world. We created a prototype of a just and compassionate society.

*As I stood with my colleagues singing songs of struggle and love at the gates of Diablo Canyon, Livermore Labs, and Fort Ord, I knew what it was like to really live — to stand shoulder-to-shoulder with other people, to boldly fight oppression and injustice, to courageously risk my career and my life for something truly important, to love people deeply, to cherish all of humanity.*

*What if everyone did this? What if the whole world were like this? What if our daily lives had this same camaraderie and loving spirit?*

While we developed an outstanding campaign around safe energy, other progressive activists had done equally admirable work on other issues. The Freeze movement to stop and reverse the nuclear arms race was growing rapidly and garnering massive support. On June 12, 1982, one of the largest political demonstrations in the United States brought together a million people who marched through New York City and vigorously advocated disarmament. Polls at this time showed about three-quarters of the public supported a bilateral nuclear weapons freeze.

At this same time, the campaign to end U.S. military and economic domination of Central American countries began to take off, and campus activity against South African apartheid was spreading. Resistance to registering for the military draft was also strong. The campaigns to end environmental destruction, racism, sexism, heterosexism, and domestic violence were developing rapidly. Cooperative grocery stores and other alternative enterprises flourished. Therapy and support groups helped thousands of people work through emotional injuries and overcome their limitations. Internationally, nonviolent movements challenged governmental domination in Iran, the Philippines, and Poland. In West Germany, the Green Party secured a place in the government and promoted political and social ideas similar to those of the Abalone Alliance.

There were, of course, many problems with change groups — flakiness, inefficiency, foolish blunders, manipulation, infighting, naïveté, cynicism, and so on. Still, our problems seemed mostly petty and solvable if we just kept plugging away, learning from our mistakes, and improving. Admittedly, we made many mistakes. And overall there were not that many people working for real progressive change. Still, we seemed to be moving in the right direction. It felt to me that we were building — slowly but surely — what Martin Luther King, Jr. called "the beloved community."

## A Promising Vision

By the early 1980s, I was expecting an even greater level of nonviolent political activity. I hoped it would lead directly to significant, fundamental change in the United States and to a much better society. I could easily imagine that our nonviolent change movements would continue to grow and involve an ever-larger number of people. I assumed our organizations would continuously develop, broaden, and mature until they were strong and wise enough to address all the important problems of society. I imagined that more and more people would have increasingly greater power to shape society, and they would be ever more sensible in exercising this power.

After watching activists employ a wide array of powerful methods to bring about change, and seeing them achieve incredible successes, transforming society seemed within reach. It appeared possible that we could eventually stop military saber rattling by the world's nations, halt destruction of the environment, and end the domination of people (and of other beings). It seemed within reach to restrain and then reform thieves, gang members, thugs, batterers, rapists, drug lords, pimps, mobsters, slumlords, corporate fat cats, power-hungry politicians, tyrannical authorities, and everyone else who made our society miserable. It seemed quite possible to end corruption, oppression, poverty, illiteracy, alcoholism, rape, battering, homelessness, racism, sexism, and all the rest.

*One man with an idea in his head is in danger of being considered a madman: two men with the same idea in common may be foolish, but can hardly be mad; ten men sharing an idea begin to act, a hundred draw attention as fanatics, a thousand and society begins to tremble, a hundred thousand and there is war abroad, and the cause has victories tangible and real; and why only a hundred thousand? Why not a hundred million and peace upon the earth? You and I who agree together, it is we who have to answer that question.* — William Morris[1]

## Two Steps Forward, Two Steps Back — The Potential Unrealized

But it did not happen that way. Instead, at every level the power structure fought back and thwarted our efforts. For example, in 1981 the Reagan administration and the New Right came to power and systematically dismantled, overturned, or undermined the alternatives we had started to build. They distorted and ridiculed our best ideas, and the news media amplified their criticism. The resources we needed to develop our projects evaporated. The economy soured and those of us who had voluntarily labored for the common good were forced to take whatever jobs we could find. Under the weight of this assault, our communities of support were stretched so thin that they snapped, flinging people apart.

Meanwhile, those who promoted and best exploited individualism, greed, militarism, racism, sexism, classism, homophobia, and hatred (people such as Dan Quayle, Patrick Buchanan, Rush Limbaugh, and Newt Gingrich) were lauded and abundantly rewarded. Those politicians who best groveled before wealthy donors were able to stay in office while those of conscience were challenged and many were turned out. Many positive accomplishments were reversed, eroded, co-opted, or forgotten, including such important, hard-fought victories as progressive income tax rates, anti-discrimination laws, access to safe abortion, pollution abatement laws, and lowered military budgets. Progressives continued to fight for positive change, but we had only limited success.

Now, at the dawn of a new century, we are still in a situation where a tiny minority of people makes most of the important decisions of society, and they generally make decisions that primarily benefit favored groups. In this era, the public passively accedes to preposterous, Far Right solutions: missile defense to solve the danger of nuclear annihilation; tax cuts for the rich and cutbacks of anti-poverty programs to solve the problem of government interference in our lives; finger-wagging moralism to solve the problems of teenage pregnancy, poverty, drug abuse, and AIDS; tougher laws and more prisons to address the problem of crime; and a massive military budget, xenophobic rhetoric, and support of murderous foreign armies to solve the "problem" of Third World countries' rejection of U.S. control. Great sums have been squandered on sordid savings and loan deals and wasted on superfluous military equipment. The rich are richer, the poor are poorer, and the crazy are crazier. Weapons abound, and our fragile world environment is more polluted and battered — natural resources consumed, the ozone layer breached, fertile topsoil washed away, groundwater depleted, and numerous species decimated.

At this time, progressives have little influence in Congress. Peace groups, social justice organizations, environmental groups, and social service agencies all scramble for limited funds. Some progressive activists who once struggled against injustice with every ounce of their being now just struggle to get by. Many who once reached for the stars now just reach for a beer. For many, hopefulness has disintegrated into bitter hopelessness.

*The world has achieved brilliance without wisdom, power without conscience. Ours is a world of nuclear giants and ethical infants.* — World War II General Omar Bradley

Even more disheartening is that this is not the first time this has happened. Looking back through history, we find similar movements for progressive change — the populist movement of the late 1800s, the socialist movement of the early 1900s, the labor struggle of the 1930s and '40s, the civil rights and antiwar movements of the '60s — faltered just when they began to have some impact.

After tallying up our limited accomplishments and many setbacks, skeptics suggest we may be engaged in a futile struggle — the issues and scenery change, but we never really get any closer to the beloved community. These skeptics suggest that creating a good society is just a hopeless pipe dream.

In analyzing history, there appears to be a cyclic pattern: we begin each new political endeavor full of hope and inspiration and struggle gallantly for several years. Then, at some point, our efforts are overturned by the established powers, subverted by competing aspirants, wrecked by our dumb mistakes, or gutted by our own infighting. Sometimes we achieve victories, but for every struggle we win, it seems we lose another. Moreover, we must zealously defend our few victories forevermore or they are snatched away from us.

*Just because everything is different doesn't mean anything has changed.*
— Irene Peter

*Why does it happen this way? What can we do about it? How can we create a good society conclusively — in a way that is not soon undone and in which those who oppose and undermine it today would instead cherish and support it?*

These are crucial questions — ones that we must answer if we are to bring about fundamental positive transformation of society.

*Sit down before fact as a little child, be prepared to give up every preconceived notion, follow humbly wherever and to whatever abysses Nature leads, or you shall learn nothing.*
— Thomas Huxley

## PERHAPS THE TIMES JUST AREN'T RIPE FOR CHANGE

Many theorists postulate that massive change can only take place when the times are right: when conditions are so horrible that almost everyone demands change and society's traditional institutions can no longer offer viable solutions. They argue that only at these times of crisis can truly revolutionary change occur and that change will *inevitably* occur at these times.

Certainly, widespread misery creates a climate for change, and critical events can then trigger a revolution. However, centuries of misery and innumerable revolutions have still not led to fundamental progressive transformation. Misery often leads only to more misery. Revolutions usually just disrupt and destroy the existing society; from the ashes, it is difficult to rebuild and establish a new, positive society.

Instead, militarists and opportunists typically rush in to restore order and seize power for themselves.

The United States seems especially adept at weathering change without transforming in any basic way. For example, successful struggles for democracy in the past now mean that fewer groups of people are excluded from voting than before, but still a privileged minority control most of society. Slavery is now illegal and women can escape the confines of their households, but poverty and wage slavery are still widespread and restrain people in many of the same ways. Roads and cars have lessened many hardships but have ravaged the environment. European powers no longer maintain colonial domination over the world, but now the United States military imposes a "sphere of influence" and multinational corporations wield economic dominance over most people of the world.

The times are never particularly fortuitous for fundamental change. Historical events induce change, but they do not necessarily lead to positive change. If we want transformation, we must take the initiative and *create* it ourselves. When historical events produce openings for change, we must be ready with positive policy measures and strong organizations that can push for their enactment.

## IS IT EVEN POSSIBLE?

Is it even possible to create a good society? Maybe it is an impossible task — like building a perpetual motion machine or remaining forever young. Perhaps human nature is so innately vile or the circumstances of reality are so austere that a good society is unachievable.

---

*Most of the things worth doing in the world had been declared impossible before they were done.* — Louis D. Brandeis

---

### Are Humans Innately Evil?

Throughout recorded history, religious leaders and philosophers have suggested that greed and belligerence are innate human characteristics — dictated by vindictive gods, a wily Satan, or the cruel dictates of evolution in a world of limited resources. Some have suggested that each of us has an inherent "dark side" that makes us greedy, irrational, angry, depressed, jealous, arrogant, and cruel.

It is true that human nature drives us to secure food, water, shelter, love, and sex and that this regularly puts us in conflict with others. Moreover, we have an aggressive side that enables us to kill prey, steal food from other animals (or people), and threaten our predators. Our hormones stimulate a sexual craving that can drive us to distraction for large parts of our lives. However, these drives certainly do not indicate that we are wicked, and they are not beyond our control. We can consciously decide how to act.

Admittedly, people can be completely out of control at times. Severe thirst, hunger, or deprivation will compel us relentlessly to find a way to satisfy our cravings, even at others' expense. Threat of mortal danger will make us fearful and stimulate a rush of adrenaline into our bloodstream, preparing us for an extremely powerful "fight or flight" response. Moreover, whenever someone attacks our sense of worth by insulting, taunting, or mocking us, we may explode with rage.

However, each of these is a defensive response to protect our bodies and our sense of worth from immediate danger. Each is an appropriate response to a particular situation and subsides when the danger passes.

Research over the past few decades indicates that extreme and enduring negative emotions — grudges, malevolence, phobias, depression, arrogance, cruelty — are conditioned responses to brutal or long-term oppression.[2] When people are severely traumatized or routinely neglected or battered, they swallow the hurt in a way that makes it come back out twisted and merciless — resulting in inappropriate reactions and intense, persistent negative feelings. In short: severe oppression induces wickedness. People who act badly are not evil — they are emotionally injured. If they had never been mistreated or if they had had a chance to heal, they would not act maliciously.

Of course, some people are truly psychotic or schizophrenic. They apparently have chemical imbalances in their brains that make them deranged. Since they are insane and not responsible for their actions, they too cannot be considered evil. Moreover, their condition can now sometimes be treated with drugs.

It is also true that children in our society are taught many evil ideas. Parents may inadvertently pass on oppressive attitudes like racism, sexism, ageism, classism, heterosexism, and so forth whenever they teach their children about the world or read them a story. Some parents, teachers, and church elders explicitly teach children to fear or detest other people based solely on their appearance, speech, beliefs, or practices.*

---

*No one is born a bigot.* — Bumpersticker

---

Many children are also indirectly taught behavior that is unsuitable in a civilized society. Society's leaders justify war, violence, and coercion if carried out by "duly appointed authorities." They often wink at acts of deception, corruption, and theft if committed by the beautiful, rich, or powerful. A great deal of advertising encourages gluttony, greed,

---

* Some people have argued that prejudice is natural and irrevocable. However, until children are taught prejudice, they have no understanding of it — they see difference, but do not judge. Many people raised in bigoted households have refused to adopt prejudice, and many others who have been deeply imbued with prejudice have overcome it. So prejudice is clearly not inherent in humans.

lust, and envy. To a great extent, our culture passively tolerates date rape and battering of women and children.

Evil ideas can be learned, and in our current society, they are learned by many people. But evil ideas can also be unlearned or never taught in the first place.

Overall, there is little evidence that humans are *inherently* evil. To the contrary, much evidence suggests that humans are naturally cooperative and loving.

• That we are usually shocked and appalled by war, violence, rape, intimidation, and terror (rather than bored, comforted, or delighted by it) attests to our good nature. When people are hurt or cry, our empathy moves us to comfort them and respond to their needs. Typically, our greatest joy comes from laughing and playing with others.

• That six billion of us can coexist on this tiny planet, mostly without incident, indicates that we are amiable beings. Every day, each of us typically encounters hundreds of people. Generally, other people are nice to us, and we courteously reciprocate. People seldom wage war against their neighbors, and when they do, it is unusual enough to be newsworthy.[3]

• That some people can endure ruthless torture extending over years and still be compassionate towards other people (sometimes even toward their torturers) indicates how great is humankind's potential for love, forgiveness, and reconciliation

Moreover, humans have many inherent traits that counter whatever bad side we might have. For example, altruism *is* probably an inherent human trait since it makes evolutionary sense: those who help their family, community, and species are more likely to ensure that their offspring survive than those who work only for themselves.[4]

This is not to say that humans are perfect. We all make mistakes, and we regularly hurt others. Nevertheless, our ability to make mistakes does not mean we are inherently evil, and it does not prevent us from creating a good society.

*Some families are not dysfunctional. Some schools nurture and support children. Some people are healthy, rational, self-assured, compassionate, and nonviolent. If some people can be this way, why not everyone?*

## Is There a Shortage of Critical Resources?

Every human requires a certain amount of resources — air, water, food, shelter, and so on — to have a good life. If there were not enough critical resources for everyone, then it would be impossible to create a good society. No matter how cooperative and compassionate we were, our society would still be miserable if, for example, we were all starving — at best, we could only share our misery equally and democratically. If there are not enough critical resources in the

world, then the best possible society might be one like our own in which some people live well, others live miserably, and powerful armed forces, working at the behest of the rich, ensure it stays this way.

There might have been times in the past when our world was constrained by critical resource shortages, perhaps in prehistoric times during ice ages or more recently during periods of prolonged drought or flood. Now, however, our world is assuredly not this way.

As an example, consider food supplies. Researchers at the Institute for Food and Development Policy (Food First) have shown that there is enough food to adequately feed every person on earth — even enough in each of the poorest countries to feed every person in that country.[5] They find that all that is missing is real democracy that would enable those at the bottom to exert control over the distribution of societal resources.

Our current world also has supplies of clean water, shelter, and basic healthcare adequate to meet the needs of every person. Shortages of these resources now only occur in those places where people are at the mercy of powerful armies. Furthermore, there are no real shortages of human interaction, community, and love — these are only in short supply when our shyness, fear, and cultural hangups get in the way. Hence, there appear to be sufficient resources to create a society that meets the basic needs of everyone in the world.

*The world has more than enough resources to accelerate progress in human development for all and to eradicate the worst forms of poverty from the planet. Advancing human development is not an exorbitant undertaking. For example, it has been estimated that the total additional yearly investment required to achieve universal access to basic social services would be roughly $40 billion, 0.1% of world income, barely more than a rounding error. That covers the bill for basic education, health, nutrition, reproductive health, family planning, and safe water and sanitation for all.*
*— United Nations Development Programme[6]*

Moreover, I believe our world is rich enough to provide more than just the basics. In 1995, $865 billion (2.8% of the world monetary economy) was devoted to producing military equipment and supporting military personnel.[7] A good society could redirect these resources to fulfilling human needs.

Moreover, we could use our resources much more efficiently. Most western European countries have high standards of living, similar to the United States, yet consume far fewer resources than here. In addition, fewer resources would be needed if products were made to last and to be recycled when they reached the end of their life. Even fewer resources would be needed if we could reduce the world's population. This should be feasible in a good society.

## Are There No Viable Solutions?

If humans are not inherently evil and if we are capable of adjusting to real world resource limitations, then why have we not yet created a good society? Are the difficulties just too large and intractable?

In this world, problems are inevitable. Humans are eternally vulnerable to weather, disease, pests, and predators. As independent individuals, we often disagree with each other. Our wants and needs frequently conflict. Clearly, there is no way we will ever be able to eliminate all problems and conflicts.

However, for centuries, social explorers have searched for ways to grapple with social problems, and they have discovered many remedies that solve or mitigate them. Over the years, these explorers have tested their solutions and recorded them for the benefit of others.

Especially in the last century, the expansion of detailed, systematic research and advances in the technology of recording and communicating ideas have enabled researchers to discover and disseminate many ingenious and practical solutions to some of the most vexing of society's problems. They have developed means to negotiate treaties between warring nations, to cooperatively resolve conflicts, to organize efficient and just economic

*No matter how cynical you get, it is impossible to keep up.* — Lily Tomlin

systems, to raise children to be self-confident, self-reliant, and emotionally healthy, to heal people from horrible emotional traumas, and to challenge injustice, repel violence, and topple oppressive governments. Figure 1.1 shows six solutions developed over the last few centuries that address some of the most difficult and seemingly intractable problems.

As an example, consider one of the more formidable problems facing humankind — the problem of "evil" people who viciously attack others. As described in the previous section, psychologists have determined that much of this evil is imbued in childhood through brutal trauma. If children are not brutalized, they do not become malicious. For those who are brutalized, intensive emotional therapy can heal much of the injury over time. Those few people whose trauma cannot be healed could be restrained so they do not hurt others. They could be kept away from society in humane homes, designed not to punish but only to prevent them from hurting anyone else.

In summary, the problem of "evil" people could be mostly solved by protecting people from brutalization, counseling those who were hurt, and humanely restraining those who could not be counseled back to health. If these solutions were applied widely, then the problem of "evil" people would shrink to insignificance and would not prevent us from creating a good society.

Other solutions are not as well known, but also exist.* Generally, the more I have searched for solutions, the more solutions I have discovered. And the more I investigate them, the more impressed I am with them.

I am convinced there are viable solutions to *every* critical, human-caused problem that plagues our world. For every type of disagreement, conflict, and confrontation in the world, no matter how unyielding it appears, invariably someone has solved a similar problem at least once somewhere, sometime.

Clearly, many problems are not always solved well. For every time an effective solution is applied well to a problem, there are hundreds of other times when the wrong solution or no solution is applied, leading to worthless or counterproductive results.

*What exists, is possible.* — Kenneth Boulding

Nevertheless, if there is a way to solve a problem once, then obviously it is not an *impossible* problem — it *can* be solved. Conceivably, we could solve it every single time if we could just apply the known solution. Nothing must be discovered or invented. No laws of physics must be overturned. We need only to learn of these solutions, pass them on to the people who need them, and then help those folks obtain the necessary resources (time, money, people-power, expertise, and so on) to apply them well. Certainly these are daunting tasks, but they are not impossible.

## Is Society Too Far Gone?

Perhaps there are so many problems intertwined so tightly into a miserable mess that it is impossible to untangle them all. If so, then we could never create a good society.

At times, I have certainly felt this was the case. There are so many problems, they are so tangled, and they are so persistent that they seem overwhelming. Fortunately, we live in a time when similarly complex problems are routinely solved.

For example, before it was done, putting a human on the moon seemed like an impossible task — one with a myriad of conflicting problems that would require tens of thousands of people to work together to create almost flawless equipment. Though extremely difficult, this task was accomplished. Achieving this goal required engineers to develop several whole new disciplines (including project management and systems engineering) and to expand others greatly — such as the field of quality control.

*It is difficult to say what is impossible, for the dream of yesterday is the hope of today and the reality of tomorrow.* — Robert H. Goddard, pioneering rocket scientist

---

* Chapter 2 describes many of these solutions. The books listed in the Methods of Changing Society section of Chapter 12 describe many more.

It also once seemed too complex to solve the problem of integrating people of vastly different cultures into a single nation. But over the last two hundred years, the United States has demonstrated that it is possible — though our society obviously still needs a great deal more work. Achieving this goal required developing and spreading two new concepts: the idea that people could integrate into another culture and then, later, the even better concept of a diverse multicultural society.

There are many problems that once seemed too complex to solve — until they were solved. To date, humans have been able to solve virtually every problem they consistently and unambiguously devoted effort to solving (within the constraints of physics). People living a few hundred years ago would consider our now commonplace technologies (like jet aircraft, computers, and the Internet) and social systems (like national healthcare and the system of libraries) to be extraordinary, almost unimaginable accomplishments. The problems we now face seem insurmountably complicated, but they too may only require systematic sorting and solving.

*Any sufficiently advanced technology is indistinguishable from magic.*
— Arthur C. Clarke, science fiction author

# Figure 1.1: Seemingly Impossible Problems and Some Viable Solutions

| "Impossible" Problem | Underlying New Paradigms | Viable Solution | Primary Methods | Some Main Developers |
|---|---|---|---|---|
| Disease, natural disasters, superstition, irrationality | Reality is consistent, understandable, testable, and changeable by humans | Scientific method of analysis (leading to technological solutions) | Hypothesis-testing, open debate and challenge | Hundreds of people including Aristotle and Plato |
| Oppressive powerholders who cannot be persuaded to change their ways and, when violently overthrown, are replaced by equally oppressive rulers | Powerholders are dependent on the support or at least passive consent of thousands of others | Nonviolent struggle | Withdrawal of support for powerholders — when the consent is withdrawn, the powerholder must change or lose power; care for and personal support of adversaries while requiring them to change their destructive behavior | Thoreau, Tolstoy, Gandhi, King, and thousands of others |
| "Evil" — aggression, malicious, wanton violence | Humans are inherently decent, but they are conditioned by destructive cultural conditioning and dysfunctional emotional conditioning | Education, loving attention, emotional therapy and healing | Education, meditation, solitude, journal writing, emotional counseling, emotional catharsis, prayer, community support, nonviolent struggle | Psychologists, religious leaders, "New Age" activists |
| Rigidity, prejudice, intolerance, dogmatism, obsession, compulsion, inhibition | In a safe environment, humans will rise to their full human potential and be powerful, loving, responsible actors | Emotional/ spiritual growth practices | Loving, respectful childrearing; emotional counseling, structured exercises, games, rituals, role-playing, and other experiences carefully designed to shake us out of our old rigid patterns and let us explore and practice new ways of acting in a safe, controlled environment | Human Potential movement, advocates of loving, respectful child-rearing, spiritual organizations |
| Conflicts over beliefs or resources | There are mutually satisfactory solutions to real problems | Consensus decision process, conflict resolution | Cooperative decision-making, principled negotiation, mediation, conflict resolution | Quakers, nonviolent activists, arms control experts |
| Mind control — human susceptibility to cults, manipulation, and propaganda; mob behavior | When raised to think for themselves, humans are intelligent and responsible | Individual empowerment and personal responsibility | Empowering childrearing and educational methods in which children are given responsibility and allowed to make mistakes without harsh criticism | Jefferson, Bakunin, radical education movement |

## REASONS FOR HOPE

After considering these arguments, I conclude that it is possible to create a good society — there are no insoluble problems, nothing that is physically impossible or culturally unachievable. Humans created this society and we re-create it every day — we can create another kind of society if we try. Of course, this does not mean it will be easy. We face strong and widespread opposition at every level. Creating a good society will require more effort than we have ever exerted before.

> *Since wars begin in the minds of men, it is in the minds of men that the defences of peace must be constructed.* — UNESCO Constitution, 1946

Still, many factors make it not only possible to create a good society but make it much easier than we might expect. Whenever I feel discouraged, I try to review these points.

### • Most People Have Experienced a Bit of a Good Society

At some point in their lives, most people experience periods of kindness or peace that provide them with an inkling of what a good society could be like. These times may only last a short while, they may involve only a spouse or a few close friends, or they may only exist in a movie or book, but they suggest what a wider good society might be like. When people experience these moments, they generally wish they could prolong them. This leads to the next point…

### • Most People Want a Good Society — We Are All on the Same Side

I have never met anyone who did not want life to be good for herself and others. Virtually all people would like to live in a just and compassionate society where they have control over their lives — a world of respect, joy, love, and laughter.

Admittedly, many people cannot imagine such a society, most do not believe it can or will ever come to pass, and everyone has different notions about how that society would be configured. Moreover, some people's ideas, if implemented, would infringe on the happiness of others. And, of course, some people would rather keep our existing society, since in their present positions of power and affluence they are doing quite well.

Nevertheless, I believe that most people do want a good society and would be willing to devote some effort to create it. Since most people want a good society, when we are truly working towards that goal, then all these people are on our side.

### • Most People Agree about the Basic Elements of a Good Society

Almost everyone agrees about the basic components of a good society. For example, no one wants to be hurt, so everyone can understand that no one else would ever want to be hurt either. Therefore, everyone understands the Golden Rule: "Do unto others as you would have them do unto you." Most people assume a good society would stand on this principle and assume that in a good society no one would be oppressed or exploited.

Similarly, most people's vision of a good society would ensure everyone had her basic needs met for air, water, food, shelter, safety, warmth, healthcare, meaningful work, leisure, exercise, community, and love. If pressed, most people would also probably acknowledge that in a good society disagreements would have to be worked out in mutually satisfying ways — no one should be able to just impose her will on another.

> *Do not do to others what you do not want them to do to you.* — Confucius, **Analects** 15.23
>
> *This is the sum of duty: do naught to others which if done to thee would cause thee pain.* — **The Mahabharata**, 5,1517
>
> *What is hateful to you, do not do to your neighbor: that is the whole Torah; all the rest of it is commentary.* — **Talmud,** Shabbat 31a
>
> *As you wish that men would do to you, do so to them.* — Luke 6:31, Matthew 7:12 (RSV)
>
> *Thou shalt love thy neighbour as thyself.* — Leviticus 19:18, Matthew 22:39 (KJ)

### • Most of the Time Most People Are Civil

Most of the time, most people obey laws and treat each other with civility. Most do not attack, rape, murder, or oppress other people or commit vandalism or arson against others' property.

### • Most People Act as Well as They Can

Most people believe they are good. Even when their behavior is less than admirable, they believe they are doing their best. When they behave badly, they believe there is some good reason for their behavior. For example, parents who abuse their children usually scold them for some real or imagined transgression that justifies the "discipline." In addition, abusive parents typically rely on their own abusive childhoods to decide what is normal or legitimate.

Even those who act according to high moral values can err. We are often confronted with moral dilemmas that have no easy solution — "damned if you do, damned if you don't." No matter which we choose, we are forced down a path that violates our standards.

Each of us must also struggle with irrational compulsions, addictions, fears, and inhibitions of which we are only vaguely aware and over which we appear to have little control. When we "knowingly" act contrary to our own moral code, it is usually due to forces beyond us.

Will Rogers once said that he never met a man he didn't like. I cannot go quite that far, but I have never met anyone whose actions seemed unwarranted once I took the time to hear her story. It appears to me that all people — given their upbringing, their education, their internalized fears and prejudices, and their current situation — act as well as they can under the circumstances in which they find themselves.

> *To understand everything is to forgive everything.*
> — French Proverb

If we were able to create a society in which there were fewer bad choices and people had more information about the negative consequences of their actions, then I believe each person's guiding morality would lead her to act well most of the time. This, in turn, would make it more likely that the society as a whole would be good.

### • Society Has Improved in Some Important Ways over the Centuries

Many efforts to improve this country have succeeded. For example:

• Women can now own property and vote. Overt discrimination against women is no longer acceptable.

• It is fast becoming indefensible for men to "discipline" their children or wives by beating them.

• Women are no longer expected to obey their husbands.

• Racial and ethnic discrimination is illegal.

• Lynchings are no longer acceptable.

> *Slavery was once considered "the American way."*

• Resolving conflicts by dueling is no longer acceptable.

• Disease is no longer considered unavoidable or interpreted as the vengeance of angry gods. Scientists have learned how to eradicate and control many diseases.

• Psychosis is now treated as mental illness, rather than moral affliction.

• Most homes are weatherproof, heated, and have running water, electric lights, refrigerators, and stainless steel silverware — luxuries that kings of yore would envy. Most people also have books, magazines, telephones, radios, televisions, VCRs, and automobiles — an abundance of material goods.

• A wide variety of basic human rights have been accepted and codified in compacts such as the U.S. Constitution's Bill of Rights and the United Nations Human Rights Charter.

These are just a few victories, but they indicate that change efforts can accomplish a great deal.

### • Movements for Progressive Social Change Are Viable and Powerful

Movements for progressive change have accomplished a great deal.* Here are just a few examples of recent successes in the United States:

• Reduced discrimination against and greatly expanded opportunities for women, racial minorities, gays and lesbians, and the disabled.

• Ended construction of new nuclear power plants and forced old ones to adhere to strict safety standards.

• Limited U.S. intervention in Central America.

• Helped to end apartheid in South Africa.

• Saved from extinction many endangered species.

• Banned or restricted many toxic substances such as asbestos, DDT, and PCBs.

### • Many People Now Work Hard to Create a Good Society

Thousands of people work diligently every day, mostly without pay or recognition, to set things right. Approximately 68% of Americans contribute money to charities and 49% volunteer their time, averaging four hours per week.[8] Though the results are not as great as we might like, this hard work shows how much desire and dedication there is for creating a good society.

> *Fortunately, many people would prefer to live a simple life in a good society than a life of riches and power in a horrible society.*

### • Even More People *Want* to Work to Create a Good Society

Many more people want to set things right. They want to live in consonance with their values, they want to work for goals they believe in, and they want to work with other kindhearted people.

Whenever social change movements illuminate an injustice and demonstrate a positive alternative, thousands of people rush forward to volunteer their time and money, even at the risk of their lives, their livelihood, or their stature in the community. Orators, like Eugene Debs and Martin Luther King, Jr., who speak directly to social problems and ask for help, often get a surprisingly positive response.

---

* Describing the history and many successes of progressive social change campaigns is beyond the scope of this book. See the Social Change History section of Chapter 12 for a list of introductory books.

## SO WHAT ARE WE DOING WRONG?

*If it is not impossible to create a good society and we have all these things going for us, then why have we not done it yet? What are we doing wrong? How can we do better?*

These are the questions I ask and try to address in the rest of this book. However, first (in Chapter 2) let me explain a bit more what I mean by a "good society."

---

*Not for ourselves alone, but for all humanity... Let us hasten to find the path that leads to liberty, safety, and peace for everyone.*
— Thomas Jefferson

---

## NOTES FOR CHAPTER 1

[1] William Morris, "Art Under Plutocracy" in *Political Writings of William Morris*, A.L. Morton, ed. (London: Lawrence and Wishart, 1984, HX246 .M72 1984), p.85.

[2] For references to the scientific literature, see the section called Dysfunctional Emotional Conditioning in Chapter 3.

[3] This may be difficult to believe after watching local television news a few evenings. However, the news media generally focuses our attention on violent spectacles. It discounts acts of compassion and loving interactions, instead fixating on the relatively few cases of hatred and destruction. This skews our perspective. See for example, Barbara Bliss Osborn, "If It Bleeds, It Leads... If It Votes, It Don't: A Survey of L.A.'s Local 'News' Shows," *Extra* 7, no. 5 (Sept./Oct. 1994): 15; and Martin A. Lee and Norman Soloman, *Unreliable Sources: A Guide to Detecting Bias in News Media* (New York: Carol Publishing Group, Lyle Stuart, 1990, PN4888 .O25 L44 1990), pp. 238–244.

[4] See Robert M. Axelrod, "The Evolution of Cooperation," *Science* 211 (March 27, 1981): 1390–1396; and Robert M. Axelrod, *The Evolution of Cooperation* (New York: Basic Books, 1984, HM131 A89 1984) for an interesting discussion of this point. Using the Prisoners' Dilemma strategic game model, Axelrod shows that cooperation based on reciprocity can evolve and remain stable even in a situation dominated by non-cooperating individuals.

[5] Frances Moore Lappé, Joseph Collins, and Peter Rosset, with Luis Esparza, *World Hunger: 12 Myths* (1986; 2nd ed. fully rev. and updated, London: Earthscan Publications Ltd., 1998, HD9000.5 .L35 1998). After studying the worldwide food situation for twenty-five years, they conclude:

• No country in the world is a hopeless case. Even countries many people think of as impossibly overcrowded have the resources necessary for people to free themselves from hunger.

• Increasing a nation's food production may not help the hungry. Food production per person can increase while more people go hungry.

• Our government's foreign aid often hurts rather than helps the hungry. But in a multitude of other ways we can help.

• The poor are neither a burden on us nor a threat to our interests. Unlikely as it may seem, the interests of the vast majority of Americans have much more in common with those of the world's hungry. (p. 1)

The world is awash with food, as chapter 1 will show. Neither are natural disasters to blame. Put most simply, the root cause of hunger isn't a scarcity of food or land; *it's a scarcity of democracy.* (p. 4)

Finally, in probing the connection between hunger and scarcity we should never overlook the lessons here at home. More than 30 million Americans cannot afford a healthy diet; 8.5 percent of U.S. children are hungry, and 20.1 percent are at risk of hunger. But who would argue that not enough food is produced? Surely not U.S. farmers; overproduction is their most persistent headache. Nor the U.S. government, which maintains huge storehouses of cheese, milk, and butter. In 1995, U.S. aid shipments abroad of surplus food included more than 3 million metric tons of cereals and cereal products, about two-thirds consisting of wheat and flour. That's enough flour to bake about six hundred loaves of bread per year for every hungry child in the United States. (p. 14)

See also Frances Moore Lappé and Joseph Collins, *Food First: Beyond the Myth of Scarcity* (1979; rev. & updated, New York: Ballantine Books, 1979, HD9000.6 .L34 1979).

[6] United Nations Development Programme, *Human Development Report 1998* (New York: Oxford University Press, 1998, HD72 .H852 1998), p. 37. This report also points out that this $40 billion cost represents about 4% of the combined wealth of the 225 richest people in the world—about $1 trillion (p. 30). It also contrasts the $40 billion figure with the money spent on cosmetics in the U.S. ($8 billion), pet foods in the U.S. and Europe ($17 billion), business entertainment in Japan ($30 billion), cigarettes in Europe ($50 billion), and worldwide military spending ($780 billion) (p. 37). <http://www.undp.org/hdro>.

[7] U.S. Census Bureau, *Statistical Abstract of the United States: 1998*, "Table 574, Worldwide Military Expenditures: 1987 to 1995" drawn from U.S. Arms Control and Disarmament Agency, *World Military Expenditures and Arms Transfers*, annual. <http://www.census.gov:80/statab/www/index.html>

[8] Independent Sector researchers estimate that in 1995, 48.8% of adults volunteered an average of 4.2 hours each week and 68.5% of households contributed money to voluntary or philanthropic organizations. Virginia A. Hodgkinson and Murray S. Weitzman, *Giving and Volunteering in the United States, 1996* (1200 Eighteenth Street, NW, Suite 200, Washington, DC 20036: Independent Sector, 1996), Tables 1.3 and 1.5. <http://www.indepsec.org/media/gv_summary.html>

# 2

# Elements of a Good Society

*What would a "good society" look like?*

Since every person has her own definition of a good society, there cannot be a single, universal standard — there are at least as many definitions as there are people. Only in a dictatorship could one person unilaterally decide what constituted the elements of a good society and impose this definition on others. Certainly, most people would agree that having one person dictate to everyone else is not acceptable in a good society.

However, this point does indicate one area of agreement: most people probably concur that a good society must be responsive to the people who live in that society. Further, most people probably agree that a good society must be an amalgam of everyone's best ideas. Hence, the first element of a good society must be rudimentary democratic consent: everyone must at least passively accept how the society is constituted and agree that it basically conforms to their own conception of a good society.

I also believe virtually everyone can endorse the principle of the Golden Rule: "Do unto others as you would have

them do unto you." A good society would treat every human being in the same way each of us would like to be treated — with fairness, kindness, consideration, forgiveness, support, generosity, and love.[1] From this fundamental principle, there are several basic elements that most people would readily agree must be present in a good society. These are described below.[2] The next section then lists a few additional elements that I believe also follow from the Golden Rule and belong in a good society though they currently are not as widely endorsed. Of course, the actual good society that would emerge from progressive transformation would be determined by everyone using consensual procedures.

> *The good of the people is the highest law.*
> — Cicero

Appendix A lists some specific, near-term policy changes that could begin the shift toward a good society.

## BASIC ELEMENTS OF A GOOD SOCIETY

### Rudimentary Democratic Consent

In a good society, everyone must at least passively endorse the basic structure. At a minimum, everyone must agree that the primary elements are configured in a sensible and just way.*

---

* I hope that in a good society, people's consent would be far stronger. Preferably, the vast majority would feel that most aspects of the society were not only reasonable, but actually desirable — they would not just tolerate their society, but actually *like* it.

## Universal Access to Human Essentials

Every human being requires certain things to live: air, water, food, protection from harsh weather (clothing and shelter), and safety from harm. In a good society, everyone would have her basic human needs met.

> *If there are homeless people on the streets while rooms in mansions sit empty, we do not have a good society.*
>
> *If children go hungry while others eat, we do not have a good society.*
>
> *If some are idle while others work too much, we do not have a good society.*

This seems elementary, but some philosophers and politicians have argued that satisfying everyone's basic human needs is not critical. They argue that some greater virtues can only be achieved by allowing or forcing some people to be destitute. They value these greater goods more than universal access to necessities.

But these thinkers are almost never themselves lacking essentials, and they do not offer to relinquish them for others. In stark contrast, those people who *are* destitute almost never believe they live in a good society — their definition requires that they rise out of poverty. Clearly, everyone needs the basics and a society that does not provide them is not very good.

## Access to Other Desirable Items

There are other basics that nearly everyone desires: tasty food, comfortable housing (with furniture, running water, and electric lights), transportation, a clean and healthy environment, healthcare, meaningful work, regular exercise, rejuvenating leisure, fulfilling relationships, family, and a close-knit community. People also want material goods like basic household appliances (such as a stove, refrigerator, kitchen tools, broom, vacuum cleaner, washing machine, clothes dryer, bathtub, shower), other basic items (like paper, pencils, books, magazines, newspapers, a bicycle), and luxuries (like an automobile, television, VCR, sound system, and a computer). People also desire good literature, music, theater, poetry, sculpture, and the other arts.

> *I'm not at all contemptuous of comforts, but they have their place and it is not first.*
> — E.F. Schumacher

None of these is essential, but life without at least a few of them is not much fun.* To me, a good society would enable most people to have most of the basic desirable items and would allow everyone to have at least a few luxuries.

---

\* Some of these items may seem essential, but consider what you would be willing to relinquish if it meant that a loved one could have enough to eat. Forced to make such a choice, all of these items would clearly be desirable, but not essential.

## Freedom and Liberty

In a good society, seldom would anyone be dominated, oppressed, or thwarted by another person or group. Whenever someone was oppressed, most everyone else in the society would immediately work to end her oppression.

---

### Society Out of Balance

**Work**

• In 1998, the average full-time worker in non-agricultural industries worked an average of 3.1 hours overtime per week — the equivalent of about 7.0 million full-time jobs.[3] In the same year, there were 6.2 million unemployed people.[4]

• The typical American worker worked 163 hours more in 1987 than in 1969 — the equivalent of one month more.[5]

• Every European economy except Italy and the United Kingdom requires employers to offer annual paid vacations to their workers of from four to six weeks. The United States requires none. U.S. workers average just over three weeks of paid vacation.[6]

• In 1990, Americans spent an average of 3.7 hours just commuting to and from work each week.[7]

**Motor Vehicle Accidents**

• In 1997, there were 13.8 million serious motor vehicle accidents in the United States, which killed more than 43,000 people. More than 6 million people were injured.[8]

**Poverty and Homelessness**

• In 1999, despite record employment, 32.3 million people (11.8 percent of the total U.S. population) lived in poverty. This included 11.5 million children under age eighteen (16.3 percent of all children). The poverty rate for African Americans was 23.6 percent. The poverty rate for American Indian and Alaska Natives was 25.9 percent.[9]

• "Even in a booming economy, at least 2.3 million adults and children, or nearly 1 percent of the U.S. population, are likely to experience a spell of homelessness at least once during a year."[10]

**Poor Health Coverage**

• In 1999, despite record employment, 42.6 million people (15.5 percent of the total U.S. population) did not have health insurance. This included 10.0 million children under age eighteen (13.9 percent of the total). Nearly one-third of Hispanics were uninsured.[11]

• The World Health Organization (WHO) reports "the U.S. health system spends a higher portion of its gross domestic product than any other country but ranks 37 out of 191 countries" in overall performance.[12]

People would also be free from intrusion into their private behavior. People would be free to think, do, and believe whatever they wanted as long as it did not hurt others.

---

*The ultimate end of all revolutionary social change is to establish the sanctity of human life, the dignity of man, the right of every human being to liberty and well-being.* — Emma Goldman

---

Of course, in any society where people live near one another and interact, they will inevitably conflict with each other. However, in a good society, people would do their best to stay out of each other's way. When people did conflict, they would use rational debate, appeals to conscience, mediation, nonviolent struggle, amiable separation, or other conflict resolution measures to resolve their differences.

In a good society, children would learn to respect others and would learn how to restrain themselves from hurting others. They would also learn how to work together cooperatively and to resolve conflicts graciously so that, when they grew up, their conflicts would be minimal.

Still, in a few cases, people's freedom and liberty must be restricted. There must be some way to prevent those who have transgressed against others from doing it again — methods like required emotional counseling, jail, or banishment. But these methods must be used sparingly and employ a bare minimum of force so as not to harm or dehumanize the transgressors.

*Don't judge a person until you have walked a mile in his moccasins.* — Proverb

## Equity and Fairness

Life is not fair and there is no way for a society to be completely equitable. But to me, a good society cannot be grossly imbalanced, and it certainly would not encourage or allow anyone to prosper at the expense of others through fraud, deception, corruption, intimidation, domination, or oppression.[13]

*If women are afraid to walk outdoors at night, we do not have a good society.*

*If dissenters fear speaking out, we do not have a good society.*

In a good society, everyone would at a minimum have equal access to information, resources, and opportunities. As much as possible, everyone would also have roughly the same amount of the material goods listed above, and no one would have significantly more than anyone else. How much is "significantly more" would, of course, need to be determined by everyone in society — again, everyone must give rudimentary consent. The methods used to ensure equitable distribution (investigation, reporting, regulation, enforcement) must also use a bare minimum of force so as not to harm anyone.

## Environmental Sustainability

Humans have evolved for thousands of years closely linked to nature. We are adapted to the earth's environment and can live quite well in it. A good society would mesh seamlessly with the natural environment, maintaining and supporting natural systems. We would live in consonance with all other species.

## Balance

There are unavoidable conflicts in society — conflicts between self-interest, the common good, the natural environment, privacy, personal liberty, and equity. Differences invariably lead to conflicts. For example, there will always be some people who want to engage in behavior that others find lewd or disgusting. A good society would balance everyone's interests and resolve these inherent conflicts in ways that a sensible person would find acceptable.

---

### Society Out of Balance (continued)

**The Environment**

• The United States represents 5 percent of the world's population and uses 26 percent of its oil. In contrast, India has 16 percent of the world's population and uses 3 percent of its oil.[14]

• In 1998, about 40 percent of U.S. streams, lakes, and estuaries that were assessed by the EPA were not clean enough to support uses such as fishing and swimming.[15]

• Eleven of the world's fifteen most important fishing areas are in decline and 60 percent of the major fish species are either fully or over- exploited.[16]

• On average, U.S. children eat a combination of twenty different pesticides daily.[17]

• Nearly 46 percent of the nation's federally subsidized apartments (870,000 units) are within a mile of factories that produce toxic pollution.[18]

**Voting**

• In the November 1996 presidential election, only 49.0 percent of adults voted. In the November 1998 federal election, only 32.9 percent of adults voted.[19]

**Foreign Policy**

• The United States has not signed a number of human rights treaties signed by most other countries of the world. These include:

◊ International Covenant on Economic, Social, and Cultural Rights

◊ Convention on the Elimination of all Forms of Discrimination against Women

◊ Convention on the Rights of the Child[20]

For example, the right of people to make loud sounds (music, construction noise, and so on) must be balanced against the needs of others for quiet. A sensible solution would allow anyone to make as much sound as she wanted when no one else was around, a certain amount of sound during the daytime when others were not likely to be bothered, and very little during the night when others were sleeping.

Similarly, people could engage in any kind of private behavior they wished as long as it did not hurt anyone else. However, in public, society might expect them to stay within certain bounds. Society might also try to limit self-destructive private behavior (like riding a motorcycle without a helmet or smoking tobacco) that would ultimately affect the society (when they needed medical care to treat their accident or illness).

In like manner, a good society would fashion a balance between the inherently conflicting needs of people for stimulation and relaxation, sensuality and propriety, spontaneity and deliberation, impulsive drive and caution, indulgence and moderation, exhibition and modesty. A good society would also reconcile end values with process values (such as justice with compassion) and would reconcile conflicting process values (such as democracy and expediency, acceptance and dissent).

Forging a sensible balance is difficult, but is almost always possible when undertaken by people of goodwill.

---

*What I mean by Socialism is a condition of society in which there should be neither rich nor poor, neither master nor master's man, neither idle nor overworked, neither brain-sick brain workers nor heart-sick hand workers, in a word, in which all men would be living in equality of condition, and would manage their affairs unwastefully, and with the full consciousness that harm to one would mean harm to all — the realization at last of the meaning of the word commonwealth.* — William Morris

---

## ADDITIONAL CHARACTERISTICS OF A GOOD SOCIETY

Beyond these basic elements, I imagine a good society would also be:

## Humane and Compassionate

People and institutions would be sympathetic towards, appreciative of, and considerate of other people, other species, and the overall environment. The primary goal of the society would be to support all people to live enjoyable lives and to achieve their full potential as human beings. Human

welfare would take precedence over money, property, and power. Society would generously offer extra help to those who had suffered from disability, poor upbringing, illness, injury, or some other misfortune. Society would also encourage altruism and cooperation.

## Democratic and Responsible

As part of their everyday daily lives, people would have permission, would be encouraged, and would actually *be* active participants in governing and controlling all aspects

---

### Society Out of Balance (continued)

**Childrearing**

• The American Academy of Pediatrics recommends that all children be breastfed for at least a year. However, in 1995, only 59.4 percent of women in the United States were breastfeeding at the time of hospital discharge, and only 21.6 percent were still nursing six months later.[21]

• "87% of parents of children aged two to seventeen feel that advertising and marketing aimed at children makes kids too materialistic." Also, "almost half of all parents report that their kids are already asking for brand name products by age 5."[22]

**Firearms**

• There are approximately 192 million privately owned firearms in the U.S. — 65 million of which are handguns.[23] An estimated 39 percent of households have a gun — 24 percent have a handgun.[24]

• The overall firearm-related death rate among U.S. children under age fifteen is nearly twelve times higher than among children in twenty-five other industrialized countries.[25]

**Prisons**

• In 1999, there were 1.3 million people in state and federal prisons — more than five times as many as in 1970. An additional 606,000 people were held in local jails.[26]

• In 1997, there were 5.7 million adults in prison or jail, on probation, or on parole — about 2.9 percent of the total adult population.[27]

• The 1999 United States' rate of incarceration of 682 inmates per 100,000 population was the second highest reported rate in the world, behind only Russia's rate of 685 per 100,000 for 1998.[28]

• If incarceration rates recorded in 1991 continued unchanged in the future, an estimated 5.1 percent of all persons in the United States would be confined in a state or federal prison during their lifetime. A man would have a 9.0 percent chance of going to prison during his lifetime, a black male greater than a 1 in 4 chance, an Hispanic male a 1 in 6 chance, and a white male a 1 in 23 chance.[29]

of their society — political, economic, social, and cultural. It would be a society truly of the people, by the people, and for the people. No person or group would dominate decision-making.

The society would value citizen involvement and would try to inform, educate, and empower each person to be a full participant in societal decision-making. Everyone in society would be encouraged and expected to take personal responsibility and initiative, not only for themselves but for the whole society — each person obligated and entrusted to look out for the common good and to set right anything that was amiss. Moreover, this responsibility and care would not be limited to a citizen's particular neighborhood, city, state, or nation, but would extend to the whole world. People would consider themselves global citizens.

*Democracy is not a spectator sport.*

To support democracy and responsibility, society would encourage people to be truthful and deal with each other in an honest and straightforward fashion. To further make democracy possible, society would also encourage people to work to heal their internalized emotional problems and overcome their fears and addictions.

Moreover, all the main institutions of society (government, schools, business, news media) would be responsive to the people in the community (not responsive only to shareholders). These institutions would treat people not just as voters, taxpayers, consumers, or spectators but primarily as citizens who ultimately "own" their society. As citizens, people have the right to be treated well and supported by all institutions. Moreover, as citizens, people have the right to know the truth about all aspects of society.

---

*We hold these truths to be self-evident, that all men are created equal, that they are endowed by their Creator with certain Unalienable Rights, that among these are Life, Liberty, and the pursuit of Happiness. That to secure these rights, Governments are instituted among Men, deriving their just powers from the consent of the governed.*

*That whenever any Form of Government becomes destructive of these ends, it is the Right of the People to alter or to abolish it, and to institute new Government, laying its foundation on such principles and organizing its powers in such form, as to them shall seem most likely to effect their Safety and Happiness.*

— The Declaration of Independence of the United States of America, July 4, 1776

---

## Tolerant and Wise

A good society would value the wisdom of every person. Every decision-making institution would invite a wide range of perspectives and truths. Society would encourage people

---

### World Imbalances

From ***Human Development Report, 1999***, United Nations Development Programme: [30]

• In 1997, the richest 20 percent of the world's population had an annual income that was 74 times that of the world's poorest 20 percent, up from 30 times as much in 1960. The most affluent 20 percent of the population of the planet consume 86 percent of the total goods and services in the world. The poorest 20 percent consume about 1 percent. [p. 3]

• In the past four years, the world's 200 richest people have seen their net worth double to $1 trillion. Meanwhile, the number of people surviving on less than $1 a day has remained unchanged at 1.3 billion. [pp. 37, 28]

• In 1998, the top 10 companies in telecommunications controlled 86 percent of this $262 billion global market. The top 10 companies in pesticides controlled 85 percent of this $31 billion global market. [p. 3]

• "In 1995 the illegal drug trade was estimated at 8% of world trade, more than the trade in motor vehicles or in iron and steel." [p. 5]

• "The traffic in women and girls for sexual exploitation — 500,000 a year to Western Europe alone — is one of the most heinous violations of human rights, estimated to be a $7 billion business." [p. 5]

• "At the root of all this is the growing influence of organized crime, estimated to gross $1.5 trillion a year, rivalling multinational corporations as an economic power." [p. 5]

• In 24 countries, life expectancy is estimated to be equal to or exceed 70 years, but in 32 countries life expectancy is less than 40 years. [31]

---

to be respectful, tolerant, and understanding of others. Society would value dissent and diversity. Schools and other institutions would not teach people to be docile or to accept dogma and authority passively, but instead would encourage them to be creative and flexible and to think rationally for themselves.

Furthermore, people would be encouraged to challenge conventional wisdom whenever they believed it was outmoded. Societal norms would also encourage people to open themselves to other beliefs and perspectives and to let go of their own limited or obsolete ideas. People would be guided and helped in their efforts to resolve their conflicts without resort to physical violence, threat, or attack and with a minimum of social coercion.

*Freedom rings where opinions clash.*
— Adlai E. Stevenson

The society would have sensible mechanisms for rationally sorting out different perspectives and disseminating the distilled wisdom to everyone, especially to young people. As a result, individuals would continually learn and grow, and society would steadily improve.

## Fun

In a good society where everyone's basic needs were met, people could devote time to endeavors such as music, theater, art, adventure, travel, and self-education. Instead of narrowly focusing on work and constantly rushing around, they could contemplate truth and beauty, they could develop their creativity, and they could build close relationships with others.

> *A good society enables and encourages everyone to practice her best behavior.*

A good society would allow and encourage people to live exciting and joyful lives. Secure and unafraid, people could be as passionate, playful, outrageous, and funny as they wanted to be. Every day, people would sing, paint, dance, write poetry, explore, lie under trees, play with children, and gaze at the stars.

Overall, I imagine that in a good society, people would labor out of their love for their fellow human beings and for the joy they derived from tackling difficult challenges, they would play because it's fun, and they would laugh for no reason at all.

---

### Lessons from Young Children

Young children are energetic and joyful. There is much we can learn from them.

• What if we enjoyed exuberant play every day, exercising and feeling our body strength — walking, running, skipping, bicycling, skating, dancing, hiking, skiing, swimming — without trying to compete with anyone else?

• What if we spent time each day exploring, investigating, and making sense of our world?

• What if we spent time each day making silly statements, telling jokes, and laughing with our friends?

• What if we spent time each day cuddling with our friends?

---

## NOT PARADISE

The good society described here may seem like a blissful paradise, completely free of suffering or discord. However, as noted in the Preface, there will always be conflict and pain in this world — we cannot escape the realities of life. Still, in the good society I envision, people's difficulties and sorrow would be greatly reduced and their love and joy would outshine their woes and disputes. It would be a far more productive and pleasant society than our current one.

## A COMPREHENSIVE MIX OF FOUR COMPONENTS

Achieving a society with these positive characteristics does not require perfection. Rather, a good society needs only a comprehensive mix of these four components:

• **Individuals** who are (1) educated and informed enough that they understand their connection and responsibility to others, and (2) emotionally healthy enough that they generally act well and seldom behave in irrational or destructive ways.

• A **culture** that largely promotes socially responsible behavior such as honesty, cooperation, tolerance, altruism, nonviolent conflict resolution, and self-education.

• **Structures of incentives** — rewards, penalties, and forms of accountability — that ensure people generally find it in their best interest to behave well.

• **Institutions** (political, economic, and social) that promote education, individual emotional health, and a socially responsible culture, and that implement structures of incentives for positive behavior.

These components can be incomplete and imperfect, as long as together they are sufficiently positive to offset their flaws and reinforce the best in the other components.

## EXAMPLES OF A GOOD SOCIETY

*Based on these principles, what would a good society look like?*

Fortunately, dreamers and visionaries have thought about this a great deal. There are many books and articles with innovative ideas about particular aspects of a good society and several novels that depict comprehensive visions of desirable societies.* Though some of these visions are ridiculous, some are truly sensible and practical. Many of the ideas have been tried successfully on a small scale.

> Reporter: *Mr. Gandhi, What do you think of Western Civilization?*
>
> Mr. Gandhi: *I think it would be a good idea!*

Below, I describe in general terms how a few important institutions might look in a good society and how society might deal with some age-old problems. Please view these descriptions only as tentative examples. Invariably, as society improves, people will come up with better ideas.

---

* See Chapter 12 for a list of visionary books.

## Family, Children, and Social Interaction

Since humans are social beings and need warm affection every day, in a good society most people would live in close connection with others. Many would live in traditional extended families (children, parents, grandparents, aunts, and uncles under one roof or living close by). Others might live in configurations more common today: nuclear families (children and one or two parents), same-sex partnerships, co-housing, cooperative households, and communes. Others might even try unusual arrangements like group marriage or line marriage.[32] Some people would live alone. But everyone would have many ways to connect intellectually, emotionally, and physically with other people whenever they wanted.

*If suicide and depression are common, we do not have a good society.*

To best provide for children's needs, they would generally live in some configuration where many able adults provided nurturance, guidance, and support (in contrast to today's single-parent and nuclear families where there are only one or two adults). By having many adults around, children would receive more attention, support, and affection, and they could learn from many approaches to life. All adults in the household would be encouraged to take on a proportional share of parenting responsibility, and they would have time in their lives to do this.

---

### Unbearable Lives

• Suicide is the eighth leading cause of death in the United States, and is the third leading cause of death for young people aged 15–24.

• Suicide took the lives of 30,535 Americans in 1997 (11.4 per 100,000 population).

• From 1952 to 1995, the incidence of suicide among adolescents and young adults nearly tripled.

— Centers for Disease Control and Prevention[33]

---

Parents and other adults who spent time with children would be taught the basics of compassionate childrearing including essential skills like how to change diapers, interpersonal skills such as counseling someone through grief, and parenting skills like how to teach and guide an inexperienced child. In addition, they would be coached by more experienced elders such as grandparents, aunts, and uncles. Trained counselors in each community would provide additional therapy and support to children or adults in distress. Conflict resolution facilitators would offer mediation for parent/child disputes.

To allow the development of normal self-esteem, parents would treat children as full human beings (albeit smaller, less knowledgeable, and less mature than adults). From

birth, each child would be allowed and encouraged to develop her own selfhood, not treated as her parent's property or servant. Parents would be encouraged to practice democracy within their household and include the children whenever possible in making decisions that affected them.

As children matured and demonstrated they could take on more responsibility, they would be given more control over their lives until they graduated into adulthood. When young adults demonstrated that they were responsible enough to nurture, guide, support, and live cooperatively with others, they would be encouraged to bear their own children.

In a good society, there would be fewer spectator events than now and many more cultural events geared toward bringing people together and participating such as dances, rituals, songfests, and cooperative games. These social events might be facilitated by trained social directors who knew how to encourage positive interaction. Young people would have special safe, structured venues for interacting with potential mates, and they would be offered clear and supportive guidance for dealing with the strong emotions and difficult issues that surround love and sexuality. In addition, people would be encouraged to perform community service tasks that would help the young, sick, or infirm and engender compassion for and connection to others in society.

A society that supported its children well, taught them personal responsibility and democracy, and preserved their self-esteem would eventually grow into a society of capable, self-assured adults who looked out for others. These adults would be emotionally healthy and could get along with their family and neighbors. If this society also provided connection and support, far fewer people than now would be isolated or feel lonely or unloved. Problems of alcoholism, drug abuse, mental illness, sexual abuse, domestic violence, suicide, and teenage pregnancy would be far less common, perhaps even rare.

## Education

Like now, schools in a good society would offer information about how to do useful things (read, write, compute, and so on). Furthermore, they would offer a range of perspectives and ideas, explain the merits and pitfalls of each, and help students evaluate each perspective for themselves. Schools and other cultural institutions would encourage people to think for themselves rather than blindly accepting what they are told.

*He who opens a school door, closes a prison.*
— Victor Hugo

Additionally, schools would address everything children need to learn to be happy and responsible citizens including human values and rights, interpersonal relationships, emotional counseling, nonviolent conflict resolution, democratic decision-making, economics, health, leisure, music, drama, visual arts, sex, and spirituality. Students would also learn about other people and their religions and cultures to help prevent racism, sexism, anti-Semitism, and so forth.

In addition, schools would teach democratic ideals by example: the schools themselves would be organized as democratically as possible, giving substantial power to students on issues that concern them. Students would work cooperatively together and teach each other.

For much of their education, students would go out into their communities and learn by watching, querying, or working with adults. When they were mature and skilled enough, students might also research critical community concerns and publicize their findings. Not only would they learn research and evaluation skills — important skills for any citizen — but they would provide a useful service to their community.

## Economics

In a good society, businesses would produce only useful goods and services, and they would produce these items in a way that is not destructive either to the people who do the work or to the environment. Businesses would prosper only when they provided useful goods or services to people, not through luck, dishonesty, corruption, intimidation, or pandering to people's addictions. Furthermore, decisions about what is produced and how it is produced would be made democratically, and the proceeds of production would be equitably distributed to everyone.

*Too many people spend money they haven't earned, to buy things they don't want, to impress people they don't like.* — Will Rogers

For example, several utopian novels describe economic systems that mostly achieve these goals:

In Edward Bellamy's 1888 novel ***Looking Backward***, everyone — whether working or not — is issued a "credit card" at the beginning of each year. Each of these cards has the same value — thus ensuring equal consumer power for every person. Each person is free to buy whatever goods and services she wants throughout the year — thus ensuring privacy and liberty. To provide these goods and services, everyone is required to work a certain amount each year until retirement at age forty-five.

In Ernest Callenbach's ***Ecotopia***, all production must adhere to strict environmental requirements. Moreover, in this people-oriented society, service workers insist that every customer treat them as peers, not as machines performing a service.

On the planet Anarres in Ursula LeGuin's ***The Dispossessed***, there is no money. Raised to value their fellow citizens and to take responsibility for their planet, everyone just takes what they need to live a simple life from storage warehouses and does the work that is required to stock the warehouses. Everyone does both manual and intellectual labor.

Most current economists see competitive markets as efficient ways for consumers to express their individual needs and desires, for producers to satisfy these requests cheaply, and for entrepreneurs to address unmet needs by starting new businesses. Markets enable individual parties to accomplish this all privately by directly bargaining between themselves. However, most progressive economists also support strong government regulation to protect the environment, to protect worker health and safety, and to prevent concentration of power in powerful monopolies. In addition, they support strongly progressive taxation to redistribute income and wealth more equitably. Most progressive economists also support worker- and consumer-owned cooperatives.

*Capitalism is the astounding belief that the most wickedest of men will do the most wickedest of things for the greatest good of everyone.* — Sir Maynard Keynes, economist

Some progressives go further. For example, Michael Albert and Robin Hahnel, in ***Looking Forward: Participatory Economics for the Twenty First Century***, propose a radically cooperative and non-hierarchical economic system that emphasizes treating everyone well. In this system, information about the value and cost of goods and services would be exchanged directly between consumers and producers. Both groups would mutually make decisions about what and how much was produced. Everyone would consensually decide the appropriate level of overall production.

In this system, every adult would be a member of two committees: a committee comprising every person at a workplace and a consumer committee made up of every person in a neighborhood. Workplace committees would decide what that workplace produced or what service it provided. The committee would also decide how people produced the product or service and who did each job task. Every person in a workplace would make work decisions on an equal footing with everyone else. Moreover, each job would consist of a balanced set of tasks — some conceptual, some manual, some fun and empowering, some boring and rote — so that everyone shared the good and bad, and everyone developed confidence and skills in all areas. Job tasks would be optimized to be efficient, enjoyable, and educational (rather than optimized for profit). Products and production would also be adjusted to reduce pollution and preserve natural resources.

At the receiving end, every consumer would get roughly equal shares of the total production of society. Each person could decide individually which of the particular goods and services produced she wanted for herself. Each person would decide with her neighborhood committee which community facilities to build (like new housing or medical facilities) and — with everyone in society — which national and international facilities to build.

Through ever-larger councils of these committees, everyone in their roles as consumers would negotiate with everyone in their roles as workers to decide for the society exactly how many goods and services would be provided each year. There would be an extensive, iterative process, guided by skilled facilitators that would start with the previous year's levels and then adjust them to reflect current desires. Proposals for particular consumption levels made by individuals, neighborhood committees, and workplaces would be summed through the councils until there was an overall societal balance between production and consumption. Then each workplace would produce or provide whatever it had agreed and consumers would receive whatever they were promised.

As a society, people could decide that everyone would work hard throughout the year and receive many goods and services or that they would all work less and have less. They could also decide to use large amounts of natural resources, or they could choose to conserve resources and minimize the impact on the environment.

As consumer desires or production techniques changed, workplaces would change the work they performed. When an item was no longer needed, the work group that produced it would switch to producing something else.

In this system, no one would be rich, and no one would be poor. Every able-bodied person would work, but no one would be exploited. Children and those who were disabled, sick, or infirm would all receive their fair share even though they might contribute less time or work. Everyone in society would have roughly equal power and wealth.

By providing the essential basics and an equitable distribution of some luxuries to everyone in society, this system would encourage cooperation, altruism, and mutual aid and discourage greed and possessiveness. Since no one would fear economic disaster, there would be no need for personal savings or insurance. Since all children would be provided for, there would be no need for inheritances. There would also be no need for advertising to convince us to buy things we do not need.

*When human rights conflict with property rights, I must choose humanity.*

No one would pay taxes since every service now provided by government would be provided by a work group just like any other important service. Also, there would be no large corporations threatening workers with job loss or manipulating government agencies.

Albert and Hahnel lay out a detailed plan covering the making of decisions and the provision of goods and some services. Less developed are their ideas about how services like long distance freight hauling, news reporting, housework, education, and emotional counseling would be provided. It is also unclear how decisions would be made about who did the work and how hard people worked. Albert and Hahnel do not even begin to address more difficult areas such as how society would decide who would do theoretical research, produce fine art, or provide entertainment. Clearly, these subjects need more development.

Still, a society based on their ideas would be far superior to our current system. It would eliminate poverty, encourage cooperation, and encourage full democratic participation in economic decisions.

The exact nature of the economic system in a good society must be decided consensually. It is possible that different regions would make different decisions and, accordingly, a good society would include a variety of cooperative economic systems.

## The Mondragon Cooperative

The large, long-lived Mondragon cooperative in Spain provides a real-world example of an alternative system that incorporates many social goals.[34] Mondragon, started in the mid-1950s, is a network of more than 170 worker-owned cooperatives serving 100,000 people and employing 21,000. It includes a worker-controlled bank, a chain of department stores, high-tech firms, appliance manufacturers, and farms as well as housing, education, and research and development organizations.

Though certainly not ideal, Mondragon has forged innovative and mostly responsive democratic decision-making structures and encouraged participation and community. For the most part, people decide cooperatively how to allocate capital and which products to manufacture.

## Resources

A good society would husband its resources carefully by re-using and recycling materials whenever possible and only mining, logging, or tilling when it was absolutely necessary. To minimize damage to the environment and to human health, a good society would only produce and apply fertilizer, pesticides, and herbicides when there were no other options. Plants would be bred primarily to be healthy, tasty, and disease-tolerant and only secondarily for appearance and long shelf life.

A society that honored good citizenship more than consumption would encourage people to spend their time helping their neighbors and looking out for the common good instead of shopping for and showing off possessions. A good society would also encourage low-impact fashions and lifestyles. For example, computers could be manufactured so that it was easy to dismantle them and recycle all their components. Clothes would inflict a much smaller toll on world resources if they were made to last for many years, they were made from easy-to-grow materials like hemp, and they were dyed only with biodegradable dyes. If designed well, these simple clothes could still have flair and flatter their wearers. People would need fewer kitchen and household items if they lived in larger households (as in extended families or co-housing) or if they shared more with their neighbors.

Video conferencing could replace a large percentage of business travel. Vacation travel would be less necessary if neighborhoods were desirable living places and work were not so onerous.

## Cities, Neighborhoods, and Transportation

Cities would be planned by city planners (with input from and ultimate control by the residents) to make them as livable as possible — rather than planned in the ways they usually are now: by real estate developers and builders who

# Figure 2.1: Good Responses to Conflict Situations

*Conflict is inevitable between people unless they are all perfect or identical. However, conflict does not necessarily mean that people must fight with each other in horrible ways. In a good society, people would employ positive responses to conflict such as the ones listed here.*

| Society Conflict Point | Assumed Root Cause | Typical Unhealthy Solutions | True Root Cause | Preferred Solutions in a Good Society |
|---|---|---|---|---|
| • Inability to produce good work<br>• Not allowed to try | • "They are stupid, lazy, or lack talent"<br>• "That's not something girls/young people/new employees, etc. can do" | • Condemnation, belittlement<br>• Domination by those with more information or skills<br>• Channeling into "jobs they can do" or "appropriate jobs" | • Youthful ignorance, inexperience, lack of skills<br>• Ignorance about other cultures<br>• Emotional hurts<br>• Prejudice, oppression | • Education (formal or informal)<br>• Skill training<br>• Apprenticeship, guidance<br>• Tutoring<br>• Travel<br>• Support, nurturance<br>• Provide equal opportunity and affirmative action to those disadvantaged |
| • Honest disagreement among those trying to work together | • "Those people had an inferior upbringing"<br>• "Those people don't know what they are talking about"<br>• "They're crazy" | • Control by leaders or patriarchs (hierarchical authority)<br>• Majority rule backed by police<br>• Abdication by those who are more easy going<br>• Individualism, isolation, escape | • Different experiences, perspectives, cultures, or insights | • Rational debate based on facts<br>• Scientific experiments to test theories of reality or to determine the best way<br>• Cooperative decision-making (problem solving and consensus)<br>• Negotiation, mediation<br>• Amiable separation |
| • Craziness (irrationality, obstinacy, inhibitions, compulsions, prejudice, addictions, depression, violence) | • Genetic inferiority<br>• Stupidity<br>• Innate personality defects (evil)<br>• Incurable emotional hurts | • Tough it out<br>• Cultural/social control (social sanctions, condemnation, belittlement)<br>• Psychiatric hospitals and asylums<br>• Laws, police, courts, jails<br>• Threats, intimidation<br>• Monitoring, surveillance, reconnaissance | • Emotional hurts (typically from childhood) | • Support, nurturance<br>• Altruism, compassion<br>• Emotional counseling therapy<br>• Appeals to conscience<br>• Nonviolent resistance or intervention<br>• Non-destructive childrearing |
| • Privilege (injustice and domination — congenital, inherited, or developed imbalances in resources or power) | • Innate destiny (birthright, luck, or reward for hard work)<br>• "There's not enough to go around" | • Promotion of myths that those who are wealthy or powerful deserve to be so and those who are poor or powerless are unworthy and deserve their poverty and lowly place<br>• Hierarchy of domination (everyone gets to dominate someone else except those at the very bottom who are powerless to do anything about it)<br>• Guilt-induced charity or pity<br>• Violent insurrection or revolution to overthrow powerholders | • Systemic forces in the society that propagate themselves (those with power or wealth have the means to maintain and increase their power and wealth)<br>• "Power corrupts" | • Altruism, compassion, gift-giving<br>• Redistributive laws (progressive income taxes, estate taxes, wealth taxes, etc.)<br>• Nonviolent struggle |

are trying to maximize their profits. Communities would be designed so that people could live near their workplaces and their friends as well as near stores, health clinics, theaters, and parks. Then most people could walk or ride a bicycle for the majority of their daily needs and desires, and they would spend much less time and far fewer resources commuting. Automobiles would only be needed to visit rural or distant places, and buses or trains could satisfy this need. Much of the half of all urban land now devoted to automobiles (for roads, parking lots, gas stations, new/used car lots, and so forth)[35] could then be used for other purposes or left as open space.

Currently, people often move to rural or suburban areas to escape from noise, pollution, and crime, or they move to rich neighborhoods with good schools and relatively low property taxes. Several changes, positive in their own right, would eliminate these reasons for abandoning cities:

• Schools would be improved so that each was as good as the best are today and all would be essentially equal in quality.

• Industrial plants would be cleaned up so that they did not emit noxious fumes and chemicals into the air and water around them. Sound-absorbing barriers or hedges would be constructed to keep industrial noise away from nearby residential areas.

# Figure 2.1 Good Responses to Conflict Situations (Continued)

| Society Conflict Point | Assumed Root Cause | Typical Unhealthy Solutions | True Root Cause | Preferred Solutions in a Good Society |
|---|---|---|---|---|
| • Conflicting wants | • Innate personality defects (envy, jealousy, greed, lust for power)<br>• Inherent reality (not enough to go around) | • Moral condemnation<br>• Channeling onto work treadmill (encourage people to work hard so they can buy what others have) | • Contempt, scorn, ridicule, disdain, and slight by those who have more<br>• Advertising that induces wants and needs | • Eliminate imbalances in wealth and power<br>• New society attitude: adjust wants and needs to what the society can reasonably produce<br>• Emotional counseling therapy and healing<br>• Non-destructive childrearing |
| • Difficult work (arduous, boring, etc.) | • Nature of reality<br>• Laziness | • Poverty (to force everyone to work)<br>• Slavery<br>• The allure of upward mobility: great wealth, privilege, and power for those who work hard | • Nature of reality (but not nearly as much as we now assume)<br>• Societal contempt for routine or repetitive work | • New society attitude: value work that is important to the creation and sustenance of a good society<br>• Reevaluate work to see if it is truly needed (all essentials can be provided with much less work)<br>• Reduce hours in the work week<br>• Rotate jobs so no one has to do the same task for too long a time<br>• Allow people to have control over their work so they do not feel hemmed in<br>• Allow people to see the results of their work so they can take pride in it<br>• Provide assistance when the work gets overwhelming |
| • Especially unpleasant or dangerous work that must be done | • Nature of reality<br>• Laziness | • Poverty or slavery (to force those who are ignorant or less powerful to do unpleasant jobs)<br>• Convince people they are unworthy to do anything but "bad" jobs<br>• Excessive incentives (excessive pay or privilege) | • Nature of reality (though not nearly as much as we are led to believe) | • As much as possible, automate all unpleasant and dangerous tasks<br>• Value all jobs that are important to the maintenance of a good society<br>• Rotate unpleasant tasks so everyone shares them equitably<br>• Provide incentives commensurate with the unpleasantness of the work |
| • Isolation, lack of community and social support | • Nature of reality<br>• Character flaws | • Hiring or coercing some people to support or entertain others (including prostitution) | • Time constraints<br>• Fear of being emotionally hurt | • Reduce the work week so people have more time to interact and support each other<br>• Emotional counseling therapy<br>• Bold, loving steps towards others (initiative and compassion) |

# U.S. Militarism

"The American military is, at this moment, more powerful relative to its foes than any armed force in history — stronger than the Roman legions at the peak of the empire, stronger than Britannia when the sun never set on the Royal Navy, stronger than the Wehrmacht on the day it entered Paris… The United States of the year 2000 is the greatest military power in the history of the world." — Gregg Easterbrook, "Apocryphal Now: The Myth of the Hollow Military"[36]

The United States has essentially no military enemies. Moreover, there are virtually no countries even capable of attacking U.S. territory. Still, the U.S. military controls vast resources — enabling it to dominate the world.

### Military Budget

• The U.S. military had budget authority of $311 billion in FY 1999 — about 41 percent of the total federal funds budget.[37]

• The United States and its close allies spend more on the military than the rest of the world combined, accounting for 63 percent of all military spending. The United States by itself spends 36 percent of the world's total military budget — up from 30 percent in 1985.[38]

• The U.S. military budget request for FY2001 is more than five times larger than that of Russia, the second largest spender. It is more than twenty-two times as large as the combined spending of the seven countries identified by the Pentagon as likely adversaries (Cuba, Iran, Iraq, Libya, North Korea, Sudan, and Syria). It is about three times as much as the combined spending of these seven potential enemies plus Russia and China.[39]

### Military Might

In 2000, the United States military included:
• 12 Navy aircraft carrier battle groups
• 10 Navy air wings
• 12 Navy amphibious ready groups
• 55 Navy attack submarines
• 12 Air Force fighter wings
• 163 Air Force bombers
• 10 Army divisions
• 2 Army armored cavalry regiments
• 3 Marine Corps divisions
• 3 Marine Corps air wings

It also included thousands of support ships, vehicles, and aircraft as well as over 5,000 nuclear warheads on submarine- and land-based ballistic missiles and thousands of conventionally armed missiles.[40]

• "The U.S. Navy boasts more than twice as many principal combat ships as Russia and China combined, plus a dozen supercarrier battle groups, compared with zero for the rest of the world. . . . America today possesses more jet bombers, more advanced fighter planes and tactical aircraft, and more aerial tankers, which allow fighters and bombers to operate far from their home soil, than all the other nations of the world combined."[41]

### Military Personnel

• At the end of FY1999, there were 1.4 million active-duty U.S. military personnel, 860,000 reservists, and 700,000 civilians.[42] Over 250,000 of the active-duty personnel were stationed in foreign countries or on ships.[43]

### Foreign Deployments

• "America is the world's sole military whose primary mission is not defense. Practically the entire U.S. military is an expeditionary force, designed not to guard borders — a duty that ties down most units of other militaries, including China's — but to 'project power' elsewhere in the world."[44]

• The U.S. Army has more than 100,000 soldiers forward stationed around the world — and more than 25,000 are deployed in over 70 countries every day of the year.[45]

• U.S. Navy deployments abroad have increased by 52 percent since 1993. Army deployments have increased 300 percent since 1989. Air Force deployments have quadrupled since 1986.[46]

• The U.S. Department of Defense (DoD) provides military training to more than 100 countries annually.[47]

### Arms Exports

• In FY1995, the federal government spent over $477 million and dedicated nearly 6,500 full-time equivalent personnel to promote U.S. arms sales overseas.[48]

• From 1995 to 1997, the United States exported $77.8 billion in arms, about 55 percent of the global total.[49]

• From 1995 to 1997, the United States exported $32 billion in military arms to developing countries. 51 percent of these arms went to non-democratic regimes.[50]

### Military Industry

• The defense industry now (1999) employs 2.2 million people, about 2 percent of the civilian workforce.[51]

### Research and Development

• In 1997, the U.S. Department of Defense spent $33 billion for research and development (R&D), while the Department of Health and Human Services, a distant second, spent about $12.2 billion for R&D.[52]

### Waste and Fraud

• The U.S. General Accounting Office reports that no major part of the DOD has been able to pass an independent audit. The DoD is not able to properly account for billions of dollars of property, equipment, and supplies, nor can it accurately report the costs of its operations.[53]

• Houses would be built solidly so neighbors could live near one another without being bothered by each other's noise.

• Street crime would be vigorously pursued so that no area became dangerous. Eliminating poverty and drastically reducing child abuse would also end the underlying impetus for most crime.

## News Media

Without solid information, citizens cannot make good decisions. In a good society, there must be a wide variety of information sources and the main sources must be held to high standards of journalistic integrity. Journalists always bring their own prejudices to their work and have a tendency to support the people they know or like. So there also must be checks and balances to minimize this influence. Some examples of news reporting in a good society:

*"The information citizens need to know to responsibly govern their society."* — Masthead Slogan of the (Fictitious) ***Daily Citizen*** Newspaper

• There would be many news organizations working independently of each another. At least two or three main news organizations would cover any particular region, and many smaller news organizations would focus on a particular issue or present a particular perspective.

• Funding for news reporting would come from sources other than advertising to eliminate dependence on sponsors. Individuals might pay for their news sources or the government might support them with tax dollars.

• The amount of resources allocated to each news organization (including the number of journalists, the number of TV channels, and the amount of radio spectrum) might be determined each year largely by how many people watched, listened, or read their newspapers and broadcasts. To ensure that dissenting voices were allocated ample resources to express themselves, a group who disagreed with the main news organizations might still be given resources for one year to launch a newspaper, TV show, or radio show. This would give them enough time to win over viewers, listeners, or readers.

---

### A Militarized World

• Since World War II, the world has spent $30–35 trillion on arms.[54]

• Global spending in 1999 on education was $80 billion. Global spending on the military was $781 billion.[55]

• In the wars of one decade, more children were killed than soldiers. Child victims of war include an estimated two million killed, four to five million disabled, twelve million left homeless, and more than one million orphaned.[56]

---

• Journalists would be prohibited from accepting gifts or favors from anyone they covered.

• Oversight groups would challenge poor, misleading, or inaccurate coverage or socially destructive perspectives.

## Foreign Policy and National Defense

In a good society, the United States would no longer exploit the resources (oil, minerals, timber, agriculture, and labor) of other countries. This would greatly reduce the need for foreign military bases and for a bloated military budget. The cost of these foreign goods would probably go up, but this would be offset by the decrease in the vast resources now consumed by the military.

*In this society, it is considered immoral to walk around wearing no clothes, but perfectly acceptable to build weapons of mass destruction.*

As much as possible, the people of the United States would cooperate with the people of other countries and treat them honestly, fairly, and compassionately. People would think of themselves as global citizens in fellowship with all other humans, not as U.S. nationals competing with other countries.

To provide defense against whatever enemies might still exist, everyone would be trained in nonviolent, civilian-based defense techniques and organized into nonviolent reserve militia units. If necessary, the country might maintain some minimally sufficient level of armaments and a small, trained military.

---

*In the councils of government, we must guard against the acquisition of unwarranted influence, whether sought or unsought, by the military-industrial complex.* — President Dwight D. Eisenhower, Farewell Address, January 17, 1961

---

## Government

In a good society, government would exist to nonviolently protect and support all people, instead of defending the property, wealth, or ideology of the wealthy and powerful. The government would be responsive and responsible to ordinary people. It would work to eliminate corruption, inefficiency, waste, and dishonesty.

To achieve these goals would require a different governmental structure than our current one — one that vastly reduced the temptations of wealth and power and that had even more checks on power. It would also need to be a more activist government that sought to restrict the concentration of power everywhere in society.

For example:

• The government would have more regulatory agencies with broader power to challenge society's institutions.

Moreover, these regulatory agencies would be regulated by independent oversight agencies that would be made less susceptible to their own misconduct by having only the power to expose corruption.

• When appropriate, decisions that are now made at a global, national, or state level would be decentralized to the local level, thus limiting the power of any individual person or group. Only those decisions challenging another large institution or those requiring a broad response would be made at high levels.

*In your public work, don't be afraid of exposure: If you do it, be proud of it. If you're not proud of it, don't do it.*

• Regulations would ban all gifts and favors to any current or past government officials. Authorities with broad power would be forced to shift to other work after a time to prevent them from becoming entrenched or susceptible to corruption.

• To prevent unsavory backroom deals, all decision-making meetings would be publicized in advance and open to journalists and citizens.

• The government would also provide a democratic forum for all of us to struggle together — providing skilled facilitators who could help us decide how we wished to balance our conflicting needs and desires with those of others, with those of future generations, and with the global environment. Currently, we are usually only spectators, relegated to watching from the sidelines while wealthy interests dictate our society's future.

## Democratic Structures

Our current democratic system relies on majority votes to elect representatives who then use majority votes to pass laws. Individuals have little input into the process. To protect them from possible oppression by the majority, minority factions are granted basic rights of privacy and well-being.

This system of "majority rule, minority rights" gives too much power to majorities and does not go far enough in protecting the rights of minorities. It assumes and encourages self-interest and competition, which often leads to selfish and anti-social behavior.

*The voice of the majority is no proof of justice.*
— Johann von Schiller

Under such a system, a group can garner a majority honestly by convincing others of the merit of their proposals. But under this system, a group can also secure a majority disingenuously by misrepresenting their motives or the impact of their proposals or by coercing, bribing, or manipulating supporters. With this ill-gotten majority, they may then grab control and secure benefits for themselves while taking no responsibility for the common good. They may deliberately or inadvertently exploit and oppress individuals or minorities. It is particularly easy for an unsavory majority to ignore or overrule

those who cannot participate in the process such as animals, plants, the natural environment, unborn generations, infants, children, and people who are mentally retarded, disturbed, senile, weak, or homeless. Because the current system rewards greed, it can rarely find good solutions or determine a fair allocation of benefits.

A good society demands a much better system — one that requires the consent of everyone and provides stewardship for those who cannot speak for themselves. Further, such a system must encourage everyone to work honestly and cooperatively with one another to meet everyone's basic needs and to support everyone fairly. Such a system would seek to provide for community needs without infringing on individuals' rights.

*A man must be both stupid and uncharitable who believes there is no virtue or truth but on his own side.* — Joseph Addison

This type of democratic system can only occur when virtually everyone in the society wants it to work and everyone attempts to look out not only for themselves but also for other individuals and for the society as a whole. They must care about the society and feel a strong sense of responsibility for others — as people often do in a tight community. They probably must also feel a strong connection to one another — much as they feel towards members of their family. Establishing such a system requires people to feel they "own" the society and reap great benefit by being part of it. People must be strong and responsible: adhering to their own beliefs and values as well as supporting community goals.

## Decision-Making System

Rather than a system of winner-take-all elections for representatives who may or may not represent a constituency or may or may not look out for the common good, a good society would have a more direct and participatory decision system. If important decisions were decentralized to the local level, people could meet in relatively small groups to discuss the issues and look for solutions that would best solve society's problems. This might require a great deal of time, but would result in much better decisions. It would also ensure that society was responsive to the needs of people.

Most issues would not require everyone's participation — only those interested in a particular issue would absolutely need to attend. Some people would likely devote much of their time to civic affairs while others would only participate when crucial issues arose or when they were concerned

*Liberty means responsibility. That is why most men dread it.* — George Bernard Shaw, *Maxims for Revolutionists*

that poor decisions were being made. To ensure accountability to the whole community, any final decision might require a 95 percent or 99 percent acceptance vote by everyone affected. This would not be a vote of desire or preference but merely an acknowledgment that the decision was tolerable and that a valid body made the decision (one with a large enough quorum and that included all those concerned).

To encourage cooperation and high principle, there might be a short community-building ritual (like standing in a circle and holding hands with others or reading an inspiring quotation) before each session. When information was needed to inform a decision, researchers would turn to a variety of sources and investigate each thoroughly. Advocates for particular positions could add their information and make their desires known. Then the group would prepare a wide range of options and delineate the advantages and disadvantages of each one. Once the group thoroughly explored all options, most people would probably see that a

---

## Ensuring Democratic Decision-Making

A good society allows everyone to have a say in the important matters that affect their lives. But to sustain a good society, they must also make decisions that are good for the whole community. This requires that everyone be included in the decision process, have access to all the necessary information to make good decisions, and take responsibility for making decisions that are good for the group. They must have the interest, time, and skills to listen carefully to everyone's perspectives and concerns, evaluate the truth of each perspective, work cooperatively with others to come up with creative solutions, and finally decide on a solution that best addresses the needs of the group. Anything less will result in poor or irrational decisions or domination by one or a few people. Bad decision processes, like our current system, often simply tally the ignorance, prejudices, and biases of the dominant group or the majority.

*Nothing is more odious than the majority, for it consists of a few powerful leaders, a certain number of accommodating scoundrels and submissive weaklings, and a mass of men who trot after them without thinking, or knowing their own minds.* — J. W. von Goethe

True democracy thus probably requires using some form of consensus decision-making process, practiced skillfully and effectively by those affected. Our current society has prepared us very inadequately for such a task. A good society must devote extensive resources to teaching everyone the skills of cooperative decision-making, providing everyone with the information necessary to make good decisions, and ensuring time to make good decisions.

few were superior and the rest could be eliminated from consideration. Most people would also recognize that none of the remaining options was perfect, but all were acceptable. Then strong preferences for a particular option or a majority vote of those at the meeting could determine the final choice. On highly controversial issues, the group might make decisions by a super majority vote (perhaps 66 percent or 75 percent), or it might defer the decision for a few months or years until a true consensus emerged.

Cooperation would be essential, but dissent would also be accepted and supported. Dissidents would be encouraged to question assumptions, criticize decisions, and closely monitor the effects of policies over time. Lobbying would be tolerated, but discouraged in favor of mutual exploration and a principled search for truth.

National or global decisions could be made by spokespeople from each local area. These spokespeople might be empowered to agree only to decisions that their local group had already endorsed. In cases of impasse, they would attempt to forge new options based on the best ideas of their local groups. Then they would take these new options back for ratification by the local groups. If ratified, they would then meet again with the other spokespeople and make a final decision. This cumbersome process might be expedited by traveling discussion facilitators, video conferencing, electronic mail, electronic bulletin board discussion groups, and other techniques.

## Safety

Unlike our current society in which war and violence are often glorified, children would be raised so that they considered the idea of assaulting another person repugnant. As adults, they would then have no desire to hurt another person, and they would recoil from any kind of violence. They would also be taught how to resist aggression nonviolently.

A good society would be safe at all times of the day and night. Men and women could walk alone anywhere without fear of assault, rape, or harassment.

Rather than relying solely on police, everyone would be encouraged to recognize destructive behavior and to interrupt it whenever it arose. Individuals working together would use the methods of rational argument, appeals to conscience, mediation, emotional counseling, and nonviolent struggle to enforce community standards. Militaristic ideas of domination, control, hatred, punishment, and revenge would be discouraged. Weapons would be restricted. To handle the worst situations, unarmed police would be trained to intervene and to subdue people without hurting them.

*It costs the same to send a person to prison or to Harvard. The difference is the curriculum.*
— Paul Hawken

Courts would primarily mediate disputes. They would provide a forum for people to explain how others' destruc-

## A Violent Society

### Percent of Persons in the United States Raped or Physically Assaulted in their Lifetime[57]

| Type of Assault | Percentage Women | Men |
|---|---|---|
| **Total Raped** | **17.6** | **3.0** |
| Attempted only | 2.8 | 0.9 |
| Completed | 14.8 | 2.1 |
| **Total Physically Assaulted** | **51.9** | **66.4** |
| *In the incident, the assailant...* | | |
| Threw something that could hurt | 14.0 | 22.4 |
| Pushed, grabbed, shoved | 30.6 | 43.5 |
| Pulled hair | 19.0 | 17.9 |
| Slapped, hit | 43.0 | 53.7 |
| Kicked, bit | 8.9 | 15.2 |
| Choked, tried to drown | 7.7 | 3.9 |
| Hit with an object | 21.2 | 34.7 |
| Beat up | 14.1 | 15.5 |
| Threatened with a knife | 5.8 | 16.1 |
| Threatened with a gun | 6.2 | 13.1 |
| Used a knife | 3.5 | 9.6 |
| Used a gun | 2.6 | 5.1 |
| **Total Raped and/or Physically Assaulted** | **55.0** | **66.8** |
| Stalked (with a high level of fear) | 8.1 | 2.2 |

Of the women who reported being raped at some time in their lives, 54 percent were under 18 years old when they were first raped.

Seventy-six percent of the surveyed women and eighteen percent of the surveyed men who were raped and/or physically assaulted since age 18 were assaulted by a current or former husband, cohabiting partner, or date.

tive behavior hurt them and ask for restoration. For malicious crimes, specially trained counselors would support and counsel the transgressors to heal them of whatever emotional disturbance drove them to hurt others. Those who could not change would be required to live and work in a special area separate from the rest of society and be continually monitored so they could not hurt anyone. Their crimes would be condemned, but they would not be tormented, rejected, or hated.

### Addictions and Drug Policy

A good society would discourage the use of mind-numbing drugs. It would also try to help anyone trapped by an addiction to drugs, alcohol, tobacco, nicotine, sugar, sports, gambling, sex, television, computers, or any other substances or practices around which people develop de-

structive obsessions. Anyone who wanted help to end her addiction would be assisted by trained counselors and supported by others trying to overcome the same addiction. Only those whose addictions caused antisocial behavior would be prevented from pursuing the addiction.

This is just a preliminary description of a few elements of a good society. The books and articles listed in Chapter 12 are invaluable in filling out this vision and suggesting other possible elements. Appendix A describes a variety of interim measures that could move the United States toward this vision.

## MAKING THIS VISION POSSIBLE

Many of the ideas described here seem impossible in our current society *and they are*. In our current society, power is much too concentrated to allow many of these ideas to work. In our current society, there is so much misleading propaganda that most people are severely misinformed. Moreover, our current society breeds large numbers of angry, misanthropic, cruel, violent, and savage people with whom it is extremely difficult to cooperate or even to co-exist. It is only as our change efforts begin to transform people and society that we could produce sufficiently favorable conditions to allow these ideas to be implemented.

The rest of this book explains how we might go about this task.

## NOTES FOR CHAPTER 2

[1] What I call "a good society" is similar to that described by many other authors and given a variety of names. For example:

Activists in the Civil Rights movement of the early 1960s, including Martin Luther King, Jr., called it "the beloved society."

Charles Derber, in *The Wilding of America: How Greed and Violence Are Eroding Our Nation's Character* (New York: St. Martin's Press, 1996, HN90 .V5D47 1996), uses the term a "civil society" and contrasts it with "wilding" (self-oriented behavior that hurts others and damages the social fabric):

> Civil society is the underlying antidote to the wilding virus, involving a culture of love, morality, and trust that leads people to care for one another and for the larger community. A civil society's institutions nurture civic responsibility by providing incentives for people to act not just in their own interest but for the common good. (p. 145)

Riane Eisler calls it the "partnership way." Riane Eisler, *The Chalice & The Blade: Our History, Our Future* (San Francisco: Harper & Row, 1987, HQ1075 .E57 1987); Riane Eisler and David Loye, *The Partnership Way: New Tools for Living and Learning* (San Francisco: HarperCollins, 1990, HQ1075 .E58

1990). The Center for Partnership Studies, P.O. Box 51936, Pacific Grove, CA 93950, (831) 626-1004. <http://www.partnershipway.org>

[2] For another list of basic elements of a good society, see Lester W. Milbrath, ***Envisioning a Sustainable Society: Learning Our Way Out*** (Albany, New York: State University of New York Press, 1989, GF41 .M53 1989), pp. 79–83. He proposes that a good society (one that would sustain a viable ecosystem) would include the following four core values:

- A high quality of life
- Security
- Compassion
- Justice

These values would be supported by eleven instrumental values:

- Fulfilling work
- Goods and services
- Health
- Peace
- Order
- Equality
- Freedom (lack of unnecessary restraints and provision of meaningful opportunities)
- Participation in community and societal decision-making
- Sense of belonging to a community
- Powerful knowledge (broad and deep)
- Variety and stimulation (recreation, education, research)

These, in turn would be supported and implemented by eight societal processes:

- Sustainable economic system (produces goods and services, provides fulfilling work, maintains economic justice, utilizes resources in a sustainable manner that preserves the eco-system)
- Health system (medicine, self-help)
- Safety system (police forces, fire protection, defense)
- Legal system (laws, courts)
- Participation system (decision-making processes, community, civic organizations)
- Recreation structure
- Research and education system
- Convenience structure (transportation, compact city design)

The thirty articles of the ***Universal Declaration of Human Rights***, adopted in 1948 by the General Assembly of the United Nations, also describe the elements of a good society. This document can be found on the United Nations' web site <http://www.un.org/Overview/rights.html> or on the site of Human Rights Watch <http://www.hrw.org/universal.html>.

Philosopher Martha Nussbaum, in "Human Capabilities, Female Human Beings," Martha Nussbaum and Jonathan Glover, eds., ***Women, Culture, and Development: A Study of Human Capabilities*** (Cambridge: Clarendon Press, 1995, HQ1236 .W6377 1994), pp. 61–104, provides a more rigorous list of eleven basic human capabilities that should be fulfilled in any good society, based especially on her study of women in developing countries:

1. Being able to live to the end of a human life of normal length, not dying prematurely, or before one's life is so reduced as to be not worth living.

2. Being able to have good health; to be adequately nourished; to have adequate shelter; having opportunities for sexual satisfaction, and for choice in matters of reproduction; being able to move from place to place.

3. Being able to avoid unnecessary and non-beneficial pain, as so far as possible, and to have pleasurable experiences.

4. Being able to use the senses; being able to imagine, to think, and to reason—and to do these things in a way informed and cultivated by an adequate education, including, but by no means limited to, literacy and basic mathematical and scientific training. Being able to use imagination and thought in connection with experiencing and producing spiritually enriching materials and events of one's own choice; religious, literary, musical, and so forth. I believe that the protection of this capability requires not only the provision of education, but also legal guarantees of freedom of expression with respect to both political and artistic speech, and of freedom of religious exercise.

5. Being able to have attachments to things and persons outside ourselves; to love those who love and care for us, to grieve at their absence; in general, to love to grieve, to experience longing and gratitude. Supporting this capability means supporting forms of human association that can be shown to be crucial in their development.

6. Being able to form a conception of the good and to engage in critical reflection about the planning of one's own life. This includes, today, being able to seek employment outside the home and to participate in political life.

7. Being able to live for and to others, to recognize and show concern for other human beings, to engage in various forms of social interaction; to be able to imagine the situation of another and to have compassion for that situation; to have the capability for both justice and friendship. Protecting this capability means, once again, protecting institutions that constitute such forms of affiliation, and also protecting the freedom of assembly and political speech.

8. Being able to live with concern for and in relation to animals, plants, and the world of nature.

9. Being able to laugh, to play, to enjoy recreational activities.

10. Being able to live one's own life and nobody else's. This means having certain guarantees of non-interference with certain choices that are especially personal and definitive of selfhood, such as choices regarding marriage, childbearing, sexual expression, speech, and empowerment.

10a. Being able to live one's own life in one's own surroundings and context. This means guarantees of freedom of association and of freedom from unwarranted search and seizure; it also means a certain sort of guarantee of the integrity of personal property, though this guarantee may be limited in various ways by the demands of social equality, and is always up for negotiation in connection with the interpretation of the other capabilities, since personal property, unlike personal liberty, is a tool of human functioning rather than an end in itself. (pp. 83–85)

[3] About 90.5 million full-time workers worked an average of 43.1 hours per week in non-agricultural industries. U.S. Census Bureau, ***Statistical Abstract of the U.S., 1999***, "Table 664: Persons At Work, by Hours Worked: 1998," drawn from U.S. Bureau of Labor Statistics, ***Employment and Earnings***, monthly, January 1999 issue. <http://www.census.gov:80/statab/www/index.html>

[4] U.S. Census Bureau, ***Statistical Abstract of the U.S., 1999***, "Table 649: Employment Status of the Civilian Population: 1950 to 1998," drawn from U.S. Bureau of Labor Statistics, Bulletin 2307; and ***Employment and Earnings***, monthly. <http://www.census.gov:80/statab/www/index.html>

[5] Juliet Schor, ***The Overworked American: The Unexpected Decline in Leisure*** (New York: Basic Books, 1991, HD4904.6 .S36 1991). For more analysis, see Barry Bluestone and Stephen Rose, "Overworked and Underemployed: Unraveling an Economic

Enigma," *The American Prospect*, no. 31 (March-April 1997). <http://www.prospect.org/archives/31/31bluefs.html>

[6] Economic Policy Institute, "European Vacations," Economic Snapshots web page, 10 May 2000 (Washington, D.C.: Economic Policy Institute, 2000). <http://www.epinet.org/webfeatures/snapshots/archive/2000/0510 00/snapshots051000.html>

[7] U.S. Census Bureau, *Statistical Abstract of the U.S., 1999*, "Table 1037: Transportation to Work: 1990," drawn from U.S. Census Bureau, *Census of Population and Housing*, 1990. <http://www.census.gov:80/statab/www/index.html>

[8] U.S. Census Bureau, *Statistical Abstract of the U.S., 1999*, "Table 1041: Motor Vehicle Accidents — Number and Deaths: 1972 to 1997," drawn from National Safety Council, Itasca, IL, *Accident Facts* and Insurance Information Institute, New York, NY, *Insurance Facts*.

[9] U.S. Census Bureau, *Poverty in the United States: 1999 (P60-210)*, March 2000 Current Population Surveys. <http://www.census.gov/Press-Release/www/2000/cb00-158.html> <http://www.census.gov/hhes/www/povty99.html>

[10] Urban Institute, "America's Homeless II: Populations and Services," slideshow released 1 February 2000 based on work by researchers Martha Burt and Laudan Aron. <http://www.urban.org/housing/homeless/numbers/sld002.htm> <http://www.urban.org/news/pressrel/pr000201.html>

For background, see Martha Burt, Laudan Aron, Toby Douglas, Jesse Valente, Edgar Lee, Britta Iwen, *Homelessness: Programs and the People They Serve — Findings of the National Survey of Homeless Assistance Providers and Clients*, Urban Institute report prepared for the Federal Interagency Council on the Homeless, 7 December 1999. <http://www.urban.org/housing/homeless/homeless.html> <http://www.urban.org/housing/homeless/homelessness.pdf>

[11] U.S. Census Bureau, *Health Insurance Coverage: 1999 (P60-211)*, March 2000 Current Population Surveys. <http://www.census.gov/Press-Release/www/2000/cb00-160.html>, <http://www.census.gov/hhes/www/hlthin99.html>

[12] World Health Organization, "World Health Organization Assesses the World's Health Systems," press release describing *The World Health Report 2000 — Health Systems: Improving Performance* (Geneva, Switzerland: WHO, June 2000). <http://www.who.int/whr/2000/en/press_release.htm>

WHO's assessment of performance compares each country's system to what experts estimate to be the upper limit of what can be done with the level of resources available in that country. It also measures what each country's system has accomplished in comparison with those of other countries. It is based on five indicators: overall level of population health; health inequalities (or disparities) within the population; overall level of health system responsiveness (a combination of patient satisfaction and how well the system acts); distribution of responsiveness within the population (how well people of varying economic status find that they are served by the health system); and the distribution of the health system's financial burden within the population (who pays the costs).

[13] Iris Young, in *Justice and Politics of Difference*, (Prince-ton, NJ: Princeton University Press, 1990, JC578. Y68 1990), defines two basic kinds of injustice:

**Oppression**: "institutional constraint on self-development" (p. 37), that is, the "inhibition of [one's] ability to develop and exercise [one's] capacities and express [one's] needs, thoughts, and feelings" (p. 40)

**Domination**: "institutional constraint on self-determination" (p. 37)

She sees oppression as having five faces:

**Exploitation**: "a steady process of the transfer of the results of the labor of one social group to benefit another" (p. 49)

**Marginalization**: excluding from the normal system of labor those that the system cannot or will not use and expelling them from useful participation in social life (p. 53)

**Powerlessness**: "inhibition in the development of one's capacities, lack of decision-making power in one's life, and exposure to disrespectful treatment because of the status one occupies" (p. 58)

**Cultural Imperialism**: "universalization of a dominant group's experience and culture, and its establishment as the norm" (p. 59)

**Violence**: "random, unprovoked attacks on one's person or property which have no motive but to damage, humiliate, or destroy the person" (p. 61)

[14] *BP Amoco Statistical Review of World Energy, 1999*, p. 9. <http://www.bp.com/worldenergy/pdf/oil.pdf>

[15] U.S. Environmental Protection Agency, Office of Water, *National Water Quality Inventory: 1998 Report to Congress* (EPA 841-R-00-001). <http://www.epa.gov/305b/98report/98summary.html>

[16] Anne Platt McGinn, "Rocking the Boat: Conserving Fisheries and Protecting Jobs," *WorldWatch Paper 142* (Washington, DC: WorldWatch Institute, 1995). <http://www.worldwatch.org/pubs/paper/142.html>

[17] 20/20 Vision, *1998-99 Biennial Report* (Washington, DC: 20/20 Vision, 2000), p. 7.

[18] Craig Flournoy and Randy Lee Loftis, "Toxic Neighbors: Residents of Projects Find Common Problem: Pollution," *Dallas Morning News*, 1 October 2000, p. 1A.

[19] U.S. Census Bureau, *Statistical Abstract of the U.S., 1999*, "Table 490: Resident Population of Voting Age and Percent Casting Votes — States: 1990 to 1998," drawn from U.S. Census Bureau, *Current Population Reports, P25-1117* and *Statistical Brief (SB/96-2)*; votes cast from Elections Research Center, Chevy Chase, MD, *America Votes*, biennial; and 1994, Congressional Quarterly Inc., *Congressional Quarterly Weekly Report*, 53, no. 15, 15 April 1995. <http://www.census.gov:80/statab/www/index.html>

[20] Human Rights Watch, *World Report 2001*, "USA Overview." <http://www.hrw.org/wr2k1/usa/index.html>

Somalia is the only other country that has not ratified the Convention on the Rights of the Child.

[21] American Academy of Pediatrics, "Policy Statement: Breastfeeding and the Use of Human Milk (RE9729)," *Pediatrics*

100, no. 6 (December 1997): 1035-1039. <http://www.aap.org/policy/re9729.html>

Michal Ann Young, M.D., "Press Statement on American Academy of Pediatrics Breastfeeding Recommendations, 17 Dec. 1997." <http://www.aap.org/advocacy/washing/brfeed.htm>

[22] Center for a New American Dream, "New Poll Shows Marketing to Kids Taking its Toll on Parents, Families," 6930 Carroll Ave., Suite 900, Takoma Park, MD 20912, July 1999. The study surveyed 400 parents. <http://www.newdream.org/campaign/kids/press-release.html>

[23] Philip J. Cook and Jens Ludwig, *Guns in America: Results of a Comprehensive National Survey on Firearms Ownership and Use* (Washington, DC: Police Foundation, 1997), p. 13 as cited by Handgun Control, Inc. (HCI), Washington, DC. <http://www.handguncontrol.org/research/progun/firefacts.asp>

[24] National Opinion Research Center, The University of Chicago, *1997-1998 National Gun Policy Survey*, September 1998 as cited by Handgun Control, Inc. (HCI), Washington, DC. <http://www.handguncontrol.org/research/progun/firefacts.asp>

[25] Centers for Disease Control and Prevention, "Rates of Homicide, Suicide, and Firearm-Related Death Among Children — 26 Industrialized Countries," *Morbidity and Mortality Weekly Report* 46, no. 5 (7 February 1997): 101–105. <http://ftp.cdc.gov/pub/Publications/mmwr/wk/mm4605.pdf>

[26] The Sentencing Project, "Facts about Prisons and Prisoners," April 2000, based on Bureau of Justice Statistics, *Corrections Compendium*. <http://www.sentencingproject.org/brief/facts-pp.pdf>

[27] U.S. Census Bureau, *Statistical Abstract of the U.S., 1999*, "Table 385: Adults on Probation, in Jail or Prison, or on Parole: 1980 to 1997," drawn from U.S. Bureau of Justice Statistics, *Correctional Populations in the United States*, annual. <http://www.census.gov:80/statab/www/index.html>

[28] The Sentencing Project, "Facts about Prisons and Prisoners," April 2000, based on Bureau of Justice Statistics, *Corrections Compendium*. <http://www.sentencingproject.org/brief/facts-pp.pdf>

[29] Thomas P. Bonczar and Allen J. Beck, "Lifetime Likelihood of Going to State or Federal Prison," U.S. Department of Justice, Bureau of Justice Statistics, Report Number NCJ-160092, March 1997. <http://www.ojp.usdoj.gov:80/bjs/pub/pdf/llgsfp.pdf>

[30] United Nations Development Programme, *Human Development Report, 1999* (New York: Oxford University Press, 1999, HD72 .H85 1999). <http://www.undp.org/hdro>

[31] World Health Organization, "World Health Organization Assesses the World's Health Systems," press release describing *The World Health Report 2000 — Health Systems: Improving Performance* (Geneva, Switzerland: WHO, June 2000). <http://www.who.int/whr/2000/en/press_release.htm>

[32] Line marriage is a type of group marriage in which members of the family range in age from children to seniors and a new young person is married into the family whenever an elder family-member dies. Robert A. Heinlein describes this arrangement in his science fiction novel, *The Moon is a Harsh Mistress* (New York: Ace Books), 1966, especially pp. 31, 209.

[33] Centers for Disease Control and Prevention, "Suicide in the United States," National Center for Injury Prevention and Control, Division of Violence Prevention, web page revised January 28, 2000. <http://www.cdc.gov/ncipc/factsheets/suifacts.htm>

The homicide rate of children aged 0–14 in the U.S. in 1990–1995 was five times the rate of twenty-five other industrialized countries, and the suicide rate was twice as great. Centers for Disease Control and Prevention, "Rates of Homicide, Suicide, and Firearm-Related Death Among Children — 26 Industrialized Countries," *Morbidity and Mortality Weekly Report* 46, no. 5 (February 7, 1997): 101–105. <http://ftp.cdc.gov/pub/Publications/mmwr/wk/mm4605.pdf>

[34] For a good description of Mondragon, see Roy Morrison, *We Build the Road as We Travel* (Philadelphia: New Society Publishers, 1991, HD3218 .M66 M67 1991).

[35] "Over 60,000 square miles of land in the United States have been paved over. That works out to about 2 percent of the total surface area, and to 10 percent of all arable land. Worldwide, at least a third of an average city's land is devoted to roads, parking lots, and other elements of a car infrastructure. In American cities, close to half of all the urban space goes to accommodate the automobile; in Los Angeles, the figure reaches two-thirds." Michael Renner, *Rethinking the Role of the Automobile*, Worldwatch Paper 84, (Washington, DC: Worldwatch Institute, June 1988, HE5611 .R46 1988), p. 46.

Renner bases the U.S. paved area figure on Richard Register, "What is an Ecocity?" *Earth Island Journal*, Fall 1987; the global average of land devoted to cars comes from Lester R. Brown and Jodi L. Jacobson, *The Future of Urbanization: Facing the Ecological and Economic Constraints*, Worldwatch Paper 77, (Washington, DC: Worldwatch Institute, 1987, HC59.7 .B79 1987). The U.S. urban land use figure comes originally from Martin Wachs, "Policy Concerns," in Susan Hanson, *The Geography of Urban Transportation*, 2nd ed. (New York: Guilford Press, 1995, HE305 .G46 1995), p. 270.

Also see Jane Holtz Kay, *Asphalt Nation: How the Automobile Took Over America and How We Can Take It Back* (Berkeley: University of California Press, 1998, HE5623 .K36 1998).

[36] Gregg Easterbrook, "Apocryphal Now: The Myth of the Hollow Military," *The New Republic*, 11 September 2000. <http://www.tnr.com/091100/easterbrook091100_print.html>

[37] Friends Committee on National Legislation (FCNL), "A Glut of Military Spending," *FCNL Washington Newsletter*, 641 (March 2000): 1 based on *Budget of the U.S. Government, Fiscal Year 2001*.

[38] Center for Defense Information, Washington, DC, "World Military Expenditures," website accessed 14 October 2000. <http://www.cdi.org/issues/wme/>

[39] Ibid.

[40] U.S. Department of Defense, *Annual Defense Report, 2000*, "Table 1: Major Conventional Force Elements, FY 2001," "Table 2: Conventional Force Structure Summary, FY 2001," and "Table 13: Reductions in U.S. Strategic Nuclear Arsenal Force Levels, FY 1990 Through 2007."

<http://www.dtic.mil/execsec/adr2000/adr2000.pdf>

[41] Gregg Easterbrook, "Apocryphal Now: The Myth of the Hollow Military," *The New Republic*, 11 September 2000. <http://www.tnr.com/091100/easterbrook091100_print.html>

[42] U.S. Department of Defense, *Annual Defense Report, 2000*, "Table C-1: "Military and Civilian Personnel Strength." <http://www.dtic.mil/execsec/adr2000/adr2000.pdf>

[43] There were 52,248 active-duty military personnel afloat and 213,270 ashore. U.S. Department of Defense, Washington Headquarters Services, Directorate for Information Operations and Reports, *Active Duty Military Personnel Strengths by Regional Area and by Country (309A)*, 31 March 2000, p. 5. <http://web1.whs.osd.mil/mmid/m05/hst0300.pdf>

There were 49,560 direct hire civilians in foreign countries. U.S. Department of Defense, Washington Headquarters Services, Directorate for Information Operations and Reports, *Selected Manpower Statistics, Fiscal Year 1999*, "Table 3-1: Total Civilian Personnel Strengths by Regional Area and by Country - Military Functions (309b)," 30 September 1999. <http://web1.whs.osd.mil/mmid/m01/fy99/m01fy99.pdf>

[44] Gregg Easterbrook, "Apocryphal Now: The Myth of the Hollow Military," *The New Republic*, 11 September 2000. <http://www.tnr.com/091100/easterbrook091100_print.html>

[45] U.S. Department of Defense, *Annual Defense Report, 2000*, "Report of the Secretary of the Army," p. 178. <http://www.dtic.mil/execsec/adr2000/adr2000.pdf>

[46] U.S. Department of Defense, *Introduction to the United States Department of Defense*, p. 15, website updated 3 July 2000. <http://www.defenselink.mil/pubs/dod101/busiest.html>

The report also boasts: "This map reflects our military's operational tempo from the end of the Cold War through last year [1999] — 99 major commitments of Americans in uniform, both active and reserve, to virtually every corner of the globe."

— This is Fact 298 gathered by PEN, the People's Education Network. <http://www.penpress.org>

[47] U.S. Department of Defense, Defense Security Cooperation Agency, International Military Education and Training (IMET) Program website. <http://www.dsca.osd.mil/programs/imet/imet2.htm> <http://129.48.104.198/introsa98/sld016.htm>.

For recent levels see the Federation of American Scientists: <http://www.fas.org/asmp/campaigns/training/IMET.html>

— This is Fact 191 gathered by PEN.

[48] William D. Hartung, *Welfare for Weapons Dealers: The Hidden Costs of the Arms Trade, 1996*, World Policy Institute, Arms Trade Resource Center. Note that these figures do not include the billions of dollars of taxpayer subsidies involved in the actual financing of foreign arms sales. <http://worldpolicy.org/projects/arms/reports/hcrep.html#unclesam>

— This is Fact 134 gathered by PEN.

[49] U.S. Department of State, Bureau of Arms Control, *World Military Expenditures and Arms Transfers, 1998*, Table 3, p. 165. <http://www.state.gov/www/global/arms/bureau_vc/wmeat98vc.html>

<http://www.state.gov/www/global/arms/bureau_vc/wmeat98fs.html>

From 1987 to 1997, the United States sold more than $280 billion in arms, about 5.2 percent of all U.S. exports for the period. The United States was one of only three countries in which arms exports represented more than 5 percent of its total exports. Israel and North Korea were the other two countries. — *Military Expenditures and Arms Transfers, 1998*, Table 2, p. 158. <http://www.state.gov/www/global/arms/bureau_ac/wmeat98/table2.pdf>

[50] U.S. Department of State, Bureau of Arms Control, *World Military Expenditures and Arms Transfers, 1998*, Table 3, p. 165. <http://www.state.gov/www/global/arms/bureau_ac/wmeat98/table3.pdf>
— This is Fact 223 gathered by PEN. The term "non-democratic regimes" is defined by the U.S. Code of Conduct on Arms Transfers and the U.S. Department of State's *Country Reports*.

[51] Center for Defense Information, Washington, DC, "Military Industrial Complex," website accessed October 14, 2000. <http://www.cdi.org/issues/usmi/complex/>

[52] U.S. National Science Foundation, Division of Science Resources Studies, *Science and Engineering Indicators, 1998*, Chapter 4, p. 4-21. <http://www.nsf.gov/sbe/srs/seind98/access/c4/c4s2.htm>

— This is Fact 435 gathered by PEN.

[53] U.S. General Accounting Office, "Department Of Defense: Financial Audits Highlight Continuing Challenges to Correct Serious Financial Management Problems," Statement of Gene L. Dodaro, Assistant Comptroller General, Accounting and Information Management Division, GAO/T-AIMD/NSIAD-98-158, 16 April 1998.

[54] United Nations Development Programme, *Human Development Report, 1994* (New York: Oxford University Press, 1994, HD72 .H85 1994). <http://www.undp.org/hdro>.

— This is Fact 279 gathered by PEN.

[55] United Nations Children's Fund (UNICEF), *The State of the World's Children, 1999*. <http://www.unicef.org/sowc99/feature3.htm> <http://www.unicef.org/sowc99/facts3.htm>

— This is Fact 84 gathered by PEN.

[56] United Nations Children's Fund (UNICEF), *State of the World's Children, 1995*, p. 2.

— This is Fact 283 gathered by PEN.

[57] Patricia Tjaden and Nancy Thoennes, *Prevalence, Incidence, and Consequences of Violence Against Women: Findings From the National Violence Against Women Survey*, U.S. Department of Justice, Office of Justice Programs, National Institute of Justice, Research in Brief Series, Report Number 172837, November 1998. <http://ncjrs.org/txtfiles/172837.txt> <http://ncjrs.org/pdffiles/172837.pdf>

This report presents the results of a nationally representative telephone survey of 8,000 women and 8,000 men about their experiences as victims of rape, physical assault, and stalking. The survey was conducted from November 1995 to May 1996.

# 3

# *Obstacles to Progressive Change*

*There are many people trying to make the world better. Why aren't they more successful?*

This chapter first addresses some popular but faulty criticisms of progressive social change efforts. Then it describes the five main obstacles that actually thwart positive change. The next few chapters then put forth a progressive change strategy that can surmount these hurdles.

## MISGUIDED CRITICISMS

When change does not come the way we would like, it is easy to blame others. Progressive activists often blame those who are not working for change — calling them apathetic, ignorant, complacent, or cynical. However, labeling people does not explain their behavior nor suggest positive solutions. These labels are also unfair — it is not at all unreasonable for people to spend their time earning a living, raising their children, living their lives, and having some fun. Rather than blaming those who are not actively working for change, it is more useful to determine why progressive activists *are* able to live their lives and work for positive change. What has inspired and enabled them to do this?

Similarly, society assigns progressive activists full responsibility for positive change and then blames them for their limitations and blunders when they fail. For example, I often hear criticisms like these:

### TOO LITTLE AND TOO MUCH EFFORT

• Progressive activists are not dedicated enough, and they do not do enough. They should care more and work harder. They should forfeit their careers, forgo having children, minimize social entanglements, and focus all their efforts on change.

• Activists work too hard, engaging in useless frenzy and then burning out. They should take better care of themselves and work at a sustainable pace. They should also remember what is important in life. They do not spend enough time supporting their spouses, children, and friends and enjoying themselves. To be effective, they must lead a sane, balanced life and regularly stop to smell the roses.

### ORIENTATION TOO ORDINARY AND TOO SPIRITUAL

• Activists are not spiritual enough. They should tune into the ecological wisdom of the cosmos and open themselves to the possibilities of mystery and magic.

• Activists are too idealistic and "airy-fairy" with their heads in the clouds. They should get down to brass tacks and do the hard, demanding work necessary to bring about change.

### TOO MUCH PLANNING AND TOO MUCH SPONTANEITY

*If we could first know where we are, and whither we are tending, we could then better judge what to do, and how to do it.*
— Abraham Lincoln

• Activists spend too much time meeting with each other to discuss how to create change and not enough time actually doing it.

• Activists do not spend enough time considering the consequences of their actions. They too often act impulsively without adequate analysis or discussion with others — then make grievous mistakes.

### TOO LITTLE AND TOO MUCH CONSIDERATION OF THE POOR

• Activists build too few organizations of working-class people and the poor — those who can easily see how they are oppressed and will fight on their own behalf.

• Activists spend too much time focusing on the underclass. The poor are too downtrodden to work coherently for progressive change. Those who do work for change only selfishly want to get more for themselves — they will not fight for the common good. Moreover, activists only want to align themselves with the victims of society because they pity them or identify with their pain.

### TOO LITTLE AND TOO MUCH CONSIDERATION OF THE ELITE

• Activists focus too little on educating members of the elite — those who are prosperous enough that they can attend to the common good and who can use their power and resources to end oppression.

• Activists spend too much time cozying up to the elite. The elite are inherently antagonistic to any substantive progressive change. Moreover, activists only want to align themselves with the elite because they envy their wealth and privilege.

### NOT ENOUGH PURITY AND TOO MUCH

• Activists should not compromise their ideals by working with others who do not share their goals. Those who share ideals should go it alone, even as a member of a small sect if necessary.

• Activists should work together in large groups and coalitions to garner enough power to create big changes instead of working in small, fragmented groups.

### FOCUS TOO NARROW AND TOO BROAD

• Activists should work on every important problem, not just their few pet issues. All issues are connected and all are important.

• Activists should all work together on one single issue instead of scattering their efforts on a thousand different projects.

### NOT ENOUGH FOCUS ON POLITICAL, CULTURAL, AND PERSONAL CHANGE

• Activists should focus pragmatically on electing progressive legislators to office by working within the Democratic Party.

• Activists should create a new political party so they can promote a truly progressive platform, even if their candidates fail to win office.

• Activists should ignore politicians and act directly to educate people and to acquire power.

• Activists should forget power and focus on shifting cultural paradigms instead.

• Activists should focus inward on their own complicity with evil and work to overcome their own power-tripping, racism, sexism, and classism.

### NOT ENOUGH ATTENTION ON THE FUTURE AND ON THE PRESENT

• Activists should strive to teach their children progressive ideals and hope that an enlightened next generation can change society.

• Activists must change the world now so their children can grow up uninjured by current problems.

## Miss the Mark

Though contradictory, these are all reasonable criticisms. Each of them reflects an important truth about the nature of society, and each may be an apt criticism of a particular change effort. Activists make many mistakes and often choose foolish or counterproductive tactics. Their understanding of the world is often incomplete or wrong and the strategies they choose are often inappropriate. However, none of these criticisms really explains why progressive change efforts do not accomplish more, and none clearly points the way to fundamental change.

These criticisms and their implied solutions miss the mark. The world is complex and diverse, so efforts to change it will also be complex and diverse. In different situations, progressive activists must act in different ways. Sometimes they must work alone — other times they must work with other groups. Depending on circumstances, they must concentrate narrowly or sweep widely, focus on highest ideals or pragmatically choose to compromise, look inward or outward, focus on the present or look to the future, work long and hard or take a much-needed vacation.

*But **why** do activists so often choose the wrong response? And why, even when they choose seemingly effective means, do they still very often lose?*

## Five Primary Obstacles

Rather than simply blaming ordinary people for not working for change or blaming progressive activists for their failures, it is better to probe much deeper to discover what actually holds back social change. Why are there so few people willing or able to work for positive change? Why do progressive activists err so often? Why is it so hard for them to succeed? What gets in the way?

I believe five main obstacles prevent progressive activists from creating a good society:

• **Adverse Power Structure**: Society's institutions and structures entice and coerce everyone into acting to perpetuate these institutions and social structures and to resist progressive change. In particular, powerful elite interests use their immense resources to thwart positive change. Regular people fear that if they stray from traditional paths they will be attacked or ruined financially.

## OBSTACLE 1: ADVERSE POWER STRUCTURE

Changing society requires changing both the way people relate to each other and changing the way societal institutions are structured. The particular way that our society is structured makes it extremely difficult to bring about fundamental positive change. Our institutions and social structures entice and coerce everyone into acting in ways that perpetuate existing institutions and social structures, even those that are quite destructive.

The people who are most hurt by the current system typically have little power to make changes. They do not have the authority to order change, the money to pay for change, nor the skills to persuade others to change. Moreover, they are taught that they deserve their fate and should passively accept it.

# A Wall of Opposition

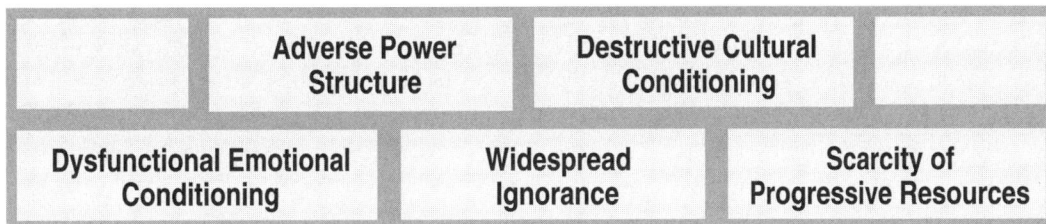

| | | |
|---|---|---|
| **Adverse Power Structure** | **Destructive Cultural Conditioning** | |
| **Dysfunctional Emotional Conditioning** | **Widespread Ignorance** | **Scarcity of Progressive Resources** |

• **Destructive Cultural Conditioning**: All of us grow up accepting societal norms, some of which are quite destructive. These norms powerfully dictate what is expected of us and what is permissible. Those who challenge or stray from the accepted norms in any significant way are usually criticized or ostracized.

• **Dysfunctional Emotional Conditioning**

All of us are hampered by internalized emotional injuries that have embedded fear and oppression deep within our psyches. This conditioning makes it difficult for us to change ourselves and often makes us resist progressive change.

• **Widespread Ignorance**: Most people do not know about progressive alternatives and do not have the skills to implement them. In addition, most progressive activists have few skills and little relevant experience working for change — which leads them to make many mistakes.

• **Scarcity of Progressive Resources**: Progressive activists have extremely limited financial resources, receive little personal support, and are too few in number.

Stacked together, these five obstacles comprise a huge barrier blocking positive change. Any serious effort to transform society fundamentally must overcome every one of these critical obstacles.

In contrast, those who have the most authority, money, and skills have a vested interest in maintaining the status quo. They are taught to believe they deserve their power and privilege and taught that they should actively fight to maintain the established order. If they feel pangs of conscience and decide to challenge the power structure or even if they just do not perform as much as is demanded by the system, they may lose their positions of power.

Most people have an intermediate level of power and awareness. They are partially hurt by the current structure, but also have a personal stake in maintaining it. They may see some of the problems caused by this structure, but they still mostly support it, often hoping that they can personally escape problems by garnering more power and money for themselves or aligning themselves with the elite.

No single person, even someone who is seemingly quite powerful, has enough power to individually bring about significant change against all the opposition generated by everyone else playing their assigned roles. Faced with broad opposition, people learn to accept the current system and to conform to its dictates, even if this means carrying out actions that oppress others.

## At the Top

Our society has developed in a way that has allowed a relatively small number of people to accumulate immense power and resources. Since they reap many benefits from the present system, these wealthy, privileged members of the "upper class" have a vested interest in maintaining the status quo. Though progressive change would greatly improve society as a whole, it would cause these affluent individuals to lose their special privileges. So typically, members of the upper class oppose progressive change, and with their immense power, they constitute a formidable obstacle.

Sociologists C. Wright Mills and G. William Domhoff call the people who fight to maintain the privileges of the upper class the "power elite." In a series of carefully documented books, they have systematically explored who constitute the power elite, how members of the elite exert power, and how they maintain their strength.[1]

To determine who constitute the power elite, Mills and Domhoff examined: (1) who garners most of the valued benefits of society (wealth, income, well-being); (2) who occupies important institutional leadership positions and makes societal decisions; (3) who wins when there are societal disagreements; and (4) who are considered by others to wield power. From this analysis, they conclude that the power elite encompasses primarily two sets of people: (1) leaders of the wealthy upper class who have the interest and ability to protect and enhance the privileged social position of their class; and (2) high-level employees of important businesses and organizations, particularly ones owned by the upper class. They find the power elite serves as the leadership group for the upper class and works largely on its behalf.

## The Upper Class

Domhoff estimates that the upper class in the United States is a relatively small group, comprising about one-half of one percent of the total population (about one million people). Though relatively few in number, members of the upper class own 20–25% of all wealth, own about half of all corporate stock, and exercise ultimate control over a significant portion of all business.[2] They sit in a large number of the seats of power in the government and the corporate community.

Members of the upper class do not all know each other and they are not monolithic in their perspectives. However, most do share similar backgrounds, share similar lifestyles, vacation at the same resorts, and socialize in overlapping social circles. They identify with each other as the "elegant, refined, sophisticated, genteel, well-bred, upper echelon, best and the brightest." Given their shared position in society, they also generally share an interest in maintaining their power and privilege.

Some people join or leave the upper class as their wealth and status grows or shrinks. Nevertheless, membership generally changes slowly, usually bequeathed from elite elders to their elite heirs. To ensure continuity over time, private boarding schools, elite colleges, and upper crust social clubs mold upper class children and up-and-coming new members of the elite into a cohesive group.

## The Power Elite and the Power Structure

The power elite is that select group with the desire and the ability to shape public policy — often with the goals of maintaining the power and wealth of the upper class and of resisting efforts to democratize society. The power elite does not include every upper class person nor is it limited to the upper class. Still, many members of the power elite are upper class and most of the rest are aligned with upper class interests.

The power elite is *not* a secret cabal conspiring to oppress other people. However, members of the power elite *are* powerful and influential. Most *do* share common interests. Many of them *do* meet together in a variety of forums (policy conferences, business meetings, trade conferences, social clubs, and friendship networks). Many *do* discuss and work out mutually satisfactory policy initiatives. Many *do* use their power to advance these initiatives.[3] Together, their efforts to "maximize profits for shareholders," "merge assets into more efficient units," "reduce labor costs," "increase productivity," "support and defend free enterprise," "overturn trade barriers," "defend property rights," "protect individual initiative," "stamp out immorality," "uphold law and order," "honor traditional family values," "maintain a strong defense," "reform government," and implement other seemingly innocuous and benevolent principles actually result in the oppression of billions of people here and abroad.

*The owners and top-level managers in large income-producing properties are far and away the dominant power figures in the United States. Their corporations, banks, and agribusinesses come together as a corporate community that dominates the federal government in Washington. Their real estate, construction, and land development companies form growth coalitions that dominate most local governments. Granted, there is competition within both the corporate community and the local growth coalitions for profits and investment opportunities, and there are sometimes tensions between national corporations and local growth coalitions, but both are cohesive on policy issues affecting their general welfare, and in the face of demands by organized workers, liberals, environmentalists, and neighborhoods.*

— William Domhoff [4]

Many members of the power elite do not feel that they are particularly powerful. Rightfully, they see tens of thousands of other powerful people and perceive that their own ability to exert control is small. Still, compared to the average person who has few resources and does not occupy a seat of authority, members of the power elite are tremendously more powerful.

Members of the power elite are not "evil" individuals. Many deeply believe authoritarian ideology and free market rhetoric and so honestly believe their actions are benign. They typically believe they are saving the world from some greater evil like "Satanism," "Communism," "terrorism," or "tribalism," or defending against domination by "politically-correct Feminazis" or "misguided Luddites."

Some members, naïve about the true nature of social processes, go along with the system and trust that their actions are benign. Other members of the power elite, ambitiously seeking monetary gain or status, feel compelled to play according to the rules of the game even though this sometimes means they must act in ways they know are destructive and immoral. Still others try to act for the social good, but discover that the economic, political, and social structures of society force them to act in destructive ways. They find that the forces they confront are so powerful that they are not allowed to choose positive solutions. If they attempt to oppose or bypass the power structure, they are barred from acting or stripped of their power — either way, they cease being members of the power elite.

> *The trouble with being in the rat race is that even if you win, you're still a rat.*
> — Lily Tomlin

No matter what their motives, desires, or ideological bent, members of the power elite control immense resources and they use these resources to advance particular policy initiatives. These initiatives generally enable, support, and defend themselves, other members of the power elite, the upper class, and the whole power structure that permits them to continue wielding their power.

Although members of the power elite shape the power structure and generally support it, they are also manipulated and oppressed by it. They are bombarded with their own rhetoric, terrorized by their own scare stories, forced to act in proscribed ways, barred from reaching out to most other people, and prohibited from considering positive solutions to social problems. Many members of the elite feel they are trapped in a terrifying world: they feel inferior to anyone with more power, money, or status; they feel besieged by liberals, people of color, the poor, and perhaps by other members of the power elite; and their lives feel empty and meaningless.

## The Might of the Power Elite

Backed by the enormous wealth of the upper class, members of the power elite own or exert dominant control over most of the important resources of society. Together, they have enormous holdings in land, mineral rights, factories, buildings, equipment, TV and radio licenses, patents, and copyrights. They control government commissions and regulatory agencies. They command military services, "intelligence" agencies, and police forces. They direct the news media, policy think tanks, universities, churches, banks, agribusiness, and most other industries, including the important information industries of publishing and entertainment. With these immense resources, they have the ability to obscure the truth and threaten anyone who attempts significant change.

---

### Are You a Member of the Power Elite?

• Were you born into a prominent family? When you were a child, did most people in your community see your parents as distinguished, sophisticated, glamorous, or eminent? Are you viewed that way now?

• Did you attend a prestigious private prep school or elite college? Did/do/will you send your children to such a school?

• When you came of age, did you receive gifts or an inheritance worth more than $50,000 (beyond college tuition)?

• Are you listed in the Social Register? Do you belong to the Bohemian Club or a local upper-crust social club? Do you vacation at posh resorts?

• Does your immediate family have an annual income of more than $200,000?

• Does your immediate family have a net worth of more than $1,000,000?

• Are you a top executive or a member of the board of directors of a large corporation, bank, law firm, foundation, university, policy-formation institute, large cultural organization, or religious denomination?

• Are you an elected or appointed official at the state or national level, a top political party official, or a top military officer?

• Do you serve on any official commissions or task forces at the local, state, or national level?

• Do your direct and indirect contributions to political campaigns, political parties, or lobbyists at the local, state, and national level total more than $5,000 annually?

• Are you a member of the board of directors or do you directly or indirectly (through a foundation) contribute more than $5,000 annually to a national policy-formation institute?

**If you answer yes to three or more of these questions, then you are probably a member of the power elite.**[5]

For example, in the area of public governance, the elite can mostly control who is nominated for office, who is elected, and who is appointed to commissions and judgeships. Moreover, they can mostly determine who lobbies legislators, how issues are portrayed, which policy questions are asked, what research information is revealed, and which solutions are considered.

> *The public be damned!*
> — Railroad baron
> William H. Vanderbilt

Consider the ways that the elite controls who is elected to public office. In the current political system in the United States, candidates for public office can usually win election only if they raise hundreds of thousands or even millions of dollars. Candidates with large amounts of money can poll voters to discover what they want to hear, then craft dazzling television advertisements filled with alluring messages, and blast them at every voter in the district. They can completely overpower honest political discussion with verbiage and spectacle. They can also blast their opponents with vicious accusations and nasty innuendo.

Candidates who cannot raise large amounts of money have no way to tell voters about themselves or their positions on policy issues and no way to counter the misinformation broadcast by opponents. Even so-called "grassroots campaigns" (with many volunteers making telephone calls and delivering literature door-to-door) typically require large amounts of money to pay for telephones, printing, and travel. Given this environment, the candidate who spends the most money usually wins.

Realistically, candidates can only raise large sums two ways. They can tap their own reserves if they are multimillionaires like Ross Perot or Steve Forbes. Alternatively, they can solicit big donors — who are usually members of the upper class. Consequently, most candidates able to win office are members of the power elite, ideologically sympathetic to elite interests, or beholden to the elite. Tellingly, the Senate is known as "the millionaire's club" for its large number of extremely wealthy members.

> *We have the best government money can buy.* — Graffiti

Once elected, these officeholders usually want to (or feel they must) propose legislation that supports and protects their elite sponsors. Hence, tax reductions for the rich are usually on the congressional agenda, but reductions for those below the poverty line rarely are.[6] To bolster their policy positions, politicians aligned with the elite can easily rely on reports generated by universities and think tanks — that are also backed by elite interests. In stark contrast, those who oppose elite domination usually have only the research of small, poorly funded public-interest groups.

Politicians who vote against elite interests are targeted by moneyed congressional scrutiny groups. These groups can distort the purpose of their legislation and rally people to flood them with calls and letters of opposition.

To ensure that Congress passes no law detrimental to their interests, large business and professional interests also hire thousands of lobbyists to visit officeholders in Washington and state capitals regularly. Besides barraging officeholders with their political arguments, lobbyists often confer lavish gifts and campaign contributions in a manner tantamount to bribery.[7]

*We have a governing system of the power elite, by the power elite, and largely **for** the power elite. Excluded from the decision arena, most ordinary people are relegated to watching silently from the sidelines as elite interests dictate the contours of their lives.*

The power elite also largely controls the news media.[8] The "major" news media, owned by large conglomerates, usually report on issues with enough dazzle to attract viewers and readers, but also in a way that does not offend their corporate owners. Top reporters for these news outlets usually have an upper middle-class background and aspire to wealth and prominence. This tilts their sympathies toward upper class and business interests. Those few reporters who challenge the elite are sometimes directly reprimanded by their editors or publishers, but more often, their editors simply do not assign them to important stories until they change their ways. They soon learn to censor themselves.[9]

Consequently, it is generally difficult to hear other than elite perspectives about anything but the most trivial topics. Most news articles approach issues from an elite perspective — pointing out how various options would affect "us" (the elite) and what the most prudent course of action is for "us" (the elite).[10]

*When politicians and pundits say the American people want free trade, capital gains tax reductions, and less government regulation, it makes no sense. Most people couldn't care less about these things. But if you substitute the phrase "the power elite" for "the American people," the meaning becomes clear.*

For example, the news media extensively cover issues concerning capital, trade, and military might. These issues are portrayed as important since they concern "our" (elite) interests. Other issues, even if they affect millions of people — like the health and welfare of children, unemployment, toxic wastes, or family violence — receive little or no coverage. Proposed solutions seldom include any that seriously challenge the power or wealth of the elite. As a result, virtually the only "controversial issues" covered by the media are those involving a struggle between different factions of the power elite.

When reporters do point out injustice, wrongdoing, or corruption by members of the elite, they typically frame it as an unusual aberration caused by a few greedy people. Alternatively, they may frame it as a larger problem, but one that occurred in the distant past and that responsible authorities have now fixed. They seldom place these problems where they belong in the larger context of ongoing, systemic corruption, chicanery, connivance, and domination by the elite.

On the local level, communities are usually dominated by bankers, real estate developers, and the owners and top managers of large local industries, law firms, and newspaper and TV stations. Members of the local power elite usually support the national elite, and members of the national elite support the local elite — or at least they passively tolerate each other.[11]

## Elite Interests Usually Win

Domhoff finds that with their immense wealth and authority, elite interests can usually exert enough power to win struggles on important societal issues — especially those concerning economic matters like tax law, consumer protection, workplace safety, and environmental standards.

As one clear example, Domhoff details how elite interests watered down a full employment bill — one that working people greatly desired — until it had virtually no substance.[12] The Employment Act of 1946 began its life as the Full Employment Act and would have made "the federal government underwrite the national investment needed each year to ensure full employment. It would be the task of government to determine what amount was needed each year, then to make available to private industry and state and local governments the loans necessary to bring total private and public investment up to the target figure. If the loans were not utilized, the Congress would authorize money for public works and other federal projects." (109)

This bill, which might have ended unemployment and poverty,[13] was fought by the Chamber of Commerce, the National Association of Manufacturers, the American Farm Bureau Federation, and others. The moderate-conservative "Committee for Economic Development" then put forward a substitute bill that "fit their conception of the limited role government should have." By the time the bill passed Congress, it "merely called for a yearly economic report to provide suggestions for dealing with threats of inflation or depression that might be on the horizon... [It] also called for a three-person Council of Economic Advisors to help the President prepare this report." (113)

*No one can earn a million dollars honestly.*
— William Jennings Bryan

*Behind every great fortune there is a crime.*
— Honoré de Balzac

Two recent cases are also telling. Elite financial interests engineered deregulation of the savings and loan industry in the early 1980s, which led to wild financial speculation. When the industry collapsed in the late 1980s, federal regulators gently slapped the wrists of those who had committed fraud. Meanwhile, the federal government bailed out the industry with hundreds of billions of dollars. The news media mostly ignored this gigantic government handout to wealthy investors and instead focused its attention elsewhere — on poor welfare cheats stealing a few thousand dollars. The federal government might have taxed the rich to pay for the bailout. Alternatively, it might have taken partial ownership of savings and loan institutions or garnered some portion of S&L's future profits in exchange for bailing them out. But these options were never considered, even though these alternatives would probably have been better for the country as a whole.

The elite agenda also governed the 1994 debate on health care reform. At the beginning of the debate, about 70% of Americans expressed strong interest in a universal, Canadian-style system of health care. In such a "single-payer" system, a government agency would serve as the single payer for all care in place of the many insurance companies that perform that role now. By avoiding the bureaucracy needed to determine who gets health care (since everyone would), a single-payer system would provide a great deal more health care at less cost to everyone. Moreover, in this kind of system, doctors would maintain their independence and would continue to decide what is appropriate care — not insurance company bureaucrats.

Though fair, efficient, and popular, the single-payer option was virtually ignored by the news media and Congress. The main options offered by the Democrats and Republicans involved expanding insurance company coverage, not replacing it. The debate — as portrayed in advertising and the news media — concerned only how much insurance coverage should expand and who should pay for it. Since the power elite did not favor it, the single-payer alternative was dismissed as "politically unrealistic." As usually happens in a battle between a large industry and the public, Congress sided with the industry.

*Progressives own or control few banks, corporations, stores, universities, think tanks, television stations, or churches. Members of the power elite own or control thousands of these institutions.*

Perhaps the clearest example of elite power is the U.S. tax structure. In *America: Who Really Pays the Taxes?*, journalists Donald L. Barlett and James B. Steele document how the wealthy are able to keep their tax rates low at the expense of the poor and middle class.[14] Barlett and Steele demonstrate the inequity of the tax code by comparing the taxes paid by two representative families in the early 1990s: Jacques Cotton, a single father of two small children living in Portland, Oregon, who earned a little less than the median family income, and then President George Bush and his wife Barbara. In 1991, the Bushes paid 18.1 percent of their $1,324,500 income for federal, state, and local income taxes, Social Security tax, personal property tax, and real estate tax. In 1992, Cotton paid 19.8 percent of his income of $33,500 for the same taxes. The tax *rate* on Cotton's moderate income was nine percent higher than the rate on the Bushes' enormous income. (17–20)

This case is not unique. The tax code allows wealthy people to write off much of their income so they only pay taxes on a small portion of the total — greatly reducing their effective rate of taxation. In 1989, more than five thousand households with income over $200,000 paid federal income tax at an effective rate of less than five percent. In contrast, over seven million households with income between $25,000 and $30,000 paid federal income taxes at an effective rate of ten percent. (46)

Barlett and Steele document how politicians change the tax code to protect the wealthy and shift the tax burden onto the middle class and poor. Summarizing, they write:

> Just what kind of a [tax] system is this?
>
> Very simply, a system that is rigged by members of Congress and the executive branch. A system that caters to the demands of special-interest groups at the expense of all Americans. A system that responds to the appeals of the powerful and influential and ignores the needs of the powerless. A system that thrives on cutting deals and rewarding the privileged. A system that permits those in office to take care of themselves and their friends. (21)

Not only have the wealthy been able to keep their taxes low, but they have also managed to mollify people by propagating several myths. Defenders of the elite contend the tax system currently soaks the wealthy and at a rate greater than ever before. They further argue that burdensome taxes discourage new investment and hinder job creation. They also maintain that American corporations cannot compete overseas because onerous taxes hobble them. (15)

Actually, taxes on the wealthy have dropped dramatically over the last five decades. An IRS study shows that the effective tax rate on the richest one percent has dropped from about 45% in 1950 to about 23% in 1990.[15] Corporations now pay much lower taxes than they did in the 1950s and at a much lower rate than corporations in other industrialized countries do.

Defenders of the elite have also routinely distorted the terms of the debate to obscure their true goals. In looking at the history of federal in-

come taxes, Barlett and Steele conclude:

> Over time, much of the debate concerning tax rates would boil down to two phrases. Tax legislation that would increase the rate on the wealthy was called "class warfare." Tax legislation that would reduce the rate on the wealthy was called "tax reform." (65)

Figure 3.1 shows how skewed is the distribution of wealth in the United States. A study by the Federal Reserve shows that in 1989 the wealthiest one percent of households — those with net worth of at least $2.3 million — owned nearly forty percent of the nation's wealth. The next wealthiest nineteen percent — with net worth of $180,000 to $2.3 million per household — owned another forty percent. This left only twenty percent of the nation's wealth for the other eighty percent of U.S. households. The United States has become the most economically stratified of industrialized nations, surpassing even countries like Britain which have moved away from their feudal pasts.

## Figure 3.1: Approximate Distribution of Wealth in the United States, 1989

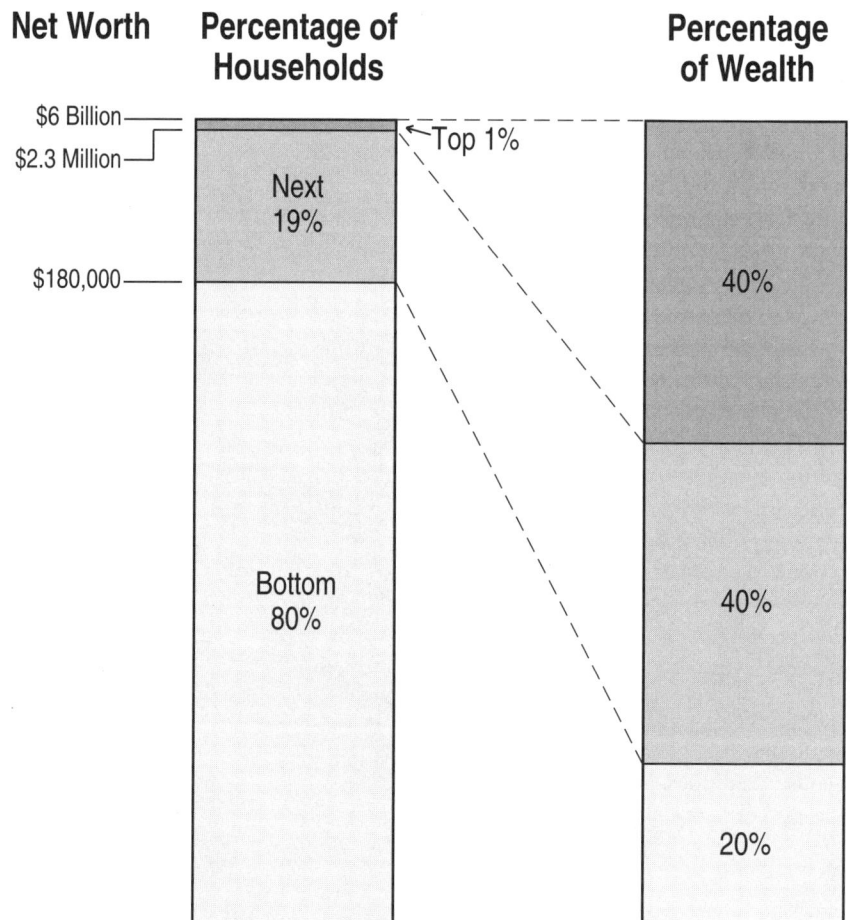

Source: *New York Times* quoting U.S. Federal Reserve data[16]

## Gross Inequity is Indefensible

*There is no reasonable justification for one person to make as much money in a few days as another earns in a lifetime. No matter how smart, beautiful, refined, charismatic, brave, clever, educated, experienced, or hard working, no human being deserves to receive five thousand times as much money as another. But billionaires in our society today typically realize more return on their investments in just two days than someone paid the minimum wage earns in fifty years of hard work.*[17]

*Our economic system rewards luck, inheritance, chicanery, and raw power. It scarcely rewards effort and usually discounts virtue. In defending this absurd system, apologists can ultimately cite only its supremacy and invincibility: it exists, and so far, no one has been able to change it, therefore it must be worthy. Skewed political and social relations rest on similarly specious logic and equally lame excuses. They too are indefensible in a civilized society.*

## Elite Interests Dictate Foreign Policy

In the realm of foreign affairs, Noam Chomsky and other critics have extensively documented how the U.S. elite supports the elite in other "friendly" countries. Atrocities committed by countries aligned with U.S.'s elite interests are usually ignored or downplayed, but those of "terrorist" countries are vociferously condemned. Indigenous peoples' struggles against exploitation by multinational corporations or local elites are usually labeled "communist aggression" or "terrorist rebellion" by U.S. elites and are subject to U.S. military intervention or covert action by the CIA.[18] But those countries that allow western corporations to operate without restriction ("free trade") are granted Most Favored Trade status.

> *When I give food to the poor, they call me a saint.*
>
> *When I ask why the poor have no food, they call me a communist.*
>
> — Dom Helder Camara, Brazilian Archbishop

For example, the United States has vigorously condemned every possible violation of human rights in Cuba and maintained a devastating blockade of this small nation for forty years. In contrast, despite the massive brutality shown in the 1989 Tiananmen Square massacre, the United States has downplayed much worse transgressions in China. Similarly, the United States launched the Persian Gulf war against Iraq when it invaded the autocratic government of Kuwait. However, when Indonesia invaded East Timor in 1975 and killed over one-third of the civilian population, the United States did nothing to stop the violence and, in fact, continued to sell weapons to Indonesia.

## Elite Power is Hidden

The extent of elite power is concealed from most people — hidden behind a pluralist facade. In a true pluralist system, individuals band together according to their interests and struggle on behalf of their group. In an ideal pluralist system, each group wins sometimes and loses sometimes. If all groups are equally powerful, then each receives approximately an equal share of resources. Even if some are more powerful than others, over time, the theory goes, victory shifts from one to another and everyone is eventually rewarded.

> *You can fool all the people all the time if the advertising budget is big enough.*
>
> — Ed Rollins, former Republican political campaign consultant

However, in our actual society, the overwhelming power of elite interests ensures that they completely win most of the battles and they strongly shape the outcome in the rest. The lower echelons — the homeless and the working poor — are virtually shut out.

Our society only resembles the pluralist ideal in those few cases when a conflict is between comparably powerful factions of the power elite. Regular people may also be able to win a battle if they are able to organize themselves into large enough groups to wield a significant amount of power.

> *I spent thirty-three years and four months in active military service as a member of this country's most agile military force, the Marine Corps. I served in all commissioned ranks from Second Lieutenant to Major-General. And during that period, I spent most of my time being a high class muscle-man for Big Business, for Wall Street, and for the Bankers. In short, I was a racketeer, a gangster for capitalism.*
>
> *I suspected I was just part of a racket at the time. Now I am sure of it. Like all the members of the military profession, I never had a thought of my own until I left the service. My mental faculties remained in suspended animation while I obeyed the orders of higher-ups. This is typical with everyone in the military service.*
>
> *I helped make Mexico, especially Tampico, safe for American oil interests in 1914. I helped make Haiti and Cuba a decent place for the National City Bank boys to collect revenues in. I helped in the raping of half a dozen Central American republics for the benefits of Wall Street. The record of racketeering is long. I helped purify Nicaragua for the international banking house of Brown Brothers in 1909-1912. I brought light to the Dominican Republic for American sugar interests in 1916. In China, I helped to see to it that Standard Oil went its way unmolested.*
>
> — Major General Smedley Butler, USMC, speech, 1933[19]

Unfortunately, even in these two circumstances, the spoils are usually divided solely among the winners, rather than allocated in a way that might be best for the common good. Weak or invisible entities like young children, future generations, and the environment have no way to compete and may completely lose out.

## Progressive Change is Subverted

Those progressive groups that play the pluralist game and work entirely within the existing political system are often manipulated by the elite and compromised. Since these groups have limited resources, they must enlist the help of more powerful, but less progressive players such as the news media, business people, congressional moderates, mainstream foundations, and moderate voters. However, in order to maintain their support from and influence with these groups, they usually must also adjust their political stance to fit within the norms of the established order. This often requires them to abandon their positions and limit their demands.

Especially in Washington, D.C., progressive organizations often must bargain, haggle, and compromise to achieve even small gains. Fair-minded activists must compete with well-funded political hacks and lobbyists. Fair and sensible solutions must compete with the vested interests of businesses, trade groups, parochial labor unions, and dog-

*A politician thinks of the next election; a statesman thinks of the next generation.*
— James Freeman Clarke

matic religious groups and with the fetishes and whims of powerful fat cats. Elite interests deliberately malign and distort reasonable solutions until these solutions seem foolish or dangerous. Those who refuse to play these power games are ignored by the influential powerbrokers and media barons or are dismissed as extremists.

As difficult as it is to play the pluralist game, it is even more difficult to bring about any truly fundamental change since this usually requires working outside the political system and challenging the core of elite power. When directly challenged, elite interests employ the full range of their formidable arsenal to resist and retaliate. Dissident groups are pointedly ignored until they grow quite large in size and stature. Then they are often slandered, harassed, belittled, infiltrated, burglarized, defrauded, and entrapped. When progressive activists are able to create some significant change, they are often threatened, jailed, fired from their jobs, assaulted, or even killed.

*Help the police. Beat yourself up!*
— Anarchist graffiti

As a pointed example, in 1990 in Oakland, California, a car bomb seriously injured Judi Bari and Darryl Cherney. These two EarthFirst! organizers had been particularly effective in bringing together environmentalists and loggers to oppose clearcutting of ancient forests, the export of mill jobs overseas, and other destructive logging company practices. In investigating the case, the Oakland police and the FBI brushed aside the many death threats directed at these activists in the previous year. Instead, the authorities accused Bari and Cherney of planting the bomb, even though the physical evidence showed this was absurd.[20]

To further distract, weaken, or disrupt effective change groups, elite interests sometimes actively encourage racism, sexism, classism, and homophobia. For example, company owners often attempt to disrupt labor unions by encouraging hatred towards new immigrants, women, or less-skilled laborers. Currently, many mainstream commercial radio stations (owned and controlled by the elite) carry incendiary "hate radio" talk shows in which hosts and callers hurl racial and sexual epithets and discuss ways to kill their enemies. Federal regulatory agencies ignore the antisocial behavior of these stations but closely scrutinize progressive, nonprofit stations, which right-wing critics accuse of airing "one-sided political diatribes" and "filth."

## Vulnerability and Fear Induce Conservatism

Given the enormous power of elite interests and their ability to crush opponents, most people are quite aware of their vulnerability. The power structure does not tolerate much dissent or divergence, and people fear being singled out as rebels. People accurately perceive that the personal risk of stepping out of line and challenging the structure is usually quite large compared to the benefits they will personally gain. The risk looks worthwhile only if there is a high probability that their efforts will somehow bring about dramatic positive change.

This fear may also feed on early conditioning. In our childhoods, probably most of us tried at least once to stand up to the oppression we saw around us. Rather than being praised and supported for our efforts, our parents or peers may have criticized, ridiculed, ignored, ostracized, or even physically brutalized us. Small and powerless in the situation, we learned not to challenge the status quo. Even now that we are adults and even in situations where we are unlikely to be punished, our painful memories and internalized fears may hold us back.

*No other offense has ever been visited with such severe penalties as seeking to help the oppressed.*
— Clarence Darrow

Not only is it difficult to rebel in this society, but even those who play strictly by the rules are vulnerable. Bad things happen to good people, and our unforgiving society provides only a minimal safety net. Multitudes of omnipresent homeless people continually remind us how much worse our lives could become if we are not careful.

Many people rightfully fear that change of any sort will just make their lives worse. Power struggles are disruptive, and those people with the fewest resources usually suffer the most. For them, though the current situation may be miserable, it is at least a known and limited misery.

Moreover, our current society is not the worst possible. Though elite powers are tyrannical and oppress billions of people here and around the world, they *do* maintain U.S. society at a certain functional level, enabling many people to have a tolerable life. Our rich society — with its free public schools, rule of law, balance of powers, and free enterprise — does a minimal job of providing for basic needs and restraining hatred, greed, and craziness. It does mitigate — at least to some extent — bigotry and other social oppressions. It does curb the most egregious corruption and domination. People still have some freedom of religion, freedom of expression, the right to vote, and the right to form and join independent organizations. They can still exert influence on some issues.

In comparison, alternative institutions proposed by progressive activists often seem paltry or pathetic, and activists do not usually have the resources to implement these alternatives. Those few times when activists *can* implement them, elite interests malign, undermine, or destroy them. Consequently, there are few viable alternatives. Many people then conclude that conventional institutions are the best ones possible.

*Under capitalism, it's dog eat dog. Under Communism, it's just the opposite. — Polish joke*

For these reasons, many people argue philosophically, as did Dr. Pangloss in Voltaire's **Candide,** that "all is for the best" in this "best of all possible worlds." Even many poor and oppressed people, believing they will never do any better, adamantly support the status quo and oppose efforts to change it.

## OBSTACLE 2: DESTRUCTIVE CULTURAL CONDITIONING

Humans are creatures of habit. Typically, we do the same things every day in about the same manner. If we did not, we would have to make decisions constantly about every facet of our lives: what to eat, when to sleep, where to go, what to do, what clothes to wear, who to talk to, what phrases to speak, what mannerisms to use, and on and on. It is much easier to find a reasonable way to act just once and then do it the same way after that.

Consequently, we adopt habitual ways of behaving, and we raise our children to act these same ways too. We socialize and civilize each other by discouraging destructive or unpleasant behavior and encouraging decorous behavior. This process establishes broad cultural norms that specify what is acceptable and expected.

All humans set up and adhere to cultural norms; it is generally a desirable way to run society. However, when cultural norms are destructive or limiting, they can block our potential as human beings.[21] For example, cultural norms dictate that young men accept their "duty" to go off to war stoically, even though they may be maimed or killed for no legitimate purpose. If young men did not accept this norm, they might refuse to fight and instead demand the end of the war system. They could save their own lives and make the world safer for everyone.

*Sometime they'll give a war and nobody will come. — Carl Sandburg*

Cultural norms include traditions, customs, religious practices, rituals, fashions, fads, peer pressure, and gossip. Some norms are codified into laws and regulations, but most are simply accepted as "normal behavior." Norms may be based on deeply held moral values or they may actually violate them. For instance, many commonly accepted sales tactics violate the ethic of honesty. Advertisements also frequently depend on (and promote) the "seven deadly sins" — especially avarice, lust, and envy.[22] Most cultural norms are relevant to our current society, but some are remnants of some ancient purpose, now long forgotten yet still passed along from generation to generation.

Cultural norms are widespread and deeply instilled. Some, like fashions, are easily recognized, but most cultural norms are so pervasive that we discount their potent influence on our lives. Frequently, what we consider personal decisions are actually dictated by strong societal norms. For instance, the dominant culture urges us to marry, bear two children, eat junk food, drink coffee and soft drinks, watch television, drive cars, shop in malls, buy presents for everyone we know for an ever-increasing number of holidays, compete with others, and scoff at the government. Women are expected to shave their legs and armpits, and wear makeup and jewelry. Men are expected to follow sports avidly, drink alcohol, and act tough around other men. Most people accept without question these and thousands of other norms, large and small. It is usually only when someone refrains from owning a car, fails to buy presents for others, or commits some other heinous cultural crime that people notice.

*People in groups tend to agree on courses of action which, as individuals, they know are stupid. — Graffiti*

Norms surround us in an extensive and mostly unseen web that profoundly affects who we are, how we act, what we believe, how we vote, what we consider pleasurable, and how we think. Cultural norms influence every aspect of our lives from superficial aspects like our music preferences and shopping patterns to important societal functions like our childrearing practices.

Cultural norms even dictate the various ways that people rebel against the dominant culture. American individualism is a cultural norm. The counterculture of the 1960s required long hair, blue jeans, work shirts, and peasant dresses. Punks today must have tattoos and body piercings. Hip artists must wear black clothes and dour expressions.

Much of our core culture and norms derive from our ethnic heritage. Because everyone in our immediate family shares the same culture and norms, they are usually invisible to us. It is only in a multicultural environment that our cultural upbringing comes into view. For example, my German and English ancestry directs me to be logical, responsible, and hard working, but also perfectionistic, emotionally impassive, and uptight around physical closeness. Living and associating with people from other backgrounds and cultures for the past thirty years — especially progressive and new age activists — has led me to notice and change some of my ways. I am now much more comfortable with mistakes, emotions, and closeness. I have also learned that when other people are not logical, responsible, or hard working in the way that I am, it is usually not because they are irrational, irresponsible, or lazy (as I was led to believe), but because they are operating from different cultural norms.

Chauvinism, prejudice, bigotry, homophobia, and other oppressive attitudes typically emanate from cultural norms. Because they are implanted at an early age and held so widely, they are difficult to identify or change.

*Children are natural mimics who act like their parents despite every effort to teach them good manners.*
— Mark Twain

For instance, classism completely infuses our culture and deeply affects how everyone thinks and acts about money and worth. Often owning-class people are arrogant and disdainful of others. They typically do not discuss money openly. Middle-class professionals frequently are uptight, insecure, squeamish, and overly polite. They usually are embarrassed to talk about money issues. Working-class people frequently are insecure, reticent, and distrustful, yet completely open about discussing money issues.

Because classism is so common and its effects so convoluted, most people do not recognize it as the source of these myriad behaviors and attitudes. Instead they accept this conduct as normal or attribute it to quirks of individual personality. This leaves classism difficult to recognize or challenge.

*The most important factor for the development of the individual is the structure and the values of the society into which he was born.*
— Erich Fromm

Most cultural norms are mindlessly passed along from one generation to the next. Norms that do not work eventually fade away, and new norms arise to deal with changes caused by weather, migration, or new technology.

However, some cultural norms are deliberately promoted. Cultural leaders such as newspaper columnist Ann Landers, talk show hosts Rush Limbaugh and Paul Harvey, and prominent religious leaders like the Pope, Billy Graham,

and Louis Farrakhan promote particular standards of acceptable behavior. Entertainers, employers, teachers, and gang leaders also establish cultural norms in their areas of influence — some positive, some destructive. Generally, the more exposure we have to these cultural leaders, the more prestige they hold with us. Also, the more they can exert power over us, the more they influence our attitudes.

With their control of society's resources, elite interests can encourage cultural norms that bolster their power and wealth. Through corporate advertising and the entertainment industry, they have the ability to steer the dominant culture in particular directions. They promote some positive norms like litter reduction, but some elite interests also promote cigarettes, alcohol, sex, violence, militarism, mindless consumerism, deference to authority, apathy towards politics and progressive change, and hatred towards racial minorities, foreigners, immigrants, homosexuals, the poor, and anyone who challenges the status quo in other than "acceptable" ways. They relentlessly promote the idea that "capitalism is good, socialism is bad" to the extent that most people fervently believe this mantra even though they have no idea what the terms "capitalism" and "socialism" mean.

Corporate advertising is especially effective in establishing cultural norms since it is slick, pervasive, and incessant. Every day, the average American is bombarded by three thousand marketing messages. No one can completely resist this torrent of ideas and images. Children are especially susceptible to advertising's influence since they have less experience and understanding of the world. Typical American children now see more than 100,000 TV commercials between birth and high school graduation.[23]

*Give me a child for the first seven years, and you may do what you like with him afterwards.*
— Jesuit Maxim

*There is no absurdity so palpable but that it may be firmly planted in the human head if only you begin to inculcate it before the age of five, by constantly repeating it with an air of great solemnity.* — Arthur Schopenhauer

Besides promoting particular products, advertising insidiously sells the idea that any need or dissatisfaction can

## A Few Examples of Destructive Cultural Norms

- Individualism, selfishness
- Materialism and consumerism
- Competition
- Drug consumption (alcohol, nicotine, caffeine, etc.)
- Classism, sexism, racism, ageism, homophobia, etc.
- Militarism

and should be rectified by buying something. Under the onslaught of consumer advertising over the last hundred years, selfish individualism has displaced traditional norms of community cooperation and support.

Because social norms are so strong, those who challenge or stray from the accepted order in any significant way are usually criticized or ostracized, even if their new ways are more reasonable and humane. There is strong pressure to conform and to pressure others to conform. This makes it difficult to create and diffuse new, positive cultural norms.

## OBSTACLE 3: DYSFUNCTIONAL EMOTIONAL CONDITIONING

As described briefly in Chapter 1, research over the last few decades has shown that when a person is severely or repeatedly traumatized, especially as a small child, the trauma is etched into her psyche. She is then much more likely to "act out" destructive or dysfunctional behavior for the rest of her life.

Severe trauma can induce rigid, patterned behavior — behavior that may have been protective at the time of the trauma but is not a rational response to current circumstances. For example, many victims of childhood sexual abuse, whose trust was severely betrayed, find it difficult to trust other people — even their supportive, loving friends.[24]

Childhood trauma also frequently induces low self-esteem or self-hatred. Victims assume they must somehow be evil enough to warrant the physical, sexual, or verbal abuse that was directed at them. This causes them to feel fearful, uncertain, docile, worthless, depressed, cynical, hopeless, and suicidal. Many people with low self-worth become addicted to alcohol or other drugs to suppress these deep, painful feelings.[25] With a low opinion of themselves, victims of abuse are also often desperate for loving attention, but incapable of loving or supporting others. This makes them poor parents.

*Many people truly believe they are stupid, ugly, or worthless because they were told this repeatedly throughout their childhood.*

Severe trauma affects some victims in a different way: they become violent and domineering. Some grow up to become violent criminals; some abuse their own children.[26]

In our society today, an alarming number of children are subjected to severe mistreatment in their homes. There are almost one million substantiated cases of child abuse or life-threatening neglect each year in the United States.[27] A federal advisory panel estimated that every year 2,000 infants and young children die from violence in the home and 140,000 (about 0.2% of all children) are seriously injured, leaving 18,000 children permanently disabled.[28]

Many parents do not physically hurt their children but still injure them psychologically by berating, bullying, fon-dling, rejecting, or ignoring them. Some children are traumatized by witnessing their parents venomously fight with each other.

Even children who grow up in stable, loving families may nevertheless face violence at school or in their neighborhoods. Children who are small, shy, or perceived as being different in some way are especially vulnerable to being ridiculed, threatened, isolated, or beaten by their peers.

*Sticks and stones can break your bones, but words can break your heart.* — Graffiti

Overall, a very large percentage of U.S. children are traumatized in some way. A recent survey of 4,000 adolescents (aged 12–17) found that 13 percent of females had been subjected to unwanted sexual contact, 21 percent of males and 13 percent of females had been physically assaulted, and 43 percent of males and 35 percent of females had witnessed firsthand someone being shot with a gun, knifed, sexually assaulted, mugged, robbed, or threatened with a weapon. An astonishing 72 percent of all the adolescents had directly observed someone being beaten up and badly hurt.[29]

## *Human Being*

**Contents**: *100% Pure Human Being*
**Care Instructions**: *Hand wash with mild soap, towel dry. Regularly shower with warm affection. Leave self-worth intact. Use no bleach. Do not tumble, squeeze, or wring dry.*

Trauma does not end with adolescence, of course. Adults suffer from domestic violence, rape, assault, murder, and war. In the United States in 1997, there were 18,200 murders, 300,000 sexual assaults, 1.8 million aggravated assaults, and 5.5 million simple assaults.[30] It is estimated that about 1.5 million women are raped or battered each year by their husbands or partners.[31]

Insults, threats, belligerence, and hostility are also prevalent in our culture. Moreover, we are all affected by the affront to dignity inherent in poverty, sexism, racism, classism, ageism, militarism, cultural chauvinism, and so on. Even relatively minor trauma can affect us — nibbling at our self-esteem, making us less flexible, inducing irrational fears and prejudices, and hindering our ability to address problems effectively.

Consequently, we all have been wounded in a variety of ways and have some emotional scars. Our injuries are buried deep within our psyches where they are difficult to fathom or remove. For example, most of us have long-term addictions of some sort — that is, we have compulsive, obsessive, fanatical, or inhibited behavior around alcohol, cigarettes, caffeine, sex, food, sweets, drugs, gambling, sports, shopping, TV, money, religion, or work that interferes with our ability to live good lives.[32]

Emotional injuries usually dissipate with time, but the worst injuries can be quite persistent. Even many decades later, our most severe emotional wounds are often still raw and tender. When poked, they stir up a swarm of intense feelings — fear, grief, and anger — that may lead us to respond in seriously dysfunctional ways. Those people who have been most severely injured typically behave the worst, terrorizing and wounding others. But in times of stress, all of us tend to behave badly, often directing our anger at those who are unable to escape or fight back: small children. In this way, the disposition toward hostility and violence is irrationally conveyed from generation to generation.

> **Common Emotional Dysfunctions**
>
> • Irrationality
> • Chronic rage
> • Depression
> • Low self-esteem
> • Inhibitions, phobias
> • Compulsions, obsessions
> • Addictions

## A Sick Society

Even worse for society, those who share the same dysfunctional behavior or attitudes sometimes band together, develop a rationalization for their warped perspective, and promote their ideas to others. For example, some women — who have been severely brutalized by men — have argued that men are inherently evil brutes and that the only solution is to imprison or castrate them all. Because this perspective is so harsh and unusual, it seems bizarre to most of us.

However, in a similar fashion, people have concocted equally irrational ideas that are now widely tolerated. They have promoted their fears (xenophobia, homophobia, gynephobia, and so on), their angry responses (lynchings, corporal punishment, vengeance, militarism, hazing, hierarchical domination, cultural chauvinism), and their compulsions (smoking, gambling, drinking alcohol, using drugs, dogmatism). All of these are twisted, misdirected, and ineffectual responses to oppression. Nevertheless, they have become so pervasive that many of them are now institutionalized in schools, fraternities, churches, business, the military, and advertising. They are accepted as cultural norms.

*The floggings will continue until morale improves.* — Office Graffiti

Consequently, we live in a "sick society" with a culture dominated by racist, homophobic, vindictive, and violent ideas.[33] We are routinely bombarded by images and stories of brutality in graphic television coverage of automobile crashes, executions, bombings, and wars. Children learn spite and prejudice from their parents, other adults, and their peers. Fears are passed along through books, movies, television, and games.

Living in a crazy society makes all of us more fearful and isolated from one another. We are afraid to talk about our troubles for fear others will criticize us for our shortcomings and reject us. We are afraid to get too close to others for fear we will be forced to bear their problems and woes. We are afraid to disagree with others for fear they will show us to be wrong or assault us. We are even afraid of working with those with whom we agree for fear they will abandon us in trying times. This isolation and fragmentation make it difficult for us to get together to solve our mutual problems or to challenge the power elite. For this reason, elite interests often encourage individualism, social isolation, and fear of others.

## Emotional Shackles

Clearly, it would be far easier to create a good society if everyone were happy and acted rationally. It would even be a bit easier to bring about positive change if just the majority of progressive activists were rational most of the time. But progressive activists share the same cultural conditioning and carry the same emotional baggage as others. Just like everyone else, activists are often self-righteous, arrogant, guilt-ridden, fearful, dogmatic, bureaucratic, irrational, depressed, dishonest, violent, vindictive, and fanatical. Many activists act out chauvinism and prejudice. They have addictions, compulsions, phobias, and deep feelings of self-doubt.*

*The greater the feeling of inferiority that has been experienced, the more powerful is the urge to conquest and the more violent the emotional agitation.* — Alfred Adler

Emotional injuries often limit activists' ability to listen to others, discern the truth, or lovingly support or even cooperate with others. Activists' behavior is often patterned and rigid, making them unable to address new situations flexibly. More than a few activists crave raw, gut-level retaliation more than they desire positive change. When they spew these feelings and behaviors at other activists or manifest them in political action, they can wreak havoc on progressive change movements.

Emotional baggage can also disempower activists. In difficult times, activists may erroneously feel their situation is as grim as it was during the worst days of their childhood when they were small, weak, and ignorant. Emotional injuries may also prevent activists from recogniz-

*Madness takes its toll. Please have exact change.* — Office Graffiti

---

\* Lest my phrasing erroneously convey that I am somehow beyond irrationality or above petty foolishness, let me assure you that I am as crazy as the next person and I have done my fair share of acting out inappropriate and counterproductive behavior.

ing positive solutions or remembering them once discovered.

Though progressive activists seek change, their internalized fears may limit how much change they can imagine or tolerate. Even those who seek to change society down to the roots often fear changing themselves if it means risking the loss of the bits of security and control they have accumulated over the years.

> *I know that most men, including those at ease with problems of the greatest complexity, can seldom accept even the simplest and most obvious truth, if it be such as would oblige them to admit the falsity of conclusions which they have delighted in explaining to colleagues, which they have proudly taught to others, and which they have woven, thread by thread, into the fabric of their lives. — Leo Tolstoy*

The nature of progressive change sometimes pushes activists towards especially bad behavior. Struggling nearly alone in a hostile world, they may huddle together for comfort, spawning the elitist and irrational behavior that Irving Janis calls "groupthink."[34] Out of desperation or self-righteousness, a small number of change organizations employ some of the techniques of mind control to recruit, indoctrinate, and manipulate their members. Some activists — those especially vulnerable to manipulation because of emotional hurts — are drawn into these organizations.[35]

---

## Some Symptoms of Groupthink

- Moral self-righteousness, elitism
- Pressure for conformity, vicious attacks on anyone who questions the group's direction
- Self-censorship
- Single-mindedness and tunnel vision
- Suppression of bad news
- Insulation from outside criticism or ideas

---

## OBSTACLE 4: WIDESPREAD IGNORANCE

Many people have limited knowledge about how society functions, and they passively accept conventional notions about democracy, free enterprise, addictions, personality disorders, and so forth. Most are also woefully ignorant of progressive alternatives. Hence, when people do learn about a useful alternative idea or method, they usually have little idea how to implement it in their own community.

This ignorance derives from many sources. Our public schools do a poor job of teaching people even the most basic

information. For example, a 1992 national survey for the Department of Education found that more than 40 million adults (about 21% of the adult population) are illiterate or only barely literate.[36] A far greater percentage of students do not learn the basics of how our government and our economy operate. Few learn even rudimentary interpersonal skills.

As noted in the sections above, this state of affairs exists in part because people tell each other erroneous ideas based on outmoded cultural norms or prejudice and pass these ideas on to their children. Moreover, elite interests actively use the news media to obscure their mechanisms of societal control and to circulate myths that perpetuate racism, sexism, classism, and so on. The elite also suppress information about progressive alternatives and belittle the ones that publicly emerge.

> *The trouble with people is not that they don't know, but that they know so much that ain't so. — Josh Billings*

Clearly, it would be easier to create a good society if everyone had basic literacy and cooperation skills. It would be easier if activists were knowledgeable and skilled, but most progressive activists are also quite ignorant. Activists typically have limited progressive change experience, only a rudimentary understanding of how the world functions, and only dim visions of possible alternatives. Their ignorance and lack of experience often lead to inefficient, ineffectual, or even counterproductive change efforts.

There are several reasons why most activists are inadequately prepared:

• Progressive change is one of the few complex endeavors in which it is assumed that, after watching others do it a few times, activists will be able do it themselves. Conceptually, progressive change seems straightforward, but to do it well requires extensive knowledge and skills. It is at least as difficult as building a skyscraper, programming a computer, performing surgery, or assembling a television. Yet it is often lumped in with other "simple" tasks like eating, washing dishes, or driving an automobile — and think how many years of our childhoods we spent mastering these tasks. Many of the skills required of activists are the same ones required of managers, planners, lawyers, social workers, and therapists — skills taught in multiyear college programs and honed through years of practice.

> *Just because you watch a television set, doesn't mean you know how to build one.*

As in the complex job of building a skyscraper, not everyone who works for progressive change needs to know how to do every task well — and some activists may only need to know how to do a few jobs. Clearly though, in each change organization, there must be *some* activists who understand and have experience performing each of the essential tasks. Furthermore, every activist must be able to work with other activists to coordinate their efforts.

• A large percentage of progressive activists have only worked for change a short time. It is often just a few months from the time an activist is first stirred to join a progressive organization and fight for change until the time she burns out and leaves.

Since activists are generally not active for long, they often have little idea how to conduct a social change campaign. Many are unaware of historical change efforts (including how other activists overcame problems) and ignorant of theoretical analyses (like socialism, anarchism, feminism, pacifism, environmentalism, multiculturalism) that help explain larger political, economic, and cultural processes. Few have a chance to learn or develop the skills they need to work cooperatively with other people. Moreover, many harbor unexamined racist, sexist, xenophobic, or other reactionary attitudes. Moreover, many activists are young and so are inexperienced in basic life knowledge and skills.

> *Experience is a hard teacher because she gives the test first, the lesson afterwards.*
> — Vernon Sanders Law

• Since progressive organizations have little money, they usually focus narrowly on their primary change work and skimp on "extraneous" education. Often the educational opportunities they do offer focus on immediate tactical skills, not strategic planning or visionary thinking.

• Activists often favor quick action over study and reflection. Our consumer culture encourages shallow, short-term, reactive thinking and discourages skill-building and long-term planning. Activists often thrash each other with stories about horrendous calamities that they feel they must immediately correct. This fosters a movement culture of desperate urgency.

## Ignorance Greatly Hinders Change

Activist ignorance creates a myriad of obstacles for progressive organizations. Here are just a few of the many ways progressive activists blunder primarily because of their ignorance:

### • Hold Low Expectations and Feel Powerless

Like others in society, many activists accept that humans are inherently evil, greedy, or crazy or believe that humans cannot change very much. Others believe the claims of invincibility made by the power elite. Without knowing

> *After suffering years of frustration, many progressive activists are content merely to "make a statement" instead of actually being heard or to be heard rather than having influence or to have influence instead of having decision-making power or to seize decision-making power rather than creating a true democracy of empowered citizens.*

that ordinary people have generated major positive changes in society countless times before, activists believe they have little power.

Activists with these beliefs are likely to feel discouraged and hopeless even before they begin — they are programmed to fail. Feeling powerless, they often content themselves with inflicting some bit of revenge against a few powerholders. This may provide some immediate personal gratification, but it usually does not create much positive change.

### • Hold Shallow Analyses or Goals

Activists often put forth simplistic, bumpersticker critiques of social problems and organize flashy, but inconsequential political demonstrations. Though these tactics can quickly generate a great deal of excitement and may seem to elicit quick responses, the potential for real, long-term change is usually limited.

If progressives can guide people to the left with shallow, flamboyant rhetoric, then manipulators like Ronald Reagan or Newt Gingrich — with their armies of propaganda specialists and immense advertising resources — can lure them even further to the far right. A progressive movement for change is quite fragile unless it can instill

> *I don't want you to follow me or anyone else... I would not lead you into [the] promised land if I could, because if I could lead you in, someone else could lead you out.* — Eugene V. Debs

into a large number of people a deep understanding both of society's problems and of progressive alternatives. There are no easy shortcuts.

### • Focus Narrowly on Superficial Change or Social Service

Elite interests continually provide assurance that everything is fine — when social problems surface, the powerholders swear they need only rein in those few people who cheat, steal, or murder. Inexperienced activists often do not understand how deep and tangled are society's problems and how extensive the changes must be to get to the root causes. These activists usually offer superficial or feeble reforms that, if implemented, would not count for much in the long run.

They may also focus on providing social services to those injured by injustice, inequity, or disaster. There is, of course, value in ameliorating present suffering: feeding the homeless, sheltering battered women, providing health care to the elderly, repairing environmental damage, and the like. However, this work does not alter the underlying structures that perpetually create and maintain suffering. It is far better to ensure

> *There are a thousand hacking at the branches of evil to one who is striking at the root.*
> — Henry David Thoreau

---

## Three Kinds of Progressive Action

• **Social Service** — helping the sick, uneducated, old, young, or poor to have a better life; or repairing damage to the natural environment.

• **Policy Change** — working to change specific policies and practices of government, business, or social organizations (such as churches).

• **Social Change** — working to fundamentally transform society so that it is more democratic, humane, just, cooperative, compassionate, and peaceful in all realms.

---

that no child is battered or malnourished than to provide support forevermore to someone with brain damage caused by battering or nutritional deficiencies.

### • Focus Narrowly on a Single Issue or an Immediate Problem

Activists often focus on a single issue that personally affects them and ignore all other issues. However, our society is extremely interconnected. If activists concentrate exclusively on a single, narrow issue, another issue will often undo or undercut their good work.

For example, the union movement of the 1930s successfully raised wages for industrial workers and made factories safer. However, because it did not make broader changes, these gains have been partially lost as the workforce has shifted more to service industries and as factory owners have automated industrial plants or moved them overseas. Efforts to make automobiles less polluting have been undercut by the increasing number of cars on the road and the increasing amount each one is driven. These increases stem partly from the greater distances people must commute after they move to the suburbs to escape from polluting factories, urban crime, and automobile noise. To be effective, activists must understand how all the problems and oppressions fit together and they must have the resources to tackle multiple problems simultaneously.

Of course, to win a campaign, activists must also focus on an accessible and immediate problem that captures peoples' imaginations. Still, if their focus is too narrow, then their solution will only address a single situation and it will only last while people are actively agitating. Members of the power elite will still hold the reins of power and will re-institute the old forms as soon as progressive activists stop pressuring them. Clearly, it is better to create an enduring democratic process and empower people to participate in that process, but inexperienced activists often do not see this or do not know how to do it.

*Whenever we try to pick out anything by itself, we find it hitched to everything else in the universe.* — John Muir

### • Focus Narrowly on Individual Powerholders

It is usually easiest to focus attention on a single powerholder who appears to be responsible for a particular problem — to persuade that person to change, force him to change, or oust him from his seat of power. However, single individuals — even wealthy or influential ones — usually have little real power. When a powerholder is persuaded to change his mind and begins to act on his new perspective, other powerful individuals and institutions usually remove him from power and step in to isolate or counteract whatever changes he may have made. Though it is more difficult, activists must fundamentally transform policies, cultural norms, and large institutions like governments, corporations, churches, and schools.

### • Focus Narrowly on Challenging Existing Institutions

Progressive activists often focus only on challenging existing institutions without creating progressive alternatives. But most current institutions serve important societal functions. If there are no alternatives that can serve these functions, then people will struggle to preserve the original institutions. Activists who seek only to eliminate these institutions will often end up fighting *against* the majority of people.[37]

### • Focus Narrowly on Progressive Alternatives

Other activists take the opposite tack and only focus on building progressive alternative institutions. However, if activists do not undercut existing institutions, then those institutions can usually use their strength to undermine or out-compete the progressive alternatives.

### • Advocate Positions to Promote a Parochial Interest

Sometimes activists argue for a position only because it helps them grab the limelight or advance their fundraising efforts. This usually does not lead to any significant progressive change.

### • Advocate Morally Dubious Positions

Sometimes — in the interest of expediency or out of sheer frustration — activists promote policies or tactics that are morally repulsive. By using tactics resembling those of their opponents, they may become similarly callous, untrustworthy, and oppressive.

For example, environmentalists concerned about toxic emissions from a factory might be satisfied if the plant were moved to Mexico. However, the workers at the factory would lose their jobs and the new factory would still emit toxics. Overall, this change would accomplish little, merely shifting misfortune elsewhere. Another example: activists might advocate murdering a police officer who routinely beats poor people and then frames them on assault charges. His

*Fanaticism consists in redoubling your efforts when you have forgotten your aim.* — George Santayana

murder would end an injustice, but it would extinguish a person's life and endorse bloodlust and killing.

### • Appeal to Prejudices or Fears

Activists often use guilt, anger, and fear to stimulate people to action. However, people charged up with intense emotions are more likely to form a lynch mob than to come up with solutions that are best for society.

For example, to attract the interest of blue-collar workers to a union, activists might raucously expose the homosexuality of a hated boss, or taunt a female manager with sexual insults. To appeal to gay professionals, activists might trash the mayor for his fundamentalist religious beliefs or blame recent immigrants for high government expenses. When encouraging business executives to promote women to top positions, activists might try to win support by snidely referring to the ethnicity of factory workers or by mocking environmentalists. All of these tactics are counterproductive in the long run.

*The road to Hell is paved with good intentions.* — Proverb

Even relatively mild tactics can have negative consequences. Every day progressive groups send direct mail funding appeals designed to scare and enrage people into impulsively supporting their causes. These simplistic fundraising letters provide little useful information and sometimes distort the policies of their opponents or exaggerate the danger of right-wing groups. Dishonest tactics frighten people, exploit their trust, perpetuate stereotypes, and foster a politics based on fear or arrogance rather than one of rational discourse. Deceptive tactics do not inform, enlighten, or empower people or advance democracy.

### • Appeal to Self-Interest

Some progressive groups attempt to advance their work by appealing to the self-interest of a group like working-class people or racial minorities. If the group eventually wins power, then it may use its newfound power to dominate others.

For example, in the early parts of the twentieth century it was considered to be in society's interest to provide cheap electricity, irrigation water, and other economic benefits to

## Figure 3.2: Various Perspectives on the Extent of One's Responsibility to Others

| Responsibility Extends To... | Interest in and Concern about Others' Situation or Plight | Phrases Describing Someone Who Acts This Way | Examples of Social Philosophies Based on this Perspective | Examples of Positive Political Activity Based on This Perspective [38] | Examples of Negative Political Activity Based on This Perspective | Who is Held Responsible When Bad Things Happen? |
|---|---|---|---|---|---|---|
| **One's Self** | None: only self-interest and self-preoccupation | Rugged individualist<br>Absorbed in daily life<br>Selfish | Free-enterprise<br>Entrepreneurialism<br>Libertarianism<br>Individualism | Self-defense (against attack or imposition) | Apathy<br>Selfishness | "Not me" |
| **One's Local Community, Neighborhood** | Empathy only with those one knows personally | Good neighbor<br>Community booster | Community cooperation<br>Anarchism | Resistance to new oppression from outside | Parochialism | "No one I know" |
| **One's Interest Group** | Empathy only with those of one's interest group or ethnic group | Team player<br>Partisan | Pluralism<br>Capitalism<br>Unionism<br>Gangsterism | Liberation from long-standing oppression | Triumph of one's group over others<br>Factionalism<br>Oligarchy | "Them" (the other group) |
| **One's Nation-State (the Government)** | Empathy only with people in one's country | Patriot<br>Citizen | Socialism<br>Statism | Democracy | Totalitarianism<br>Xenophobia<br>Isolationism<br>Imperialism | "Foreigners" |
| **The Whole World** | Empathy with everyone in the whole world | Statesperson<br>World citizen | Environmentalism<br>Internationalism | Stewardship | World domination | "God"<br>"No one" (all of society) |

rural farmers who made up a large part of the population. These subsidies helped poor farmers and ensured a steady source of cheap food for everyone. However, farmers now constitute a small percentage of the public, and many of these subsidies go to wealthy corporate farms that cause massive environmental damage. The subsidies are no longer good for society.

Figure 3.2 summarizes the ways people typically view their responsibility toward others. Narrowly focused perspectives tend toward selfishness, parochialism, factionalism, isolationism, or imperialism. Activists can avoid these problems only by adopting a broad orientation in which they look out for the interests of the whole world (including other species and the environment).

To bring about truly progressive change, activists must embody statesmanship, stewardship, self-sacrifice, and policies that help everyone. They must seek inclusive democracy, not just power or control for the activist camp or for a particular constituency.

### • Focus on Blame and Punishment

Many progressive activists share the dominant societal ideology that the way to stop oppression is to find out who is to blame and attack, immobilize, destroy, or "retrain" them. But this perspective can easily lead to more oppression. In fact, this punishment-revenge-control model of change is the same one used by those who originally set up prisons, military schools, mental hospitals, and police forces. Though the founders of these institutions may have had good intentions, the institutions they created are now frequently bastions of oppression.

*Might doesn't determine who is right, only who is left.* — Bumper sticker

Punishment-revenge-control is also the essence of gang warfare and clan feuding — conflicts in which victory usually comes to those who are most ferocious and who have the most firepower. Since progressive activists usually have less firepower than our opponents, we usually lose these battles. It is in our interest to fight in other ways.

## OBSTACLE 5: SCARCITY OF PROGRESSIVE RESOURCES

Fundamentally transforming society is an enormous enterprise. Millions of people must change their personal behavior as well as work in concert to change major societal institutions and transform cultural norms. This effort would require them to spend a significant amount of time and effort outside their daily routines.

However, the vast majority of people spend all their time just coping with immediate problems and living their daily lives. Immersed in a sick society and besieged by their own daily traumas, most scurry from one task to another as best they can and then retreat to distracting entertainment (TV, movies, sports, travel) in their bits of spare time. Most of their money goes to essentials — or to things they consider essential for a decent life.

Under these circumstances, it is not unreasonable that so many people choose to delegate political responsibility to others. As long as their lives are tolerable — that is, as long as they feel they have some degree of economic opportunity, security, and liberty — then most people will passively allow the power elite to maintain control.

*The mass of men lead lives of quiet desperation.* — Henry David Thoreau

This passivity then builds on itself: when people pay little attention to societal problems and political activities, they do not feel competent to make responsible decisions. They deliberately make a commitment to everyday life and delegate their political responsibility to leaders (the power elite) who "know more."[39]

As discussed above, members of the power elite mostly work to maintain the power and privileges of the upper classes, not to advance the common good. Since most people cannot and the elite will not, the burden of developing positive alternatives and moving society toward democracy falls on those few people willing and able to make the effort: progressive change activists.

However, the elite control the vast majority of society's assets (other than simple household items), so there is not much left for activists to tap.[40] Consequently, progressive organizations are usually underfunded and overburdened. Many progressive activists volunteer time and money and

### Who Is Politically Active?

One researcher estimates "about 10–15 percent of the electorate may be counted as political activists — that is, people who are informed and active participants in organizations, parties, or campaigns — people who take some ongoing political responsibility as a feature of their lives." Another scholar believes only five percent of the U.S. population is politically sophisticated and involved.

Who are these informed and politically active people? Research indicates they are likely: (1) to have attended college; (2) to be part of the high-status, powerful part of society (wealthy, older men); (3) to have parents who inculcated a sense of civic duty, provided a model of political responsibility, and suggested one was capable of effectively acting in the political sphere; and/or (4) to be a member of an ethnic group, political party, or other social group with a political bent. They are typically people who have the skills and resources to make change and believe that either individually or collectively, they *can* have influence.[41]

receive nothing for their efforts beyond the satisfaction of working for a good cause. Paid activists typically work long hours and receive low wages and poor benefits.

## Living in the Cracks

In times past, some activists managed to live on part-time work, disability payments, or Social Security. Others lived in cheap crash pads and grazed on the discards of our affluent society by dumpster diving for food and castoff clothes. Though poor, they had time to work for progressive social change. Other activists found a safe niche in the church, in academia, or by working for nonprofit organizations. However, recent conservative government policies have drastically shifted the nation's wealth to the rich and defunded social services and education — severely constricting these alternative sources of livelihood. In these tough times, there are few ways for activists to support themselves.

In the past, progressive activists also relied on liberal institutions for financial support as well as encouragement, education, office equipment, research materials, and safe places to meet, rest, work out strategy, and resolve internal problems without harassment. These institutions included liberal foundations, liberal churches (such as Quaker Meetings, Unitarian churches, and various black churches), progressive labor unions, progressive businesses, alternative schools, liberal colleges, and some government agencies. Unfortunately, most of these institutions are now wracked with their own internal problems and money woes and can no longer offer much support.

Activist poverty and scarce resources impose many limitations on progressive change organizations:

• Low-income activists are often immobilized by layoffs, transportation breakdowns, housing troubles, health or dental problems, injuries, crime, and family crises. They do not have the money that wealthier people use to avoid or overcome these problems.

---

### Financial Independence

To avoid financial dependence on the Southern white elite, the Black Freedom struggle of the 1960s relied instead on the financial and organizational self-sufficiency of independent black people such as church ministers and hairdressers. The struggle also relied on donations from white liberals in other parts of the country. Martin Luther King, Jr. spent much of his time speaking and raising funds around the country.

Some activists in the anti-war movement in the late '60s sold alternative newspapers to finance their activities. In the '70s and '80s, food co-ops, the progressive therapeutic community (therapists and body workers), and other alternative businesses provided employment and financial support for many activists. Colleges and universities have often provided a safe haven for a small number of progressive faculty and staff.

---

• Activists are continually tugged by other commitments to work, family, and friends. These obligations limit the time they can devote to progressive change and to developing the knowledge and skills necessary to do good work.

• Progressive activists are often drawn to more enticing work. Many activists in the United States have the opportunity to live adequate lives without involvement in change work. So activists voluntarily choose to work for change and to endure the hardships that accompany this work. If the work becomes too tedious or difficult for them, they can just stop. Those activists with the most skills are also usually the ones with the best opportunity to pursue lucrative and supportive conventional careers and hence have the greatest disincentives to devoting their lives to progressive change.

• Activists often burn out from overwork. Volunteer activists are especially vulnerable if they must also work full-time at a conventional job to support themselves.

• Progressive organizations must devote a great deal of their efforts to recruiting volunteers and raising funds. In

---

### Conflicts, Turf Battles, and Infighting

Coming from different backgrounds and with different experiences, activists have diverse ideas about what needs to be changed and how to go about it. Immersed in a competitive culture and lacking the skills to work with others from diverse backgrounds, activists create a multiplicity of small groups. These groups sometimes duplicate each other's efforts, compete with other groups for limited funds and supporters, or even work at cross-purposes. Some activists believe they are the sole "vanguard of the revolution," and believe they must crush competing ideologies. Frustration at meager results — exacerbated by activists' internalized emotional wounds — leads some activists to bludgeon others for their real or imagined mistakes.

Conflict among human beings is inevitable and, when dealt with well, can be quite useful. Conflict can shine a light on fuzzy thinking and reveal the flaws in proposed solutions. But unless activists have the knowledge and skill to debate rationally and spar gently with each other, their conflicts can escalate into nasty feuds.

Struggles among progressives can destroy organizations and dishearten activists. Turf battles and infighting can create painful and long-enduring enmity among activists who might otherwise work effectively together. Since progressive resources are so scarce, squandering them on internecine battles is especially unfortunate.

my experience, progressive groups typically expend between one-quarter and one-third of all their time and money just raising funds.

• Progressive institutions that might be able to pass on the lore and practice of social change to new activists — such as progressive political parties, libraries, museums, and activist schools — are almost nonexistent. Progressive groups, focused as they usually are on current change efforts, usually devote scant resources to these long-term organizational resources. Thus, the solutions they work out are often lost, and new change movements must painfully re-learn or re-invent them.

## Scrambling for Money

This desperate scramble for scarce resources has several other negative consequences:

• It encourages progressive groups to compete for resources rather than cooperate with one another.

• It entices progressive groups to use obnoxious fund-raising methods like the inflammatory direct mail appeals mentioned above.

• It entices progressive groups to focus their outreach on people already supportive of change — "preaching to the choir" — instead of toward those they might sway to a new, progressive understanding.

• It forces progressive groups to cater to their supporters and volunteers. This is positive when it pushes organizations to be more democratic, accountable, and responsible. However, when donors and volunteers are ignorant or more conservative, it may bind groups to a simplistic analysis or a watered-down solution and stifle their most creative and effective work. Groups are especially sensitive to the desires of their most powerful and wealthy supporters who are often the least progressive.

• It entices progressive groups to shift their political stance to enlist the help of more powerful, but less progressive people like reporters, businesspeople, Congressmembers, and foundation directors. Groups cannot advocate fundamental change when their politics must fit within the norms of the established order.

## Inadequate Personal Support

Besides financial resources, progressive activists also need cultural and personal support, but our society is not very sympathetic to them or their mission. Television, movies, and advertising generally laud those with a sharp wardrobe, cool accessories, and a sarcastic attitude who individually rebel (in proscribed ways) against square "family values." However, they typically belittle those who work for democracy, compassion, and real community or those who challenge militarism, consumerism, inequality, or domination.

Progressive activists also tend to get minimal personal support for their change work. Parents and friends often oppose their efforts. To obtain support, some activists immerse themselves in a tight community with other progressive activists, but then they risk losing touch with the rest of society.

To secure the emotional and financial support they need, some activists try to build their own hierarchical fiefdoms, manipulating and controlling less powerful activists. Others seek ego-enhancing fame by carrying out wild stunts. These actions usually accomplish nothing and may actually undermine real progressive change.

Some activists invoke one of the several glamorous images that society sometimes allows activists — that of morally pure saint, strident rebel, or wise sage — to attract disciples and admirers. But creating a just and humane society requires ending dependence and domination in all its forms, so this is not a good, long-term solution.

---

### Lost Heritage

Society seldom acknowledges the contribution of progressive activists, even when they bring about far-reaching social change. At best, society may extol the work of a single individual like Martin Luther King. Newspapers and history books usually only record the steps taken by the elite when they finally *respond* to social movement demands.

For example, years of progressive struggle won both the forty-hour workweek and the Social Security program, but most people assume these things have always existed or attribute them to the generosity of President Franklin Roosevelt.

Most people are unaware of progressive history or its importance in forcing the government to respond. New activists often have no idea how their activist forebears struggled and what they accomplished.

---

### Advice from Friends and Relatives

Rather than being praised for their virtuous efforts and encouraged to do even more, activists are often given advice like this:

• *"The world is full of problems and it's always been that way. Why do you think you're so smart that you can change everything?"*

• *"If you want to be noble, why don't you become a doctor — you could help people and make a good living too."*

• *"Why do you feel you have to be the one to take on the world's problems? Leave it to the bigshots and the politicians who think they know what is best for us."*

• *"How can you be a good parent if you're running around the country saving the world?"*

• *"Hey dude, mellow out and be cool. Life's a beach."*

## Burnout

If a change organization includes many activists suffering from these afflictions, it generally becomes ineffectual — plagued by lack of direction, fruitless activities, poor follow-through, and infighting. Exhausted or cynically disgusted, activists then drop out of the organization. Those few who keep plugging along feel powerless and exude hopelessness. Naturally enough, potential new activists are reluctant to join a group populated by such dreary people.

*We, the unwilling, led by the unknowing, are doing the impossible for the ungrateful. We have done so much, for so long, with so little, we are now qualified to do anything with nothing.*
— Office Graffiti

After many tough battles, progressive organizations sometimes consist entirely of activists desperately trying to extract support from each other, but with none able to give to the others. These organizations accomplish little and soon collapse.

## OVERCOMING THESE FIVE OBSTACLES

In summary, the reason that progressive activists have not yet created a good society is not that they are unworthy to bring about positive change, they do not care enough, or they have impossible goals. Rather, it is simply that they lack the knowledge, skills, strength, and endurance to overcome the sizable opposition they face from the power structure, destructive cultural norms, dysfunctional emotional conditioning, and widespread ignorance. The size and breadth of these obstacles make them seem overwhelming. It is easy to feel hopeless when faced with this gigantic wall of opposition.

Still, though these obstacles are huge and intertwined with each other, they *can* be understood, untangled, and surmounted. The next seven chapters describe a way we could build a powerful and skillful counterforce capable of systematically addressing and overcoming every one of these hurdles.

## NOTES FOR CHAPTER 3

[1] Of their many books, see especially C. Wright Mills, *The Power Elite* (Oxford: Oxford University Press, 1956, E169. 1.M64); G. William Domhoff, *The Powers that Be: Processes of Ruling Class Domination in America* (New York: Vintage-Random House, 1978, HN90 .E4D65 1979b); and G. William Domhoff, *Who Rules America Now?: How the "Power Elite" Dominates Business, Government, and Society* (New York: Touchstone-Simon & Schuster, 1983, HN90 .E4D652 1986). In his recent books, Domhoff uses the term "power structure" to denote the network of powerful people along with the powerful institutions they control.

[2] In a 1995 government survey, the majority of financial assets were owned by the 1% of households with the greatest net worth:

| Asset Type | Top 1% | Next 9% | Bottom 90% |
|---|---|---|---|
| Stocks and Mutual Funds | 51.4% | 37.0% | 11.6% |
| Financial Securities | 65.9 | 23.9 | 10.2 |
| Trusts | 49.6 | 38.9 | 11.5 |
| Business Equity | 69.5 | 22.2 | 8.3 |
| Non-Home Real Estate | 35.1 | 43.6 | 21.3 |
| **Total for Group** | **55.5** | **32.1** | **12.5** |

Of those in the top 1%, 77.3% were 45 years old or older; 95.3% were non-Hispanic White and 3.9% were Asian. Most had attended college (16.5% had attended but not graduated, 29.1% had graduated, and 40.1% had graduated and also attended graduate school). The overwhelming majority were self-employed (71.1%) or professionals, managers, and administrators (23.5%). More than half (55.0%) rated their health as excellent.

Edward N. Wolff, "Recent Trends in the Size Distribution of Household Wealth," *Journal of Economic Perspectives* 12, no. 3 (Summer 1998): 140, 146. This data is based on the Survey of Consumer Finances conducted by the Federal Reserve Board.

[3] Michael Parenti has made this point and documented it quite well in several of his books.

[4] Domhoff, G. William, *Who Rules America: Power and Politics in the Year 2000,* 3rd ed. (Mountain View, CA: Mayfield Publishing, 1998, HN90 .E4 D654 1998), p. 1.

[5] Clearly, these questions are not absolutely definitive. The power elite is an amorphous group with no clear line separating its members from others. These questions are merely suggestive of the amount of prestige, wealth, and authority typically held by members of the power elite and of the level of influence they exert.

[6] Kevin Phillips, in *The Politics of Rich and Poor: Wealth and the American Electorate in the Reagan Aftermath* (New York: Random House, 1990, HC110 .W4 P48 1990), documents the massive redistribution of wealth from the poor to the wealthy during the Reagan administration.

[7] There are various estimates of the size of the lobbying effort in Washington, DC:

"About 5,000 to 6,000 lobbyists are registered out of a total Washington lobbying population that has been estimated as high as 80,000." Washington Post Wire Service, "Senate OKs Tighter Rules for Lobbyists," *San Jose Mercury News*, 7 May 1993.

"…more than two-thirds of Washington's nearly 14,000 lobbyists [are] unregistered, according to the General Accounting Office." Washington Post Wire Service, "House Takes Up Lobbying Reform Bill," *San Francisco Chronicle*, 25 November 1995.

Associated Press, "Special Interests' Spending Disclosed," *San Francisco Chronicle*, 23 September 1996:

> Corporations, trade groups, unions and other special interests spent at least $400 million trying to influence the federal government in the first half of 1996, according to an analysis of the first disclosures under a new lobbying law…
>
> The figure is the most comprehensive estimate yet of amounts special interests spend on lobbying official Washington, but experts say it is probably conservative.
>
> "I don't think you're at all out of bounds with the thought of a billion-dollar-a-year-industry," said Ron Shaiko, an American University professor who teaches lobbying.

This article further reports the top 10 spenders among groups that reported lobbying expenses for the first half of 1996:

| | $ Millions |
|---|---|
| Philip Morris | 11.3 |
| American Medical Association | 8.5 |
| U.S. Chamber of Commerce | 7.5 |
| General Motors | 6.9 |
| Christian Coalition | 5.9 |
| General Electric | 5.3 |
| Chemical Manufacturers Association | 4.5 |
| AT&T | 4.3 |
| Pfizer | 4.2 |
| Citicorp | 4.2 |
| **Total for Top Ten:** | **62.6** |

[8] Ben Bagdikian, in *The Media Monopoly*, 5th ed. (Boston: Beacon Press, 1997, P96 .E252U625 1997), reports that ten corporations now control most of America's daily newspapers, magazines, radio, television, books, and movies. He also documents the many ways this restricts coverage of important issues.

[9] Randolph T. Holhut, in "A Horrible Year for Journalism," opinion column, *San Francisco Bay Guardian*, January 6, 1999: 11, summarizes the problem by describing what happened to four reporters: Gary Webb, who reported on the CIA-backed Nicaraguan contras' role in introducing crack cocaine into South Central Los Angeles; Mike Gallagher who reported on the abuses in Honduras of Chiquita Brands International (poisoning, bullying, and sometimes killing farmworkers); and April Oliver and Jack Smith, who reported that U.S. forces used sarin nerve gas to kill American defectors in Laos during the Vietnam War:

> The fates of Webb, Gallagher, and Oliver and Smith have one common thread. They all took on powerful institutions, the essential facts of their stories were all true, and all of their bosses abandoned them and discredited their work when the powerful institutions in those stories raised a fuss.
>
> The message this sends to other reporters is clear: stick to safe, innocuous stories and stay away from anything that might cause

trouble for the military-industrial complex or multinational corporations.

[10] Jeff Cohen, Executive Director of Fairness and Accuracy in Reporting (FAIR) explores this "propaganda of the center" in "Propaganda from the Middle of the Road: The Centrist Ideology of the News Media," *Extra!* 2, no. 4 (October/ November 1989).

[11] Philip J. Trounstein and Terry Christensen, in *Movers and Shakers: The Study of Community Power* (New York: St. Martin's Press, 1982, JC330 .T86), describe the reputational methodology for determining the identity of the elite in a community. As an example, they conducted a study of the elite in San Jose, California.

[12] G. William Domhoff, *The Powers that Be: Processes of Ruling Class Domination in America* (New York: Vintage-Random House, 1978, HN90.E4D65 1979b), pp. 109–117. This account relies on Stephen K. Bailey, *Congress Makes a Law* (New York: Columbia University Press, 1950), pp. 23–24.

[13] Marxists would argue that capitalism requires a reserve army of the unemployed, but the very low rates of unemployment found in many European countries challenges this argument.

[14] Donald L. Barlett and James B. Steele, *America: Who Really Pays the Taxes?* (New York: Simon and Schuster, Touchstone, 1994, HJ2381 .B37 1994). Barlett and Steele also document the history of tax law and detail recent changes: who wrote each piece of legislation, who lobbied for changes, who made campaign donations, and so forth.

Another good summary of the history of income taxes can be found in Sam Pizzigati, *The Maximum Wage: A Common-Sense Prescription for Revitalizing America by Taxing the Very Rich* (New York: Apex Press, 1992, HC110 .I5P59 1992).

[15] Quoted in "Beautiful Dreamer: Is Phil Gramm Right About 1950?" *Too Much*, Summer 1995: 2, Council on International and Public Affairs (Suite 3C, 777 United Nations Plaza, New York 10017).

[16] Federal Reserve data for 1989 quoted in Keith Bradsher, "Gap in Wealth in U.S. Called Widest in West," *New York Times*, April 17, 1995, p. A1.

More recent figures indicate that the share of all wealth owned by the bottom 80 percent dropped to 16.1 percent in 1995. In this year, the top 1 percent of the population had about the same amount of wealth (38.5 percent) as the bottom 95 percent (39.7 percent); 18.5 percent of households had zero or negative net worth.

| Percentage Share of Net Worth Held by | Percent of All Wealth | Percent of All Financial Wealth |
|---|---|---|
| Top 1% | 38.5% | 47.2% |
| Next 4% | 21.8 | 24.6 |
| Next 5% | 11.5 | 11.2 |
| Next 10% | 12.1 | 10.1 |
| Top 20% | 83.9 | 93.0 |
| 2nd 20% | 11.4 | 6.9 |
| 3rd 20% | 4.5 | 1.4 |
| Bottom 40% | 0.2 | -1.3 |

Subtracting net equity in owner-occupied housing, the top 1% owned 47.2% of all financial wealth in 1995 and the top 20% owned 93.0% of all financial wealth; 28.7% of households had zero or negative financial wealth.

In 1995, each of the families in the top 1% had a net worth of $2.4 million or more, and each of the families in the top 10% had a net worth of $352,000 or more. Each of the families in the top 20% had a net worth of $177,000 or more.

Edward N. Wolff, "Recent Trends in the Size Distribution of Household Wealth," *Journal of Economic Perspectives* 12, no. 3 (Summer 1998): 131–150, especially p. 136.

[17] An annual return of 10% on a billion dollars yields $100 million/year or about $548,000 in two days. Someone earning $5.15/hour (the minimum wage in 1999) makes $206/week or $10,712 in a year. In fifty years she would make about $535,600.

"The assets of the [world's] top three billionaires are more than the combined GNP of all least developed countries and their 600 million people." United Nations Development Programme, *Human Development Report, 1999* (New York: Oxford University Press, 1999, HD72 .H85 1999), p. 3. <http://www.undp.org/hdro>

[18] See, for example, Edward S. Herman and Noam Chomsky, *Manufacturing Consent: The Political Economy of the Mass Media* (New York: Pantheon Books, 1988, P95.82 .U6H47 1988).

After studying U.S. military and covert intervention in over seventy nations since World War II, William Blum concludes:

> The engine of American foreign policy has been fueled not by a devotion to any kind of morality, but rather by the necessity to serve other imperatives, which can be summarized as follows:
>
> • making the world safe for American corporations;
>
> • enhancing the financial statements of defense contractors at home who have contributed generously to members of congress;
>
> • preventing the rise of any society that might serve as a successful example of an alternative to the capitalist model;
>
> • extending political and economic hegemony over as wide an area as possible, as befits a "great power."

William Blum, "A Brief History of U.S. Interventions: 1945 to the Present," *Z Magazine* 12, no. 6 (June 1999): 25–30. This article is based on his book, *Killing Hope: US Military and CIA Interventions Since World War II* (Monroe, ME: Common Courage Press, 1995, JK468 .I6B59 1995), revised and expanded edition of: *The CIA: A Forgotten History* (London: Zed Books, 1986). <http://members.aol.com/bblum6/American_holocaust.htm>

[19] Excerpt of a speech posted on the Federation of American Scientists web site: <http://www.fas.org/man/smedley.htm>

[20] Brian Glick, *War at Home: Covert Action Against U.S. Activists and What We Can Do About It* (Boston: South End Press, 1989, HV8141 .G57 1988) summarizes how the government's COINTELPRO program waged covert action against activists in the 1960s and how similar efforts were directed against activists working on Central America issues in the 1980s.

David Helvarg, *The War Against the Greens: The Wise Use Movement, the New Right, and Anti-Environmental Violence* (San Francisco: Sierra Club Books, 1994) recounts recent terrorism directed at environmentalists including the Bari/Cherney example.

For a history of government and business harassment of progressive activists from the beating of Wobblies to the blacklists of the 1950s and the COINTELPRO program in the 1960s, see Robert Goldstein, *Political Repression in Modern America: 1870 to the Present* (Cambridge, MA: Schenkman Publishing, 1977, JC599 .U5G58).

Also, see the books listed in Chapter 12 under the heading of Suppression of Activists.

[21] For an extensive discussion of norms and cultural change, see Robert F. Allen with Charlotte Kraft and the staff of the Human Resources Institute, *Beat the System!: A Way to Create More Human Environments* (New York: McGraw-Hill, 1980, HM101 .A574).

[22] Lewis Mumford observed that industrial society transformed all these sins except sloth "into a positive virtue. Greed, avarice, envy, gluttony, luxury, and pride [are] the driving forces of the new economy." Lewis Mumford, *The Transformations of Man* (1956; reprint New York: Harper & Row, Torchbooks, 1972, CB53 .M82 1956), p. 104.

[23] The 3,000 marketing messages per day statistic comes from the Media Foundation, Adbusters web site, accessed January 12, 1999: <http://www.adbusters.org/campaigns/media-index.html>

The Media Foundation can also be reached at 1243 West 7th Avenue, Vancouver, BC V6H 1B7 Canada, (604) 736-9401.

"One analyst estimates that the typical American is exposed to 50–100 advertisements each morning before nine o'clock. Along with their weekly 22-hour diet of television, American teenagers are typically exposed to 3–4 hours of TV advertisements a week, adding up to at least 100,000 ads between birth and high school graduation." Alan Durning, "Asking How Much is Enough," *State of the World, 1991: A Worldwatch Institute Report on Progress toward a Sustainable Society*, Project Director, Lester R. Brown (New York: Norton, 1991, HC59 .S733 1991), p. 163. For ads in the morning, he cites Andrew Sullivan, "Buying and Nothingness," *The New Republic*, May 8, 1989; for the data on teenagers (aged 12–17), he cites John Schwartz, "Stalking the Youth Market," *Newsweek Special Issue*, June 1990; his childhood total estimates were based on Action for Children's Television, Boston, MA, private communication, October 17, 1990.

TV-Free America estimates children watch 30,000 TV commercials each year. They also report that the average American child sees 200,000 violent acts on TV by age 18 including 16,000 murders. TV-Free America web site, accessed January 12, 1999: <http://www.tvfa.org/stats.htm>

TV-Free America can also be reached at 1611 Connecticut Avenue, NW, Suite 3A, Washington, DC 20009, (202) 887-0436.

[24] A review of 27 studies on the impact of sexual abuse of female children found that "long-term effects include depression and self-destructive behavior, anxiety, feelings of isolation and stigma, poor self-esteem, difficulty in trusting others, a tendency toward revictimization, substance abuse, and sexual maladjustment." Angela Browne and David Finkelhor, "Impact of Child Sexual Abuse: A Review of the Research," *Psychological Bulletin* 99, no. 1 (1986): 66–77.

A more recent review of 32 studies found that "adult women with a history of childhood sexual abuse show greater evidence of sexual disturbance or dysfunction, homosexual experiences in adolescence or adulthood, depression, and are more likely than nonabused women to be revictimized. Anxiety, fear, and suicidal ideas and behavior have also been associated with a history of childhood sexual abuse but force and threat of force may be a necessary concomitant." Joseph H. Beitchman, Kenneth J. Zucker, Jane E. Hood, Granville A. daCosta, Donna Akman, and Erika Cassavia, "A Review of the Long-term Effects of Child Sexual Abuse," ***Child Abuse & Neglect*** 16 (1992): 101–118.

[25] One study found that children who experience severe violence in the home are approximately three times as likely as other children to use drugs and alcohol, get into fights, and deliberately damage property. This study also found that abused and neglected children are four times as likely to steal and to be arrested. Richard J. Gelles and John W. Harrop, "The Nature and Consequences of the Psychological Abuse of Children: Evidence from the Second National Family Violence Survey," paper presented at the Eighth National Conference on Child Abuse and Neglect, Salt Lake City, Utah, October 24, 1989.

In this same 1985 survey of 3,346 U.S. parents, 63% of parents reported they used verbal aggression — such as swearing at or insulting their child — at least once in the previous year. More than a third of parents who used verbal aggression reported they did so more than eleven times during the year. Researchers found that the more parents used verbal aggression, the greater was the probability of their child being physically aggressive, delinquent, or having interpersonal problems. This relationship applied both to children who were physically punished as well as those who were not. Yvonne M. Vissing, Murray A. Straus, Richard J. Gelles, and John W. Harrop, "Verbal Aggression by Parents and Psychosocial Problems of Children," ***Child Abuse & Neglect*** 15, no. 3 (1991): 223–238.

Another study of 4,000 adolescents aged 12–17 found that nearly 30 percent of sexual assault victims developed Post-traumatic Stress Disorder (PTSD) and 20 percent still suffered from it. Typical symptoms of PTSD are anxiety attacks, nightmares, and difficulty sleeping. Of those physically assaulted, 23% developed PTSD and 15% still suffered from it. Of those who had witnessed serious violence, 15% developed PTSD. Dean Kilpatrick and Benjamin Saunders, "The Prevalence and Consequences of Child Victimization," U.S. Department of Justice, Office of Justice Programs, National Institute of Justice, NIJ Research Preview, Report Number FS 000179, April 1997, 2 pages. <http://www.ncjrs.org/pdffiles/fs000179.pdf>

The studies cited in the note above and the note below also document the consequences of childhood abuse or neglect.

[26] Psychotherapist Alice Miller, in ***For Your Own Good: Hidden Cruelty in Child-Rearing and the Roots of Violence***, Hildegarde and Hunter Hannum, trans. (New York: Farrar Straus Giroux, 1983, HQ769 .M531613 1983; originally published in German as ***Am Anfang war Erziehung***, 1980), convincingly argues that oppressive childrearing practices — employed to beat the willfulness out of children ("spare the rod and spoil the child") — lead to adults who are docile, servile, and unfeeling. Repressing their feelings of anger, pain, and fear, they often are completely unaware of what was done to them. They are then ripe for exploi-

tation by dictators like Adolph Hitler who can easily manipulate their obsequiousness and suppressed anger and induce them to fight wars and engage in mass murder:

> People with any sensitivity cannot be turned into mass murderers overnight. But the men and women who carried out "the final solution" did not let their feelings stand in their way for the simple reason that they had been raised from infancy not to have any feelings of their own but to experience their parents' wishes as their own. These were people who, as children, had been proud of being tough and not crying, of carrying out all their duties "gladly," of not being afraid — that is, at bottom, of not having an inner life at all. (p. 81)

A growing body of research supports the concept of an intergenerational transmission of violence (also called the "cycle of violence") that begins with child abuse and neglect.

For example, one recent national study of 900 people who had been victims of physical and sexual abuse or neglect before the age of 12 were compared with 670 non-victims. It found that victimization increases the chances of later juvenile delinquency and adult criminality by 57%. It also found that physical abuse almost doubles the chances of later being arrested for a violent crime and severe neglect increases the chances by 55%. Michael G. Maxfield and Cathy Spatz Widom in "The Cycle of Violence Revisited 6 Years Later," ***Archives of Pediatric and Adolescent Medicine*** 150 (April 1996): 390–395.

Another analysis of the same data found that the 153 children who had been sexually abused were 27.7 times more likely to be arrested for prostitution as an adult than non-victims. Cathy Spatz Widom, ***Victims of Childhood Sexual Abuse — Later Criminal Consequences***, NIJ Research in Brief Series, U.S. Department of Justice, Office of Justice Programs, National Institute of Justice, Report Number NCJ 151525, March 1995, 8 pages. <http://www.ncjrs.org/pdffiles/abuse.pdf>

Another study found that 68 percent of 300 incarcerated male felons in a New York State medium security prison reported they had been subjected to some form of harsh victimization in early childhood (before age 12). The study found that about 35% reported severe childhood physical abuse, 14% reported sexual abuse, 16% reported life-threatening neglect, and 23% reported experiencing multiple forms of abuse and neglect. About 26% of the sex offenders reported sexual abuse. Robin Weeks and Cathy Spatz Widom, "Self-Reports of Early Childhood Victimization Among Incarcerated Adult Male Felons," ***Journal of Interpersonal Violence*** 13, no. 3 (June 1998): 346–361. This report is also summarized in Robin Weeks and Cathy Spatz Widom, ***Early Childhood Victimization Among Incarcerated Adult Male Felons***, NIJ Research Preview, U.S. Department of Justice, Office of Justice Programs, National Institute of Justice, Report Number FS 000204, April 1998. <http://www.ncjrs.org/txtfiles/fs000204.txt>

Many older studies provide additional evidence that physical abuse, sexual abuse, and neglect of children as well as children witnessing violent behavior in person or on television causes some — perhaps many — of them to be aggressive in infancy and childhood, to be delinquent in adolescence, to be abusive and violent in adulthood, or to be withdrawn and suicidal in adolescence and adulthood. Unfortunately, most of these older studies have methodological flaws that prevent drawing any firm conclusions. Cathy

Spatz Widom, "Does Violence Beget Violence?: A Critical Examination of the Literature," **Psychological Bulletin** 106, no. 1 (1989): 3–28.

27 U.S. Census Bureau, **Statistical Abstract of the U.S., 1998**, "Table 373: Child Abuse and Neglect Cases Substantiated and Indicated — Victim Characteristics." <http://www.census.gov:80/statab/www/index.html>

28 U.S. Department of Health and Human Services, "A Nation's Shame: Fatal Child Abuse and Neglect in the United States — A Report of the U.S. Advisory Board on Child Abuse and Neglect," Administration for Children and Families, April 1995, HE23 .1002:AB 9, pp. xxiii–xxv. I calculated the percentages from census data showing there are about 65 million children aged 17 or younger.

29 Dean Kilpatrick and Benjamin Saunders, "The Prevalence and Consequences of Child Victimization," U.S. Department of Justice, Office of Justice Programs, National Institute of Justice, NIJ Research Review, Report Number FS 000179, April 1997. <http://www.ncjrs.org/pdffiles/fs000179.pdf>

30 Michael Rand, **Criminal Victimization 1997: Changes 1996-97 with Trends 1993-97**, National Crime Victimization Survey, Bureau of Justice Statistics, U.S. Department of Justice, Report NCJ 173385, December 1998, p. 3. The Crime Victimization Survey interviews about 80,000 people aged 12 and over each year. <http://www.ojp.usdoj.gov/bjs/pub/pdf/cv97.pdf>

31 Patricia Tjaden and Nancy Thoennes, **Prevalence, Incidence, and Consequences of Violence Against Women: Findings From the National Violence Against Women Survey**, U.S. Department of Justice, Office of Justice Programs, National Institute of Justice, Research in Brief Series, Report Number NCJ 172837, November 1998. <http://ncjrs.org/pdffiles/172837.pdf>

32 For exploration of this point, see Anne Wilson Schaef, **When Society Becomes an Addict** (San Francisco: Harper & Row, 1987, BF575 .D34S33 1987).

33 Erich Fromm convincingly makes this point in **The Sane Society** (New York: Rinehart, 1955, reprinted New York: Henry Holt, First Owl Book, 1990 HM271 .F75 1990), especially in Chapter 2, titled "Can A Society Be Sick? — The Pathology of Normalcy."

34 Irving Janis, "Groupthink," **Psychology Today**, November 1971: 43–46, 74–76; Irving Janis, **Groupthink: Psychological Studies of Policy Decisions and Fiascoes**, 2nd ed. (Boston: Houghton-Mifflin, 1982, E744 .J29 1982).

35 Steven Hassan, a former member of the cult known as the "Moonies," provides an excellent analysis of mind control, including a list of mind control techniques.

Steven Hassan, **Combating Cult Mind Control** (Rochester, Vermont: Park Street Press, 1988). <http://www.shassan.com>

36 A 1992 survey by the U.S. Department of Education's National Center for Education Statistics estimated that about 21 percent of the adult population — more than 40 million Americans over the age of 16 — had only rudimentary reading and writing skills. Most adults in this "Level 1" category could pick out key facts in a brief newspaper article, for example, but could not draft a letter explaining an error on their credit card bill. A sub-group in this category — representing roughly 4 percent of the total adult population, or about 8 million people — was unable to perform even the simplest literacy tasks.

Many factors help to explain why so many adults demonstrated English literacy skills in the lowest proficiency level defined (Level 1). Twenty-five percent of the respondents who performed in this level were immigrants who may have been just learning to speak English. Nearly two-thirds of those in Level 1 (62 percent) had terminated their education before completing high school. One-third were age 65 or older, and 26 percent had physical, mental, or health conditions that kept them from participating fully in work, school, housework, or other activities. Nineteen percent of the respondents in Level 1 reported having visual difficulties that affect their ability to read print.

Irwin S. Kirsch, Ann Jungeblut, Lynn Jenkins, and Andrew Kolstad, **Adult Literacy in America: A First Look at the Findings of the National Adult Literacy Survey**, (Washington, DC: National Center for Education Statistics, Office of Educational Research and Improvement, U.S. Dept. of Education, 1993, LC5251 .A6437 1993). <http://nces.ed.gov/nadlits/naal92/>

37 For a good example of "functional analysis" and finding alternatives that fulfill necessary functions, see George Lakey, **Powerful Peacemaking: A Strategy for a Living Revolution** (Philadelphia: New Society Publishers, 1987), Chapter 1.

38 Richard Flacks, in **Making History: The American Left and the American Mind** (New York: Columbia University Press, 1988, JK1764 .F57 1988), discusses self-defense, resistance, liberation, and democracy.

39 For a good discussion of this point, see Flacks, **Making History**, pp. 51–53.

40 A Merrill-Lynch study based on 1995 census data shows that half of all U.S. families have less than $1,000 in net financial assets (excluding their equity in a home or car). Joseph M. Anderson, **The Wealth of U.S. Families in 1995** (127 Hesketh Street, Chevy Chase, MD: Capital Research Associates, June 1, 1998). <http://www.ml.com/woml/forum/wealth1.htm>

41 The quote comes from Flacks, **Making History**, p. 26.

The 5 percent estimate comes from W. Russell Neuman, **The Paradox of Mass Politics: Knowledge and Opinion in the American Electorate** (Cambridge, MA: Harvard University Press, 1986, JK1967 .N48 1986), p. 170. Neuman finds that 20 percent of the public are unabashedly apolitical. He finds the remaining 75 percent are only marginally attentive to politics and are mildly cynical about the behavior of politicians but still feel a duty to vote.

The characteristics of politically active people comes from Flacks, **Making History**, pp. 25–27, and Neuman, **The Paradox of Mass Politics**, pp. 112–131.

# *4*

# *Elements of an Effective Strategy for Democratic Transformation*

## In This Chapter:

**Some Strategies of the Past**

**Crucial Characteristics of Fundamental Change Efforts**

**A Strategy for Democratic Transformation**

**Mass Education and Powerful Social Change Movements**

**Six Essential Components of an Effective Strategy**

*How can we surmount the five obstacles to fundamental progressive change described in the last chapter? What is an effective strategy for creating a truly good society?*

Since we have never created a truly good society before, the best route is unknown.[1] Still, we can learn from the past. This chapter examines the historical efficacy of several approaches and identifies a few crucial characteristics of a strategy to bring about fundamental change. It also describes six specific components that an effective strategy must incorporate.

## SOME STRATEGIES OF THE PAST

In the past few hundred years, activists have employed many strategies in an effort to bring about fundamental change. All of these strategies have been effective at various times and to various degrees, but each has drawbacks.[2] As I see it, an effective strategy for bringing about fundamental transformation would include the best of each of them while avoiding their limitations.

## Violent Revolution

As it is usually understood, a revolution is a violent struggle for control of a society — a struggle that may involve mass uprisings, civil war between competing armies, drawn-out guerrilla warfare, or a quick coup d'état. A revolution usually involves a series of complex processes progressing through many stages. These include the breakdown of the existing order, competition among all the new claimants for central authority, and the building of new institutions.[3]

Revolutions are riveting spectacles that attract wide attention, interrupt people's daily routines, and jar their sensibilities. If successful, revolutions expeditiously replace old powerholders with new ones. Even if not completely successful, revolutions forcefully challenge the existing order and raise the profound question "What is the proper governance of society?" By risking their lives for a cause, revolutionaries provide an inspiring model of action that compels others to examine themselves. All of these aspects of revolution are valuable characteristics of an effective change strategy.

However, because of their violent nature, revolutions are usually bloody, chaotic, and terrifying. Typically, large numbers of people experience horrible personal tragedies that deeply affect them for life. The victors — often those who fought most savagely — are typically shell-shocked, arrogant, and filled with hatred and bloodlust. The revolutionary process has taught them how to kill and destroy but not how to build anything positive. Over the course of the struggle, they may have come to value secrecy, trickery, and duplicity if this knavery led to victory. After the revolution, they seldom want to share their hard-won power with others. Instead, they typically brandish their weapons at anyone who challenges their absolute control.

> *If we don't change direction, then we're likely to end up where we're headed.*
> — Graffiti

Rather than democratizing power, revolutions typically just shift authority from an old oppressive elite to a new oppressive elite. When old institutions are destroyed, new institutions must be cobbled together hastily and so are often built on the same reactionary assumptions as the old.

For example, following the French Revolution of 1789, members of the old elite were executed in a "Reign of Terror." The resulting power vacuum led to a major struggle among the revolutionary leaders, which was ultimately resolved when Napoleon Bonaparte crowned himself emperor and launched a military conquest across Europe. This new dictatorship was no more democratic or enlightened than the old monarchy.

The American Revolution of 1776 was more successful in democratizing political relationships — giving common people some voice in the government and offering a greater chance of fair treatment — but it did not end rule by plutocrats. Instead, it transferred control from the old, British elite to a new, American elite principally composed of rich men of English background. Women, slaves, the poor, and Native Americans were still excluded from the halls of power. Similarly, the Russian revolution of 1917 deposed the Czar, but it did not democratize the political system. Within ten years, control was concentrated in the bloody hands of Joseph Stalin.

> *The surface of American society is covered with a layer of democratic paint, but from time to time one can see the old aristocratic colors breaking through.*
> — Alexis de Tocqueville

## Historical Materialism

In the mid-1800s, German intellectual Karl Marx wrote several books that radically influenced progressive change strategies.[4] Marx believed in historical destiny, specifically that capitalism had naturally displaced feudalism and eventually socialism would displace capitalism. He believed that when conditions deteriorated enough, oppressed industrial workers would see the contradictions in capitalist control. He assumed they would rise up, overthrow capitalism, and create a powerful workers' state that would then, after a time of consolidation, wither away and give rise to a good society.

Though Marx's critiques of capitalist society have been quite useful, his ideas about social change are less valuable. A century and a half after he first promoted his ideas, the workers' revolution he foresaw has still not come about.[5]

## A Vanguard Party

In the early part of the twentieth century, Vladimir Lenin developed a strategy to bolster and accelerate Marx's historical destiny and ensure it took place sooner rather than later — even under the harsh conditions of czarist Russia. Lenin urged radical intellectuals and workers to build a vanguard party of disciplined cadre who could then educate and "revolutionize" industrial workers to overthrow the owning class. This strategy largely worked and helped to ensure the success of the Russian revolution.

> *Power tends to corrupt, and absolute power corrupts absolutely.*
> — Lord Acton

However, as demonstrated so poignantly in the Soviet Union, when a vanguard party successfully wins a revolution, it often becomes as oppressive as the regime it overthrew: democracy is cast aside and replaced by overbearing bureaucracy and Stalinist purges. The strict obedience demanded by most vanguard parties is inherently dangerous and easily abused.

## Countercultural Transformation

In the 1830s and 1840s, utopian intellectuals in the United States started a number of small, socialist communes that practiced and promoted various "countercultural" ideas. Since these communes were started by diverse groups of Christian and secular communalists, spiritualists, and sensualists, their ideals ranged widely. For instance, some — like the Shakers — promoted strict celibacy, whereas others promoted group marriage, and still others advocated free love.

Though diverse, these communities each sought to infuse their ideas and morality into society. This change strategy was somewhat successful: their ideas influenced the campaigns of the time for educational reform, women's rights, and the abolition of slavery. They also inspired several popular utopian visions such as Henry George's ***Progress and Poverty***, Edward Bellamy's ***Looking Backward***, and William Dean Howell's ***A Traveler from Altruria***.

However, these visionaries were naïve about social, political, and economic realities. They overestimated the skill of their members and underrated both the depth of cultural socialization and the depth and severity of their members' emotional conditioning. They could not successfully insulate themselves from the pressures of capitalism or the influences of the dominant culture. By shunning political parties, labor organizations, churches, and the professions, they disengaged themselves from political and social life and excluded themselves from the councils of power. Eventually, their communes disintegrated from internal or external pressures or faded into bland, conventional institutions.

The counterculture movements of the 1920s and 1960s met a similar fate. Though influential, most of the communes spawned by these movements eventually unraveled. Counterculture ideas were largely drowned or distorted beyond recognition by the dominant culture.

## Alternative Institutions

The Populist Movement of the late 1800s sought to establish people-controlled banks and cooperative ventures to avoid or undermine the economic elite who controlled conventional banks and railroads.[6] They were able to create some alternative institutions — a few of which still survive such as the State Bank of North Dakota.

However, without changing the fundamental nature of society, these institutions were left vulnerable to constant attack. Over time, most fell to the wayside or were destroyed by economic competition. Most of the many cooperative retail stores founded in the 1930s and 1960s, which were owned by consumers or employees, met the same fate. For example, in the San Francisco Bay Area, the Berkeley Co-op Markets, with ten stores in the East Bay, collapsed in the 1980s.[7]

## Mass Advertising

Beginning in the 1830s, steam-powered printing presses and an expanding railroad network made it possible to disseminate information quickly throughout the country. Nationally distributed newspapers and magazines provided a medium for national advertising, which could sell brand-name products at a premium price. Soon the same advertising techniques developed for selling Ivory soap nationwide were employed to convey political and cultural ideas.

In the 1930s, President Roosevelt used broadcast radio to sell his New Deal programs to the public. At the same time in California, conservatives used propaganda films to help defeat Upton Sinclair's progressive End Poverty in California (EPIC) campaign. Using similar means, Hitler's propaganda minister, Joseph Goebbels, created a variety of appealing messages to ignite support for Nazi nationalism.

*In an age of universal deceit, telling the truth is a revolutionary act.*
— George Orwell

Political campaigns today rely heavily on advertising to influence public opinion. Using polling and focus groups to determine what people want to hear and what messages they will accept, politicians then formulate clever advertisements and broadcast them widely and relentlessly.

Presumably, mass advertising could also be used to promote progressive change. However, progressive activists seldom have the financial resources to mount a large advertising campaign. Even if the money were available, most media outlets — controlled as they are by the power elite — will not broadcast messages advocating fundamental progressive change. Furthermore, by its very nature, advertising is much better suited to disseminating inflammatory propaganda and mindless rhetoric than at presenting thoughtful commentary on the value of progressive change.

---

### Progressive Change, Inc.

If a large corporation, with vast resources, decided to create a good society, it might go about it like this:

First, the company would hire thousands of employees to do all the necessary work. Researchers would design and test alternative institutions, and engineers would develop plans to implement them. Thousands of well-paid employees would build and deploy them.

The company would hire an advertising agency to craft clever messages extolling the virtues of these alternatives and the defects of existing options — then massively advertise on television, in magazines, and in newspapers. To attract attention to the campaign, it might mail calendars, refrigerator magnets, and plastic ice scrapers, imprinted with change messages, to every household.

The company would contract with consulting firms to prepare reports that proved the superiority of progressive alternatives, and then mail these reports to opinion leaders in every community. It would hire prominent citizens to personally lobby in Washington and pay thousands of citizens to call or personally lobby their government representatives. It would finance progressive candidates to challenge officeholders who resisted change. It would also hire scores of slick lawyers to sue for change.

It would hire an army of attractive young salespeople who would present alternatives at gala events in fancy hotel ballrooms or even demonstrate them door-to-door. It would encourage people to "test drive" the alternatives.

In reality, there is no large corporation with the goal of creating a good society, and progressive activists do not have the resources to mount such an expensive change campaign. Even if it were possible, this description shows that this process might very well fail anyway. A top-down approach might disempower and corrupt people as much as it promoted progressive change, creating a mere caricature of a good society. At the end, we might have only an imprinted refrigerator magnet to hint at what might have been.

## Technological Advances

Throughout history — especially in the last few centuries — many people have hoped that advances in technology would naturally generate a good society. They have believed that advances in medicine would reduce illness and mortality and that development of new devices (like automobiles, airplanes, and computers) would make life easier and more enjoyable. They assumed that automation would enable people to work less. With more leisure time, people could better support their friends and neighbors, and they would educate and improve themselves.

Technology has fulfilled some of this promise. We have better food and medicine than our ancestors, and we live longer. We travel more and farther. We can easily communicate around the world. We can read books, listen to beautiful music, watch movies any time we want, and access a wealth of information through the Internet. We have many more dazzling toys — delights that the richest nobles of a few hundred years ago would envy.

Still, as implemented in this society, technology has also caused great problems. The environment has been ravaged. Noise has increased. Our lives have sped up, leaving us frantic and exhausted. Many people work as hard as ever while others have no job and live in poverty. Some people live in palaces, but others have been driven into the streets. Inane advertisements intrude into every facet of our lives. Technology amplifies the power of crazy people who now have the means to kill hundreds of innocent victims with weapons of incredible firepower. People halfway around the world can now threaten us with nuclear-tipped missiles. Technology also makes it much easier for the police — or other agents — to spy on us in a variety of ways.

Clearly, by itself technology does not create a good society. Rather, technology appears to accelerate and intensify both good and bad social trends.

## Conventional Electoral Politics

Since the founding of the United States, activists have lobbied and pressured officeholders and attempted to elect advocates of progressive change to office. They have been somewhat successful in both endeavors, but they have not been able to bring about fundamental change. The founders of this country structured the political system to impede rapid or radical change. Winner-take-all elections favor bland centrists and opportunists. Judges with lifetime appointments can block significant change for decades. Moreover, as described earlier, the control exercised by elite interests over elections and their domination of lobbying ensures the dilution or derailing of most progressive initiatives.

*If voting could change anything, it would be illegal.*
— Anarchist graffiti

Conventional politics also has limited influence on the economic, social, or cultural aspects of society. As currently structured, the economic system is mostly immune to progressive political intervention. Instead, large corporations and trade groups largely shape it. Corporate advertising influences our culture more than do government, schools, or churches. The distribution of real estate — that is, affluent white people living in one neighborhood separated from poor people of color living in another — more effectively molds social interaction than any government policy.

Hence, though progressives have used government to make some changes, they have not been able to use it to bring about fundamental progressive transformation. Without major changes in the election and governing systems, progressives will probably fare no better in the future.

## Mass Social Movements

Periodically, mass social movements have arisen and challenged the established order. Some have been quite large and powerful. For example, the civil rights movement of the 1960s ended discrimination in housing, transportation, and education and eliminated most barriers to voting in the South.

Typically, these movements have used a variety of tactics — such as leafleting, public speaking, strikes, boycotts, and sabotage — to pressure and undermine the power of authorities. Because social change movements rely on large numbers of people for their strength, the divergent perspectives of participants about goals and tactics can tear the movement apart. They are also vulnerable to the ignorance and conditioning of participants. In addition, they are vulnerable to infiltration and disruption by authorities. So far, no social movement has been large enough to bring about fundamental transformation of society.[*]

## Incremental Change

In the last century, progressive change theorists in the United States have generally advocated one or a combination of these strategies. However, the limitations and historical failures of each loom large. While theoreticians have argued about the hypothetically best strategy for fundamental change, most contemporary activists have ignored them. Instead, activists have pragmatically focused on a particular injustice and used whatever change tactics seemed to work best in the short run, hoping that eventually it would lead to fundamental change.

This strategy has typically included limited advertising (direct mail, leaflets), grassroots canvassing, lobbying, and supporting liberal politicians — spiced up with occasional civil disobe-

*No matter how far you've gone down the wrong road, turn back.*
— Turkish proverb

---

[*] The rest of this book describes a project for overcoming these limitations.

dience, strikes, and boycotts. This strategy has brought about some positive changes, but clearly, it has not yet created a good society. With only limited resources, it probably never will.

# CRUCIAL CHARACTERISTICS OF FUNDAMENTAL CHANGE EFFORTS

The deficiencies of these historical strategies and the obstacles discussed in the previous chapter offer some important lessons for developing an effective strategy for fundamental progressive transformation. The effort to bring about change must be:

## Powerful and Inspiring

The forces maintaining the current society are extremely powerful. As described previously, members of the power elite control vast resources that they actively deploy to thwart progressive change efforts. Moreover, all of us carry counter-progressive tendencies induced by dysfunctional aspects of the dominant culture and by emotional conditioning. These tendencies are difficult to identify, challenge, or change.

*The meek shall inherit what's left of the earth.*
— Graffiti

To counter these powerful forces requires equally powerful counter-efforts. A large number of people must work assiduously and skillfully for progressive change, probably for many decades. Eventually, the vast majority of people in our society must be involved in progressive change efforts. They must vigorously challenge the power elite, the dominant culture, and their own internalized emotional demons. Strategies that rely only on new technology, individual goodwill, or "working within the system" are not powerful or direct enough to dislodge the elite or dissolve calcified social norms.

## Focused on Broad, Fundamental, and Enduring Change

Society is an agglomeration of individual people. Individual people staff institutions, and individuals transmit cultural norms. However, individuals are not entirely autonomous agents: cultural norms shape individuals and large institutions pressure and constrain them.

An effective strategy must therefore change all three of these entities: institutions, individuals, and our culture. It must fundamentally transform each of them so they do not revert to the old ways after a short time. Change must be deep and broad enough and it must coincide with other changes so that a change in one area is not undone by still unchanged individuals, institutions, or norms in another realm.

Specifically, an effective strategy must bring about large-scale, long-term, **structural change** on all levels and transform all aspects of people's lives:
- **Individual values, beliefs, and temperament**
- **Personal interaction**
- **Small and large group dynamics**
- **Society-wide**

Changes must come in all realms that determine how people work and interact as consumers, producers, providers, parents, teachers, students, clergypeople, laypeople, politicians, soldiers, and citizens:
- **Political system**: laws, voting; local, state, and national government; executive, legislative, and judicial branches
- **Economic system**: production, consumption, storage, transportation, property relations, trade, markets, money, investments, taxes, rents, profits, businesses, cooperatives, corporations
- **Social connections**: families, kinfolk, cliques, communities, racial and ethnic groupings, clubs, workplaces, cities, nations
- **Institutions**: schools, businesses, churches, associations, military forces, and government agencies
- **Culture**: language, values, beliefs, education, religion, ceremonies, work, play, stories, humor, literature, music, theater, television, movies, the Internet

## Reliant on Ordinary People

Progressive activists must rely primarily on themselves and ordinary people in their communities, not on members of the elite, the news media, politicians, or liberal foundations. Though these entities are potent and sometimes provide useful help, more often they steer change toward token reform rather than fundamental transformation.

On Politics: *When our people get to the point where they can do us some good, they stop being our people.* — M. Stanton Evans

## Democratic and Responsive

To achieve the goal of deep democracy, a viable strategy for change must be democratic in its processes and it must foster a broad democratic structure that is responsive to all people. A good strategy must also be responsive to criticism and include a positive way for people to question change methods. Throughout the change process, activists must continually evaluate their own efforts and be open to outside criticism.

*I know of no safe depository of the ultimate powers of society but the people themselves; and if we think them not enlightened enough to exercise their control with a wholesome discretion, the remedy is not to take it from them, but to inform their discretion by education. This is the true corrective of abuses of constitutional power.* — Thomas Jefferson

## Focused on Ending Oppression, Not Toppling Individual Oppressors

A strategy for thorough change must eliminate the real, structural sources of oppression — not just attempt to topple current authorities and replace them with progressive activists. Activists are inherently no more moral than the present rulers are. Every person is capable of oppressing others, no one is so virtuous that she is immune to temptation, and no one is so perfect that she will never err.

Everyone is vulnerable to the corrosive effects of power. In fact, given the way leaders are idolized and indulged in our society, taking the reins of power often corrupts even those who are most caring and conscientious. Moreover, because of the way humans react to emotional injuries, those who have suffered the greatest oppression are often those most likely to "act out" the same kind of oppression if they are given the chance.

The particular role we play in our life — saint, sinner, member of the power elite, ordinary person, progressive activist — mostly depends on circumstances beyond our control. None of us chose our parents or our life experiences, they just happened to us. It is ridiculous to fault someone for having cruel parents, growing up deprived of necessities, or being immersed in racism. It is equally silly to commend someone else for having loving parents, having all her needs met, and being immersed in tolerance.

*Only the truth is revolutionary.* — Graffiti, Paris uprising, May 1968

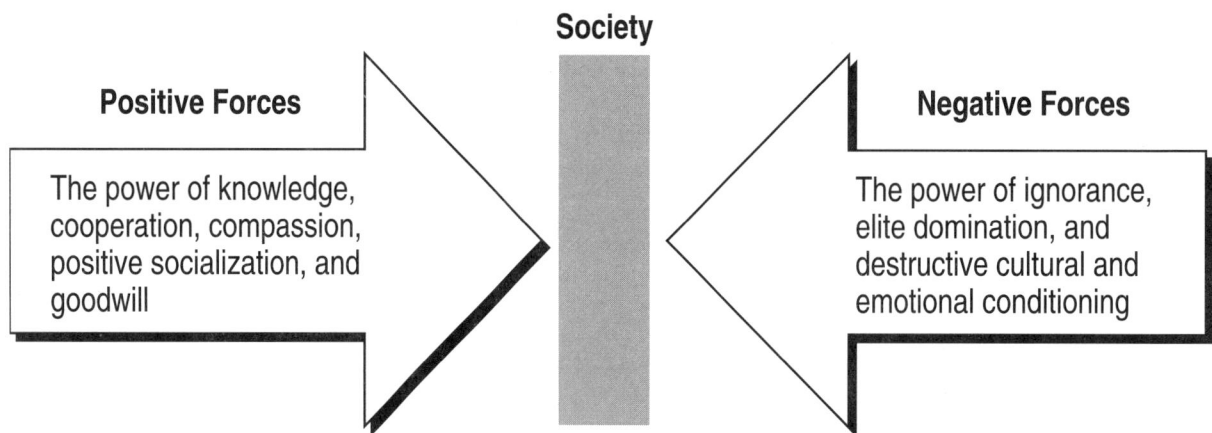

**Figure 4.1: The Struggle to Create a Good Society**

**Positive Forces** — The power of knowledge, cooperation, compassion, positive socialization, and goodwill

**Society**

**Negative Forces** — The power of ignorance, elite domination, and destructive cultural and emotional conditioning

People often conceive of the struggle to create a good society as a giant battle with evil people on one side and saints on the other. Alternatively, they imagine powerful government or business leaders on one side and regular people on the other. However, it is not that simple.

Even the most tyrannical or corrupt authorities are human beings who love their families and friends. Just like everyone else, they want to live gratifying lives of joy and worth. They are not the stereotypical evil enemies depicted in melodramas. On the other side, the downtrodden are not all virtuous heroes. A thoroughly trampled and relatively powerless person can still abuse others: an elderly, homeless alcoholic may scream at a passerby, molest a child, or ignite a destructive fire. Moreover, regular people

who oust a tyrant and assume the mantle of power can easily become as tyrannical as the previous authorities.

Creating a good society requires ending all oppression, not just changing the identity of the oppressor and oppressed. It also means creating positive and supportive institutions, not just tearing down oppressive structures.

As the figure above shows, it is more useful to view the effort to create a good society as a struggle to influence society and its people, institutions, and cultural norms. The positive forces of knowledge, cooperation, compassion, constructive socialization, and goodwill push in the direction of a good society as the negative forces of ignorance, domination by elite interests, and destructive cultural and emotional conditioning push the other way.

With this understanding, the struggle to create a good society can be seen in a new way. It is not a competition between good and bad people. Rather it is competition between degrading and damaging tendencies on the one hand and nurturing and cooperative tendencies on the other (see Figure 4.1).

## Nonviolent

Violent strategies typically produce a great deal of destruction and heartbreak, and do not end domination — they usually only shift oppression from one place to another. Violent strategies also do not usually overcome destructive cultural norms or alleviate dysfunctional emotional conditioning.

A strategy for fundamental progressive change must therefore use nonviolent means that nurture people and bring out their best behavior. Effective change efforts must not demean or dehumanize people. Instead, change efforts must either persuade people or sensitively coerce them to stop their harmful behavior. Change efforts are most potent when they penetrate deeply into opponents' hearts, dissolving rigid, patterned behavior and kindling compassion and goodwill.

*There are only two forces in the world, the sword and the spirit. In the long run the sword will always be conquered by the spirit.*
— Napoleon Bonaparte

## Moral, Principled, True to Ideals, with the Means in Harmony with the Ends

More generally, a good strategy for change must rely only on means that are harmonious with the good society we seek to create. Many strategies for change are clearly unsuited to creating or maintaining a good society and cannot be used. Even seemingly innocuous change efforts can veer off in a counterproductive direction if they are not strictly aligned with morality and principle.

Laudatory goals and courageous, selfless action are valuable in inspiring people — motivating them to accomplish more than they could imagine under ordinary circumstances. Reaching toward high ideals encourages people toward selfless generosity.

*Always do right. This will gratify some people, and astonish the rest.*
— Mark Twain

Figure 4.2 contrasts several important progressive behaviors and attitudes with non-progressive ones.

## Direct and Personal

A face-to-face interaction is more human and more effective in touching someone than an impersonal mass appeal. People are influenced much more by members of their immediate family, their friends, or their neighbors — those they have long experience with and have developed trust in — than by strangers or distant institutions. In addition, smiles, hugs, and physical warmth can convey love, support, and comfort much better than any words. Furthermore, while some people are motivated to work for change solely by noble passion or individual self-interest, more are attracted to the fellowship and solidarity they feel working in concert with their friends.

# Figure 4.2: Progressive Behavior and Attitudes

| Progressive* | Not Progressive |
|---|---|
| Belief in the possibility of a better society | Belief that not much can or should be changed |
| Honest | Deceitful, manipulative |
| Moral, principled, conscience-driven | Immoral, unscrupulous, expedience-driven |
| Democratic (political, economic, and social) | Dominating, oppressive |
| Respectful, caring, loving, compassionate | Self-righteous, vindictive, punitive, hateful |
| Giving, generous | Demanding, greedy, stingy |
| Seeking the common good | Seeking self-interest |
| Cooperative | Competitive |
| Oriented toward mutual problem solving | Oriented toward defeating others |
| Flexible, open, responsive | Rigid, closed-minded, suspicious, intransigent |
| Nonviolent | Threatening |
| Sensible, reasonable, wise | Irrational, prejudiced |
| Passionate | Shutdown, alienated |
| Responsible, committed | Irresponsible, capricious |

---

* Throughout this book, when I refer to *progressive activists*, I mean they adhere or aspire to all of *these* characteristics.

## A STRATEGY FOR DEMOCRATIC TRANSFORMATION

Because it is so often misunderstood or downplayed, let me emphasize one important point: creating a good society is quite different from grabbing control of society's power structure or manipulating the masses. To create a good society, progressive activists must transform deeply held cultural norms, overcome emotional blocks, redistribute power from the elite to everyone in roughly equal measure, and ensure people use their newly-acquired power responsibly and compassionately for the common good. To create a truly good society, activists must make these sweeping changes without establishing another coercive power structure.

*As the twig is bent, so grows the tree.* — English Proverb

I can see only one way to bring about this transformation democratically: activists must prepare people to take power and prepare them to assume power responsibly once they have taken it. In order not to be dictatorial, activists can challenge people, offer information, and provide support, but they cannot force people to act in any particular way. Therefore, **the main activities of progressive activists must be to develop and consistently convey alternative ideas to large numbers of people and help them integrate these ideas into society as they see fit.**

If people find these ideas valuable, they will eventually adopt them, just as progressive activists have adopted them for themselves. If people do not like these ideas, then as free citizens, they must be able to reject them.

*One cannot **impose** a cooperative, democratic society on people — they must adopt it and claim it as their own. Activists who are truly progressive cannot use force or trickery; we can only serve as mentors and midwives, showing the way and facilitating the birth of a new society. Our means must reflect our desired ends if we want our means to lead to those ends.*

## MASS EDUCATION AND POWERFUL SOCIAL CHANGE MOVEMENTS

As this discussion indicates, an effective strategy for progressive transformation depends on educating and transforming virtually everyone in this country so they can then *democratically choose* a good society. Since the mass media are not suitable for broadcasting ideas about fundamental progressive change, and progressive activists have little con-trol over the media anyway, activists must instead use more direct means.

As I envision it, advocates for progressive change would personally reach out to people — one by one when necessary — until they have touched essentially every person in this country. Activists would spend much of their efforts interacting directly with people — listening, talking, and discussing ideas, promoting the desirability of progressive change, showing how progressive ideas could work, and counseling and supporting people as they changed.

*A popular Government, without popular information, or the means of acquiring it, is but a Prologue to a Farce or a Tragedy; or, perhaps both. Knowledge will forever govern ignorance: and a people who mean to be their own Governors, must arm themselves with the power which knowledge gives.* — James Madison

However, this would not be a completely individual activity. Progressive activists would join together in grassroots change organizations that would provide them with mutual support, greater visibility, and collective power. Some of these organizations would directly challenge institutions while others would build alternative institutions that would eventually displace conventional institutions. In this way, each grassroots organization could directly reach hundreds of people and indirectly affect thousands with little interference from the power elite. With enough organizations spanning the country, they could influence everyone.

### Changing People's Perspectives

Some people are persuaded by reading an article or book, others by watching a television show. However, most people change their perspectives on important issues only after a series of convincing experiences:

• They witness horrible events and see that current institutions or authorities are unresponsive.

• They learn about better alternatives.

• They see that others are working to implement these alternatives.

• They watch authorities ignore problems, repress dissent, crush positive alternatives, and lie. They discover the truth and realize they have been fooled.

• They ponder the situation for a time and talk the issue through with a trusted friend. New ideas settle into their consciousness.

• They see how they might work with others to implement alternatives.

• They believe their efforts working for change are likely to succeed.

• They see people they know who are happy in similar post-change institutions.

Each change organization would not only communicate with people in its community, but it would also offer a safe, supportive environment for educating its own members. Surrounded by a progressive subculture, members would have a chance to learn new ideas and behaviors, plumb the depths of these ideas over an extended period, try them out in interactions with others, and thoughtfully consider how to integrate them into their own lives — all with little fear of retribution.

If hundreds of these grassroots organizations were networked or allied together by an issue or constituency, they would comprise a social movement potentially capable of influencing millions of people, undercutting the existing order, and bringing about large-scale change. If a large number of these progressive movements were working for change collaboratively (in coalition, federation, or alliance), they could fundamentally transform society using completely democratic and minimally coercive means.

## SIX ESSENTIAL COMPONENTS OF AN EFFECTIVE STRATEGY

As briefly outlined here, this mass education strategy seems quite simple. However, it encompasses more than is first apparent. To be effective, this strategy includes these six essential components:

## 1. Clear Conceptions of Progressive Change

Without knowing what a good society might be like or knowing feasible methods to create one, most people will never consider working for change. Moreover, without a clear understanding, they probably will not even passively endorse the work of progressive activists. Therefore, it is essential that a great many people believe it is possible to transform society and understand how to do it. Initially, only progressive activists must understand, but eventually almost everyone must have a clear sense.

Progressive activists must develop and convey both an inspiring vision of a truly good society and a comprehensive and workable plan for realizing that vision.[8]

*"Would you tell me, please, which way I ought to walk from here?"*

*"That depends a good deal on where you want to get to," said the Cat.*

*"I don't much care where," said Alice.*

*"Then it doesn't matter which way you walk."*
— Lewis Carroll,
**Alice in Wonderland**

### A CLEAR VISION OF A GOOD SOCIETY

Chapter 2 listed the basic elements that I believe should be part of a good society and detailed a few particular as-

# Figure 4.3: Essential Components of an Effective Strategy

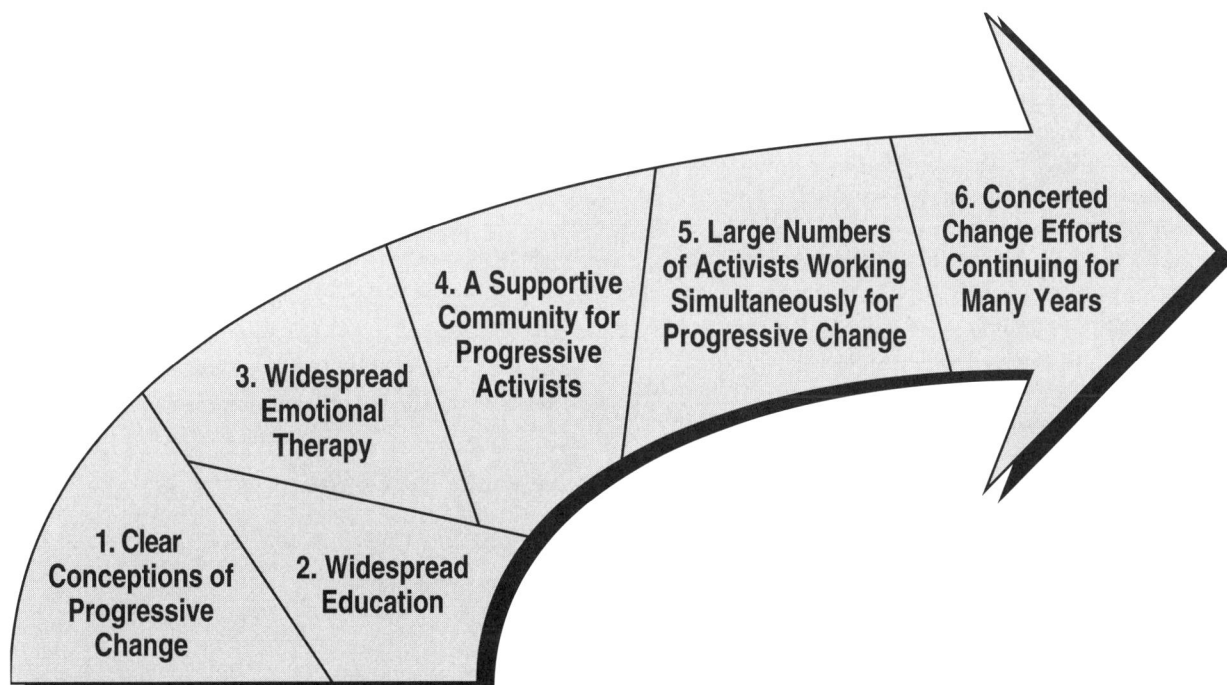

1. Clear Conceptions of Progressive Change

2. Widespread Education

3. Widespread Emotional Therapy

4. A Supportive Community for Progressive Activists

5. Large Numbers of Activists Working Simultaneously for Progressive Change

6. Concerted Change Efforts Continuing for Many Years

pects of such a society. I hope this skeletal framework can serve as the basis for a more comprehensive vision. As we move towards a good society, this vision must be expanded to address all parts of society and refined in light of new experience and the desires of every person.

### A COMPREHENSIVE AND FEASIBLE STRATEGY FOR CHANGE

A comprehensive and feasible plan for social transformation would galvanize many people to action. Such a plan would attract and excite those who are now discouraged by the apparent ineffectiveness of current progressive change efforts. It would alleviate newcomers' fear that progressives might lead them over a cliff or down a slow, winding path to nowhere. Moreover, a comprehensive plan would provide a reassuring context for the work of current progressive activists when their efforts seem inconsequential or unimportant. A clear plan could also help keep activists on track and bolster their fervor at those crucial times when frustrating setbacks might otherwise lead them to try unsavory shortcuts or give up.

For a progressive change plan to be comprehensive and feasible, it must be:

• **Realistic** — Since fundamental change of society is an enormous goal, an effective change strategy must be grounded in a realistic assessment of all the political, economic, social, and cultural forces in society. Like a strategy for war, it must consider the forces favoring and opposing progressive change and the power and resources (people, weapons, money, and influence) each side has at its command. A realistic plan must show how to overcome the obstacles described in the last chapter and incorporate the lessons from history listed above.

• **Thorough** — Just as a general contractor might plan construction of a building, each step must be laid out in a clear way — who does what first, how that step leads to the next step, what we can expect to follow, and so forth. Not every particular has to be specified completely, but the plan must be detailed enough that skeptics (potential supporters) find it realistic after careful scrutiny.

• **Encompassing** — The plan must seek to transform all aspects of society fundamentally, from humanizing the ways that people interact with each other to democratizing the large institutions of society. It cannot merely shift power from one group of elite power brokers to another. Rather, it must empower citizens to take charge of societal institutions and to operate them equitably and compassionately for the common good.

The plan must also consist of many, diverse campaigns for change that affect a wide range of people and effectively address a variety of important issues so that, in total, they comprise a comprehensive change strategy.

• **Practical** — The plan must be practical. It must rely on techniques and tactics of demonstrated effectiveness. Furthermore, these methods must be within the realm of experience and the bounds of morality of the people who will use them.

• **Honorable, Lofty, Inspiring** — To garner widespread support, the plan must rely on actions that most people in society consider morally sterling. Furthermore, to have a chance of working, the plan should inspire people to their best behavior — bringing out the compassion, empathy, and concern for the common good that usually emerge only in times of disaster or war.

• **Consistent with Goals** — If it is to bring about truly fundamental change, the plan must employ the tools of a good society as it creates that society. The plan itself must be inclusive of all people, cooperative, just, and democratic. All aspects of the plan must build towards a good society.

• **Flexible and Adaptable** — Mistakes and changing circumstances require that evaluation, correction, and change be built into the plan. Otherwise, change efforts will more than likely become rigid, inappropriate, and possibly even tyrannical.

Since creating a good society is a long process — stretching over decades — the change process will likely evolve through several distinctive stages: building a foundation in the early years, making critical changes in the middle years, and consolidating the changes in the later years. It will encompass a variety of large campaigns, each with many smaller sub-campaigns.

This book is my attempt to formulate a preliminary plan for change that meets these criteria. The plan outlined here must, of course, be expanded and refined over time to accommodate changes and new understandings.

## 2. Widespread Education

Somehow progressive activists must convey a vision of a good society to the vast majority of people and help them develop the skills necessary to create and maintain a good society. This requires an educational process capable of reaching virtually everyone.

In addition, progressive activists must acquire the knowledge and skills they need to bring about change. This requires another educational process geared specifically to current and future activists.

*Since a democratic society repudiates the principle of external authority, it must find a substitute in voluntary disposition and interest; these can be created only by education.* — John Dewey

### LEARN HOW SOCIETY ACTUALLY FUNCTIONS

People must learn how to recognize the myths that obscure understanding of our society. They must begin to see how destructive and cruel our society really is. They must learn the truth about how it actually functions and who really has power: who makes decisions and how they implement them. People must also learn that it is possible for ordinary people to gain power and struggle for positive change.

## LEARN TO PRACTICE DEMOCRACY AND COOPERATION

To create and maintain a good society, the vast majority of people must also have a vision of a good society and be able to practice democracy, cooperation, and other progressive means for working and living together. Many people have never seen these methods practiced at all, and most have never seen them practiced well. Of those few people who have any experience with these methods, most have not learned how to use them well.

Instead, people practice what they know: They boss their children and spank them when they do not obey. They tolerate schoolyard bullying. They support rabid sports competition. They endorse schools that rely on rote memorization and mindless regurgitation. They accept undemocratic voting procedures. They acquiesce to domination by people up the hierarchy. They pass along to their children their misconceptions, prejudices, fears, and addictions.

*Enlighten the people generally, and tyranny and oppressions of body and mind will vanish like the evil spirits at the dawn of day.* — Thomas Jefferson

Skills required for a good society include the ability to:
• Read, write, and do arithmetic at a basic level
• Think critically and sort out conflicting claims
• Listen well and empathize with others' positions
• Convey ideas to others by speaking clearly
• Cooperate with others and work in a team
• Solve problems creatively
• Make decisions cooperatively and democratically
• Share equitably with others
• Resolve conflict well
• Stand up to prejudice
• Nonviolently challenge injustice and imbalances of power
• Rear children in a way that preserves the child's self-esteem and inculcates responsibility

Schools in the United States address some of these areas and impart a rudimentary level of skill, but far more is needed.

For example, our society is ostensibly democratic, but the democracy most people first see is the charade practiced by their school Student Council. Student Councils are usually impotent bodies populated by ambitious students who run for office mainly out of the desire to build up their résumés or to impress their parents. Student Council members are typically elected by a small minority of students who voted primarily because of their candidate's popularity or flamboyant campaign tactics. Council members are generally ignorant about policy issues, and the Council usually has no real power to change any important policies anyway.

Seeing this, students learn that democracy is a silly game played primarily by attention-seekers. Their cynicism towards democracy then extends to local, state, and national government, especially when they learn that corruption and fraud are commonplace.

Real democracy is, of course, quite different from this. It requires knowledgeable and assertive citizens who can debate real issues and come up with decisions that best address the common good. People must know how to research issues, how to formulate positions, and how to explain their perspective to others. They must know how to hear others' perspectives, how to ask penetrating questions, how to develop solutions, and how to work together to integrate various perspectives into a good decision that truly addresses community needs and to which everyone can consent. They must also know how to implement these decisions in a fair and timely manner.

*Which is the best government? That which teaches us to govern ourselves.* — Johann Wolfgang von Goethe

Since people have not grown up in a good society and learned these skills by watching others, everyone must be shown or taught them more directly. Since the public schools do not teach these skills, progressive activists must. So an effective change strategy must include an educational process that can convey these ideas and skills thoroughly enough that most people can acquire them.

## LEARN TO OVERCOME DESTRUCTIVE CULTURAL CONDITIONING

As described in the last chapter, every society has strong cultural norms, most of them benign. However, some norms are destructive and must be changed before a good society can flourish.

Societal norms change slowly, but individuals often adopt new cultures quite readily. Robert F. Allen and the staff of the Human Resources Institute discovered, to their dismay, just how quickly young people could adopt delinquency culture.[9] In their research in the early 1950s, they followed black families that had recently moved from the South or Puerto Rico to urban areas in the Northeast. Many black youngsters who had never been involved in delinquency were transformed into full-fledged miscreants in just six to eight months. Clearly, urban ghettos provided an effective training program. Moreover, the process took place in such a way that the young boys only barely noticed what was happening to them.

*Habit is habit, and not to be flung out of the window by any man, but coaxed downstairs a step at a time.* — Mark Twain

In a similar fashion, a person will adopt a more positive culture if immersed in a favorable environment. Allen and his colleagues found that to develop positive behavior such an environment should include these seven elements:

• Direct communication of what behavior is acceptable and expected and why.

• Modeling of this positive behavior by others, especially those with the most influence.

• Commitment of time and resources to good behavior.

• Training and practice of positive behavior so a person can actually do it when she tries.

• Rewards for positive behavior (attention, praise, awards, money) and penalties for destructive behavior (confrontation, condemnation).

• Constant contact with people who act well and limited contact with people who act badly. When it is impossible to change the larger culture, this contact can be provided by a positive mini-culture in which everyone acts well within the local environment.

• Immediate contact with people who act well when a person first comes into the environment since a person is especially receptive to new norms when she first tries to establish friendships and fit in.

---

*The great law of culture is to let each become all that he was created capable of being; expand, if possible to his full growth; resisting all impediments, casting off all foreign, especially noxious adhesions, and show himself in his own shape and stature, be those what they may.* — Thomas Carlyle

---

Generally, people take several steps to overcome their destructive cultural conditioning:

• **Open Up** — They expose themselves to other cultures and new ideas. Many people learn through travel or by meeting travelers from other places. Some people attend lectures, workshops, theater, or concerts to expose themselves to new ideas. Others survey local churches or social clubs, looking for unique perspectives. Books, magazines, movies, radio, and television can also provide a window into other worlds.

• **Observe** — They become aware that cultural norms shape their beliefs, values, and feelings. They notice the ways these norms are taught and the ways they are enforced. They recognize that other people have different ideas and different ways to do things.

• **Evaluate** — They compare their own beliefs, values, and feelings to those of other people to see which are more humane and useful.

• **Decide** — They decide to adopt more humane beliefs and feelings and decide to act in new, more appropriate or useful ways.

• **Act** — They behave more like their ideal. They restrain their hurtful behavior and change their relationships with others.

• **Practice** — They practice their new behaviors and beliefs repeatedly until these behaviors and beliefs feel "normal."

• **Create a Subculture** — They find other people who also want to adopt new cultural norms and interact with them in the new ways, thus creating their own subculture with its own positive norms.

To deliberately adopt and adhere to new cultural norms, a group should ensure that all aspects of the group are oriented toward the new norms. Each individual must be supported and encouraged to adopt the new culture, and the group as a whole must explicitly choose the new cultural norms and try to move towards them. Moreover, the leaders of the group must adopt the new norms and allocate resources to move the group towards them. The policies, procedures, and programs of the group must also be brought into alignment with the new norms.

Changing our whole society's cultural norms will require changing the culture of the society's leadership as well as societal policies and institutions.

### LEARN TO CHANGE SOCIETY

As detailed in the previous chapter, progressive activists now usually learn how to create change by watching other activists. Since these other activists are seldom very knowledgeable about theory, strategy, and tactics or skilled in effective change techniques, new activists are often taught poorly. They generally learn slowly through trial and error. Consequently, many new activists burn out long before they have a chance to learn much.

To be effective, activists must learn to design powerful and exciting campaigns that move toward fundamental change, and they must learn how to develop and promote positive cultural norms. They must learn how to avoid and overcome dysfunctional patterned behavior, infighting, groupthink, and hopelessness. They must also learn how to support other activists and how to arrange emotional support for themselves.

Moreover, activists must learn — even better than everyone else — how to practice democracy and cooperation. Obviously, activists cannot show the way to others unless they have already traveled the path and know it well. An effective change strategy must therefore include an educational process that can expeditiously pass on to most activists all the knowledge and skills they need.

## 3. Widespread Emotional Therapy

A good society cannot exist if everyone suffers from emotional trauma and regularly acts out in inappropriate ways. Moreover, progressive activists cannot work effectively to create a good society if they continually carry around their own emotional baggage.

To reduce emotional trauma, an effective strategy for change must offer effective emotional therapy to most people. It must include ways for people to learn how to stop inflicting their dysfunctional behavior on others and help them learn means to interrupt other's inappropriate behavior. They must also learn how to overcome their addictions and inhibitions. Moreover, an effective strategy must provide a way for progressive activists to work through their emotional conditioning and heal enough so they can think clearly in stressful situations, confront other peoples' worst behavior, and quickly rebound from attacks.

> *One will rarely err if extreme actions be ascribed to vanity, ordinary actions to habit, and mean actions to fear.*
> — Friedrich Nietzsche

### STEPS TO EMOTIONAL HEALTH

Generally, people take several steps on the way to emotional health:

• **Observe** — They notice the ways their behavior is inappropriate or unproductive, especially the ways it is hurtful to themselves or others. They observe the ways other people act that are more appropriate, effective, or compassionate.

• **Digest** — They ponder and analyze their emotional responses. They think, talk, and write about their life and the traumas that they have suffered in childhood (and more recently). They consider how past traumas affect their current behavior. They notice the decisions they have made over the years and how those decisions have led to the life they now have.

• **Explore Possibilities** — They envision new ways to feel and behave that are more appropriate and self-affirming.

# Autobiography
# in Five Short Chapters

by Portia Nelson[10]

**Chapter One**: *I walk down the street. There is a deep hole in the sidewalk. I fall in. I am lost... I am helpless. It isn't my fault. It takes forever to find a way out.*

**Chapter Two**: *I walk down the same street. There is a deep hole in the sidewalk. I pretend I don't see it. I fall in again. I can't believe I'm in the same place. But it isn't my fault. It still takes a long time to get out.*

**Chapter Three**: *I walk down the same street. There is a deep hole in the sidewalk. I see it is there. I still fall in... It's a habit... but, my eyes are open. I know where I am. It is my fault. I get out immediately.*

**Chapter Four**: *I walk down the same street. There is a deep hole in the sidewalk. I walk around it.*

**Chapter Five**: *I walk down another street.*

They consider other ways to live, other decisions they might make, and new directions they might go.

• **Decide** — They decide to act in new, more appropriate or useful ways, and they work to change their conception of themselves to reflect their true self-worth.

• **Plan and Arrange** — They arrange for other people to help them act in these new ways. They plan ways to escape or change their violent or degrading home life or workplace. They consider who can provide support and encouragement as they move forward.

• **Act** — They behave more like their ideal. They avoid or escape from hurtful situations, restrain their hurtful behavior, change their relationships with others, and begin to feel good about themselves. They focus on pleasant activities and their successes. They seek out supportive friends.

• **Emote** — As feelings of anger, frustration, fear, and confusion arise, they express these feelings in a safe and supportive environment — either with a counselor or with family or friends.

> *A hearty laugh gives one a dry cleaning, while a good cry is a wet wash.*
> — Puzant Kevork Thomajan

• **Move On** — They avoid hurtful situations, and they focus on the future. They move on to a better life and continue working through any other emotional barriers they discover in themselves.

Some people can work through their emotional wounds and choose positive new directions without any help. They typically use several techniques. Some think over their life while walking in the woods or sitting on a mountaintop. This allows them to sort out the truth without intrusive interference by others, and it costs nothing. Others write their thoughts in a journal. Some people give themselves daily affirmations and encouragement to move forward.[11] Some people immerse themselves in science fiction, fantasy stories, role-playing, spiritual explorations, or even hallucinogenic drug experiences to kick themselves out of their rigid patterns and to push themselves towards alternative perspectives and activities. Though these methods are effective for many people, there is always a danger that they will cause some people to veer off into a fantasyland instead of staying grounded in the reality of their lives.

To surmount severe emotional trauma, most people need assistance. Skilled therapists or members of the clergy can help people by:

• providing a safe, compassionate environment
• providing nurturance and encouragement
• providing an objective, uninvolved point of view
• providing solid information about emotional traumas, their sources, and how to overcome them
• suggesting alternative behaviors and activities
• serving as a role model of emotional health and appropriate behavior

Since good therapists are expensive and members of the clergy have limited time, many people rely instead on mutual support and cooperative counseling with their friends or colleagues. To work well, peer counselors must devote at least as much energy as, and develop skills comparable to, beginning therapists.

Through emotional therapy, activists can overcome many negative feelings and behaviors and thus act intelligently, flexibly, and passionately. Good emotional therapy can dramatically improve an activist's ability to perform social change work. It can also make her much happier.

---

*By starving emotions we become humorless, rigid and stereotyped; by repressing them we become literal, reformatory and holier-than-thou; encouraged, they perfume life; discouraged, they poison it.* — Joseph Collins

---

My own counseling experience is quite positive. For ten years, I was involved with a peer counseling organization. Each week I attended a two-hour class taught by a more experienced counselor. Every week I also had two or three counseling sessions, each with a different class member. In these sessions, I would counsel my partner for an hour, then we would switch, and she would counsel me for an hour. Since leaving this organization, I still have a weekly counseling session and attend a support group every three weeks. With this support, I have overcome many of my limitations. Stormy emotions no longer run my life, and I am now able to redirect this energy into positive change activity.

Still, even with good counseling and solid support, emotional injuries are difficult to heal. It often takes years to sort through the emotions and more years for their intensity to subside. The only long-term solution is prevention — raising children in a loving and supportive environment. When efforts to create a good society begin to succeed (especially in eliminating childhood traumas like child abuse, neglect, and poverty), there will be more emotionally healthy people

*Do the best you can — you can't do any better than that.*

### The Healing Power of Positive Change Work

Powerful, positive social change work can be very effective in helping people overcome their dysfunctional emotional conditioning. The camaraderie that comes from working with others and the ennoblement that comes from working for a righteous cause can counter feelings of loneliness, low self-esteem, alienation, purposelessness, and hopelessness.

around. In the meantime, we must accept that many people will have emotional wounds.

## 4. A Supportive Community for Progressive Activists

Activists thrive best when immersed in a supportive community that practices positive cultural norms. Such a group can push each activist to act her best. In such an environment, activists can also try out innovative ideas without fear of condemnation.

When times are rough, progressive activists must get both practical and emotional support from others. A supportive community can furnish this assistance, offer nurturance, and provide a safe space to heal from attacks. When activists know they have access to such a safe, supportive community, they are less afraid of being attacked by powerful interests or being abandoned by unsupportive family or disgruntled friends. This results in happier, clearer-thinking activists who are more compassionate and can take bolder and wiser action.

*People are more fun than anybody.* — Dorothy Parker

A strong, supportive community of activists, in which everyone is usually in good emotional health, is also more resistant to infighting. Whenever an activist exhibits signs of stress or trauma, others can move in with loving support. They can interrupt that person's destructive behavior and guide her back to emotional health before she hurts anyone else. In this way, no one ever goes overboard, and the community can remain harmonious.

In addition, a supportive community can provide:
- Shared resources (such as computers, automobiles, tools, and so on)
- Financial aid (including loans and grants)
- Help with basic life maintenance (help with housework, food preparation, transportation, childcare, eldercare)
- Help in learning skills or acquiring knowledge
- Companionship for shared leisure activities (including singing, massage, and play)
- Supportive interaction (active listening, encouragement, provocative questioning, cuddling, support for nonconforming behaviors and dissenting ideas)
- Help in dealing with conflicts
- Long-term social interaction (providing stability and commitment)
- Help with progressive change efforts
- Help in fending off outside attacks or threats
- Connection to more distant activists who can help in difficult times

Traditionally, support for activists has been provided by lovers, secretaries, subordinates, or hired consultants (such as mediators and bookkeepers), but these resources are generally not available to progressive activists who are dedi-

## Living Simply

By living simply, activists can reduce their dependence on society, escape many pressures to conform to the dominant culture, and free up more time and resources for progressive change. Simple living is also more ecologically responsible.

Activists can live more simply by:
• Sharing housing, vehicles, tools, books, equipment, facilities, and so on
• Ignoring fashion trends and beauty regimens
• Limiting purchases to essentials — hand-making gifts, toys, and the like instead of buying them
• Fixing and mending items instead of buying new ones
• Substituting simple pleasures like hiking, conversation, storytelling, shared play, music, and reading for expensive luxury goods and tourist travel
• Reducing health care needs by exercising regularly, eating a healthy diet, receiving massages, and engaging in meditation, counseling, and sufficient leisure

cated to equality or too poor to hire assistants. A supportive community in which activists voluntarily and mutually support one another offers a better way.

## 5. Large Numbers of Activists Working Simultaneously for Progressive Change

As explained above, both morality and practicality dictate that a good strategy must use democratic and non-coercive means to bring about fundamental change. This means the vast majority of people in this country must at least passively tolerate each of the major changes.

To reach and influence the vast majority of people requires that large numbers of progressives become advocates for fundamental change. Only when there are large numbers of activists can they personally inform, persuade, encourage, inspire, and support each person to learn and change at her own pace.

*Light is the task where many share the toil.* — Homer

Moreover, only large numbers of activists can simultaneously challenge scores of harmful existing institutions, build alternative institutions to replace them, and resist the immense might of the power elite. With large numbers, activists could challenge elite interests from so many directions at once that they would be overwhelmed and their capacity to retaliate would diminish. This, in turn, would offer hope that real change was possible, which would inspire even more people to join the effort and would energize activists to work harder.

Currently in the United States, millions of progressive-minded people desire positive change. However, only a relatively small percentage of these people actively work for comprehensive, fundamental change.

Based on my experience and research, I estimate about 50,000 people work a sizable number of hours each week for fundamental progressive change. Probably an additional 300,000 progressive advocates talk with their family and friends about fundamental change and occasionally work for it. Perhaps several hundred thousand more people desire fundamental change, but do little beyond contributing small amounts of money to progressive organizations.*

Based on my experience, I estimate that fundamental change will require at least three times as many progressive activists and advocates — at least a million people working actively for fundamental, comprehensive change. To transform society, these activists and advocates must also be more experienced, skilled, and capable than their counterparts are today.

## 6. Concerted Change Efforts Continuing for Many Years

To provide sufficient time to reach the vast majority of people in this country and enough time to sway most of them profoundly, these progressive activists must maintain a high level of change activity over many years. Moreover, enough decades must go by so that those people who are unable to change can grow old, pass away, and be replaced by young people more receptive to progressive ideals. It also takes decades to design and build alternative structures. Therefore, I estimate it would take at least forty years of concerted effort to bring about a comprehensive transformation of society.

*By the fall of drops of water, by degrees, a pot is filled.*
— The Hitopadesa

## AN EFFECTIVE STRATEGY THAT INCORPORATES THESE COMPONENTS

If carried out well, I believe the change strategy outlined here, encompassing these six essential components, would be sufficient to overcome the five main obstacles to fundamental progressive change described in the previous chapter. This strategy — based on mass education and powerful social change

*Energy and persistence conquer all things.*
— Benjamin Franklin

---

* These estimates take into account all the employees and volunteers of change and service organizations, political officeholders and their staffmembers, government employees, public-interest lawyers, labor organizers, teachers, students, and ministers. Figure C.4 in Appendix C provides more details about these estimates.

movements — would also enable progressive activists to bring about fundamental transformation of our society in a principled way consistent with participatory democracy and other progressive ideals.

The next six chapters expand on this general strategy and detail a specific program for implementing it.

---

# NOTES FOR CHAPTER 4

[1] A few scholars have argued that some prehistorical societies were gentle, compassionate, equitable, and pacifistic, that is, good societies. See, for example, Riane Eisler, *The Chalice and the Blade: Our History, Our Future* (San Francisco, Harper & Row, 1987, HQ1075 .E57 1987). Even if this is true, they assume that these societies evolved naturally from small hunter-gatherer societies, so no one had to transform a bad society into a good one, as we must do.

[2] For an excellent summary of many historical change movements and theories, see David Miller, ed., *The Blackwell Encyclopedia of Political Thought* (Oxford, UK: Blackwell Publishers, 1987, JA61 .B57 1987). For a good summary of the history of leftist movements in the United States in the twentieth century, see John Patrick Diggins, *The Rise and Fall of the American Left* (New York: W. W. Norton, 1992, HN90 .R3D556 1992).

[3] Jack Goldstone, "Revolutions, Theory of," *The Blackwell Encyclopedia of Political Thought*, pp. 436–441.

[4] See, for example, Karl Marx and Friedrich Engels, *Communist Manifesto* (1848), and Karl Marx, *Capital* (1867), in Lewis S. Feuer, ed., *Marx and Engels: Basic Writings on Politics and Philosophy* (Garden City, NY: Anchor, Doubleday, 1959, HX276 .M27736).

[5] Marxist Ronald Aronson persuasively argues that capitalism has changed in ways not anticipated by Marx. After careful study, he concludes that

> Marxism as a revolutionary project, compelling as it has been, belongs to an earlier age. Any new radical project, for all its continuing commitment to emancipation and social justice, will look and feel very different.

Ronald Aronson, *After Marxism* (New York: Guilford Press, 1995, HX44.5 .A78 1994), p. 39.

[6] See Lawrence Goodwyn, *The Populist Moment: A Short History of the Agrarian Revolt in America* (Oxford, UK: Oxford University Press, 1978, E669 .G672 1978).

[7] Michael Fullerton, ed., *What Happened to the Berkeley Co-op? A Collection of Opinions* (Davis, CA: Center for Cooperatives, University of California, 1992).

Note that some co-ops are still doing well, and the co-op movement is still strong in some places.

[8] Marxist Ronald Aronson argues this point clearly:

> No new radical project is possible that is not constructed around a unifying and compelling vision of a different social order. Any new movement, to be effective, will have to provide a convincing account of the major problems caused by the existing order, principal structures to be changed, and groups of people likely to struggle for such changes. It will have to nourish powerful convictions about the kinds of changes being pursued and about its participants' ability to achieve them. It will have to mobilize people — by generating wide solidarity, giving people a sense of political and personal direction, and by simultaneously promoting self-confidence and realism. Its members will have to be sustained by a clear understanding of being wronged, deep convictions about being right, an awareness of being strong, a sense of building a new future, an effective understanding of the present, and a sense of hope and possibility.

Ronald Aronson, *After Marxism* (New York: Guilford Press, 1995, HX44.5 .A78 1994), p. 231.

On page 244, Aronson describes some essential features of a powerful movement. The people in it must:

- Have the **will** to achieve their goal of changing the social order
- Feel they have the **right** to that change
- Feel they are **capable** of achieving and enjoying that change
- Believe it is historically **possible** to achieve the change

[9] Robert F. Allen, *Beat the System!: A Way to Create More Human Environments* (New York: McGraw-Hill, 1980, HM101 .A574), pp. vii, 56–57.

[10] Portia Nelson, "Autobiography in Five Short Chapters," *There's a Hole in my Sidewalk: The Romance of Self-Discovery* (Hillsboro, OR: Beyond Words Publishing, 1993), 2–3. Used with the permission of Beyond Words Publishing.

[11] I have found a guided meditation audiotape to be quite useful in helping me relax and visualize overcoming barriers and moving toward my highest ideals. Prepared by Dr. Emmett Miller and called "Healing Journey," it is available for $12 from: Source Cassette Learning Systems, Inc., 131 East Placer St., P.O. Box 6028, Auburn, CA 95604, 800-528-2737, dmae@drmiller.com <http://www.drmiller.com/manage.html>.

# 5

# *A Strategic Program to Create a Good Society*

*The strategy for fundamental change described in the last chapter provides a general outline, but how can we implement it?*

This chapter details a strategic program for progressive transformation — a strategy that possesses the crucial characteristics and incorporates the six essential components described in the last chapter. Relying heavily on a broad educational process, this strategic program would persuade an ever-larger number of people to support fundamental progressive change. Then, working primarily in small, local organizations, progressive activists would use their collective strength to nonviolently challenge and undermine destructive institutions while developing new, progressive institutions.

This chapter provides an overview of the strategic program. The next five chapters offer a specific project to implement this strategy.

## A STRATEGIC PROGRAM

Building on models developed by historians, sociologists, and social change theoreticians over the last century, this strategic program involves several major parts.[1] For the sake of clarity, I have divided this program into four main stages with several sub-stages. Though described here as if they are distinct and sequential, these stages would blend and intertwine.

> *The wind and the waves are always on the side of the ablest navigators.*
> — Edward Gibbon

Note that progressive activists are already working in all the stages described here, though at a level that appears to be insufficient to bring about fundamental change. The program I envision would augment this current work. Also, note that unlike most earlier strategies, which typically assume historic change occurring over a few years, this strategy would extend over many decades.[*]

## 1. Lay the Groundwork

In the first stage, the public is largely ignorant of ways to bring about comprehensive change. Virtually everyone feels either content with the current society or hopeless about the prospects for significant change (as most people do now).

---

[*] As a conceptual aid, I think of these stages as each lasting roughly twenty years and being sequential. However, as noted in the section below entitled "Overlapping Stages," these stages overlap and intertwine and may take many more or many fewer years to implement.

---

# Four Stages of Societal Transformation

## 1. Lay the Groundwork
   A. Find Other Progressives
   B. Learn How Human Affairs are Now Organized
   C. Learn and Practice Change Skills
   D. Form Supportive Communities

## 2. Gather Support
   A. Raise Consciousness
   B. Build Organizational Strength

## 3. Struggle for Power
   A. Challenge the Power Structure through Conventional Political and Legal Methods
   B. Illuminate Domination and Oppression
   C. Fight Oppression Using Nonviolent Action
   D. Develop Popular Alternative Institutions

## 4. Diffuse Change Throughout Society

---

During this time, people desiring positive change would locate each other. They would also learn what they need to know to bring about powerful change, and they would build strong communities for mutual support.

### A. FIND OTHER PROGRESSIVES

Those people of goodwill who desire positive change would first seek out other like-minded people. When they found each other, they would discuss and develop their ideas for change. They would encourage each other to ask difficult questions and would search together for real answers, even if that meant looking beyond conventional progressive wisdom.

### B. LEARN HOW HUMAN AFFAIRS ARE NOW ORGANIZED

These progressive-minded people would then learn all about our current society. They would learn how elite interests control the social, economic, political, and cultural institutions of society and how the power structure entices and forces us all to support the status quo. They would explore issues such as why sales taxes are charged on almost every commodity, but not on the sale of stocks and bonds. They would study progressive change campaigns of the past and examine change methods that might be effective now. They would investigate alternative institutions of the past and decide which might be useful now.

*The penalty good men pay for indifference to public affairs is to be ruled by evil men.* — Plato

In addition, these progressive people would observe the ways that socialization, oppression, and emotional trauma affect human beings and find ways to overcome destructive conditioning. They would explore their own dysfunctional socialization and emotional conditioning, notice the ways they currently behave ineffectively, and learn better ways.

### C. LEARN AND PRACTICE CHANGE SKILLS

These progressives would then begin to think of themselves as "activists." They would learn the skills necessary to launch campaigns for change and practice their skills by joining current efforts to challenge the power structure and harmful social norms. They would research issues, circulate petitions, boycott destructive companies, and help progressive politicians run for elective office. They would support existing alternative institutions (like cooperatives) and explore ways to build new ones.

### D. FORM SUPPORTIVE COMMUNITIES

These activists would also establish supportive change communities with other progressive activists. As much as possible, they would treat each other well and live as if they already had a good society: they would "live the vision now" in their everyday lives. They would also find ways to support each other physically, financially, and emotionally. They would begin to work through their own negative socialization and emotional conditioning, and they would work to develop the determination and self-discipline necessary to bring about significant positive change.

At the successful end of Stage 1, hundreds of thousands of progressive activists would have developed a great deal of experience and change skill — more than most activists have today. They would have a deep understanding of how large, impersonal forces shape our society. They would also have changed their work and home lives to minimize the worst pressures of conventional society on themselves. When possible, they would live in a mutually supportive community with other activists.

## 2. Gather Support

In the second stage, activists would reach out to millions of regular people — raising awareness and building powerful organizations.

### A. RAISE CONSCIOUSNESS

To raise awareness about the need for change, activists would speak to members of existing organizations (church and civic organizations groups, labor unions, professional associations, and so forth), distribute leaflets at community events (festivals, county fairs, concerts) or door-to-door, and publish newspapers, magazines, books, and web pages on the internet. They would produce radio and TV shows and speak out on street corners. They would petition, vigil, march, parade, and picket. They would perform political theater and sing inspiring songs of change.

Through these means, activists would identify a variety of societal problems and explain (or directly demonstrate) that existing institutions cannot or will not solve these problems. They would contrast these flawed institutions with progressive alternatives that *do* address and solve these problems.* They would paint a vision of a good, non-oppressive society and describe a viable strategy for getting there. They would cite the immediate and long-term material, emotional, and spiritual benefits of a good society for all of humankind and the immediate benefits of working for change to activists (such as enhanced self-respect and warm fellowship). In addition, they would urge people to learn more and to join in the effort to create a good society.

*Ideas are the factors that lift civilization. They create revolutions. There is more dynamite in an idea than in many bombs.*
— John H. Vincent

To raise consciousness, progressive activists would first encourage people to talk with their friends about their troubles and fears. This interaction would likely reveal that each person's problems are not unique, but are actually shared by many others. Activists would also point out that many of these problems are the result of large social and political forces that can only be addressed through society-wide change. They would further explain that society is structured in such a way that it often supports oppression and perpetuates personal dysfunction. For example, activists might point out that schools often teach students to think they are stupid instead of helping them to learn.

Activists would explain how people are socialized to accept cultural norms and show that many of these norms do not serve us well. They would describe new cultural mores that were more humane and suitable. They would model these values with their own behavior, and they would help others unearth their own positive social skills. They would also demonstrate various ways to develop positive social norms and spread them to other people.

*You cannot teach a man anything; you can only help him find it within himself.* — Galileo

In addition, activists would explain how humans internalize their emotional injuries and demonstrate potent ways to heal these hurts. They would make it clear that many "immutable personality traits" are actually just the lingering manifestations of emotional trauma. They would help people to develop complete respect for themselves and encourage them to accept others.

Progressive activists would encourage people to look at their own lives, ask questions, and discuss their ideas with others. They would encourage people to develop a broad environmental, humanistic, and global consciousness and strive for the elimination of all oppression of all people (and other species and the natural environment) in all ways at all levels. They would explain the limitations of simple reforms and point out the need for deep systemic transformation to end all oppression. Above all, they would encourage people to take action.

*Ye shall know the truth, and the truth shall make thee mad.*
— Aldous Huxley

During this stage, there are several specific societal myths, propagated by the power elite and conservatives, that activists would need to challenge and debunk:

- **Myth**: Your troubles are your own fault.
- **Myth**: Your troubles are caused by racial minorities, immigrants, women, poor people, drug addicts, fuzzyheaded liberals, or haughty professors.
- **Myth**: It is impossible to have a good society — so this is the best for which we can hope.
- **Myth**: Like the weather, society's institutions and processes are natural phenomena that human beings cannot affect. Society has always been like this, and it always will.
- **Myth**: Running the country is a difficult job that is best left to the smart people who now run it. Ordinary people are too dumb or screwed up to run it.
- **Myth**: Elite interests (or cultural norms or emotional conditioning) are so powerful that ordinary people cannot overcome them. "You can't fight City Hall."
- **Myth**: Progressive activists are impractical idealists.
- **Myth**: Progressive activists are dangerous radicals, influenced by weird, un-American ideas.
- **Myth**: Progressive activists are strange, deranged people trying to lure others to join their bizarre cults.

These societal myths are widely held across society. A stirring speech or a well-written leaflet may convince some people these myths are false. But most people will require much more persuasion at a deeper and more personal level with people they trust. Some will reject these myths only when they are disproved repeatedly through demonstrated activity.

Activists would thus need to spend considerable time talking directly with people. They must also create alternatives that thoroughly expose and contradict these myths. To persuade the staunchest skeptics, activists might need to model these alternatives personally for many years.

At the successful end of this sub-stage, a majority of the public would be both hopeful and justifiably upset. They would desire a good society, understand they do not currently have one, see that it is possible to have one, and realize there are no acceptable reasons they cannot have one. They would understand how the power structure, cultural

---

* To show people that existing institutions are unresponsive, activists might use some of the techniques described below in Stages 3A and 3B. Demonstrating alternatives is classified as Stage 3D.

socialization, and emotional conditioning preserve the status quo, and they would find this state of affairs disturbing. They would be ready for significant change and sympathetic to those who were working for positive change. Large numbers would be inclined to devote some effort to work toward a good society. Many would be willing to join a progressive change organization.

### B. BUILD ORGANIZATIONAL STRENGTH

In this stage, progressive activists would also build a network of thousands of progressive organizations that would develop extensive analyses and programs for change. As I see it, activists would work primarily with four kinds of organizations:

> *We must learn to live together as brothers or perish together as fools.*
> — Martin Luther King, Jr.

(1) Most activists would form local groups dedicated to working for fundamental progressive change in their community. These groups would raise the public's consciousness (as described above) and prepare to struggle with the power structure (as described below in Stage 3).

Like current grassroots organizations, these groups might be completely independent or, more likely, they would be loosely allied with state, national, or international organizations. However, by being relatively small and locally controlled, these groups would allow extensive dialog among their members and encourage democratic participation in determining the direction of the group. Through participation in their governance, each member would learn how to work with others and would develop the skills necessary for direct democracy.

As I envision it, these groups would also provide a basic support network for their members, capable of supplying physical, economic, or emotional aid. They would offer a sympathetic environment for people to overcome their emotional blocks and patterns of submission. They would also serve as a friendship community, allowing people to play and celebrate together.

Like grassroots groups today, some of these groups would probably focus on a single progressive issue, chosen because it best illuminates an important problem or offers the best opportunity for fundamental change. Other groups would have a broader focus, working for fundamental transformation on many issues. Some groups might constitute local chapters of a progressive political party.

(2) Some activists would work primarily with state, national, or international organizations, researching issues, lobbying officeholders to vote for progressive measures, or coordinating the work of local organizations.

(3) Other activists would work primarily with existing mainstream organizations (churches, labor unions, professional societies, civic clubs, service organizations, political parties). They would push these organizations to work for fundamental reforms. Within these organizations they might form study groups, social action committees, or pro-

gressive caucuses. They would work to persuade individual members to adopt a more progressive outlook and would work to shift the organization toward a more progressive stance.

(4) Still other activists would devote their efforts to establishing a variety of alternative institutions inspired by progressive ideals: cooperative businesses, cooperative households or communities, humane social service agencies, volunteer police, fire, or rescue groups, alternative radio stations, community television stations, and so forth. To bring about fundamental change, they would choose to build alternatives that undercut the control of the power elite and redirected resources toward progressive change. For example, the currently existing company, Working Assets Long Distance, provides long distance telephone service. However, unlike its competitors, it places its advertising in alternative magazines and contributes one percent of its total revenue to progressive organizations.

---

## Small, Grassroots Organizations

To create a good society, some activists must work in Washington, DC, New York, and other centers of political and economic power where they can directly influence decision-makers. However, to build a widespread, democratic movement for progressive change, most activists must work at the local level where they can involve large numbers of ordinary people and steadily build broad organizations. Ideally, some activists would live in every community in the United States so they could personally engage and influence every person in the country. Moreover, to build democracy, activists must be free to pursue their own political interests and work for change in whatever diverse ways they choose.

Activists could accomplish these two objectives if they worked primarily in small, locally based organizations. By keeping their groups autonomous and relatively small, they could evade outside interference and avoid stifling bureaucracy.

These small, grassroots groups would need to work with each other only when larger campaigns demanded collective strength. At those times, they could come together in loose coalitions and confederations. Each local group might affiliate with several different regional or issue-oriented alliances and work closely with or more independently of each depending on circumstances.

Eventually, to form a cohesive force capable of society-wide transformation, a large number of coalitions and alliances would need to coordinate their activities. Weaving these many diverse threads into a coherent tapestry would require, of course, a great deal of communication and cooperation. But this is exactly what a good society would also require, so this arrangement would serve as a precedent and prototype of a good society.

Over time, these activists would work together to build large networks, alliances, or political parties connecting these many grassroots groups and counter-institutions.[2]

At the successful end of Stage 2, hundreds of thousands of progressive activists would be working for fundamental change as members of thousands of organizations all over the country. Together, these groups would be large and strong enough to challenge vigorously the power structure and destructive social norms.

Built on the strong base established in Stage 1, these groups would be more numerous and more powerful than progressive change organizations were in the 1960s and 70s. They would also be considerably more stable. Having significantly affected most of the public in this stage, they would be poised to work for much deeper and broader change in Stage 3.

## 3. Struggle for Power

In the third stage, activists would use their organizational strength to undermine oppressive institutions and replace them with viable alternatives.

### A. CHALLENGE THE POWER STRUCTURE THROUGH CONVENTIONAL POLITICAL AND LEGAL METHODS

Progressive activists and their supporters would elect progressive candidates to office and pass referenda that enacted progressive legislation. They would lobby legislators and administrators to enact progressive measures and they would sue oppressive institutions. With an understanding of the need for fundamental and systemic change, they would demand reforms that created more democracy and less oppression. They would do their best to avoid diversions, unpalatable compromises, token reforms, and counterproductive measures. Whenever the existing political system was unresponsive, activists would push more directly, as described in the next sub-stage.

### B. ILLUMINATE DOMINATION AND OPPRESSION

Just as in the civil rights movement of the early 1960s, activists would directly challenge the status quo in ways that dramatized the inadequacy and cruelty of present norms and institutions while demonstrating the superiority of alternatives. When possible, they would stage dramatic demonstrations that placed opponents in a no-win dilemma: forcing their opponents to make substantive progressive change or showing them to be unresponsive and oppressive, which would undercut the legitimacy of their authority.

For example, thousands of people could publicly refuse to pay that part of their taxes that goes to subsidize large corporations. Instead, they could pay an equivalent amount directly to alternative organizations that provide social services for children or battered women. If the government harassed these people, it would show the government is more interested in subsidizing corporations than helping needy people. If the government left them alone, they could continue to redirect money to truly beneficial uses.

Demonstrations like this would also shatter societal myths that hide oppressive realities. As an example, consider the relatively mild demonstrations of the early 1960s when black people quietly stood in line at voting booths. As they waited to vote, they were ignored, driven away, or beaten. Their simple act contradicted the societal myth that they did not want to or were too lazy to vote. Moreover, it revealed the truth that the local authorities did not allow them to vote and often harshly repressed them if they tried. Their responsible, nonviolent action stood in stark contrast to the violent and immoral response of the authorities.

*As long as our social order regards the good of institutions rather than the good of men, so long will there be a vocation for the rebel.* — Richard Roberts

By nonviolently promoting freedom, compassion, and other progressive ideals, activists would illuminate the possibilities and inspire others to action. When elite interests fought back, their actions would highlight the moral bankruptcy of the existing order and the greed, tyranny, cruelty, and violence at its core. By boldly standing up for what is right, activists would also grow emotionally stronger and see more clearly how their own socialization and emotional conditioning held them back.

If carried out in ways that clearly contrasted progressive ideals and alternatives with the violence and inequity of current norms and institutions, these actions would likely win support from large numbers of people. These people would then increase the pressure for change. Many defenders of the status quo would begin to withdraw their support. Some might deliberately carry out their duties inefficiently, or they might stop doing them altogether.

After years of constant agitation, even those most intensively indoctrinated and those paid well to prop up the power structure would begin to waver and defect. Without their support, the power of the elite would erode.

### C. FIGHT OPPRESSION USING NONVIOLENT ACTION

As organizations working for fundamental progressive change grew in size, they would mount mass boycotts, strikes, and blockades to challenge thoroughly the power of elite interests. Ever larger numbers of people would refuse to support or tolerate the existing order. Organized crowds would banish drug dealers and thugs from their neighborhoods. Citizens would refuse to pay taxes that sustained exploitation or corruption. People would boycott useless or low-quality products and products or services offered by exploitative companies. They would picket and blockade factories and offices and denounce unresponsive managers. Workers

*Power concedes nothing without a demand, it never has and it never will.* — Frederick Douglass

would strike for fair wages, reasonable working conditions, control over what they produce and how they produce it. People would confront racism, sexism, classism, and other forms of oppression at the personal, community, state, national, and international level.

Millions of people refusing to provide support would severely undermine existing structures. These structures either would collapse or be forced to change dramatically.

### D. DEVELOP POPULAR ALTERNATIVE INSTITUTIONS

In this stage, a large number of people would also embrace counter-institutions and drop their support for old institutions. As alternative institutions grew, they would provide essential services and displace current institutions. These alternative institutions would eventually become the primary institutions.[3]

Alternative institutions would probably include organic farms, cooperative businesses (consumer- or worker-owned), publicly-controlled free hospitals and medical clinics, co-housing, publicly financed mass transportation, bicycle

lanes, progressive schools, reuse and recycling centers, local currencies (like Ithaca Dollars), and so on.

In the early years of this stage, most efforts for change would probably have minimal effect. Much of the activity would be symbolic in nature, designed primarily to raise consciousness and erode support of destructive conventional institutions. However, over time, with enough support at enough levels, change activities would begin to challenge the existing order. Workers would refuse to work until their demands were met. Police officers would refuse to arrest strikers and blockaders, enabling activists to shut down oppressive and exploitive institutions. Troops would refuse to back up the police.

*You see things, and you say "Why?" But I dream things that never were, and I say "Why not?"*
— George Bernard Shaw

News reporters would demand to cover important news from the perspective of citizens (not the elite) and to report the unvarnished truth. Voters would oust corrupt and reactionary politicians, replacing them with honest progressives.

Eventually, alternative institutions would be large enough to provide all necessary services. Drug rehabilitation centers would grow capable of serving every addict. Alternative banks would provide capital to those who truly needed funding. Progressive doctors and clinics would provide care to those who most needed it, not just to those who could pay. Consumers would buy from progressive businesses that provided useful and well-made products, produced by well-paid workers in factories that produced no toxic wastes. People would only support churches that acted in harmony with their ideals. They would only attend sporting events that encouraged cooperation and esteem building. Muckrakers and police would focus on eradicating corruption in high places. People would divert their taxes directly to useful services. Progressive officeholders would raise taxes for the wealthy and lower them for the poor.

At the successful end of Stage 3 (after several decades), progressive activists would be able to shut down large parts of society with broad boycotts, mass blockades, and general strikes. Existing institutions would collapse and vast numbers of people would shift their allegiance to alternative institutions. Politicians would scramble to implement progressive measures or be replaced by those who would.

## 4. Diffuse Change Throughout Society

In this last stage, progressive change would spread to every corner of society. Alternative institutions and progressive cultural norms would completely replace the old. Young people would expect and demand honesty, fairness, and democracy. Outmoded attitudes would fade away as the few remaining people who clung to them eventually died.

Society would shield children from oppression and violence. Virtually every child would grow up without experiencing horrible emotional trauma. They would learn the

---

## Practical Alternatives

*Few things are harder to put up with than the annoyance of a good example.* — Mark Twain

Nothing undercuts justifications for the status quo better than the vivid demonstration of practical alternatives. To effectively promote fundamental change, an alternative must address the real needs of people. It must fulfill all the functions of a current practice or institution at least as well as the existing one, but do it more fairly, compassionately, and democratically. For example, most people would be reluctant to drop their support for the police, the prison system, and the military until progressives could show humane alternatives that were still as effective in protecting people from crime and tyranny.

To dispel myths of powerlessness, good alternatives must clearly demonstrate that ordinary citizens can responsibly assume power and run society's institutions better than the elite now do.

Building alternative institutions and demonstrating alternative behavior is, of course, quite difficult. In the beginning of the transformation process, activists can demonstrate only their own personal behavior, their own cooperative ways of interacting, their own nonviolent methods of struggle, and the few small-scale alternative institutions they have built. However, as progressive movements grew, activists would be able to develop and implement new laws, new kinds of relationships, and impressive alternative institutions. Once implemented, these more exciting and inviting models would attract a great deal of attention and acceptance.

skills necessary to practice democracy, freedom, and citizenship. Everyone would learn nonviolent change skills as part of her normal education, and any efforts to re-institute oppressive institutions would be countered by large numbers of people using these skills. People would also travel to other countries to help activists in other places overcome oppression, build alternative institutions, and transform their societies.

# Figure 5.1: Leadership Roles in Each Stage of Transformation

| Stage | Primary Leadership Roles for Activists |
|---|---|
| **1A. Find Other Progressives** | **Personal Networker**: Help concerned people find others of like mind<br>**Discussion Leader**: Help people talk about their concerns |
| **1B. Learn About Change** | **Teacher**: Educate concerned people about the world and how to change it<br>**Visionary**: Communicate visions of a good society |
| **1C. Learn and Practice Change Skills** | **Guide**: Teach and demonstrate specific progressive change skills |
| **1D. Form Supportive Communities** | **Community Builder**: Help activists build supportive and joyous communities<br>**Therapist**: Help activists work through their emotional conditioning |
| **2A. Raise Consciousness** | **Lecturer/Writer/Performer/Artist**: Teach people the truth about the way the world works and how to change it<br>**Agitator**: Encourage people to challenge and question<br>**Firebrand**: Amplify and direct discontent<br>**Trailblazer**: Demand a good society and demonstrate what it would look like by zealously living it |
| **2B. Build Organizational Strength** | **Organizer**: Build cohesive cooperative organizations, establish democratic procedures, develop programs<br>**Mentor**: Teach and demonstrate how to work with others<br>**Organization Networker**: Help organizations find each other and work together |
| **3A. Challenge the Power Structure through Conventional Political and Legal Methods** | **Researcher**: Investigate existing structures and alternative possibilities<br>**Lobbyist**: Lobby officeholders for progressive change<br>**Campaign Worker**: Campaign to elect progressive candidates to office or to pass referenda<br>**Politician**: Run for office and, if elected, develop and promote progressive legislation<br>**Litigator**: Prepare, file, and litigate lawsuits against harmful institutions |
| **3B. Illuminate Domination and Oppression** | **Strategic Planner**: Design effective demonstrations and campaigns<br>**Demonstrator**: Picket and blockade organizations to illuminate oppression<br>**Supporter**: Provide physical, emotional, and financial support to demonstrators |
| **3C. Fight Oppression Using Nonviolent Action** | **Resister**: Boycott, strike, and blockade oppressive organizations<br>**Coordinator**: Coordinate the work of many progressive organizations |
| **3D. Develop Popular Alternative Institutions** | **Entrepreneur**: Build alternative institutions<br>**Pioneer**: Patronize alternative institutions |
| **4. Diffuse Change Throughout Society** | **Manager**: Synthesize diverse ideas into workable policies; re-orient institutions<br>**Administrator**: Implement policies through alternative institutions |

## OVERLAPPING STAGES

Like other models, this development framework presents a simple outline of what would be an extremely complex reality. Though largely flowing in the order presented, the four stages of this grand strategy for fundamental transformation would overlap.

Note, too, that within this strategic program, each campaign for change, focused on a particular issue, constituency, institution, or goal, would also go through stages. These intermediate stages would probably be similar to the four described here, with people learning, raising others' consciousness, forming organizations, challenging the status quo, building alternatives, and implementing changes.[4]

Each progressive change organization might also go through similar overlapping stages over the course of its existence. Moreover, a single organization might simultaneously have committees involved in different stages. For example, a group might have an outreach committee focused on bringing in new activists and raising consciousness, a direct action committee focused on confrontation, a committee focused on building alternatives, and a transnational committee trying to carry the transformation process to other countries. In addition, each activist might go through similar overlapping stages of personal understanding and activity.[5]

This book focuses on the overall level of grand strategy. It concentrates primarily on the earlier stages, assuming that with the foundation in place, activists would further develop and implement the rest of the strategy.

## LEADERSHIP ROLES FOR EACH STAGE

Leadership is essential for collective action. Through these different change stages, the kind of leadership required would vary. Figure 5.1 lists the primary leadership roles most needed in each stage.

*A leader is best*
*When people barely know he exists.*
*Not so good when people obey and acclaim him,*
*Worse when they despise him.*
*"Fail to honor people,*
*They fail to honor you."*
*But of a good leader, who talks little,*
*When his work is done, his aim fulfilled,*
*They will say, "We did this ourselves."*
— Lao-tzu

## TIERED STRUCTURE

This model of democratic transformation provides an outline, but who would actually initiate and sustain it? How would they work with each other?

As discussed in the last chapter, only a small number of people have the desire, skills, and resources to devote most of their time to positive change. Most people spend their time raising children, making a living, and living their daily lives. They can spend only a few hours each week learning about issues, learning how to bring about change, or actually working for it.

Consequently, change movements inevitably have a tiered structure. Typically, the leaders are well educated, skilled, and experienced, but few in number. They usually work long and hard for a small salary. Below them are a larger number of volunteers with less knowledge and fewer skills. They typically work a few hours a month and have a small amount of influence on the direction of the organization. A much larger number of people contribute money to change organizations, occasionally show up at educational meetings, events, and rallies, and call or write letters to elected officials. They usually have no control over the change organization.

Paralleling traditional political and business structures, those at the top of this hierarchy have the most power and those at the bottom have little. This hierarchy is not democratic and actually undermines efforts for democratization of society since people do not learn democratic methods, only how to follow and obey.

*Power without responsibility is oppressive.*

*Responsibility without power is depressing.*

### Very Active Vernal Graduates

Figure 5.2 shows an alternative structure. The most involved activists would be at the bottom. As I envision it, this tier would consist of very active graduates of the Vernal Education Program (described in Chapter 6) who have agreed to work at least twenty hours per week for fundamental progressive change. Highly educated and skilled, these activists would provide leadership. However, because their overall focus would be building a broad, powerful, nonviolent, democratic grassroots movement, they would provide "leadership from below" — they would primarily support, inform, and inspire their progressive colleagues. They would participate in the decision-making process of their change organizations, but strictly on an equal footing with others or, perhaps, even from a behind-the-scenes position. This would allow less-experienced colleagues to take the lead.

## Figure 5.2: A Democratically Structured Movement for Progressive Transformation

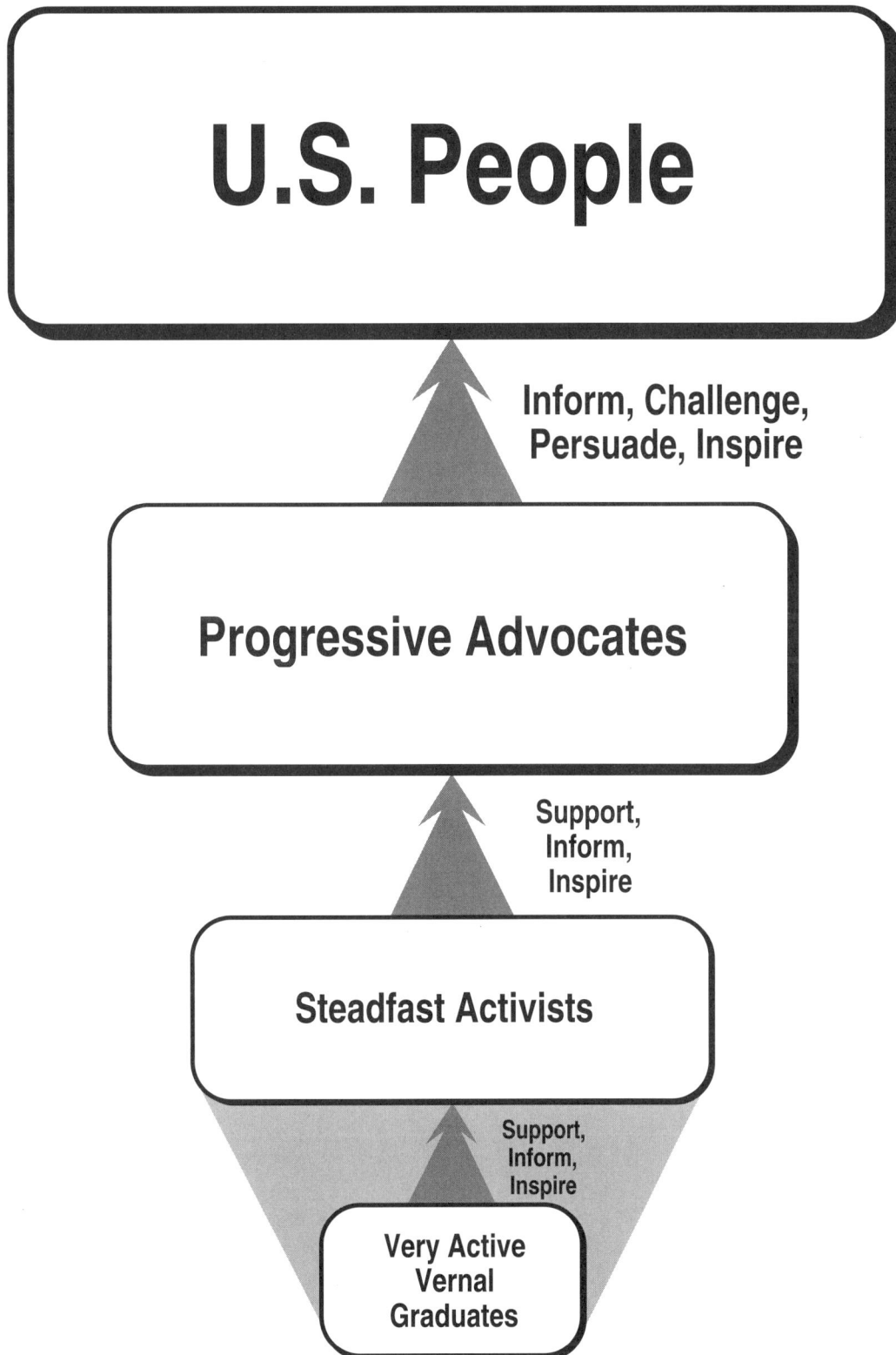

**U.S. People**

Inform, Challenge, Persuade, Inspire

**Progressive Advocates**

Support, Inform, Inspire

**Steadfast Activists**

Support, Inform, Inspire

**Very Active Vernal Graduates**

As much as possible, these skilled activists would mentor less-experienced activists and offer timely educational workshops on topics related to the work at hand. They would also provide emotional support and counseling to other activists to minimize infighting. Since these skilled and dedicated Vernal graduates might be the most active members of their organizations, they might also do much of the mundane work that others did not have the time or skills to do. Overall, they might devote as much as half of their change effort to supporting other activists.

## Steadfast Activists

A larger number of steadfast activists, as shown on Figure 5.2, would work at least several hours per week for fundamental change. They would comprise the core of organizations working for progressive transformation. As described above in Stage 2B, I expect most of these activists would work with small, largely autonomous local organizations.

These steadfast activists would devote most of their time to active change work: persuading the public, lobbying public officials, lobbying church, labor, professional, and civic organizations, challenging political parties, building alternatives, confronting reactionary institutions, and so forth. However, they too would devote a substantial amount of their time to support, inform, and inspire progressive advocates (described below), especially by teaching democracy and change skills. They might spend a significant amount of their change time teaching and mentoring the progressive advocates associated with their organization.

> *Trust men and they will be true to you; treat them greatly and they will show themselves great.*
> — Ralph Waldo Emerson

## Progressive Advocates

Progressive advocates would be a much larger number of people who were members or supporters of these many change organizations. Limited by family obligations, work obligations, a low level of skill or experience, or their fears of deeper commitment, progressive advocates would work at most a few hours per week for fundamental change. They might only occasionally attend their organization's meetings. However, because of their much larger numbers, these advocates would carry out a significant portion of progressive change activity. They would also provide much of the financial support for their group. In addition, they would likely constitute the main supporters of alternative institutions and would do much of the lobbying of public officials. They would comprise most of the people who attended rallies and engaged in other nonviolent activities.

However, their most critical change work would be simply talking with their relatives, friends, and neighbors about the need for fundamental progressive change and how to go about it. They would inform, challenge, persuade, and inspire their acquaintances and the larger public. Many would hand out leaflets at county fairs and speak to school children, church groups, labor unions, and civic organizations on behalf of their progressive organization. Others might show progressive videos in their homes or set up study groups for their friends and neighbors.

In this model, small, local groups, comprised completely of very active Vernal graduates, steadfast activists, and progressive advocates, would be largely autonomous. They could work together with other local groups, forming coalitions and democratically structured alliances whenever advantageous. This decentralized structure would be much more democratic than most current progressive organizations and would promote democratic ideals.

Steadfast activists and very active Vernal graduates would have complete and equal governance over their small organizations. Progressive advocates would have an amount of control commensurate with the amount of responsibility they took on. Small groups would have ultimate power over larger alliances (instead of the other way around), and they would be free to disassociate from these alliances or even challenge them using the techniques of nonviolent struggle.*

## Everyone

At the top of this structure would be all the people of the country — those who would ultimately make democratic decisions in a good society. As larger and larger numbers of people became involved in progressive change, the democratic structures of progressive groups would constitute the skeleton of a democratic structure for general governance of the country. When this progressive structure became the predominant structure, regular people would then govern our country democratically, not only in the political sphere, but also economically and socially.

Let me emphasize this point: In this model, progressive organizations would be governed democratically — with participation by all members and supporters. As these organizations grew in number, size, and influence, they would collectively wield increasing amounts of power over the important institutions of society. Eventually (at the end of Stage 4), they would exert influence over most aspects of society. Since they would operate democratically and in the common interest and they would support only democratic institutions, as they exerted increased power, the society as a whole would become more democratic and responsive to people's needs.

---

* Progressive caucuses within mainstream organizations that have hierarchical structures would be forced to play by the larger organization's rules. Still, internally, the caucuses could be egalitarian and democratic.

## IF NOT NOW, WHEN?

When would this process of transformation begin? I believe it could start whenever we decide to begin.

Many sociologists who have studied the history of social movements argue that movements arise only under certain favorable conditions. Figure 5.3 lists some of the conditions and events these scholars have found historically precipitate social upheaval. However, one or another of these events occurs almost every year, yet major social upheavals occur much less often.

Other scholars argue that social movements come in cyclical waves, rising and falling as the pendulum of public opinion swings back and forth. They argue that a swing to the left frightens moderates, shifting them more to the right. Then the implementation of right-wing policies frightens moderates, causing them to swing to the left. These swings seem to occur on a regular basis, every thirty or forty years. This provides an explanation for the regular appearance of strong progressive political movements such as the Populist movement of the 1880s, the Progressive movement in the early part of the Twentieth century, the radical labor movement of the 1930s, and the civil rights/anti-war/youth movement of the 1960s.

Both of these perspectives focus on the take-off stage of social movements when they are most visible. However, most social movements have long preparatory stages when nothing appears to be happening, but important groundwork is being laid. For example, the civil rights movement emerged in the mid-1950s when most of the country had shifted towards conservatism. Historians can see that the powerful Montgomery bus boycott of 1955–56 — which led directly to the larger civil rights movement of the 1960s — was a probable next step after a decade of steady, grassroots organizing, but it was a surprise for most people at the time.[6]

Preparatory work must be done long before social change movements become visible. Once they have taken off, there is little time to build important maintenance structures (like communities of support), for activists to learn important skills, or for activists to work through their cultural and emotional limitations. If we wait until the take-off stage, then it is usually to late to lay the groundwork.

Moreover, a fundamental transformation of all aspects of society will necessarily take decades to occur. During this long period, many social change movements will probably arise and fade. Waiting for a time when the political winds are blowing in a progressive direction could mean waiting a long time unnecessarily. There is no reason to wait — we can start the process of transformation whenever we want. We can start the process now.

Certainly, over the course of the transformation process activists will accomplish more when conditions are favorable and less when conditions are inhospitable. Particular progressive movements may stagnate or falter in unfavorable periods — when most people are content with the status quo or feel hopeless, when elite interests are strong and united, or when

> *This time, like all times, is a very good one if we but know what to do with it.*
> — Ralph Waldo Emerson

---

### Figure 5.3: Some Conditions and Events that May Trigger Political or Social Upheaval

**Economic Conditions**
Adversity
Prosperity
Adversity Preceded by Prosperity

**Psychological Conditions**
Discontent, Frustration (relative deprivation of achievements compared to aspirations)
Alienation (loss of community)

**Political Conditions**
Foreign Domination and Exploitation
Governmental Inefficiency (deficits, corruption)
Disintegration of the Ruling Elite (ineptitude, in-fighting)
Elite Intransigence and Repression

**Social Conditions**
Ideological Decay (social norms and values are no longer accepted)
Institutional Decay (rigid institutions thwart people and groups)
Social Disequilibrium (racial, gender, or class antagonism)
Defection of Intellectuals (away from the elite)

**Specific Events**
Power of Elite is Undermined (an election defeat, war, coup d'état, an army mutiny, etc.)
Straining Event (economic disaster, famine, sudden growth or technological change, severe weather)
Crackdown on Dissidents
Terrorist Act
Historical Accident

SOURCES: This list is based on a summary of many scholars' work provided by Mostafa Rejai, *The Strategy of Political Revolution* (Garden City, NY: Doubleday, Anchor Press, 1973, JC491 .R381), pp. 24–26, supplemented with the discussion in Anthony M. Orum, *Introduction to Political Sociology: The Social Anatomy of the Body Politic*, 2nd ed. (Englewood Cliffs, NJ: Prentice-Hall, 1983, JA76 .O78 1983), pp. 318–337.

# Figure 5.4: Representations of Societal Change Over Time

### Normal (Cyclic) Shifts in Power Between Progressive and Anti-Progressive Forces

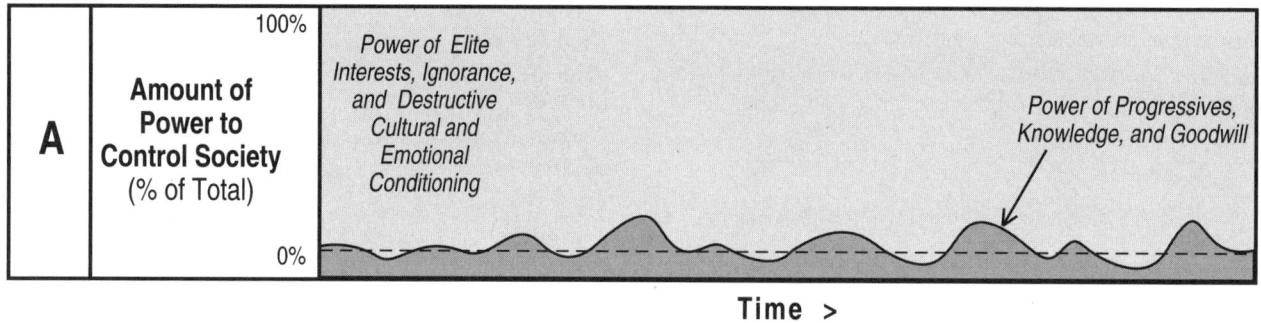

**A** — Amount of Power to Control Society (% of Total) — 100% / 0%

*Power of Elite Interests, Ignorance, and Destructive Cultural and Emotional Conditioning*

*Power of Progressives, Knowledge, and Goodwill*

**Time >**

### Fundamental Transformation Created by Massive Progressive Social Movements

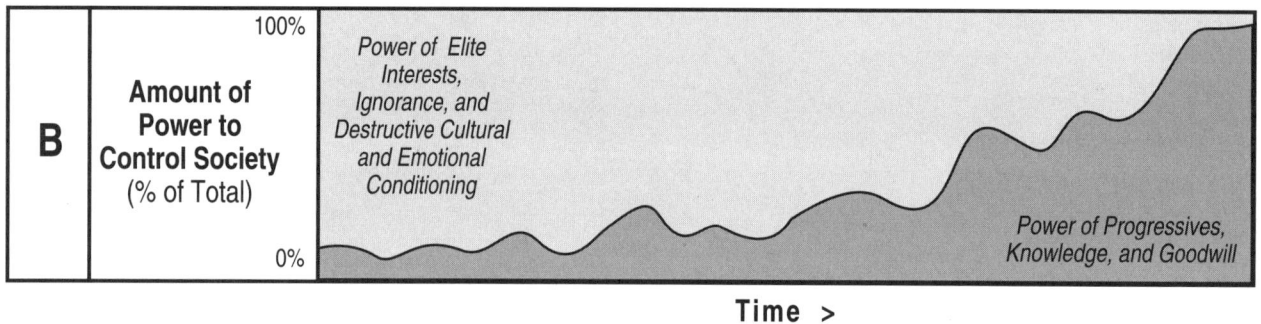

**B** — Amount of Power to Control Society (% of Total) — 100% / 0%

*Power of Elite Interests, Ignorance, and Destructive Cultural and Emotional Conditioning*

*Power of Progressives, Knowledge, and Goodwill*

**Time >**

### Fundamental Transformation Created by Massive Movements   Idealized Smooth Transition

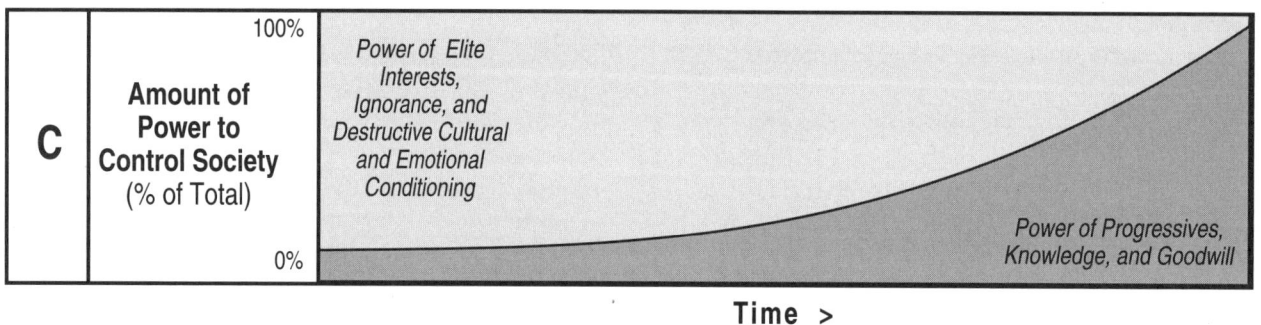

**C** — Amount of Power to Control Society (% of Total) — 100% / 0%

*Power of Elite Interests, Ignorance, and Destructive Cultural and Emotional Conditioning*

*Power of Progressives, Knowledge, and Goodwill*

**Time >**

progressive resources are scarce. During these periods, activists may have few victories. They may be forced to devote virtually all of their efforts to defending gains and minimizing losses. Still, if they have the skills, strength, and endurance to continue to work for change through these periods, then when conditions grow more favorable, their progressive social movements can soar. If activists' overall efforts over the decades are sufficiently strong, then eventually they can bring about a complete transformation of society.

The three diagrams in Figure 5.4 portray this perspective. The area under the line in each diagram represents the percentage of all power held by the forces working towards a

good society. The area above the line represents the relative power held over people by elite interests, by people's ignorance, and by destructive cultural and emotional conditioning. These diagrams indicate the potential shift between these forces over the decades.* When the line is near the bottom, it indicates that elite interests, ignorance, and destructive cultural and emotional conditioning dominate society. When the line is near the top of the diagram, it

---

\* Note that I have not established the scale on the time axes of these diagrams. Conceivably, the duration of the diagrams might be as little as fifty years or as much as a thousand years.

indicates that we have achieved a democratic and non-oppressive society.

The top diagram shows "normal" changes caused by cyclic forces and by various triggering conditions and events. The fluctuations in the line indicate all the shifts due to technological changes, political elections, regular progressive reform movements, elite repression, right-wing movements, and so forth. When conditions are ripe, progressive social movements arise and cause some positive change. Later, when conditions grow unfavorable, these movements falter and the power of progressive forces declines. Though power shifts back and forth, progressive forces never have enough strength or skills to overcome the opposition, so the line oscillates near the bottom of the diagram (above and below the dotted line).

The middle diagram shows a similar oscillation, but in this case, progressive social movements are strong enough to create fundamental change. In this representation, the power of progressive forces eventually grows to almost one hundred percent, indicating a complete transformation of society. The curve has bumps and dips — analogous to those in the top diagram — caused by "normal" cyclic and triggered changes. However, because progressive social movements are more effective, they gain much more during the favorable periods and lose far less during the unfavorable periods. Over time, the curve shifts ever higher. Since the curve is generally rising, the percentage of power held by progressive forces after major setbacks in the later years is still greater than the highest peaks in the early years.

The middle diagram is probably a realistic rendering of the complexity of fundamental transformation since it indicates the actual successes and failures year to year. But clearly, it is impossible to predict the exact course of future events, what conditions and triggers might accelerate or decelerate progressive change, when these changes might occur, and the extent of their impact. So any diagram like this would necessarily have the bumps and dips in the wrong places and would show them with the wrong magnitude. The bumps and dips would also mask the overall shift.

For these reasons, I created the bottom diagram, which is an idealized version of the middle one.* It shows the same fundamental transformation over time, but omits "normal" cyclic and triggered changes and ignores the jumps and starts that characterize real change. Hence in this diagram, the line moves smoothly upward. Like the middle diagram, this one indicates that, at the beginning, the relative power of the forces working toward a good society is low. But as time goes on, it grows steadily to almost the entire total. Since earlier victories make it easier to bring about change, the line slopes a bit upward to show that change accelerates over time.

---

* Think of it as subtracting the top diagram from the middle. (To create the middle diagram, I actually added the bumps and dips from the top diagram to the bottom one.)

## STRONG ENOUGH?

Historically, social change has followed the oscillatory pattern described in the top diagram. How can we ensure that it follows the path of progressive transformation described by one of the two bottom diagrams instead?

The next few chapters describe one practical way. But first let's look in more depth at the dynamic of effective nonviolent struggle since it plays a crucial role in this program, and it is often misunderstood.

## NONVIOLENT STRUGGLE

Many people equate nonviolence with passivity or capitulation. They consider it too gentle and weak to challenge the might of elite interests, the viciousness of soldiers trained to kill mindlessly, or the cruel malice of rapists and torturers. However, when practiced by a small group of dedicated and skilled activists, nonviolent action can disarm opponents, vividly expose injustice, and inspire people far and wide. When practiced by large numbers of people working together in a bold, incisive campaign, nonviolent engagement can undermine all support for powerholders and force sweeping change.

By its nature, principled nonviolent struggle promotes fairness, democracy, and compassion. When planned by skilled and conscientious leaders like Mohandas Gandhi or Martin Luther King, Jr. and carried out well, it has the extraordinary ability to overturn oppression without creating an oppressive counterforce. It de-escalates hostility, violence, and fear, reduces polarization, and ennobles both participants and opponents. It also promotes mutual problem solving based on real needs and reasonable desires, making it possible to develop appealing win-win solutions for everyone involved.

> *In this age of the rule of brute force, it is almost impossible for anyone to believe that anyone else could possibly reject the law of the final supremacy of brute force.*
> — Mohandas Gandhi

Nonviolent struggle, at its best, cuts through old behavior patterns and touches the caring human beings trapped inside. Like cathartic theater, nonviolent struggle can unearth buried hearts, rejuvenate shriveled souls, and awaken the playful and loving sides of people.

### The Power of Nonviolent Struggle

Nonviolent struggle is effective because it ingeniously undercuts the power of oppressors. Even the most powerful tyrants hold very little power as individuals — most of the power they wield is dependent on the support of thousands of others who actually carry out their desires and the passive acquiescence of millions of people who could intervene but do not.

For example, police have power because society imbues them with authority and grants them the right to use force. The courts and city hall back them up. Their commanders and fellow police officers support their daily actions.

Soldiers have power because society values their might, praises their willingness to fight, and authorizes their killing. Society also pays to support them using tax money. Their officers train them, lead them, command them, and supply them with weapons.

> *I am your king, and you'd better do what I say or else I can't be king anymore.*
> — cartoonist B. Kliban

Torturers may seem to be inhuman miscreants acting outside the bounds of sanctioned authority. However, they too are supported by a martial sub-culture and their actions may be covertly authorized by the government. Moreover, the larger society may passively support their actions if most people consider cruelty necessary to defeat "terrorists" or "subversives."

Individuals have little power without institutional backing — only the power of their own muscles and wits plus whatever personal weaponry they may have acquired. To visualize the extent of this dependency, imagine the weakness of even the most powerful and affluent people if no one in society would provide them food. They would be forced to hunt, forage, or farm just to feed themselves. It is only because others agree to supply them with food that these "powerful" people do not live an enervating, hand-to-mouth existence.

Moreover, all people rely on others for reassurance that their actions are reasonable and morally justified. Even rapists rely on a general climate of misogyny to condone their conduct.

A well-designed nonviolent campaign undermines support for oppressors and challenges their destructive behavior. It encourages other people to stop passively consenting to oppressors' demands and instead to actively dissent and intervene. It encourages ethical leaders and the public to condemn their unsavory actions. It encourages the oppressors' own family and friends to criticize them (as happened during the Vietnam War with Defense Secretaries Robert McNamara and Melvin Laird). A good campaign even attempts to awaken the consciences of the oppressors so that whatever dormant empathy they might have for others will steer them toward more compassionate behavior. For example, McNamara actually resigned.

> *Let me say, at the risk of seeming ridiculous, that the true revolutionary is guided by great feelings of love.* — Ché Guevara

When large enough numbers of people condemn oppressors' actions and refuse to cooperate with them, they are forced to capitulate. In like manner, when many people refuse to act according to harmful social norms or to act out their own harmful behavior patterns, they undercut the strength of those norms and dissolve the power of destructive patterns. Over the course of a nonviolent campaign, as principled resistance grows, more and more people take control of their own lives and take back control of their society. Power shifts from oppressive tyrants to cooperative and compassionate people and from oppressive norms and institutions to ones that are more humane.

To be effective, nonviolent struggle must induce enough people to dissent, refuse, and intervene.

Some people can be persuaded by rational discussion, compelling leaflets, passionate speeches, vigils, marches, parades, rallies, and similar activities. For example, in a campaign to stop production of land mines, activists might stage a rally at the gates of the land mine factory with poignant speeches from prominent moral leaders and moving testimonials from people who had lost limbs to land mines. This might stir the consciences of some workers in the factory to seek other employment.

Small, symbolic boycotts and physical interventions can illuminate injustice and inspire people to end their support. For example, a die-in and mock funeral with hundreds of wailing widows dressed in black would dramatize the misery caused by land mines.

Larger, more personal actions can place key players in a pivotal situation where they must either sever their support for oppressors or exert extra effort to go on. Continuing this example, thousands of activists might blockade the gates of the land mine factory by lying closely together on the ground. This would force workers to decide whether going to work was worth having to walk on the protesters' bodies. Many would not take this hurtful step.

> *He that complies against his will Is of his own opinion still.*
> — Samuel Butler

In this example, progressive activists directly sway workers to stop producing land mines. But nonviolent struggle more often brings about change indirectly. For example, the demonstration against the land mine factory may directly influence only a few workers, but it might induce friends and neighbors of the workers to criticize them. This might prod them enough that they would seek new jobs. More likely, such a demonstration might induce thousands of people across the country to call their congressional representatives, pressuring them to cut funding for the land mine factory. Alternatively, the demonstration might induce people to boycott other products of the company that makes land mines. This might put enough economic pressure on the company to force it to convert the factory to another use.*

Just as a stool with a broken leg topples over, a power structure collapses without the support of the people who formerly sustained it. Nonviolent campaigns that appear to target powerholders are more often aimed at cracking their support, so they will tumble off their thrones of power.

## Elements of Effective Nonviolent Campaigns

Nonviolent struggle campaigns can only induce large numbers of people to dissent and refuse if those campaigns seek to move society in a direction that people find appealing. Nonviolent struggle requires that activists stand up for what is right, take risks, bear suffering without retaliation, and act honestly and openly, even when secrecy might seem desirable. They must avoid being hostile, arrogant, or self-righteous.

Effective nonviolent struggle campaigns include these elements:
- They have fair and just goals, inclusive of everyone.
- They rely on compassion and a desire for democracy and fairness — not on malice or vengeance.
- They boldly and openly stop oppression without demeaning or physically injuring the oppressors. They support every person involved in the campaign as an individual human being.
- They address the root causes of problems and suggest far-reaching remedies that can actually solve them.
- They illuminate a wide spectrum of facts and perspectives and convey them to the larger community in an understandable fashion.
- They promote rational dialog.
- They encourage people to think for themselves.
- They embrace a multiplicity of truths.
- They accept the possibility that everyone may be misguided or wrong (including progressive activists).
- They are experimental and tentative, oriented toward finding the best solution among many possible choices rather than imposing a preconceived answer.

The best nonviolent actions are playful, joyous, and inspiring. They use creative activities that break through rigid behavior patterns and open people up to new modes of thinking and acting. They forcefully challenge oppression and offer superior alternatives.

## Steps in Nonviolent Campaigns

Effective nonviolent campaigns often span many years, require immense preparation, and proceed through many steps. Typically, activists will first investigate a persistent social problem and research a variety of possible solutions. They will then communicate their findings to the public and build organizations to lobby or sue authorities for change. Next, to build widespread understanding and support, they speak out, distribute leaflets, publish newsletters, post websites, perform guerrilla theater, debate their opponents, and so forth. While most activists usually press for change through conventional channels, others may illuminate the oppression through public protest or symbolically enact an alternative to demonstrate its superiority.

If opponents are not responsive, activists prepare for more intensive nonviolent struggle. Typically, they first educate even more people about the issue and build an action organization. They inform their opponents of their intentions and attempt to negotiate a solution. If their opponents are still unresponsive, then activists may picket, fast, and hold large marches or rallies to dramatize the issue and expose their opponents' unresponsiveness. They may also pressure their opponents' colleagues and friends.

As part of their effort, activists might also perform community service to exhibit their compassion and demonstrate they are willing to do concrete tasks necessary to create a good society. They may praise opponents' positive efforts or even offer them gifts to express goodwill, show integrity, and allay opponents' fears of being attacked.

It is usually only after all these steps — preparation that bolsters the strength and resolve of activists and undercuts the rationale and legitimacy of their opponents — that activists engage in coercive strikes, blockades, or boycotts to force authorities to capitulate.

---

* There are several other ways to increase the effort required to produce land mines: if workers could find jobs nearby that paid higher wages, they would probably choose to take those jobs. If the land mine company could make larger profits by producing some other product, then it would probably stop production. Development of an effective nonviolent national defense program would undercut the rationale for building land mines.

---

## Typical Steps in a Nonviolent Campaign

1. Background research and investigation

2. Widespread education

3. Negotiation with the powerholders

4. Demonstrations that illuminate the oppression and offer alternatives

5. Outreach to enlist the support of more people

6. Community service and goodwill gestures towards the powerholders and the larger community

7. Nonviolent noncooperation and intervention

Naturally, these strong challenges to the status quo often stimulate a violent backlash. However, if activists remain true to their ideals and respond nonviolently, then public opinion tends to swing behind them. An organized public then lobbies authorities, and this broad and strong pressure finally forces positive change.

## Preparing for a Nonviolent Action

A large nonviolent action can take many months of preparation. Activists must persuade large numbers of peo-ple to attend, arrange transportation to the demonstration site, and provide for their basic needs for food, water, toilet, and shelter.

Even more important, activists must ensure that the action is purposeful, creative, and potent so it will be effective in swaying the public. If the goal is to illuminate injustice and foster public pressure for change, then activists try to expose the social myths that obscure reality and sustain conventional beliefs. They devise actions to counter these myths.

---

# Creative Nonviolent Action

**Mr. Skeptic**: Ok, Ms. Promoter of Nonviolence, how would you deal with a real-world situation. Let's say I'm walking down a dark street late at night in the grungy part of town, and a big man pulls a knife on me and demands I hand over my wallet. What should I do?

**Ms. Promoter of Nonviolence**: Well, you might do many things. What options do you see?

**Mr. Skeptic**: I don't see any possibilities at all. It's a scary situation. I guess I could fight him and try to knock the knife out of his hand. If I knew karate or some other martial art, I might be able to overpower him. But these aren't very nonviolent. The only nonviolent option I see would be to just give in and hand over my wallet.

**Ms. NV**: Well, actually there are many other nonviolent options. For example, perhaps you could run away, or you could scream at the top of your lungs. Let's be more creative. Maybe you should shout that there is a fire, point at this imaginary fire, and run towards it. The mugger might be surprised just long enough for you to get away. Or perhaps you could introduce yourself to him and try to shake his hand. Maybe you could run up to him and give him a big hug. Or maybe you should fall to the ground and act like you're having an epileptic fit.

What if you said some crazy things about the Queen forcing you to use drugs and then sprinkled imaginary pixie dust on your head? Or what if you got down on your hands and knees and crawled between his legs. What if you started to sing Mary Had a Little Lamb and did a little jig? What if you complimented his clothing and gave him a gift — what if you wrote him a poem and gave it to him? Maybe you should ask him for his autograph.

**Mr. S**: None of those seem like good ideas to me.

**Ms. NV**: Well perhaps not, but the point is that there are a lot of options — a lot more than you came up with. They may seem crazy, but some of them might be useful in re-arranging the situation. Creative nonviolent action often works by transforming a bad situation where everyone is playing a conventional role into a new situation where everyone has to play by new rules. It forces people to step out of their normal, patterned behavior. Once people are thinking, they may discover a more appropriate way to act.

There may even be some sort of mutually satisfactory solution. Perhaps this mugger has never been given a poem before and your gesture would open his heart. Maybe introducing yourself would transform the situation from "mugger robbing victim" to a situation more like two friends talking together on the street. Robbery would then seem out of place and impolite. Perhaps not. But the point is to come up with a lot of ideas and then evaluate whether they would work. If you don't, then you have already surrendered to your fear. You are forced to play by the rules of a bad game...

Let me tell you a story: once, at a demonstration at the Rocky Flats nuclear bomb trigger factory, the police, with their nightsticks drawn, started to rush towards a group of demonstrators. The demonstrators, realizing they might be beaten, began to play the hokey-pokey. The police, when confronted by a bunch of people playing a children's game, did not know what to do. In their eyes, the demonstrators had transformed from "dirty communists" to young people just like their sons and daughters. Before the demonstrators played the hokey-pokey, it didn't seem like a very good idea to avoid being beaten; but after it worked, it seemed brilliant.

**Mr. S**: These ideas still don't seem workable to me.

**Ms. NV**: Well perhaps not. The situation you described is a tough and scary one. There may be no good solutions. Perhaps the mugger is deranged and desperate for money to buy drugs. Perhaps he will rob and kill you no matter what you do.

Maybe the only solution is for you not to be there late at night — or even better, for there not to be a grungy part of town at all. Perhaps the real solution is to work now to ensure that no part of town is grungy and there are no deranged drug addicts desperately stalking the streets looking for victims they can rob for drug money.

For example, to counter the myth that the military is starved for funds, activists could create a giant physical chart on a downtown street with the percentage of income taxes going to the military represented by hundreds of rifles lined up end-to-end for hundreds of yards. They might represent the much smaller percentage of taxes that go to education with books lined up for a few feet. After displaying this proof of misplaced priorities, activists might pick up these props. Those who picked up rifles could pretend to shoot those holding books who would dramatically "die." This action would graphically depict the priorities and predictable consequences of current government policy.

If the goal is to coerce powerholders to change directly, then activists determine whom they can most feasibly compel and how they can best pressure them. For example, activists might seek to stop a company from producing a product that it sells only overseas, like infant formula. They might determine that they could coerce the influential marketing vice-president to discontinue the product by launching a broad consumer boycott of another product that it sells domestically.

> *The most common way people give up their power is by thinking they don't have any.* — Alice Walker

To be effective, progressive activists must ensure that participants refrain from harsh or vindictive behavior and focus instead on challenging their opponents boldly and compassionately. Toward this goal, organizers of a nonviolent direct action often draw up guidelines for behavior. They may require participants to join an "affinity group" — like-minded people who support each other and can ensure that each member adheres to the guidelines. Organizers usually require all activists to attend a workshop to learn bold, nonviolent responses to conflict by practicing these skills in simulations and role-plays.

## Tips for Action

*Redirect your anger into positive action. Convert your fear into excitement. Stand tall on your principles. And don't forget to have fun!*

An effective action is thus well planned and the participants are well prepared. Activists often choreograph the whole demonstration like a theater or dance performance. They carefully craft it to bring out everyone's best character, touch hearts, illuminate destructive behavior, and pose alternatives that are more effective and humane.

Structure and planning do not preclude individual spontaneity or initiative. To the contrary, innovative responses will arise freely in a safe, alternative environment. In such surroundings, people are more likely to step out of their patterned behavior and address the situation at hand with compassion and intelligence. This fresh thinking is exciting and energizing.

At its best, a powerful nonviolent action profoundly affects all participants — activists, opponents, and bystanders. An effective action often feels new, magical, and unique, yet ageless and just right. Participants and observers may suddenly see new possibilities and imagine new vistas. They may feel a compassionate understanding of others — even those who have oppressed them. Participants may even feel — for the first time — genuine joy and delight in the world.

## The Danger of Nonviolent Struggle

If planned and carried out well, nonviolent struggle can be effective against even the most hardened and highly armed troops. By demanding change in ways that do not endanger anyone, nonviolent struggle reduces opponents' hostility and undercuts justifications for violent response. Hence, compared to warfare, nonviolent struggle is relatively safe.

Still, struggle of any kind can be deadly. Current institutions are dedicated to resisting substantive change with the full range of their arsenals. When challenged, they may respond with deadly force — remember the killings at Kent State and Tiananmen Square.

> *Life shrinks or expands in proportion to one's courage.* — Anaïs Nin

Moreover, since nonviolent actions are designed to jiggle people's rigid patterns, even a mild action can evoke an intense reaction. Some opponents and bystanders may respond with tears, elation, or excited realization when they see high ideals and practical solutions visibly demonstrated. But others may react with fear or fierce rage. By anticipating the latter, activists can sometimes counteract it with compassion, logic, or creative maneuvers, or they may be able to stand to the side so that the rage goes harmlessly past them (like an aikido move). Still, at times, activists must take the full brunt of the fury. The best actions are planned with a deep understanding of human dynamics and carried out skillfully to keep responses within bounds and minimize casualties.

### *The Goal is Positive Change*

*Something seems wrong to most people engaged in struggle when they see more people hurt on their own side than on the other side. They are used to reading this as an indication of defeat, and a complete mental readjustment is required of them. Within the new terms of struggle, victory has nothing to do with their being able to give more punishment than they take (quite the reverse); victory has nothing to do with their being able to punish the other at all; it has to do simply with being able, finally, to make the other move... Vengeance is not the point; change is.*

— Barbara Deming[7]

# Twelve Principles of Strategic Nonviolent Struggle

Recently, two scholars studied six historical society-wide battles to determine the major factors, subject to activists' control, that contribute to success or failure of a nonviolent struggle.[8] Since their analysis was not oriented towards the particular goal of creating a good society, they did not conclude that nonviolent campaigns must be morally consistent with a good society or that campaigns must garner widespread support. Still, the results of their study are notable. They concluded that a nonviolent struggle would be more likely to succeed if it conforms to these twelve strategic principles:

**Development** (prior to the conflict, create a favorable environment)

1. Formulate Functional Objectives — Choose a clear, specific goal towards which all decisions are made.

2. Develop Organizational Strength — Build an efficient struggle organization with strong and flexible leadership, a skilled and dedicated activist operational corps, and a sympathetic and supportive civilian population.

3. Secure Access to Critical Material Resources — Ensure that activists have food, clothing, energy, medical supplies, computers, and so on.

4. Cultivate External Assistance — Get other countries or outside groups to support your cause and provide aid.

5. Expand the Repertoire of Sanctions — Prepare a large number of possible tactics in advance and evaluate their strengths and weaknesses for various circumstances.

**Engagement** (during the struggle, maximize the effect of your actions)

6. Attack the Opponents' Strategy for Consolidating Control — Refuse to obey whatever your opponents want obeyed. Subvert the enforcers (police, troops).

7. Mute the Impact of the Opponents' Violent Weapons — Get away, disable their weapons, prepare your supporters for the worst so they are not terrorized or demoralized when it comes, and so on.

8. Alienate Opponents from Expected Bases of Support — Make your opponents' violence and their goals appear unconscionable so they are condemned internally, by their allies, and by other countries.

9. Maintain Nonviolent Discipline — Keep your behavior (and that of your allies) within acceptable limits to reduce any justification for your opponents' violence and to undermine their support. Distance yourself from those who use violence to "help" you.

**Conception** (as the struggle continues, evaluate what is happening)

10. Assess Events and Options in Light of Levels of Strategic Decision Making — Realistically assess the struggle on the appropriate level (policy, operational planning, strategy, tactics, and logistics) and respond accordingly. Especially, do not confuse a tactical win with an overall victory or a tactical loss with an overall defeat.

11. Adjust Offensive and Defensive Operations According to the Relative Vulnerabilities of the Protagonists — Depending on the circumstances, focus on undercutting your opponents, or switch to defending your own support structures. Also, strike in many places with many tactics or focus on a few vulnerable spots.

12. Sustain Continuity Between Sanctions, Mechanisms, and Objectives — Use appropriate methods to steer your opponents to the desired end: conversion, accommodation, coercion, or disintegration of their power base.

## SUMMING UP

The previous chapter specified crucial characteristics of democratic change efforts and six essential components of an effective strategy. By relying on broad educational efforts, mass change movements, a decentralized and democratic organizational structure, and nonviolent struggle, the strategic program described in this chapter includes all of these characteristics and components. If thoroughly implemented, I believe this strategic program would produce a good society.

The next five chapters describe a practical way to implement this strategic program over eighty years. Chapters 6, 7, and 8 focus on the first two stages. These chapters describe a specific endeavor — the Vernal Education Project — to increase greatly the strength, knowledge, skills, and endurance of progressive activists and their organizations. Chapter 9 shows that with this increased capability, activists could realize the third and fourth stages and actually bring about fundamental transformation of society. Chapter 10 lays out a specific timeline for developing and implementing the Vernal Education Project.

## NOTES FOR CHAPTER 5

[1] I have drawn on several previous works that examine revolutionary change and major paradigm shifts.

Rex D. Hopper, "The Revolutionary Process: A Frame of Reference for the Study of Revolutionary Movements," *Social Forces*, 28, No. 3 (March 1950): pp. 270–279, synthesizes the research of several earlier scholars on the "natural history" of revolutionary change. He divides the process into four main stages, based primarily on the psychological state of the public:

• The Preliminary Stage of individual restlessness.

• The Popular Involvement Stage of collective unrest and excitement.

• The Formal Stage when people develop a collective opinion about the new social order and try to implement it.

• The Institutional Stage when the new order is successfully implemented.

The Formal stage covers the dramatic part of a revolution — the phase generally considered "the Revolution." My stages 2A, 2B, 3, and 4 roughly correspond to Hopper's four stages, though again note that my model focuses on the work of activists while Hopper's model focuses on the psychological state of the public.

William H. Friedland, et al., *Revolutionary Theory* (Totowa, NJ: Allanheld, Osmun, 1982, JC491 .F73), pp. 126–130, lists four basic elements of revolutionary mobilization:

• Raising Consciousness

• Increasing Participation

• Undermining the System

• Building and Sustaining the Revolutionary Organization

In the introduction to his stirring history of the Populist Movement of the 1880s and 1890s, *The Populist Moment: A Short History of the Agrarian Revolt in America* (New York: Oxford University Press, 1978, E661 .G672 1978), pp. xviii–xxii, Lawrence Goodwyn suggests four stages for democratic movement building:

• Formation

• Recruitment

• Education

• Politicization

In the Formation stage, the movement creates an autonomous institution where new interpretations of how to live can materialize that run counter to those of the prevailing authority — a "counterculture." In the Recruitment stage, the movement finds a tactical way to recruit large numbers of people. In the Education stage, the movement educates its constituents and inculcates a high level of social analysis. In the Politicization stage, the movement expresses its power in an autonomous political way such as through a powerful political party able to win elections.

Goodwyn points out that a successful movement must be initiated by people who have individually attained a high level of personal political self-respect — people who are not resigned and cannot be intimidated. Then, in the last three stages, there must be democratic methods for widespread communication within the mass movement to counter the misinformation and propaganda put out by elite interests and the dominant culture. This democratic communication is necessary to allow participants to develop collective self-confidence in their new way of doing things. With individual self-respect and collective self-confidence, people then make their own "movement culture."

Goodwyn sees the Populists' development of extensive bottom-up farming cooperatives as an essential first step because it let large numbers of people see a workable democratic alternative to the status quo. These cooperatives were subsequently undermined by the power elite, providing a deep political lesson for all those involved. The Populists' lecturing system — which involved up to 40,000 lecturers traveling across the country — offered an excellent (though clearly not sufficient) means of communicating these political lessons to large numbers of people.

In the Populist Movement example, Goodwyn's four stages appear to correspond to my stages 3D (or perhaps 1D), 2B, 2A, and 3A. But actually, the entire populist movement probably represents a single individual campaign (admittedly an enormous one) within my Stage 3 (see my discussion in the section called "Overlapping Stages").

In contrast, his four theoretical stages roughly correspond to my Stages 1, 2B, 2A, and 3. My Stage 1 also addresses Goodwyn's observation that a movement must be initiated by individuals with a high level of understanding and self-respect. My Stage 2 includes his observation about the need for democratic methods of internal communication and the need to develop collective self-confidence.

The strategic program specified in this chapter most closely follows the nonviolent revolutionary process described by George Lakey in *Powerful Peacemaking: A Strategy for a Living Revolution* (Philadelphia: New Society Publishers, 1987); revised version of *Strategy for a Living Revolution* (New York: Grossman Publishers, 1973, HM278 .L32 1973). He devotes a chapter to each of his five stages. I consider the ideas in his chapters 1 and 8 as additional developmental stages, making seven in all. Lakey's chapters correspond to the stages in this book approximately as follows:

| Stages in this Book | Lakey's Chapters |
|---|---|
| 1. Lay the Groundwork | 1. Empowering Ourselves for Peace |
| 2A. Raise Consciousness | 3. Cultural Preparation |
| 2B. Build Organizational Strength | 4. Building Organizational Strength |
| 3A. Challenge the Power Structure through Conventional Political and Legal Methods | — |
| 3B. Illuminate Domination and Oppression | 5. Propaganda of the Deed |
| 3C. Fight Oppression Using Nonviolent Action | 6. Political and Economic Non-cooperation |
| 3D. Develop Popular Alternative Institutions | 7. Intervention and Parallel Institutions |
| 4. Diffuse Change Throughout Society | 8. The World in Revolution |

Note that Lakey's Chapter 2 provides several excellent historical examples of successful nonviolent struggles.

My ideas about nonviolent revolution have also been greatly influenced by Susanne Gowan, George Lakey, William Moyer, and Richard Taylor, *Moving Toward a New Society* (Philadelphia: New Society Press, 1976, HN65 .M65).

2 Marxist Ronald Aronson points out that a society-transforming movement must be quite diverse, but everyone must also have a deep understanding of all the many kinds of oppression:

> Perhaps the various forms of oppression can still be located within some single world-historical dialectical spiral, but the movements opposing them are autonomous and plural by nature, each seeking to undo specific, however interrelated, forms of oppression, each requiring an understanding that respects its specificity. The fundamental fact is that any large-scale movement today or in the future, if it is to be *a* movement, must be kaleidoscopically diverse in principle. To be politically effective, it will be a radical coalition — or nothing at all. And although such a coalition is the single conceivable force capable of transforming contemporary society to its roots, it can only take on the systemic source of each of its components' specific struggles by developing a communal vision in which each struggle is joined to every other.
>
> Any movement that would aim at transforming the most basic contemporary oppressions, any such radical coalition, will have to strive for socialism *and* an end to patriarchy *and* an end to racism *and* gay liberation *and* a transformed relationship to nature *and* nuclear disarmament *and* a profound settling of accounts with the once-colonized and native peoples — *without prioritizing one struggle over another*... This post-Marxist universalism must differ from that of Marxism by placing on the agenda the liberation of all oppressed peoples, of the overwhelming majority — *in their specificities* as well as in their commonality. Or it will not happen.

Ronald Aronson, *After Marxism* (New York: Guilford Press, 1995, HX44.5 .A78 1994), p. 36.

3 This strategy parallels that proposed by André Gorz, *Socialism and Revolution* (Garden City, NY: Anchor Press/Doubleday, 1973, HX44 .G613), p. 137:

> A socialist strategy of progressive reform does not mean that islands of socialism will emerge in the sea of capitalism. But it does mean the building up of working-class and popular power; it means the creation of centers of social management and of direct democracy, particularly in the major industries and co-operatives of production; it means the conquering of positions of strength in representative bodies; it means free products and services fulfilling collective needs; and this must inevitably result in intensified and deepened antagonism between the social production required by the needs and aspirations of the people, on the one hand, and the requirements of capital accumulation and power on the other.

Gorz also describes this strategy in André Gorz, *Strategy for Labor: A Radical Proposal* (Boston: Beacon Press, 1967, HD8431 .G613). For example, on page 8, he writes:

> Seizure of power by insurrection is out of the question, and the waiting game leads the workers' movement to disintegration. The only possible line for the movement is to seize, from the present on, those powers which will prepare it to assume the leadership of society and which will permit it in the meantime to control and to plan the development of the society, and to establish certain

limiting mechanisms which will restrict or dislocate the power of capital.

4 See, for example, Bill Moyer's detailed *Movement Action Plan: A Strategic Framework Describing the Eight Stages of Successful Social Movements* (San Francisco: Social Movement Empowerment Project [721 Shrader Street, 94117], 1987).

5 See, for example, my paper "Rising Consciousness: Typical Steps People Take in Recognizing the Need to Work for Fundamental Social Change." <http://www.vernalproject.org>

6 Stewart Burns, *Daybreak of Freedom: The Montgomery Bus Boycott* (Chapel Hill, NC: University of North Carolina Press, 1997, F334 .M79N39), pp. 1–37, and personal communication with Burns, May 30, 1999.

7 Barbara Deming, "On Revolution and Equilibrium," *We Are All Part of One Another: A Barbara Deming Reader*, ed. Jane Meyerding (Philadelphia: New Society Publishers, 1984, PS3554 .E475W38 1984), p. 179. First published in *Liberation Magazine*, February 1968.

8 Peter Ackerman and Christopher Kruegler, *Strategic Nonviolent Conflict: The Dynamics of People Power in the Twentieth Century* (Westport, CT: Praeger, 1994, JC328.3 .A28 1994). Their six case studies offer detailed descriptions of both successful and unsuccessful nonviolent campaigns:

- Nonviolent Efforts in the First Russian Revolution, 1904–1906
- The Ruhrkampf: Regional Defense Against Occupation, 1923
- The Indian Independence Movement, 1930–1931
- Denmark Resistance to Nazi Occupation, 1940–1945
- El Salvador: The Civic Strike of 1944
- Solidarity Versus the Polish Communist Party, 1980–1981

# 6

# The Vernal Education Project

*Human history becomes more and more a race between education and catastrophe.*
— H.G. Wells

The last chapter described a four-stage strategic program for bringing about fundamental transformation of society. This chapter specifies a project to implement the first stage by developing a network of fifty educational centers across the United States. These centers would bolster the knowledge, skills, strength, and endurance of thousands of dedicated progressive activists each year, enabling them to support and educate hundreds of thousands of other activists (as described in Chapters 7 and 8). Together, all these activists would then be able to carry out the rest of the strategic program for fundamental change (as described in Chapter 9).

In order to discuss this project and distinguish it from other education programs and other progressive change efforts, I have named it the Vernal Education Project. I chose the term "vernal" to evoke the image of a new, vibrant effort to revitalize society in a fresh, lively way, reminiscent of springtime.

Please note that I have formulated this education program and the plan for its development in some detail to show that it is feasible to create such an enterprise.* I have spent a great deal of time considering all the necessary elements and testing many combinations of size and cost factors to come up with a self-consistent set that also seems both realistic and desirable. I believe this particular plan is sound, and I hope to work with others to implement it. However, this design is only one possible scheme among innumerable alternatives, and it is not set in stone. As the other developers and I work together to create the first education center and replicate it, we will invariably modify this plan in a variety of ways, probably changing it substantially.

Moreover, other activists might admire some aspects of the Vernal Education Project but have other ideas about

**ver•nal** \vûr′ núl\ adj. 1. Of, relating to, or occurring in the spring. 2. Fresh or new like the spring; youthful; energetic.

---

* This chapter summarizes the design. Appendix B includes many additional figures that provide more extensive detail. Chapter 10 lays out a specific timeline for developing and implementing the design.

how to implement them. They might create their own independent endeavors. Inevitably, what actually unfolds will surely be quite different from what is described here. I present this plan simply to show there is at least one way to carry out such a project and to offer it as a first draft for a project.

## DESIGN CRITERIA FOR THE VERNAL EDUCATION PROGRAM

There are many classes, workshops, internships, and schools for progressive activists, but they are generally oriented toward beginning activists, toward a particular organization and its needs, or toward specific issues.* With its unique goal of fundamental societal transformation, the Vernal Education Project has a distinct orientation. To successfully implement Phase 1 of the strategic program for change outlined in Chapter 5, it must meet these criteria:

• **Offer a Wide-Ranging Education to Progressive Social Change Activists**

*When the only tool you own is a hammer, every problem begins to resemble a nail.*
— Abraham Maslow

The Vernal Education Project must offer activists a broad and diverse education that lets them truly understand how the world now functions and shows them ways to transform all aspects of society.

• **Vastly Increase the Skills, Strength, and Endurance of Activists**

The project must provide a deep education to a large number of progressive activists. It must provide enough skills and offer enough support that activists have the strength and knowledge to effectively transform society. It must offer activists practical skills and useful information they can directly apply to their progressive change work. It must also provide enough support so that activists can carry on their work for many years.

• **Facilitate the Development of a Cooperative Community**

The project must support a cooperative community of progressive activists.

• **Operate Efficiently**

The project must produce substantial results, yet consume few resources. The overall cost must be quite low. The project must also supplement and bolster existing progressive change efforts, not detract from them or compete with them for funding or activist energy.

---

* A few of these educational programs are described at the end of this chapter.

• **Span the Country**

The project must reach large numbers of activists all across the United States.

• **Integrate with Activists' Lives**

The project must not disrupt activists' lives. In particular, it must educate them without diverting them from their change work.

• **Grow Rapidly and Continue for Decades**

The project, starting from square one, must grow rapidly so that it can quickly reach a large number of activists. It must then be able to continue providing education and support to many activists for many decades.

• **Conform to Progressive Ideals**

The project must be consistent with progressive ideals in its structure, operation, and methods.

## Philosophy of Education for Progressive Change

The last design criterion is especially important. Not only must the Vernal Education Project offer extensive education to thousands of activists, but it must do so in a way that is consistent with a good society. Traditional schools often view students as empty vessels into which wise teachers pour knowledge, filling them with The Truth. But this approach is actually more conducive to fostering a dictatorship of docile slaves than to building a democratic, cooperative society of empowered, responsible citizens. It assumes students are not only ignorant, but unable to think for themselves. It also assumes there is a single, absolute truth which teachers know and students must learn.

*The function of education is to teach one to think intensively and to think critically… Intelligence plus character — that is the goal of true education.* — Martin Luther King, Jr.

*Education is not filling a bucket but lighting a fire.*
— William Butler Yeats

The world is infinitely complex. Important truths conflict with other truths, each valid in its way. For students truly to learn, they must have exposure to the full spectrum of ideas. They must also have the opportunity to weigh each new idea — evaluate its merits and flaws, relate it to their previous experiences, compare it to other ideas, explore its ramifications — and then wrestle with it to find an appropriate place for it in their own worldview. Furthermore, to become powerful citizens, students must practice using their own judgment, choosing their own directions, working cooperatively with others, and taking responsibility for their individual and collective choices.

I have tried to design the Vernal Education Program to offer a supportive environment for activists to explore a broad range of ideas about society and social change. Vernal students would be free to envision the kind of world they seek to create and free to choose whatever means they believe are best to get there. They would also have a safe place to try out their ideas and to practice using them with each other.

## OVERVIEW OF THE VERNAL EDUCATION PROGRAM AND NETWORK

As I envision it, the Vernal Education Network would consist of fifty Vernal centers spread across the United States. Each Vernal center would be operated locally, but each would use a similar curriculum and similar educational methods. Each center would also coordinate with the others regionally and nationally.

The Vernal Program would be oriented toward activists with at least a year of social change experience and a desire

to support other activists. It would offer Vernal students a wide variety of information, skills, and ongoing support so that after graduating they could do effective, powerful, progressive social change work. Each one-year session, about as intensive as the combination of two semesters of college and a summer job, would consist of these main parts:

- Student-run study groups
- Internships with existing social change groups
- Some independent social change work
- A small amount of social service work
- Self-study of current affairs
- A series of five staffmember-facilitated workshops
- Student-run emotional support groups or individual therapy
- Special events for Vernal students to socialize and network with each other

In addition, Vernal staffmembers would provide information about other educational resources and encourage students to partake of the ones they needed. Students would also be encouraged to maintain good physical health and to exercise regularly.

The first three months of the yearlong session would

---

# Some Definitions

**Vernal Education Program** — an educational program that would use a particular curriculum and methods to educate progressive activists

**Vernal Session** — a one-year course of study and mutual support that would involve thirty students who learned together

**Vernal Staffmembers** — experienced activists who would administer and facilitate Vernal sessions

**Vernal Team** — four full-time equivalent (FTE) Vernal staffmembers who would facilitate and administer four different Vernal sessions at a time; they would assist the study groups, arrange internships, research and prepare materials, facilitate workshops, mentor and support students, hire and prepare new staffmembers, and administer the whole program; typically, a team would launch a new session every three months

**Vernal Center** — another name for a Vernal team located in one metropolitan area; note that a Vernal center would be conceptual, not physical — the Vernal team might not even have an office

**Vernal Education Network** — the network of fifty Vernal centers around the United States.

**Regional Administrators** — Vernal staffmembers who would provide additional administrative help to Vernal centers and provide coordination between centers; they would not be associated with a particular center, but would work with all the centers in a region

**New Staff Preparers** — Vernal staffmembers who would help to hire, support, and teach new staffmembers how

to do their jobs; these staffmembers would also not be associated with a particular center, but would work wherever necessary across the country

**Vernal Students** — activists who enrolled in a Vernal session

**Vernal Graduates** — activists who graduated from a Vernal session

**Very Active Graduates** — Vernal graduates who saw progressive social change as their primary focus and worked at least twenty hours per week for fundamental change

**Less Active Graduates** — Vernal graduates who spent less than twenty hours per week working for progressive change — these people would probably spend some time working for social change, but their *primary* focus would be on some other activity (such as pursuing a traditional career or raising a family)

**Vernal Activists** — all Vernal students, very active graduates, and less active graduates who were working for progressive change

**Vernal Education Project** — the effort to create and sustain the Vernal network and to support Vernal activists in their progressive social change work

Note that I have deliberately chosen not to use the term "school" since this word often conjures up images of classrooms, grades, and obedience to authority — the Vernal Education Program would have none of these. I have also chosen to avoid traditional terms like "training," "instruction," and "teachers" to escape the negative connotations sometimes associated with these words.

emphasize academic study of theory and history, though it would also include practical, hands-on learning. The next six months would include less theory and be more practical. The last three months would emphasize direct social change work. This last period would also pave the way for Vernal students to make a smooth transition to the change work they would do after graduating.

Students would live at home and do most of their studying, internships, and social change work in their home communities. In this way, their learning would be directly related to the change work they chose to do, and they would not incur any costs of going away to school. This would also significantly decrease the overall cost of the Vernal Program.

Each yearlong Vernal session would enroll about thirty students who lived near each other, learned together, and supported each other. Each session would be largely independent of others, though students would periodically socialize with students from other local sessions.

Four full-time Vernal staffmembers would work together in a team to simultaneously facilitate four sessions in the same area. Vernal staffmembers would provide overall guidance to students, arrange internships, facilitate the workshops, develop and update the curriculum, develop and update lists of local resources, and ensure that students were offered what they needed to become effective activists. Staffmembers would also provide administration for the whole program including recruitment and admission of students, collection of tuition, accounting, hiring new staffmembers, and so on.

To ensure the resources of the Vernal Program were used wisely, admission would be limited to activists who were already knowledgeable and experienced with social change and were committed to long-term progressive change. In particular, the program would be limited to those who intended to devote most of their time to nonviolent, fundamental social change for at least seven years after they graduated from the session and who were willing to support and educate other activists. The program would also be limited to activists who agreed to work to end their own addictive and oppressive behavior and to conduct all their social change work in an exemplary manner so as to serve as positive role models for other activists and the general public. In selecting students, Vernal staffmembers would also seek to assemble a group that reflected the diversity of the region in age, race, ethnicity, class, gender, sexual orientation, and so forth.

Once again, note that I have outlined a specific format for the Vernal program here, but it is likely to change as the developers of the Vernal Project test a variety of possibilities and see what works best.[1]

## Mission of the Vernal Education Program

The main mission of the Vernal Program would be:
• To pass along the lore of social change to activists — including social change history, social change skills, political

theories, critiques of current society, visions of alternatives, and methods for imparting change skills to other activists
• To develop activists' critical thinking skills
• To provide progressive activists with a chance to experience and practice the skills of direct democracy, consensus decision making, individual and collective responsibility, cooperation, conflict resolution, systematic problem solving in a group, nonviolent struggle, and other methods of progressive social change
• To spread social change skills widely across the entire range of movements for progressive change and across the United States
• To create a community of activists sympathetic with one another's perspectives who could support one another emotionally and physically
• To provide a safe forum for diverse activists to discuss and debate social change ideas with their colleagues
• To sustain progressive activism, especially during hard times
• To inspire hope by serving as a bright beacon of progressive ideals, exemplary moral values, and effective social change shining out through the darkness of conventional society and politics
• To inspire hope by producing enough Vernal graduates who would work assiduously for change so that each graduate would know she was not alone

*We have come out of the time when obedience, the acceptance of discipline, intelligent courage and resolution were most important, into that more difficult time when it is a person's duty to understand the world rather than simply fight for it.*
— Ernest Hemingway

## DETAILS OF THE VERNAL EDUCATION PROGRAM

After studying a variety of progressive change schools, I have tried to craft the Vernal Education Program to convey the greatest amount of social change knowledge to new activists using the fewest resources possible. To ensure the program would be both useful and inexpensive it relies on: (1) having students teach each other, (2) tapping the educational resources of existing social change groups, and (3) avoiding the costs of renting, buying, and maintaining campuses or buildings. The design also incorporates a wide variety of educational methods.

At the heart of the Vernal Program would be direct, hands-on social change work, supplemented by reading, discussion, research, writing, experiential exercises (role-plays), and some lecture presentations. Though the program would include social change theory, it would focus primarily on the practical aspects of applying this theory to real social change work — especially to the work that Vernal students were presently engaged in or would be soon after graduating. As I envision it, the program would have these ten main parts:

## 1. Study Groups

Study groups would be the primary means for Vernal students to acquire basic knowledge about the history and theory of progressive social change. Students would conduct study group meetings in their own homes. Each study group would comprise five to nine students who lived in the same neighborhood or city. The students in four or five study groups located near one another would comprise a Vernal session of about thirty students.

Students would meet in their study groups for three hours at a time (see Figure 6.1 for a typical meeting agenda). They would meet four times a week for the first three months of their session (the first quarter), three times a week for the next six months, and twice a week for the last three months except when they were attending workshops (as described below) and during holiday and vacation periods. Following this schedule, Vernal students would meet 116 times in their study groups.*

During the first nine months, students would mostly follow an established curriculum of study topics prepared by Vernal staffmembers (see the illustrative outline of topics below in the section entitled "Study Group Topics"). In preparation for most meetings, students would read an appropriate book or set of articles. Then they would discuss these readings at the study group meeting. Some readings would be introductory in nature for those relatively new to the topic, while others would appeal to those who were already knowledgeable.

Students would focus on several different major topic areas, spending a few weeks on each one. At the beginning of each major topic area, every student would read the same book or set of articles. For the rest of the time devoted to the topic area, each student would choose and read a different set of materials and make a concise five minute presentation to the other students describing the reading and its most important ideas.[2] In some meetings, students would choose an article or two from a recent magazine or newspaper that covered some current event (on any topic), read it, and present it to the other students.

*Interest is the greatest teacher.* — Proverb

Each student would read approximately 50–150 pages (and, perhaps, listen to a recording, watch a video, or ex-

### Figure 6.1: A Typical Agenda for a Study Group Meeting

| | |
|---|---|
| 10 min. | **Check-in** (each person briefly says how things are going, especially anything new and good) |
| 5 | **Agenda Review** |
| 15 | **Business** (choose facilitator for next meeting, arrange any important logistical matters related to readings, meeting place, and so on) |
| 50 | **Presentation of Reports** and Clarifying Questions on the readings |
| 15 | **Break** — Refreshments, stretching, games, informal discussion |
| 75 | **Discussion** — What are the useful or interesting ideas in these readings? *or* How can we reconcile the diverse ideas in these readings? *or* How could we use this information to bring about progressive change? *or* something else decided by the group |
| 10 | **Evaluation** — Good aspects of the meeting process, bad aspects, ways to improve the process |
| 3 hours | |

plore a web site) in preparation for each study group meeting. Every few weeks, students would also read supplementary materials and prepare brief written summaries for the other students. On average, students would probably spend about six hours preparing for every study group meeting.

During some study group meetings, students might analyze a particular problem using a force-field chart, web chart, or problem-solution-action chart.† Alternatively, they might engage in a values clarification exercise, do a campaign simulation exercise, or play a simulation computer game. At other meetings, students might listen to recordings, watch videos, or invite experienced activists to talk about their work. Students might also take field trips to visit nearby social change organizations. At some meetings, particularly when world events were especially exciting, stu-

---

* In each thirteen-week quarter, students would have one week of vacation and two weeks of workshops (three in the first quarter). Hence they would meet in their study groups for nine weeks the first quarter and ten weeks in each of the other three quarters. Figure B.3 in Appendix B has more detail.

---

† **Force-field chart**: a brainstormed list of the forces supporting and opposing a particular change campaign.
**Web chart**: a diagram of the various causes of a particular social situation and the causes of those causes, extending out to all the root causes.
**Problem-solution-action chart**: a brainstormed list of social problems (in a particular issue area), then possible solutions to one of the problems, then possible actions to realize one of the solutions.
For a more detailed description of these exercises, see Philadelphia Macro-Analysis Collective of the Movement for a New Society, ***Organizing Macro-Analysis Seminars: Study and Action for a New Society*** (Philadelphia: New Society Publishers, 1981).

dents might decide to forgo the regular topic and instead discuss current affairs.

For the last three months of the session, each study group would research a particular issue area of interest and then cooperatively create a reading list on this topic. Students would be encouraged to choose a topic related to the social change work they were doing or were planning to do. After graduating, they could then use this list as the basis for self-study groups for other (non-Vernal) activists working on this topic as well as by other Vernal groups.

## Figure 6.2: A Possible Study Group Schedule

| Qtr | Week of Pair* | Meeting in Week | Source of Readings | Students Read Same Materials? |
|---|---|---|---|---|
| 1 | A | 1st | Prepared List | Same |
| | | 2nd | Prepared List | Same |
| | | 3rd | Prepared List | Different |
| | | 4th | Special Activity | — |
| | B | 1st | Prepared List | Different |
| | | 2nd | Prepared List | Different |
| | | 3rd | Prepared List | Different |
| | | 4th | Current Events | Different |
| 2 | A | 1st | Prepared List | Same |
| | | 2nd | Prepared List | Different |
| | | 3rd | Special Activity | — |
| | B | 1st | Prepared List | Different |
| | | 2nd | Prepared List | Different |
| | | 3rd | Current Events | Different |
| 3 | A | 1st | Prepared List | Same |
| | | 2nd | Prepared List | Different |
| | | 3rd | Special Activity | — |
| | B | 1st | Prepared List | Different |
| | | 2nd | Prepared List | Different |
| | | 3rd | Current Events | Different |
| 4 | A | 1st | Self-Generated List | Same |
| | | 2nd | Self-Generated List | Different |
| | B | 1st | Special Activity | — |
| | | 2nd | Current Events | Different |

* For each quarter, study groups would first follow the schedule listed as Week A, then Week B, Week A, and so on: A B A B A B A B A B.

During the last three months, students might also spend some time helping to facilitate other beginning Vernal sessions held nearby and to mentoring new students. This would give them a chance to practice what they had just learned from their Vernal studies about helping others learn.

Figure 6.2 shows a possible study group schedule. In this schedule, students would focus on each topic for two weeks. For the first part of the first week (designated week "A" here), all of the students would read and discuss the same materials. For the rest of the two week period, each student would study a different reading, present it to the other students, and discuss it. At the last meeting of the second week (week "B"), each student would choose a recent article on a current event, present it to the other students, and facilitate a discussion of it. One meeting of each two-week period would be completely devoted to a special activity such as doing an exercise, watching a video, having a guest speaker, going on a field trip, or playing a simulation game.

Following this schedule, students would cover fifteen staffmember-chosen topics (the first topic for only one week) and one topic they had chosen on their own. Of the total 116 meetings, they would read and discuss staffmember-suggested readings at 67 meetings, read and discuss readings they had put together themselves at 10 meetings, read and discuss articles on current events or issues at 19 meetings, and do a special activity at 20 meetings. They would all read the same materials at 24 meetings, and they would read different materials at 72 meetings.

Please note again that this is just a possible plan — Vernal students could adjust the schedule to whatever best suited them, or they might choose to arrange a completely different program of study.

Note also that students would learn not only from reading, discussing social change ideas, and engaging in exercises, but also by working cooperatively to plan their study group activities. A Vernal staffmember would periodically attend study group meetings to see how things were going and to offer information, support, and direction. As I see it, a staffmember would typically visit once a week at the beginning and then once or twice a month for the rest of the year.

## 2. Internships

A second key part of the Vernal Program would be internships with several existing social change organizations in or near the students' home community. Internships would offer Vernal students practical, real-world experience and regular contact with experienced mentors.

Students would have a different internship in each of the second, third, and fourth quarters of the session. Each internship would require twelve hours of work per week for ten weeks (skipping weeks with workshops). If possible, sponsoring organizations would pay students a modest stipend. However, most groups could probably not afford to do so.

Groups offering internships would be encouraged to allow students to read the group's literature, attend its planning meetings, and participate in the group like any volunteer or new employee. Students would perform day-to-day work for the organization and also work on at least one instructive project. Typical projects might be:

• Researching and writing an article for publication or a leaflet to be used in canvassing
• Sending out press releases and following up with reporters
• Arranging to speak to several student, labor, church, or civic groups and then doing it
• Arranging a series of film showings
• Helping plan a rally, conference, or fundraising event
• Lobbying for a bill

By carrying out a real project, students would advance the work of the sponsoring group, gain a direct understanding of the work that the group performs, and learn the skills necessary to do their project. After ten weeks, students should have a good understanding of how the organization works, why it is configured the way it is, and why it works for change in the way that it does.

Many organizations would probably seek to offer internships. Vernal staffmembers would select groups that could provide a good learning experience for students, including a supervisor/mentor who could meet regularly with the student to review the student's work and learning experience. To ensure internships were educational and satisfying, each student would also have a designated Vernal staffmember to confer with about any problems. Whenever problems arose, the Vernal advisor would advocate for the student and negotiate solutions with the sponsoring group.

Typical organizations offering internships might be locally based peace, justice, or environmental groups; neighborhood groups; local groups working against racism, sexism, ageism, or heterosexism; chapters or affiliates of national groups such as the ones listed in Figure 6.3; public-interest law firms; church social action committees; labor unions; social change funding foundations; political campaigns; and progressive publications. Students might also work for social service agencies that have a social change component such as battered women's shelters. Students would work primarily with locally based groups but might have one internship with a national- or state-level organization if it were nearby.

In areas where there were no suitable organizations to offer internships, students might work with an individual activist who agreed to serve as a mentor. Alternatively, stu-

# Figure 6.3: Some Progressive National Organizations with Local Offices, Chapters, or Affiliates

• War Resisters League (WRL)
• Peace Action (formerly Sane/Freeze)
• Jobs with Peace (JwP)
• Women's Action for Nuclear Disarmament (WAND)
• 20/20 Vision
• Democratic Socialists of America (DSA)
• The New Party
• The Greens / Green Party
• Women's International League for Peace and Freedom (WILPF)
• The National Organization for Women (NOW)
• The American Friends Service Committee (AFSC)
• Fellowship of Reconciliation (FOR)
• Clergy and Laity Concerned (CALC)
• New Jewish Agenda
• Interfaith Impact for Justice and Peace
• Common Cause
• The American Civil Liberties Union (ACLU)
• Alliance for Democracy
• National Lawyers Guild
• The Association of Community Organizations for Reform Now (ACORN)

• Fairness and Accuracy in Reporting (FAIR)
• Student Environmental Action Coalition (SEAC)
• Greenpeace
• The Sierra Club
• Citizens Clearinghouse for Hazardous Wastes
• The Toxic Waste Coalition
• Citizen Action
• Public Interest Research Groups (PIRGs)
• The National Association for the Advancement of Colored People (NAACP)
• The National Urban League
• The Gray Panthers
• The National Council of Senior Citizens
• Children's Defense Fund
• Stand for Children
• Act Up
• Food Not Bombs
• Bread for the World
• Amnesty International
• United Nations Association
• Physicians for Social Responsibility

dents might start a new organization to fill the obvious void in their area.

Students would be encouraged to work both with familiar organizations they found especially interesting and with those that were unfamiliar. By choosing three dissimilar groups, students would see several ways of working for social change, observe a variety of internal processes, and hear a range of social change philosophies. By discussing and comparing their experiences with other students, they would have exposure to even more perspectives.

For example, a student especially interested in legislation to advance women's issues might intern first with the local NOW group and speak before civic groups about the need for day-care centers and battered women shelters. In the next internship, she might choose a very different area and work with a group trying to stop weapons shipments to repressive countries by blockading the local port. Finally, she might work with a campaign to elect a progressive Congressmember. At study group meetings she might learn from the experience of one student who helped a lawyer draft a lawsuit to force the clean-up of a local toxic waste dump and from another student who worked with a community organization demanding a police review board. At a workshop, she might compare her experiences with her support buddy who researched progressive tax-code legislation for a progressive party.

Internships would benefit both students and the sponsoring organizations. Students would have direct, personal exposure to a variety of groups and their different social change styles and philosophies. In turn, students would contribute a great deal of inexpensive assistance to the sponsoring organizations. The 120 hours of work students would contribute should be quite valuable since students would already be somewhat skilled and experienced — they would have had at least a year of prior experience before enrolling plus whatever they had learned from the Vernal Program up to that point.

Moving from one internship to the next and discussing their experiences with students who were interning in other places would produce another benefit: students would informally "crossbreed" ideas from one group to another. This could help create bonds between groups and might expedite formation of a broad coalition at some later juncture. Through their internships, students might also discover organizations with which they wanted to continue working after completing their Vernal education.

## 3. Social Change Work

In addition to their internships, students would work for progressive social change as a regular, ongoing member of a local change group. Typically, this would be a small, self-governing, grassroots group working on a particular issue of great interest to the student, such as reducing military spending, increasing funding for poverty programs, cleaning up toxic wastes, changing the local tax code, or exposing

racist bank policies. For many students, this group would be the one with which they were working before enrolling in the Vernal Program or the one that they intend to work with after graduating. In areas where there were no suitable social change groups, students would start one.

As I envision it, students would work with their local group about three hours per week for the first three quarters and then, to help prepare them to work for change after they graduated, for nine hours per week during the last quarter. Working for only three hours a week, students would probably not be the most active or effective members of their groups. Still, they would probably partake of the full experience. Grappling with concrete problems in a real group would provide students with countless questions for discussion in study group meetings, workshops, and support group meetings. Working with a group would also provide students with an opportunity to immediately try out ideas and techniques as they learned them. During the last quarter, when they would be working nine hours per week, students should have time to accomplish a good deal of social change work.

## 4. Social Service Work

Besides their social change internships and work for change, students would volunteer a small amount of time during the first quarter (a total of 24 hours) for a social *service* organization helping poor, homeless, disabled, sick, hurt, or emotionally disturbed people, providing assistance to children or infirm elders, or repairing damage to the natural environment. Direct service would introduce students to some of the unmet needs of society and to the organizations that provide assistance. Direct service would also encourage understanding of and altruism towards people in need. Moreover, this service work would help to establish a positive reputation for the local Vernal center.

*To be in good moral condition requires at least as much training as to be in good physical condition.*
— Jawaharlal Nehru

Though important to society, this part of the Vernal Program would be restricted to a relatively small amount of time in just the first quarter since the program primarily focuses on social *change* and there is not time to do more.

## 5. Self-Study of Current Affairs

As part of their Vernal education, students would be expected to stay informed about current affairs and social change movements through reading, listening to the radio, and browsing the internet for a total of six hours per week. Students would typically read a good daily newspaper or a weekly news magazine as well as three to six weekly or monthly progressive and alternative newspapers, newsletters, or magazines. They might also listen to a daily news program on the radio or read articles and action alerts on web pages or receive them through email. As described above, students would also spend some time in their study groups discussing current affairs.

## 6. Workshops

As I envision it, over the course of the yearlong Vernal session, the thirty students enrolled in that session would attend together a series of five staffmember-facilitated workshops: a five-day orientation workshop plus four ten-day workshops. Every day of each workshop would have two or three class periods each two-and-one-half hours long. During these classes, Vernal staffmembers would present basic

---

### Figure 6.4: A Typical Agenda for a Workshop Class — Canvassing

| | |
|---|---|
| 5 min. | **Gather and a Quick Game** |
| 5 | **Agenda Review** |
| 15 | **Presentation**: Purpose and techniques of canvassing to raise funds |
| 5 | **Demonstration**: Canvassing to raise funds |
| 20 | **Role Play**: Canvassing to raise funds — groups of 2: 1 canvasser, 1 person at home — play roles for 5 min., discuss for 5 min. (what works and what doesn't?), then switch |
| 15 | **Presentation**: Purpose and techniques of canvassing to garner support |
| 5 | **Demonstration**: Canvassing to garner support |
| 20 | **Role Play**: Canvassing to garner support — groups of 2: 1 canvasser, 1 person at home — play roles for 5 min., discuss for 5 min., then switch |
| 10 | **Break** — Refreshments, stretching, games, informal discussion |
| 15 | **Presentation**: how to talk with someone who strongly disagrees |
| 5 | **Demonstration**: Talking with someone who strongly disagrees |
| 20 | **Role Play**: Canvassing someone who strongly disagrees — groups of 2: 1 canvasser, 1 person at home — play roles for 5 min., discuss for 5 min., then switch |
| 5 | **Wrap-up Discussion/Questions** |
| 5 | **Evaluation** — Good aspects of the class, bad aspects, ways to improve the class |

2.5 hrs

---

information on important social change topics, answer questions, facilitate discussions of ideas and solutions, and facilitate experiential exercises (role plays, simulations, games). Experiential exercises would take up the bulk of the time in each class. Figure 6.4 shows an example of a typical agenda for one of these classes. The five workshops would include a total of eighty of these classes.

For each of the classes, students would receive an extensive set of notes — a simple textbook of two to ten pages — on the topic covered. These notes are described more fully below.

One class time during each workshop would be devoted to a structured discussion and evaluation of study group topics, internships, social change work, and the rest of the Vernal Program. Based on this evaluation of the session, Vernal staffmembers would then address any problems and, in conjunction with the students, modify the program as necessary.

Some time each day would be left open for students to relax, play, exercise, study, and informally discuss social change and swap their experiences. There would be a social party held one evening during each workshop for students to dance and sing together. Students would also have a designated time each day to confer and commiserate with a "support buddy" about how things were going for them — a chance for each student to express her joys, fears, and emotional upsets.

These workshops would provide an efficient way for Vernal staffmembers to quickly convey to students a great amount of knowledge and skills. They would also bring Vernal students and staffmembers together in a close, structured, yet relaxed environment — facilitating friendship, bonding, and honest political discussion. This would help to spawn a true community of activists.

> *He that is taught only by himself has a fool for a master.* — Ben Jonson

Workshops would be held in rented or donated facilities — preferably inexpensive retreat centers in beautiful, natural environments. These retreat centers might be summer camps, ski lodges, or college campuses. To hold down costs, students would help with food preparation and cleaning. Also, if possible, students and staffmembers would perform some physical labor for the retreat center (construction, maintenance, cleaning) in exchange for reduced rent. Besides lowering costs, this work would help strengthen bonds between students and teach cooperation skills.*

## 7. Health and Exercise

Social change work is difficult and often physically demanding. It usually requires great energy and stamina. Many activists are hindered in their work by health prob-

---

* If there were no work available for students to do, they might engage in some other group activity such as a group hike.

lems, especially as they grow older. The most effective activists are vigorous, healthy, and fit.

As I see it, staffmembers would set a good example with their own behavior, and they would also encourage students to exercise regularly, eat healthy food, get adequate sleep, bathe, clean their teeth regularly, and otherwise maintain a healthy lifestyle. At workshops, staffmembers would ensure that students had ample opportunities to engage in vigorous physical activity. They would prepare nutritious meals from healthy ingredients and ensure healthy snacks were always available. Every workshop class and study group meeting might also include some stretching or light exercise.

*True enjoyment comes from activity of the mind and exercise of the body; the two are ever united.* — Humboldt

## 8. Support Groups/Therapy/Body Work

Social change work usually requires a great deal of intense, personal interaction — cooperating with, challenging, caring for, and struggling with all kinds of people. To be effective, activists must maintain good emotional health and minimize their own ineffectual, inappropriate, or oppressive behavior. The most effective activists are energetic, confi-

### A Possible Support Group Meeting Agenda

Members of a support group typically divide up the total time they have together so each person has a specific period in which to engage in whatever activity she finds most useful. In her designated time, a member might talk about a recent difficult experience or a problem she is struggling to overcome. She might ask the other members to support her by simply listening attentively, or she may want the others to ask questions, to give her suggestions, to challenge her ideas, or to praise her for her hard work. For comfort, she might want to be complimented, touched, or held.

To focus specifically on achieving her social change goals, she may find it useful to answer the following set of questions:

1. How have I worked for positive social change since the last meeting? What worked well? What hasn't worked so well? How might I have done it better?

2. Considering the current situation, what should be done next to bring about positive social change?

3. What are my specific plans to bring about change in the next few days, weeks, or years?

4. What concerns, fears, or inhibitions do I have about implementing these plans?[3]

dent, clear thinking, focused, and humorous, even in difficult circumstances. To provide emotional sustenance, students would have a chance to meet weekly or bi-weekly in support groups to talk about how things were going and to get encouragement and nurturance from other students in a safe atmosphere.

Early in the year, students would learn about a variety of personal transformation techniques (such as journal writing, solitude, meditation, yoga, massage, peer counseling, therapy with a counselor). Staffmembers would encourage each student to choose a helpful personal transformation practice and engage in it regularly.

*Let him that would move the world, first move himself.* — Socrates

## 9. Socializing and Networking

Once a month, students and staffmembers would plan a potluck dinner for all the students in all the local sessions in the area. At these dinners students could meet each other and socialize, sing, dance, and discuss their change work. Students would also be encouraged to set up additional social networking meetings, parties, or celebrations every three or four months with other students and other activists with whom they worked. "Gathering the clan" would remind them that they are not alone in their change work and would provide a chance for activists with diverse backgrounds and orientations to meet in a friendly, informal atmosphere.

After graduating, Vernal activists would likely want to continue to socialize with, support, and learn from each other. They would probably stay in touch by arranging social events, meetings, conferences, or reunions with other graduates.

## 10. Other Resources

Most communities have many additional educational resources that are useful for activists. These include:

• Workshops for nonprofit organizations concerning fundraising, office management, board development, computer use, and so on

• Workshops on mediation and conflict resolution

• Various classes and workshops focused on personal transformation and emotional counseling therapy — assertiveness training, Parent Effectiveness Training, 12-Step Programs for overcoming alcoholism and other addictions, Re-evaluation Counseling, meditation, yoga, aikido, tai chi, and hundreds of others.

Rather than trying to duplicate any of these resources, Vernal staffmembers would try to evaluate, list, and briefly describe a wide range of local resources. They would recommend resources that seemed especially pertinent, useful, and inexpensive and offer tips on how to evaluate them so students would not waste their time or money.

# Figure 6.5: A Vernal Student's Typical Week
## (when not attending workshops)

| | 1-Year Vernal Program | | | | Ongoing |
|---|---|---|---|---|---|
| | 1st Qtr | 2nd Qtr | 3rd Qtr | 4th Qtr | Yrs 2 —> 8 |
| Hours in a Week (24 hours x 7 days) | 168 | 168 | 168 | 168 | 168 |
| **Life Maintenance and Social Life** | | | | | |
| Sleeping (8 hours/day) | 56 | 56 | 56 | 56 | 56 |
| Cooking, Eating, Bathing, Cleaning House, Shopping, Commuting, Paying Bills, Exercising, Attending Church, Socializing, Relaxing, Etc. (avg. 7 hours/day — or 5 hours/day on weekdays and 12 hours/day weekends) | 49 | 49 | 49 | 49 | 49 |
| Total | 105 | 105 | 105 | 105 | 105 |
| **Vernal Program** | Very Intensive Study | Intensive Study + Internship | Intensive Study + Internship | Study + More Change | Paid Work & Social Change |
| Study Group Meetings | 12 | 9 | 9 | 6 | 2 |
| Studying for Study Group | 24 | 18 | 18 | 15 | 3 |
| Studying Current Affairs (newspapers, magazines, web pages, etc.) | 6 | 6 | 6 | 6 | 6 |
| Social Change Internships | | 12 | 12 | 12 | |
| Social Change Work with local change group | 3 | 3 | 3 | 9 | 20 |
| Social Service Work | 3 | | | | |
| Support Group / Therapy / Body Work | 2 | 2 | 2 | 2 | 2 |
| Total | 50 | 50 | 50 | 50 | 33 |
| **Paid Work** | | | | | 20 |
| **Other Time in Week Available** For Additional Study, Social Change Work, Social Service, Gardening, Other Hobbies, Leisure, and so on | 13 | 13 | 13 | 13 | 11 |
| **Total Time Working for Social Change** (local change group + internship) | 3 | 15 | 15 | 21 | 20 |

**Note**: There is probably not enough time for extensive travel, childrearing, and so on.

## Synergistic Learning

Individually, each component of the Vernal Program would enable students to learn and practice crucial social change skills. Combined, these components should be even more educational. Students could immediately apply what they learned from study groups, self-study, and workshops to their social change efforts and see how these ideas worked in practice. They could bring questions and problems from their internships, social change work, and social service work to study group meetings and workshops where staffmembers and other students could provide insight and guidance. Students could compare their experiences in different internships and social change groups. Throughout, they would be surrounded by other activists offering insight, support, and encouragement.

## A Vernal Student's Time

Would there be enough time for Vernal students to fit all these activities into their lives? Figure 6.5 shows how a typical student might spend her time each week of the Vernal session (excluding the weeks spent attending workshops).* Throughout the session, students would devote about fifty hours each week to Vernal activities — with this time allocated in somewhat different ways during each of the four quarters of the year.

As I imagine it, during the first three months (the first quarter), students would spend twelve hours each week meeting with their study groups. They would spend another twenty-four hours each week studying and otherwise preparing for their study group meetings. Students would spend six hours each week reading about current events. They would spend three hours each week working with their social change group and three more hours performing social service. They would also spend two hours per week meeting with an emotional support group or with a personal therapist (or engaging in some other similar activity). During this first quarter, they would devote most of their fifty hours each week to reading and discussing social change information.

For the next six months, students would meet with their study group less often and do no social service work. Instead, they would spend these twelve hours per week in internships. During the last three months, they would meet with their study group even less often and spend these six hours per week working with their local social change group.

I assume that basic life maintenance activities like sleeping, eating, bathing, cooking, shopping, exercising, relaxing, commuting to meetings and internships, and so on would take about 15 hours per day or 105 hours per week. Based on these figures, Figure 6.6 shows what a typical student's week in the third quarter of the session might be like. This is a busy and full schedule, but should not be overly stressful.

The last column of Figure 6.5 shows how Vernal graduates might spend their time during their seven years of intensive activism after they graduate. Here I assume they work twenty hours each week doing unpaid social change work and another twenty hours each week at an income-producing job. They continue to read progressive publications and get emotional support for the same number of

hours they spent during the Vernal session. They also continue to meet with a study group, but only once every other week and they spend much less time preparing for it.

As outlined here, this lifestyle is intensive. There is not much time for activities other than education and social change. Students generally only have about thirteen hours per week for other activities and graduates only have about ten or eleven hours per week. This would probably be enough time for socializing and simple hobbies, but not enough time for extensive travel, childrearing, or other time-intensive activities.

Although this lifestyle would be somewhat limited, it should also be quite fulfilling. Based on my own experience and what I have seen of other activists, I believe many Vernal activists could live this way without becoming weary or disgruntled for eight years (one year as students plus seven more years as very active graduates). I believe they could willingly embrace such an eight-year period of intensive education and social change work since this would comprise only about ten percent of their lives — they would still have time for many other activities in the rest of their lives.

## A Possible Vernal Curriculum

It is important for progressive activists to learn about a variety of specific topics. But it is equally important — if not more so — for them to learn how and where to get information, how to learn, how to think, how to wrestle with ideas, and how to debate ideas productively with other people. As I envision it, the Vernal Education Program would devote at least as much time to these important learning processes as it would to offering specific information.

This section first describes a possible curriculum in terms of general areas of knowledge covered, then specific topics that might be covered in the study groups and workshop classes. Finally, it covers the educational methods the Vernal staffmembers would probably use to help students learn to wrestle with diverse ideas and perspectives.

### General Areas of Knowledge

There are a zillion things that are useful for progressive social change activists to learn, and they cannot all be learned in just one year. However, certain basic areas of knowledge seem essential:

#### • Current Reality

How does the world function? What is the conventional way to view social, cultural, political, military, and business affairs? What criticisms do conventional groups have of society?

---

* Figure B.3 in Appendix B shows an even more detailed week-by-week analysis of time spent in each of these categories including time spent in workshops, time spent studying for the workshops, and the week-long vacation periods at the end of each quarter. Holidays are not shown, but Vernal students would, of course, observe all the major ones — this would reduce the total hours. Overall, students would devote about 2,300 hours to the Vernal Education Program over the course of the year.

# Figure 6.6: Laura's Week — Representative of Vernal Students During the Second Quarter

| | Sunday | Monday | Tuesday | Wednesday | Thursday | Friday | Saturday |
|---|---|---|---|---|---|---|---|
| 7:00 AM | Slept in | Slept | Slept | Slept | Slept | Slept | Slept in |
| 8:00 AM | | Ate, showered, and read the newspaper | Exercised | Ate, showered, and read the newspaper | Exercised | Ate, showered, and read the newspaper | |
| | | | Ate, showered, read paper | | Ate, showered, read paper | | |
| 9:00 AM | Ate, showered, and read the newspaper | Study Group Meeting | Studied for Study Group | Study Group Meeting | Studied for Study Group | Study Group Meeting | Ate, showered, and read the newspaper |
| 10:00 AM | | | | | | | |
| 11:00 AM | Church | | | | | | |
| Noon | Ate lunch | Ate lunch, read "Ms." | Ate lunch | Ate lunch with Kim | Ate lunch | Shopped and ate lunch | Hiked and picnicked with Kim |
| 1:00 PM | Called parents | Commuted | Commuted | | Commuted | Read "The Nation" | |
| 2:00 PM | | Internship at Peace Center | Internship at Peace Center | Washed Clothes | Internship at Peace Center | | |
| 3:00 PM | Went swimming | | | Studied for Study Group | | Studied for Study Group | Went shopping |
| 4:00 PM | | | | | | | |
| 5:00 PM | | | | | | | Vacuumed |
| 6:00 PM | Made dinner and ate with housemates and Michelle | Commuted | Commuted | Made dinner and ate | Commuted | Cleaned bathroom | Made dinner and ate with Jennifer |
| | | Ate dinner with housemates | Ate dinner with housemates | | Ate dinner with housemates | Made dinner and ate | |
| 7:00 PM | | | | Citizens for Equitable Taxes (CET) Meeting | | | |
| 8:00 PM | Studied for Study Group | Support Group Meeting | Paid bills | | Made calls for CET | | |
| 9:00 PM | | | Studied for Study Group | Read "Extra" | Read "Z Magazine" | Went to a movie with Naomi and then talked | Went to a Party at Zachary's |
| 10:00 PM | | Read a novel | | Wrote a letter to Yuhong | Watched TV | | |
| 11:00 PM | Brushed teeth | Brushed teeth | Brushed teeth | Brushed teeth | Brushed teeth | | |
| Midnight | | | | | | | |
| 1:00 AM | | | | | | Brushed teeth | Brushed teeth |
| 2:00 AM | Slept | Slept | Slept | Slept | Slept | Slept | Slept |
| 3:00 AM | | | | | | | |
| 4:00 AM | | | | | | | |
| 5:00 AM | | | | | | | |
| 6:00 AM | | | | | | | |

• **Alternative Perspectives**

What criticisms do progressive activists have of current society? What are their alternative visions?

---

*The Ignorant know nothing. The Provincial know only the perspective of their own community. Traditionalists hear new ideas, but cling to those of their ancestors. Conformists learn of alternative perspectives, but embrace only the most conventional. Zealots know of other ideas, but accept only what they already believe. The Confused stumble across many perspectives, but don't know what to believe. It is only the Explorers, the Curious Students, the Free-thinkers, the Scholars who seek out many perspectives and thoroughly investigate each one to dig out its truth.*

---

• **Multiple Perspectives**

Why do people disagree? Why does each group believe its way is best? What criticism does each group have of every other perspective? What problem does each group's solution solve and how does it solve it? What are the values and assumptions behind each group's perspective? What material conditions or philosophical values underlie each group's perspective? How do you decide who is right?

---

*Until you can see the truth in at least three sides of an issue, you probably don't understand it. And until you can convincingly argue all three perspectives, you probably can't work with a diverse group of people to find a mutually satisfactory solution.*

---

• **Bringing About Change**

How have activists tried to bring about change in the past? What was effective and what was not? Who opposes progressive change and why? What are the methods usually proposed to bring about social change? How do you design an effective campaign for fundamental social change? What factors make success more likely? How do you sustain yourself and others through a long, difficult campaign? What empowers and inspires others to action?

Below I have outlined a possible preliminary curriculum that covers these basics from a multiplicity of perspectives. This curriculum is only an example — staffmembers and students would develop the actual curriculum, and it would evolve over time.

## Study Group Topics

Following the schedule of study groups outlined above, students would spend two weeks on each of fourteen topics and a single week on another topic. These topics would cover a variety of social change issue areas and a wide range of theoretical and practical aspects of social change. Each topic would have a list of twenty to thirty different sets of staffmember-chosen readings from which students could choose. Students could also find their own readings. These fifteen main topics might be:

• **The Environment**
  • Natural systems
  • Consuming natural resources (mining, drilling, logging, ranching, farming, hunting)
  • Renewable resources
  • Land development
  • Population growth, sustainability
  • Pollution, garbage, toxic wastes

• **Economics**
  • Self-sufficiency, individualism
  • Agriculture
  • Producing goods, providing services to others
  • Ownership, property
  • Wealth distribution
  • Feudalism, slavery, capitalism, socialism, privatization
  • Government regulation
  • Transnational corporations, globalization
  • Cooperatives, worker-, community-, or government-controlled businesses, locally owned and controlled businesses, non-profit businesses
  • Wages, working conditions, occupational safety
  • Unemployment, poverty
  • Taxes

• **U.S. International Relations**
  • Colonialism, domination
  • Armed military force
  • Diplomacy
  • Citizen exchanges
  • Global communication

• **Social Institutions**
  • Schools
  • Churches
  • Libraries
  • Police
  • Prisons
  • The military
  • The healthcare system
  • The welfare system
  • Community organizations

• **Culture**
  • Education
  • Religion, spirituality
  • Entertainment
  • Sports
  • Mass media, the Internet

- Personal communication
- Ethnicity, racism, sexism, classism, ageism, homophobia, and so on

- **Personal Relationships**
  - Family, childrearing
  - Paternalism
  - Battering, dysfunctional families
  - Sexual abuse, rape
  - Health and healing
  - Emotional counseling therapy
  - Cooperation
  - Feminism
  - Sex, hetero- and homosexuality

- **Politics**
  - Democracy
  - Elections, voting
  - Theory of government, anarchism
  - Libertarian pluralism
  - The U.S. governmental system of making and enforcing laws

- **History of Movements for Progressive Change**
  - Anti-slavery
  - Populist
  - Socialist (1910s and '20s)
  - Conservation (National Parks)
  - Women's suffrage
  - Labor union
  - Consumer
  - Conscientious objectors to war
  - Black freedom struggle
  - Anti-Vietnam war
  - Anti-nuclear power and weapons
  - Environmental
  - Women's liberation
  - Anti-racism
  - Gay and lesbian freedom
  - Anti-globalization
  - Other movements around the world

- **Visions of a Better Society**
  - Utopian visions
  - Nonviolence
  - Participatory democracy, citizenship
  - Appropriate technology, simple living
  - Multiculturalism
  - Cooperation, community

- **Theory and Practice of Social Change**
  - Analyzing power structures
  - Choosing issues
  - Strategic planning
  - Stages of a movement
  - Political, social, and cultural change

- **Movement Building**
  - Developing visions of a good society
  - Researching an issue
  - Educating and persuading others
  - Lobbying
  - Lawsuits
  - Campaigns for political office
  - Demonstrations, struggling for change
  - Designing effective campaigns

- **Organizational Development**
  - Starting and developing an organization
  - Recruiting volunteers
  - Supporting and empowering people, team building
  - Facilitating meetings
  - Addressing racism, sexism, and so on
  - Resolving conflicts
  - Fundraising
  - Administration

- **Being an Activist**
  - Personal growth and emotional therapy
  - Critical thinking
  - Internalized oppression and liberation
  - Building a supportive community
  - Personal finances

- **Repression of Activists**
  - Spy and intelligence agencies
  - Police, red squads, FBI
  - National Guard, Marine Corps
  - Private security agencies
  - Death squads, Ku Klux Klan, other terror groups
  - Public relations firms
  - Movement-breaking consultants
  - Honesty, trust
  - Building a safe community

- **Teaching Others**
  - Theories of adult education
  - Teaching styles
  - Mentoring activists
  - Developing curricula

*Everyone thinks of changing the world, but no one thinks of changing himself.*
— Leo Tolstoy

## Workshop Class Topics

As I see it, the eighty workshop classes (each two and one-half hours long) would cover many of the same topics as listed above, but would focus on aspects that are more easily learned through workshop presentations and experiential exercises than through reading and discussion. Below is a possible list of topics. The numbers in parentheses indicate how many classes might be devoted to each topic. Note that topics are listed in logical categories. However, classes would probably not be conducted in this order but in an order that matched the study group schedule, students' needs, or staffmembers' schedules.

- **Choosing One's Values (4)**
  - Personal change, social change, and values clarification, developing a vision of a good society (1)
  - Becoming informed — newspapers, magazines, radio, TV, the Internet, and other news and communication media (1)
  - Deciphering and overcoming media propaganda (1)
  - Appreciating other perspectives and developing truths to live by — creating, testing, and challenging models of reality, thinking clearly, debating different perspectives, critical argumentation (1)

- **Being an Activist (12)**
  - Self-esteem and assertiveness — being bold and non-violent (1)
  - Internalized oppression and liberation (2)
  - Emotional and physical sustenance in tough times (1)
  - Building a supportive community — daily interaction, concern, support, humor, singing, massage (2)
  - A range of counseling therapy and personal growth techniques (1)
  - Living lightly on the earth every day (1)
  - The many roles of an activist — rebel, citizen, reformer, social changer, scholar, manager, facilitator, worker, secretary, counselor, minister, spokesperson, teacher (1)
  - Personal finances — toward financial independence (1)
  - Money and class on a personal level (2)

- **Developing a Social Change Organization (15)**
  - Starting and developing a social change group (1)
  - Organizational forms and structures (1)
  - Discussing, debating, and struggling with ideas (1)
  - Encouraging diversity and dissent, avoiding group-think, mind-control, and cult-like behavior (1)
  - Addressing racism, sexism, homophobia, ageism, and other prejudices (2)
  - Addressing classism and money issues (2)
  - Dealing with emotional trauma and craziness — emotional support (2)
  - Resolving conflicts (2)
  - Dealing with infiltration, provocateurs, harassment (1)
  - Helping other activists learn new skills (2)

- **Meeting Together and Making Decisions (7)**
  - Leadership and management theories (1)
  - Parliamentary procedure and voting (1)
  - Making cooperative decisions (1)
  - Facilitating a group meeting (2)
  - Effective problem solving in groups (1)
  - Working in large, dispersed organizations (1)

- **Running a Social Change Office (4)**
  - Basic office management skills — filing, accounting, communication, computer use (2)
  - Basic organization maintenance skills — fundraising, membership, personnel management (2)

- **Social Change Methods (17)**
  - Researching an issue (1)
  - Developing visions of alternatives (1)
  - Writing, publishing, and distributing leaflets, pamphlets, newspapers, books, and web pages (1)
  - Persuasion techniques and methods (1)
  - Speaking out publicly (1)
  - Canvassing (1)
  - Outreach to the news media (1)
  - Political film and video (1)
  - Political music, art, and theater (1)
  - Protest demonstrations — rallies, vigils, fasts, pickets, marches, confrontations (1)
  - Strikes and boycotts (1)
  - Civil disobedience and direct action (2)
  - Risking arrest and going to jail for a cause (1)
  - Electoral politics and lobbying (2)
  - Lawsuits, referenda, and other legal action (1)

- **Social Change Campaigns (6)**
  - Strategic planning for social change — force field analysis (2)
  - Designing effective campaigns — constituencies, issues, and action (2)
  - Campaign simulation (2)

- **Working with Others (7)**
  - Addressing special constituencies — racial/ethnic minorities, religious groups, elders, young people, labor union members, lesbians and gays, women, rural folks, and so on (3)
  - The diversity of social change groups — their ideas and practices (2)
  - Working in coalitions and federations (1)
  - Local grassroots groups and how they relate to national social change organizations (1)

- **Social Change Movements (3)**
  - Types of change movements and their goals: resistance, liberation, democracy, and stewardship (1)
  - Evaluating and choosing ten important areas of focus for social change in the next few decades (2)

- **History of Social Change Movements (4)**
  - Overview of world movements for change (1)
  - Oral history of recent local movements presented by active participants (2)
  - Lessons we can learn from earlier social change efforts (1)

## Reading Lists

Vernal staffmembers, working in conjunction with students, would continually revise the list of reading materials for study groups, adding new books and articles and retiring weak and outdated materials. They would also maintain a library of all these materials to loan to students.

---

**The Vernal Education Program Curriculum Checklist:**

• Why are we studying this?
• Why are we using these methods?
• Is there a more educational or empowering way?

---

## Workshop Notes and Agendas

Vernal staffmembers would also prepare detailed workshop notes on the topics outlined above. Generally, for each topic, the notes would include major points of interest and discussion, the range of perspectives held by progressive activists (and others), active areas of contention and debate, and references to books, articles, web pages, and other sources of information. They would also include lists of questions and discussion topics to challenge and stimulate students to learn and explore new ideas. They might include provocative quotations or koans (paradoxical Zen Buddhist riddles to ponder in order to attain intuitive knowledge). For some topics, the notes might simply be annotated bibliographies of important books, articles, and web pages. Some notes might include a sample workshop agenda.

The notes would give students more information than they could absorb in workshop classes. After graduating, Vernal activists could review the notes when they were actually faced with difficult situations in their change work. Graduates could also use the notes and agendas to develop evening or weekend workshops for other activists, and when appropriate, they could pass copies of the notes to others. Moreover, these notes would be broadly distributed outside of activist circles — posted on the Vernal Project web site <http://www.vernalproject.org> — to help advance social change more widely. "Information is power," and these short, clear, and understandable summaries of progressive change theory and practice could be very powerful.[4]

## Researching and Developing the Curriculum

With help from students, Vernal staffmembers would continually update the curriculum, incorporating new social change issues, new social change methods, and new change philosophies. They would draw on magazine articles, books, web pages, their own social change experience, and the experiences of other activists.[5] Vernal staffmembers would share their research and coordinate the development of new curricula with other Vernal teams around the country.

## Educational Methods and Style

The curriculum of the Vernal Program would be very important, but the way that it was presented would be just as important — students learn as much by watching their teachers and mentors as they do from studying. I expect that the Vernal Program would refrain from using the cruel and disempowering techniques common in many traditional schools.

Though public and church schools have the admirable goal of educating children, they also usually have a more sinister goal: to mold students so they will conform to societal norms and accommodate themselves to the ruling authorities. To accomplish this unsavory goal, schools usually employ four main processes:

*What you are speaks so loudly I can't hear what you say.*
— Ralph Waldo Emerson

• **Selective information**: Schools present a limited amount of information, usually from a narrow spectrum of perspectives and declare "this is the way it is." If mentioned at all, alternative ideas are usually explained badly and belittled. Standardized textbooks ensure that everyone receives the same one-sided information.

• **Indoctrination**: Schools repeatedly present the same information as fact until "the Truth" seems self-evident and all other ideas seem ludicrous.

• **Manipulation**: Schools use grading and tracking to control and steer students into acceptance of the status quo. Those who best adopt conventional dogma are encouraged and rewarded; those who do not are held back, criticized, and even ostracized.

• **Demoralization**: Students are controlled and restricted. They are forced to attend (often boring) lectures. This steals their initiative and demoralizes them.

Social change schools teach a more progressive ideology, but some actually employ the same mind-numbing and manipulative teaching processes as conventional schools. As I see it, the Vernal Program would empower students to explore a variety of ideas and develop their own ideology by using these alternative methods:

• **Comprehensive Information, Diverse Perspectives**

The Vernal Program would present a wide array of information and perspectives including age-old wisdom, conventional thought, and a range of alternative perspectives: "Here's what different people think and their reasons for thinking it."

### • Questioning

The Vernal Program would encourage questioning: "How do we know this is true? How do we find out? How else do people look at things? Why do some people disagree? Whom can we believe? Are there other ways of looking at an issue that no one has ever considered?"

*Take from others what you want, but never be a disciple of anyone.*
— A. S. Neill, director of Summerhill School

### • Discussion and Problem Solving

The Vernal Program would show students how to gently and productively discuss divisive topics and resolve conflicts by clearly summarizing all perspectives, sorting ideas into categories, and synthesizing new, more comprehensive perspectives.

### • Scientific Method

The Vernal program would encourage students to ascertain truth by evaluating evidence — not to accept dogma based on blind faith. "What works? What doesn't? What is useful? What might work better? How can we test this? Do our hypotheses seem to predict future events accurately? If not, what new postulate can we test that might predict it better? Which entities and postulates seem useless and can be discarded?"

*An ideology that cannot withstand intense challenge is invariably anti-progressive. Through questioning, ideas grow to be more robust and compelling.*

## Question Authority!

### • Open Education, Collegial Atmosphere

The Vernal Program would have no requirements for participation in any activities. Students would not be graded, and every student who completed the session would receive a diploma. Staffmembers would assist students to learn whatever the students thought was best for themselves (within the constraints of the overall Vernal Program). Staffmembers would strive to maintain their role as helpful resource people rather than as leaders or controllers of students.

Students would be encouraged to collaborate with, help, and teach each other — passing on what they had learned through their years of experience or what they just learned the day before. Staffmembers would also ask students to help them to evaluate and modify the curriculum, materials, and educational methods.

The Vernal Program would in no way be value-free — the curriculum would clearly be quite progressive and the staffmembers' various progressive views would permeate the program. But as much as possible, when staffmembers expressed their perspectives, they would try to make their ideological bent explicit, allow it to be discussed, and encourage it to be challenged.

### • Humane, Gentle Struggle

The Vernal Program would also encourage staffmembers and students to acknowledge that they are each human beings with feelings, desires, and limitations. The program would encourage them to respect their differences and to treat each other well even as they struggled over ideas.

*The true teacher defends his pupils against his own personal influence.*
— Amos Bronson Alcott

## VERNAL STAFFMEMBERS

### Background and Skills

Vernal staffmembers would be chosen for their experience as social change activists and for their educational skills, especially their ability to use alternative, student-centered education methods. When hiring new staffmembers, existing staffmembers would try to recruit people with whom they could easily work. They would also seek demographic and ideological diversity.

Each staffmember in a Vernal team would have similar responsibilities, differing according to need and according to each staffmember's interests. Those with more experience and skill in education might focus more on facilitating workshops; those with more administrative skill might work more on setting up internships, handling finances, and hiring. Optimally, every staffmember would be skilled in all the areas required for educating students and administering the program. More likely, though, staffmembers of each Vernal team would have complementary skills that could address everything necessary.

### Staff Hiring and Pay

Given all that would be expected of them, staffmembers would likely work quite hard. The work should be rewarding, but the amount of it might still be exhausting. Since staffmembers would be experienced and skilled in many areas, disgruntled staffmembers could probably find other lucrative jobs without much effort. In order to induce staffmembers to work for years without burning out or leaving, they would need to be paid reasonable wages and benefits. On the other hand, wages could not be too generous or the cost would threaten the overall viability of the Vernal Project.

Aiming for a prudent balance, I assume the Vernal Program would pay full-time Vernal staffmembers $24,000 per year (in 1995 dollars) and offer generous benefits that included paid vacation, holidays, and health and dental care coverage.[6] In addition, the Vernal Program would put $2,000 per year into a retirement account for each staffmember. Part-time staffmembers would earn a proportional share of salary and benefits.

Dedicated Vernal staffmembers with few obligations should be able to live reasonably well on this salary. However, it would probably be too small an amount for staffmembers to support a spouse and children or for them to save much during their tenure. Still, I expect many activists would be eager to work as Vernal staffmembers since the work would be quite satisfying and the organization would be very supportive.

Hiring and integrating new staffmembers would require a great deal of effort, so people would be hired who planned to stay with the Vernal center for at least five years. But staffmembers who stayed too long could become stale and stodgy, so they might be encouraged to move on to other endeavors after ten or fifteen years. Staffmembers would be evaluated each year by their peers and the local center's board of directors (see below).

## VERNAL STUDENTS

## Admission Requirements

The main purpose of the Vernal Project would be to bring about fundamental progressive transformation of society. However, it is possible that over time the Vernal Program might be seen as a surrogate business school by those seeking an inexpensive entrance to the executive ranks of corporate America or as an inviting intellectual sandbox for those seeking an inexpensive place to play with philosophical ideas.

Admissions must therefore be quite selective to ensure that the limited resources of the Vernal Project would be used wisely. The program must be available only to those most open to learning and most interested in using what they learn to work for progressive change. These would be the minimum requirements:

### • One-Year of Experience with Active Social Change Work

It would be important that applicants already have some activist experience so they would know the joys and disappointments of working for change and how this work affected them. After doing it for a while, many activists discover that social change work frustrates, bores, or frightens them. Other activists realize that other activities are more important to them, at least at that particular point in their lives.

After a year of social change work, applicants should have a good sense of what social change work is all about, and they could knowledgeably decide if they wanted to work long-term for fundamental change. In addition, by having at least a year of experience, students would have a much better idea of what they needed or wanted to learn. Moreover, they would have accumulated some valuable experience to share with other students.

### • Academically Capable

The Vernal Program, as I envision it, would be similar to college, requiring extensive reading and studying. Students would need to handle a fairly heavy academic workload. Many people do not enjoy this kind of academic work and the Vernal Program would be inappropriate for them. Non-academically oriented activists would probably learn better with an activist mentor who could assist and guide them "on the job."

### • Willing and Able to Work Primarily for Fundamental Social Change for Eight Years

Applicants would have to seriously intend to make social change work their highest priority for eight years (one year in the Vernal session plus seven years after graduating). During this eight-year period, they would be expected to work at least twenty hours per week for fundamental change. They must also be willing to work to end their own oppressive and addictive behaviors, support and encourage other nonviolent activists, and as much as possible, serve as a good role model for others by living in an exemplary way.

By making fundamental change their highest priority, Vernal activists might be forced to delay for eight years many of the pleasures and activities of their peers: partying nightly, traveling, raising children, pursuing a conventional career, saving money for a house and retirement, and so on. Older activists who had already done most of these things might find it easier to make this commitment, though some might have a difficult time adjusting after years of a more conventional lifestyle.

*Respectable men and women content with good and easy living are missing some of the most important things in life. Unless you give yourself to some great cause you haven't even begun to live.*
— William P. Merrill

Also, since social change work usually pays little or nothing, Vernal students and graduates would likely need to live modestly and inexpensively. Since they would probably be able to work no more than half-time at a non-social change job or full-time at a change job, most could probably earn only $10,000 to $30,000 per year. This limitation would probably not be very important for those financially supported by spouses or family members, those living on retirement funds, or those relying on independent wealth.

However, those relying only on their earned income would be forced to have a frugal lifestyle: living in shared housing; riding a bicycle, taking public transportation or having an older car; doing without fancy clothes, expensive furniture, and expensive appliances; and so on.

### • Oriented Toward Behind-the-Scenes Support of Other Activists

Priority for admission would also be given to applicants who indicated interest in doing the kind of basic support work that the Vernal Program most encourages. Vernal graduates would generally be helpers, facilitators, and supporters — providing leadership from below — rather than designated powerholders or leaders who controlled or directed others.

### • Able to Pay Tuition and Support Themselves

Applicants for admission would have to indicate how they would plan to pay Vernal tuition and how they would sustain themselves during the one-year session. The nature of the Vernal Program would probably prevent students from tapping conventional Federal and State education grants or loans. Loans of any kind might be problematic since most Vernal graduates would earn little money.

Some of the students' internships might pay stipends, and some internally generated scholarships would be available (see below). However, most students would need to tap their savings or rely on their spouse, parents, grown children, friends, or other supporters for financial support. As part of the application procedure, each indigent student would be encouraged to assemble a group of personal supporters who could contribute financially to her education and could then share in the glory of her accomplishments.

### • Positive Recommendations

Applicants would need to have very positive written recommendations from three activists, professors, clergypeople, or others who knew them well and could honestly evaluate

---

### Some Notes on Political Sophistication

Political scientist Russell Neuman finds that less than five percent of the U.S. population (perhaps 10 million adults) is highly sophisticated politically.[7] Neuman defines political sophistication to include three components:

• **Political salience** — interest, concern, and attentiveness toward political issues

• **Political knowledge** — familiarity with major issues, prominent political figures, and events and accurate knowledge about the forces that shape political decisions

• **Political conceptualization** — the ability to evaluate, relate, differentiate, integrate, and form abstract mental models about political forces and their interaction.

---

how well they work as progressive social change activists.

Applicants who did not meet these criteria would be encouraged to wait until they could satisfy them or would be directed to other educational programs (including on-the-job mentoring). The Vernal Program would not be appropriate for everyone. Moreover, even if the Vernal Project becomes wildly successful, most activists working for fundamental change (even those working more than twenty hours per week) would never attend a Vernal Program. So being rejected would in no way imply that applicants were stupid, lazy, politically incorrect, or in any way inferior to those who did attend.

## Likely Applicants

The Vernal Program would be most appealing to those who were politically sophisticated enough to understand social problems and solutions, progressive enough to work for a positive vision of a good society, dedicated enough to commit to work primarily for change for many years (and forgo other major commitments), and prosperous enough to attend a Vernal session and then work mostly for change for a seven-year period.

After considering the nature of our society, the Vernal Program would likely be most accessible and attractive to five types of people:

### • Career Activists

Some activists have dedicated their lives to social change. They either work full-time for progressive organizations or work part-time at a conventional job and devote the rest of their time to social change. Some of these activists might decide to take a year off from their change work to attend a Vernal Program.

*The purpose of life is a life of purpose.*
— Robert Byrne

### • Progressive Organization Staffmembers

A subset of the above group are staffmembers of enlightened social change organizations that value skilled staffmembers and can afford to let them take most of a year off to further their change knowledge and skills. These organizations might partially or fully pay their staffmembers while they attended a Vernal session. In exchange for this support, these students might spend all their social change time (three hours per week for the first three quarters, nine hours per week the last quarter) working for their sponsoring organization. Note, though, that students in this circumstance should have internships with other social change groups so they could experience a range of activist philosophies and work styles.

### • People Financially Supported by their Spouses

Some activists have sympathetic spouses who can support them while they do social change work. In the past, "housewives" — financially supported by an employed

# Figure 6.7: Rough Guesstimates of the Age Distribution of Vernal Students

| | % of Total | Age at Time of Enrollment | | | | | | |
|---|---|---|---|---|---|---|---|---|
| | | 18–25 | 26–35 | 36–45 | 46–55 | 56–65 | 66–70 | 71+ |
| Progressive Organization Staff | 5% | 20% | 25% | 25% | 20% | 10% | 0% | 0% |
| Other Career Activists | 25% | 10% | 25% | 20% | 20% | 20% | 5% | 0% |
| Supported by Spouses | 10% | 5% | 15% | 20% | 30% | 30% | 0% | 0% |
| Vigorous Retirees | 20% | 0% | 0% | 0% | 14% | 65% | 20% | 1% |
| Bright-Eyed Young People | 40% | 60% | 40% | 0% | 0% | 0% | 0% | 0% |
| **Everyone** | 100% | 28% | 25% | 8% | 12% | 22% | 5% | 0% |

**Average Age =    39.7**

husband — often devoted much of their time to charity or civic groups. Women in this situation have traditionally been the backbone of many change organizations like the League of Women Voters (LWV) and Women's International League for Peace and Freedom (WILPF). In these economically-constrained but more gender-liberated times, there are a lot fewer women who are financially supported by their spouses, but perhaps a few more men supported by theirs.

### • Vigorous Retirees

Some older people, who have already completed a conventional career and raised children, are still healthy and vigorous. Typically in their fifties or sixties, they have worked enough of their lives to have accumulated substantial savings and are also still healthy and hearty enough to do intensive social change work. Many of these people might have been activists earlier in their lives but pulled back when family or other life commitments took precedence. These people might decide to refresh and update their social change skills by attending a Vernal session. Others are "late bloomers" who are just beginning to work for social change.

### • Bright-Eyed Young People

Many young people are new to social change, often having gotten involved in high school or college. These adventurous and idealistic young people might decide to attend a Vernal session instead of more traditional paths like going to college, graduate school, or a trade school, starting a conventional career job, joining the Peace Corps, hitchhiking around the world, joining a rural commune, working at a crisis hotline, or volunteering at a social service agency. Those from more affluent backgrounds might receive financial support from their parents or other relatives to attend a session.

Because of the heavy academic component of the Vernal Program, I assume a relatively high percentage of applicants would be college-educated. Because of its cost, it would probably attract more activists from middle-income and wealthy families. Still, the Vernal Program should appeal to a wide variety of people. When possible, Vernal staffmembers would select a group that reflected the diversity of the region in age, race, ethnicity, economic class, gender, sexual orientation, and so on.

Vernal staffmembers would make a special effort to attract and support students from oppressed groups who might otherwise feel intimidated. To make it less difficult for these people to attend, some Vernal sessions might consist entirely of students who were all poor, all non-white, all rural, all elders, or whatever. In addition, to increase the number of poorer students, the Vernal Program would offer scholarships and stipends (see below).

Figure 6.7 shows my rough guesstimate of the age distribution of Vernal students. Based on my experience with activists and my projection of who would be interested in the Vernal program, I expect there would be a large number of young people in their early twenties and also a large number of people in their late fifties and early sixties. I assume that the average age would be about forty, but relatively few students would actually be that age.

## THE VERNAL EDUCATION NETWORK

### Vernal Centers

As I envision it, when the Vernal network had reached full size, it would consist of fifty centers, each with a team of four full-time equivalent (FTE) staffmembers. Each Vernal center might have a small office, but more likely, the staffmembers would just work out of their own homes. Centers would be based in the most populous metropolitan areas in the country. Every year, each team would facilitate four sessions of about thirty students. The Vernal network would therefore offer education to about six thousand students each year.

Each session would consist of four or five study groups of five to nine students each — totaling 28 to 32 students. A typical session might consist of five separate study groups with six students apiece. Each study group would include students who all lived very close to one another (a few miles at most) so they could easily meet. The study groups comprising a session, however, might be very spread out, so that students could attend from many widely scattered communities. Typically, a Vernal team would work with study groups within a reasonable driving distance of 75 miles in each direction from its central base (within 150 miles from

each other). However, in sparsely populated regions, study groups might be scattered even wider. In such situations, Vernal staffmembers would travel far from their home metro area to distant communities and stay for several days at a time to set up and monitor internships and to confer with students at meetings of their study group.

This arrangement would enable the fifty Vernal teams to reach a very large number of potential students. As detailed in Figure B.11 in Appendix B, if the fifty Vernal centers were located in the most populous cities, about two-thirds of the U.S. population would be close enough to a center that they could attend a Vernal session.

In the early years, when the Vernal network was just beginning to grow, each Vernal team would recruit, hire, teach, and support all the new staffmembers it needed. However, when the network grew large enough, the number of new people required each year to cover expansion and to replace retiring staffmembers would be quite large. To ex-

# Figure 6.8: A Possible Vernal Geographical Structure

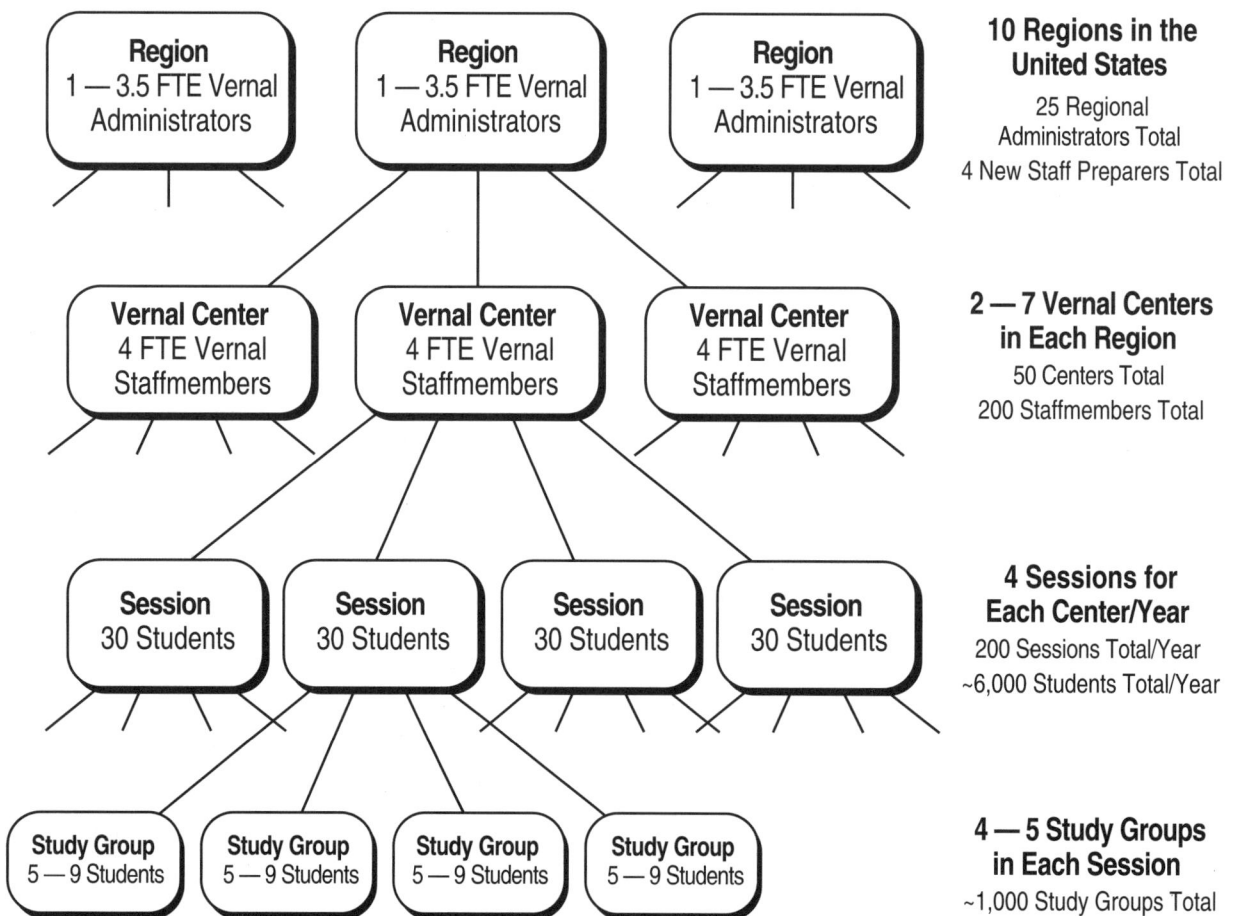

**Region**
1 — 3.5 FTE Vernal Administrators

**Region**
1 — 3.5 FTE Vernal Administrators

**Region**
1 — 3.5 FTE Vernal Administrators

**10 Regions in the United States**
25 Regional Administrators Total
4 New Staff Preparers Total

**Vernal Center**
4 FTE Vernal Staffmembers

**Vernal Center**
4 FTE Vernal Staffmembers

**Vernal Center**
4 FTE Vernal Staffmembers

**2 — 7 Vernal Centers in Each Region**
50 Centers Total
200 Staffmembers Total

**Session**
30 Students

**Session**
30 Students

**Session**
30 Students

**Session**
30 Students

**4 Sessions for Each Center/Year**
200 Sessions Total/Year
~6,000 Students Total/Year

**Study Group**
5 — 9 Students

**Study Group**
5 — 9 Students

**Study Group**
5 — 9 Students

**Study Group**
5 — 9 Students

**4 — 5 Study Groups in Each Session**
~1,000 Study Groups Total

Students in a study group would usually live within a few miles of each other. Students in a session would generally live within 75 miles of a Vernal center and within 150 miles of each other.

**Note**: This is **not** the decision-making structure!

pedite this process, I envision that some experienced activists would be hired solely to recruit, hire, teach, and support new staffmembers. With special assistance from these "new staff preparers," newcomers would be better prepared to join their Vernal team.

As the number of Vernal centers grew, it would be advantageous for the centers in the same part of the country to work together in a regional alliance and to have additional help. They would hire regional administrators to take over much of the administrative work of the centers, including record-keeping, accounting, and payroll. This would free up the Vernal team staffmembers to focus more on education. Charged with supporting the needs of the region and the whole network, the regional administrators would also work to facilitate communication and cooperation between the

centers in the region and with centers in the rest of the country.

Figure 6.8 summarizes a possible geographical structure of the Vernal Project when it had reached full size. Four to five nearby study groups of five to nine students each would comprise a Vernal session (about thirty students in all). Each team of four (full-time equivalent) staffmembers would facilitate four sessions. Two to seven teams would work in each of ten regions throughout the country (fifty teams total), and there would be one regional administrator for every two centers (twenty-five total). Four new staff preparers would help to recruit, teach, and support new staffmembers around the country. Overall, Vernal teams would conduct two hundred sessions each year for six thousand students.

# Figure 6.9: A Possible Vernal Decision-Making Structure

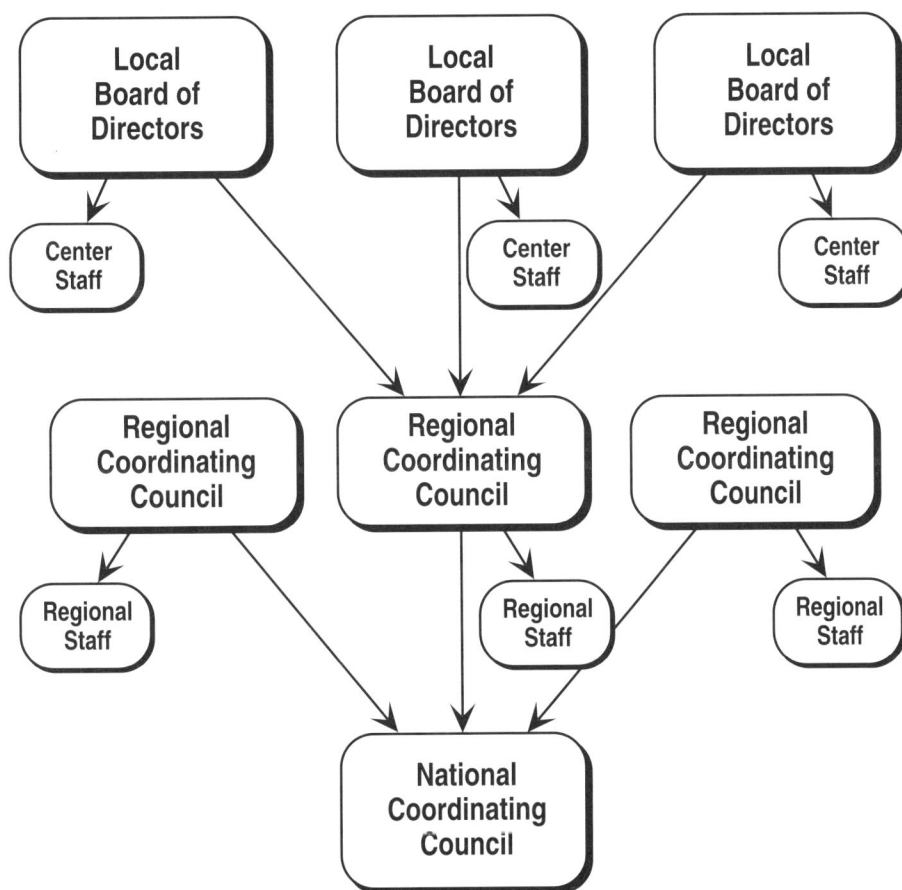

**50 Local Boards**
(one for each center)

Supervise center staff

6 — 12 members

Members chosen from staff, students, graduates, and local activists

Meet 12 times/year

Send 2 representatives to regional council

**10 Regional Councils**

Supervise regional staff and coordinate activities of all centers in region

2 representatives from each local board of directors

Meet 3 — 4 times/year

Send 1 — 3 representatives to national council

**1 National Council**

Coordinates activities of regional staff and all centers

~ 21 members: 1 — 3 from each regional council

Meets 1 or 2 times/year

A local board of directors would supervise each Vernal center. Boards would be responsible for all decisions (including curriculum, admissions, and hiring) though Vernal staffmembers would probably make most everyday decisions. Regional coordinating councils would coordinate publicity and recruitment for the local centers. The national coordinating council would gather articles for a national alumni newsletter, coordinate national publicity, coordinate curriculum changes, and ensure a reasonable balance of salaries and tuition across regions.

**Note**: In this model, there are no national staffmembers. All national work would be carried out by regional or local staffmembers.

## Network Governance

To be consistent with progressive ideals, the Vernal Education Network must be governed in a decentralized, democratic, cooperative way. Figure 6.9 shows a possible decision-making structure for the network when it had reached full size.

Each Vernal team would make most of the decisions regarding the day-to-day running of its sessions. For important policy decisions, each center would be governed by a board of directors. This board might have six to twelve members consisting of perhaps roughly equal numbers of Vernal staffmembers, active graduates, current students, and interested local activists. Working in conjunction with the Vernal team, the board would chart overall direction and make important policy decisions concerning the following:

- Personnel — recruiting, hiring, salary levels, evaluation
- Student recruitment and admissions
- Levels of financial support for students — scholarships and stipends
- Curriculum
- Coordination with other centers

I assume the board would use a cooperative consensus decision-making process for all decisions. They would meet once a month and meetings would be open to any interested member of the Vernal community (and perhaps the larger community). Observers would be allowed to participate as long as they were not disruptive, though final decisions would be made by the official members. Boardmembers would be chosen by their peer constituency (staffmembers, students, graduates, community activists). They would serve staggered terms lasting three years (one year for students).

*Make yourself an honest man, and then you may be sure there is one less rascal in the world.*
*— Thomas Carlyle*

I envision that all of the Vernal teams in a region would cooperate to maintain and support the centers in that region. Each center's board would send two representatives to a regional coordinating council that would meet three or four times each year. The Regional Council would coordinate publicity and recruitment in the region to reduce duplication of effort. It would also hire and supervise the regional administrators.* Regional Council meetings would also provide a forum for discussion of curricula and a place to share innovative education methods, study lists, and so on.

To coordinate the overall affairs of the nationwide Vernal Education Network, I envision a governing board consisting of representatives from each of the regional coordinating councils — perhaps, one to three from each region

proportionate with its size. This Council would meet once or twice a year and coordinate the following work:

- Publish an alumni newsletter twice each year and distribute it to every Vernal graduate, perhaps via e-mail.
- Maintain a Vernal Project web site.
- Arrange periodic visits or exchanges of staffmembers from one center to another so they could learn from each other and get a sense of current issues in other regions.
- Coordinate Vernal curricular development, publicity, and so on to reduce duplication of effort.
- Monitor each center to ensure the curriculum and facilitation at each were first rate.

Note that, as I envision it, there would be no national staffmembers. All national work would be delegated to regional administrators or center staffmembers.

By being highly decentralized and narrowly focused on education, the Vernal Education Network should be relatively impervious to attacks and less susceptible to infighting. As I see it, neither the network as a whole nor any of its parts would take official stands on any political issues or attempt to force anyone to do or believe anything. This would lessen internal disharmony and shield the network from outside criticism. Also, the total resources of the Vernal network would be small and divided almost evenly among all the centers, so it would not be a very desirable target for powermongers seeking to control, exploit, or plunder it. Since all Vernal staffmembers, students, and graduates would have extensive skill and experience working cooperatively, the network should operate well and serve as an exemplary model of good governance.

*Concentrated power can easily be captured and diverted to pernicious ends; democratic power, because it is dispersed, is more secure and resilient.*

## Affiliation with Other Organizations

As outlined here, the Vernal Education Network would be independently controlled and operated. However, the network might be fiscally sponsored by a nonprofit organization (like Agape Foundation or A. J. Muste Foundation) to provide a means for tax-exempt donations. To establish name recognition and a positive reputation, the network as a whole or some individual centers might also be loosely associated with a small progressive group like the War Resisters League or ACORN. The network might even be directly affiliated with some larger group like the American Friends Service Committee or an existing school like Antioch College, which already has a strong reputation, a complete administrative and fundraising structure, and tax-exempt status. The advantages of an established organization's support for the Vernal Project would, of course, need to be weighed against the possible disadvantages of being controlled or influenced by another organization that might

---

* Note, though, that it would not control the Vernal Centers in any way.

seek to impose its own ideas regarding the curriculum or structure.

# THE GROWTH OF THE VERNAL EDUCATION NETWORK

## Three Steps

The main goal of the Vernal Education Network would be to produce enough skilled and knowledgeable graduates in all parts of the United States to bring about fundamental progressive transformation of society in a few decades. To accomplish this goal, the network would eventually need to be quite large and extend across the country. To get from the current situation of no Vernal centers to this large network of fifty centers using a minimum of resources, I envision three distinct steps:

### (1) Set up the first center and determine the best way to conduct high-quality sessions

This step would require hiring several staffmembers and having them learn to work together as a team. They would develop the curriculum and educational materials, identify progressive organizations that would be willing and able to offer internships, attract potential students, conduct a few sessions, and then adjust all the components until the whole process worked well. In this step, the emphasis would be on developing a quality educational process and developing a positive reputation in the progressive community so that it would then be easier to attract students and find internship organizations. Once the team was cohesive and had figured out how to conduct high-quality sessions, it would be time to:

### (2) Rapidly replicate the center to fifty locations around the country

This would be a very energy-intensive process of hiring new staffmembers in other locations, imparting to them the necessary skills and knowledge to conduct high-quality sessions, identifying internship organizations in those distant locations, and recruiting students in all those locations. During this step, the emphasis on rapid growth would mean that the quality of the sessions would probably suffer somewhat. Existing centers would devote much of their resources to spawning new centers, which would likely detract from their efforts to conduct good sessions. Moreover, the new centers would be experiencing growing pains, so the quality of their sessions would probably not be the best.

When the network had reached full size, then it would be time to:

### (3) Conduct a large number of high-quality sessions steadily for many years

In this third step, the network would not grow in size. Innovation would be limited. All energy would be devoted to conducting high-quality sessions and ensuring students were adequately prepared to work for fundamental change.

## Three Phases

To implement these three steps, I assume the Vernal Project would have three main phases. The initial creation phase (Phase 1) would last five years, the expansion phase (Phase 2) would last fifteen years, and the steady phase (Phase 3) would last forty years. To prepare for the first main phase, there would also be two development phases (Phases D1 and D2). In Development Phase D1, the initiators of the Vernal Project would develop the curriculum and test it in several short workshops. In Development Phase D2, they would further develop and test the curriculum in a six-month pilot session. They would also publicize the program and recruit students in preparation for the first actual session.[*]

At the end of the development phases, the initiators of the Project would become the first Vernal staffmembers and begin the first actual session in Vernal Year 1. Comprising three (full-time equivalent) people, these staffmembers would recruit students, arrange internships, facilitate workshops, research and prepare study group materials, counsel and support students, hire and teach any new staffmembers, and provide all the necessary administration for this session. They would probably make a number of mistakes and have to learn how to overcome them.

Over the next four years of Phase 1, the first center would grow from holding a single session to holding four sessions each year. During this phase the staffmembers would devote a great deal of time to developing procedures and methods, further refining the curriculum, and publicizing the center more widely. The number of staffmembers would grow to a complete team of four plus one more staffmember who would make preparations for a new center in another region. In Vernal Year 5, this additional staffmember would recruit and hire new staffmembers, arrange internships in the new location, and recruit students in the new location.

In the sixth year, at the start of Phase 2, staffmembers would start an additional center in another region. Some of the original staffmembers might move to the new location to provide guidance in establishing procedures and administration or they might rely completely on staffmembers hired at the new location. This style of growth would be repeated at a rapid pace throughout Phase 2 (Vernal Project Years 6 through 20) across the United States until there

---

[*] The development phases are discussed in much more detail in Chapter 10. Appendix B provides more detail for Phases 1, 2, and 3.

were a total of fifty Vernal teams facilitating two hundred sessions each year. During this Phase, Vernal staffmembers would also set up regional administration offices.

Phase 3 would begin in Vernal Project Year 21 and continue for forty years. During this period, the network would remain the same size with all efforts devoted to educating students and supporting the graduates.

In Project Year 61 the Vernal Project would end. By this time, society might have been transformed enough that the Vernal program would no longer be needed. Or if the Vernal Project had not yet been successful, then it would be time to try a different approach.

## A Political Education Movement

As stated earlier, the main goal of the Vernal Education Network would be to produce skilled and knowledgeable activists who could then work to bring about fundamental progressive transformation of society. The Vernal Project would be primarily oriented towards supporting various progressive social change movements.

Still, if the Vernal Education Project proceeded as described here, it would, by itself, form the backbone of a specific social change movement: a political education movement dedicated to informing people about the need for fundamental change, about the ways and means of working for positive change, about productive ways of wrestling with diverse ideas, and about gratifying ways to work together with other people. In convincing activists to attend a Vernal session, Vernal staffmembers would be building this movement. When these students graduated and then encouraged their friends and colleagues to attend a Vernal session, they would also be building this movement. Moreover, when Vernal graduates taught their fellow activists, they would be further building this movement.

Widespread political education is a crucial part of fundamental progressive social change, but it is not the only part. In the first twenty years of the Vernal Project, it would be essential that this political education movement grow and spread across the country. However, once it had reached a certain size, activists would need to put much more emphasis on challenging the power structure, challenging entrenched cultural and social norms, building alternative institutions, and providing support to those working for positive change. The political education movement would continue its important work, but other, larger movements to bring about specific societal changes would arise and the overall focus would shift to them. The Vernal Education Project would assume its proper place as a support project bolstering the work of other movements.

## A Note on Overall Size

Eventually, the number of Vernal centers must be large enough to ensure that graduates could transform society. However, the number of centers should not be so large that the Vernal network would pull resources away from other endeavors (such as the actual effort to transform society). The size of the Vernal network would also be constrained by the number of viable applicants for admission, that is, the total number of activists who were serious about long-term progressive social change and also eager and able to devote a year to study in a Vernal program.

I believe a network of fifty centers, educating 6,000 students each year, would be about the right size. As I show in Chapters 7 and 9, this should be large enough to ensure a reasonable chance of overall success. I also believe that Vernal staffmembers could, without excessive effort, attract 6,000 activists with the necessary interest and resources to attend a Vernal session each year once the Vernal network had established a positive reputation and demonstrated its value.

To provide some context for this figure of 6,000 Vernal students annually, consider that about 4,000 people have joined the Peace Corps every year since its inception in 1961. In the 1998–1999 school year, about 40,000 young people served in the AmeriCorps domestic volunteer program. In 1995, about 1,186,000 college students received bachelor's degrees, and in 1997, about 2,500,000 people turned 55 years old.[8]

# VERNAL PROJECT FINANCES

## Expenses

By relying mostly on study groups, self-study, and internships, the Vernal program would have relatively few expenses. The greatest costs would be for staffmember support and retreat center rental. I assume that for the first few years, while the Vernal network was developing, full-time staffmembers would be paid just $18,000 per year (in 1995 dollars and adjusted periodically for inflation*). As the centers became established, salaries would rise and finally stabilize at $24,000. Assuming an additional cost of 33% to cover health care, pensions,

*If you think education is expensive, try ignorance.*
—Derek Bok, President, Harvard University

---

* All these costs and salries are specified in 1995 dollars — they would be adjusted in the future to account for inflation. For example, in 2000 the cost of living is up about 13% from 1995, so $18,000 in 1995 dollars would be adjusted to $20,400 in 2000 dollars; $24,000 (1995) would be adjusted to $27,200 (2000).

# Figure 6.10: Summary of Assumed Vernal Expenses

| | Expenses Per Student | Expenses Per Session (30 Students Per Session) | Expenses Per Center Per Year (4 Sessions Per Center) |
|---|---|---|---|
| Retreat center rental, cook's fee, food costs | $ 1,000 | $ 30,000 | $ 120,000 |
| Salaries and benefits for Vernal team (4 FTE/center) | 1,067 | 32,000 | 128,000 |
| Vernal center administrative expenses | 125 | 3,750 | 15,000 |
| Salaries and benefits for regional administrator (0.5 FTE/center) | 133 | 4,000 | 16,000 |
| Regional administration expenses | 42 | 1,250 | 5,000 |
| Salaries and benefits for new staff preparers (0.08 FTE/center) | 21 | 640 | 2,560 |
| New staff preparer expenses | 12 | 360 | 1,440 |
| **Total** | **$ 2,400** | **$ 72,000** | **$ 288,000** |

**Assumptions**:

Retreat center expenses include rental of the retreat center, the cook's fee, and the cost of food. Assume this costs $25/day/student for 40 days (35 full days, 10 half-days) = $1,000/student.

Assume a salary of $24,000/staffmember plus $8,000 more to cover benefits and taxes = $32,000/staffmember.

Administrative Expenses include office rental, office equipment (file cabinets, computers, office materials), phone, mailings (paper, printing, postage), and travel.

Assume center administrative expenses would be $15,000/center (probably a tiny office or none).

Assume regional administrative offices would cost $10,000/administrator.

Assume administrative costs for each new staff preparer would be $18,000 (probably no office, but high phone and travel costs).

All figure are in 1995 dollars.

other benefits, and the employer share of taxes, total expenses would be $32,000 for each staffmember.

I assume that each yearlong Vernal session would cost about $30,000 to cover retreat center rental, the cook's fee and food costs at the retreat center. I assume each Vernal center would also require $15,000 per year to pay for books, printing, postage, computers, travel, and so on. I have assumed that each regional administrator would spend $10,000 per year for office rent, equipment, printing, mailing, and travel. I also assume each new staff preparer would spend $18,000 per year, primarily for travel and long-distance phone calls. Figure 6.10 summarizes the cost of these items for each student, each session, and each center.

## Tuition

For students to be able to attend a Vernal session, the cost cannot be too great. Most students attending a Vernal session would probably not be wealthy, and after graduating, most would probably have little earning potential. Also, because of the political nature of the Vernal program, it would probably be difficult to secure government accreditation, so students would most likely not be able to qualify for education grants or loans. Even if they could get loans, most graduates would probably find it difficult to pay them off.

So, tuition must be kept to a minimum, and there must be scholarships and stipends available to cover living expenses for the least well-off students.

Still, all the expenses must be paid somehow. Since students would be the primary beneficiaries of the Vernal program, it makes sense to charge a reasonable amount for what they are receiving (rather than, for example, reducing the salaries and benefits of staffmembers). Moreover, many students from wealthy or middle-class backgrounds would be able to pay relatively high tuition.

Aiming for a prudent balance, I have assumed a moderate tuition with substantial scholarships and stipends for those who could not afford it. I assume that tuition for a Vernal session would be $5,000 (in 1995 dollars and adjusted periodically for inflation).* For comparison purposes, the average tuition and required fees for public, four-year colleges in the United States in 1995 was about $3,000 for an academic school year (two semesters or three quarters) and about $14,500 for private colleges.[9]

---

* For example, adjusting for 13.3% inflation from 1995 to 2000, tuition would be $5,650 in year 2000.

## Tuition Income

At the beginning of the Vernal Project when expenses would be higher and income lower, I assume that scholarships would be smaller and students would pay closer to the full amount of tuition, averaging about $3,600 per student per year. The fourth column of Figure 6.11 shows a possible distribution of tuition, scholarships, and stipends that would produce an average of $3,600 income to the Veral Project per student. In this distribution, fifty percent of the students (fifteen students) would pay full tuition, twenty percent (six students) would pay $3,500, twenty percent (six students) would pay $2,500, and ten percent (three students) would pay no tuition and receive a $1,000 stipend to help with their living expenses.

one session. After students had learned about and discussed economic class and money issues and after they had gotten to know and trust each other well, staffmembers could facilitate a special meeting at one of the retreat center workshops. At this meeting, each student could present her own personal money situation. Then the group could collectively and consensually decide how much each student would pay.

This group process would allow much more flexibility of outcome and compel students to honestly address real money issues in a practical way. Some wealthy students might find themselves offering to pay even more than $5,000 while those who were especially poor might receive a larger stipend. Every student would likely learn a great deal about money and economic class in our society and how these important issues affected her personally.

## Figure 6.11: A Typical Distribution of Tuition in Phases 1 and 3

| Situation | Annual Tuition Paid | Stipend Received | Percentage of Students | |
|---|---|---|---|---|
| | | | Phase 1 | Phase 3 |
| Full Tuition | $5,000 | | 50% | 30% |
| Partial Tuition | $3,500 | | 20% | 20% |
| Half Scholarship | $2,500 | | 20% | 15% |
| Large Scholarship | $500 | | | 5% |
| Full Scholarship | $0 | | | 10% |
| Full Scholarship + Stipend | $0 | $ 1,000 | 10% | 20% |
| | | | 100% | 100% |
| **Avg. Income Collected Per Student =** | | | **$3,600** | **$2,400** |

As the Vernal network grew and expenses declined, more scholarships and stipends could be offered. I calculate that the average income to the Project per student per year could drop to $2,400 by Vernal Project Year 21. The last column of Figure 6.11 shows a distribution of tuition, scholarships, and stipends that would bring in an average of $2,400. In this distribution, thirty percent of students would pay full tuition, twenty percent would pay $3,500, fifteen percent would pay $2,500, five percent would pay $500, ten percent would receive full scholarships, and twenty percent would receive full scholarships and also receive a $1,000 stipend for expenses.

Figures B.8 and B.9 in Appendix B show other distributions that also deliver an average of $3,600 and $2,400 per student.

The initial tuition amount that each student would pay would be determined by the Vernal team and the board of directors for the center. But this amount might later be adjusted by a collective decision of all the students attending

## Net Finances

Using these expense and tuition assumptions, it is simple to calculate the finances of the Vernal Project. As shown in Figure 6.12, tuition income and overall expenses would each be about $100,000 in Vernal Year 1 and would grow to a steady $14.4 million in Phase 3. After the development phases, the Vernal network would bring in more income than it would cost in every year except one: only in Year 9, when a relatively large number of centers would be starting up, would expenses exceed income, and then only by $5,000.*

In the development phases, startup costs not matched by income would result in a deficit of $103,000.† However, if this amount were borrowed, the loan could be paid back from subsequent tuition income by Vernal Year 5. Figure 6.13 shows the projected net income for each of the first thirty years of the Vernal Project. Note that in Years 21 and beyond, the net is exactly zero.

---

* See Figures B.13, B.15, B.16, B.17, and B.18 in Appendix B for details on the number of sessions, students, and paid staffmembers that underlie this summary.

† I assume the average tuition collected for the two ten-day test workshops in Development Phase 2 would be $300, and I assume expenses (other than staffmember salary) would be one-fifth of a regular session. For the six-month pilot session, I assume an average of $1,800 tuition collected per student and expenses of one-half of a regular session.

# Figure 6.12: Summary of Vernal Project Characteristics and Finances

| Phase | Year | Number of Students Enrolled | Average Tuition Income /Student ($) | Total Number of Paid Staff | Staff Salary ($) | Total Yearly Tuition Income ($ in 1,000s) | Total Yearly Expenses ($ in 1,000s) | Total Net Income ($ in 1,000s) | Running Total Net Income ($ in 1,000s) |
|---|---|---|---|---|---|---|---|---|---|
| D1 |  | 0 | 0 | 0.5 | 18,000 | 0 | 12 | *-12* | -12 |
| D2 | Prep-1 | 30 | 300 | 1.0 | 18,000 | 9 | 31 | *-22* | -34 |
|  | Prep-2 | 30 | 300 | 2.0 | 18,000 | 9 | 55 | *-46* | -80 |
|  | Prep-3 | 30 | 1,800 | 2.5 | 18,000 | 54 | 77 | *-23* | -103 |
| 1 | 1 | 30 | 3,600 | 3.0 | 18,000 | 108 | 106 | 2 | -101 |
|  | 2 | 30 | 3,600 | 3.0 | 18,000 | 108 | 106 | 2 | -99 |
|  | 3 | 60 | 3,200 | 3.0 | 24,000 | 192 | 163 | 29 | -70 |
|  | 4 | 90 | 3,200 | 4.0 | 24,000 | 288 | 229 | 59 | -11 |
|  | 5 | 120 | 3,200 | 5.0 | 24,000 | 384 | 313 | 71 | 60 |
| 2 | 6 | 150 | 3,200 | 8.0 | 24,000 | 480 | 443 | 37 | 97 |
|  | 7 | 180 | 3,200 | 11.0 | 24,000 | 576 | 572 | 4 | 101 |
|  | 8 | 240 | 3,200 | 14.0 | 24,000 | 768 | 736 | 32 | 133 |
|  | 9 | 390 | 3,200 | 24.0 | 24,000 | 1,248 | 1,253 | -5 | 128 |
|  | 10 | 630 | 2,900 | 32.5 | 24,000 | 1,827 | 1,800 | 27 | 155 |
|  | 11 | 870 | 2,800 | 41.0 | 24,000 | 2,436 | 2,347 | 89 | 244 |
|  | 12 | 1,110 | 2,650 | 49.5 | 24,000 | 2,942 | 2,894 | 48 | 292 |
|  | 13 | 1,440 | 2,650 | 64.0 | 24,000 | 3,816 | 3,762 | 54 | 346 |
|  | 14 | 1,950 | 2,650 | 88.0 | 24,000 | 5,168 | 5,134 | 34 | 379 |
|  | 15 | 2,550 | 2,550 | 107.5 | 24,000 | 6,503 | 6,458 | 45 | 424 |
|  | 16 | 3,150 | 2,550 | 132.5 | 24,000 | 8,033 | 7,981 | 52 | 475 |
|  | 17 | 3,840 | 2,550 | 161.5 | 24,000 | 9,792 | 9,743 | 49 | 524 |
|  | 18 | 4,620 | 2,550 | 193.5 | 24,000 | 11,781 | 11,684 | 97 | 621 |
|  | 19 | 5,340 | 2,500 | 216.5 | 24,000 | 13,350 | 13,260 | 90 | 711 |
|  | 20 | 5,820 | 2,450 | 229.0 | 24,000 | 14,259 | 14,197 | 62 | 773 |
| 3 | 21 | 6,000 | 2,400 | 229.0 | 24,000 | 14,400 | 14,400 | 0 | 773 |
|  | 22 | 6,000 | 2,400 | 229.0 | 24,000 | 14,400 | 14,400 | 0 | 773 |
|  | 23 | 6,000 | 2,400 | 229.0 | 24,000 | 14,400 | 14,400 | 0 | 773 |
|  | 24 | 6,000 | 2,400 | 229.0 | 24,000 | 14,400 | 14,400 | 0 | 773 |
|  | 25 | 6,000 | 2,400 | 229.0 | 24,000 | 14,400 | 14,400 | 0 | 773 |
|  | 26 | 6,000 | 2,400 | 229.0 | 24,000 | 14,400 | 14,400 | 0 | 773 |
|  | 27 | 6,000 | 2,400 | 229.0 | 24,000 | 14,400 | 14,400 | 0 | 773 |
|  | 28 | 6,000 | 2,400 | 229.0 | 24,000 | 14,400 | 14,400 | 0 | 773 |
|  | 29 | 6,000 | 2,400 | 229.0 | 24,000 | 14,400 | 14,400 | 0 | 773 |
|  | 30 | 6,000 | 2,400 | 229.0 | 24,000 | 14,400 | 14,400 | 0 | 773 |
| Total for first 30 years |  | 92,610 |  |  |  | 228,057 | 227,181 | 876 | 830 |

| Phase | Years | Students |  |  |  | Income | Expenses | Net |  |
|---|---|---|---|---|---|---|---|---|---|
| D1 |  | 0 |  |  |  | 0 | 12 | -12 |  |
| D2 | P-1->P-3 | 90 |  |  |  | 72 | 163 | -91 |  |
| 1 | 1-> 5 | 330 |  |  |  | 1,080 | 917 | 163 |  |
| 2 | 6->20 | 32,280 |  |  |  | 82,977 | 82,264 | 713 |  |
| 3 | 21->30 | 60,000 |  |  |  | 144,000 | 144,000 | 0 |  |
| Total = |  | 92,700 |  |  |  | 228,129 | 227,356 | 773 |  |
| including Phases D1 & D2 |  |  |  |  |  |  |  |  |  |

All figures are in 1995 dollars.

# Figure 6.13: Vernal Project Projected Net Income
## (thousands of 1995 dollars)

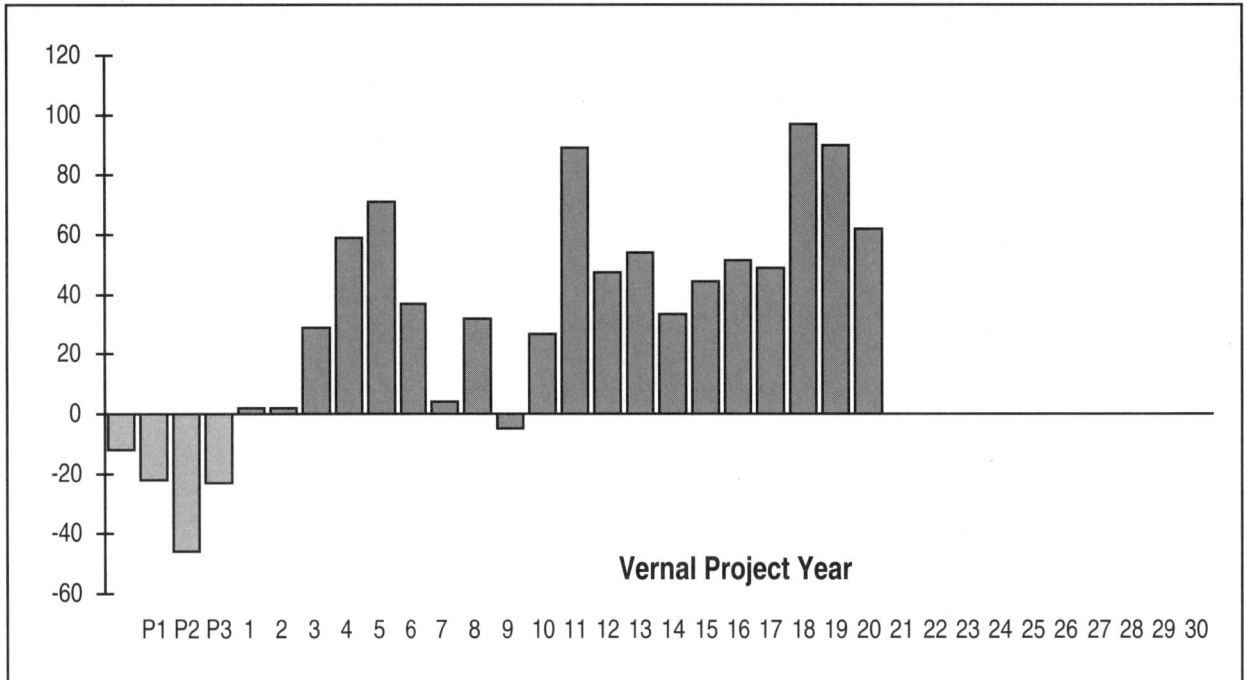

## MEETING THE DESIGN CRITERIA

The beginning of this chapter listed eight design criteria that the Vernal Education Project must meet to effectively transform society. Here is how its design specifically meets each of these criteria:

• **Offer a Wide-Ranging Education to Progressive Social Change Activists**
• The Vernal program would have ten diverse components that address different aspects of an activist's life and involve different kinds of learning (lectures, readings, discussion, experiential role-plays, internships, direct "on-the-job" experience, personal mentoring, counseling).
• The program would cover both abstract theory and actual practice. Students would immediately practice what they learn in their internships, their change work, and the governance of their study group.
• The curriculum would cover a wide diversity of topics including social change history, current affairs, current change efforts, visions of the future, barriers to change, and personal aspects of becoming and being an activist. It would cover all aspects of political, economic, social, and cultural change.

• Students would have three internships with different change organizations. They would also work with a social service agency and with their own change group. Working with these many organizations, they would meet a variety of people with a variety of perspectives and styles.
• Students would learn together with thirty other activists from their metropolitan area. These activists would likely be a diverse group — including men and women, poor residents of the city and richer residents of the surrounding suburbs, and people from a variety of cultural backgrounds.*

• **Vastly Increase the Skills, Strength, and Endurance of Activists**
• The program's yearlong session would provide enough time for students to learn the skills they needed to do effective social change work.
• The program's emphasis on practical skills and direct learning (in internships and social change work) would ensure students learned information useful to their future change work.
• The program would offer practical skills to thousands of progressive activists every year. After graduating, they would immediately be part of a vast network of skilled

---

* Admittedly, Vernal students would connect only with other students from similar *geographic* backgrounds since they would continue to live in their home communities while attending a Vernal session.

activists all working simultaneously for fundamental progressive change (see Chapters 7 and 9).

• The program would provide strong personal support for every student from many sources. Students would learn how to develop a personal support network for themselves and how to effectively support others.

• The program would facilitate strong bonding between students so they could continue to provide solid support to one another for many years after graduating.

*They may forget what you said, but they will never forget how you made them feel.* — Carl W. Buechner

### • Facilitate the Development of a Cooperative Community

• The program would teach cooperative skills and demonstrate them in the operation and governance of the Vernal program.

• The students in a session would have many opportunities to develop strong connections and to practice working cooperatively with each other. The program would bring the six (or so) students in a study group together on an almost daily basis for a year. It would bring them together with the other twenty-four (or so) students in their session for a total of forty-five days at retreat center workshops. Students would be cooperatively learning, discussing ideas, working, and making decisions together for the whole year.

### • Operate Efficiently

• The program would be limited to those activists who could make the most of it and could best support and educate other activists.

• By encouraging Vernal graduates to educate and support other activists, the program would greatly multiply the number of activists it could reach, educate, and support (see Chapter 7).

• The program would require little capital by relying on existing infrastructure: student's homes, existing change groups, and established retreat centers.

• The program would require relatively few staffmembers by relying heavily on peer education and internships with existing change groups.

• The program would pay the staffmembers a relatively small salary (but still enough to attract skilled activist-teachers).

• The whole Vernal Project would be self-supporting. After receiving a small start-up loan, it would rely completely on tuition income for funding. It should also be a net provider of activist energy: students would contribute to their internship group as much as or more than they would require in support.

### • Span the Country

• Vernal centers would be located in fifty locations across the country and each one would reach out to students in a wide area. Students from almost every part of the country could attend while continuing to live at home.

• As soon as they graduated, Vernal graduates could immediately start working for change all across the country since they would already be living in the communities where they intended to work.

### • Integrate with Activists' Lives

• Students' activities in the Vernal program would be similar to their normal activities as activists. In particular, the mode of working and living in the last three months of the program would guide students towards sustainable social change activism.

### • Grow Rapidly and Continue for Decades

• The Project's three phases would allow the first center to develop a quality program, then encourage rapid growth to full size with fifty centers, and finally continue providing a quality education at this level for forty years. Once developed, the curriculum, methods, and materials of the Vernal program could be easily transported and adapted to other places or situations (including other countries).

### • Conform to Progressive Ideals

• The Project would encourage and practice honesty, compassion, cooperation, democracy, support, respect for each person, and nonviolent methods of resolving conflict. No student would be forced or coerced to think or do anything.

• By being decentralized and focused exclusively on progressive education, the program would not be particularly attractive to those who wanted to dominate or control others. This would make it easier to implement and sustain practices that adhere to high ideals.

• The size of the Project would ensure that graduates, working in conjunction with hundreds of thousands of other progressive activists, would have enough strength to bring about fundamental change without having to sacrifice their ethics for expediency (see Chapters 7 and 9).

*The greatest sign of success for a teacher is to be able to say, "The children are now working as if I did not exist."*
— Maria Montessori

## OTHER EDUCATIONAL PROGRAMS

The idea of an educational program for progressive activists is not new. The Vernal program was inspired in part by the many schools and training programs across the United States that have contributed so much to progressive change. Below, listed roughly in chronological order, are brief descriptions of some of the recent ones that have influenced the design of the Vernal program.

• From 1921–1936, the Brookwood Labor College in Westchester County, New York, with A.J. Muste as director, taught a two-year program in labor organizing for about twenty or thirty students. Students lived on campus, but also attended meetings of their labor unions and participated in labor activities. The college was quite successful for several years. In 1928, the American Federation of Labor attacked it, and during the Depression, it suffered from money troubles. In 1933, Muste left after an internal conflict.[10]

• Myles Horton set up the Highlander Folk School in Tennessee in the 1930s to teach and empower the poor rural people of Appalachia and the South. Highlander has played an extremely important role in stimulating and supporting the labor movement, the civil rights movement, and almost every other progressive social change effort in the South since then.

• After organizing the Back of the Yards area of Chicago, Saul Alinsky founded the Industrial Areas Foundation in 1940 which organized and taught organizers across the country. In 1969, Alinsky began a training school for organizers with a fifteen-month full-time program.

• Conscientious objector prison camps for those refusing to fight in World War II served as a fertile breeding ground for radical pacifists. "Internment in the Civilian Public Service camps or in federal prison was a formative experience for a new generation of pacifist leaders, providing them with the equivalent of a postgraduate education in applied Gandhianism. . . . Outside they would have found themselves a tiny minority committed to unpopular beliefs and unable to have any measurable effect on national policy. Inside they found themselves surrounded by political comrades, with their opponents equally close at hand."[11]

• As part of the Civil Rights movement in the South, activists established "Citizenship Schools" that taught literacy and the basic concepts of democratic government.

• In the 1960s, the New England Committee for Nonviolent Action had a school/community in Voluntown, Connecticut. Here activists shared their experiences and organized peace walks, civil disobedience, and anti-war and draft resistance speaking tours. They also learned how to live nonviolently with other people by actually doing it.

• In the late 1960s, a plethora of alternative education programs for adults sprang up across the nation. In the area where I now live, the Free U provided a way for students to connect with those willing to teach them. Classes ranged from guitar lessons to Marxist economics. Some of these classes were eventually formalized and absorbed by community adult education programs.

• The "consciousness raising groups" or "rap groups" of the early women's liberation movement allowed women to understand their oppression. By sharing their personal experiences and noting the similarities in their stories, they were able to formulate a more general analysis of patriarchal oppression and develop political strategies for ending it.

• The Movement for a New Society (MNS) taught activists the skills of nonviolent action and cooperative organization and living from 1970 until about 1985. Their Life Center in Philadelphia had weekend workshops, two-week long workshops, and a two-year long training program. MNS trainers traveled around the country offering nonviolence trainings for a variety of activists. Activists trained by MNS constituted the core of the nonviolent direct action anti-nuclear power and weapons movements. In December 1977, I attended a five-day workshop conducted by MNS activists and held at the Quaker Center in Ben Lomond, California. Many of my ideas about the staffmember-facilitated workshops come from this workshop.

• MNS activists also developed a formal study group model (called a "Macro-Analysis Seminar") with an extensive reading list and recommendations for ways people could read the materials and study together. Thousands of people organized these seminars across the country.

• In the mid-1970s, Heather Booth and other New Left activists formed the Midwest Academy to teach people how to organize grassroots groups to fight for progressive change in their communities. The Midwest Academy has been instrumental in developing a network of progressive "citizen action" organizations in several states, primarily in the Midwest and Northeast.

• Nonviolence training/preparations conducted for most civil disobedience and direct actions since the civil rights movement have given hundreds of thousands of activists their first deep exposure to the lore and practice of nonviolent social change. Knowing they will soon be at a demonstration with the potential for violent repression, attendees often learn an incredible amount in these brief workshops.

• Political education classes conducted by arrestees in jail during almost every large progressive demonstration in the last few decades have also been instrumental in expanding the knowledge base of activists. In jail, seasoned activists have often been able to share their experiences and philosophies with an interested and "captive" audience. For example, during the two weeks that Clamshell Alliance activists were held in National Guard armories in 1977, experienced activists conducted numerous workshops on nuclear energy, alternative energy, and all aspects of organizing.

• The War Resisters League offers a ten-day workshop for about twenty activists every August in western Massachusetts. Many pacifists and war tax resisters attend these workshops and go on to organize for peace.

• The Fellowship of Reconciliation, in its Peacemaker Training Institute, offers several week-long training programs around the country for young people. These workshops focus on nonviolence and cultural diversity.

• Greenpeace has a week-long training class for its employees who engage in nonviolent direct action demonstrations (such as hanging banners from polluting factories and intercepting whaling ships).

• The Ruckus Society conducts weeklong Action Training Camps for activists who engage in nonviolent direct action demonstrations, especially hanging banners and sitting in the top of endangered old-growth trees.

• The Center for Third World Organizing in Oakland, California, offers three-day workshops and a five-week apprenticeship program primarily for community activists of color.

• The Green Corps offers internships to young activists working on environmental issues. The yearlong program begins with one month of classroom training. For the rest of the year, students work on a series of five different environmental campaigns separated by four week-long trainings.

• The two-year long Community Studies program at the University of California at Santa Cruz is an experiential program oriented toward social change. In addition to extensive classroom education, students complete two internships — one three months long and one six months long. They then write a thesis or carry out a large project.

There are also currently a variety of other training centers for community organizers.[12]

Though inspired by these educational programs, the Vernal program would have a different focus and scope than any of them. Being a full-time program for a full year and addressing a wide variety of issues, the Vernal program would be much broader and deeper than most of the currently operating programs. It would also be directed toward more experienced activists and toward those who could devote years of their lives to fundamental progressive change. Therefore, the Vernal program should generally complement, rather than compete with, these other programs.

## CARRYING OUT STAGE 1 OF THE STRATEGIC PROGRAM

The previous chapter described a four-stage program for fundamentally transforming society. In the first stage, a large number of progressives would find each other, would learn how society functions, would learn and practice the change skills they needed to transform society, and would form supportive communities. I believe the Vernal Education Project, as described in this chapter, could successfully accomplish the goals of Stage 1. If carried out as described here, the Project would result in a large number of progressive activists, willing and able to work for fundamental change.

The next chapter describes how these activists could develop powerful communities of support and build powerful social change movements. Then Chapter 8 tells a story that illustrates what this might look like in a single community.

## NOTES FOR CHAPTER 6

[1] I have outlined a specific format to give a feel for what is possible, but it is merely illustrative. As the Vernal Project develops over time and more centers are formed, the best way to educate activists in these skills will surely evolve. Here are a few examples of some possible alternatives we might consider:

• Some Vernal centers might create a stretched out two-year program. Such a program could be more compatible with part-time employment, thus opening the program to students of more limited financial means.

• Some Vernal centers might affiliate with local colleges, community colleges, or alternative institutions of higher education to offer more widely recognized certifications (perhaps, a masters degree in Applied Social Change).

• While the live-at-home model described here minimizes costs and ensures that graduates understand their community, some Vernal centers might encourage activists to move nearby for the duration of the program. Such residential programs could be particularly important for activists from rural areas.

• As new technologies develop and the costs of using older technologies declines, the centers will probably develop a number of tools for distance learning. These efforts start with the already existing web site <http://www.vernalproject.org> and the resources posted there. In the future, tools for distance learning might include such items as video games that help teach nonviolent action and online tools that facilitate online meetings and group problem-solving processes.

• Some centers might combine distance learning with intense three-week onsite programs twice a year. There are several innovative MBA programs for fully employed managers that follow this model.

• Some centers might focus on global issues and bring in multinational students (or locate classes on several continents).

• Some centers might try to build a stronger connection between alumni and students, perhaps relying on alumni to do much of the teaching. Vernal staffmembers might then focus almost exclusively on administration, and it might be possible to have fewer staffmembers.

• Centers might also do more to support the alumni community, perhaps sponsoring annual retreats that would encourage mutual support and sharing of experiences.

• There might be a regional follow-on program geared to a small subset of the graduates of Vernal sessions, especially those graduates who might eventually become Vernal staffmembers. This second tier program might consist of three-week-long workshops held twice a year for two years and be facilitated primarily by a new staff preparer. The program might focus on advanced topics in social change and methods for teaching social change skills. This would provide opportunities for continued learning and community building even if these activists did not become Vernal staffmembers.

[2] For more on the philosophy and practical organization of social change study groups, see Philadelphia Macro-Analysis Collective of Movement for a New Society, ***Organizing Macro-Analysis Seminars: Study & Action for a New Society*** (Philadelphia: New Society Publishers, 1981).

[3] These four questions are based partly on Harvey Jackins, ***The Enjoyment of Leadership*** (Seattle: Rational Island Publishers, 1987), p. 40.

For an excellent article describing support groups and how to make them effective see Tova Green, "Support Groups" in Tova Green and Peter Woodrow, ***Insight and Action: How to Discover and Support a Life of Integrity and Commitment to Change*** (Philadelphia: New Society Publishers, 1994, HM133 .G7 1994), pp. 7–52.

[4] The notes and agendas that I have prepared for workshops on consensus decision-making and nonviolent direct action are examples of the kind of papers I would expect staffmembers to prepare (see <http://www.vernalproject.org> for a list). Virginia Coover, et al., ***Resource Manual for a Living Revolution***, 2nd ed. (Philadelphia: New Society Press, 1978, HN65 .R47 1978), Neil Wollman, ed., ***Working for Peace*** (San Luis Obispo, CA: Impact Publishers, 1985, JX1963.W72 1985) and other organizing manuals are also examples of such notes.

[5] For example, in their September 1997 annual meeting, the National Organizers Alliance debated the advantages and disadvantages of seven tenets of Alinsky-style political organizing: democracy, simplicity, quantity, winning, pragmatism, diversity, and harmony. For a description of the process and some of the perspectives that were illuminated see Kim Fellner, "Is Nothing Sacred?!," in ***The Ark***, Newsletter of the National Organizers Alliance, no. 10 (January 1998): 12–16; or Joel Bleifuss, "Sacred Cow, Or Bull?: Questioning the Tenets of Political Organizing," in ***In These Times*** 21, no. 25–26 (November 23, 1997): 16–17.

[6] A salary of $24,000/year in 1995 was relatively good for a full-time social change activist, but for an activist with many years of experience it is low. Compared to conventional jobs, it is quite low. Salaries for classroom teachers in 1995 averaged $37,264 and for public college professors averaged $49,100. U.S. Census Bureau, ***Statistical Abstract of the U.S., 1998***, "Table 276: Average Salary and Wages Paid in Public School Systems: 1980 to 1998" and "Table 314: Average Salaries for College Faculty Members: 1995 to 1997," drawn from American Association of University Professors, Washington, DC, ***AAUP Annual Report on the Economic Status of the Profession***.
<http://www.census.gov:80/statab/www/index.html>

Still, I believe these jobs would be quite desirable. I do not think it would be difficult to find qualified candidates.

[7] W. Russell Neuman, ***The Paradox of Mass Politics: Knowledge and Opinion in the American Electorate*** (Cambridge, MA: Harvard University Press, 1986, JK1967 .N48 1986). The five percent figure is on page 170; the definition of political sophistication is on page 54.

Note that Neuman mostly focuses on politics in the traditional sense: elections, politicians, and the issues discussed in the conventional news media. This point of view overemphasizes the two major parties and the issues they find important, and it overlooks most of the work of progressive and conservative activists. My own definition of political salience, knowledge, and conceptualization is broader than just electoral politics and includes economic, social, and cultural aspects of society.

[8] According to an October 16, 1998, Peace Corps press release, "Budget Agreement Allows Peace Corps To Expand; Gearan Says 8 Percent Increase Puts Agency on Path to 10,000 Volunteers," there have been 150,000 volunteers and trainees from the time the program was established in March 1961 through Fall 1998 (37.5 years). This averages about 4,000 per year.
<http://www.peacecorps.gov/news/index.html>

The AmeriCorps data appears on this web page dated October 1998: <http://www.americorps.org/100k/history.html>

AmeriCorps volunteers work with organizations such as the American Red Cross, Habitat for Humanity, Big Brothers/ Big Sisters, and Boys and Girls Clubs. After completing a year of service, they receive an education award to help pay for college or vocational training.

The number of college graduates comes from U.S. Census Bureau, ***Statistical Abstract of the U.S., 1998***, "Table 252: School Enrollment, Faculty, Graduates, and Finances, With Projections: 1985 to 2008," drawn from U.S. National Center for Education Statistics, ***Digest of Education Statistics***, annual, and ***Projections of Educational Statistics***, annual.
<http://www.census.gov:80/statab/www/index.html>

The number of people turning age 55 comes from U.S. Census Bureau, ***Statistical Abstract of the U.S., 1998***, "Table 16: Resident Population, by Sex and Age: 1997," drawn from U.S. Bureau of the Census, ***Population Paper Listings PPL-91***.
<http://www.census.gov:80/statab/www/index.html>

[9] U.S. Census Bureau, ***Statistical Abstract of the U.S., 1998***, "Table 312: Institutions of Higher Education — Charges: 1985 to 1997," drawn from U.S. National Center for Education Statistics, ***Digest of Education Statistics***, annual.
<http://www.census.gov:80/statab/www/index.html>

[10] A. J. Muste, ***The Essays of A. J. Muste***, Nat Hentoff, ed. (Indianapolis: Bobbs-Merrill Co., 1967, JX1963 .M8455), pp. 84–154.

[11] Maurice Isserman, ***If I Had a Hammer: The Death of the Old Left and the Birth of the New Left*** (New York: Basic Books, 1987, HN90 .R3187 1987), p. 132.

[12] For a list of 17 community training centers see Center for Third World Organizing, "Training Centers & Organizing Networks," ***Third Force***, Special Section published in conjunction with ***The Neighborhood Works*** 5, no. 1 (March/April 1997): 32.

# 7

# *Building a Powerful, Democratic Social Change Movement*

other activists. This would greatly increase the strength and endurance of progressive change organizations, thereby achieving the goals of the second stage of the strategic program (Gather Support).[1]

*To get the bad customs of a country changed and new ones, though better, introduced, it is necessary first to remove the prejudices of the people, enlighten their ignorance, and convince them that their interests will be promoted by the proposed changes; and this is not the work of a day.* — Benjamin Franklin

Chapter 5 outlined a specific, four-stage program for fundamentally transforming society based on education and mass social change movements. Chapter 6 presented the Vernal Education Project as a means to achieve the goals of the first stage of this strategic program. If carried out, the Vernal Project would produce a network of thousands of skilled and dedicated activists working all across the United States for fundamental progressive change — a solid core of hardworking activists that could both reassure other activists that their efforts would not be wasted and energize everyone to do the hard tasks necessary to succeed.

This chapter further explores the role and influence of Vernal activists. It first describes some likely characteristics of Vernal activists, the ways they would probably support themselves, their likely numbers and influence, and their likely focus of activity. It then describes the many ways these activists might support, inform, and inspire over one million

## *About Vernal Graduates*

### Characteristics of Vernal Graduates

Those activists who met the entrance requirements for a Vernal program would be more likely than most activists to have certain characteristics. Attending a Vernal session would tend to bolster these characteristics and add a few more. As a result, most Vernal graduates would probably have the following attributes:

• **Highly Motivated Activists**

Those people attracted to a Vernal program would probably already be highly motivated progressive activists. To be accepted into a session, they would express a desire to work primarily for progressive change for at least eight years.

In attending the program, they would learn about the horrendous problems of our current society and about effective ways to overcome them. This would probably increase their interest in working for change, and being surrounded by other dedicated Vernal students and graduates would likely inspire them even more. Therefore, Vernal graduates would likely be enthusiastic.

Vernal graduates would likely also understand the importance of basic routine work to bring about change. Knowing its importance, they would probably be more willing to do this under-appreciated work even when it was difficult, boring, or tedious.

### • Familiar with Visions of a Good Society

Vernal students would read and discuss a wide variety of ideas about what should characterize a good society. They would consider and evaluate many possibilities. By the time they graduated, they would likely have their own informed and principled perspective on most aspects of a good society — from how people should relate to one another to how the economy should function.

### • Dedicated to Working for Fundamental Change

Vernal students would learn about the extent of society's problems and how much society must change to fulfill their vision. Hence, most graduates would probably desire broad, wide-ranging, fundamental social change. They would understand the many steps required to bring about comprehensive change and why an immense effort would take decades to succeed. Hence, most graduates would probably dedicate themselves to working long-term for fundamental change.

### • Dedicated to Using Bold, Nonviolent Methods

Vernal students would learn the moral and strategic benefits of nonviolent struggle and the pitfalls of revenge and feuding. Knowing the checkered history of revolution and war, they would probably be skeptical of activities that promised instant results through use of intimidation or violence. Consequently, most graduates would probably appreciate and use bold, nonviolent methods to bring about change.

### • Dedicated to Supporting and Educating Other Activists

Knowing that to bring about democratic change it is essential to persuade and mobilize large numbers of people, Vernal graduates would probably commit themselves to supporting and educating many other activists. In the Vernal program they would learn a variety of ways to encourage and support other activists.

### • Highly Skilled and Experienced

Activists applying to a Vernal program would already have had at least one full year of social change experience. The yearlong Vernal session would expand their knowledge in all aspects of progressive change. With a few more years of experience after graduating, they would probably be much more skilled and experienced than most other activists.

In particular, Vernal graduates would likely have a broader understanding of issues than most activists — for example, they would probably understand and appreciate at least two sides of most important controversies. Vernal graduates would also have much greater skills than most activists for developing change campaigns and for dealing with their fellow activists' emotional conditioning, addictions, and interpersonal conflicts. Moreover, they would probably understand the social inculcation process, understand the basis of their own native culture, appreciate the benefits of other cultures, and know how to transform the culture around them in positive directions.

> *God, give us grace to accept with serenity the things that cannot be changed, courage to change the things which should be changed, and the wisdom to distinguish the one from the other.*
> — Reinhold Niebuhr

### • Life-Long Learners

Those who attended a Vernal session would likely be particularly interested in education. Presented with many valuable, yet diverse and contradictory perspectives, Vernal students would probably realize the importance of continually questioning and learning. After graduating, most Vernal activists would probably therefore continue to read a wide variety of materials and attend workshops, seminars, and discussion groups where they could learn and ponder new ideas. They would likely seek out opportunities to discuss and debate ideas with their friends, colleagues, and opponents.

### • Physically and Emotionally Healthy

Encouraged to eat well, exercise daily, and maintain a healthy, balanced lifestyle and taught how to overcome destructive emotional and cultural conditioning, Vernal graduates would probably be much more physically and emotionally healthy than most activists. They would probably have far fewer addictions, compulsions, obsessions, fears, or phobias than most people, and they at least would be aware of and might be mostly free of prejudices. Most of the time they would probably feel fulfilled and lighthearted.

When confronted with other people's prejudices, anger, depression, or low self-esteem, they would be much more likely than most people to remain calm, clear-headed, confident, and loving. Most of the time they would probably be able to respond intelligently, compassionately, maturely, and perhaps even joyfully.

Vernal graduates would probably be relatively open to new ideas, flexible in their thinking, and playful. They would also have at least a basic understanding of how to challenge their own and others' rigid and dysfunctional behavior through gentle banter and loving support.

### • Principled, Trustworthy, Honorable

Vernal students would likely know they could only persuade other people to a progressive perspective if their own personal behavior conformed to high political ideals. As a result, they would probably strive to be extremely honest, honorable, trustworthy, and straightforward in all their dealings. I expect most would also try to be strong, gentle, courageous, altruistic, and humble.

*May you live your life as if the maxim of your actions were to become universal law.* — Immanuel Kant

### • Inspiring and Appealing

With their knowledge, skills, experience, and dedication to change, Vernal graduates would probably be quite inspiring and appealing both to other activists and to the general public. People would appreciate their expertise and their commitment to making the world better.

I expect most Vernal graduates would be exemplary role models of empowered and responsible citizens. Moreover, most graduates would probably seek jobs in which they could do satisfying and ethically responsible work. Most would probably live simply (reduce their material desires to a low level) to minimize their consumption of natural resources and their impact on the natural environment. I also expect most would establish positive relationships with a variety of people. They would likely be caring, generous, honest, and joyous — they would probably share, laugh, and play with others.

*Nothing astonishes men so much as common sense and plain dealing.* — Ralph Waldo Emerson

### • Hopeful

Vernal graduates would have the opportunity to work regularly with other skilled and dedicated activists. Knowing they were part of a large and solid effort to build a powerful, long-term force for positive change would give Vernal graduates hope that fundamental transformation of society is possible. I expect they would be rousingly optimistic about the prospects for comprehensive social change.

## Financial Support of Vernal Graduates

To be able to spend at least twenty hours each week working for fundamental social change, very active Vernal graduates would need some way to meet their basic needs for food, housing, transportation, health care, and so on. Many would probably live simply and share housing, tools, bicycles, and automobiles with others to reduce their expenses. Nevertheless, most graduates would still need some

kind of income. I expect that Vernal graduates would rely on one or several of the following financial sources:

### • A Social Change Job

Some Vernal graduates would be able to find jobs doing direct social change work. Social change organizations typically pay low wages, but usually pay enough to support activists who are willing to live simply. Change organizations are often focused on narrow, near-term goals, and they devote much of their time to fundraising, but Vernal graduates might be able to configure their job tasks so they could devote at least twenty hours each week to fundamental progressive change.

*Hey buddy, can you spare some social change?* — Bumpersticker

### • A Conventional Part-time or Temporary Job

Some Vernal graduates might take part-time jobs or a series of short, temporary jobs that would provide them with a reasonable income but would not limit or distract them from their primary social change activity. Vernal activists might be drawn particularly to part-time jobs at social change organizations doing non-program work such as administration, canvassing for funds, grant writing, publication production, or bookkeeping. Or they might work part-time for social service agencies or other nonprofit groups.

These jobs are usually much more available than social change jobs, they typically pay better, and they are usually more stable. Though not directly oriented toward fundamental social change, these jobs would allow graduates to do socially beneficial work, earn a living, and still leave them time to work for change.

Some graduates might choose flexible jobs such as temporary office work, waiting tables in a restaurant, catering, substitute teaching, conference or event organizing, or freelance carpentry, painting, or landscaping. Others might do contract writing, typing, editing, graphic design, web design, publication production, theater production, video production, or computer programming. Still other graduates might take seasonal work as forest firefighters, retail sales clerks (during the Christmas buying season), river raft guides, ski instructors, or tax form preparers. Though not change-oriented, these jobs pay reasonably well, are not oppressive, and allow time for other pursuits.

### • Independent Wealth

Vernal graduates who had worked all their lives in a conventional career and then retired might be able to rely on a combination of their savings, a pension, and Social Security payments. Those who owned their homes might have relatively modest expenses, and if their children had moved out of their house, they might rent out rooms to generate some additional income. Those Vernal graduates

# Figure 7.1: Typical Careers of Vernal Activists

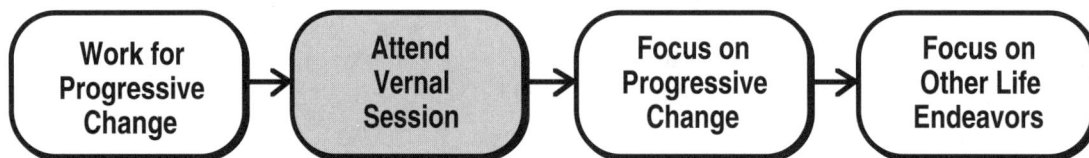

| Work for Progressive Change | → | Attend Vernal Session | → | Focus on Progressive Change | → | Focus on Other Life Endeavors |
|---|---|---|---|---|---|---|

| | Prospective Vernal Students | Vernal Students | Very Active Vernal Graduates | Less Active Vernal Graduates |
|---|---|---|---|---|
| **Time in this Role** | At least 1 year of prior social change work | 1 year | 7 year intention (but for most, actual would be less) | For most graduates: the rest of their lives |
| **Social Change Activity Level** | Variable | First nine months: about 3 hours/week working for fundamental change<br><br>Last three months: about 9 hours/week | Work at least 20 hours/week for fundamental progressive social change | Probably most would work at least 1 hour/week for fundamental progressive change |
| **Social Change Expertise** | Probably most would have 1–3 years of prior experience working for change | Somewhat more experienced | Experienced/very experienced | Very experienced |

born to wealthy families might be able to rely on gifts from their parents or an inheritance.

**• A Supportive Spouse**

Some Vernal graduates would likely be supported by their working spouses.

**• Sponsors**

Many graduates would probably rely on the benevolence of one or more friends who agreed to support their social change work. For example, a graduate might have five friends who were each willing and able to give her $20 each week. Such gifts would total more than $5,000 annually. Other friends might offer free room and board in their homes or the free use of an automobile.

People with a direct, personal connection to a Vernal activist would typically be family members (siblings, parents, grandparents, aunts, uncles, grown children), close neighbors, fellow churchmembers, old family friends, old friends from high school or college, or former colleagues at a conventional job.

## THE TOTAL NUMBER OF VERY ACTIVE AND LESS ACTIVE GRADUATES

When enrolling in a Vernal program, students would commit to working for fundamental change at least twenty hours per week for seven years after they graduated. Many

would do exactly that — they would work primarily for fundamental change for seven years and then would shift their primary focus to other endeavors. Some especially dedicated graduates might devote themselves to change work for more than seven years, and those few graduates completely dedicated to social change would do so for their whole lives.

*The average person puts only 25% of his energy and ability into his work. The world takes off its hat to those who put in more than 50% of their capacity, and stands on its head for those few and far between souls who devote 100%.* — Andrew Carnegie

However, for one reason or another, a large percentage of graduates would not work at this pace for the full seven-year period. Inevitably, some would be pulled away by other obligations or interests. Some would be swamped by work demands, childrearing responsibilities, or other family obligations (such as caring for their aging parents). Others would incur injuries or develop health problems, and some would die from accidents, illness, or old age. Some Vernal graduates might become disillusioned with their change work, some might burn out from overwork, and some might become frustrated by living on a low income. Still others might simply decide that progressive change work had too few rewards compared to other enticing opportunities.

# Figure 7.2: The Rate Vernal Graduates Would Become Less Active

| Years After Grad | Baseline Assumption | | | Optimistic Assumption | | | Details |
|---|---|---|---|---|---|---|---|
| | Very Active at Beginning of Year | Shift to Less Active Status During the Year | Shift Rate (%) | Very Active at Beginning of Year | Shift to Less Active Status During the Year | Shift Rate (%) | |
| | 30 | 4 | 13% | 30 | 2 | 7% | Thirty students attend a session |
| 1st | 26 | 4 | 15% | 28 | 1 | 4% | Graduates begin change work |
| 2nd | 22 | 3 | 14% | 27 | 1 | 4% | |
| 3rd | 19 | 3 | 16% | 26 | 1 | 4% | |
| 4th | 16 | 3 | 19% | 25 | 2 | 8% | |
| 5th | 13 | 2 | 15% | 23 | 1 | 4% | |
| 6th | 11 | 2 | 18% | 22 | 1 | 5% | |
| 7th | 9 | 2 | 22% | 21 | 1 | 5% | Last year of commitment |
| 8th | 7 | 5 | 71% | 20 | 10 | 50% | Many remaining very active grads would |
| 9th | 2 | 2 | 100% | 10 | 2 | 20% | become less active |
| 10th | 0 | 0 | — | 8 | 2 | 25% | |
| 11th | 0 | 0 | — | 6 | 2 | 33% | |
| 12th | 0 | 0 | — | 4 | 1 | 25% | |
| 13th | 0 | 0 | — | 3 | 1 | 33% | |
| 14th | 0 | 0 | — | 2 | 2 | 100% | |
| 15th | 0 | 0 | — | 0 | 0 | — | |
| Total | 125 | 30 | | 225 | 30 | | |
| | 3.7 | | | 7.0 | | | |

Average number of years Vernal graduates would be very active

**Note**: The commitment to be very active would end after the 7th year. Consequently, many very active graduates would probably become less active at the beginning of the 8th year after they graduated.

Some of these Vernal graduates would continue to work for change at a reduced pace; others might stop working for change completely. Eventually, every graduate would either shift to other activities or grow old and die.

In order to estimate how much progressive change work Vernal graduates might do, I have chosen to group them into two categories: those "very active graduates" who would be working primarily for fundamental progressive change (twenty hours per week or more) and those "less active graduates" who would be focused primarily on some other activity and whose progressive activism would thus be a smaller part of their lives. Please note that I draw this line only for the purpose of analyzing the overall contribution of Vernal graduates, not to glorify those who work more for fundamental progressive change nor to denigrate those who work less.

*Expect people to be people.*
— Graffiti

Figure 7.1 shows the typical progression of Vernal activists' social change careers. Before attending a session, they would have at least one year of activist experience — most would probably have one to three years. They would then attend a Vernal session for one year. After graduating, they would be very active for several years, and then they would shift into the less active category — most for the rest of their lives.

Estimating how long Vernal graduates would be very active is extremely difficult so I have made two estimates — a very conservative baseline estimate and a more optimistic estimate. In the base case (shown at the left side of Figure 7.2, I assume that an average of four of the thirty students who would begin each session (13 percent of the total) would drop out sometime during the year-long session. Another four (15 percent of those remaining) would become less active in the first year following their graduation. I

# Figure 7.3: The Number of Vernal Students and Very Active Vernal Graduates
## — Baseline Scenario —

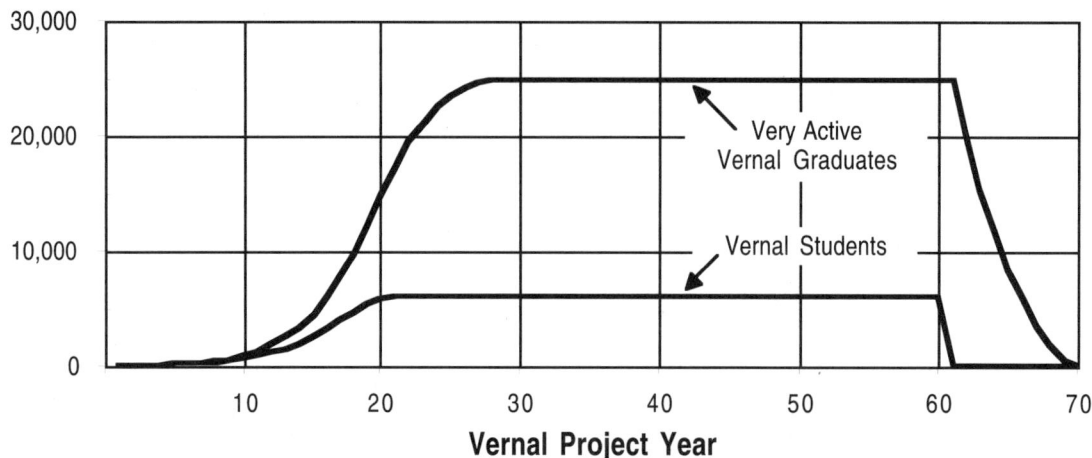

assume another three graduates would become less active during each of the next three years after that, and two more in each of the following three years.

In this conservative baseline scenario, only seven graduates would still be very active at the end of the seventh year after they graduated. Then at this point, having fulfilled their commitment, I assume most of these seven would turn to other activities during the eighth year, and I assume they would all be less active by the end of the ninth year. In this baseline scenario, Vernal graduates would be very active for an average of only 3.7 years after they graduated.

The optimistic scenario (shown at the right side of Figure 7.2) follows a similar track, but assumes graduates would shift to less active status at a slower rate. At the end of the seventh year (the beginning of the eighth), twenty graduates would still be very active. Two would still be very active until sometime during their fourteenth year after graduating. In this scenario, graduates would be very active for an average of 7.0 years after graduation.

To some, this optimistic scenario may still seem too pessimistic. I hope that the knowledge and support that students would receive in a Vernal session would enable them to continue working longer than the times shown here. But I also know how difficult progressive change work is, how poorly it pays, and what a great toll it can take on even the most dedicated activist. Moreover, for the purposes of this analysis, I want to be quite conservative in my estimates.

Combining these assumptions with my previous assumptions about the rate of growth of the overall Vernal Education Project (described in Chapter 6), it is possible to calculate the total number of Vernal graduates who would be very actively working for change each year. Figure 7.3

shows the results for the baseline scenario throughout the sixty years of the Vernal Project and the ten years after it ended.* In the baseline estimate, the number of very active graduates would rise to 25,000 by Vernal Project Year 30 (thirty years after the session officially begins) and then would remain at this level until the session ended in Year 60. From Years 30 to 60, the number of new very active graduates would be offset by a comparable number of graduates shifting to less active status.

The number of less active graduates would grow steadily as very active Vernal graduates shifted their focus to other endeavors. However, after a time, many graduates would die or completely drift away from progressive change work. For this analysis, I assume graduates would die or completely end their social change work an average of twenty-five years after they graduated from a Vernal session.† With this assumption, the number of less active graduates would grow to about 125,000 by Vernal Year 60 in the baseline scenario.

The optimistic scenario traces a similar trajectory except the number of very active graduates rises to a steady level of 45,000, and the number of less active graduates grows to about 105,000.

---

* Figure C.3 in Appendix C shows the same values in tabular form for both scenarios. Figures C.1 and C.2 show the intermediary calculations that generate these values.

† I assume the rate that graduates would die or drift away from progressive work would follow a Normal curve with a mean of twenty-five years and a standard deviation of seven years. See the note at the bottom of Figure C.3 in Appendix C for more detail.

## THE INFLUENCE OF VERNAL ACTIVISTS

For the first few years of the Vernal Project, the small number of Vernal graduates means they would probably contribute relatively little to overall progressive change efforts. If the Vernal Project proceeded as described by the baseline scenario, at the beginning of the last year of Phase 1 (Vernal Year 5), there would be only 157 very active Vernal graduates, 53 less active graduates, and 120 students. Moreover, they would be concentrated in just a single metropolitan area. Since their numbers would be so small, their efforts would not be earthshaking (except perhaps in that metro area).

However, in Phase 2, the number of very active graduates would grow to almost 15,000 (in the baseline scenario). The number of less active graduates would grow to almost 12,000, and the number of students would grow to 6,000. Together, these Vernal activists would constitute a substantial force of dedicated, skilled, and experienced activists working all across the United States Undoubtedly, they would contribute a considerable amount to progressive change efforts, and they could offer extensive support to other activists.

In Phase 3 (Years 20 to 60), the Vernal Project should be able to significantly affect progressive change efforts. To understand its impact, consider Vernal Year 40 in the middle of Phase 3 as representative. If the Vernal Project proceeded as described by the baseline scenario, there would be 6,000 Vernal students, 25,000 very active graduates, and about 104,000 less active graduates in this year. This large number of skilled activists could directly influence a large percentage of the total population. In this year, there would be one graduate for about every 2,000 people (including children) in the United States — perhaps one graduate for every 100 politically aware and active adults. If each of these graduates just spent a few hours each week talking to a different friend or neighbor about progressive change, Vernal activists could influence a sizable proportion of the total population each year.

Moreover, as described in the section below, it is likely these graduates would do much more than just discuss politics with their friends. I expect that Vernal activists would work for change primarily in two ways:

(1) By helping other activists to build powerful, grassroots citizen movements that educate people about the need for progressive change, use nonviolent methods to challenge the power structure and oppressive cultural norms, and construct alternative institutions.

(2) By helping themselves, other activists, and the public overcome destructive cultural and emotional conditioning through education, skill building, counseling, community building, and practicing alternative behavior.

*It is from numberless diverse acts of courage and belief that human history is shaped. Each time a man stands up for an ideal, or acts to improve the lot of others, or strikes out against injustice, he sends forth a tiny ripple of hope, and crossing each other from a million different centers of energy and daring those ripples build a current which can sweep down the mightiest walls of oppression and resistance.* — Robert F. Kennedy

## VERNAL ACTIVISTS' FOCUS OF ACTIVITY

Vernal activists would be free agents — they would be completely at liberty to do whatever kind of social change work they wanted to do (or none at all). However, with their background and the education they would receive in a Vernal session, I expect they would be dedicated activists and particularly inclined to do certain kinds of social change work. This section describes the methods and tactics they would probably use, the kind of social change campaigns they might develop, the goals for which they might strive, and the work they would probably do to help people overcome destructive cultural and emotional conditioning.

### General Methods of Change

Figure 7.4 shows several general methods typically used to maintain or change society. With an orientation toward long-term, fundamental progressive change, I expect most Vernal activists would reject methods like physical force and propaganda and instead use more nonviolent and democratic methods like rational persuasion, appeals to high ideals, fellowship, structural engineering (changing the environment in which people operate), and nonviolent confrontation.

# Figure 7.4: Some General Methods for Changing Society

| Method | Description | Assumption | Appeals to * | Primary Users | Main Strengths | Main Dangers |
|---|---|---|---|---|---|---|
| **Physical Force** | Coerce people with threats of physical harm | People are best swayed by physical threats | Control; security; status; confrontation; hierarchy | Military; police; armed rebels; thugs; gangs; intelligence agencies; militant unionists | Usually quite effective for those with the most strength | Coercive; violent; elitist; anti-democratic; often gives control to militaristic or bloodthirsty leaders |
| **Political Force** | Use political authority to implement policies | Change authorities and the people will follow along | Status; attention; hierarchy | Political authorities | Lawful; seemingly democratic and moral; relatively good at implementing decisions | Elitist; anti-democratic (involves only political leaders); usually gives control to those with charisma or great wealth |
| **Economic Force** | Hire people to implement policies or hire agents to use physical or political force | People are best swayed by economic threats or offers | Control; material possessions; hierarchy | Corporations; the very wealthy; organized crime syndicates | Usually quite effective; seemingly democratic and moral; good at implementing decisions | Elitist; anti-democratic; gives control to the rich |
| **Advertising, Propaganda** | Persuade people by bombarding them repeatedly with the same message | Say the same things enough times in enough ways and people will be swayed | Control | Corporations; politicians | Often quite effective | Manipulative; anti-rational and anti-democratic |
| **Engineering** | Change people's physical or social environment to affect their views | People will adapt their perspective to their environment | Rationality; control | Urban planners; corporate managers; management consultants | Good at rectifying destructive or inefficient environments | Relies on those with specialized knowledge and expertise; can be manipulative |
| **Rational Persuasion** | Persuade people with arguments based on facts and research | People are rational and will change their minds when presented with reliable evidence | Rationality; autonomy | Scholars; lawyers; lobbyists; activists | Good at finding root causes, illuminating relevant information | Relies on those with specialized knowledge; time consuming; analytical and detached |
| **Emotional Appeals to Ideals** | Appeal to people's ideals or consciences | People are best swayed by emotional appeals to their ideals | High ideals | Religious/spiritual people; nonviolent activists | Uplifting, focuses on the positive | May be anti-rational; may give control to charismatic leaders |
| **Emotional Appeals to Anger, Hatred, or Fear** | Appeal to people's anger, fears, or prejudices | People are best swayed by invoking their fears or prejudices | Directness; anger | Lobbyists; lawyers; militant activists | Taps into gut emotions; good at mobilizing people | Often anti-rational and manipulative; may give control to charismatic leaders; often unstable |
| **Fellowship and Personal Support** | Bring people into a warm community | Kindness and community can persuade people to resolve their differences | Warmth, love, joy | Religious/spiritual people; therapists; activists | Uplifting; makes people feel good; effective in bringing new people in | Often ignores or suppresses differences and conflicts |
| **Nonviolent Confrontation** | Force people to deal with problems by directly confronting them | Confrontation can cut through emotional blocks and sway people in remarkable ways | Directness; confrontation | Nonviolent activists | Effective, uplifting, empowering | Can be manipulative |

SOURCE: Inspired by and partially based on Kurt E. Olmosk, "Seven Pure Strategies of Change," *The 1972 Annual Handbook for Group Facilitators* (La Jolla, CA: University Associates, 1972, HM134 .A55): 163–172.

* **Appeals to** = This method typically appeals to those who value…

# Figure 7.5: Characteristics of Some Typical Social Change Tactics

| Type of Activity | Politi-cally Based? | Organ-ized? | Mass Partici-pation? | Consis-tent w/ Good Society? | Chal-lenges Oppo-nents? | Direct? | Sends Clear Message? | Sends Loud, Public Message? | Builds Democ-racy? |
|---|---|---|---|---|---|---|---|---|---|
| Apathy, Ignorance | No | No | — | No | No | — | No | No | No |
| Utopian Withdrawal | Yes | Yes | No | Maybe | No | No | Maybe | No | No |
| Right Living | Yes | Yes | Maybe | Yes | No | Yes | Yes | No | Maybe |
| Personal Counseling | Maybe | Yes | No | Yes | No | Yes | No | No | Yes |
| Vandalism | Maybe | No | No | No | Yes | Yes | No | No | No |
| Riots, Looting | No | No | Yes | No | Yes | Yes | No | Yes | No |
| Sabotage | Maybe | Maybe | Maybe | No | Yes | Yes | Maybe | No | No |
| Terrorism, Assassination | Yes | Yes | No | No | Yes | Yes | Maybe | Yes | No |
| Guerrilla Warfare | Yes | Yes | No | No | Yes | Yes | Maybe | Yes | No |
| Advertising | Yes | Yes | No | Maybe | Maybe | Yes | Yes | Yes | No |
| Lobbying Authorities | Yes | Yes | Maybe | Yes | Yes | No | Yes | No | Maybe |
| Electoral Campaigns | Maybe | Yes | Yes | Yes | Yes | No | Maybe | Yes | Maybe |
| Lawsuits | Yes | Yes | No | Yes | Yes | Yes | Yes | Maybe | Maybe |
| Personal Persuasion | Yes | Yes | Maybe | Yes | No | Yes | Yes | No | Yes |
| Public Speaking | Yes | Yes | No | Yes | No | Yes | Yes | Maybe | Yes |
| Street Theater | Yes | Yes | No | Yes | No | Yes | Yes | Yes | Yes |
| Rallies, Pickets, Marches | Yes | Yes | Yes | Yes | Yes | Yes | Yes | Yes | Yes |
| Boycotts | Yes | Yes | Yes | Yes | Yes | Yes | Yes | Yes | Yes |
| Strikes | Yes | Yes | Yes | Yes | Yes | Yes | Yes | Yes | Yes |
| Sit-ins, Blockades | Yes | Yes | Maybe | Yes | Yes | Yes | Yes | Yes | Yes |

SOURCE: Inspired by and partially derived from Martin Oppenheimer, *The Urban Guerrilla* (Chicago: Quadrangle Books, 1969, JC491 .O6), pp. 30–33.

NOTES:

• **Politically Based?**: Are participants politically aware and savvy, and does the activity grow out of this awareness (rather than being based mostly on raw anger, hatred, prejudice, or fear)?

• **Organized?**: Is the activity highly organized and coordinated (rather than unplanned and undirected)?

• **Mass Participation?**: Does the activity involve large numbers of people and encourage bottom-up organization (rather than involving just a few activists and encouraging top-down organization)?

• **Consistent w/ Good Society?**: Is the activity consistent with a good society?

• **Challenges Opponents?**: Does the activity challenge powerful opponents and force them to respond?

• **Direct?**: Do participants directly bring about change (rather than appealing through others)?

• **Sends Clear Message?**: Does the activity convey a clear political message that might persuade other people?

• **Sends Loud, Public Message?**: Does the activity convey a message loudly and widely so that other people will hear it?

• **Builds Democracy?**: Does the activity encourage people to get involved? Does it give them the power to make decisions? Does it encourage them to think for themselves?

The **Yes** cells are shaded to make the patterns of characteristics more visible.

## Tactics for Changing Society

People use a variety of tactics to bring about change. Some of these activities effectively promote positive change, others accomplish nothing, and some others are actually counterproductive. Figure 7.5 lists twenty of the more common tactics and shows whether they have several characteristics that promote positive change.

For example, rallies, pickets, and marches are organized ways to bring together large numbers of people for a social change purpose (rally support for a cause and pressure opponents). These three tactics are generally nonviolent and are acceptable in a good society. Typically, they directly challenge opponents of positive change and send out a loud, clear political message. They also build toward democracy by encouraging the participants (and observers) to think about an issue, take a stand, and get more involved.

In contrast, vandalism is usually carried out by a single individual or a small number of people who are angry, but not particularly politically aware. Typically, they act spontaneously, without much planning or organization, which means their efforts are often poorly directed. By its nature vandalism is destructive and not consistent with a good society. It directly challenges opponents but, at best, usually sends out a muddled and muted political message so it does not build understanding or democracy.

I would expect that Vernal activists, and the organizations in which they worked, would primarily use tactics that promoted long-term positive change, that is, the ones with many "Yes" entries in Figure 7.5.

## Building Citizen Movements for Progressive Change

Being free individuals, Vernal activists could choose to work for progressive social change in any way they liked.

*You can never have a revolution in order to establish a democracy. You must have a democracy in order to have a revolution.*
— Gilbert K. Chesterton

Some Vernal activists would probably work in cities, others in rural areas. Some would direct their efforts towards people who already understand the workings of society and attempt to mobilize them to action. Other Vernal activists would probably work to help people with less knowledge learn the true workings of society and help them imagine better structures. Some Vernal activists would work with community groups (like neighborhood associations, tenants' unions, homeowner associations, or parent associations), some with religious or civic groups, some with professional groups (like teachers, doctors, or engineers), some with working people and labor unions, and others with students and faculty at colleges and universities. Some would focus on a single issue, others on a wide variety of issues. Some Vernal

activists would likely work in the halls of political power in Washington or state capitals, lobbying for specific legislation. Some would devote their efforts to electing progressive legislators. Some might work for public interest research groups writing reports to influence the news media and authorities. Others would work with public interest law firms that sought to win change through litigation.

However, as I mentioned above, I expect that most Vernal activists would choose to work at the grassroots level and would attempt to build large, democratically governed citizen movements oriented toward fundamental progressive change. To build these movements, they would probably come together with other activists in their community and develop specific change campaigns focused on major societal problems of interest to large numbers of people in their community.

If designed properly, these campaigns would:

• Reach out to large numbers of people.

• Promote positive visions of a good society and demonstrate positive and powerful means to create it.

• Teach people how to live in consonance with their ideals, especially how to solve their mutual problems collectively and make decisions together in a cooperative, caring, and democratic way.

• Illuminate current injustices and demonstrate positive alternatives in a clear way.

• Empower people to take action against injustice.

• Teach people the skills necessary to challenge opponents and tackle dysfunctional cultural norms.

• Help people form organizations, networks, federations, and political parties with other concerned citizens to muster enough strength to overcome opposition.

• Force major, structural changes in critical societal institutions using methods of nonviolent struggle.

### SOCIAL CHANGE CAMPAIGNS

Successful change campaigns typically have many components and proceed through several distinct stages, each involving somewhat different constituencies. Based on his more than twenty-five years of experience participating in and planning nonviolent social change campaigns, Bill Moyer has developed a detailed eight-stage framework for understanding the progression of successful change campaigns.[2]

Moyer's eight stages are:

**1. Normal Conditions**

During politically quiet times the public mostly supports or acquiesces to the status quo.

**2. Prove Failure of Institutions**

Activists — working mostly in established progressive organizations and using mostly mainstream tactics like preparing and publicizing research reports — show that powerholders violate the public's cherished values (such as honesty, democracy, and freedom). Activists prove and document that a problem exists and that official institutions do not respond properly.

### 3. Ripening Conditions

A small number of concerned activists engage in prototype nonviolent actions and prepare for a larger movement. A network develops of grassroots activists willing to push for change.

### 4. Social Movement Take-Off

A trigger event publicly dramatizes the reality that social conditions and powerholder policies violate the public's values. Thousands of people become passionately involved and engage in various acts of opposition (such as marches, rallies, vigils, pickets, strikes, and blockades). The news is filled with stories of people protesting the status quo. Activists work to inform larger numbers of people and to bring people into social change organizations. They design powerful demonstrations that expose societal myths and illustrate positive alternatives.

### 5. Identity Crisis of Powerlessness

After a time, the excitement wanes, and the number of visible demonstrations decreases. Seeing few immediate results from their efforts, many inexperienced activists despair or burn out even though the campaign is proceeding well and is simply shifting into a different mode as described in the next stage.

### 6. Majority Public Support

Change activity shifts from nonviolent actions carried out by a small number of activists to a larger, broad-based movement that uses more conventional methods (like lobbying and lawsuits) to pressure powerholders. Activists seek to inform large numbers of people, encourage them to oppose the status quo, and urge them to support alternatives.

### 7. Success

The great majority of the public demands change. This, then, finally forces the authorities to acquiesce. The social change movement wins one or more of its demands but usually through conventional channels such as changing a law or winning a legal settlement. Often those in power claim credit for the changes and deny that the social change movement influenced them in any way.

### 8. Continuing the Struggle

Activists work to assure that the successes won are actually realized (laws are implemented and enforced). The movement continues to fight for more and stronger measures or shifts to other issues and begins another round of the eight stages.

With their broad understanding of social change dynamics, Vernal activists could help other activists understand these eight typical stages of a campaign and success-

fully maneuver through them. They could especially help inexperienced activists understand that campaigns take years to succeed, that the focus of activity shifts from one arena to another over time (and requires different kinds of social change work), and that victories are seldom clear-cut. They could especially help discourage activists who work in different arenas from fighting with each other and help them weather the crisis of powerlessness in Stage 5.

### SUCCESS, DEFEAT, REFORMISM, AND CO-OPTATION

Through the many steps of a social change campaign, pressure weighs on activists to be satisfied with meager gains or with mere cosmetic changes. Without a clear goal and the strength to achieve it, campaigns are often stymied or sidetracked. Instead of transforming society, they may only force modest reforms or bring about temporary changes.

Figure 7.6 lists seven distinct levels of success activists may achieve in a campaign. These successes range from simply gaining access to an existing institution to broad, structural transformation of societal institutions. In the early stages of a campaign, it may be a major victory simply to get existing authorities to listen to a new perspective. As a progressive organization grows in strength and influence, it may push for acceptance of progressive ideas, then for reform that includes these ideas, and finally for fundamental transformation of the institution. When an institution has been fundamentally transformed, its policies and practices adhere to progressive ideals like honesty, democracy, and equity without constant prodding by progressive activists.

For example, if schools received funding at a uniform rate per student throughout the nation, many current efforts would be unnecessary. Wealthy parents would have an incentive to support improvement of all schools, not just those in their neighborhoods. Other parents would have less incentive to move to wealthy suburban neighborhoods (that now have well-funded schools). With better schools and more supportive teachers, juvenile delinquency in poor neighborhoods would decline.

Faced with fierce opposition, progressive change campaigns seldom achieve the seventh level of success. Besides being thwarted by powerful opponents, progressive activists may also be led astray by sympathetic activists or politicians who believe that simple relief or reform is sufficient. Ambitious politicians or activists also frequently "co-opt" a progressive effort by adopting the rhetoric of activists or assuming the mantle of leadership, but failing to push for truly fundamental progressive change.

With their understanding of social change campaigns, Vernal activists could help other activists understand the differences between weak reforms and fundamental change. They could encourage their colleagues to celebrate limited successes but also to stay focused on long-term goals. They could push for "transformative reform" — that is, reform that allows and facilitates greater reforms later by democratizing underlying structures — rather than "reformist reform" that relieves the immediate problem but undercuts

# Figure 7.6: Levels of Activist Success

| Level | Example: Newspaper Coverage | Example: Government Policy Change |
|---|---|---|
| 1. Access to an Existing Institution | A reporter reads a progressive organization's press release and agrees to talk with activists. | Progressive activists testify at a Congressional hearing. |
| 2. Agenda-Setting in the Institution | The reporter understands the activists' perspective and considers it when writing articles. | A Congressmember introduces a bill that includes progressive measures. |
| 3. Policy Change in the Institution | The reporter includes the progressive perspective in articles on the issue. | Congress enacts legislation that includes the progressive measures. |
| 4. Desired Output from the Institution | The editor prints these articles with the progressive perspective intact. | The legislation is enforced. |
| 5. Desired Impact Achieved | The public reads the articles and understands the activists' perspective. | The legislation is enforced enough that it has the intended consequences. |
| 6. Reform of the Institution | Activists are offered a regular newspaper column in which they can present their perspectives on many issues. | People elect a more progressive Congress that is inclined to enact progressive policies and will ensure the policies are implemented. |
| 7. Structural Transformation or Replacement of the Institution | Activists produce their own newspaper with wide circulation and regularly publish their views on many issues. | Changes in the constitution lead to a more democratic process for electing Congress. Congress is then continually more inclined to enact and implement progressive policies. |

SOURCES: This seven-level model is based on a six-level model in Paul Burnstein, Rachel L. Einwohner, and Jocelyn A. Hollander, "The Success of Political Movements: A Bargaining Perspective," in J. Craig Jenkins and Bert Klandermans, eds., *The Politics of Social Protest: Comparative Perspectives on States and Social Movements* (Minneapolis: University of Minnesota Press, 1995, JA76 .P6235 1995): 282–284, which is, in turn, based on a five-level model in Paul D. Schumaker, "Policy Responsiveness to Protest-Group Demands," *Journal of Politics*, no. 37 (May 1975): 494–495. I have added the last row and the newspaper example.

further progressive action.[3] In addition, they could explain why it is necessary to build organizations with enough strength to achieve sweeping victories.

## Overcoming Emotional and Cultural Obstacles

As described in Chapter 3, widespread ignorance, emotional conditioning, and dysfunctional cultural norms significantly hinder progressive change. With their extensive skills and knowledge, Vernal activists would likely be especially adept at helping people overcome these obstacles and become more knowledgeable, clear-thinking, compassionate, and self-confident citizens.

I expect Vernal activists would work first to clear themselves of their own emotional and cultural limitations so they could behave well and serve as role models for others. Then they would help other activists overcome personal blocks and be more effective. Finally, working in conjunction with other activists, Vernal activists could assist the larger public. Figure 7.7 details some emotional and cultural obstacles and the specific contributions Vernal activists might make to help people surmount them.

## THE DISTRIBUTION AND TASKS OF VERNAL ACTIVISTS

### Very Active Vernal Graduates

To get a better sense of the extent that Vernal graduates might influence society in Phase 3 of the Vernal Project, this section presents a more detailed and numerical analysis based on a few simplifying assumptions.*

---

* Obviously, even if the Vernal Education Project proceeded exactly as I suggest (and this is very unlikely), the number and distribution of very active Vernal graduates would not match these assumptions. Every community is different, every social change organization has its own flavor and style, and every Vernal graduate would choose her own path. There is no way to know where Vernal graduates would live, what organizations they would join or create, whether they would work with other graduates, what work they would do, nor what impact they might have on the world. I have made these assumptions *only* to illustrate some possibilities and to indicate the kind and quantity of social change we might expect from the Vernal Project.

## Figure 7.7: Overcoming Emotional and Cultural Obstacles

| Typical Emotional and Cultural Obstacles | What Vernal Activists Could Contribute to Help Overcome these Obstacles |
|---|---|
| Ignorance Misinformation | Clear and accurate information Provocative questioning Cooperative problem solving methods |
| Prejudice (racism, sexism, ageism, and so on) Mistrust | Clear and accurate information Personal counseling Cooperative problem-solving methods |
| Addictions, compulsions, phobias, and other dysfunctional behavior | Clear and accurate information Personal counseling Support and encouragement Gentle prodding |
| Uncertainty, self-doubt, conceit, arrogance | Clear and accurate information Personal counseling Support and encouragement |
| Isolation | Cooperative community Personal support |
| Hopelessness | Clear conceptions of a good society Knowledge of positive alternatives Skill and experience working for positive change Dedication to working for change |

First, I assume graduates would be spread throughout the country in numbers proportionate to the general population. I also assume that most would work with small, democratically governed grassroots organizations. For the purposes of this analysis, I assume the 25,000 very active graduates (in Vernal Years 25–60 in the baseline scenario) would be distributed as follows:

• I assume fifty very active graduates would work in each congressional district.* They would work with grassroots organizations focused on the local community. Since there are 435 congressional districts in the U.S., this would involve a total of 21,750 very active graduates nationwide.

• I assume an average of forty-five very active graduates would work in each of the fifty states. They would work

with progressive organizations focused on a state or regional level. This would involve a total of 2,250 graduates nationwide.

• I assume one thousand very active graduates would work with progressive organizations focused on the national and international level.

Note that many of these organizations — especially those working at the local level — would have only volunteer members and staff since probably only the largest could raise enough funds to be able to pay staffmembers.

### GRASSROOTS ORGANIZATIONS

I assume that the fifty very active graduates in each congressional district working at the local level would work with several types of grassroots organizations: Issue-Oriented Advocacy Groups, Alternative Institution Development Groups, Progressive Political Parties, and Progressive Caucuses within mainstream organizations. To further detail the analysis, I assume they would be distributed in the following way:

• **Issue-Oriented Advocacy Groups: Twenty-Four Very Active Vernal Graduates**

I assume four very active graduates would work together in each of six separate community- or college-based advocacy groups campaigning on a particular issue.† These might be existing organizations or ones that the Vernal graduates would create. Each might be an independent organization or it might be a single committee or task force of a larger organization.

As I see it, these 2,610 advocacy groups dispersed across the country would focus on a local aspect of an important, pivotal issue like corporate domination, environmental destruction, weapons production, poverty, crime, police brutality, corruption, inadequate childcare, inadequate healthcare, destructive U.S. foreign policy, racism, sexism, domestic violence, wealth inequality, or drug abuse. Some might push for favorable treatment of cooperative enterprises, a more humane tax code, reform of election campaign financing, a more democratic decision-making structure, or some other worthy endeavor. In all their efforts, these organizations would push for democratic and cooperative control of society.

Some of these groups would probably work with a single constituency (such as doctors, high school students, environmentalists, mothers of small children, residents of a single poor neighborhood, members of a labor union, or owners of small retail stores). Others would probably try to reach a broad, general audience.

---

* I focus on congressional districts since CDs each have approximately the same population (currently about 600,000 people) and they roughly conform to geographic and social boundaries. I think it is easier to understand the influence that Vernal activists might have by imagining a single congressional district (for me, the one where I live), and envisioning these activists working here.

---

† As I see it, these groups would work for broad, fundamental change, but focus on one issue at a time and emphasize local aspects of this issue. Members of the group would "think globally, but act locally" and "think broadly, but act tightly focused" on one issue.

To build a powerful social change movement focused on their chosen issue, members of these groups would do some or all of the following:

• Research and write factual leaflets about the issue, describing the problems with the current situation, what created and sustains these problems, possible alternative solutions, and how to implement these alternatives. Effective leaflets would expose societal myths and reveal the web of power-brokering and corruption that maintains the status quo.

• Inform and persuade people by distributing these leaflets at public events, showing videos, sending e-mail, speaking at schools, churches, and civic groups, canvassing door-to-door, circulating petitions, writing letters to local newspapers, staging vigils, rallies, and marches, and performing guerrilla theater. They would encourage people to withdraw their support from those conventional institutions and authorities responsible for problems and instead support alternative institutions that would solve them.

• Track local news stories covering the issue and challenge and persuade reporters to adopt a more progressive perspective.

• Press for change by lobbying authorities, filing lawsuits, and/or organizing boycotts, strikes, and blockades. They might focus their attention particularly on local business leaders, government officials, or civic leaders.

• Actively encourage new activists to join their organization and work to inform and support them.

• Build an inspiring and effective organization that practiced cooperative democracy and mutual support in its internal processes.*

• Publish a newsletter for supporters.

• Reach out to other progressive groups in the area and, when appropriate, work in coalition or affiliate with them.

With four very active Vernal graduates essentially serving as steady, part-time staffmembers, these organizations would likely be much more capable than most current or past grassroots social change groups. Linked or allied with other similar groups working on the same issue in every part of the country, these focused groups would have tremendous power to bring about change in their chosen issue area. I expect they would be similar to — but stronger than — the alliances of local groups recently working against nuclear power, nuclear weapons, U.S. military support of dictatorships in Central America, toxic waste, the death penalty, and sweatshops.

As I see it, the four very active Vernal graduates would help their organizations in these ways:

• Devoting at least twenty hours per week to their organization, the four very active Vernal graduates could do much of the basic day-to-day grunt work, ensuring that the basic task and internal maintenance functions of their groups were adequately performed.

---

* See also the section below titled "Cooperative Activist Communities."

## Seven Principles for a New Organizing Model

*Based on her many years of organizing the multiracial Piedmont Peace Project in a poor, rural area of North Carolina, Linda Stout[4] proposes that organizing efforts adhere to these seven principles:*

*1. Focus on social change (not on social service).*

*2. Work across race and class lines.*

*3. Include indigenous organizers and leaders (empower members of the community to be the organizers and leaders).*

*4. Encourage diversity (racial, class, and so on) with ongoing outreach and training — include diversity and leadership training in every staff meeting, board meeting, and retreat.*

*5. Focus on the connections between local and national issues.*

*• Groups should educate themselves on how economic justice, peace, environmental, and women's issues are interconnected.*

*• Translate national issues into local language and issues so they appeal to people in the community.*

*6. Develop and maintain personal empowerment while working for organizational power by doing the following:*

*• Listen to people.*

*• Help them look at various options.*

*• Help them see themselves in a position of power.*

*7. Be flexible and ready to create new models to adapt to the needs and leadership styles of participants.*

---

• Their steady, long-term presence would provide much-needed stability and continuity of experience. They could convey the history and practices of their organization to new members. This would be of particular value to organizations based at colleges since students come and go so quickly.

• With their deep understanding of society and of change methods, the graduates could help their organizations choose penetrating issues, strategies, tactics, and goals; they could guide their organizations toward effective work. I expect they would push their groups to champion strong reform measures that democratized society and led to deep, fundamental change. They would steer their groups away from feeble compromises, measures based on narrow self-interest, or measures that might infringe on others. They would also point out the connections between issues and offer a broad perspective on social change. Most important, they would encourage their

> *Leadership is getting someone to do what they don't want to do, to achieve what they want to achieve.* — Tom Landry

colleagues to investigate thoroughly all aspects of their chosen issue and act responsibly in all their change efforts.

• They would help connect and weave diverse people and groups together in coalitions and alliances.

• To increase understanding of the group's primary issue or to bolster their colleagues' social change skills, I imagine the four Vernal graduates would offer their colleagues a variety of educational materials: books, articles, notes, movies, videos, and web pages. At strategic times, they would facilitate educational workshops tailored to the interests and needs of the group's members. They might conduct workshops on a particular issue, or they might teach change skills such as how to develop strategic campaigns or how to use a particular change tactic. They might present personal transformation techniques, various ways to overcome cultural barriers, cooperative meeting processes, and positive ways to resolve conflict. They might present information on how their chosen issue fits with other progressive issues.

I imagine the Vernal graduates would also spend a significant amount of time every day individually mentoring other activists in their group — imparting their relevant knowledge and skills about every aspect of changing society and being an activist. Moreover, I expect they would help set up self-study groups to further educate themselves and their social change colleagues.

• The four graduates would probably devote a great deal of time to encouraging and supporting other members of their organization. I expect they could inspire their colleagues with their excitement and high expectations.

*Nothing great was ever achieved without enthusiasm.*
— Ralph Waldo Emerson

• As I envision it, they would also be playful and loving, offering hugs and compassionate counseling to their colleagues during difficult periods. Whenever interpersonal conflicts erupted, the Vernal graduates could calm the combatants and use their negotiation skills to mediate. Furthermore, they would help members of their groups understand and celebrate (rather than fret and fume about) their differences in age, gender, race, ethnicity, class, sexual orientation, and culture.

• Towards the goal of creating a democratic society of empowered citizens, I expect the Vernal graduates would encourage newcomers to take responsibility for the organization and to take initiative. To avoid disempowering other activists, I imagine Vernal activists would mostly aid and support others — working largely behind the scenes and only occasionally stepping out front into the limelight. I imagine they would try to let their colleagues make mistakes and learn from the consequences, without scolding them or taking control away from them.

• I also imagine the four graduates would expect the best of their fellow activists, prodding them to strive towards their highest ideals. They would encourage their fellow activists to boldly challenge conventional ideas, their own

perspectives, and each other's views. They would push them to struggle and learn from each other while they also supported and cared for one another. This would help to prevent their organizations from degenerating into wishy-washy feel-goodism or achieving only lowest common denominator accords.

With a reliable core of experienced, hard-working Vernal graduates, these local advocacy groups would likely do effective change work and make relatively few mistakes. Each group's integrity, effectiveness, and democratic procedures would impress both its members and outside observers, inspiring outsiders to join the group and members to work diligently towards its goals.

Based on my experience, I believe four very active graduates working together would be able to attract, mentor, encourage, and support about twenty-four other dedicated activists, and they could do it well enough that these twenty-four steadfast activists could work energetically for many years. If this were the case, each of these grassroots organizations would have twenty-eight active members who regularly attended meetings and carried out its projects. With this strong core, I believe each organization could attract and support about one hundred fifty active supporters (progressive advocates) who would regularly attend the group's events (presentations, hearings, demonstrations) or volunteer a few hours of work.* [5]

With so many active members and supporters, each of these grassroots organizations could probably reach several thousand more people each year — persuading them that society could be improved and convincing them of the value of a few specific positive alternatives. By having long and repeated conversations with large numbers of people, they probably would *profoundly* touch a certain number — perhaps fifty or one hundred individuals each year — and persuade them to radically alter their thinking about the nature of society and their role in it. Deeply affected by these conversations, many of these people would become activists eventually.

Note that I have assumed that the very active graduates would be most effective by working together as a group of four within each organization. If they worked individually, in pairs, or as a group of three, the twenty-four graduates in a congressional district could work with a larger number of organizations. However, they would also be more likely to become isolated or to go astray. I believe each Vernal graduate could more easily stay on track if she were continually working with three other experienced activists who had a similar understanding of the need for fundamental progres-

---

* Chapter 5 has more detailed definitions of steadfast activists and progressive advocates. In Appendix C, I further define steadfast activists as those who work from three to sixty hours each week for fundamental change and progressive advocates as those who work less than three hours each week, but at least ten hours per year.

Note that some of the steadfast activists and progressive advocates working with very active Vernal graduates would probably be less active Vernal graduates or Vernal students.

sive change. Knowing that the other three very active Vernal graduates were working skillfully and diligently with her for change would inspire her to her best work and hearten her in tough times. Furthermore, when one (or two or three) of them blundered or fell into despair, the others could use their well-developed support skills to comfort or heal her back to wholeness. Each graduate would know she could count on the other Vernal graduates to be honest, understanding, and caring even if other activists in the group defaulted.

### • Alternative Institution Development Groups: Eight Very Active Vernal Graduates

In each congressional district, I assume four very active graduates would work with each of two different groups striving to develop an alternative institution such as a community bank, a land trust, a cooperative food store, a farmer's market, a childcare cooperative, a tool sharing cooperative, a collectively owned and operated business, an alternative school, a battered women's shelter, a co-housing community, or a community garden. I expect the very active graduates would work to ensure that the alternative institution was fair, honest, open, democratic, cooperative, egalitarian, and powerful. They would work to build an institution that truly provided a progressive alternative to a conventional institution, which probably means that, as it grew over time, its existence would challenge the power structure or conventional cultural norms. If elements of the power structure fought back by attacking or undermining the alternative institution, the developers would then organize large numbers of supporters to resist the attacks and sustain the alternative institution.

I imagine that each of the 870 Alternative Institution Development Groups dispersed across the country would be similar in size to the Issue-Oriented Advocacy Groups described above — with twenty-four steadfast activists and several hundred progressive advocates. I also assume the four very active Vernal graduates would provide a similar level of support and guidance to the other members of the group and to each other.

### • Progressive Political Parties: Six Very Active Vernal Graduates

In each congressional district, I assume six very active graduates would work together with a progressive political party like the New Party or the Green Party that has a multi-issue agenda. I expect they would do the same kind of education, advocacy, and recruitment work as activists in the Issue-Oriented Advocacy Groups. They would probably also:

• Work with others to develop the party's platform.

• Work to elect progressive party members to public office.

• Coordinate efforts with the party's state and national offices.

With six hard-working very active graduates at its core, the local party chapter would likely be a vibrant organization. It would also be more likely to stay on a progressive track. Progressive political parties are always tempted to moderate their perspectives and soften their stances to appeal to large numbers of mainstream people or to attract big funders. Understanding how this might co-opt their efforts or compromise their integrity, the Vernal graduates could work to keep the party honest and its policies consistent with fundamental progressive change.

By reaching out to a large number of other organizations, including the Issue-Oriented Advocacy Groups and Alternative Institution Development Groups, a progressive party should be able to attract many members and win elections, especially locally. Since most congressional districts currently have no organized progressive parties, having a large and vigorous one in all 435 CDs across the country would be a major breakthrough.

*Democracy is based upon the conviction that there are extraordinary possibilities in ordinary people.*
— Harry Emerson Fosdick

### • Progressive Caucuses: Twelve Very Active Graduates

In each congressional district, I assume four very active graduates would work together in each of three mainstream groups (a total of 1,305 groups across the country) such as conventional political parties, churches, labor unions, professional associations, civic organizations (like the Lions Club, Rotary Club, or Parent-Teacher Association), or social clubs. They would work to democratize the organization, to persuade members of the group to adopt more progressive perspectives, and to make the official policies of the organization more progressive.

If there was an existing progressive caucus within the organization, they might join it, or if there was none, they might create one. More often though, they would just gather informally to express their views. To sway the other members, they would present progressive ideas and circulate articles or papers that explained and promoted their positions. They would also seek out people in the organization who were open to progressive ideas, discuss issues with them, support them, inform them, and encourage them to learn more. Furthermore, in all their interactions with others, they would try to be models of honesty, integrity, and compassion.

Since these twelve very active graduates would work in only three mainstream organizations, it might seem that they would have little overall influence. In every community, there are hundreds of mainstream organizations including many that are quite large. However, these twelve very active graduates would be particularly skilled, knowledgeable, experienced, and active in their groups, making them more influential than most people. Each graduate would be a powerful voice for progressive ideas and a dependable ally for other people who backed progressive measures. I also imagine they would be especially willing to work with coalitions like the local Council of Churches or Central Labor Council. This would greatly expand their influence.

### Additional Work

Besides their primary work with the groups described above, each of these fifty very active graduates working in a single congressional district would probably devote some time to other change-related activities.

• As I mentioned earlier, they would all probably talk with their families, friends, and neighbors about progressive change.

• Many graduates might attend a weekly or monthly progressive study group, discussion group, video-watching group, eating club, singing group, or theater group. With the participation of fifty very active graduates in every congressional district, every community in the country might have several such camaraderie-building associations of progressive activists.

• Many graduates would likely also join mainstream organizations that matched their personal interests such as churches, civic organizations, or social clubs. Within these groups, they might periodically advocate for progressive change. Some activists might even deliberately join an organization with dissimilar interests as a way to reach out to conservatives in the community. For example, an activist who worked primarily with a group advocating for better community childcare facilities might join a conservative civic organization. As the members got to know her on a personal level, she could discuss her advocacy work and its importance. Conservative members who would scornfully reject her political arguments might be swayed by her personal integrity and her principled behavior. Eventually, they might be willing to consider her political ideas.

• These fifty very active graduates would serve as local examples of responsible and caring citizens. Some would likely visit schools to talk about the crucial role of an informed and active citizenry in a democratic society and present themselves as exemplary role models.

• Whenever a crucial issue or political campaign in their area came to a critical juncture, many of these activists would probably focus their efforts on it for a short time. With their deep understanding of progressive ideas and methods, there would usually be no need to persuade them to support the campaign, to convince them of the value of the change effort, nor to teach them particular tasks. Rather, they could jump right in and do effective work.

For example, the fifty very active graduates in a congressional district might write fifty letters-to-the-editor to the local paper calling for a particular change, make fifty phone calls to a political officeholder, or be fifty people attending a rally, vigil, picket, or blockade. In the time immediately before an election, each might do a week of campaigning and canvassing for a progressive political candidate, empha-

sizing the issues and talking to the constituencies they knew best. By focusing intensive effort on a particular spot, they might enable a group to make a decisive breakthrough.

Clearly, fifty very active Vernal graduates in a single congressional district could contribute an incredible amount to bringing about progressive social change. If, as described here, each very active Vernal graduate could support, inform, and inspire six steadfast activists and if each of these six steadfast activists could support, inform, and inspire six progressive advocates, each congressional district would have fifty very active Vernal activists, three hundred steadfast activists, and eighteen hundred progressive advocates. Together, these 2,150 activists would constitute a powerful force in their community.

## STATE ORGANIZATIONS

As I envision it, the very active graduates working at the state level would work with existing statewide progressive organizations, or they might start new ones. They would carry out such work as the following:

• Research important local, state, and regional problems and develop possible solutions. They would write reports, papers, and pamphlets and distribute these documents to local progressive activists. They would also prepare model legislation for state or local governments that embodied the best solutions.

• Investigate corruption and power brokering among powerful people, corporations, and government institutions. They would publish exposés and issue press releases describing their findings.

• Serve as a reliable and ready source of progressive information and commentary to journalists on important issues.

• Maintain information resources (such as newspaper clipping files and web pages) on important progressive issues, especially those on which local change groups were working.

• Coordinate the efforts of local activists. For example, an organization might collect information from various local groups and pass it on to others, arrange regional tours for prominent speakers, or organize large, cooperative events such as benefit concerts or large, regional rallies.

• Collect information about members of the state legislature and executive agencies and pass this on to local activists to aid them in their local lobbying.

*The trouble with practical jokes is that very often they get elected.*

— attributed to Will Rogers

• Watchdog, inform, lobby, and challenge state legislators, state administrators, and federal legislators from their state. The power of these activists in lobbying authorities would be greatly enhanced by working in conjunction with grassroots groups.

• Coordinate large, class-action lawsuits.

I expect the very active Vernal graduates working in these state-level organizations would take on the same roles as those working with the grassroots groups described above. Very active graduates would work in groups of four, and they would devote much of their effort to supporting and educating the other members or employees of their organizations.

I assume the number of very active graduates working in a state would be proportional to the state's population, so in the smallest states, there might be only five very active Vernal graduates working at this level. In the largest state, California, I assume there would be about two hundred. Overall, I assume there would be very active graduates working in a total of 562 statewide organizations across the country.

### NATIONAL AND INTERNATIONAL ORGANIZATIONS

As I imagine it, the thousand very active graduates working at the national level would perform the same kind of work as the activists working at the state level, but their focus would be on the national and international arena. Many would probably work in Washington, DC, and focus on the federal government. Others would probably work in important business centers like New York or Los Angeles and focus on transnational corporations. Some might even work overseas, perhaps with international organizations like the United Nations, Bread for the World, or War Resisters International.

At the national level, progressive activists confront powerful and sophisticated politicians, business executives, and public relations flacks who are skilled at deceiving and manipulating people. Activists at this level are usually under intense pressure to negotiate, bargain, log-roll, pander, fawn, toady, compromise, or just give in. For this reason, it would be especially important for these progressive activists to have a strong support group in which they could encourage each other to maintain high ideals and adhere to high standards. Very active graduates could arrange these support groups, encourage activists to stand up for their principles, and help sustain their vision of a good society. They could also arrange regular visits by principled activists from grassroots groups who could remind and encourage the activists working in this arena to focus on fundamental, progressive change.

Like those working at the local and state level, I assume these very active graduates would also mostly work in groups of four. In large organizations, they might work in groups of six. I assume there would be very active graduates working in a total of 225 national and international organizations.

Overall, as described here, very active Vernal activists would be working in groups of four or six in a total of 6,007 local, state, national, and international organizations across the country.

## Less Active Vernal Graduates

Most Vernal graduates, even after their primary focus had shifted to some other endeavor, would probably continue to do some social change work. With their extensive skills and long experience, these activists could contribute a great deal to change efforts. In the baseline estimate, the number of less active graduates would steadily rise from about 15,000 in Vernal Year 21 to 125,000 in Year 60 and would average about 90,000 over this forty year period. In Vernal Year 40, there would be about 104,000 less active graduates.

Many less active graduates would probably continue to work with the change groups they had worked with before — they would just devote less time each week than before. They would therefore fall into my category of steadfast activist or progressive advocate. Others might have little social change involvement, but would occasionally work on a particular issue or political campaign. Most would likely vote for progressive political candidates and continue to influence their families, friends, neighbors, and co-workers.

Since most would probably continue to want to bring about fundamental change and would now have reasonably well paying conventional jobs, they would likely donate relatively large amounts of money to social change groups. This could provide a significant resource. For example, if 100,000 less active Vernal graduates contributed an average of $1,000 each year, this would amount to $100 million — enough to support more than 3,000 full-time activists.*

## Vernal Students

The six thousand Vernal students would also contribute a great deal to social change efforts. For the first nine months of their Vernal session, students would be working with a grassroots change group for about three hours each week. In the last quarter, they would work nine hours per week, putting them in my category of steadfast activist. Since they would each have at least one year of social change experience prior to enrolling in a Vernal session, they would probably be more skilled than many of their colleagues in these groups.

For the last nine months of the Vernal session, each student would also be serving in an internship with progressive organizations for twelve hours per week. With six thousand Vernal students each doing three internships, most progressive organizations in the country could have at least one intern each year. This would provide an immense amount of skilled labor for these organizations.

---

* Figure C.5 in Appendix C shows more detailed estimates of monetary contributions that might be made by all progressive advocates.

## An Example

To provide a sense of how much all these Vernal activists might contribute to progressive social change efforts, let's consider a particular campaign — the effort to significantly reduce U.S. military spending and redirect these funds to socially beneficial endeavors. Since this is an important and fundamental issue, let's assume that one-tenth of the grassroots Issue-Oriented Advocacy Groups supported by very active Vernal graduates (a total of 261 groups) would decide to devote themselves to this single campaign.* With this many groups, perhaps half of the people in the country would have a grassroots group working specifically on this issue in or near their community. With 28 active members (very active Vernal graduates and steadfast activists) and about 150 progressive advocates, each group would be as big and effective as the largest current local social change groups.

I imagine that each of these groups would regularly show films and videos, speak to church and civic groups, distribute leaflets, hold vigils and rallies, canvass door-to-door, and send out e-mail. In all these ways, they would tell people that a large percentage of the federal budget goes to support the military and explain how this robs important social services of much needed funds. They would also point out that the U.S. military does not defend the United States from outside threats (of which there are virtually none now), but instead violently enforces the current oppressive world economic order. They would argue that a much reduced military force, working in conjunction with the military forces of other countries under the direction of the United Nations' General Assembly, would be better at ensuring world peace and prosperity. They could also argue that nonviolent peacekeeping teams would be even more effective in establishing a democratic and just world than a massive military force.

Vernal activists in these communities working with Alternative Institution Development Groups would likely discuss how money redirected from the military could be used to bolster their alternative institutions. Perhaps five percent of the Alternative Institution Development Groups supported by Vernal activists across the country (43 groups) might attempt to form nonviolent peacekeeping teams for deployment in world hotspots. Other Vernal activists working in these same communities with mainstream groups would likely raise this issue with their constituencies, generating more and broader discussion as well as generat-

> *Our country, right or wrong. When right, to be kept right; when wrong, to be put right.*
> — Carl Schurz

ing more pressure on elected officials. Other Vernal activists working across the country with a progressive political party would likely push for reduced military spending and be able to get this policy adopted into their party's platform. By presenting accurate information and well-reasoned arguments directly, face-to-face to thousands of people in these hundreds of different communities, these many groups should be able to drastically shift the perspective of much of the public.

At the national level, there might be ten or twenty organizations containing four or six very active Vernal graduates focused on this issue (such as Peace Action, Friends Committee on National Legislation, and the Council for a Livable World). They would research and document this issue and prepare reports and leaflets for distribution in Washington and across the country. These organizations would also raise this issue with Congressmembers and urge progressive members to sponsor legislation. Vernal activists would work to ensure that any proposed legislation was strong and fair.

Military contractors, military personnel, military hawks, defense industry workers, and other advocates of military spending would, of course, argue the importance of U.S. military operations overseas, the contribution to the economy provided by military contractors, the job losses associated with military cutbacks, and so on. Vernal graduates could then use these arguments to deepen the discourse and discuss militarism, global capitalism, lobbying by military contractors, and economic conversion.

At strategically appropriate times, the grassroots groups would organize simultaneous rallies or send large numbers of people to a rally in Washington. Some would probably also organize local nonviolent direct actions of various kinds to emphasize the critical need for change, demonstrate the depth of their commitment, and increase the visibility of the issue. With so many large, powerful local groups constantly staging events and reaching out to their communities, this issue would become so prominent that the national media would be forced to address it. This would then stimulate even greater citizen discussion, more rallies, larger demonstrations, and finally, votes for military cutbacks. Congressmembers would feel intense, constant pressure to address this issue. Progressive parties would run candidates to challenge intransigent Congressmembers and might win in a few districts.

Eventually, this anti-military/pro-nonviolent cooperation movement would grow large enough to force substantial change. With tens of thousands of activists insisting that legislation not be compromised and vigilantly tracking the results (both in Washington and at the grassroots), the government would be forced to make far-reaching changes.

During the entire time these Vernal activists were working on this issue, the other 2,349 grassroots Issue-Oriented Advocacy Groups and 827 Alternative Institution Development Groups supported by very active Vernal graduates would be doing similar work on other issues. For

---

* Note that in addition to these 261 groups, there would probably be many other organizations also working on this issue that had no very active Vernal graduates as members. For the purposes of this discussion, I focus here only on these 261 communities.

example, another 300 groups might attempt to challenge the prison-industrial complex. Some of these groups might lobby state legislators to cut funding for prisons and shift money to other uses in rural areas. Others would push for release of prisoners sentenced for drug possession and for rehabilitation services. Some groups might focus attention on how prison guards finance conservative legislators and work to sever this connection. Another 300 groups might seek to overhaul the political election system — advocating universal registration, campaign finance reform, informative voter pamphlets, proportional representation of parties in Congress, or other measures.

Meanwhile, hundreds of other groups might focus on comprehensive health care, toxic waste, police brutality, child abuse, income and wealth redistribution, land ownership, sweatshops, and all the other issues that must be addressed to bring about comprehensive progressive change. They would be supported by Vernal activists within progressive parties, progressive caucuses in mainstream organizations, and state and national organizations. By linking issues and supporting each other at crucial times, these independent efforts, focused on many issues, would comprise a massive movement for sweeping progressive change — a movement larger than has ever been seen in this country.

As victories were won and changes enacted, these many groups could push for deeper and broader change or shift their focus to other issues that needed attention. After decades of work, they would be able to address all the major issues and force significant change in every realm.

by being convinced of the truth of progressive ideas or she might just be attracted to the people in a change organization and their considerate ways of relating to each other — a refreshing reprieve from the fear and loathing of the dominant society.

Either way, when this person attended the change organization's meetings, she would begin to learn the group's procedures for conducting its business. By participating in cooperative decision making, she would learn how to work cooperatively and democratically with others. She would learn how to take responsibility for herself and learn the importance of looking out for others in her community. By observing the group's process, she would learn how to encourage positive dissent and constructive conflict. She would also learn how to resolve conflicts using gentle means that led to mutually satisfying results.

Other members of the change group would support her as well as encourage her to be loving and compassionate. They would expect the best of her and help her to develop a positive self-image. Whenever her previous socialization or emotional wounds led her to feel depressed or unworthy, to become greedy, narrow-minded, or immobile, or to insult or hurt other people, the other members would gently guide her back on track. They would teach her ways to overcome her self-destructive or uncivil behaviors through means of meditation, positive goal setting, journal writing, or other techniques, and they would offer counseling to help her heal her emotional wounds. Moreover, in this supportive envi-

*It's the not me in thee that makes thee so valuable to me.*
—Quaker Proverb

## CREATING COOPERATIVE ACTIVIST COMMUNITIES

These examples indicate that Vernal activists could have an immense impact in their efforts to bring about political, economic, social, and cultural change in society. Still, their greatest contribution might actually be to help build larger and stronger communities of activists. By reducing the amount of bickering and in-fighting, Vernal activists could help progressive organizations adhere more closely to progressive ideals and be more effective in accomplishing their change goals. Progressive organizations would then be more attractive to outside observers and more effective in developing and spreading a new, cooperative culture.

*Together we stand, divided we freak out.*

### Supportive and Educational Change Organizations

As an illustration, imagine a new person interested in progressive change. She might be drawn to progressive work

---

**Becoming a Social Change Activist**

There are several reasons people typically decide to become social change activists: [6]

• **Morality**: They want to do the right thing and act in consonance with their values.

• **Altruism/Empathy**: Out of an unselfish sense of concern for others' welfare, they seek to help other people.

• **Identity**: They seek to maintain the image they have of themselves as ethical and altruistic people.

• **Self-Interest**: They gain social or economic gains for participating, or they are subject to sanctions (including social pressure) for not participating.

• **Fun**: They enjoy the process of working for change. They get to be part of a fun group of like-minded people with whom they experience community, caring, and support. Or they enjoy challenging authorities and working to end oppression.

ronment, she could learn how to joyfully and lovingly play with other people — and she would have ample opportunity to do so.

By building these strong, cooperative change organizations, Vernal activists would not only act in consonance with their ideals, they would also lessen the amount of discord and ill-will in their groups — making the groups more resistant to attack or infiltration. Participating in a positive model of a good society every day would inspire hope for the future in each member.

## Communities of Support

Besides working in their own supportive change organizations, Vernal activists would also likely set up additional support links with other activists. Some would probably form tight support communities in which a small number of like-minded activists lived together, shared meals, food preparation, and maybe even their possessions and money (just like a family). Others would form looser friendship connections with activists who lived nearby, perhaps sharing a meal once a week. Some of these support communities might emphasize simple living, and some might hold ceremonies or engage in rituals that helped to bond them together. Some would likely tie together activists who all shared a particular philosophy or style. Physically remote activists might use e-mail and other electronic means of communication to connect and share with others.

No matter how loosely or closely bound, these congenial communities would provide a place for activists to interact with others who shared their perspectives and activities, and they would provide a safe environment in which activists could learn to love others openly and without fear. Within such a community, activists could build trust and develop and practice their skills of interpersonal interaction, active listening, problem solving, conflict resolution, counseling, cooperative decision-making, and leadership. In such a safe, supportive atmosphere, activists would be more likely to remember their ideals and would find it easier to stay true to them. Feeling secure in their home space, activists could venture out more courageously — tackling bigger problems, delving into riskier areas, and using more difficult or dangerous tactics.

> *We must all hang together, or most assuredly we shall all hang separately.*
> — Benjamin Franklin

These communities could also provide a source of help and a safe haven for activists when they encountered harsh opposition. By maintaining a high level of caring and understanding, such a supportive community could ensure there were always at least one or two people who could think clearly and give lovingly. If opponents crushed the spirits of some activists, those who were still in good emotional shape could nurture and counsel the rest back to health. Similarly, if some activists were physically hurt, the others could carry on the work of their fallen colleagues while helping to nurture them back to health.

### Cohesive Communities

A cohesive community is characterized by:[7]

• **Common beliefs and values**: People agree about a large number of things and are not divided too much by economic inequality or cultural heterogeneity — such as linguistic, ethnic, or religious cleavages.

• **Direct and many-sided relations**: People deal directly with each other and they relate to each other in many ways: as neighbors, friends, co-workers, fellow members of churches, kinfolk, and so forth.

• **General reciprocity and mutual aid**: People give to one another and help each other out, without any immediate expectation of a returned favor (sharing, hospitality, help, generosity, fraternity, solidarity).

• **Stable relations**: People expect to continue to interact with one another in the future so they keep each other's needs in mind.

• **Collective action**: People know how to work together and do so regularly.

• **Communal self-governance**: People decide together how to act, especially in ways that promote the common good.

• **Collective regulation**: People promote socially desirable behavior and discourage destructive behavior by offering social or economic benefits (approval, companionship, warm embraces, money, food, desirable employment, and so on) or invoking sanctions (disapproval, censure, shunning, and so on).

• **Collective mediation and conflict resolution**: People effectively mediate and resolve conflicts.

## Interconnected Communities

As the number of activist communities increased and the bonds between them grew, activists could spend more and more of their time with other supportive people who shared their worldview. They could listen to alternative radio stations, watch alternative television shows, read alternative publications, and patronize alternative businesses. Surrounded by an alternative culture, they would be less subject to conventional norms and the propaganda disseminated by elements of the power structure. This would make it even easier for them to adopt alternative perspectives and demand a good society. Moreover, their everyday actions as consumers would provide crucial support to alternative institutions and would reduce their support of conventional institutions.

## Figure 7.8: A Possible Distribution of Vernal Graduates, Steadfast Activists, and Progressive Advocates

| | Num of Orgs | Very Active Vernal Graduates | | Other Steadfast Activists | Progressive Advocates |
| --- | --- | --- | --- | --- | --- |
| | | Num/Org | Total | | |
| **Total** | | | 25,000 | 150,000 | 900,000 |
| **Local Organizations** | 5,220 | | 21,750 | 130,500 | 783,000 |
| Total in each congressional district | 12 | | 50 | 300 | 1,800 |
| *Issue Advocacy Groups* | *6* | *4* | *24* | *144* | *864* |
| *Alternative Institution Development Groups* | *2* | *4* | *8* | *48* | *288* |
| *Progressive Political Parties* | *1* | *6* | *6* | *36* | *216* |
| *Progressive Caucuses* | *3* | *4* | *12* | *72* | *432* |
| **State Organizations** | 562.5 | 4 | 2,250 | 13,500 | 81,000 |
| Average per State | 11.3 | | 45 | 270 | 1,620 |
| **National and International Organizations** | 225 | | 1,000 | 6,000 | 36,000 |
| Small | 175 | 4 | 700 | | |
| Large | 50 | 6 | 300 | | |

## THE OVERALL CONTRIBUTION OF VERNAL ACTIVISTS

Overall, with their large numbers and well-developed skills, Vernal activists should be able to greatly increase the strength, skill-level, and endurance of progressive change organizations.

### • Strength

As described above, I assume Vernal graduates and students would work many hours and do much of the actual mundane work of progressive social change groups. They would persuade people to adopt a progressive perspective and inspire people to work for change. Vernal activists would also support and encourage other progressive activists to work harder and longer, take bigger risks, stay in better physical and emotional health, and fight less with their fellow activists.

On average, I expect each very active Vernal graduate could support and encourage six other steadfast activists, each working at least three hours per week for fundamental progressive change. Assuming there were 25,000 very active graduates, they could therefore support a total of 150,000 steadfast activists (about 300 working locally in each con-

gressional district, an average of 270 working at the state level, and 6,000 working nationally).

I assume each very active Vernal graduate, working in conjunction with six steadfast activists, could support and encourage an additional thirty-six progressive advocates, each working one or two hours each week for fundamental progressive change. This would make a total of 900,000 progressive advocates working across the nation. Figure 7.8 summarizes these numbers.

If my assumptions are sound, through most of the forty years of Vernal Phase 3 there would be an average of over one million people working simultaneously for fundamental, progressive change. This would be a tremendous force of dedicated activists. I estimate this is about three times as many activists as are now working for fundamental change. Together, I estimate they would work about 3.6 times as many hours each week for comprehensive change as activists do now.*

---

* See Figure C.4 in Appendix C for the details behind these estimates.

# Figure 7.9: A Large Progressive Movement with Vernal Graduates and Other Steadfast Activists Constituting the Base

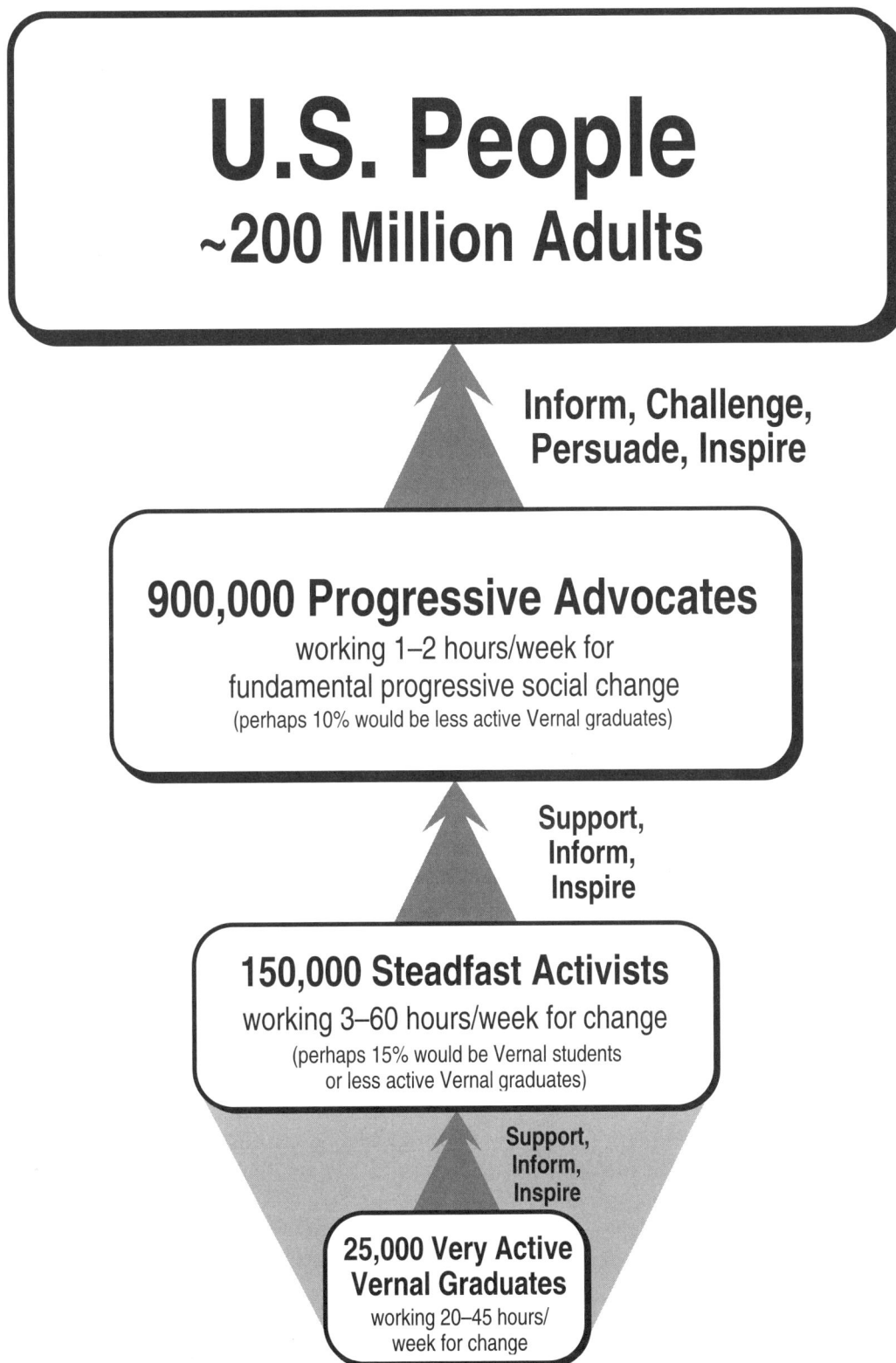

## U.S. People
### ~200 Million Adults

**Inform, Challenge, Persuade, Inspire**

## 900,000 Progressive Advocates
working 1–2 hours/week for
fundamental progressive social change
(perhaps 10% would be less active Vernal graduates)

**Support, Inform, Inspire**

## 150,000 Steadfast Activists
working 3–60 hours/week for change
(perhaps 15% would be Vernal students
or less active Vernal graduates)

**Support, Inform, Inspire**

## 25,000 Very Active Vernal Graduates
working 20–45 hours/
week for change

A million activists and advocates promoting fundamental, progressive change would be enough to personally reach a significant portion of society. These activists and advocates could also greatly bolster the progressive infrastructure and culture necessary to sustain activists. Furthermore, this many activists would provide a strong base of subscribers for progressive magazines and newspapers, a steady funding base for community-sponsored radio and television stations, and a steady base of support for political musicians, comedians, and other artists.

Figure 5.2 showed a tiered structure with very active graduates at the bottom. Figure 7.9 is identical to Figure 5.2, but includes the number of activists who I assume would be working for change in the middle of Vernal Phase 3 (Year 40) as discussed in this chapter. At the bottom of this structure would be about 25,000 very active Vernal graduates working between twenty and forty-five hours each week for fundamental progressive change.* They would support, inform, and inspire about 150,000 steadfast activists working from three to sixty hours per week for fundamental change.† Perhaps fifteen percent of these steadfast activists (22,500) would be Vernal students or less active Vernal graduates. These steadfast activists would support, inform, and inspire another 900,000 progressive advocates working one or two hours each week for fundamental change. Perhaps ten percent (90,000) of these advocates would be less active Vernal graduates.

Together, these million activists would inform, challenge, persuade, and inspire all the rest of the people of the United States. Their efforts would be directed at transforming every person in society into an empowered, responsible citizen so that we can all live together cooperatively.

### • Skills and Knowledge

Vernal activists would be much better educated than most activists today. By devoting much of their efforts to educating and personally mentoring the activists with whom they worked, they should be able to greatly increase the knowledge and skills of their colleagues. With their relatively large numbers, it would be feasible for Vernal activists to personally mentor all 150,000 steadfast activists and a significant portion of the 900,000 progressive advocates. As a result, the average knowledge and skill level of all progressive activists would likely be much greater than now, and activists would probably be significantly more effective in accomplishing their goals.

### • Endurance

By providing a solid core of activists for a large number of progressive organizations, Vernal activists would also likely increase the stamina and endurance of other activists. With good support, activists would enjoy working with their organizations more, and they would therefore persevere longer. There would probably be far less infighting and more effective work. Activists would stick around long enough to become knowledgeable and skillful and long enough to teach what they had learned to new activists.

Knowing there were a million other dedicated and skilled activists working for fundamental change would also inspire activists to work harder and remain truer to their highest ideals. It would provide the hope and inspiration that activists have long desired and needed.

*Victory belongs to the most persevering.*
— Napoleon Bonaparte

### Total Contribution

In Phase 3, the Vernal Education Project — constituting 25,000 very active Vernal graduates, around 100,000 less active Vernal graduates, and 6,000 Vernal students — would likely provide a tremendous boost to progressive organizations. They would make it possible for every community in the United States to have a large number of powerful grassroots organizations working every day for change. They could ensure that their fellow activists were well versed in the theory and practical techniques of progressive change and that their change organizations stayed on a truly progressive path. They would likely increase the skills, strength, and endurance of progressive change organizations severalfold.

In Vernal Phase 3, the combined efforts of progressive activists might add up to a force perhaps three or four times more powerful than current progressive change work. This would be an unprecedented increase in the overall power of progressive forces.

# REALIZING STAGE 2
# OF THE STRATEGIC PROGRAM

Chapter 5 described a four-stage strategic program for fundamentally transforming society. Chapter 6 outlined an education program that could realize the goals of the first stage (Lay the Groundwork).

This chapter demonstrated that if the Vernal Education Project were implemented as described in Chapter 6, it would generate a large number of skilled and experienced activists working diligently for change. These Vernal activists would greatly bolster the work of other progressive activists, increasing the strength, knowledge, skill, and endurance of progressive change organizations, especially at the grassroots. By raising awareness about the need for change and building organizational strength, Vernal activists — working with over a million other activists — could

---

* I assume, to avoid burnout, Vernal graduates would work no more than forty-five hours per week.

† Since most steadfast activists would not be Vernal graduates, some would likely work at a burnout rate of up to sixty hours per week.

successfully implement Stage 2 of the strategic program (Gather Support).

Chapter 9 shows how the million activists supported by Vernal graduates — working together over several decades — could successfully implement Stages 3 and 4 of the strategic program and fundamentally transform society.

But first, in Chapter 8, let me try to make this all seem a bit more real by telling a story about a single community organization and a few activists who make it an effective force for progressive change.

---

# NOTES FOR CHAPTER 7

[1] My thinking about the role of Vernal activists in social transformation has been greatly influenced by the Populist Movement of the 1880s and 1890s especially as portrayed by Lawrence Goodwyn, *The Populist Moment: A Short History of the Agrarian Revolt in America* (New York: Oxford University Press, 1978, E669 .G672 1978). At its peak, the Populists had 40,000 lecturers who spoke directly to people and propounded practical ideas about building alternative institutions (like cooperative banks). They provided an alternative source of information which were outside of elite propaganda channels and were less influenced by the dominant culture. Populist organizations also provided a crucial support base for the members. The long line of wagons extending across the countryside on the way to each of the mass meetings of the National Farmers Alliance and Industrial Union in the 1880s showed all the participants that they were not alone.

The movements of the 1960s also showed me the ways that universities, Black churches, rap groups, teach-ins, and the whole "counterculture" offered support and alternative education to large numbers of people and how useful this was in bolstering social change movements.

[2] Bill Moyer, *The Movement Action Plan: A Strategic Framework Describing the Eight Stages of Successful Social Movements* (San Francisco, CA: Social Movement Empowerment Project [721 Shrader Street, 94117], 1987). Moyer describes each stage and the level and kind of public support for powerholders and opposition activists in each one. He also cites the goals, tasks, and pitfalls for activists in each stage. See also Tom Atlee, "How Nonviolent Social Change Movements Develop: An Interview with Bill Moyer," *ThinkPeace* (Oakland, CA) 6, no. 2 (March/April 1990): 3–6.

[3] By "transformative reforms" I mean changes in political, economic, social, or cultural institutions that advance fundamental transformation of society. In contrast to reforms conceived on the basis that they can be won and implemented readily within the current system, transformative reforms are those required to satisfy true human needs and desires. They often require changing the current system. Furthermore, transformative reforms enable and foster even greater reform — they win the immediate goal but also

reshape the playing field to make it easier to win further victories. They build progressive infrastructure, engender an enlightened consciousness, and empower people. Moreover, they equip people with the means to make decisions democratically and the means to ensure that the reforms are implemented properly.

André Gorz, *Strategy for Labor: A Radical Proposal* (Boston: Beacon Press, 1967, HD8431 .G613), pp. 6–8, uses the terms "non-reformist reform," "revolutionary reform," "anti-capitalist reform," and "structural reform" to convey this same idea.

[4] Linda Stout, *Bridging the Class Divide and Other Lessons for Grassroots Organizing* (Boston: Beacon Press, 1996, HN65 .S75 1996), pp. 105–116.

[5] My assumptions here are based on observations of effective social change activists and organizations. The really skilled activists I have known attract many other people to their organizations, and many of those who are attracted become activists and begin to work for change. Skilled activists know how to support people, teach them, and encourage them.

I assume that Vernal graduates would approach their level of skill and so would have comparable levels of success in encouraging other people to become activists. In considering several of these outstanding activists, I estimated that they are able to bring in and support roughly four to ten other people who then work significant amounts of time for change (and are therefore "steadfast activists"). I believe a skilled activist should be able to support at least four or five other people, but generally, it is difficult for an activist to give personal attention to more than nine or ten. So here, I assume that each very active Vernal graduate would be able to support an average of six other steadfast activists.

From my observations of social change organizations, it appears that effective organizations typically have many times as many "advocates" (people who are mostly busy with other parts of their lives, but who provide financial support and a bit of volunteer energy to the organization) as active members (steadfast activists). In considering these organizations, it appears that they attract somewhere around three to ten times as many advocates as steadfast activists. Here, I assume there are six progressive advocates for every steadfast activist (not counting the very active Vernal activists). This estimate is also very rough, but seems reasonable.

[6] I derived these five reasons from two sources: (1) Michael Taylor, "Rationality and Revolutionary Collective Action," in Michael Taylor, ed., *Rationality and Revolution* (New York: Cambridge University Press, 1988, HX550 .R48R37 1988): 63–97 (especially pp. 85–87). His analysis draws on Howard Margolis, *Selfishness, Altruism and Rationality: A Theory of Social Choice* (New York: Cambridge University Press, 1982, HB846.8 .M37), Tibor Scitovsky, *The Joyless Economy: An Inquiry into Human Satisfaction and Consumer Dissatisfaction* (New York: Oxford University Press, 1976, HB801 .S35), and Stanley Benn, "The Problematic Rationality of Political Participation," in Peter Laslett and James Fishkin, eds., *Philosophy, Politics and Society,* 5th series (New Haven: Yale University Press, 1979, JA71 .L27); (2) Michael Albert, *Why Radicalism?*, a lecture recorded at Z Media Institute, Summer 1998, Boston, MA, available from *Z Magazine.*

[7] I derived these points from Michael Taylor, "Rationality and Revolutionary Collective Action," in Michael Taylor, ed., ***Rationality and Revolution*** (New York: Cambridge University Press, 1988, HX550 .R48R37 1988): 63–97 (especially pp. 68, 71). Taylor discusses the first three points in more detail in Michael Taylor, ***Community, Anarchy, and Liberty*** (New York: Cambridge University Press, 1982, HX833 .T39 1982), pp. 26–32.

In these works, Taylor convincingly argues that cohesive communities, able to provide a strong social foundation, are crucial for bringing about fundamental change and maintaining a good society.

Michael Taylor and Sara Singleton, "The Communal Resource: Transaction Costs and the Solution of Collective Action Problems," ***Politics & Society*** 21, no. 2 (June 1993), 195–214, argue that the transaction costs (search costs, bargaining costs, and monitoring and enforcement costs) of reaching and implementing an optimal collective solution are greatly reduced in a cohesive community.

For a more general discussion of collective action, see Mancur Olson's defining work, ***The Logic of Collective Action: Public Goods and the Theory of Groups*** (1965; revised edition, New York: Schocken Books, 1971, HM131 .O55 1971). Olson explores the factors that encourage and prevent people from working together. In particular, he describes the "free rider" problem in which non-contributors have little incentive to work collectively with others since they receive the same benefits from a public good as do hard-working contributors. For a good review of the literature on collective action since 1965, see Pamela E. Oliver, "Formal Models of Collective Action," ***Annual Review of Sociology*** 19 (1993): 271-300.

# 8

# Melissa's Story:
## A Tale Illustrating Some Aspects of the Vernal Education Project

## A BAD MEETING GETS BETTER

A group of twenty caring people gathers on this Tuesday night at Linda's house. They are concerned that a growing number of pre-teens in their town seem to be heading toward juvenile delinquency. They hope to formulate a proposal for positive action to present to the town council. They are a diverse group: a dozen concerned parents, an anti-drug crusader, a librarian at the public library where teens often gather after school, an owner of a local business that was vandalized by teens, a social worker who often works with teens, some good-hearted humanitarians, and a few people who seem to come just for the opportunity to hear themselves talk. Once again they are faced with a difficult decision.

This time around the group seems to be divided into three distinct camps aligned around specific positions, plus a few people who are unaligned and a few who are very con-

fused. The gulf between their many positions seems enormous and impossible to bridge. Evidently believing that the best defense is a good offense, members of each camp have rehearsed their invectives, and they now sarcastically ridicule each other's positions. People begin to interrupt each other and make snide comments under their breaths. As the meeting grinds on and everyone's frustration mounts, subtle insults give way to direct attacks. What seemed at the beginning to be a simple problem is now a convoluted tangle, poisoned by personal venom.

After forty-five minutes, the group seems further than ever from reaching a solution. Moreover, a great deal of ill will has developed among these people — enough to poison every other agenda topic, too. It looks like this will be another disastrous meeting — perhaps the one that finally splinters the group into oblivion.

\*　　　　\*　　　　\*

*You have probably seen this before. Business meetings, club meetings, congressional debates, informal discussions — everywhere the same scenario plays out. The United States Senate — idealized as the greatest deliberative body in the world — frequently looks more like a playpen filled with ignorant and insecure children squabbling with each other over nonsense. Even in meetings of caring people who are trying to make the world more cooperative, loving, altruistic, and fair, the same dynamics usually arise: posturing, defensiveness, attacks, ridicule, anger, frustration, disempowerment, and disintegration. It happens so often, it seems as natural and as inevitable as rain. Fortunately, it is not.*

*        *        *

Suddenly Melissa, an assertive young woman new to the group, interrupts the wrangling. Diplomatically she says, "Let me try to summarize what I've heard." She then carefully restates every idea presented — often more clearly, more objectively, and less melodramatically than it was originally presented — and points out where each idea agrees or conflicts with every other. It is evident that by doing so, she is validating every perspective and implicitly validating the people holding that perspective. She is also drawing a clear map of the issues.

"We seem to all agree about this one point, but several people disagree about this other one. Let's explore this disagreement. Why do we hold these different perspectives? What life experience has led you to hold your view?"

She then encourages them all to speak in turn — relating their history and how it has led them to their current outlook. In this context, people's perspectives no longer seem to be incompatible descriptions of reality, but more like an array of flowers — each lovely in its own way, each as valid as the next, and each uniquely valuable.

"There appear to be several ways of looking at this issue. Perhaps every one of them is true. How can we resolve these seeming contradictions? Is there some solution that can encompass them all?"

By now, everyone is feeling much safer and more inclined to be cooperative. They feel considerably more amenable to solving this puzzle together. People begin suggesting possible solutions and exploring whether the solutions would address everyone's concerns. A few solutions emerge that seem to address most of the major concerns. New concerns arise, and people suggest further modifications to the solutions that might resolve these concerns. Rather than impediments to progress, doubts and objections now seem valuable — like warning signs that might prevent the group from swerving into a ditch.

After a while, several solutions evolve into one that seems satisfactory. This solution excites many people and doesn't appear to have any major drawbacks. A few people admit they can accept it even though to do so they must back away from their earlier strong positions. A few others are still reluctant to adopt the solution, but realize it is probably the best one this group could ever come up with. They agree to go along with the decision too.

The meeting progresses well and the group tackles and resolves one issue after another. Melissa's purposeful, yet cheerful demeanor encourages others to act the same way. The frustration and disillusionment that permeated the room just an hour before has now been replaced with eager excitement.

Melissa is clearly leading the process, but no one feels she is manipulative. Rather, they feel she is supporting them all and helping them work together to clear away obstacles.

When someone expresses amazement at her skill, Melissa explains that she attended an educational program — called the Vernal Education Program — where she observed good meetings, learned basic process skills, and was allowed to practice with other students until she could facilitate meetings well. "It's really pretty easy — as easy as learning to drive a car."

*        *        *

*Human interaction is learned behavior. Like growing vegetables, fixing a car, or programming a computer, anyone can learn the basics of these tasks and some people have learned how to do each one well. The more we learn and the more we practice, the better we can perform these tasks.*

*Yet, our society treats human interaction as if it is mysterious — unknowable and uncontrollable. It is astounding that our society — a melting pot of diverse people and ideas and dedicated to democracy — has done such a poor job of teaching these basic skills of peaceful interaction and democratic process. Our schools spend more time teaching children to obey than they do teaching them how to cooperate. Most books and television shows teach us that conflicts can only be resolved through violence, intimidation, or sexual manipulation, and then bombard us with particularly dreadful examples of these techniques.*

*Only in the last few decades have schools begun to teach cooperative interaction skills. Unfortunately, most of these classes are oriented toward business and psychology students as if only business leaders and their therapists needed to know these important skills.*

*        *        *

## AN EMOTIONAL SNAG

The entire group agrees this is the best meeting they have ever had. Moreover, they admit they are actually having fun. Everything is going along great until Steven makes one careless remark. Unbeknownst to the group, Melissa is extremely sensitive about rape. When Steven offhandedly scoffs at a rape incident reported in the news, Melissa unexpectedly responds with a sharp comment. Then Mark attempts to smooth things out by dismissing the importance of Steven's original remark, but this makes Melissa see red. She turns toward Mark, her rage beginning to leak through her normal calm, and almost makes a nasty retort. She controls herself but clearly is disturbed. A dark cloud hangs over the room. Everyone knows the peace has been broken, and many people begin preparing themselves for another dirty battle. Melissa tries to get things back on track, but she is distracted and upset. The bond of cooperation has been shattered.

\*          \*          \*

*Each of us has been hurt by other people, and many of our old wounds remain unhealed. Whenever someone pokes our open wounds, we are likely to react with irrational fear, grief, anger, or violence. Sometimes we realize our feelings are inappropriate and stop, but often we cannot see it or stop it — especially when we feel isolated or powerless. Then we are likely to lash out at others.*

\*          \*          \*

Lester, a quiet, elderly man also new to the group, stands up, walks over next to Melissa, and addresses the group. "Rape is not a joking matter. It devastates women and dehumanizes us all. I want us all to agree we won't say things like that — things that hurt other people." He then turns to Melissa and offers his shoulder. Melissa hugs him and begins crying softly. Lester gently holds her. This makes the other people uneasy, so Lester speaks calmly to them over Melissa's shoulder. "Don't worry; it's OK. People cry sometimes when they're hurt. Then they stop, and it's all OK." Lester continues to hold Melissa. "Melissa knows me and trusts me not to hurt her or make fun of her."

Then while Melissa softly cries, he continues talking over her shoulder to the group, explaining that when people have been hurt, they need to express all their feelings in a safe environment. "Every week Melissa and I get together and support one another. When I was a child, my father used to criticize me constantly and whip me with his belt whenever he thought I disagreed with him. It made me angry, resentful, and afraid. Melissa has helped me overcome these feelings. I'm no longer afraid to speak out, and I'm no longer so furious or bitter. She reassures me that I didn't cause my father's rage, holds me while I cry, and encourages me to step outside of these old hurts and move forward. Then I do the same for her." As he speaks about his hurt, his voice begins to falter and his lower lip trembles just a bit. He pauses momentarily, looking somewhat uneasy and uncertain. Melissa then hugs him tighter. This seems to refocus his attention and bolster his resolve. He clears his throat and continues in a strong voice. "Like many women, Melissa is very sensitive about rape."

He then describes how rape affects women — how horrible it is to be terrorized and controlled by a rapist, how long it takes for a woman to feel safe again and to feel comfortable again with her body. As he talks about particularly painful aspects of rape and oppression of women, Melissa sobs deeply and he holds her closer. He continues for several minutes and everyone else sits in stunned silence. Several people have tears in their eyes and Rachel coughs uncomfortably. Melissa stops crying and reassures everyone

she is all right. She is still shaken, but asks the group to continue with the meeting as she sits down.

Lester checks that she is OK and then begins facilitating the meeting right where Melissa had left off. Though not as adept as Melissa, he clearly is also quite skilled. At first, there is some awkwardness in the discussion, but after a few minutes everyone relaxes, especially when Melissa's clear, calm voice rejoins the discussion.

By the end of the meeting, Melissa is once again cheerful and open. As people begin to leave, she makes an effort to reconnect with both Steven and Mark. They are a bit cautious, expecting her to lash out at them, but clearly, she feels no ill will. They are relieved by her demeanor. Still a bit anxious, they clumsily apologize to her for their statements and Melissa graciously accepts their apologies.

Impressed by what she saw in the meeting, Rachel approaches Lester. She asks him where he learned to facilitate and how he learned to deal with emotional upheavals so well. He says he attended the same Vernal Education Program as Melissa and learned how to support people there. It was also where he first tackled his own deep emotional hurts.

\*          \*          \*

*In difficult times, it helps a great deal to be able to retreat to a safe place with someone to comfort us — while someone else carries our workload. Then, in this safe environment, we can let our emotions out and take some time to understand what inflamed us. Unfortunately, in our current society, when we show fear or grief, we are more often belittled, ridiculed, or even beaten. We quickly learn to hide our feelings and pretend we are not injured, driving the hurt deeper inside. Forced to swallow our hurts, we may decide it is best to avoid any potentially dangerous situation so we will never risk being hurt again. Or we may come to believe we can only be safe if we dominate and control others.*

\*          \*          \*

## MELISSA'S REVELATION

As they leave the meeting, Lori tells Melissa how upset she was by Steven's insensitive comment about rape and by Melissa crying. Melissa reassures Lori that she is OK, but that she is still recovering from a brutal rape. "I'm still emotionally tender," she says, "but I'm getting better and better at standing up for myself and other women."

"Yes, we've got to stick together," Lori agrees. "I was raped by my uncle when I was just twelve. That's when I realized you can never trust men — even if they act like they're kind. My uncle hurt me horribly. It took me a long time to realize that I wasn't to blame — he kept telling me my innocence and beauty made him do it. He made me hate myself for being pretty. But I finally figured out it was his fault — not mine. *He* did it to me.

"Sometimes, I wish I could inflict as much pain on him as he has caused me — I wish I could slowly torture him to death and watch him writhe in pain. It's time we women stood together and stood up to men. Don't you think it would be better if we started our own group with just women? Then we wouldn't have to deal with guys like Steven and Mark and their neanderthal ideas about women."

\*       \*       \*

*When we are deeply traumatized, we may seek revenge against the people who hurt us. We often blame a particular individual or generalize to a large class of people. At best, this can be divisive. At worst, it can spread the violence and trauma, engulfing others in the same vicious pattern of fear and hatred.*

\*       \*       \*

Melissa is startled by Lori's forthrightness. She feels she must respond in kind, so she takes Lori's hand and looks into her eyes. "I certainly understand how much your uncle must have hurt you. After I was raped, I was afraid to be around any men. I felt horrible and dirty. For quite a while I was deeply depressed, and I wasn't sure I wanted to live in this world. When I finally felt my strength return, I was so angry I wanted to kill every man who looked at me. For months, I stomped around, filled with rage, snarling at everyone until even my friends were afraid of me. I knew my rage was justified and it felt like the more anger I had, the stronger I was. But eventually, I came to realize that I was becoming as full of hatred as that rapist — he was winning because he was turning me into a monster as vile as himself. Just as he hated women and desired to crush my spirit, I was beginning to hate men and wanted to crush them. And I realized I couldn't go on hating everyone or it would just rot me from the inside out. I knew hating like that would eventually destroy me.

"Finally, I saw that I could only really win if I stood for love and compassion against his hatred. I realized I could only respect myself again if I started acting like a civilized human. And I knew I could only do *that* if I forgave myself for being overcome by hatred. It was then that I realized that the rapist might also have been overcome by hatred that was induced by some traumatic experience, and I did my best to feel compassion for him. I didn't forgive him for what he did to me, but I tried to understand why he was so full of hatred — what must have happened to him to make him hate women so much that he could methodically rape

and terrorize me. Whatever it was must have been horrible — maybe it was even worse than what he did to me.

"That's how I came to realize that I had to work against *all* injustice, against *all* hatred, against *all* oppression wherever I find it — in myself or in others. I wasn't sure exactly how to go about it or where to start. I was still very wary of men.

"But then I attended this wonderful education program — the Vernal Education Program — and met some men like Lester — gentle, loving men who are also completely dedicated to ending the oppression of women. I discovered other people who had also realized that hatred just generates more hatred in a stupid, endless cycle. I found they had a better way to transform society that didn't rely on hatred. So that's what I am trying to do now."

\*       \*       \*

*It is often difficult to see the humanity in those who have hurt us badly. But if we can see the ways we sometimes hurt other people, we can begin to understand the origins of hatred and cruelty. We can begin to recognize the forces that drive us, and we can start to empathize with others, even those who appear completely hardened and depraved. Rather than focusing narrowly on revenge or on defending ourselves, we can broaden our perspective and consider how to transform ourselves and our society so no one is hurt, oppressed, or exploited.*

\*       \*       \*

## A BEAUTIFUL VISION

Melissa continued: "I'm working now towards completely eliminating rape. I intend to change the world until rape and all other forms of sexual abuse of women are no longer part of it."

This statement astounded Lori. "No more rape or sexual abuse? How could you possibly eliminate these things? As long as men are running around loose they're going to rape women and abuse girls, aren't they?"

"No, I don't believe so," Melissa replied. "Most men don't abuse women — most men find it abhorrent. If we accept abuse as natural male behavior or inevitable, we are actually providing brutal men with an excuse for their violent acts. By doing so, we make it more likely they'll be violent. I think we have to emphatically insist that sexual abuse isn't natural and we won't tolerate it anymore.

"Also, in looking carefully at this, I realized that some women are much more vulnerable to being abused than others. Some women have been hurt so much, they just expect to get hurt more. And some are so poor or weak they cannot protect themselves. If they were stronger, less vulnerable to domination and exploitation, and more self-assured, they would be safer.

"I'm working to empower women to stand up to male violence. I think we can force men to stop raping and abusing women. I'm also committed to changing our culture until rape is considered even more detestable than slavery is now viewed. And I intend to find out what it is that makes men rape so we can change things enough that no boy will ever grow up to become a rapist. I know it sounds incredible, but I'm convinced it's possible. Human beings learn how to be cruel and vicious, and they can just as readily learn how to be kind and compassionate. I think we just have to change the conditions that lead men to rape.

"I'm convinced it is possible, and I'm committed to making it happen. I want to live in a world where rape is unthinkable. I want to walk down the street unafraid. I want every woman to be able to walk wherever she wants without fear. And I intend to make it that way."

\*           \*           \*

*Oppression is not inevitable. The idea of hurting another person is a concept that children learn. Motivation for hurting others comes from the anger and fear of unhealed emotional wounds. Opportunity for hurting another arises when people are so poor or beaten down that they cannot defend themselves. Oppression can be ended by teaching children how and why not to hurt others, by healing people's emotional wounds, and by building everyone up so they cannot be easily victimized.*

\*           \*           \*

Lori is completely flabbergasted. Melissa's ideas seem to make sense, but they are so new to her that she can't accept them. "But it just doesn't seem possible. You're saying we could change boys so they never grow up even thinking of raping women. I can't imagine that ever happening."

Melissa tries to convince her. "Just because something exists now doesn't mean it has to always exist. Women were once accused of being witches and burned at the stake. Now they aren't. For centuries, girls were considered the property of their fathers and women were considered the property of their husbands. It was considered acceptable for men to use and abuse women however they wanted. But now this is unacceptable. If people could change those terrible practices, then we can stop other kinds of oppression, too."

"But it just doesn't seem possible," Lori scoffs. "If we could do that, then why don't we end poverty, war, and disease while we're at it? We could just live perfect lives forever."

Melissa responds passionately: "Well, I'm not convinced we can eliminate disease or aging, but I see no reason for poverty or war. Our world is rich enough that there's no good reason for poverty. And war doesn't accomplish any-

thing useful. Why not eliminate them both? I'd like to live in a world where brutality and violence of all kinds are rare oddities — a world where no one fears bodily harm from others. And more than that — where no one lacks food, shelter, medical care, or loving support. I would like everyone in the world to be at least as powerful, as assertive, and as loving as I have learned to be — or rather, even *more* so — as much as I hope to be. I think it is possible, and I'm working toward making it a reality."

"But how could we possibly do this?" Lori asks skeptically.

"I think the first step is just to imagine a better society. We have to envision the kind of world we want to live in. I've been fortunate to hear and read some extraordinary ideas."

When Lori asks Melissa where she heard these ideas, Melissa tells her she learned of them in the same Vernal Education Program.

\*           \*           \*

*Our vision of what could be is often limited to what currently exists. The first step to improvement is to conceive of a better world. If we can imagine it, then there may be a way to create it. A clear image of a positive future can also inspire us to do the hard work required to make it a reality.*

\*           \*           \*

## THINGS GO BETTER WITH GOOD SUPPORT

Lori likes hearing Melissa describe her vision, but she is still cynical about the prospects for change.

"Well that sounds great, but it's not so easy to make changes. I once tried to stand up to some men in the plaza who were making sexist remarks and lewd gestures towards the women there. Those jerks just laughed at me, made nasty comments, and then threatened me. As I walked away, one of them followed me for a while, and I was afraid he might hurt me. They harassed me just for challenging their remarks. What would happen if I really stood up to sexual violence? I might get killed."

\*           \*           \*

*When we challenge oppression, we often become a target for that oppression. This can be terrifying — sometimes even deadly.*

\*           \*           \*

"I know," Melissa assured her. "Making significant change can be dangerous. I think the man who raped me may have done it partly to punish me for my efforts to protect women from male violence. Oppression is very powerful, and it is pervasive throughout our society. Especially in the situation you described, you were there by yourself, a single individual trying to stand up to a whole group of men. You were trying to confront not only their ideas, but also the whole culture behind those ideas. It's no wonder that you weren't able to accomplish very much.

"But what if you were there with a hundred other women and you were only confronting a few guys? And what if there were tens of thousands of other women and men all over the country confronting sexism at the very same time — at the very same moment in hundreds of places? In those circumstances, you would be much more likely to have an impact.

"And what if beforehand, you had met with the other hundred women and you had given each other encouragement and support and then practiced techniques to challenge sexist behavior in a powerful way? What if afterwards you all got together and talked about what had happened, how it felt for you, and how you might do better in the future? With that kind of love and support, it would probably be a whole lot easier. That's what I'm trying to do: to set it up so we can be powerful and also reasonably safe as we vigorously challenge oppression.

"Especially since I was raped, it is very difficult for me to stand up to angry men. But I am determined to do it, and with enough good support, I know I can do it. When I know what I am getting into — when I've practiced my response beforehand, and I'm well supported — it is much easier for me to act courageously. And I think that's true for everyone."

*   *   *

*It is always easier to do tasks when you have solid support from others and you have the necessary skills and experience to do a good job. This is especially true of a difficult task like working for comprehensive social change.*

*   *   *

## POWERFULLY CHALLENGING OPPRESSION

Melissa paints a pretty picture, but Lori is still skeptical. At the next meeting, Lori has a chance to put Melissa's vision to the test. She describes a recent incident that begs for an immediate response.

The previous Saturday night, a prominent businessman in the community beat his wife nearly to death while they were arguing about their relationship. On Monday, while she was lying in a coma, the local newspaper ran an opinion column by a senior staff editor that tried to justify his action by arguing that although the beating was deplorable, it was understandable because she had had an affair with another man. Sentiments in town are now split, largely along gender lines. Many men feel that she got what she deserved, and most women are horrified by the violence and worry about the fate of the woman.

"What should we do about this?" Lori asks Melissa, wondering if she could come up with a response as bold and captivating as her vision. "Here's a perfect example of male oppression supported by the good ol' boys at the newspaper. We should do something."

"You're right," Melissa replies without hesitation. When the meeting begins, she raises the issue for the group to discuss. Lori and Melissa relate their direct experience of gender oppression and insist there must be a strong, pointed response by both women and men. Lester vociferously backs their perspective and points out that oppression of any person degrades everyone.

However, some people are afraid to take a public stand. Mark argues that this has little to do with juvenile delinquency and will just divert their attention from their goal. Melissa replies that standing up for what is right directly addresses juvenile delinquency by demonstrating how moral people should act and providing a model of good behavior for teenagers.

Steven then argues that perhaps the newspaper editor knows more about what really happened, and he speculates that the wife may have attacked her husband first. This makes Lori extremely angry. At first, she is filled with bitter disgust. Then, as other men nod agreement, she collapses into disheartened resignation and slumps in her chair. Sensing the group will find it difficult to reach any kind of consensus, Margot tries to end the discussion and have the group move on.

*   *   *

*Many people are afraid to take a stand on contentious issues. They may feel they don't know enough, they may be afraid of making a mistake, or they may fear being hurt. People are especially afraid of divisive issues that fissure along lines of gender, race, ethnicity, and religion since people may find themselves in bitter conflict with their friends.*

*   *   *

Melissa points out that the newspaper article says nothing about the wife attacking the husband. Further, she insists that no matter what happened, there is *never* any justification for hurting another person. She then declares that this is an extremely important example of oppression. "We are here because we care about teenagers and don't want them to be hurt. Don't we also care about women? Don't we also want *women* not to be hurt? I am opposed to all oppression wherever I see it. This is an outrageous example of oppression, and I feel we must speak out. Standing aside would tacitly endorse domination of women."

Lester then joins her in arguing that everyone must take a principled stand against violence and against the newspaper's attempt to exonerate the husband and his brutality. With both of them advocating the same position, both speaking clearly and eloquently, they are finally able to persuade everyone in the group to act. They are so persuasive that even Steven finally comes around.

The group decides to organize a march of both women and men who oppose domestic violence. The march will begin at noon on Thursday of the following week. They decide to march from the hospital to the front of the newspaper office where they will demand a retraction of the opinion column. They all agree to call everyone they know who might be sympathetic, tell them how important it is to come, and ask them to call their friends. Everyone in the group does this, and it appears that the march will be quite large.

Melissa and Lester show themselves particularly proficient at organizing a political event and ensuring every important preparatory task is accomplished. When Lori asks them where they learned to argue for a position so well and to organize demonstrations, they reply that they learned and practiced these skills in the Vernal Education Program.

\*                    \*                    \*

*A lone voice can easily be drowned out or ignored, but when several people back each other up, they can have much greater influence. This is especially true when they are knowledgeable and well spoken. People are often willing to join with anyone who can clearly articulate high-minded action. Sometimes, it seems, people are just waiting for the right encouragement — then they will jump in.*

\*                    \*                    \*

## BUILDING A BROAD ALLIANCE

Preparations for the march are going well until the town's police chief threatens to arrest everyone who marches unless they have a parade permit. He also refuses to issue a permit, claiming the event will be disruptive. The newspaper then reports that the mayor and several members of the city council are supportive of the police chief's position.

When it becomes clear this will discourage many people from attending, Lori confesses her frustration to Melissa. "Suddenly everyone I talk to has a prior engagement for Thursday at noon," she moans. "The whole town structure

is circling the wagons to protect this jerk. This morning, the head of the Chamber of Commerce — a woman! — issued a statement commending the generosity of the husband as an employer and benefactor of nonprofit social organizations. She also implied that anyone who wanted to have a job in this town should keep her mouth shut.

"Everyone is now afraid to come to the march. We may end up with just a few people — the same handful of people who always work against oppression of women.

"I am so angry. You know, I wouldn't be unhappy if the windows of the newspaper and all those other businesses downtown were smashed into a thousand pieces. I wouldn't even be sad if some of those guys got hurt when their windows shattered. It would serve them right for acting like such asses!"

\*                    \*                    \*

*In this country, there has developed a circle of powerful people who control important societal institutions. They are implicitly supported by employees of those institutions. Often, when members of this elite are challenged, they use their positions of power to protect themselves and to crush their opposition. They also regularly use their power to enrich themselves at the expense of others.*

*When ordinary people see how difficult it is to challenge the power structure, they often give up. Those who are especially frustrated and angry may consider violent responses or misdirect their anger towards less powerful people who can't fight back.*

\*                    \*                    \*

Melissa takes Lori's hand. "I know how this upsets you. It's so clearly wrong. They know they're wrong, so they use their might to intimidate people and thwart our efforts. Still, I don't want to resort to their tactics. I don't want to brutalize people in the same way they do. And we don't need to do that: I have another plan that should work much better."

She then tells Lori that she has contacted several dozen people of goodwill in neighboring cities and all across the country. "These people are willing to make an issue of our situation in their communities. They are writing letters to the editors of their local newspapers, calling radio and TV stations, leafleting, and planning rallies for the same day. They are trying to focus critical attention on the elite in this town and embarrass them into behaving properly. Their support should also embolden people in this town to take a stand. We need to alert everyone that we have support from across the country."

Melissa, Lori, and Lester then spread the word to their group and throughout their community. When people learn of this support, they feel less isolated and realize they might actually have enough power to win this struggle. Most agree to defer their other "plans" and come to the march. Members of the city council and the mayor are bombarded with calls and letters from townspeople and from people all over the country condemning their stance and their cowardice. Sensing the changing atmosphere, one of the more progressive members of the city council, who has been silent up to this point, denounces the police chief's action in a radio interview. Melissa, Lori, and Lester quickly spread the word about this interview to everyone they can in town.

By the day of the demonstration, several hundred people are willing to defy the police chief and risk arrest. Just before the march is to begin, the police chief backs down and issues a parade permit. The crowd then marches to the newspaper office and engages in a festive picket at the front doors. Most are wearing yellow sashes — made by women in the garden club — as a symbol of their support for the battered woman. Many people vow to boycott the newspaper unless it changes its position. Melissa and Lester lead the group in singing "We Shall Overcome." Then Rachel stands up and leads the crowd in a group moan, which grows into a group yell of love and support. People leave feeling energized and excited.

The next day, the newspaper runs an editorial partially apologizing for running the opinion column and pointing out the need for more investigation of the issue. The editor also commissions a female reporter — who had been asking for years to write articles on issues of concern to women — to write an in-depth series of articles on the situation and the larger issue of domestic violence.

At the next meeting, everyone is excited about being part of this successful campaign. They are energized and willing to work even harder on the issue of teenage delinquency.

Lori asks Melissa how she was able to garner so much support so quickly for their cause from all across the country. Melissa tells her that she contacted other people she met at the Vernal Education Program and other graduates of the Vernal network. She said they all had a long-standing agreement to help each other out whenever possible. Many of these activists were already working on the issue of domestic violence so it was easy to mobilize support. Lori then asks Melissa if it might be possible for her to attend the Vernal Education Program.

"Certainly," she answers. "I can loan you a book that describes it and then you could apply for admission to the local center."

# 9

# *Transforming Society*

Chapter 7 described how Vernal activists could support and educate hundreds of thousands of other activists and greatly increase the strength and endurance of progressive change organizations. If the Vernal Project developed as projected here, in forty years Vernal activists would generate a force for progressive change that would be perhaps three or four times greater than now — with about one million activists working for fundamental change.

This chapter shows how all these activists, working together, could fundamentally transform society.

## THE DYNAMICS OF SOCIETAL CHANGE

A progressive movement that is three or four times more powerful than now would have a profound impact on society. Presumably, it would be three or four times as effective in challenging the power structure and overcoming the barriers of widespread ignorance, oppressive cultural norms, and dysfunctional emotional conditioning. However, because of the particular dynamics of social change, if this powerful progressive effort were sustained over many decades, it would likely have an even greater impact — dramatically increasing the chances for ultimate success.

This section first discusses the general dynamics of the diffusion of new ideas or practices through society. Then it explores how conflictive social change enhances these dynamics. Finally, it describes how skilled and dedicated Vernal activists could help other progressive activists take advantage of these dynamics.

### Diffusion of Innovations

Progressive social change activists seek to shift the consciousness of large numbers of people so that they will accept creative new ideas, engage in fresh, positive behaviors, and support alternative institutions. In short, activists seek to spread progressive innovations until they are adopted across society.

It takes time for any innovation to be widely adopted, even a non-controversial one such as a new technology like the telephone. Social researchers have studied the "diffusion of innovation" process extensively. They have learned what it takes to communicate new ideas (including political and cultural ideas) and effective ways to encourage people to adopt them.[1]

### STAGES IN ADOPTING AN INNOVATION

Generally, in adopting an innovation, people go through six main stages.

**1. Need**: People experience a problem and feel a need for a new idea or practice that solves the problem.

"Early needers" — those who first experience the problem and feel a need for an alternative — are those who are injured or stymied by the current situation and desire something better. But it is not just anyone who is injured or stymied. The poor and downtrodden experience the problems of our society most strongly, but they often believe these problems are inevitable. People who feel a need must believe that there is some possible solution to their problem.

**2. Gain Knowledge**: People learn about an innovation and gather information about it.

People may learn about an innovation by traveling to another place where the innovation is used or from a visitor who has already used the innovation. One-way, mass information channels such as television, radio, and newspapers are often effective means to let people know that an innovation exists and that it might solve a problem.

Progressive activists, who are unable to pay for advertising and find it difficult to obtain favorable media attention, can instead use alternative mass media like newsletters, street speaking, tabling, e-mail, web pages, and dramatic protest demonstrations that the news media will cover.

Generally "early knowers" have higher education and are more tuned into affairs outside of their own lives — they are more cosmopolitan, they travel more, they have a greater exposure to the mass media, they have greater social contact with other people, and so on.

**3. Shift Opinion**: People are persuaded that the innovation is one they should adopt.

Once they learn about an innovation, people are curious and seek more information about the new idea. They evaluate the new idea and mentally try it out in their own lives. They want to know what benefits and drawbacks it may have in their situation.

Generally, they are most persuaded to adopt the innovation if:

• The innovation appears to have a large relative advantage over their existing practice — it is cheaper, saves time or effort, is more convenient, is more satisfying, is more ethical, or bestows higher prestige.

• The innovation is compatible with their needs, existing values, and past experiences.

## Figure 9.1: Typical Steps in the Adoption of an Innovation

| Typical Steps | Role of Change Agent to Accelerate Adoption |
|---|---|
| 1. **Need**: People experience a problem and feel a need for an innovation that solves the problem. | Change agents can help people recognize their need for change or show them an innovation that illuminates how difficult their lives are without it. |
| 2. **Gain Knowledge**: People learn about an innovation and gather information about it. | Change agents can broadcast information that describes the new innovation and extols its benefits. Change agents should present the innovation within the context of existing ideas and practices and explain the innovation using familiar terminology. |
| 3. **Shift Opinion**: People are persuaded that the innovation is one they should adopt. | Change agents can arrange for people to meet with their peers who have already adopted the innovation. They can also provide samples or arrange opportunities for people to experiment with the innovation. |
| 4. **Decide**: People decide to adopt (or reject) the innovation. | Change agents can encourage people to adopt the innovation. |
| 5. **Implement**: People implement the innovation and adapt it to their own circumstances. | Change agents can ensure that people understand how to use the innovation and how to modify it sufficiently to meet their particular needs. |
| 6. **Confirm**: People confirm that the innovation works well for them and integrate it into their normal routine (or they realize it does not work for them and discontinue using it). | Change agents can arrange for adopters to hear from other satisfied adopters so they do not feel isolated or wrongheaded in their decision to adopt. |

• The innovation is not too difficult to understand or use.

• Before they try it, they can observe other people using the innovation in an environment similar to their own — they can watch "early adopters" or see a demonstration project.

• They receive positive evaluations from their peers who have already tried it in a situation similar to their own.

• They can experiment with the innovation for a short time in a limited way — they can try out a sample or perform a small trial.

• Their peers encourage them to adopt the innovation.

• Society encourages them (via the mass media) to adopt the innovation.

Generally, in shifting their opinion, people are influenced more by face-to-face discussions with their peers than they are by mass media pronouncements. People seek solid information, especially from peers whom they have already judged to be trustworthy, sensible, and a good source of accurate information and opinion on other innovations ("opinion leaders"). People are also persuaded more by a two-way discussion that addresses their specific concerns and uses familiar terminology. This is especially true if the innovation is difficult to understand, difficult to implement, or dangerous.

Sometimes a timely event helps to promote the innovation. For example, being laid off from her job may encourage someone to question the current system of employment that is dominated by large corporations. It may encourage her to look favorably on employee-owned businesses or other kinds of cooperatives.

**4. Decide**: People decide to adopt (or reject) the
    innovation.

People generally adopt an innovation sooner if it has a low initial cost, provides immediate rewards, and has a catchy name with positive connotations. People are also more inclined to adopt an innovation if they are offered an incentive, though they may discontinue the innovation as soon as the incentive ends.

Compared to later adopters, early adopters generally:
• Are better educated.
• Have higher aspirations (for education, occupation, and so on).
• Have higher social status and greater resources (they can risk more without fear) *or*
• Have fewer resources (they have less to lose and a greater incentive for change).
• Are better able to cope with uncertainty and risk.
• Are less fatalistic.
• Are more open-minded (less dogmatic, more open to change, more imaginative).
• Are more likely to be opinion leaders for their peers.
• Are better at dealing with abstractions (such as innovations they have never seen).

**5. Implement**: People implement the innovation and adapt
    it to their own circumstances.

In this stage, people seek information about how to obtain the innovation, how to use it, what problems might arise when using the innovation, and how to resolve those problems.

**6. Confirm**: People confirm that the innovation works well
    for them and integrate the innovation into their
    normal routine (or they realize it does not work for
    them and discontinue using it).

People are more likely to continue with the innovation if they receive supportive messages from their peers and from the larger society.

Figure 9.1 summarizes the typical steps in the adoption of an innovation and what a "change agent"* can do to accelerate adoption.

### RATE OF ADOPTION OF INNOVATIONS

Not all innovations are universally adopted. Some innovations — like fads and fashions — blossom briefly and then fade away. Others are adopted by a subset of the population, but are never accepted by everyone.

For those innovations that eventually *are* adopted universally, the number of people adopting it over time generally traces an S-shaped curve as shown in Figure 9.2.[2] At first, there are just a few venturesome people willing to adopt the innovation. Then the idea catches on and a steadily increasing number of people adopt it. Finally, after a time, the last few recalcitrant people adopt it.

The first few percent of people who adopt a new idea, the innovators, are usually quite adventurous. They typically like to be on the cutting edge of innovations, so they are usually tuned into many sources of information and are open to new ideas. Generally, they must have the resources and self-confidence to boldly go where no one has gone before. They are often daring risk-takers, willing to accept setbacks and social disapproval if the innovation does not work out.

However, because they are so daring, innovators are often viewed as crackpots in their home communities. Because they are seen as being unusual, they often have few personal connections with other local people and only have friendships with other innovators in distant locales. Isolated and with little social status in their home communities, they typically do not influence the people around them very much, so it takes a while for the innovation to spread to others.

Following the innovators, the early adopters are typically more integrated into the local social system. Though they are not quite as open to new ideas as the innovators, they are regarded by their peers as more sensible and reasonable — more likely to offer accurate knowledge and sage advice. With their high status and numerous social connections,

*All truth passes through three stages:*
    *First, it is ridiculed.*
    *Second, it is violently*
        *opposed.*
    *Third, it is accepted as*
        *being self-evident.*
— Arthur Schopenhauer

---

* "Change agent" is a sociology term for someone who tries to bring about change.

# Figure 9.2: Typical Adoption Rate of Innovations

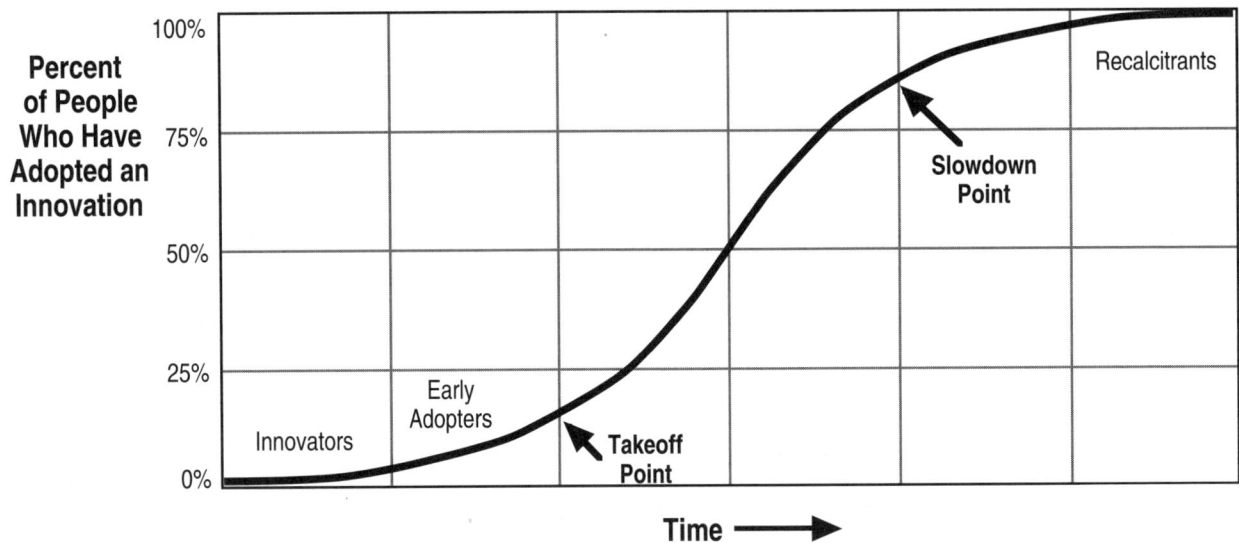

early adopters often serve as role models and opinion leaders for others: when they adopt a new idea, other people turn to them for their evaluation. If their assessment is positive, then others are inclined to adopt the innovation too.

In general, new ideas spread primarily from peer to peer or from near-peer opinion leaders to those people who share similar traits. The tighter the interpersonal connections, the faster an innovation will typically spread. Generally, people seem to be influenced by others only if they have a direct link to them or only have a single intermediary. Typically, those who have the most connections to other people will pick up an innovation sooner.

A person is more likely to adopt an innovation as the number of people in her peer network who have already adopted the innovation increases and the norms of her social system shift more towards adoption. Usually when about 15 to 30 percent of the population have adopted an innovation (which is also usually when the opinion leaders in a system have begun to favor it), the adoption rate accelerates rapidly.* The adoption process then continues at a rapid pace until almost everyone has adopted it. At the end, there are typically a few recalcitrant people who hold out. It may take many years before they all adopt the innovation.

Figure 9.2 illustrates each part of this typical S-curve dynamic. If we assume — just for the purposes of this discussion — that the time scale at the bottom of the figure covers a total of sixty years, then in the first ten years, only about two percent of the population (the innovators) adopt the innovation. In the next ten years, only another fourteen

percent (the early adopters) adopt the innovation. So, after twenty years, just 16 percent of the population have adopted the innovation. However, once the take-off point is reached in the twentieth year, the rate goes much faster. In each of the next two decades, thirty-four percent of the population adopt the innovation — more than two-thirds of the whole population in this twenty-year period. Then the rate slows down again, and in the fifth decade, fourteen percent more adopt. Finally, in the sixth decade, the last two percent (the recalcitrant people) adopt the innovation.

Because of this dynamic, the most difficult part of the innovation adoption process typically comes at the beginning. A few innovators may quickly adopt the innovation, but it may take many more years of hard work to persuade the early adopters and opinion leaders. However, once these critical people have adopted the innovation, then the vast majority may soon adopt the innovation with little additional prodding.

## The Dynamics of Conflictive Societal Change

This tendency for the cumulative number of people who adopt an innovation to trace an S-curve is usually even more pronounced for social change that requires arduous struggle against determined and dangerous opponents. While activists attempt to persuade people to adopt an alternative, their opponents actively work to persuade people that the alternative is unfashionable, useless, destructive, or too costly. Opponents may smear and ridicule proponents of the alternative or even threaten harm to anyone who adopts it. This makes it much more difficult for innovators and early

---

* Note that in a relatively isolated community, the take-off point may come when 15 to 30 percent of the *local* community (not the larger population) adopts the innovation.

# Figure 9.3: Activists' Dilemma:
## Success Breeds Success, Failure Breeds Failure

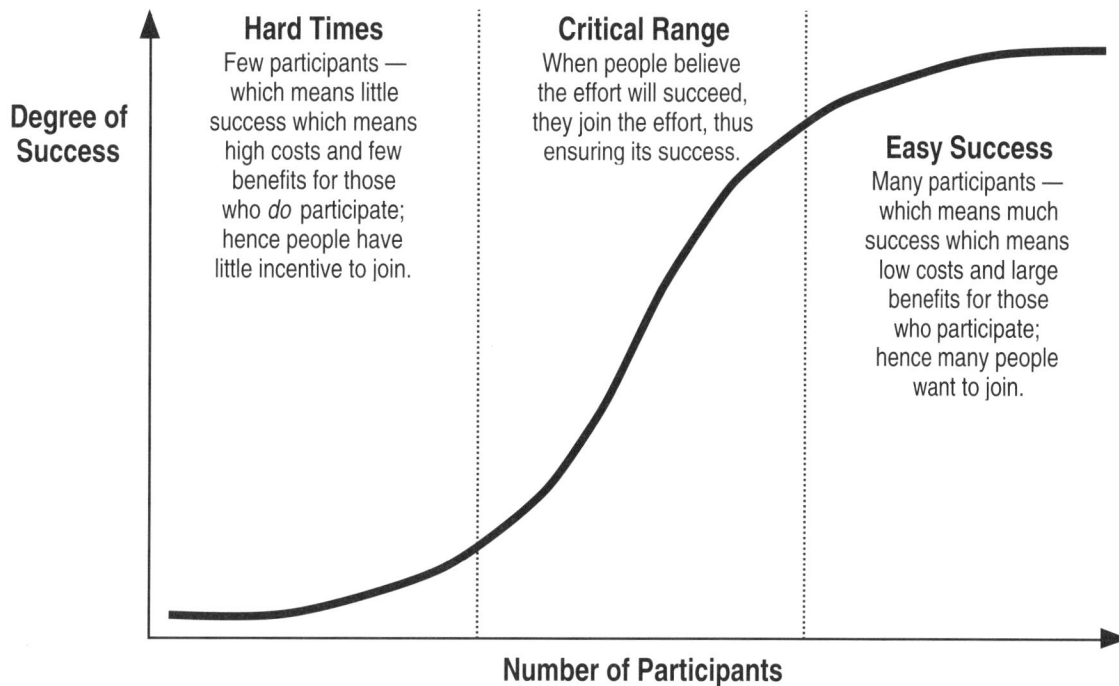

**Hard Times**
Few participants —
which means little
success which means
high costs and few
benefits for those
who *do* participate;
hence people have
little incentive to join.

**Critical Range**
When people believe
the effort will succeed,
they join the effort, thus
ensuring its success.

**Easy Success**
Many participants —
which means much
success which means
low costs and large
benefits for those
who participate;
hence many people
want to join.

**Degree of Success** (vertical axis)

**Number of Participants** (horizontal axis)

---

adopters to decide to adopt the alternative and makes it much less likely that others will even consider adoption.

### AN ACTIVIST PREDICAMENT

Moreover, for progressive activists challenging the power structure, another critical factor exaggerates the S-curve phenomenon even more.[3] Since progressive activists usually have minimal access to other resources (like money or authority), they typically must rely on rallying large numbers of people to their cause in order to have enough strength to succeed. However, in the early stages of a campaign for change, there are typically just a few activists willing to participate, and consequently their efforts usually fail to have much impact. Moreover, as long as success looks doubtful, other people are quite reluctant to get involved since no one wants to join a hopeless cause. Only when success seems assured will others join the fight. However, until they join, the number of activists remains too small to ensure success.

Figure 9.3 shows this predicament graphically. When the number of people involved in the change effort is small (depicted on the left side of the figure), the power they can exert is small and their efforts to bring about change typically fail. The cost to activists is high — long, grueling work, low pay, and sometimes violent repression — with little to show for it. So naturally, few people want to join the effort.

In contrast, when large numbers of activists are willing and able to work together in an organization, they constitute a powerful force for change. It is therefore much easier to win. As shown on the right side of the figure, the cost to any particular activist is then low and the rewards are great. Activists not only reap a share of whatever benefits come from achieving the goal, but they have the excitement of working on a successful campaign. For their efforts, they also typically get wide recognition as well as admiration and lavish praise from their fellow activists (and historians). So naturally, near the end of a campaign, many people want to be involved.

Between these two states, there is usually a critical range where a small increase in the number of activists will greatly increase the degree of success. In this critical range, people may see that their participation — if joined simultaneously by others — will lead to success. Therefore, at this crucial point, many people will join the effort.

This dynamic leads to an exaggerated S-curve: a campaign may dawdle at a very low level of effort for many years. Then at some point, it will grow to a critical size or

*In the beginning of a change, the patriot is a scarce man, and brave, and hated and scorned. When his cause succeeds, the timid join him, for then it costs nothing to be a patriot.*
— Mark Twain

some trigger event will encourage a surge in participation. With this influx of people, the campaign will suddenly take off. With enough people involved, activists are then able to win victory quickly. This victory leads to greater participation, which then produces even more victories.

The demise of the government of East Germany and the other Eastern Bloc countries around 1990 superbly illustrates this dynamic. For decades, people in these countries were afraid to challenge their governments and little changed. The situation only began to shift with the emergence of the Solidarity movement in Poland and the ascendance of President Gorbachev in the Soviet Union. Solidarity experienced less repression than people expected, and at the same time, it became clear that the Soviet Union would not invade Poland. Suddenly, hundreds of thousands of people poured into the streets. With so many protesting, they were virtually immune to government repression. People escalated their efforts, and all of these unpopular governments soon collapsed.

### PROBLEMS CAUSED BY THIS DYNAMIC

This exaggerated S-curve dynamic causes several major problems for progressive activists. In the difficult early years of a campaign, the activist burnout rate is typically very high and recruitment of new members is extremely difficult. Activists are often frustrated by their repeated failures and cynical about future prospects. Those dedicated activists willing to work for little reward during this bleak time are often obsessive and rigid.

During the take-off stage, with the influx of many people, success suddenly seems possible, but the change organization may collapse under the burden of so many new people. Processes that worked well in a small, intimate organization of dedicated activists often fail when it grows to include a large, diverse group of people who do not know each other well. Quick growth also means that the organization is comprised mainly of inexperienced activists who are more likely to make serious mistakes. Through their ignorance, they may be diverted from their goals, fooled by phony solutions, or drawn into counterproductive infighting.[4]

In the later stages of a campaign, with success just ahead, the organization may be filled with people whose commitment is quite low. Those who join only when victory is near may leave again at the first sign of renewed opposition or internal difficulty. They may also simply grow bored over time and drift away.[5]

### ENHANCING THE PROSPECTS OF A NEW CAMPAIGN

In the early segment of a campaign, people are more likely to join and persevere if they believe it is worthwhile. The following situations increase the likelihood of people joining a new campaign:

• If people believe the benefits they will personally reap (their share of the collective benefits — that is, the improvements in their lives that come from making society better — plus whatever individual benefits might come to them) are higher than the cost of participation (the amount of effort required of them and the danger they face).

• If they believe enough other people will join with them to ensure success.

• If they believe the campaign will be successful even if others do not join them.

• If they believe they should join the campaign for other reasons (moral, communitarian) even though they are not sure it will be successful.

There are several conditions that encourage these beliefs and several means that activists can use to create or enhance them:

• **Strong Social Networks**

People with bonds of kinship, friendship, or common membership in an organization are more committed to and trusting of each other. Feelings of solidarity and affection induce an obligation to participate in their friends' projects. Social ties also facilitate communication so people have reliable information about other peoples' desires and likely behavior.

• **Appealing Goals**

Only if the goals are important and likely to confer extensive benefits will people be willing to exert strong effort and subject themselves to risk. People are also much more willing to work together in concert if the objective is simple and clear.

• **Respected Leaders**

Visible leaders with a record of success (in social change or other endeavors) convince people that the campaign will be focused and well run.

• **Persuasive Activists**

Activists can help people develop a common understanding of their problems and help them develop a common solution. They can persuade people that the issue is vital and worth working on, that collective action is possible, that others will join with them, that the opposition is not as powerful nor as dangerous as it seems, and that the campaign will lead to victory. Alternatively, they can persuade people that to be morally virtuous, they should work for positive change — even if their effort is ultimately futile.

• **Personal Benefits**

Activists can offer participants benefits other than victory such as empowerment, prestige, companionship, a loving community, or feelings of belonging.

• **A Strong Reputation**

If an organization has a reputation for dedication, persistence, resilience, and success, people are more likely to believe it will be competent and successful in any new endeavor.

• **Strong Traditions**

Planning events or demonstrations at traditional places or on significant anniversary dates can remind people of past successes or invoke traditions of resistance to oppression.

• **Energetic Early Participants**

If there are enough participants and they work hard enough, they can constitute the critical mass necessary to win early victories. Even before they achieve any significant gains, other people can see that they are likely to be successful.

• **Confidence**

If early participants appear confident in their success, they are more likely to convince others. Of course, they must eventually win some victories or others will feel they were misled.

• **Early Victories**

A few early victories can convince others that an organization will be successful and they should jump on the band-wagon. Victories may also convince the opposition of the likelihood of change and that further resistance will only waste their resources.

*Pick battles big enough to matter, small enough to win.*
— Jonathan Kozol

• **Demonstrations of Strength**

Large rallies or marches show participants and the public that the organization enjoys great support.

• **Projections of Strength**

Inflated estimates of the size of the organization, attendance at demonstrations, or polling numbers can convince the public that the change effort enjoys wider support than it really does. However, if the strength is revealed to be inflated, then this can destroy the reputation of the organization.

• **Favorable Mass Media Coverage**

Through news media coverage, the public can learn about the plans of a change organization, the size and impact of its demonstrations, how authorities are responding, whether other people are sympathetic or hostile to the campaign, and other relevant information that enables them to evaluate the campaign's prospects. Favorable coverage can encourage people to join. Moreover, if the news media broadcast the successes of the group, then everyone knows that everyone else is aware that the campaign is succeeding.

• **Innovative Tactics**

A new, creative, or fun tactic can entice people with its novelty or its potential to surprise, befuddle, or disconcert the opposition.

• **Sympathetic, Lax, or Inept Opposition**

Signs that the opposition will not or cannot respond with heavy sanctions encourage people to participate.

### THE CONTRIBUTION OF VERNAL ACTIVISTS

With their extensive knowledge, considerable skill, and dedication to change, Vernal activists should be able to create or strengthen many of these conditions. Vernal activists would probably be energetic early participants in change campaigns across the country. They would be skilled at persuading other activists of the moral and practical worth of these campaigns and the value of working together. Most would project confidence grounded in their own social change experience.

As graduates of a Vernal program, they would probably have a strong personal reputation, and they would likely build a strong reputation for their organizations. They would be adept at building a supportive organization culture that would offer appealing personal benefits (like hugs, unconditional love, and solid support) to their colleagues. They would also likely be adept at fostering feelings of camaraderie.

From their experience and relevant education, they should be able to design effective campaigns with appealing change goals, innovative tactics, and effective means to win early victories. They would be good at exploiting the mistakes of their opponents. They would also know how to obtain favorable media coverage and how to accentuate the strength and morality of progressive efforts.

In the take-off and final stages of a campaign, Vernal activists should be especially helpful. Their Vernal education would enable them to facilitate the rapid growth of their change organization and avoid destructive mistakes. In addition, they would probably know how to prudently conclude one campaign and launch the next without losing supporters.

By creating and enhancing all these conditions, Vernal activists would ensure that a large number of campaigns for progressive change were spawned, moved into the critical range (in which the effort is large enough that participants believe they will succeed and so even more people join the effort), and finally took off. They would help progressive campaigns successfully navigate the S-curve dynamic instead of languishing endlessly at a low level of activity or crashing and burning as a campaign took off. As more and more of these campaigns succeeded, it would become even easier to garner interest and support which would lead to even greater growth and more change.

## TRANSFORMATION SCENARIOS

If the Vernal Project proceeded the way I imagine, it would generate an unprecedented force of about a million dedicated activists working steadily for progressive change for several decades. They would be able to build powerful organizations and generate massive campaigns for social change. They would help many of these campaigns grow large enough to reach the critical range so they would then rapidly grow even greater in size and impact.

This would generate a growing snowball effect: as change campaigns began to succeed, an ever-increasing number of people would be attracted to join the effort to create a good society. They would win important victories, which would then stimulate even more people to join the effort. This would inspire an ever-increasing number of people to tackle a wider range of problems, to push for more and deeper changes, and to reach for even higher ideals.

*I'm not going to spend my time or risk my neck working with a bunch of bozos so we can ultimately elect some mealy-mouthed, blow-dried politician or so we can make some minor change in the status quo while 99.9% of our sick society continues unchanged. But I'll work hard for years and risk my career and even my life for a truly just cause — especially if I can work with wonderful, supportive people. And especially if it looks like we might have some reasonable chance of bringing about real, lasting change.*

Because of this snowball dynamic, I believe progressive activists, supported and guided by Vernal activists, could bring about comprehensive and fundamental change of society in as few as eighty years. The transformation would start slowly, but would grow steadily, and then would accelerate to a final fundamental shift of power and consciousness.

I conceptualize the process proceeding through four distinct periods, each roughly twenty years long. Note that I have given these four periods the same names as the four stages of societal transformation described in Chapter 5 since the primary focus during each period would be to implement the corresponding stage of societal transformation. Note also that the Vernal Project would exist only through the first three periods — the first sixty years — and would end before the transformation was complete.

## Lay the Groundwork: Vernal Project Phases 1 and 2

As I envision it, over the first twenty years of the Vernal Project (Vernal Phases 1 and 2), the number of Vernal students would grow from 30 attending a single session to 6,000 attending two hundred sessions across the country. In the baseline case, the number of very active graduates would grow at an ever-increasing rate to about 17,000 at the end of Year 20. The number of less active graduates would grow to about 15,000 by the end of this year.

During this twenty-year period, Vernal activists would begin to assist thousands of progressive organizations. They would strengthen these groups and increase the skills and knowledge of their fellow activists. They would help their fellow activists overcome their harmful cultural and emotional conditioning. They would also begin to convey basic information to the public about progressive ideas and alternatives. Their efforts would bolster progressive change organizations and help to lay the foundation for later work.

For the first ten years of this period, the number of Vernal activists would be relatively small. Outside of progressive circles, the work of Vernal activists would probably go almost unnoticed. During this period, I expect that the overall impact of progressive organizations on society would be about the same as it is now.

*I walk slowly, but I never walk backward.*
— Abraham Lincoln

Only in the second decade (from Vernal Project Years 11 to 20) would the support of Vernal activists enable progressive organizations to begin to grow significantly. In this second decade, progressive organizations would just begin to have enough strength to noticeably challenge the power structure and the dominant culture.

## Gather Support: first half of Vernal Project Phase 3

For the next twenty years (Vernal Project Years 21 to 40), tens of thousands of Vernal activists would continue to support grassroots progressive organizations and help them grow larger and stronger. With a strong base, these organizations would begin to demonstrate positive alternatives and to win some campaigns. They would reach out to millions of people, convincing them of the need for fundamental change and painting a picture of a good society. They would teach the basics of democratic governance and nonviolent struggle to large numbers of people. They would also show people how to overcome destructive cultural and emotional conditioning and how to live joyful lives. Their impressive organizations — powerful, yet also adhering to high principles — would rapidly grow until they involved a total of about one million activists and progressive advocates and were supported by tens of millions more people.

# Three Important Early Goals

Early in the transformation process, Vernal activists would probably choose to exert some effort towards three goals that would make the change process easier and increase the chances of eventually transforming society:

## Create Safe Havens for Activists

Activists are usually forced to work and play within current economic and social systems. Moreover, if they hope to be effective in reaching out to regular people, they must remain connected to mainstream society. However, when activists are immersed too deeply in the dominant culture of competition, prejudice, and consumerism, they may become as frustrated, cold, angry, critical, and materialistic as everyone else in society. Moreover, the culture and the power structure continually thrash progressive activists. Constantly besieged by derogatory propaganda about their social change work, many activists find it difficult to remember why they want to work for progressive change or how to go about it.

Therefore, early in the transformation process, progressive activists probably need to create safe, nurturing havens where they can encourage and support each other to act their best, to strive for their highest ideals, and to heal from attacks. In such an environment, activists could also learn the skills necessary to joyously cooperate and gently struggle with each other.

Vernal centers, with their experienced staffmembers skilled in supporting other activists, would provide one safe haven. Activists might create other havens by living together in a supportive community, or they might meet periodically with other activists for a support weekend at a retreat center. Social change organizations could also become safe havens when they grew strong enough and the members learned enough skills to support each other well.

## Shift Resources to People of Goodwill

Our society's economic and social systems regularly reward greed, dishonesty, corruption, and thuggery. The rich steadily amass more wealth and power, and banks, corporations, government, the police, and the military ensure this process continues in an orderly fashion. At the same time, social workers, teachers, counselors, progressive activists, and other people of goodwill working to make the world better are typically poor and overworked.

Progressive activists would probably seek ways to use their time and money so that these precious resources went mostly to other honest and caring people, not to those who make life more difficult and oppose progressive change. Activists unintentionally support domination and dysfunction whenever they pay rent, buy groceries, buy alcohol and other drugs, buy gasoline, attend sporting events, movies, or other entertainment venues, and purchase most commodities and services. Activists also inadvertently support the status quo by supporting conventional politicians and by paying taxes that are used to train soldiers, build prisons, and subsidize mammoth corporations.

Whenever possible, activists would probably seek to keep resources within the progressive community. To achieve this goal, while still living a reasonable life, they might live simply and give gifts of service and support instead of store-bought goods. Whenever possible, they might also patronize alternative businesses, support progressive politicians, and boycott conventional corporations and organizations.

## Reduce Childhood Trauma

Fundamental change requires a citizenry capable of understanding political, economic, and social processes and able to make decisions cooperatively with others. People who grow up in loving homes in which they are supported and guided toward positive social behavior usually learn, as part of their everyday experience, how to work cooperatively with others. As adults, they are typically healthy, clear thinking, happy, and able to secure and keep a job. They are compassionate towards other people and find it relatively easy to cooperate with others.

In contrast, people who are raised in abusive, dysfunctional, loveless, or poverty-stricken families and neighborhoods typically find life extremely difficult. Even if they receive love, support, and favorable opportunities later in life, they are often plagued with depression, deep-seated anger and fear, addictions, health problems, muddled-thinking, and deeply-ingrained prejudices. They are often angry, belligerent, and sullen and find it hard to work with others. They are more likely to mistreat their families, neighbors, and co-workers.

Therefore, early in the process, activists working for fundamental transformation of society would probably seek ways to reduce childhood emotional trauma so that the next generation would have more adults who are functional. Eventually, to transform society, a whole generation of children must grow up in favorable circumstances and experience only minor childhood emotional trauma. Since it takes so long for a generation to grow up, live their lives, and pass on, activists should seek to achieve some success in this realm early in the process.

Therefore, in addition to their other work, activists would probably offer parents information about ways to rear their children with love and support.[6] Activists might also offer parents information about how to support and counsel each other through their worst emotional problems so they would be less likely to abuse their children. Activists would probably also work for the protection of physically and emotionally battered children.

During this period, progressive organizations would begin to win some important reforms. This would embolden them to work harder and to struggle for changes that are more comprehensive. However, it would also induce elite elements of the power structure to fight back vigorously in order to maintain their control and privilege. The power elite would probably belittle, attack, and infiltrate progressive organizations even more than they do now. They would attempt to disrupt progressive organizations, inflame the public's prejudices and fears, and pit people against one another. They would do their best to assign blame for all social problems to poor people, drug addicts, immigrants, and progressive activists (as they do now).

Like the 1930s and 1960s, this would be a period of intense excitement and activity, but most of the actual changes in society would be relatively shallow and hotly contested. Most societal power would still be firmly controlled by elite interests and would be locked in place by the dominant culture and everyone's ignorance and conditioning. Progressives would win the hearts and minds of many people, but they would not hold the levers of societal power or be able to free most people from their emotional or cultural indoctrination. The struggle that is difficult today would likely grow even harder during this period.

## Struggle for Power: second half of Vernal Project Phase 3

However, if the Vernal Project were successful in helping progressive organizations persevere at the same high level of intensity for two more decades (Vernal Project Years 41 to 60), they would be able to bring about much deeper and broader change. This would extend the period of intensive change and struggle for a period of forty continuous years. In my reading of history, there has never been such a strong effort for progressive change sustained over such a long period. Every previous period of intensive progressive change in the United States has faded to quietude after just ten or twenty years. The Vernal Project would make the difference — providing the support, skills, and continuity to ensure that positive, progressive change continued at a high level for four decades.

With such a solid effort sustained all across the nation, almost every person in our society would eventually be able to hear a clear presentation of progressive ideas. Activists would have the chance to change millions of hearts and minds one by one. They could explain unfamiliar concepts and address people's fears. They could show people how to work through their emotional hurts and adopt new behaviors. They could invite people to embrace new cultural norms and to patronize alternative institutions. They could call on people to assert themselves and take responsible control of society.

During this period, tens of millions of people would have the opportunity to try out alternative ways of acting and to test alternative institutions. Many would find these new concepts and institutions attractive, and they would embrace them and promote them to their friends.

As I see it, individuals and families would come together and form small cooperative communities (neighborhood associations, community groups, labor unions, communes, co-housing projects, and so on). Then these communities would collaborate with others to form self-governing neighborhoods and businesses. In time, these would unite to form self-governing cities.

Simultaneously, hundreds of well-planned and well-executed campaigns for change, carried out by large numbers of participants and supported by millions more, would successfully force the power structure to change. Progressives would secure many positions of authority in government and business. Desiring greater democracy, they would then use their authority to disperse information, power, and wealth more widely.

Over time, clear and balanced information would begin to displace misinformation and deceptive propaganda. People of goodwill would be able to establish and propagate virtuous cultural and social norms. Efforts to challenge people's prejudices and counsel them through their emotional tangles would begin to free them from their irrational behavior patterns and dysfunctional conditioning.

*A new scientific truth does not triumph by convincing its opponents and making them see the light, but rather because its opponents eventually die, and a new generation grows up that is familiar with it.* — Max Planck

Older people, many unalterably wedded to the old order, would grow old and die, while young people, influenced by and accepting positive ideas, would take their places. Over eighty years, almost the entire populace would pass away and be replaced by their more progressively minded children and grandchildren.*

As public support shifted to more compassionate and democratic institutions, the control wielded by the power elite would erode. This would make it much easier to bring about additional change. As more people were liberated from their conditioning and emotional injuries, they would no longer exude hate and prejudice, but would instead spread goodwill. Those working for the common good would support and cooperate with one another, which would free up even greater love and support. Though the effort to bring about progressive change would be very difficult at first, it would finally become easier.

---

* Appendix C explores in much more depth how aging and population turnover could accelerate progressive social change.

I expect that by the middle of this period, a majority of people would favor fundamental progressive change. By the end of this period (Vernal Project Year 60), most people would feel capable of participating in civic activities and running society's institutions.

## Diffuse Change throughout Society
### (after the Vernal Project had ended)

For the next twenty years (Vernal Project Years 61 to 80), alternative institutions would replace society's conventional institutions in every part of the country. A new, compassionate culture would replace the current culture of greed and competition. Young people would expect and demand a good society, and they would grow up in an environment conducive to emotional health and socially benign behavior. Resistance to progressive change would fade. Though the Vernal Education Project would have ended, Vernal graduates would continue to work for progressive change and to model principled behavior.

As clear knowledge, a compassionate culture, and genuine democracy spread ever wider and ignorance, the adverse power structure, and dysfunctional cultural norms wielded less control, the effort needed to bring about positive change would steadily decrease. The pace of change would accelerate until democracy, compassion, altruism, and cooperation flowed into every corner of society.

At the end of this period, the transformation would be essentially complete. Power and wealth would no longer be concentrated in the hands of the power elite. Instead, institutional power would be dispersed among a very large number of goodhearted people working honestly for the common good. Though still not a completely democratic system, the public would tolerate only those leaders who worked to spread power and wealth more widely. There would be little possibility that the old power elite could reverse this trend or that another power elite could develop since the new culture and institutions would encourage ethical behavior. After several more generations, power would be completely dispersed and true democracy would reign.

By the end of this period, most people's destructive cultural and emotional conditioning would no longer dictate their actions. Most children would be raised in ways that developed their intelligence, rationality, altruism, and love. Consequently, they would have fewer dysfunctional behavior patterns and emotional limitations, and they would be able to live cooperatively with other people. By the end of this period, a new culture of compassion and cooperation would be the norm. Instead of hopelessly accepting indifference and cruelty as innate human traits, people would joyfully help each other.

## A Possible Scenario for Fundamental Change

Figure 9.4 graphically details this possible transformation process.* Each of the six diagrams shows a different aspect of the process over time. As indicated at the bottom of the figure, the diagrams begin in Vernal Project Year 1, continue through all three Vernal Project Phases, and extend beyond to Vernal Year 80. The top diagram (Diagram A) is identical to Figure 7.3. It shows that the number of very active Vernal graduates (in the baseline scenario) would grow to about 25,000 over the first thirty years of the Vernal Project, then would remain constant until the project ended at the end of Vernal Year 60.

Since there would not be many Vernal graduates for the first twenty years of the Vernal Project (Phases 1 and 2), society would remain much as it is now. Diagram B shows only about 350,000 people (about 0.13% of the adult population) actively working for fundamental progressive change during most of this time, as many as I estimate are currently working for change. These activists would be laying the groundwork, but having only the same limited impact that they do now.

However, at the beginning of Phase 3, as large numbers of Vernal graduates assisted and supported change efforts, progressive social change movements would grow rapidly and the number of activists and advocates would shoot up. The number of activists and advocates would begin to grow rapidly around Vernal Year 20, swelling threefold to about one million (0.5% of the adult population) by Year 40.

After Vernal Project Year 40, I assume that the number of people working for fundamental change would level off at about one million since I presume that only a small segment of the public would ever have the desire and be able to devote time to change efforts. The number of activists would reach a steady state — the same number of people would be taking up progressive activism each day as existing activists and advocates would be returning to their everyday lives. Still, such a large body of progressive activists working continuously for such a long time would be unprecedented.

---

* Though grounded in my understanding of social change and supported by estimates which I believe are realistic and self-consistent (as discussed above and in Appendix C), this figure portrays a model of change based entirely on my assumptions about how progressive change movements influence people and about the extent they can influence people. It depicts a kind of societal transformation that has never occurred before. It also shows intangible qualities (like "public support") that are almost impossible to measure.

Even if my assumptions are mostly correct, reality will surely play out very differently than this figure indicates. All of these curves are smooth, and as pointed out in the discussion of Figure 5.4, if they truly described reality, they would be quite jagged. Real change occurs in jumps and starts, accelerated and delayed by various unpredictable events. So please accept this figure only for what it is — an idealized representation of what could occur if my understanding of change dynamics is accurate and the Vernal Project has the impact I think it would.

They would generate a tremendous amount of change activity every year and each activity could build on previous efforts. Also, though the number of activists would remain constant, I expect that the participants in these movements would become more and more knowledgeable and skilled over time, and consequently, their efforts would become ever more directed and effective. This qualitative change does not show on this figure.

Though progressive social movements would be quite large and prominent by Vernal Project Year 30, it would likely take a while for them to have much influence on most people. As described above, people are set in their ways and do not change their ideas or their activities until directly confronted with new situations. People usually only hear about ideas or events through the filter of the conventional news media, which typically characterizes alternatives as silly or distasteful. Embedded cultural conditioning and deep-seated emotional injuries are also difficult to recognize and eradicate. Therefore, it would take many years to significantly influence the majority of adults.

Diagram C indicates how Vernal graduates and movements for fundamental progressive change might affect the public. At first, these movements would have little impact. The vast majority of the public would hardly be affected (shown here by the lightly shaded area).*

However, as progressive movements grew in size, skill, and power, more and more of the public would be swayed. By Year 40, approximately fifteen years after progressive change efforts took off, I estimate more than half of the adult public would be at least moderately affected by progressive movements.

I use the term "moderately affected" to mean that people have heard progressive ideas and found them persuasive. Consequently, they would want to make their lives and their society better, and they would see that it might be possible to do so. They would also have at least some understanding of how society shapes their perspectives, how emotional and cultural conditioning constricts their behavior, and how societal institutions steer their lives. Many of them might only partially understand the implications of progressive ideas and might not fully support fundamental transformation of society. Still, they would try to act ethically and responsibly in accordance with progressive ideals, they would teach their children progressive ideas, they would usually vote for liberal or progressive candidates for political office, they would contribute money to progressive causes, they would patronize alternative institutions, and they would consider themselves liberals or progressives.

As progressive movements continued to push for change over the next few decades, the number of people they would influence would continue to grow. By the end of Vernal Phase 3 in Year 60, perhaps 90% of adults would be at least moderately affected and 45% would be strongly affected (shown here as the darkly shaded area).

By "strongly affected" I mean people would be deeply connected to progressive ideas and activity, and they would expect and demand a good society. They would consider themselves strong progressives, and they would fully understand and support fundamental progressive transformation as well as nonviolent social change methods. They would have a deep and clear understanding of how society affects their perspectives and lives. They would strive to live up to progressive ideals at all times, and they would actively try to overcome their dysfunctional conditioning and emotional blocks. They would teach their children progressive ideas, they would consistently vote for progressive politicians, they would avidly support alternative institutions, they would conscientiously boycott destructive enterprises, and they would regularly contribute money to progressive change organizations. They would try to convince their family, friends, colleagues, and neighbors to do likewise. Some of them might also campaign for progressive politicians, lobby legislators, speak out, circulate petitions, attend hearings, attend rallies, and so on.

By Year 70, I estimate more than half of the adult population would be strongly affected, and most of the rest would be moderately affected. Only a small percentage would remain unaffected.

Based on the influence levels in Diagram C, Diagram D indicates the overall level of public support for fundamental transformation of society. At first, only a small percentage would even be aware of alternatives that differed significantly from conventional ideas or institutions. As progressive movements pushed for change and acceptance grew, support for fundamental change would grow. By Year 50, when about a third of the adult population was strongly affected by progressive movements and another third was moderately affected, I assume a majority would finally favor fundamental change and would actively support alternative institutions. By Year 80, after most of the transformation was complete, I estimate that more than 95% of adults would support fundamental change.

Diagram E tries to quantify who controls the major institutions of society. In this diagram, I indicate that even after five decades of powerful progressive social movement activity, the power elite, ignorance, the dominant culture, and everyone's destructive emotional and cultural conditioning would continue to rule society. Although most of the public would support fundamental change by Year 50, it would take another decade of hard work for societal power to shift.

---

* In Figure C.8 in Appendix C, I estimate the extent to which fundamental movements for change would affect various age cohorts over this eighty-year period, including the effect of elders dying and new generations growing up in a changing world. The values of the curves displayed in Diagram C come from this analysis. The terms "hardly affected," "moderately affected," and "strongly affected" are described in more detail in Figure C.7.

# Figure 9.4: A Possible Scenario for Transformation of Society

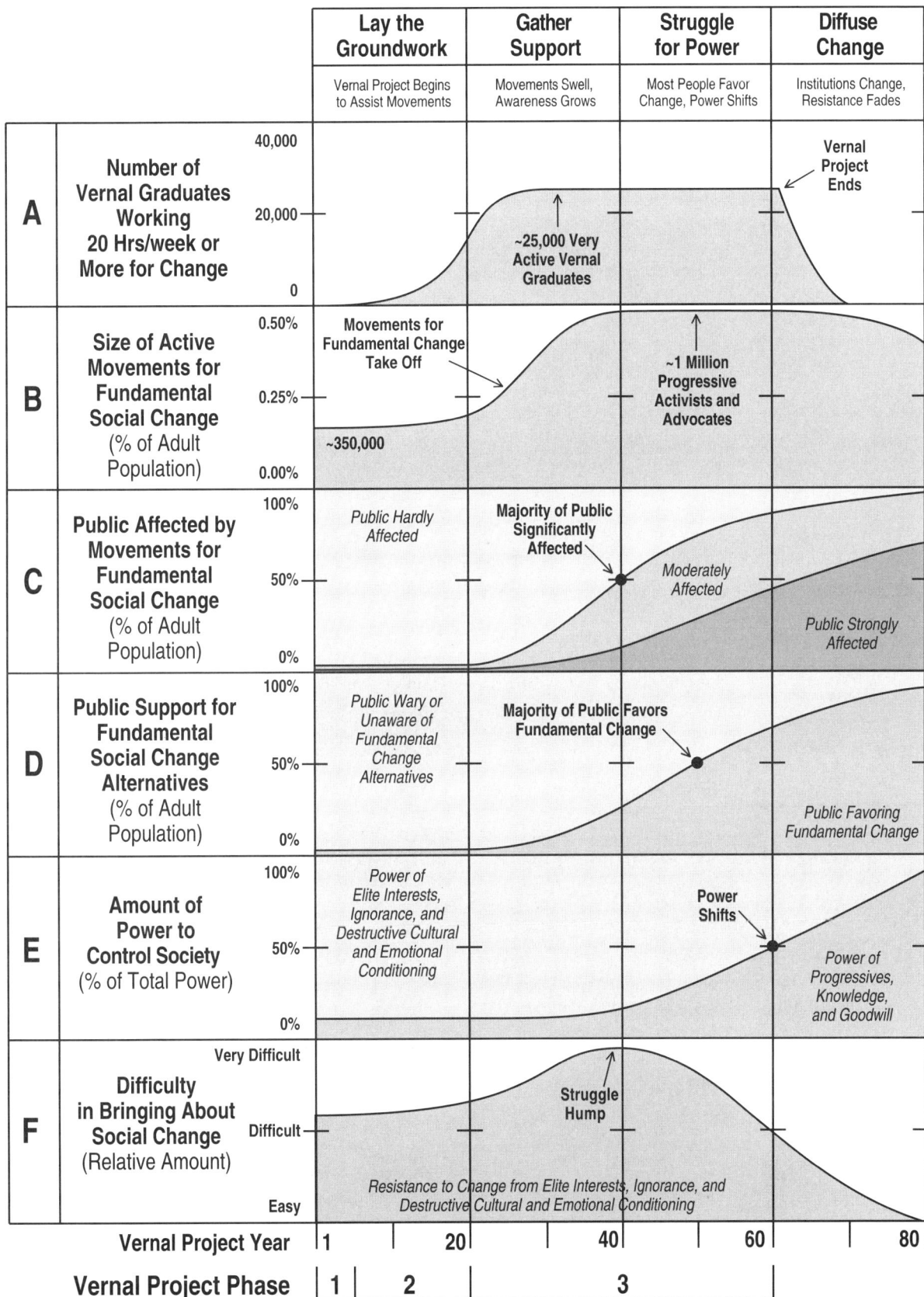

| | Lay the Groundwork | Gather Support | Struggle for Power | Diffuse Change |
|---|---|---|---|---|
| | Vernal Project Begins to Assist Movements | Movements Swell, Awareness Grows | Most People Favor Change, Power Shifts | Institutions Change, Resistance Fades |

**A — Number of Vernal Graduates Working 20 Hrs/week or More for Change**
(40,000 / 20,000 / 0)
~25,000 Very Active Vernal Graduates
Vernal Project Ends

**B — Size of Active Movements for Fundamental Social Change (% of Adult Population)**
(0.50% / 0.25% / 0.00%)
Movements for Fundamental Change Take Off
~350,000
~1 Million Progressive Activists and Advocates

**C — Public Affected by Movements for Fundamental Social Change (% of Adult Population)**
(100% / 50% / 0%)
Public Hardly Affected
Majority of Public Significantly Affected
Moderately Affected
Public Strongly Affected

**D — Public Support for Fundamental Social Change Alternatives (% of Adult Population)**
(100% / 50% / 0%)
Public Wary or Unaware of Fundamental Change Alternatives
Majority of Public Favors Fundamental Change
Public Favoring Fundamental Change

**E — Amount of Power to Control Society (% of Total Power)**
(100% / 50% / 0%)
Power of Elite Interests, Ignorance, and Destructive Cultural and Emotional Conditioning
Power Shifts
Power of Progressives, Knowledge, and Goodwill

**F — Difficulty in Bringing About Social Change (Relative Amount)**
(Very Difficult / Difficult / Easy)
Struggle Hump
Resistance to Change from Elite Interests, Ignorance, and Destructive Cultural and Emotional Conditioning

**Vernal Project Year**   1    20    40    60    80

**Vernal Project Phase**   1    2    3

Only after large numbers of people raised in the old society had grown old and died, large numbers of children had grown up surrounded by progressive alternatives, and a strong majority favored and pushed for fundamental change, would the power of progressive institutions, clear knowledge, and altruism grow to exceed the power of the power elite, ignorance, and destructive cultural conditioning. Once this shift occurred, by about Year 60, progressives would be able to refashion society's institutions more quickly and power would then shift even faster over the following few decades. Transformation could then be largely completed by Vernal Year 80.

Notice that the shift in power (in Year 60) would occur more than thirty years after the take-off of progressive movements. I estimate it would take more than three decades of sustained effort at a very high level of intensity to bring about this shift in power.

Diagram F shows my estimate of how difficult it would be to bring about change. When progressive change movements first began to have a significant impact, elements of the power structure would fight back vigorously. Moreover, everyone's fears about change, concerns about progressive alternatives, and internalized emotional injuries would arise. During this time (shown as a "struggle hump" on the diagram), it would become even more difficult than it is now to bring about progressive change. Only after a majority of the public was significantly affected (in Vernal Year 40) would it begin to get easier to bring about progressive change and we would begin to "slide over the hump." Only after a majority of the public supported fundamental change (in Year 50), would the level of difficulty drop back to the current "difficult" level. Only after the balance of societal power had shifted to progressive forces in Year 60 would it become somewhat easier to make changes.

> *Few things are impossible to diligence and skill... Great works are performed, not by strength, but endurance.*
> — Samuel Johnson

## A Typical Failing Scenario

In contrast to this transformation scenario, Figure 9.5 shows my understanding of how progressive change movements typically fail to transform society. Each of the six diagrams shown here mirrors those in Figure 9.4. I have modeled these diagrams on the history of progressive change movements in the United States, especially the period from the 1950s to the 1990s. At the bottom of the figure, I indicate the historical years that resemble this scenario.

Diagram A indicates there is nothing equivalent to the Vernal Project in this scenario, so there are no Vernal graduates. Still, progressive movements periodically do take off whenever enough good organizing has laid the groundwork and some event (the Depression, the Vietnam War) fuels their growth. For example, the 1950s were relatively quiescent, dominated by consumerism, militarism and McCarthyism. Long-term efforts in the Black community led to an upsurge in the Civil Rights Movement in the mid- to late-1950s. Pacifists were able to launch the Ban-the-Bomb Movement in response to the Cold War, and the Beat Generation advocated a hip culture as an alternative to the dominant culture of "Father Knows Best" home life and "Organization Man" work life.[7]

In Diagram B, I show that social change movements take off and grow rapidly (mirroring the early and mid-1960s). However, as they grow, internal problems and external opposition beset these movements. Police infiltrators and provocateurs disrupt and discredit them, the conventional news media attack them, commentators belittle them, and infighting erupts within (just as it did in the mid- and late-1960s). Without the knowledge and support of Vernal activists, these progressive movements are victims of these corrosive effects. After ten years, there are as many people abandoning these movements in discouragement and disgust as are joining them. As the external attacks mount and internal dissension grows, the movements wither (as they did in the mid-1980s). After twenty or thirty years, they shrink back to about the same number of hardcore activists as before (as the movements of the 1960s and 1970s did by 1990).

Diagram C again indicates that it would take time for progressive movements to affect the public. Even as progressive movements begin to falter (as they did in the early 1970s), the public continues to be affected by them. However, without continued activist energy, conservative counter-movements undermine the effects (as the Reagan Revolution did in the 1980s). After progressive movements begin to shrink, their effect on the public also dwindles.

Overall, I estimate that less than half of adults are moderately or strongly affected by progressive movements before these counter forces shift public opinion back towards a conservative viewpoint. Many children are influenced during the time of expanded progressive movements (as many of us were in the 1960s and early 70s), but as they enter adulthood their expectations shrivel in the arid conservative climate of that time.

Diagram D shows that the percentage of adults who know about and favor fundamental change begins to grow with the rise of progressive movements. It grows as large as perhaps 25% of the population, but then, in the re-emerging conservative environment, it declines.

Since the percentage of people favoring fundamental change in this scenario never rises above 25%, movements for fundamental change are never able to wrest power from the power elite or seriously challenge people's emotional and cultural conditioning. As shown in Diagram E, the total power of progressive movements remains relatively low throughout this period and eventually sinks back to about the same level as before. The power elite, ignorance, cultural domination, and emotional conditioning remain firmly in control throughout the entire period.

# Figure 9.5: A Typical Failing Scenario Without the Vernal Project

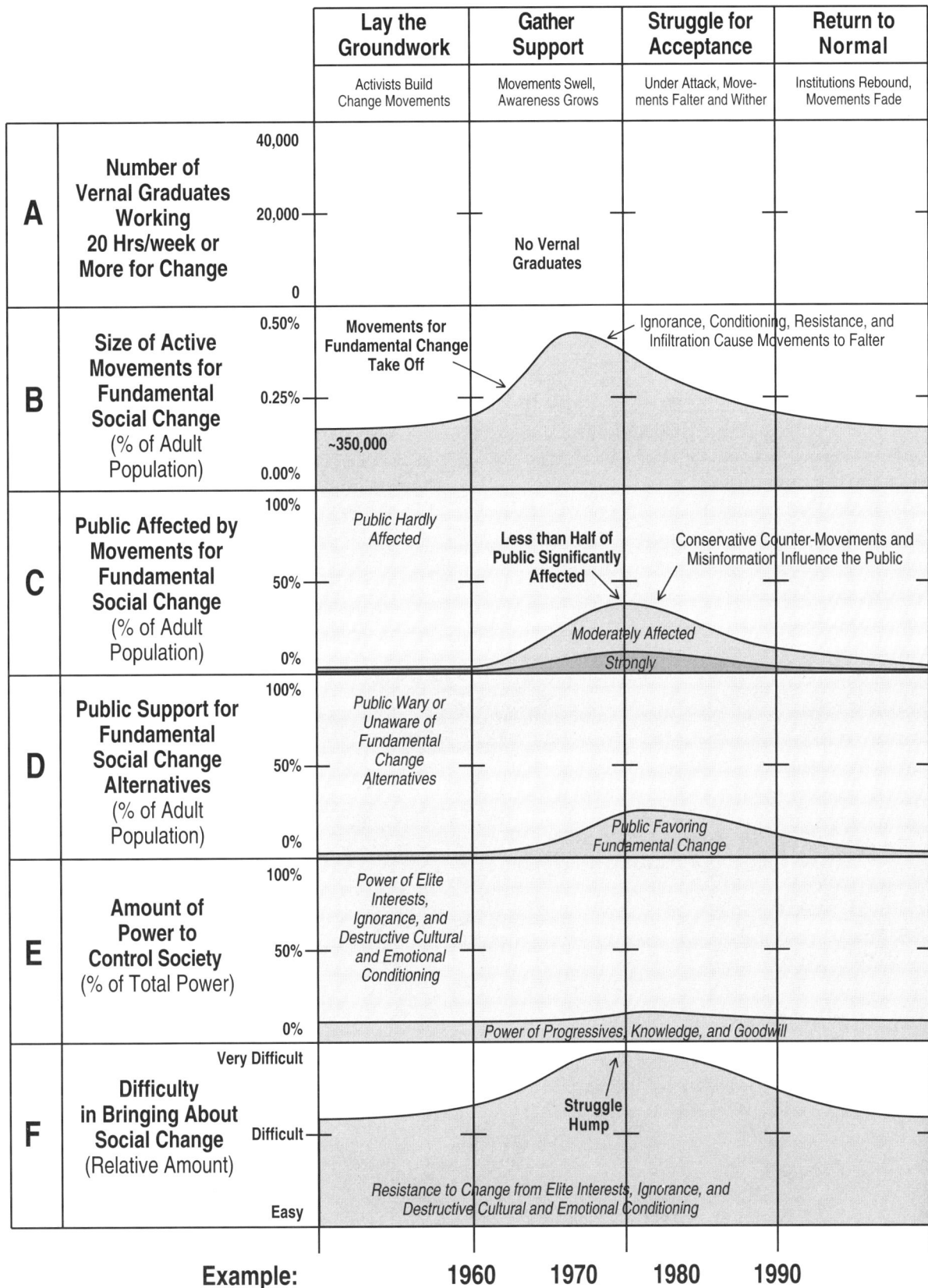

| | | Lay the Groundwork | Gather Support | Struggle for Acceptance | Return to Normal |
|---|---|---|---|---|---|
| | | Activists Build Change Movements | Movements Swell, Awareness Grows | Under Attack, Movements Falter and Wither | Institutions Rebound, Movements Fade |
| **A** | **Number of Vernal Graduates Working 20 Hrs/week or More for Change** | 40,000 — 20,000 — 0 | No Vernal Graduates | | |
| **B** | **Size of Active Movements for Fundamental Social Change** (% of Adult Population) | 0.50% — 0.25% — 0.00% — ~350,000 | Movements for Fundamental Change Take Off | | Ignorance, Conditioning, Resistance, and Infiltration Cause Movements to Falter |
| **C** | **Public Affected by Movements for Fundamental Social Change** (% of Adult Population) | 100% — 50% — 0% | Public Hardly Affected | Less than Half of Public Significantly Affected · Moderately Affected · Strongly | Conservative Counter-Movements and Misinformation Influence the Public |
| **D** | **Public Support for Fundamental Social Change Alternatives** (% of Adult Population) | 100% — 50% — 0% | Public Wary or Unaware of Fundamental Change Alternatives | Public Favoring Fundamental Change | |
| **E** | **Amount of Power to Control Society** (% of Total Power) | 100% — 50% — 0% | Power of Elite Interests, Ignorance, and Destructive Cultural and Emotional Conditioning | Power of Progressives, Knowledge, and Goodwill | |
| **F** | **Difficulty in Bringing About Social Change** (Relative Amount) | Very Difficult — Difficult — Easy | Resistance to Change from Elite Interests, Ignorance, and Destructive Cultural and Emotional Conditioning | Struggle Hump | |

Example:      1960     1970     1980     1990

Diagram F shows that the resistance to change during the peak of movement activity increases the difficulty of bringing about change (the "struggle hump"). Then as progressive movements wane, resistance also wanes and the level drifts back down to the difficult level.

At the end, society is in about the same place as before. The situation then continues until the next set of social change movements arises.

The cyclic process depicted in this figure stands in stark contrast to the continually improving process shown in Figure 9.4. It illustrates the difference that I believe the Vernal Project could make. If the Vernal Project produced as many skilled and experienced activists as I assume, and if it could bolster progressive movements for change as much as I expect, then it would enable people of goodwill to finally overcome the combined power of elite interests, ignorance, destructive cultural conditioning, and dysfunctional emotional conditioning. The repetitive cycle of progressive change activity followed by failure and inactivity could shift to a dynamic of change activity leading to more positive change, then leading to even more positive change, and finally leading to a good society.

# HOPE

## Another Major Obstacle: Hopelessness

In Chapter 3, I described five main obstacles to progressive change. Throughout this book, I have hinted at another obstacle that stems from the others and may be more important than all the rest: deep and widespread hopelessness. Whenever progressive activists try to bring about far-reaching, positive change, they discover how difficult it is to accomplish their goals. Opponents — who they thought might have some integrity — instead lie, cheat, steal, and attack them relentlessly. People they thought would join them instead stand to the side in ignorance or confusion — or turn away in fear. Friends they counted on often flake out, burn out, or run away in fear or frustration.

*More than any other time in history, mankind faces a crossroads. One path leads to despair and utter hopelessness. The other, to total extinction. Let us pray we have the wisdom to choose correctly. — Woody Allen*

In the face of such difficulties, it is easy for activists to become discouraged. As hopelessness grows, more activists give up and drift away, which makes it even more difficult to bring about positive change. Eventually, only the most hardened activists are left — only those who have steeled themselves to the seeming impossibility of their task and carry on anyway.

## The Hope Factor

As you can see, the Vernal Project powerfully tackles this obstacle by painting a powerful vision of a good society and delineating a practical means of creating it. It also ensures there would be enough activists with enough skills and strength working for change over a long enough time to challenge effectively even the most entrenched, powerful, and unscrupulous opponents. With the Vernal Project in full swing, activists would know that there would be more than a million dedicated and skilled activists working for fundamental positive change at the same time that they were. They would see that, together, they had the wisdom and strength to overcome opposition. They would see that their efforts were steadily bringing about positive change.

I expect this knowledge would fill them with profound hope — probably more than most current activists have ever experienced in their entire change careers. This hope would likely excite and empower them to do their best work. It would help them persevere for decades through seasons of drought as well as plenty. I expect it would energize them enough and sustain them long enough so that they could finally achieve their goals.

It would also inspire many people that today are not particularly interested in working for social change to step out of their conventional lives and become activists, thus providing the large numbers necessary to bring about comprehensive change.

*It is stupid to be naïvely hopeful, but it is also a mistake to underestimate the power of the human heart. When touched deeply and ignited to a feverish passion, people can hurl rivers into the air and entice mountains to dance.*

## SUMMING UP

Chapter 7 showed that if the Vernal Project were implemented as described in Chapter 6, it would generate a large number of skilled and experienced activists working diligently for decades. These Vernal activists would greatly bolster the work of other progressive activists, increasing the strength, knowledge, skill, and endurance of progressive change organizations, especially at the grassroots. I estimated they could generate a force for positive change that would be three or four times greater than now — with about a million activists working for change.

This chapter shows that by working steadily for many decades, Vernal activists would enable change organizations to inform, inspire, excite, and support millions of people to

# Models/Precedents for Massive Social Change Movements

In considering how to bring about transformation of the United States, I have considered most of the large progressive movements of the last century including the following:[8]
- The Populist movement of the 1880s and 1890s.
- The Progressive movement from 1900 to 1920.
- The labor movement of the 1930s.
- The Civil Rights movement of the 1950s and 1960s.
- The Ban-the-Bomb movement of the early 1960s.
- The Free-Speech movement of 1964.
- The welfare rights movement (late 1960s to early 1970s).
- The anti-Vietnam war movement (late 1960s to early 1970s).
- The anti-nuclear movements of the 1970s and 1980s.
- The anti-U.S. intervention in Central America movement of the 1980s.
- The anti-toxic waste movement (late 1980s and 1990s).
- The women's liberation, men's liberation, and gay liberation movements since the 1970s.
- The current anti-globalization movement.

I have investigated some of the large cultural movements of the last century including the following:
- The religious awakening movements of the early part of the twentieth century.
- The free-love movement of the 1920s.
- The Freudian psychotherapy movement of the first half of the twentieth century.
- The human potential movement since the 1940s.
- The Beat movement of the 1950s.
- The counterculture of the 1960s.
- The New-Age spiritual movement since the 1960s.
- The ethnic identity movements since the 1960s.

I have also studied several previous networks of activists as possible models for the Vernal Project. Though instructive, none of these networks was as large or as comprehensive as the vision described here.
- In India, Mohandas Gandhi established a group of satyagrahis ("truth-seekers"), many of whom lived together in ashrams (spiritual communities). Gandhi exhorted them to adhere to a strict regimen of exemplary behavior and inspired them to courageous actions. By adhering to strict guidelines of action, the satyagrahis were able to inspire deep respect among their adversaries, and they were able to bring about significant changes in Indian society including ending British colonial control. Though very inspiring, serious differences between the culture of India and the United States limit this model for our purposes.

- The Committee for Nonviolent Action (CNVA), the Atlantic and Pacific Life Communities, Peacemakers, and Plowshares are networks of mostly religious pacifists who have engaged in courageous acts of nonviolent social change over the last five decades. Because of their religious nature (or, in the case of Peacemakers, their intense individualism) they have been limited in their numbers and whom they are able to influence.
- The Movement for a New Society in the 1970s and 1980s created a loose network of dedicated and experienced nonviolent activists working for social change. They were influential in inspiring and directing the anti-nuclear power and weapons movements and they built a strong base in their Philadelphia Life Center. However, the total number of MNS activists never exceeded a few hundred.
- Labor union officials and shop stewards comprise a large network of activists, many of them quite progressive. However, their field of focus and methods of change generally are limited to labor issues.
- Similarly, some progressive clergy serve as important organizers, but usually only within their church constituency.
- Greenpeace has several teams of activists that engage in powerful nonviolent direct actions. The activists who carry out these actions are trained extensively and their actions are carefully organized to create a big impact. Because of the nature and style of the actions, however, the number of Greenpeace activists is small. Their actions focus only on illuminating a situation, not on involving large numbers of people.
- Similarly, small numbers of EarthFirst! activists have engaged in intensive nonviolent actions in the last decade. These actions, suggestive of nonviolent guerrilla warfare, have also involved relatively few people.
- Ruckus Society trains activists to engage in nonviolent blockades, tree-sits, and banner hangings. Though some of their actions have been larger in scope (for example, the blockade of a World Trade Organization meeting in Seattle in 2000), these actions are still relatively small.
- Peace Brigades International sends trained volunteers into conflict areas of the world to stop conflict by nonviolent means (primarily by their presence and witness). Though effective, their efforts involve few people.
- There are also various networks of activists based on Marxist-Leninist ideologies or religious dogma. Though they espouse freedom, fairness, and compassion, provide some camaraderie for their members, and invoke the sanctification of Marx or God, they are often cultish, anti-democratic, intolerant, and violent. Though sometimes successful on their own terms, they are not particularly good models for this project.

work for progressive change. They would enable an unprecedented number of progressive campaigns to grow large enough and strong enough to win solid victories and to implement real change. This would stimulate even more effort and more victories. At the same time, Vernal activists would also help large numbers of people overcome their ignorance, dysfunctional emotional conditioning, and destructive cultural conditioning, enabling them to become self-confident, capable citizens. Over time, older conservative people would die and young people who expected and demanded progressive change would take their place. If the Vernal Project proceeded this way and it was as successful as I predict, it could fundamentally transform society in eighty years. We could create a good society.

The next chapter describes a specific timeline for initiating and implementing the Vernal Education Project.

---

# Notes for Chapter 9

[1] This summary is based on Everett M. Rogers, *Diffusion of Innovations*, 3rd. ed. (New York, The Free Press, Macmillan, 1983, HM101 .R57 1983), which, in turn, summarizes the results of over 3,000 studies in this field.

[2] The number of people adopting an innovation over time typically corresponds to a bell-shaped Normal curve — at first, only a few adopt, then there is a rush to adopt until half of the people have adopted, then the rate slows until the last few individuals adopt. The cumulation curve that corresponds to this Normal curve is S-shaped.

Theorists postulate that the number of new adopters traces a Normal curve because it is proportionate to the (multiplied) product of two values: the number of people who have already adopted and the number of people who are still potential adopters. Intuitively, this makes sense: as more people adopt an innovation, there are more people available to demonstrate the innovation to others and convince others to adopt it, so the number of adopters grows rapidly. However, after many people have adopted the innovation, there are fewer people available to be convinced. The adopters mostly interact with each other, not with potential adopters, so the rate slows.

An alternative explanation is that the change in growth rate corresponds to the degree that people are open to innovation. Like most other human characteristics, this tendency probably corresponds roughly to a Normal curve: some people want to be on the cutting edge of every trend, some people do not like to change at all, and most people are in between.

Note that the adoption of innovations does not *always* follow such a curve.

[3] This section is based largely on Dennis Chong, "Coordinating Demands for Social Change," *Annals of the American Academy of Political and Social Science* 528 (July 1993): 126-141.

See also Dennis Chong, *Collective Action and the Civil Rights Movement* (Chicago: University of Chicago Press, 1991, HB846.5 .C48 1991).

[4] The main student organization of the New Left, Students for a Democratic Society (SDS), experienced this exact problem from 1965 to 1969, which led to its demise. See Kirkpatrick Sale, *SDS: Ten Years toward a Revolution* (New York: Random House, 1973, LB3602 .S8363 .S24) for a detailed description.

[5] Also, as Bill Moyer points out, during the take-off stage, activists may keep raising their goals so that by the time they achieve their original goal, they discount its value and focus only on what they have still not accomplished. Inexperienced activists may then grow demoralized and leave just when their change effort is most successful. See Bill Moyer, *The Movement Action Plan: A Strategic Framework Describing the Eight Stages of Successful Social Movements* (San Francisco, CA: Social Movement Empowerment Project [721 Shrader Street, 94117], 1987).

[6] Currently, 61 percent of parents condone spanking as a regular form of punishment for young children despite research indicating that corporal punishment is harmful. Moreover, 57 percent of parents believe that even a 6-month-old child can be spoiled — a belief that is incorrect. Zero to Three: National Center for Infants, Toddlers and Families, "Year 2000 Parent & Public Survey," (734 15th St., NW, Suite 1000, Washington, D.C. 20005, 202-638-1144), October 2000. Their study surveyed 1,000 parents with children 6-years-old and younger. <http://www.zerotothree.org/2000poll-results.html>

[7] "Father Knows Best" was a 1950s situation comedy television show that depicted a staid, middle-class lifestyle in the suburbs. William Hollingsworth Whyte's popular book, *The Organization Man* (New York: Simon and Schuster, 1956, BF697 .W47), critiqued corporate culture and mass consumption.

[8] For a list of references that describe these movements, see Chapter 12.

# 10

# *Implementing the Vernal Project*

*Right now, the Vernal Education Project is just an idea. How could we turn this dream into reality?*

As I currently envision it, the Vernal Project would have five phases — two development phases to launch the project (and nurture it through the difficult first years), and then three main phases to carry it out. Aspects of each phase are summarized in Figure 10.1 and described in more detail below.*

In the first development phase, the initiators of the project conceptualize it, plan it, and interest others in it. A major part of this effort is writing, publishing, and publicizing this book (an effort that began in 1988 and will continue for a few years after publication of this book). By discussing the idea with interested activists, we would develop a core group of two or three volunteer staffmembers. Assuming that we collectively decided to proceed with a project similar to the one described here,† we would then develop and facilitate a few prototype one-day workshops for activists.

In the second development phase, lasting three more years, we would raise sufficient funds to pay staffmembers, develop a small organization of 2.5 full-time equivalent (FTE) paid staffmembers and a board of directors, develop a preliminary curriculum for the Vernal program, arrange internships with local social change organizations, attract students, and test the curriculum in one-day workshops and in a six-month pilot session. In the last year, we would prepare for Phase 1 by attracting more students for the first full Vernal session.

In Phase 1, lasting for five years, we would create and develop a Vernal center in one metropolitan area. We would facilitate the first eleven sessions — one each year for the first two years and several during each of the last three years. This would require attracting about 300 paying students and hiring more staffmembers. In the last year of this phase, we would also prepare to

> *Thunder is good, thunder is impressive, but it is the lightning that does the work.*
> — Mark Twain

---

* Note that I have chosen to set Vernal Project Year 1 to be the first year of Phase 1. I have designated the three years of Development Phase D2 as Prep-1 to Prep-3. The years before Prep-1 have no special designation.

† Once a group assembled, we would make decisions consensually, incorporating the best ideas of everyone and proceeding accordingly. What we would come up with might differ significantly from what is described here.

# Figure 10.1: Summary of Vernal Phases

| Phase | Name | Project Years | Main Tasks |
|---|---|---|---|
| *Development Phase D1* | *Conceptualize, Plan, and Generate Interest* | | *Generate interest and attract volunteer Vernal Project staffmembers* |
| *Development Phase D2* | *Develop and Test the Curriculum in a Pilot Session* | *Prep-1 to Prep-3* | *Generate wider interest, develop and test the curriculum, raise start-up funds, hire staffmembers, attract the first students* |
| **Phase 1** | Launch the first Vernal Center and Prepare for Expansion | 1 to 5 | Generate wider interest, attract students, facilitate the first eleven sessions, build the organization, prepare for expansion |
| **Phase 2** | Replicate the Vernal Center across the United States | 6 to 20 | Replicate the center in 49 other locations across the United States, conduct several thousand sessions for thousands of students |
| **Phase 3** | Maintain at a Stable Level and then Evaluate/End | 21 to 60 | Conduct 8,000 sessions for 240,000 Vernal students |

replicate the program to another region of the country by hiring additional staffmembers.

In Phase 2, lasting fifteen years, we would replicate the center across the United States until there were fifty centers facilitating 200 sessions each year.

In Phase 3, lasting for forty more years, the Vernal centers would continue to facilitate 200 sessions per year. At the end of this phase, we would evaluate and then probably end the Vernal Project.

Please note that I have formulated this preliminary proposal in some detail to show that there is at least one feasible way to launch and sustain the Vernal Education Project. I have spent a great deal of time considering what steps would be required to implement the project and how long each would take, and I believe this particular proposal could work. However, this is not a final blueprint. As the other initiators and I work together to launch the Vernal Project, we will develop a new, more detailed plan. This plan will include the best of all the initiators' ideas and address the social change environment we find ourselves in at that time.

# *FIVE PHASES*

## Development Phase D1: Conceptualize, Plan, and Generate Interest

For the Vernal Project to come into existence, we must first develop the idea and then excite enough people to make it viable. Development Phase D1 began in January 1988 when I first began to write this book, and it will continue until there is sufficient interest and involvement to move on to the second development phase. I hope we can

reach this milestone within two years after publication of this book.

By necessity, this first development phase has an indefinite length and the time frame for each task is uncertain. Once we have enough interest to move into Development Phase D2, then the schedule should adhere more closely to a specific timeline as shown in Figure 10.2.

### A. DEVELOP THE PROJECT AND GENERATE INTEREST AMONG A SELECT GROUP OF ACTIVISTS

### *1. Write, Publish, and Publicize this Book*

The main task of this phase is to write, publish, and publicize this book. I began writing this book as a way to explore the concept of creating a good society and to solidify my ideas about social change. It seemed that it might be possible to create a good society through the means I had learned from my work as a change activist, but I was not exactly sure how to go about it. I decided that writing a book would force me to specify each step, to critically evaluate each aspect of the process, and to assess whether the overall effort could be successful. I also assumed a book would provide a relatively clear document for conveying these ideas to others.

After three years of thinking and writing, I was convinced that it is possible to create a good society and that this could best be accomplished through mass education and grassroots social change movements. In December 1990, I circulated a draft of this book to dozens of people including many experienced activists. I received extensive

> *Every new opinion, at its starting, is precisely in a minority of one.*
> — Thomas Carlyle

# Figure 10.2: Vernal Project Timeline

| Vernal Phase —> | D1 | | | D2 | | | 1 | | | | | 2 | 3 |
|---|---|---|---|---|---|---|---|---|---|---|---|---|---|
| **Vernal Project Year —>** | ... | ... | ... | P1 | P2 | P3 | 1 | 2 | 3 | 4 | 5 | 6–20 | 21–60 |
| **Phase D1** — Conceptualize, Plan, and Generate Interest | | | | | | | | | | | | | |
| A. Develop the Project and Generate Interest | | | | | | | | | | | | | |
|    1. Write, Publish, and Publicize this Book | — | | | | | | | | | | | | |
|    2. Write Articles and Have Them Published | — | — | — | | | | | | | | | | |
|    3. Discuss the Project Idea with Other Activists | — | — | — | | | | | | | | | | |
| B. Assemble a Core Group of 2–3 Volunteer Staffmembers | | | — | | | | | | | | | | |
| C. Set Up and Facilitate One-Day Workshops | | | – – | | | | | | | | | | |
| D. Raise Sufficient Funds to Proceed | | | — | | | | | | | | | | |
| **Phase D2** — Develop and Test the Curriculum | | | | | | | | | | | | | |
| A. Develop a Complete Curriculum and List of Readings | | | | — | — | – | | | | | | | |
| B. Set Up and Facilitate Ten-Day Workshops | | | | | | | | | | | | | |
|    1. Secure a Facility | | | | – – | | | | | | | | | |
|    2. Attract Students | | | | – | – | – | | | | | | | |
|    3. Choose Students and Collect Tuition | | | | – | – | | | | | | | | |
|    4. Facilitate the Ten-Day Workshops | | | | – | – | | | | | | | | |
| C. Develop a Small Organization | | | | | | | | | | | | | |
|    1. Hire Staffmembers | | | | — | | | | | | | | | |
|    2. Set Up a Small Office | | | | – | | | | | | | | | |
|    3. Develop Office Procedures and Staffing | | | | – | – | | | | | | | | |
|    4. Develop a Board of Directors and Governance | | | | — | | | | | | | | | |
|    5. Raise Sufficient Funds to Proceed | | | | | | | | | | | | | |
| D. Facilitate a Six–Month Pilot Session | | | | | | | | | | | | | |
|    1. Secure Facilities for the Workshops | | | | | | | | | | | | | |
|    2. Attract Students and Accept Applications | | | | | – | | | | | | | | |
|    3. Choose Students and Collect Tuition | | | | | | – | | | | | | | |
|    4. Arrange Internships | | | | | | – | | | | | | | |
|    5. Facilitate the Pilot Session | | | | | | — | | | | | | | |
|    6. Evaluate | | | | | | — | | | | | | | |
| E. Prepare for Phase 1 | | | | | | | | | | | | | |
|    1. Secure Facilities for the Workshops | | | | | | — | | | | | | | |
|    2. Attract Students and Accept Applications | | | | | | — | | | | | | | |
|    3. Choose Students and Collect Tuition | | | | | | — | | | | | | | |
|    4. Arrange Internships | | | | | | — | | | | | | | |
| **Phase 1** — Launch First Vernal Center & Prep for Expansion | | | | | | | | | | | | | |
| A. Prepare for the Vernal Sessions | | | | | | | | | | | | | |
|    1. Attract Students and Accept Applications | | | | | | | — | — | — | — | — | | |
|    2. Choose Students, Arrange Scholarships, Collect Tuition | | | | | | | — | — | — | — | — | | |
|    3. Arrange Internships | | | | | | | — | — | — | — | — | | |
| B. Facilitate and Administer the Vernal Sessions | | | | | | | | | | | | | |
|    Session 1 (revise curriculum extensively) | | | | | | | — | | | | | | |
|    Session 2 (revise curriculum some) | | | | | | | | — | | | | | |
|    Session 3 (curriculum mostly stable) | | | | | | | | — | | | | | |
|    Session 4 | | | | | | | | | — | | | | |
|    Session 5 | | | | | | | | | — | | | | |
|    Session 6 | | | | | | | | | | | | | |
|    Session 7 | | | | | | | | | | — | | | |
|    Sessions 8–11 | | | | | | | | | | — | – | | |
| C. Build the Vernal Organization and Prepare for Replication | | | | | | | | | | | | | |
|    1. Hire More Staffmembers | | | | | | | | | — | | | | |
|    2. Examine and Assess Good Locations in Other Regions | | | | | | | | | — | | | | |
|    3. Hire Staff for One New Region and Prepare Them | | | | | | | | | | — | | | |
| **Phase 2** — Replicate the Vernal Center across the U.S. | | | | | | | | | | | | — | |
| **Phase 3** — Maintain at a Stable Level — Then Evaluate/End | | | | | | | | | | | | | — |

critical feedback that spurred me to revise and expand the book. I distributed this revised draft to about twenty activists in 1997 through 2000 and then incorporated their comments and criticism.

I plan to publish this book in 2001 (if you are reading it, then I must have succeeded). Over the following two years, I intend to engage in an extensive book tour to generate interest in the Vernal Project. As much as I am able and can arrange speaking engagements, I will make presentations to bookstore patrons, community groups, college students, and activists.* To generate more interest, I will send a press release describing the book and the Vernal Project to about one hundred progressive organizations. I may place a small advertisement in progressive magazines such as *The Nation*, *In These Times*, *Z Magazine*, *The Progressive*, and *Mother Jones*. I will also publish the book on the Vernal Project web site and invite discussion of the Vernal Project idea. I also plan to send email announcements to a variety of activists.

### 2. Write Articles and Have Them Published

To stimulate greater interest in the project, I plan to write several articles summarizing the ideas in the book.† I will try to have these articles published in progressive journals such as *The Nation*, *Z Magazine*, *The Progressive*, the *Nonviolent Activist* (published by the War Resisters League), *Fellowship* (Fellowship of Reconciliation), *Peacemakers*, *The Ark* (National Organizers Association), *Deep Democracy* (Alliance for Democracy), *Peace and Change*, *Socialist Review*, and similar publications as well as educational journals. I will also post articles on the Vernal Project web site.

> *The worst thing is to get involved with people who aren't passionate about what they're doing.*
> — Willem Dafoe

### 3. Discuss the Project Idea with Other Activists

Since 1989, I have discussed the idea of the Vernal Project with a large number of people. Many are intrigued by the concept and a few are very excited by it. Several long-term activists and educators have expressed interest in working on the project, but none has yet made a commitment. Once this book is completed, I will work vigorously to attract more activists to the Vernal Project by having extended discussions with those who express interest in it.

### B. ASSEMBLE A CORE GROUP OF TWO OR THREE VOLUNTEER STAFFMEMBERS

Before Development Phase D2 can begin, we must gather a core group of several staffmembers who are willing

and able to volunteer more than ten hours per week for several years. I hope that the work of Task A above will generate enough interest that we can assemble a core group of volunteer staffmembers within two years after publication of this book.

Starting a large project like this from scratch is difficult. The initiators of the Vernal Project must be strongly committed to bringing it to fruition. Also, since there will be little or no money to pay these staffmembers for the first few

> *The man who goes alone can start today; but he who travels with another must wait till that other is ready.*
> — Henry David Thoreau

---

## Essential Traits of the Initiators of the Vernal Project

The initiators of the Vernal Project (two or three people) must be very committed to progressive social change and have strong abilities in a variety of areas. Specifically, they should have these qualities:

• Knowledgeable about social change theory and practice.

• Knowledgeable about a variety of current progressive issues.

• Experienced working for progressive social change: researching issues, educating the public, building social change organizations, challenging dysfunctional institutions and cultural norms, and building alternative institutions.

• Skilled at developing educational materials: workshop agendas, notes, and papers.

• Experienced working in a cooperative organization or living in a cooperative household.

• Physically and emotionally healthy.

• Experienced in working through emotional hurts.

• Experienced supporting other people through their hard times and emotional injuries.

• Aware of their own cultural upbringing, especially its negative aspects.

• Able to work with a wide variety of people and a wide variety of cultures.

• Willing and able to adopt new cultural norms.

• Willing to relocate to the location where we decide to launch the project.

• Willing and able to work without pay for several years to develop and build the Vernal Project (enough savings, a part-time job that pays well enough to provide support, and/or a willingness to live simply).

---

* My first public presentation, long before publication of the book, was on January 29, 1998 at the offices of Bay Area Action, Palo Alto, California. I presented the ideas to about forty environmental activists and friends.

† One short article was published as a letter to the editor in *Z Papers*, 1:2 (April–June 1992), (Boston: South End Press), pp. 55–56.

years, they will need to have savings or some other part-time job to cover their living expenses.

Naturally, if we are unable to find enough other activists qualified and eager to initiate the Vernal Project, then we would be forced to abandon the idea.

### C. SET UP AND FACILITATE ONE-DAY WORKSHOPS

As I envision it, once the core group convenes, we would develop several evening and one-day workshops for educating activists. These prototype workshops would cover a few selected topics from the full Vernal program. They might be in various locations around the country or all in one location. Students would pay a small fee to cover the cost of the meeting room and preparation expenses.

These workshops would give us experience facilitating, give us a chance to practice working together, and begin to establish our credibility as activist educators. During this time, we would also develop workshop notes, lists of readings, and an outline of a preliminary curriculum.*

This would also be a time for each of the initiators to identify her strengths and weaknesses and learn to support each other. We would work together to develop our skills and minimize our cultural and emotional blocks. In addition, we would discuss and modify the plans for the Vernal Project. In this process, we would grapple with our different perspectives, and learn to cooperate and struggle gently with one another.

### D. RAISE SUFFICIENT FUNDS TO PROCEED

To ensure there would be sufficient energy to facilitate these short workshops and prepare for Development Phase D2, I assume we would pay one or several staffmembers a small stipend in the last year of Development Phase D1. This small sum, totaling $12,000†, would only partly pay for the staffmembers' effort — they would still mostly be volunteering their time. In order to pay this small stipend, we would need to raise $12,000 in donations, foundation grants, or long-term loans sometime near the beginning of that year. I feel certain we could secure this relatively small amount of money.

By the end of this last year of Development Phase D1, we would also need to be sure we had sufficient resources to proceed to Development Phase D2. In Phase D2, we would be formally hiring several staffmembers, so expenses would rise significantly. Before we could proceed, we would either need to raise sufficient funds or we would need to generate enough interest in the Vernal Project that we felt confident we could soon raise enough money. If interest or funding were insufficient, then we would need to halt or delay the project until circumstances were more favorable.

---

* As a model, we could use the notes and agendas developed for the workshops I have facilitated over the past twenty years on consensus decision-making and nonviolent action. These papers are available on the Vernal Project web site: <http://www.vernalproject.org>.

† All monetary figures in this book use 1995 dollars. The actual amounts would include inflation since 1995.

We would also probably want to secure nonprofit status to make it easier to receive grants from foundations and individual donations.

## Development Phase D2: Develop and Test the Curriculum

Assuming the work in Phase D1 went well and there was sufficient interest in the Vernal Project, we could then begin Development Phase D2. In this three-year phase (in the years designated Prep-1, Prep-2, and Prep-3), we would develop the curriculum and test it — first in two ten-day workshops and then in a six-month pilot session. During this phase, we might also continue to offer evening and daylong workshops to test newly developed parts of the curriculum. We would continue to publicize the Vernal Project to attract interest and support. In this phase, we would also secure enough funds, through grants or loans, to hire several staffmembers.

### A. DEVELOP A COMPLETE CURRICULUM AND LIST OF READINGS

We would develop the curriculum mostly during the first two years of this phase in conjunction with the two ten-day workshops. Developing the detailed materials for the curriculum would require several steps:

• Interview experienced activists for their views on the information activists need to know to be effective.

• Locate and review existing materials and curricula used in other activist schools and workshops.

• Research books and magazines looking for additional information.

• Draw up a detailed plan of workshop and study group topics.

• Prepare detailed workshop agendas, notes, figures, and annotated bibliographies.

• Circulate these materials to experienced facilitators and activists for review.

### B. SET UP AND FACILITATE TEN-DAY WORKSHOPS

In each of the first two years of this phase, we would facilitate a ten-day workshop. In the timeline (Fig. 10.2), these workshops are shown taking place in the third quarter of Vernal Year Prep-1 and the second quarter of Year Prep-2. These two workshops would help us refine the curriculum notes and gain additional experience educating activists. Each of the thirty students would pay a fee of $500 to cover the basic expenses of the workshops. With scholarships, I estimate the average collected would be $300 ($9,000 total).

Setting up and facilitating these workshops would involve four main tasks:

#### 1. Secure a Facility

We would need to find a good facility for the workshops — preferably a retreat center in a beautiful location. We probably would need to reserve the facility at least six months before the workshops took place. We would also need to hire a cook to prepare meals for the workshop. The timeline shows these tasks taking place in the first quarter of Vernal Year Prep-1 for the first workshop and the fourth quarter of Prep-1 for the second workshop.

### 2. Attract Students

To provide enough time for participants to learn about the workshops and apply for admission, we would need to start publicizing each workshop at least six months before it began. We would send mailings to activist organizations, talk with individual activists we knew, and make presentations in as many forums as possible. The timeline shows these tasks taking place in the first and second quarters of Vernal Year Prep-1 for the first workshop and the fourth quarter of Prep-1 and the first quarter of Prep-2 for the second workshop.

Because the Vernal program would be new and have no reputation, it might be difficult to attract students. Those most likely to be interested would probably be activists with direct personal connections to the Vernal staffmembers and with each other. If we could not find enough interested students, then we would need to delay or end the project.

### 3. Choose Students and Collect Tuition

For these initial workshops, we would probably accept most of the activists who applied for admission. Only if there were many applicants could we be more selective and choose a more diverse mix of activists. Sending out acceptances and collecting tuition would probably take about six weeks.

### 4. Facilitate the Ten-Day Workshops

These workshops would give us additional facilitation experience, give us more practice working together, and establish our credibility as activist educators. At the end of each workshop, we would ask the students to criticize the curriculum and facilitation process so we could make improvements.

### C. DEVELOP A SMALL ORGANIZATION

To accomplish the work required in this phase, we would need a small paid staff and a formal organization.

### 1. Hire Staffmembers

In this phase, we would hire several staffmembers to facilitate and administer the first Vernal center. Those hired would probably be the same activists volunteering in Development Phase 1. I assume that in Vernal Year Prep-1 there would be one full time equivalent (FTE) paid staffmember, in Prep-2 there would be two FTE paid staffmembers, and in Prep-3 there would be 2.5 FTE paid staffmembers.

By the third year of this phase (Prep-3), the team (which might be composed of four or five people) must have enough expertise to facilitate the six-month pilot session. Optimally, at least one staffmember would also have prior

experience administering a school or other nonprofit organization, and at least one would be experienced in raising funds.

Even though the salaries would be modest ($18,000/year plus benefits) and the workload high, I believe it would be possible to find enough staffmembers. There are not many other good social change jobs, so these would probably be desirable positions. However, if we could not find enough skilled staffmembers, then we would need to delay or end the project.

### 2. Set Up a Small Office

We would need to establish an office to handle the administration of the pilot session and to prepare for the first complete session. During this phase, the office could be minimal — probably just a room in someone's home, a computer, an answering machine, and a post office box for a mailing address.

### 3. Develop Office Procedures and Staffing

In this phase, we would also need to develop administrative procedures and coordinate staffing. As the center grew, we would need to continually develop and refine our procedures.

### 4. Develop a Board of Directors and Governance

At the beginning of this phase, we would need to find seven or eight people willing to serve on a board of directors for the first Vernal center. We would try to assemble a board with a diverse mix of activists and educators. I think it would be relatively easy to assemble a strong board comprising people who were excited about the Vernal Project and committed to making it succeed. Again, if we could not, then it would probably be best to delay or end the project rather than proceed without the necessary support.

**Steps in a project:**
*1. Wild enthusiasm*
*2. Disillusionment*
*3. Total confusion*
*4. Search for the guilty*
*5. Punishment of the innocent*
*6. Promotion of non–participants*
— Office Graffiti

### 5. Raise Sufficient Funds to Proceed

Expenses in this phase would be significant. The two ten-day workshops and six-month pilot session would require renting a retreat center and paying a cook. As described above, we would also hire several staffmembers and pay them a modest salary.

I assume expenses for retreat center rental, food, and a cook for the six-month pilot session would total half as much as a regular session and salaries would be $18,000/year for full-time work plus benefits. As described above, the ten-day workshops should bring in about $9,000 each. As described below, the pilot session should bring in tuition income of about $1,800 per student ($54,000 total).

With these assumptions, expenses would exceed income by $22,000 in Year Prep-1, by $46,000 in Prep-2, and by $23,000 in Prep-3, resulting in a total deficit of $103,000 by the end of this development phase (see Figures 6.13 and B.18 for details). The slight excess of income over expenses in the early years of Phase 1 would not make up this shortfall until Vernal Year 5.

Before we could hire staffmembers, we would need to secure sufficient funds through grants or loans to cover this anticipated shortfall. We would probably seek grants from progressive foundations and donations or loans from supportive individuals.

I am reasonably confident that we could raise this money if everything else were on track.* However, if the funds did not materialize, then it would probably be wise to end the project at this point rather than attempt it without the necessary capital. Lacking these relatively minimal resources, we would probably be unable to launch the project satisfactorily, and it is likely the project would ultimately stumble and fail.

### D. FACILITATE A SIX-MONTH PILOT SESSION

At the beginning of the third year of this phase (Vernal Year Prep-3), we would offer a six-month pilot session to thirty students. This pilot session would have approximately the same schedule as the first six months of a full Vernal session. It would include study groups, social change work, social service work, a single internship in the second quarter, an introductory five-day workshop and two ten-day workshops.

This pilot session would allow us to develop the enrollment and administrative procedures, test the curriculum, and work out solutions to the problems we encountered. This pilot session would involve six main tasks:

### 1. Secure Facilities for the Workshops

We would need to secure the facilities at a retreat center for the three workshops.

### 2. Attract Students and Accept Applications

Since the pilot session would require a six-month commitment from the students, we would need to start recruiting at least nine months before the session began. As before, we would send out mailings and talk to individuals and organizations.

If we were unable to attract enough students, then we would probably end the Vernal Project at this point. For the project to succeed, it must generate sufficient interest (and tuition income) during this critical development phase.

### 3. Choose Students and Collect Tuition

Once we had received applications, then the board of directors and staffmembers would need to choose a class of thirty students, notify them of their acceptance, arrange scholarships, and collect tuition fees. This process would probably take about eight weeks.

### 4. Arrange Internships

We would need to arrange an internship with a local progressive organization for each of the thirty students. To find sufficient opportunities, we would need to begin this process at least six months before the session began. Good internship opportunities would be critical to the success of the Vernal Project. If we could not find enough high-quality internships, we would probably have to delay or end the Vernal Project.

### 5. Facilitate the Pilot Session

Finally, we would need to facilitate all aspects of the pilot session.

### 6. Evaluate

After the pilot session concluded, we would evaluate the whole process by asking students, internship agencies, and everyone else involved to give feedback about what worked well and what did not. This would allow us to modify the whole program to serve students better.

### E. PREPARE FOR PHASE 1

While the pilot session was underway, we would begin preparing for the first full session. As before this would require four main preparation tasks:

### 1. Secure Facilities for the Workshops

### 2. Attract Students and Accept Applications

### 3. Choose Students and Collect Tuition

### 4. Arrange Internships

We would also need to increase the number of paid staffmembers to three (full-time equivalent) by the end of this phase.

At the end of this development phase, we would critically evaluate the prospects for continuing. If the pilot session had gone well and if we had a strong organization, a good reputation in the community, wide interest and support from progressive activists, and sufficient resources, then we would proceed. If we did not, then we would probably end the project and shift our efforts to some other worthy endeavor.

---

* Based on drafts of this book, a very generous individual has offered an interest-free, 10-year loan of $100,000 as soon as a core group of Vernal staffmembers has assembled and other key parts of the project are underway. Assuming this person's offer is still available when we reach this point, we should be able to proceed without additional fundraising effort.

## Phase 1: Launch the First Vernal Center and Prepare for Expansion

Once we had developed, tested, and evaluated the program in the pilot session, we could begin the first true phase of the Vernal Project. In Phase 1, lasting five years, we would facilitate eleven year-long Vernal sessions — one each year for the first two years, then two in the third year, three in the fourth year, and four in the last year. All of these sessions would probably be in the same metropolitan area.

### A. PREPARE FOR THE VERNAL SESSIONS

As before, we would spend the nine months before each session preparing for it. As the Vernal Project became better known, finding students would probably get easier.

### 1. Attract Students and Accept Applications

### 2. Choose Students, Arrange Scholarships, Collect Tuition

### 3. Arrange Internships

### B. FACILITATE AND ADMINISTER THE VERNAL SESSIONS

For the first two years, we would begin one new session each year. This would leave ample time for the three staffmembers to refine the whole process of facilitating sessions, arranging suitable workshop facilities, finding good internship opportunities, attracting students, and working out logistical and operational bugs. By Vernal Year 3, we should have a stable and effective process and could start facilitating two sessions per year — the second starting six months after the first. By Year 5, we would be facilitating four sessions each year, with a new one starting every three months.

At the beginning of this phase, we would still be making major revisions to the study guides and reading lists. However, by the fourth year we would probably need to revise the curriculum only in minor ways — with new materials that reflected changes in the world (new political issues, new world hotspots, changing U.S. government policy, and so forth). As I envision it, over the next fifty-six years, the basic curriculum would remain mostly stable — evolving slowly to encompass new issues, new ideas, and new educational methods.

### C. BUILD THE VERNAL ORGANIZATION AND PREPARE FOR REPLICATION

Once the first Vernal center was established and growing, we would need to develop a more formal organization that could find and oversee internships, guide the study groups, plan the logistics for workshops, copy materials, arrange publicity, send correspondence, handle admissions, maintain financial books (including payroll), hire new staffmembers and prepare them, manage other personnel matters, and create new Vernal centers around the country.

### 1. Hire More Staffmembers

By Year 4, we would need to hire a fourth staffmember to help facilitate and administer the greater number of sessions being facilitated. This person might be a recent graduate of the Vernal program. We would also need to establish a more formal office and furnish it with desks, file cabinets, computers, and so on. We would also probably want to set up a small library of books for use by Vernal staffmembers and students for research.

In anticipation of even more rapid growth in the future, we would need to hire a fifth staffmember in Year 5 whose primary work would be hiring, preparing, and supporting new staffmembers. This new staff preparer would need to have previous experience hiring, aiding, and guiding new personnel.

### 2. Examine and Assess Good Locations in Other Regions

In the fourth year, we would look for a good location for a new Vernal center in another region of the United States. We would try to choose a city with a large progressive community so that attracting interest and support would not be hard.

### 3. Hire Staffmembers for One New Region and Prepare Them

Once we had chosen the new region, we would need to replicate all the Vernal center functions there. During the last year of Phase 1 (Vernal Year 5), we would need to hire three staffmembers for the new center and prepare them to manage it. The new staffmembers would probably be hired in the new location and then brought to the old center for a few months of orientation.

Staffmembers in the new region would need to develop their own board of directors for the new Vernal center. They would also need to arrange internships and attract students for their first session, which would begin in Vernal Year 6.

## Phase 2: Replicate the Vernal Center across the United States

Over the next fifteen years (Vernal Project Years 6 to 20), we would replicate the Vernal program all across the United States until there were fifty active centers, each with a full team of four FTE staffmembers and each facilitating four sessions each year (200 total sessions per year).

### FIFTY VERNAL CENTERS IN TEN REGIONS

As I envision it, each new Vernal center in a region would facilitate just a single session for the first year or two. This would give the new staffmembers a chance to establish themselves, develop office procedures and staffing patterns, develop a strong board of directors, set up good internship opportunities, and attract students. It would also allow some time for the reputation of the center to grow. Over the next three years, the number of sessions facilitated each year would increase to four and the team would grow to four FTE staffmembers.

In the following year, this lead center would be strong enough that it could hire three staffmembers to start another complete center in another city within the same region. With a great deal of support from the lead center, I assume each one of these new centers would be strong enough to immediately facilitate two sessions in its first year and four sessions in its second and subsequent years.

In order for the Vernal network to grow to fifty centers this quickly, each lead center in a region would need to help start a new center within its region every year until it had launched the full number of centers for that region. Moreover, the lead center in the first region would also need to help launch new centers in all the other regions (see Figures B.13 and B.14 in Appendix B for details). According to this plan, almost half of the centers would be fully operational (facilitating four sessions each year) by Vernal Year 17, and all would be at this level by Year 21.

This rapid expansion would probably be tumultuous and the first few sessions conducted by each center might be substandard. However, by the end of this phase, most of the fifty centers should have robust programs.

### A GROWING NUMBER OF STAFFMEMBERS

As shown in Figure B.16 in Appendix B, the number of staffmembers facilitating sessions would grow from eight in the first year of this phase (Vernal Year 6) to 200 by the end of the last year (Year 20). As the Vernal network grew, we would hire additional people to help administer the programs within each region. I assume we would hire a regional administrator as soon as two centers opened in a region and then would hire an additional half-time administrator whenever another center in that region opened. Hence, by Year 21, there would be twenty-five FTE regional administrators. We would also hire special new staff preparers to hire, prepare, and support new staffmembers. I assume we would need one new staff preparer for about every ten new staffmembers hired.

Following this plan, the Vernal network would grow until there were 229 FTE staffmembers in Year 21 (see Figure B.18 in Appendix B for details).

# Phase 3: Maintain at a Stable Level, Then Evaluate and End

For the next forty years (Vernal Project Years 21 to 60), the fifty Vernal centers would continue to facilitate four sessions each year. As before, this would include attracting applicants, accepting applications, choosing students, arranging scholarships, collecting tuition, arranging internships, guiding study groups, facilitating workshops, and

administering the centers. The fifty Vernal centers would enroll a total of 6,000 students each year. Together, they would have an annual budget of about $14 million.

At the end of this phase in Vernal Project Year 60, we would end the project. By then we would have either succeeded in fundamentally transforming society or the Vernal program would seem antiquated. If we had succeeded, then much of the Vernal curriculum would likely be an integral part of the public school system (in whatever form that system had evolved). If we had not yet succeeded, then we should probably develop new strategies more in keeping with the times and shift the resources of the Vernal network to those new projects.

Like many ideas and projects, the Vernal Project might have gone astray sometime over the course of these sixty years. It is also possible that by that time the United States would no longer dominate the rest of the world, or there might be new forces of oppression which we cannot even imagine now. Whatever had occurred, it would be time to carefully evaluate the whole project and choose new directions. The project would be discontinued and all the staffmembers encouraged to find other opportunities. Another project could then arise that is more appropriate to the end of the twenty-first century.*

*If your contribution has been vital, there will always be somebody to pick up where you left off, and that will be your claim to immortality.*
— Walter Gropius

## A NOTE ON SPEED

If everything proceeded according to this timeline, the Vernal Project would be quite small for many years. To all appearances, little would happen throughout the many years of Development Phase D1 and not much during the three years of Development Phase D2. Even through the five years of Phase 1, the Vernal Project would only educate a few hundred activists. Not until several years into Phase 2, perhaps fifteen years from now, would there be sizable numbers of Vernal graduates. Only then would the Vernal Project begin to have a noticeable effect on society.

*Take time for all things: great haste makes great waste.*
— Benjamin Franklin

*Everything should be made as simple as possible, but not simpler.*
— Albert Einstein

---

* If it seemed the project was going well but required a few more years to complete, then perhaps it could be continued for another set period. However, this extension should be limited to five or ten more years at most. It is imperative that the Vernal Project not become another perpetual institution that could lose its way or be captured and manipulated by the power elite. The project should do its task and then end.

It may seem like this is too long a time. I have tried to design a timeline that moves along as quickly as possible, but is still realistic. My experience indicates that it takes time to create a new project, figure out the details, and develop workable procedures. Moreover, it takes time to build relationships, to understand other activists, and to struggle through differences. Most importantly, it takes time for people to hear about a new project, evaluate it, decide that it has merit, and decide to support it. Since students would be making a major commitment of time and money, it would probably take a great deal of time to convince them of the value of their participation in the project. I think this timeline proceeds as fast as is prudent to enable ultimate success.

In fact, the timeline may seem too rapid. We will have to work diligently and skillfully to accomplish all the necessary tasks in the time specified. Nevertheless, I think it is critical to move at least this fast. Otherwise, activists may come to believe that the project will never really take off. They must feel confident that their efforts will lead to further efforts, and the total effort will lead to creation of a good society in a reasonable amount of time.

## NEXT STEPS: LAUNCHING THE VERNAL PROJECT

Since you are reading this book, I have successfully completed the first part of Development Phase D1. Still, much must be done before the Vernal Project can proceed.

### Requirements Before Proceeding

Of the many requirements that must be satisfied for the Vernal Project to sprout and grow, two are particularly crucial:

(1) At least two experienced activists (and preferably three) must commit themselves to making the project succeed. For several years, these initiators of the Vernal Project must work long hours as unpaid volunteers and then for several more years for relatively low wages. I have made this commitment, so I only need to find one or two others who are also willing and able to dedicate themselves to this project through the initial development phases.

*People can be divided into three groups: those who make things happen, those who watch things happen, and those who wonder what happened.*
— John Newburn

(2) There must be a large number of activists interested in becoming Vernal students. From now through the end of Phase 1, we would need to attract about 450 activists who would be willing to spend a year attending a yearlong program that is practically unknown. These students would also need to be willing and able to pay an average of $3,600 tuition (in 1995 dollars) and be willing and able to work half time for social change for seven years after graduating.

This book, the articles that the initiators of the Vernal Project will write, and the speeches we will make must be sufficiently enticing to attract widespread interest and support. A large number of potential students must believe that it is possible to create a good society and that the Vernal Project will greatly assist this process. They must be eager to make the project happen. To determine if there is sufficient interest, we might survey the activist community near the site of the first Vernal center. As soon as we received a large enough number of favorable responses, we would know we could proceed.

## My Role

I fervently hope this project will proceed, and I plan to work vigorously to make it succeed. Over the last decade, I have striven to expand my skills so that I am capable of doing the tasks necessary to carry out the project. I have also worked assiduously to increase my physical, emotional, and financial health so that I have the ability to make it succeed. I plan to work long and hard on it, and I believe my contribution will be valuable.

Because I have invested so much time and energy in designing the Vernal Project and preparing this book, it has unavoidably become "my" project. However, for the project to succeed, it must be owned by an ever-growing number of people — first a few initiators, then the early Vernal staffmembers and students, and finally everyone connected with the project. As much as I am able, I will try to let go of the project and let it become "our" project. Once the team of initiators has assembled, I assume we would work collectively on an equal footing.

I look forward to discussing all aspects of the Vernal Project and working cooperatively with others to reshape it in whatever ways make sense. I will do my best to support and encourage others to take responsibility and credit for all that we do. I am open to changing every aspect of the Vernal Education Project. I am even willing to hand the project over to others to carry out if they are more capable than I am. My greatest desire is to create a good society, and I will play whatever role seems best to accomplish that goal.

Some activists may be inspired by this book, but feel the Vernal Education Project is not the best way to proceed. They may have very different ideas about how to bring about fundamental change, and they may launch their own separate projects. I hope they do, since their projects may succeed where this one fails. Over the long run, those projects that do well will grow and prosper, while those that go astray will die from their own weaknesses or be superseded by better projects.

## What You Can Do

If you like the Vernal Education Project and would like to help it proceed, here are some things you can do:

### • TELL OTHERS

Loan this book to your friends and family members. Tell others about the Vernal Project web site. Send an email message to your colleagues. Inform everyone who might support this vision. Discuss the ideas and the assumptions. Do they make sense? Is it possible for the Vernal Project to succeed? Would enough people join the project and could they overcome the obstacles that stand in the way? Is this an exciting vision that inspires hope? Is it a project with which you would like to be a part?

---

### What You Can Do Right Now to Learn Activist Skills

If you are reading this before the Vernal Project has reached Phase 3, there probably is not yet a Vernal center in your area. Until there is, you can learn activist skills on your own. Here are some suggestions:

• Read the books and magazines, and explore the web pages listed in Chapter 12 and on the Vernal Project web site. Talk with other people who have thought about social change issues. Question your assumptions about current reality. Explore possible paths to create a better society. What would a good society look like? What institutions and cultural norms would need to change? How would they be different? What stands in the way of positive societal change? What is the best way to create a good society? What can you do to move society in that direction? What do you need to know? What do you need to teach others?

• Find a personal transformation technique with which you feel comfortable (such as meditation, counseling, massage, or a support group) and engage in it regularly. What emotional injuries have you incurred? What destructive cultural conditioning have you absorbed? In what ways do you act out dysfunctional behavior? How can you act better? Who could help you? How could they help you? How can you help others?

• Contribute resources (time, money) to activists working for positive social change. What resources do you have? What can you give?

• Work for positive change with other activists. Make a commitment to work at least half time for seven years for fundamental progressive transformation of society.

---

### • BECOME ONE OF THE INITIATORS OF THE PROJECT

If you have the necessary skills and experience and you are excited enough to devote a significant amount of your time over the next few years, then become one of the initiators of the project. Let's work together to create a strong project.

Critically evaluate the Vernal Project and work with us to make it even better. What has been overlooked? How could we make the project stronger?

### • CREATE YOUR OWN BETTER PROJECT

Critically evaluate the Vernal Project and design a better one: What experiences have you had that contradict my assumptions? What kind of project would make more sense? Start a project that you believe would be more likely to succeed. Go for it! May the best project succeed! Every effort for progressive social change contributes to our ultimate success.

> *If a better system is thine, impart it; if not, make use of mine.* — Horace

### • WORK WITH OTHER SOCIAL CHANGE EFFORTS

If you do not have the necessary desire, skills, or experience to become an initiator of the Vernal Project and you do not plan to launch your own project, then join an existing social change effort. There is much work to do, and many good organizations with which to work. Find a group that appeals to you and do what you can to make the world better.

## SUMMING UP

This chapter describes a preliminary plan for implementing the Vernal Education Project and presents a detailed timeline. This tentative scenario seems feasible, and I intend to do my best to carry it out. Please join me in making it a reality.

---

*We are face to face with our destiny and we must meet it with a high and resolute courage. For us is the life of action, of strenuous performance of duty; let us live in the harness, striving mightily; let us rather run the risk of wearing out than rusting out.*
— Theodore Roosevelt

# *11*

# *Some Objections and Concerns*

Reviewers of this book have raised many concerns about this proposal for creating a good society. Before addressing these concerns, let me first summarize the main points made in this book.

## SUMMARY

In **Chapter 1**, I described how my personal experience as a progressive activist and my study of historical social change campaigns led me to believe it is possible to create a truly good society. I argued that people are sufficiently intelligent and humane to live in a good society and that there are enough resources to support one. I further asserted that there are viable solutions to all of society's worst problems and backed up this assertion with a list of several seemingly impossible problems that actually have solutions. This chapter also listed some important factors that increase the chances for successfully creating a good society:

- Most people have experienced a bit of a good society.
- Most people want a good society — we are all on the same side.
- Most people agree about the basic elements of a good society.
- Most of the time, most people are civil.
- Most people act as well as they can.
- Society has improved in some important ways over the centuries.
- Movements for progressive social change are viable and powerful.
- Many people now work hard to create a good society.
- Even more people *want* to work to create a good society.

**Chapter 2** described the basic elements I believe must be part of a good society. Built on the foundation of the Golden Rule, these include:

- Rudimentary democratic consent — Everyone must at least passively endorse the society; otherwise, it is oppressive.
- Universal access to human essentials (air, water, food, protection from harsh weather, and safety from harm).

• Access to at least some other desirable items (such as good housing, running water, electric lights, meaningful work, fulfilling relationships, bicycles, computers, health care) and some luxuries.

• Freedom and liberty — Everyone is protected from oppression and can do what they want as long as it does not infringe on others.

• Equity and fairness — Everyone has equal opportunity and roughly equal access to societal resources.

• Environmental sustainability — Society is in consonance with the natural environment.

• There is balance between conflicting wants and needs.

This chapter also described some additional elements that would characterize a good society:

• Humane and compassionate

• Democratic and responsible

• Tolerant and wise

• Fun

**Chapter 3** described the five main obstacles that stand in the way of creating a good society:

1. Adverse power structure — Society's institutions and structures entice and coerce everyone into acting to perpetuate these institutions and social structures and to resist progressive change.

2. Destructive cultural conditioning — Outmoded or harmful traditions, customs, religious practices, prejudices, and advertising images impede progressive change.

3. Dysfunctional emotional conditioning — Emotional traumas condition people to act in rigid and dysfunctional ways (irrational behavior, inhibitions, compulsions, phobias, addictions, depression, low self-esteem, et cetera).

4. Widespread ignorance — Most people have a limited understanding of the workings of society. Few people know about progressive ideals or change methods.

5. Scarcity of progressive resources — Most progressive activists are financially poor and receive meager personal support.

**Chapter 4** briefly evaluated various historical strategies for overcoming these obstacles and transforming society: violent revolution, historical materialism, a vanguard party, countercultural transformation, alternative institutions, mass advertising, technological advances, conventional electoral politics, mass social movements, and incremental change. Learning from their limitations and failures, I then compiled a list of eight crucial characteristics of fundamental change efforts. To be both progressive and effective, these efforts must be:

• Powerful and inspiring enough to overcome strong opposition.

• Focused on broad, fundamental, and enduring change (to transform individuals, institutions, and the culture enough that they do not revert to the old ways).

• Reliant on ordinary people (since the elite usually will not help).

• Democratic and responsive — not dictatorial.

• Focused on ending systemic oppression, not toppling individual oppressors (since anyone has the potential to become an oppressor).

• Nonviolent — not oppressive or destructive.

• Moral, principled, true to ideals, with means in harmony with the ends (so efforts do not go astray).

• Direct and personal (so they can deeply touch and transform people).

Based on this analysis, I argued that the only viable way to bring about fundamental progressive change is to educate and liberate the imagination of every person in society so that everyone can collectively and democratically choose to create a good society. To transform all of society also requires powerful social change movements capable of challenging entrenched power.

I then asserted that an effective strategy should be based on mass education and social change movements and include these six essential components:

1. Clear conceptions of progressive change including
   • A clear vision of a good society
   • A comprehensive and feasible strategy for change

2. Widespread education in which people can
   • Learn how society actually functions
   • Learn to practice democracy and cooperation
   • Learn to overcome destructive cultural conditioning
   • Learn to change society

3. Widespread emotional therapy

4. A supportive community for progressive activists

5. Large numbers of progressive activists working simultaneously for change

6. Concerted change efforts continuing for many years

**Chapter 5** described a four-stage strategic program for creating a good society that incorporates these characteristics and components. Progressive activists would:

1. Lay the groundwork
   A. Find other progressive activists
   B. Educate themselves — learn how human affairs are currently organized and other ways they might be organized
   C. Learn and practice change skills and overcome destructive and dysfunctional conditioning
   D. Form supportive communities with other people of goodwill

2. Gather support
   A. Raise others' awareness about the possibility of creating a good society and the means to do it
   B. Build powerful political and social organizations

3. Struggle for power
    A. Vigorously challenge the power structure and destructive cultural norms through conventional political and legal methods
    B. Illuminate domination and oppression using various methods of nonviolent action
    C. Resist oppression using nonviolent action
    D. Develop appealing alternative institutions based on progressive ideals
4. Diffuse change throughout all of society

This chapter further argued that this program could best be carried out with a democratic, bottom-up change movement structure in which a small number of dedicated activists would personally inform, support, and inspire a larger number of steadfast activists. These activists would, in turn, inform, support, and inspire a much larger number of progressive advocates. Together, these activists and advocates would inform, persuade, and inspire everyone in society.

In this model, the most skilled and experienced activists would constitute a stable and reliable core. These experienced activists could support other activists, broaden their understanding of society, suggest innovative and effective ways to tackle difficult problems, and continue doing tedious or grueling work when other activists strayed or faltered. This would help to ensure that progressive organizations would grow and prosper, not go off course, stagnate, or erupt in infighting.

This chapter concluded by explaining the dynamics of nonviolent struggle, since nonviolent action would play a crucial role in the project and is often misunderstood.

To begin to implement this four-stage strategic program and the bottom-up activist structure, I proposed the Vernal Education Project in **Chapter 6** (and **Appendix B**). This project would establish fifty Vernal centers around the United States that would provide education and support for a large number of dedicated progressive activists.

Designed to be practical and inexpensive, the yearlong Vernal education program would consist of these main components:
- Student-run study groups
- Internships with existing social change organizations
- Independent social change work
- A small amount of social service work
- Self-study of current affairs
- A series of five ten-day-long, staffmember-facilitated workshops
- Student-run emotional support groups or individual therapy
- Social events that enable students to connect with each other

This program would offer activists a chance to experience and learn direct democracy, cooperation, emotional therapy, personal support, and a variety of social change methods while building strong bonds with other nearby activists. Students in this program would be encouraged to work for fundamental progressive change at least twenty hours per week for seven years after they graduated.

If the Vernal Project proceeded as described, after about a twenty-five year period of development and growth, the fifty Vernal centers would be providing a quality education covering the basics of fundamental social change to six thousand students every year.

**Chapter 7** (and **Appendix C**) showed how this education project could greatly bolster and support progressive change organizations. Based on reasonable assumptions about the growth of the project and the number of activists who might participate, I determined that after twenty-five years there would be 25,000 graduates of the education program working at least twenty hours per week for fundamental change. There would also be 150,000 other steadfast activists working at least three hours per week and an additional 900,000 progressive advocates working a few hours per week. Together, they would constitute an unprecedented force of over one million progressive proponents.

This many activists — most of whom would have much greater knowledge and skill than activists today — could generate an effort perhaps three or four times more powerful than current efforts for fundamental change. Dispersed all across the country, they could create an immense and sustainable movement for progressive change.

**Chapter 8** told Melissa's story to illustrate the various ways the Vernal Education Project could inform, support, and inspire activists.

**Chapter 9** (and **Appendix C**) first described the unique dynamics of social change and then showed how the Vernal Education Project could affect those dynamics and actually bring about fundamental transformation of society over eighty years.

Graduates of the education program — working with and supporting hundreds of thousands of other progressive activists — would build communities in which they could support each other and learn to work together cooperatively. They would build alternative institutions based on progressive values as well as nonviolently challenge institutions and cultural norms that stood in the way of creating a good society. By struggling steadfastly for decades, I predicted they could influence most people in the United States to adopt a more progressive perspective and help them to become more responsible and active citizens.

After about fifty years of sustained struggle — with a majority of the public favoring fundamental progressive change — transforming society would then begin to be easier. The change process would accelerate and could be largely completed in just thirty more years.

**Chapter 10** laid out a timeline for implementing the Vernal Education Project, especially the tasks required to launch it and carry it through the first five years. I concluded that the project could begin once a large number of activists expressed interest in and support for the project and three initiators — who were willing and able to launch the project — have come together.

# QUESTIONS AND CONCERNS

Reviewers of this proposal have questioned both its premises and its viability. Below are some of their concerns and my responses.

## Is It Possible to Create a Good Society?

### IT SEEMS TOO GOOD TO BE TRUE

*Your good society sounds like some kind of unreachable fairyland. Are you trying to create a perfect world?*

No matter how wonderful society might eventually be, I am sure there will always be many problems. Human beings will continue to be born with physical deformities. People will still get sick, have accidents, and incur injuries. Lightning will continue to strike, floods will inundate us, earthquakes will shake us, and tornadoes and hurricanes will ravage us. Moreover, people will continue to make mistakes and accidentally hurt others. They will also continue to disagree and get angry at each other. Even if people could act their best, we will still invariably hurt one another. I do not believe there is any way to abolish these aspects of life and achieve perfection. If we ever could, our lives would probably be very boring.

> *In the long run, men hit only what they aim at... they'd better aim at something high.*
> — Henry David Thoreau

However, I believe our society could be vastly better than it is now. Some people routinely act in caring, cooperative, and responsible ways that nourish those around them and promote a supportive society. If most people behaved this way instead of just a few, our society would be tremendously better. Gone would be most of the current strife and repression of human spirit. Without all this human-imposed suffering, I believe joy and a sense of solidarity with others could be as common as hopelessness and alienation are now.

### IS PERFECTION REQUIRED?

*In your good society don't you assume that everyone would be perfect?*

> *Aim for excellence, not perfection.* — Proverb

I assume only that most people would be in reasonably good psychological shape — as emotionally healthy and capable as many people are now. People could still make mistakes, and they could still occa-

sionally be irrational and hateful. However, I assume that most people would be rational and compassionate most of the time. I assume they would be able to rebound from depression or hurt quickly in the same way many people can now.

### MUST PEOPLE CHANGE THEIR PERSONALITIES?

*How do you expect to change people's personalities?*

I do not believe that people have rigid, unchangeable personalities. My own feelings and reactions change drastically from day to day depending on the situation in which I find myself. When surrounded by gentle, loving people, my tender side comes out. When attacked, hurt, or stifled, I am more defensive and surly. When I walk in the woods on a beautiful day, watch a heart-touching movie, or have a good cry with a loving friend, my heart opens with joy and compassion. When threatened by authorities, thwarted by obstinate bureaucracy, scorned by friends, or impeded by poorly designed technology, I usually become angry or withdrawn. Encouragement boosts my intelligence and creativity. Ridicule lowers my responsiveness and self-esteem. I assume that circumstances affect other people in these same ways. If so, then a good, compassionate society would bring out the best in all of us and make it much easier to create and maintain a good society.

I also assume people would be more capable and compassionate if they were not raised in poverty, pushed around by alcoholic parents, sexually abused, raped, or battered by adults, taunted and humiliated by their peers, forced to go to war by the government, and in other ways traumatized as they grow up. I further assume that caring support and good emotional therapy would help them to become less neurotic and more resilient.

## Is Democracy Possible and Desirable?

### IS DEMOCRATIC DECISION-MAKING POSSIBLE IN A LARGE SOCIETY?

*Is it really possible to practice participatory democracy in a large society? How could we make cooperative decisions among millions of people?*

We have only begun to use the knowledge and technology developed over the last few centuries that should make widespread democracy much more viable. At the time of the American Revolution, large distances and slow travel made direct face-to-face decision-making impossible for the large and dispersed U.S. population. At that time, electing a representative who could go to the capital and fashion legislation with other representatives by majority vote seemed like the best democratic process possible. The founders of this country presumed that people would elect wise men who would, in good faith, represent them. Now, two hundred years later, it is easy to see the limitations of this system: advertising, money, and hype distort both the electoral and legislative processes. Even the worthiest representatives are flawed human beings, subject to the lure of power, wealth, and fame. They often act on their own behalf or that of their sponsors, not on behalf of the common good.

However, we now have available to us incredibly powerful communication technologies — including telephones, mass-distribution newspapers, radio, television, email and the Internet — that allow us to communicate with people all over the world. If these technologies were used to convey solid information and to allow citizens to exchange opinions, then everyone could be far better informed. Moreover, if everyone knew the basics of cooperative discussion (speaking clearly and succinctly, listening carefully, summarizing agreements and disagreements, and synthesizing solutions), people could work together more effectively to fashion consensual agreements.

As I envision it, a good democratic process would be based on small discussion and decision groups. People would meet face-to-face with people who lived nearby to make all decisions affecting their local group. They would also appoint one or two representatives who would attend neighborhood-wide council meetings and ratify decisions on neighborhood issues. These representatives would be held strictly accountable to the will of their local group: they could only agree to measures that their local group endorsed. If a proposal at a neighborhood council meeting were not endorsed by every representative of every local group, then the representatives would formulate new proposals that each representative would then take back to her local group for more discussion and approval. Discussion of proposals would shift back and forth between local groups and the neighborhood council until all of the local groups consented to a final proposal.

In a similar manner, representatives from the neighborhood councils — who were similarly held accountable to the neighborhood councils — would make community-wide decisions in community councils. Councils of representatives at the city, region, nation, and world level would make decisions in the same fashion. Such a tiered decision-making process would enable everyone in society to have control over all decisions that affected them with a minimum of hierarchy and bureaucracy.[1]

*It won't work. We know because we haven't tried it.*
— English Proverb

This process could only work if there were effective means for discussing proposals, making cooperative decisions, and resolving conflicts, and only if everyone were skilled in using these techniques. Fortunately, great advances have been made in the fields of interpersonal communication, mediation, conflict resolution, and cooperative decision-making. Currently, few people know these techniques, but in a good society, I imagine that everyone would learn them in grade school and would be adept at using them by the time they reached adulthood.

## IS THERE ENOUGH TIME FOR REAL DEMOCRACY?

*How would people find the time to learn about a variety of issues, discuss them with others, and make good societal decisions?*

Currently, many of society's resources are devoted to producing unimportant (sometimes totally useless) consumer items and then advertising them enough to attract buyers. In a good society, I expect we could eliminate most of this waste. This would free up vast resources of time and effort.[2]

In addition, in our current society, much effort is devoted to determining who is entitled to own goods or property and who is entitled to receive services. Additional effort is devoted to enforcing these property rules. Much of the banking, insurance, and real estate industries is devoted to these tasks as well as much of the judiciary system, prison system, police, military, and private security firms. In a good society in which everyone had all her basic needs met and no one owned much more than anyone else, these tasks would require far less effort and far fewer resources.

Moreover, I expect that in a good society there would be no idle rich people and no unemployed poor people. Every able-bodied person would work throughout her life. In such a fully employed society, people would be able to work fewer hours each week than they do now. Consequently, they would have more time for childrearing, visiting with friends, and engaging in civic affairs.

I also expect that in a good society civic responsibilities would be more evenly distributed. Right now, only business managers and government officials spend much time making decisions, and they often spend all their working time attending meetings and making far-reaching decisions. Most ordinary people — overworked and disempowered — spend little time on management or civic affairs. Instead, they spend their free time entertaining themselves and trying to recover from the stress of their jobs. In a good society, I expect no one would spend all her time making societal decisions and everyone would spend some time doing so.

Moreover, decision-making would probably be a lot easier than now. Currently, many issues are raised only to inflame people so they will support particular politicians or endorse particular measures that enrich a special interest group. In a good society in which everyone had her basic needs met and in which the culture encouraged frugality, sharing, and cooperation, there would probably be much less of this needless wrangling. People would strive to find mutually acceptable solutions to conflicts, not constantly bludgeon their opponents. Better decisions would be made with more input from more people. Once a decision was made, it would probably not have to be revisited for a long time.

*Would people want to spend so much time on decision-making? Wouldn't some people decline to participate?*

Most people currently find civic affairs boring or trifling. However, in a good society in which people made important decisions, they would likely have much greater interest. The process could also be a lot more fun. Decision-making would give people a chance to interact with their neighbors, to work toward meaningful goals that directly affected their lives, and to develop creative solutions. If practiced well, I imagine decision-making could be as enjoyable as sporting events. Certainly, the results would be much more meaningful to everyone involved. Still, some people would probably decline to participate. This would be fine; no one would be forced to participate.

## Are the Five Obstacles Enumerated the Real Obstacles to Positive Change?

### WHAT ABOUT OTHER OBSTACLES?

*Philosophers and activists have posed many other obstacles to positive change. In your list of the five main obstacles, why don't you include obstacles like people's stupidity or their fear of change?*

The dumb things that people do are amazing. However, foolishness is not limited to certain people: we all make mistakes and act stupidly at times. Unquestionably, this does hinder positive change, but I do not see this as a major obstacle.

Human beings have incredible intellectual abilities, and most of the time we think remarkably well. In a good society, people would be squelched much less than they currently are, so I expect even more of everyone's intellectual capacity would be available. Overall, I believe we are smart enough to create a good society.

Clearly, some people are *more* skilled at thinking about issues or solving problems than others just as some are more physically or musically adept than others. But when people want to work together cooperatively, these differences *enhance* the process. In a cooperative atmosphere, those people who have less knowledge or understanding turn to those with more knowledge or understanding for guidance. In a cooperative group, when someone is able to come up with a good solution, everyone is happy to endorse it.

A cooperative society would draw on those who can easily perform mathematical calculations when that is required, and it would draw on those who can make music when that is desired. A cooperative society would thus function at the level of the smartest and most skilled rather than sinking to the lowest common denominator.

There are many other obstacles — like hopelessness and fear of change — that I see as subsets or combinations of the five main obstacles I described. In choosing obstacles, I tried to choose ones that were broad enough to encompass every other obstacle and that did not overlap with each other. I believe these five cover all the significant obstacles to positive, fundamental change.

### IS THE POWER ELITE MONOLITHIC?

*Is the opposition from the "power elite" a single unified force?*

Members of the power elite are not monolithic in their composition or perspective, but the interests of the elite frequently overlap and their efforts often coalesce. There is not a secret conspiracy, but there is a confluence of affluent and powerful interests who find it to their advantage to cooperate in such efforts as restricting government regulation and lowering taxes for the wealthy. These interests are centered in the corporate community and the social upper class. Institutions like the Chamber of Commerce, the Business Roundtable, the American Enterprise Institute, the Trilateral Commission, the Council on Foreign Relations, and the Bohemian Club help to solidify the perspective and culture of the elite and align their actions.

> *Washing one's hands of the conflict between the powerful and the powerless means to side with the powerful, not to be neutral.* — Paulo Freire

One sign of widespread agreement among members of the elite is that seldom does anyone in any position of wealth or power criticize capitalism, competition, property rights, wealth accumulation, or U.S. military domination of other countries (protecting "our national interests"). Most members of the elite agree on these important, fundamental tenets. Their disagreements usually involve only the details of when and how to apply these basic principles.

### ARE SOME CULTURES BETTER THAN OTHERS?

*Do you assume that some cultures are better than others? How do you decide which ones are better?*

I do not assume that any particular culture is bad or that any culture is better than another. I suspect every culture has dysfunctional and destructive aspects, as well as useful and empowering parts. For example, the perfectionism that I got from my German and English ancestors has some positive aspects, but it mostly makes me feel like I am worthless unless I do everything perfectly — which is not particularly useful. I hope that we can develop a variety of interacting cultures that draw on the best of all current cultures but have fewer destructive and dysfunctional parts.

As a social change strategy, I think it is generally best to let people criticize their own culture rather than attacking others' cultures. Most people are defensive about their culture and do not want other people to criticize it publicly. Moreover, people often already know the parts of their culture that are irrational and oppressive since they have been bludgeoned by them all their lives. When I find it necessary to criticize someone's culture, I try to put the criticism in a constructive context by listing the positive as well as negative aspects of their culture as well as my own.

### WHAT KNOWLEDGE IS ESSENTIAL?

*There are many kinds of knowledge. Who is ignorant and of what are they ignorant?*

For a good society to exist and persist, I believe people need to know how to practice democracy and cooperate with each other. They also must know how to overcome their dysfunctional cultural and emotional conditioning. Moreover, a large number of people (progressive activists and advocates) must know how to change society in a positive way. Parents and those who work with young people must know positive childrearing practices.

It would be useful if everyone were knowledgeable about nature, technology, psychology, sociology, history, culture, art, and all the other fields of knowledge, too, but this is not essential.

## Is This the Right Strategy for Change?

### WHAT DO YOU MEAN BY "FUNDAMENTAL PROGRESSIVE SOCIAL CHANGE"?

*What do you mean by the term "fundamental progressive social change"?*

By "fundamental," I mean getting to the root of problems and completely changing whatever needs to be changed to create a good society. "Progressive social change" means any activity that moves positively toward a good society. Figure 4.2 lists several behaviors and attitudes I consider progressive.

It is difficult to write about fundamental progressive social change because all the conventional terminology is either vacuous and unclear or suggestive of practices I do not endorse. I have chosen words that I think best convey what I mean and do not carry too much extraneous baggage. I have also tried to use simple, straightforward language whenever possible. Still, many people inevitably misunderstand or misinterpret these terms.

*We are getting into semantics again. If we use words, there is a very grave danger they will be misinterpreted.* — Nixon aide H.R. Haldeman testifying in his own defense at the Watergate hearings

### WHY ARE PROGRESSIVE ACTIVISTS NEEDED?

*Why do we need activists to create a good society? Why isn't the current system of private business and representational government with two parties adequate to create a good society? Shouldn't we leave the job of helping the unfortunate to churches and social service agencies?*

Our current society is based on narrow self-interest and fierce competition. It sets up an endless succession of win-lose contests. Our educational system encourages individu-alism and callous rivalry. Business is based on furious, cold-hearted competition. Any business that does not play brutally enough risks losing to others that do. Moreover, the whole economic system is structured so there will always be unemployment and unmet consumer needs (scarcity).

*The American system of ours, call it Americanism, call it Capitalism, call it what you like, gives each and every one of us a great opportunity if we only seize it with both hands and make the most of it.* — Al Capone, American gangster

As a natural consequence of this competitive and savage environment, many people — usually those beset by accident, illness, disability, physical or emotional battering, or just bad luck — end up losing one or more of these contests. Those who lose many rounds of this pernicious game usually fall so far behind that they (and their descendants) continue to lose in every future round. Even those who win can never rest since there is always the danger that someone stronger, prettier, smarter, shrewder, healthier, luckier, or more brutal will surpass them.

Our society also encourages winners to blame those who have been defeated — self-righteously calling them stupid or lazy. Moreover, our society sanctions the use of bullying to force losers to accept their miserable fate.

Such harsh institutions and such a callous culture cannot possibly produce a good society of toleration, compassion, fairness, equity, balance, democracy, and joy. At best, good-hearted individuals and church groups can alleviate some of the worst suffering created by this system, but they cannot end the misery if they only focus on helping individual victims.

Government could provide more support for those who have lost these battles and it could work toward establishing fairer competition. It could even change societal institutions to downplay competition and support compassionate alternatives. However, since the winners control government, government generally works to perpetuate competition and usually takes the winners' side.

The problem is structural and institutional. It involves the essence of our economic, political, and social systems. It can only be solved by totally transforming all aspects of our society — replacing the underlying ideology of greed and competition with one of compassion and mutual support, and replacing inhumane institutions with compassionate alternatives. The current structures are inadequate to accomplish this task.

## ARE ACTIVISTS THE ONLY ONES WHO CREATE A GOOD SOCIETY?

*Is it only "activists" who will create a good society? What about schoolteachers, ministers, social workers, planners, architects, nurses, doctors, hairdressers, and grocery store clerks? Is it only when we explicitly call ourselves "activists" and work outside existing institutions that we contribute to a good society?*

Activists are people who *actively* work to create a good society. Hence, by definition, they are the ones who will create a good society. I consider anyone of goodwill who works toward a good society to be an "activist" whether they consider themselves one or not.

In this book, I focus particularly on those who work steadfastly for fundamental, comprehensive progressive change at least a few hours each week (labeled in this book as steadfast activists and progressive advocates) because they take a leading role — they are more involved and more progressive than other activists. I hope we can greatly increase their skills and increase their numbers to more than a million. Nevertheless, in a society of several hundred million adults, these million activists cannot transform society unless they are working in conjunction with many more less-involved activists who each do their own small part. Still, if all people just live their everyday lives and only promote a good society through their normal work and relationships, then I do not believe we will have the strength to overcome the obstacles and create a good society.

## WHY ARE SO MANY ACTIVISTS REQUIRED?

*Is it really necessary to educate and organize so many activists?*

There are people with wealth and in positions of authority who currently have a vast array of powerful means to coerce or threaten anyone who tries to change society. Most of the gigantic institutions that dominate our society also have built-in mechanisms for perpetuating themselves and for preventing significant change. Our culture, including its destructive aspects, also perpetuates itself. Moreover, each of us has a multitude of internalized hurts and fears that stifle us and limit our ability even to see what is happening.

Effectively challenging the power elite, the institutions they control, and everyone's cultural and emotional conditioning requires an extremely strong counterforce. To keep this counterforce from getting out of hand and itself becoming oppressive, it must be widely dispersed and of a relatively benign nature.

For these reasons, I believe we need a large and broad movement of activists supported by the vast majority of the adult population. Since most people do not have the skills, knowledge, or desire to participate in this movement, there must be a smaller number of activists who deliberately devote time and energy to create this movement and generate interest in it. These activists must carry out a large-scale, sustained campaign to inform and inspire millions of people

to understanding and action. Likely, they will not have the money, prestige, or authority to carry out this campaign using conventional means (national advertising, massive news coverage, televised publicity stunts, celebrity endorsements, slick teacher packets, research grants to university professors, grants to social service agencies, and so on). Instead, they must rely on their own personal integrity, their large numbers, and their resolute efforts to persuade other people, one by one.

To reach a majority of the people in a country the size of the United States using direct face-to-face methods requires a very large number of activists — I assume one for every 200 adults or so. This means there must be around a million progressive activists in the United States, each working for change at least a few hours every week.

## DOES IT MAKE SENSE TO ACT WITHOUT GREATER UNDERSTANDING?

*There are many ways to think about our world and society. People have proposed many ways of solving our problems. By choosing a particular orientation and a particular solution, aren't you excluding other possibilities? How do you know this is the right strategy? Does it make sense to choose one strategy and act on it without greater understanding?*

The world is certainly multifaceted and complex. No perspective can ever be completely correct. Being open to multiple perspectives is essential if we are to avoid falling into an ideological rut. There is always a danger of believing one perspective too single-mindedly and consequently making terrible errors.

At the other end of the spectrum, however, there is always the danger of being so open to multiple perspectives that we can never make a decision or act. Paralysis of analysis can relegate us to the sidelines. Then, by doing little or nothing, we unwittingly support the status quo.

I believe we have enough understanding to act. Certainly, we will make mistakes, but if we do our best to stay true to our ideals, our worst mistakes will be minor compared to the horrors of current oppression, destruction, and war.

Like a surgeon, we must be careful not to harm the patient by intruding needlessly. Nevertheless, if the patient is severely ill, then we must operate, even if surgery is risky. We must be as careful as possible, but we must proceed.

*All that is necessary for the triumph of evil is that good men do nothing.*
— Edmund Burke

## WHY AN EDUCATION PROGRAM?

*The Vernal Project would require a large amount of time and effort — most of it devoted to education, not action. Wouldn't it be better to use these resources to support activists in their efforts to bring about change?*

My experience working in a variety of change campaigns has convinced me we need to find a better way to bring about fundamental social change. Too much of our current efforts are devoted to struggling with each other (infighting) and pursuing ineffective strategies. This wastes much of our effort and drives away many people who might support us. It saps the strength and energy we need to succeed.

I believe the time and effort required by the Vernal Education Project is worth the cost. By greatly increasing the knowledge, skill, and endurance of activists, I think it would generate far more useful effort, over the long run, than it would consume.

---

*Today the world is the victim of propaganda because people are not intellectually competent. More than anything, the United States needs effective citizens competent to do their own thinking.* — William Mather Lewis

---

### IS IT POSSIBLE TO BRING ABOUT FUNDAMENTAL CHANGE WITHOUT A FIGHT?

*Most strategies for progressive change have called for armed struggle. But the Vernal Project focuses mostly on supporting, educating, and inspiring people, not on struggle. Is it possible to bring about fundamental change without a fight?*

As I envision it, the Vernal Education Project would involve a great deal of struggle with those who stand in the way of positive change (the power structure). It would also involve a great deal of struggle to overcome destructive cultural norms and dysfunctional emotional conditioning. I see a fierce fight, sometimes dangerous and intense, spanning eighty or more years and extending into every realm of society. Some people will probably die and many more will be injured physically, mentally, and spiritually. I do not see any way around this.

However, if this battle is to lead to a good society, it must proceed in certain ways. Democracy, wisdom, and compassion typically fare poorly in savage wars. Civilians are massacred and truth vanquished. Repression, bigotry, and hatred typically do much better — often thriving — in such an environment, and they end up winning out in the end.

Therefore, we must find a way to exert massive power without undercutting our own efforts and ultimately undermining our victory. We must fight in a way that is effective, but does not destroy the things we are fighting for: truth, freedom, fairness, compassion, sustainability, tolerance, balance, and joy. To do this, activists must have the knowledge and skill to employ suitable methods in useful ways at appropriate times. The Vernal Education Program would offer this essential information to activists.

Even if we are very skilled, it seems impossible for us to bring about massive change against a deeply entrenched opposition without them causing devastating destruction. Fortunately, there are many nonviolent techniques that actually undermine our opponents in a way that restrains their response. We may also be able to outflank our opponents by educating large numbers of people, inspiring them to their best behavior, and supporting them as they shift their support from conventional institutions to alternative institutions. When large numbers of people withdraw their support from our opponents, the strength of our opponents diminishes, reducing their ability to fight back, and therefore rendering them less dangerous.

### ARE THESE THE CORRECT METHODS?

*The Vernal Project relies heavily on education, nonviolent struggle, emotional therapy, and consensus decision-making. These tactics have their limitations, and they have often been used poorly and abused. Are you sure these are the best methods?*

Education, nonviolent struggle, emotional therapy, and consensus decision-making are certainly not perfect methods of change. Still, they are usually benign and generally better than most other methods. If practiced well, they prevent activists from making too many grievous mistakes. Each of these processes encourages understanding, dissent, questioning, and challenge. They build people up so that they can speak their minds clearly and forcefully against oppression. They also promote honest interaction and compassionate embrace of other people.

---

*There are two ways for me to win an argument: I can convince my opponents that I am right. Or they can convince me they are right; then when I adopt their perspective, I also become right.*

---

Even when these methods fall short of ideals, I think they have much more potential than hierarchical authority processes or processes based solely on tradition. Such processes have aspects that squelch dissent and questioning, so they are more likely to lead to groupthink and self-righteous oppression of others.

There are still other processes — bargaining, mediation, ministering, prayer, meditation, and so on — that have potential for moving toward a good society, and I do not oppose them when they do. However, I am more wary of these processes since they do not necessarily steer people toward boldness, honesty, openness, questioning, dissent, and compassion.

### WHAT KIND OF EMOTIONAL COUNSELING DO YOU ADVOCATE?

*To improve their emotional health, do you recommend that people should talk about their childhoods and how bad they feel? If people are happier when they talk about making music, why not help them set up their lives so they make more music instead?*

I believe people can overcome their emotional obstacles in many ways. When I am depressed, confused, or emotionally stuck, I typically do the following things:
- Listen to music
- Sing, whistle, or play music
- Go for a hike or a bicycle ride
- Exercise or stretch

- Read a good book
- Go to a movie
- Go for a drive in the countryside
- Get a massage
- Talk to my friends
- Help someone out
- Ask someone to help me out
- Write in my journal
- Write a political treatise
- Have an intense political discussion with someone
- Work on an exciting project
- Make love with my partner
- Go to a therapist who can help me see a perspective I do not already have
- Think positive thoughts about better ways to act and then try to act that way
- Feel sorry for myself, then get angry and decide to fight back
- Cry or laugh intensely

Other people often do the following things (which I usually do not do):
- Watch TV
- Go to a party and dance
- Drink alcohol or take mind-altering drugs
- Play card games, board games, or video games
- Engage in competitive sports like basketball, golf, or bowling
- Watch other people play sports (on television or directly)
- Go to a store and shop
- Work in a garden
- Drive fast, skydive, river raft, etc. (engage in a mind-absorbing activity)
- Attend church
- Pray
- Gamble
- Take anti-depressant drugs
- Yell at someone, start a fight, attack someone

As far as I can tell, all of these activities help people deal with their emotional upsets and limitations to some extent. I am not opposed to any of them practiced in moderation (except the last one). Some of them are probably more efficient in helping get someone back on an even keel than others, and some of them can be destructive at times. Still, it differs for every person, so it is difficult to prescribe a single method.

When I counsel people, I try to encourage them to do what seems to work best for them. Sometimes I encourage them to be bolder. Sometimes I encourage them to be mellower. Sometimes I hold them and stroke their hair softly. Sometimes I challenge them. Usually, I try to see how they are hurt and where their limitations are, and then encourage them to overcome those limitations.

I do not care which kind of therapy or activity people use to overcome their emotional problems as long as the method they choose enables them to act intelligently and compassionately and it does not hurt anyone else.

## WHAT ABOUT ACTIVISTS IN RURAL AREAS?

*As described here, the fifty Vernal centers would be located in metropolitan areas and would generally only admit students who lived within a 75-mile radius of a center. What provision is there for activists who live in rural areas or in metropolitan areas other than these fifty?*

In developing the idea of the Vernal Education Project, I felt it essential that activists learn in their own home environment. I also felt that to minimize resource costs, the Project could not have more than fifty centers. By putting centers in the largest metropolitan centers (and having them reach out to a few metropolitan areas that are not within 75 miles of a center), I found that they could accommodate about two-thirds of the U.S. population. I think this is about as good as can be hoped. Still, in this arrangement, one-third of the population would not have direct access to a Vernal center.

However, this does not mean that one-third of the country would have no progressive activists. I see the Vernal Project as a *supplement* to progressive change movements, not a replacement for them. There are now progressive activists in almost every city, town, and rural area in the United States, and I assume this would continue throughout the time of the Vernal Education Project. As I envision it, the Vernal Project would simply increase the number of skilled and experienced activists in these fifty metropolitan areas.

Moreover, just as now occurs, I expect that the efforts of Vernal activists would spill over into other areas. The news media would report positive, powerful change activities, and activists across the country would learn of these actions and duplicate them in their own communities. Natural migration would also lead many Vernal activists — and the steadfast activists and progressive advocates they support — to move to regions where there were no Vernal centers. They would bring their knowledge and expertise to their new communities.

Furthermore, I assume Vernal activists would not focus exclusively on their own communities. Since they would be interested in creating a good society, they would want progressive change to occur in all parts of the United States (and the world). I expect they would publish their strategy and skill papers on the Internet and distribute them to anyone who wanted them. Furthermore, I expect many of them would deliberately work to reach out to activists in the outlying areas around their centers. They might periodically travel to these areas and facilitate skill-training workshops for the activists there. They might also provide telephone or email consulting to activists in these outlying communities.

### WON'T EXCLUDED ACTIVISTS BE RESENTFUL?

*Won't those activists who do not live near a Vernal center be resentful? Won't some of them move to a city with a Vernal center so they can attend a Vernal Program?*

Some activists may be discontent and move, but I hope they are not and do not. Activists are needed everywhere to bring about the transformation of society. If an activist moved close to a Vernal center and lived there for a year while attending a Vernal Program, her focus of attention and her connections would likely shift. There is a good chance she would not move back after graduating. Therefore, the community she moved away from would no longer benefit from her activist energy.

> *We fight not to enslave, but to set a country free, and to make room upon the earth for honest men to live in.*
> — Thomas Paine

To prevent this, I would expect that Vernal centers would generally be reluctant to accept applicants from outside their focus area. Instead, they would encourage Vernal graduates to facilitate educational workshops for activists in outlying areas.

I also hope that activists would understand why the Vernal Education Project was limited to fifty centers. I hope they would see that their change work in their own communities was more important than attending a Vernal Education Program.

### WHY FOCUS ON ONE NATION?

*Why do you focus on the nation-state of the United States? Why not the whole world or smaller areas like a single state or bioregion?*

By focusing on the United States, I do not mean to imply that I accept the inviolability of the system of nation-states. If we were able to create a good society, political boundaries would likely decrease in importance. Nevertheless, they are currently very important. Crucial decisions regarding the military, tax policy, civil rights, and regulation of corporations are made on the federal level. These decisions often supersede local, state, and international decisions. People frequently move from place to place within the United States, but usually do not move outside its borders. So culturally, we are more alike than different.

Still, the world is changing. Transnational entities like multinational corporations, the World Trade Organization, the United Nations, and NATO are becoming more important. Immigration, especially in California, Texas, and Florida, is significant. Over time, it will be increasingly important to address world issues.

However, for this project, it seemed prudent to choose an entity large enough to make a difference, but not so large that it was overwhelming. That is why I chose the United States as the focus of the Vernal Education Project.

### WHY FOCUS ONLY ON THE UNITED STATES?

*Why do you focus only on the United States? We live in a highly interdependent world. Multinational corporations go wherever labor is cheapest and wherever it is easiest to pollute and dispose of toxic wastes. The financial influence of countries like Kuwait, Saudi Arabia, and Venezuela greatly affects the economic and political systems in the United States. Drugs from countries like Colombia and Cambodia also greatly affect us. We should be working with The Greens in Europe and working in solidarity with struggling movements for change in Central America, Eastern Europe, Africa, Australia, Canada, Mexico, and elsewhere.*

I completely agree with these sentiments. It is essential for contemporary change movements to be aware of international issues and to work with other progressives around the world. I assume that Vernal-supported change movements would devote significant amounts of their energy toward changing conditions worldwide, just as many progressive movements do today.

As I stated in the Preface, I have focused on the United States not because I am xenophobic or parochial, but for these three reasons:

(1) This is my country, and I feel responsible for the way it works. It seems proper for me to work to clean up my home country before addressing the ills in other countries.

(2) I have lived here all my life. I understand this country much better than any other place. Immersed in this culture, I have some sense of how to change the United States. Any strategy or program I might develop for another country would likely have serious flaws.

(3) Fundamentally changing the United States would probably have more impact on the world than changing any other single country. The United States dominates the world militarily, economically, and culturally. Elite interests in the United States can and do impose their policies on most other countries. If the U.S. elite stopped dominating other countries, they could implement more programs that address the needs of their citizens instead of supporting "U.S. interests."

Also, please note that the Vernal Project is only an education and support project. The social change movements that Vernal graduates supported would probably focus on a wide variety of issues including U.S. foreign policy and economic trade with other countries. Many Vernal graduates would probably decide to travel oversees and work with groups like Doctors without Borders or Peace Brigades International at some point in their change careers.

### WOULD THE VERNAL PROJECT GO INTERNATIONAL?

*If the Vernal Project were successful in the United States, would it spread to other countries?*

As I envision it, the Vernal Project is limited to fifty Vernal centers in the United States. However, once it grew to noticeable size in Phase 2, the *concept* of the Project would likely spread around the world. If the Project were effective, I am sure that activists in other countries would replicate it in their own countries, adapting it as appropriate to fit their own cultures.

### IS IT REALLY POSSIBLE TO ATTRACT SO MANY ACTIVISTS TO JOIN THE VERNAL PROJECT?

*When the Vernal Project reaches full size, you expect 6,000 activists to attend the program every year. Is it reasonable to assume so many activists would be willing and able to attend?*

It will not be a trivial task to attract 6,000 students every year, especially in the years before Vernal graduates have had much impact on society. This is a large number compared to current change efforts. However, this figure is comparable to the number of people entering the Peace Corps each year (about 4,000). If the Vernal Project is doing well, I expect staffmembers should be able to generate enough interest and excitement in the Project to attract that many applicants.

I believe there are many people who really want to create a good society — they just do not believe it is possible, and their cynicism keeps them away. If the Vernal Project were proceeding as described in this book, these doubters would see thousands of other activists working for change. This would dispel their concerns and fears. Energized and hopeful, they would be ready and eager to attend a Vernal program. Recruiting them would only require locating them, informing them of the program, encouraging them to apply for admission, and helping them find enough money to cover their tuition and living expenses.

> *If you think you can do a thing, or think you can't do a thing, you're right.*
> — Henry Ford

### WHAT SECULAR SENTIMENT WOULD INSPIRE SO MANY ACTIVISTS TO JOIN?

*Working for progressive change is hard work and can be very dangerous. It requires a great deal of effort and usually provides little in return. Capitalism attracts adherents by appealing to self-interest. Conventional politics often attracts those who desire power and fame. Many religions attract large numbers by threatening damnation and offering salvation. What positive secular philosophy or sentiment can attract so many activists?*

As I see it, people would be attracted to the Vernal Education Project for several reasons:

(1) Some people, appalled by our current destructive and dysfunctional society, feel compelled to do something to change it. They would see the Vernal Project as a powerful, practical way to end oppression, alienation, prejudice, corruption, deceit, violence, war, strife, and destruction of the environment. They would join the Project in response to their feelings of anger, guilt, fear, or hopelessness.

(2) Some people are inspired by the noble progressive ideals of honesty, integrity, respect, compassion, generosity, democracy, equity, fairness, tolerance, responsibility, coop-

eration, community, and so on. They would see the Vernal Project as a moral and effective way to implement these ideals.

(3) Some people are inspired by their own selflessness and altruism to do the right thing and work for positive change. They would see the Vernal Project as a suitable means.

(4) Some people work for change with the hope that they can create a better world for their children and grandchildren. They too would see the Vernal Project as a suitable way to accomplish this goal.

(5) Some people would be attracted to the supportive and life-affirming atmosphere of the nascent communities of activists where progressive ideals were already partially implemented. They would join the Project to be treated well, to feel supported, and to be able to act according to progressive ideals without being exploited or ridiculed.

Each of these is a powerful motivator that I believe could attract thousands of people of goodwill and sustain them for many years as they worked for progressive change.

## Would the Vernal Project Distort Progressive Change Movements?

### WOULD THE VERNAL PROJECT CREATE AN ELITIST VANGUARD?

*Would Vernal activists become an elitist vanguard?*

Because of their greater experience and higher level of skills, Vernal activists would naturally be prominent in many movements for social change. Still, I hope that Vernal activists would see themselves only as being *different* from other activists, not particularly *special* or *privileged*.

Nevertheless, because of their unusual situation, they might have a tendency to overtly or subtly assert their "superiority" over others, to huddle with others like themselves, to become rigid in their political dogmas or actions, or to dominate others. This would be detrimental to positive social change. It is essential that they *not* be elitist or oppressive.

To minimize inappropriate behavior, I expect Vernal staffmembers would constantly remind Vernal students of the dangers of deliberate or inadvertent domination or rigidity. Staffmembers would encourage graduates to provide "leadership from below" rather than to assume prominent leadership positions. I hope graduates would develop and promote a strict code of responsible behavior and an effective feedback system to restrain any tendency toward elitism, domination, rigidity, or self-righteousness.

### WOULD THE VERNAL PROJECT FOSTER A WHITE, MIDDLE-CLASS MOVEMENT?

*If the purpose is to improve society for all people, a large-scale project must include all people (not just token representatives of minority groups). Would the Vernal Education Project actively recruit and involve a racially diverse group of staffmembers and students? Isn't the Vernal Project oriented toward white, middle-class people?*

I expect each center would be committed to diversity. I assume that Vernal staffmembers would actively recruit and involve a cross-section of all people in their community including racial minorities, men and women, rural people, working-class people, gay, lesbian, and transgendered people, younger, older, and middle-aged people, and so on. Scholarships and stipends would make it possible for low-income activists to attend a Vernal session.

Nevertheless, because the program would charge tuition and would require students and graduates to support themselves, I imagine that it would appeal more to those who were financially better off. Thus, it might attract a disproportionate number of activists from financially stable, middle-class and working-class backgrounds. There might also be a relatively higher proportion of students from wealthy backgrounds, though the number of rich people — especially those who desire fundamental progressive social change — is not large.

Still, I do not expect the imbalance to be large. I expect the students and staffmembers of the Vernal Project would be reasonably representative of the larger population.

More importantly, I assume Vernal graduates would be able to reach out to all parts of the American public. I assume the social change movements they worked with would cover a broad cross-section of society. Remember that the Vernal Education Project is not a social change movement, but a *support* program for other social change efforts. I believe the social change movements supported by the Vernal Project would be very diverse and representative of the U.S. population.

### WOULD THE VERNAL PROJECT CREATE A CULT?

*In many ways, the Vernal Education Project sounds like an indoctrination program for a cult. Would the Project be a cult? How would you prevent it from becoming cultish?*

People working primarily as social change activists have a tendency toward cult-like behavior. Working long hours and earning little money, believing themselves to have a better answer to how to live, and constantly attacked or ignored by regular people, activists can easily become separated from the mainstream. Under these circumstances, it is easy for them to fall into cultish or "groupthink" behavior. Furthermore, to actually accomplish significant social change, activists often admonish each other to be "disciplined" — which often means to adhere to a strict code of behavior that may or may not be rational or ethical.

The Vernal program would not endorse or support isolation, overwork, or other cult-inducing activity. Staffmembers would teach students about cult mind-control and groupthink, and they would do their best to interrupt rigid, elitist, or sectarian behavior. They would point out the dangers of being dogmatic "true believers" in a cause.

Moreover, Vernal staffmembers would strongly encourage Vernal activists to:

- Practice humility and abstain from self-righteousness
- Value every person
- Stay connected to relatives, friends, neighbors, and co-workers
- Think for themselves and value their own opinion
- Speak openly and keep few or no secrets
- Look at things from many different perspectives
- Seek information from varied sources and view all information skeptically
- Critically evaluate every idea, no matter its origin or promoters
- Encourage dissent and multiple points of view
- Avoid mystifying jargon
- Realistically accept bad news or setbacks (not naively deny or avoid it)
- Not dwell on bad news, setbacks, or apocalyptic visions
- Not buy into paranoia or excessive fear
- Avoid conspiratorial thinking
- Be realistic and avoid fantasizing about impossible scenarios
- Express their emotions
- Avoid guilt tripping, shaming, or humiliating themselves or others
- Refrain from attacking or demeaning others
- Avoid making irrevocable commitments
- Accept uncertainty
- Continually think — flexibly and open-mindedly

### DO YOU THINK YOU KNOW WHAT EVERYONE SHOULD DO?

*You seem to think you know what everyone should do. Do you have an agenda for us all?*

Since I am trying to create a good society, I would like a large number of people to do many things. I promote my ideas and hope that others will pick them up for the same reasons I picked them up from other people — because they seem to make sense and they might work. That is the essence of my social change strategy and why I have structured the Vernal Project as a dispersed educational program instead of as a hierarchical cult, religion, or army.

*Insanity without ambition is like a machine gun without bullets.* — Graffiti at Stanford University, 1990

I am open to changing my ideas. I hope this book starts a dialog about the best way to bring about progressive change. As we discuss these ideas, I hope that we all learn and grow and that we come up with increasingly better ideas.

### ISN'T THE VERNAL EDUCATION PROGRAM RIGID AND DOGMATIC?

*With the level of control you seem to intend in the Vernal education program, won't it be hierarchical, rigid, dogmatic, and propagandistic?*

I have tried to design an education program that has some structure so that it can contribute something valuable to the effort to create a good society. However, I also intend it to be very flexible. I have tried to build democracy and openness into every aspect of the structure. I have tried to avoid rigidity and dogmatism of every kind.

In this design, everyone who attended an education program would do so voluntarily. As I conceive it, the program has much less structure than a typical undergraduate degree program, and it only lasts a year. It would have no graduation requirements and every activity would be completely voluntary. Many of the study topics would be student-generated and the rest could (and probably would) be altered to suit the students' interests and concerns. If students wanted to revamp the program totally, I would support them as long as they understood the implications of their actions.

As I envision it, the study group readings would be diverse and include both mainstream and conservative perspectives — though the readings would emphasize a variety of progressive perspectives. Students would be exposed to a large number of perspectives by working with three separate and diverse internship organizations, their own social change organization, as well as a social service organization. They would also interact with twenty-nine fellow students and at least four different staffmembers. Students would choose all their internship programs and social service activities.

I hope that the staffmembers would spend less than a quarter of the time in which they interacted with students making presentations to them. When they did present lectures, I would expect them to lay out multiple perspectives (albeit, most of them probably progressive perspectives). I hope the staffmembers would spend most of their time asking strategic questions, setting up roleplays that enabled students to consider many perspectives, and challenging students to develop their own ideas.

I developed a detailed education program to show that it is possible to meet all of my design criteria with a reasonable one-year program. I am open to changing the curriculum, the format, or even the whole concept. I only desire that, however the program eventually develops, it meets the design criteria.

Note that graduates of the education program would be *completely* free to do whatever they wanted to do. I hope they would work assiduously and passionately for fundamental progressive change — at least for a few years — since I expect that society can only be transformed if most of them do so. Still, they could do whatever they pleased. No matter what they chose, I hope that the staffmembers

would be understanding and supportive, though we might be frustrated if graduates chose activities we thought were frivolous or counter-productive.

## Will This Strategy Take Too Long?

### WHY DOES THIS STRATEGY TAKE SO LONG?

*Most revolutions take only weeks or months to succeed — a few years at most. Why does this strategy take eighty years?*

Most revolutions make only superficial changes in society: usually just substituting one ruling group for another. The Vernal Education Project seeks democratic transformation of all of society down to its roots. This requires the vast majority of people to change significantly. They must learn a large amount of new information and develop a vast array of new skills. They must change their perspectives about most aspects of society, and they must understand and overcome a large portion of their dysfunctional and destructive cultural and emotional conditioning. All these changes take time, especially since — for many decades — the power elite and the dominant culture would continue to bombard them with misleading propaganda and advertising.

Moreover, many institutional and structural changes take decades to implement. For example, our society's severe income stratification and reliance on automobiles have led to widespread suburban sprawl, ghettoized central cities, and a car-oriented society. Reconfiguring the layout of cities to reflect the principles of sustainability, equity, and human-orientation would take many decades.

> *To reform a man, you must begin with his grandmother.*
> — Victor Hugo

The social transformation outlined here would actually entail rapid change. I assume that social change movements are relatively quiet when the Vernal Project begins. Yet, after only a few decades of development and growth (by Vernal Year 25 or so), progressive social change movements would be at least as large and strong as even the most powerful previous social change movements in this country's history — maybe much stronger. Just fifteen years after that, a majority of people all across the country would be significantly affected by these movements in all realms of their lives — political, economic, cultural, and personal. This would be an unprecedented feat — comparable to other massive socioeconomic transformations such as the industrial revolution or the computer revolution. Most historical shifts of this magnitude take many decades or even centuries to evolve.

## COULDN'T TECHNOLOGY SPEED TRANSFORMATION?

*The Internet and other technologies make it possible for activists to communicate rapidly around the world and to reach billions of people. Won't these technologies make it possible to speed the transformation process?*

Communication technologies have the potential to accelerate the process greatly. However, the power elite would likely continue to control most communication channels throughout most of the transformation process. Progressive communications would probably continue to be buried in an avalanche of banalities and advertising. Most people would not hear about (or even think of searching for) alternative ideas for many years. Only when the power to control society shifted (around Vernal Year 60 in my projections), would progressives be able to regularly promote their ideas to the majority of people.

Moreover, I believe that deep, personal change in people's perspectives and psyches take many years. These changes usually come as the result of direct and personal change experiences. Most people do not change their fundamental beliefs after merely reading an enlightening article on the Internet, hearing an alternative radio program, or receiving an email from a progressive activist. They must hear alternative perspectives many times from many sources, especially from sources they trust.

Developing new skills takes even longer. Most people must practice for weeks, months, or years before they are proficient at counseling friends, cooperating with co-workers, facilitating cooperative meetings, mediating conflicts, struggling nonviolently with opponents, and building alternative institutions. Technology can help people learn these skills, but it probably cannot accelerate the process much.

## BUT WE DON'T HAVE EIGHTY YEARS…

*The natural environment is rapidly deteriorating. Species are going extinct at a dizzying pace. Elite interests are consolidating their power globally and undermining democratic governments. Weapons of war are becoming ever more deadly and increasingly available to combatants and terrorists throughout the world. We do not have much time. We can't wait eighty years. We must act now.*

Just because there is a need for faster change does not mean that it is possible. Positive change can only come as fast as it can come.

There may be faster ways to bring about change, but many of those ways would probably be more negative than positive. I believe the Vernal Project is the best and fastest way to bring about *positive, enduring* change and to create a truly good society. I hope we can do it before the natural environment is irrevocably destroyed and before a fascist or militaristic regime engulfs and enslaves us all.

> *The only time you do not fail is the last time you try anything — and it works.*
> — William Strong

## AND WE'LL ALL BE DEAD IN EIGHTY YEARS…

*Eighty years seems like a long time. Most adults now living will be dead by then. Why should people work on a project that would not produce a result until long after they were gone?*

The Vernal Education Project focuses on a long-term goal, but this goal is quite similar to the goals that many people already have: making life better for their children or making a difference for posterity. In striving toward these goals, people know they will never see the fruits of their work, but they still work to enable future generations to have a good life.

Moreover, if the Vernal Project proceeds as I envision, there would be a great deal to see and experience after only a few years. The growth and development of the Vernal Project would be exciting in itself. Graduates of the Vernal Project would help generate social change movements comparable to those in the 1930s or 1960s within twenty to thirty years. I believe most activists could be motivated by these more short-term events along the way to the larger, more distant goal.

> *Give the gift that keeps on giving: a good society. Your grandchildren will be glad you did.*

Part of the reason I wrote this book was to lay out a realistic transformation scenario so people would understand it, believe it, and want to work toward making it happen even though they would probably not see it completed. If the Project developed in the early years as I describe it here, readers of this book would have reason to believe that it would proceed to the conclusion described.

## What About…?

### RESISTANCE TO ATTACK AND SUBVERSION?

*The power elite regularly sabotages social change movements through various kinds of surveillance, disruption, and attack. Agents of the elite spread disinformation about activists, provoke infighting among activists, encourage activists to be belligerent, promote violent change tactics, and assassinate movement leaders. How would the Vernal Project resist infiltrators, provocateurs, and assassins from disrupting or discrediting progressive change movements?*

There is no way to safeguard movements from infiltration and disruption, but the Vernal Project would foster social change movements that were less susceptible to these efforts in a variety of important ways.

The Vernal Education Project would create and promote:

• **Savvy activists**: Vernal activists would know the history of movement sabotage, and they would probably be able to recognize disruptive techniques. They could warn their fellow activists about and would know how to respond effectively to sabotage, character assassination, and disruption.

• **Decentralized leadership**: By empowering and building leadership skills among thousands of people, movements supported by the Vernal Education Project would be much less vulnerable to assassination or co-optation of a few leaders. Likely, there would be hundreds or thousands of people who could step forward and carry on whenever any single person was killed, disabled, or co-opted.

• **Geographical decentralization**: Change movements supported by Vernal activists would be dispersed all over the country. This would make them less vulnerable to charges of regional elitism (such as "Yankees are trying to run our lives" or "Washington bureaucrats are trying to dictate what we do"). It would also make the overall change movement less vulnerable to local or regional attacks.

• **Homegrown activists**: Generally, Vernal students would live in their home communities while attending a Vernal session and would continue to live there after graduating. This would make them less vulnerable to community concerns about "outside agitators." By building direct and personal connections with many people in the community, each progressive activist could garner broad support whenever she was unfairly attacked. Because each activist would be working in her home community, she would probably also be better at understanding and dealing with her antagonists.

• **Network of support**: Vernal activists would probably have strong connections to other Vernal activists. If attacked locally, they could ask for support from other Vernal activists outside their locality.

• **Focus on diverse issues**: Vernal-supported change movements would address a wide variety of issues. This would force opponents to challenge these movements on many fronts, which would likely reduce the extent of opposition or reformist co-optation on any particular issue. Also, by working on all kinds of economic, racial, social, and cultural issues simultaneously and taking a broad progressive perspective, Vernal-supported movements would be less vulnerable to accusations of elitism, classism, racism, sexism, ageism, homophobia, and so forth.

• **Strong progressive community**: Vernal-supported change movements would develop a strong community spirit. Activists would probably know and like each other, which would make them less vulnerable to character assassination. I expect each activist would also have much greater personal support from her friends and colleagues than most activists do now. This would make each one less vulnerable to intimidation.

• **Emotionally healthy activists**: Vernal activists and those they supported would probably be much more emotionally healthy than current activists. This would mean they would be less susceptible to manipulation by guilt-, hate-, and fear-mongers.

• **Greater understanding of conflict and how to resolve it**: Members of Vernal-supported change groups would know that conflict is inevitable and that it can be positive if handled well. Hence, they would be less likely to suppress conflict. Vernal activists would also be skilled and knowledgeable in mediating and resolving conflict.

• **Practice of progressive ideals**: I expect Vernal-supported social change groups would attempt to adhere to progressive ideals. Their change actions would strive toward goals of fairness, equity, and democracy and their tactics would be open, forthright, democratic, and nonviolent. In this context, secretive, manipulative, or offensive tactics or shortsighted shortcuts advocated by provocateurs would have little appeal. In addition, by adhering to these ideals, progressive movements would be widely admired. It would be much harder for opponents to criticize or stigmatize them.

• **Clear understanding of fundamental progressive change**: Members of Vernal-supported change groups would probably have a clear understanding of the need for long-term, fundamental progressive change. Consequently, they would be less susceptible to calls to accept limited reform or to use unsavory tactics.

• **Alternative means of communication**: Vernal-supported change groups would lilely build robust alternative means of communication between their organizations such as face-to-face meetings, internal newsletters, frequent phone calls, and email. They would also build effective means to communicate to the public such as publications, community radio, and web sites. These communication channels would be less susceptible to disinformation and rumors propagated through conventional media or through infiltrators. Movement supporters could hear directly from activists instead of hearing interpretations disseminated by a hostile mainstream press.

*In Germany they came first for the Communists, and I didn't speak up because I wasn't a Communist. Then they came for the Jews, and I didn't speak up because I wasn't a Jew. Then they came for the trade-unionists, and I didn't speak up because I wasn't a trade-unionist. Then they came for the Catholics, and I didn't speak up because I was a Protestant. Then they came for me and by that time no one was left to speak up.*
— attributed to Rev. Martin Niemoller

### DOES THE PROJECT PROVIDE RESISTANCE TO TAKEOVER?

*What would prevent the Vernal education network from being taken over by infiltrators with the intention of disabling or discrediting the whole Vernal Project?*

Because each Vernal education center would not actually do any social change work, I assume it would be a less inviting target for infiltration than a change organization. Also, by being extremely dispersed geographically and with little national structure (there would be no national office or national staffmembers and the regional administrators would make no important decisions), it would be difficult to take over the Vernal network.

Furthermore, since the Vernal Project would produce relatively few graduates and would have little influence throughout Phases 1 and 2 (through Vernal Year 20), I hope that it would not attract much attention until it was firmly established.

The nature of the Vernal Education Project should also protect it from infiltration. To become a Vernal staffmember (or a new staff preparer), an activist would have to demonstrate a long history of positive change activity. Hence, it would not be easy for infiltrators to become staffmembers. The board of directors for each Vernal center would consist of Vernal staffmembers, students, and graduates as well as a few activists from the local progressive community. Each would have to demonstrate a relatively long history of progressive change work. Consequently, it is unlikely that infiltrators could take over the board.

If a few infiltrators did make it onto the board of a Vernal center, they could be disruptive. However, the other members of the board would be skilled and knowledgeable. They would likely spot an infiltrator who tried to disrupt the center. They could use their skill and knowledge for resolving conflict, and their ability to counsel activists, to confront anyone who was disruptive. Moreover, since the board would use a cooperative consensus decision-making process, those who were not open, cooperative, and oriented toward problem solving would stand out. If a boardmember refused to work honestly with others to resolve conflicts, it would be relatively easy to develop a consensus among the other members to remove that person from the board.

### DOES THE PROJECT PROVIDE RESISTANCE TO DOMINATION?

*What would prevent the Vernal education network from being dominated by progressive activists with big egos?*

Again, I assume that the emotional health of the Vernal staffmembers would be relatively good, and they would be knowledgeable and skilled. I expect they would rarely act arrogantly or try to dominate others. When one did, her colleagues (usually three others) could quickly intervene. I expect these other staffmembers would be strong and skilled enough to challenge, support, and counsel the errant staffmember until she stopped acting out.

## Still…

### IT JUST SEEMS IMPOSSIBLE…

*The whole undertaking just does not seem possible. The goal is so ambitious. The ideas have to be wrong. It has to be too simple or too naïve or missing something. How do you know this will work?*

Honestly, I do not know if it will work. However, just because something has never occurred before does not mean it can never happen. Slavery was common 150 years ago, but is now mostly gone. Capital punishment is considered barbaric in most of the world and only a few countries still allow it (unfortunately, one being the United States). The

computers, telecommunication satellites, and jet aircraft we take for granted now were just the imaginings of a handful of crazy dreamers a few decades ago.

In our current society, it is especially difficult to imagine any genuine positive change. Television news assaults us every day with a stupefying brew of dreadful images of disasters and tragedies, inane reports on trivial events, and titillating but useless gossip. Politicians regularly drown us with deceptive blather and disingenuous promises that they seldom keep. Advertising constantly bombards us with splashy images and clever appeals that tempt us to purchase worthless products. At the same time, most things of true value to human beings are ignored, mocked, or repackaged into banal commodities. So our whole culture repeatedly and pervasively informs us that significant positive change is impossible. Hopelessness permeates our society like a thick cloud of poisonous gas, numbing our senses and killing our spirits. The heavy weight of despair keeps us down.

*That which seems the height of absurdity in one generation often becomes the height of wisdom in another.*
— Adlai Stevenson

Moreover, cynics incessantly cite innate human frailties like greed and arrogance, and they recount the many previous failed efforts for positive change. But these are really more excuses than reasons for failure. For every way in which humans are warped or weak, there is a way in which we are noble and strong. For every promising initiative that has failed, another soared beyond anyone's expectations.

*Every noble work is at first impossible.*
— Thomas Carlyle

I believe there are only five main obstacles to creating a good society and none of them is insurmountable. We can overcome each by applying skilled effort methodically and patiently over time. It may seem impossible — but I believe our hopeless feelings indicate only how difficult it has been in the past for us to succeed and how painful it has been for us to fail repeatedly.

Still, I may be wrong. It may be impossible to create a good society, or this particular way of getting there may be the wrong path.

I am heartened by the responses of the many experienced activists who critically evaluated the draft of this book. Most expressed general skepticism that it would work, but almost none offered specific reasons why it could not work. Almost all of them encouraged me to continue working on this project.

*The whole problem with the world is that fools and fanatics are always so certain of themselves, and wiser people so full of doubts.* — Bertrand Russell

I do not know if this effort will work or not, but I believe it is the best chance we have.

### YOUR ASSUMPTIONS MAY BE WRONG...

*You make a large number of estimates and projections about how things might evolve. Are you sure these are all reasonable?*

Writing this book forced me to specify concretely how everything might work. Consequently, I am aware of the considerable number of assumptions and assertions I make and how large some of them are. Each is subject to challenge and criticism. In fact, *I* can formulate powerful arguments against almost every assumption and assertion that I make. Then again, I also have strong and persuasive arguments in support of each of them.

*Only those who attempt the absurd can achieve the impossible.* — Graffiti

Overall, after carefully evaluating each one, I am convinced these assumptions are sensible, reasonable, and compelling. Still, they may be wrong. As the Vernal Project proceeds, we can check these assumptions to see how reliable they are and revise the Project accordingly.

### WILL THIS REALLY WORK?

*If your assumptions are faulty, this project will probably not work out. What happens if the Vernal Education Project never happens?*

If the Project failed to take off, it might be because my ideas were faulty — my understanding too naïve, my projections for the future too utopian, or my plans just plain misdirected. If so, then I would need to reconsider all my assumptions and reasoning and then start over.

*A cynic is an idealist turned inside out.*
— Graffiti

It may be that the analysis is correct, but that the forces arrayed against positive change are just too strong. Then the Project would ultimately fail. This would be disheartening. Still, I believe the effort would have been worthwhile. It is far better to strive for a grand goal and fail than never to have striven at all.

If we proceed yet fail, our efforts will not go to waste: whatever curriculum we develop, workshops we facilitate, and positive change we are able to bring about will be valuable and will contribute to progressive transformation. I believe it is worth making the attempt.

*In great attempts, it is glorious even to fail.* — Cassius

*The probability that we may fail in the struggle ought not to deter us from the support of a cause we believe to be just.*
— Abraham Lincoln

*Defeat is not the worst of failures. Not to have tried is the true failure.* — George E. Woodberry

For more objections and concerns, and to join a discussion of the Vernal Education Project, see:
<http://www.vernalproject.org>

---

## NOTES FOR CHAPTER 11

[1] I imagine a local group might encompass about 10 families (roughly 20 adults). A neighborhood might then include 20 of these local groups (400 adults in all), and a typical community might have 25 of these neighborhood groups (10,000 adults). A typical city might encompass 20 of these communities (comprising 200,000 adults). Fifty cities (totaling ten million adults) would constitute a district, state, or bioregion. With just two more levels (seven levels in all), everyone in the world could be included.

Kirkpatrick Sale in **Human Scale** (New York: Coward, McCann & Geoghegan, 1980, HC106.7 .S24 1980), p. 179–208, investigates the optimal size for human groups. He discovers that a face-to-face association — a tribe, village, or neighborhood in which everyone knows everyone else — typically has about 500 members. Communities typically have about 5,000–10,000 people. This is large enough to provide all necessary services, but still enables people to live within easy walking distance of each other. The most desirable cities typically have 50,000–100,000 people.

Note that people would likely form additional groupings — based on their common jobs, interests, hobbies, lifestyles, ethnicity, gender, or age — to discuss issues that affect particular facets of themselves. These cross-connections would further foster consensus across society.

[2] A few obvious examples of items that would be unnecessary in a good society: most advertising and junk mail; cigarettes and other destructive drugs; symbols of conspicuous wealth like mansions, luxury yachts, luxury autos, backyard swimming pools, and expensive jewelry.

In a good society, people would live closer to their work and would spend less time commuting, and there would be much better mass transportation and fewer cars. This would result in many fewer collisions thus reducing the need for health and rehabilitative care. In addition, the environment would be much less polluted so there would be less need for health services to repair the damage to our bodies caused by pollutants and toxic waste.

# *12*

# *Resources*

**In This Chapter:**

**Books and Articles**

**Book Publishers**

**Magazines**

**Radio Programs**

**Web Sites**

This chapter describes a large number of resources for learning about progressive ideas and social change efforts. It includes books, articles, publishers, radio programs, and web sites. Those resources that are accessible on the Internet include email addresses and web references.

## *BOOKS AND ARTICLES*

This section lists a few of the books and articles used to develop the ideas in this work. Some of the references are annotated. References cited in the text include the chapter number in brackets [ ] indicating where they are cited. In addition, references include a Library of Congress catalog number to make them easier to locate in a research library.

Resources are grouped in these categories:

• **Visions of a Good Society**
  • Utopian Novels
  • Socialism
  • Anarchism
  • Other Visions

• **Critiques of Society**
  • General
  • The Power Elite
  • Corporations
  • Distribution of Wealth
  • Economics
  • The Environment
  • Communication Media
  • Hunger
  • Racism
  • Prisons
  • Suppression of Activists
  • Competition
  • Feminist Critiques
  • Children
  • Childrearing
  • Schools
  • Other Destructive Cultural Norms
  • Groupthink and Cults

• **Social Change History**
  • General
  • The Populist Movement (1870s–1890s)
  • Early Twentieth Century Efforts
  • The Labor Movement
  • Efforts in the 1950s
  • The 1960s Movements
  • Movements in the 1970s, 1980s, and 1990s

*The books which help you most are those which make you think the most.*
— Theodore Parker

• **Methods of Changing Society**
  • General
  • Theory and Analysis
  • Simple Living
  • Overcoming Destructive Cultural Norms
  • Overcoming Dysfunctional Emotional Conditioning
  • Education
  • Persuasion and Lobbying
  • Building Social Change Movements
  • Community Organizing
  • Organizing Manuals and Handbooks
  • Nonviolent Struggle
  • Building Social Change Organizations
  • Cooperative Decision-Making
    • Theory and Analysis
    • Consensus Decision-Making
    • Problem Solving
    • Conflict Resolution
  • Building Activist Finances
  • Other

• **Other Cited Works**

## Visions of a Good Society

### • *UTOPIAN NOVELS*

Bellamy, Edward. *Looking Backward, 2000–1887*. 1888; edited with an introduction by Cecelia Tichi. New York: Penguin Books, 1982, PS1086 .L6 1982.

In 1887, a young man falls into a trance. He awakens 113 years later in a world of peace and plenty. In this utopian society, everyone attends school until age 21, performs unskilled labor for three years, then works in a skilled career job until retirement at age 45. Housework is treated like all other work. Workers in arduous and dangerous trades work fewer hours than those performing easier tasks — the rate determined by how many people choose each profession. All people are expected to work to their ability.

Everyone in society, whether working or not, receives equal payment at the beginning of each year to spend as he/she chooses. This total economic equality among people completely eliminates poverty and greatly reduces crime. It also encourages cooperation and goodwill, ending the impetus for dishonesty, political wrangling, and war.

Workers are induced to high production by incentives of social rankings and through military-like discipline in the "industrial army" — which I find a bit objectionable. Otherwise, this socialist vision seems workable and persuasive. The system for publishing books and periodicals and for producing art is particularly innovative.

Bryant, Dorothy. *The Kin of Ata are Waiting for You*. New York: Moon Books/Random House, 1971, PS3552 .R878 .K5.

A violent and alienated man is transformed by his unexpected visit to an island inhabited by simple people who live peacefully, guided strictly by their dreams. The book begins with a violent murder, but then creates a genuinely uplifting spirit that touches one's soul and makes the softening and socializing of a violent man seem clearly possible.

Callenbach, Ernest. *Ecotopia: The Notebooks and Reports of William Weston*. Berkeley, CA: Banyan Tree Books, 1975, PS3553 .A424 E2.

At a time in the future (1980), Washington, Oregon, and Northern California secede from the United States and create a positive, ecologically sustainable society. Twenty years later, a journalist visits Ecotopia and reports on all aspects of this attractive society.

This novel abounds with interesting and innovative ideas.

_____. *Ecotopia Emerging*. Berkeley, CA: Banyan Tree Books, 1981, PS3553 .A424 E3.

A prequel to *Ecotopia* that describes how the revolution came about. Though improbable, it offers more stimulating ideas about social change and visions of a good society.

Gilman, Charlotte Perkins. *Herland*. 1915; reprint: New York: Pantheon Books, 1979, PZ3 .G4204He 1979.

In this utopian novel, three male adventurers stumble across an all-female society hidden high in a large valley in the mountains. Though suffering from antiquated, racist ideas and Victorian notions about sexuality and perfectionism, Gilman's feminist and communitarian vision makes perceptive observations about sexism, classism, childrearing, education, criminality, and religion. It also offers positive alternatives.

*As recent students of utopia have articulated, vigorous utopian thinking sketches models of a peaceable kingdom, points us toward society's repressed possibilities, enables us to see more clearly actual tendencies, both positive and negative, strengthens our grounds for rejecting existing social forms, reactivates lost dreams and longings, and encourages political action.*
— Ronald Aronson[1]

Heinlein, Robert A. *The Moon is a Harsh Mistress*. New York: Ace Books, 1966, PS3515 .E288 M66. [Chap. 2]

This science fiction novel shows that it is relatively easy to overthrow a dictatorship when most vital functions of society (a penal colony underneath the surface of the moon) are run by a supercomputer that is so large it has awakened into consciousness — and this conscious computer sympathizes with the revolutionary cause.

Though completely improbable, this novel does summarize conventional ideas about organizing a violent revolution through secret cells. It also offers some interesting alternatives to nuclear families.

Huxley, Aldous. *Island*. New York: Perennial/Harper & Row, 1962, PR6015 .U9I8.

This novel champions Eastern religion and hallucinogenic drugs too much for my tastes, but it has several interesting ideas about education and recovery from traumatic emotional experiences.

LeGuin, Ursula K. *The Dispossessed*. New York: Harper & Row/Avon, 1974, PZ4 .L518Di.

A planet much like the Earth (called Urras) has exiled members of a nonviolent, anarchist change movement to its very desolate moon (Annares). After two hundred years of almost complete separation, a physicist from Annares travels to Urras and observes the differences between the two societies.

Urras is extremely stratified with the rich dominating the poor, men dominating women, and a few countries dominating the rest. In sharp contrast, Annares has almost no status distinctions (and hence no racism, sexism, classism, or nationalism). Everyone performs both manual and intellectual labor. Money is not used — instead each person takes what she needs and offers what she can. Still, in this attractive society, bureaucracy, rigidity, and personal fiefdoms develop and must be resisted.

> *There is nothing like dream to create the future. Utopia today, flesh and blood tomorrow.* — Victor Hugo

This wonderfully engrossing novel makes a communitarian-anarchist society seem very possible and desirable.

Morris, William. *News from Nowhere*. 1890; reprinted in *Three Works by William Morris*. New York: International Publishers, 1968.

The morning after a Socialist League meeting in 1890, a man awakens one hundred twenty years later. He discovers that a general strike led to a successful revolution in 1952 and that society is now egalitarian and environmentally oriented.

Gender roles in this utopian vision are somewhat traditional, but otherwise it is amazingly forward looking as it explores architecture, love, work, economics, ecology, and revolution.

Piercy, Marge. *Woman on the Edge of Time*. New York: Knopf, 1988 [1976], PS3566 .I4 W6 1988.

Held against her will in a mental hospital, a woman is visited telepathically by a woman from the year 2137 who describes her world. This novel contrasts the horrors of 1960s mental wards with the gentle egalitarianism of a future world. Though depressing overall and somewhat dated in its perspective, it presents many innovative ideas including gender-blind terminology: "person" and "per" instead of "he" and "his."

Starhawk. *The Fifth Sacred Thing*. New York: Bantam, 1993, PS3569 .T33565 F54 1993.

This vision relies too much on goddess magic for my tastes, but it does provide a nice description of nonviolent resistance to armed attack.

## • SOCIALISM

Aronson, Ronald. *After Marxism*. New York: Guilford Press, 1995, HX44.5 .A78 1994. [Preface, Chapters 4, 5, and 12]

Long-term Marxist philosopher and theorist Ronald Aronson persuasively argues that the Marxist Project as described by Marx has not yet and never will occur. He argues for a new, radical change project that differs from the Marxist project in several ways:

First, it will be without historical certainty…

Second, a movement aiming at significant change will be a politics of identity as well as a politics of social structures and power. . . .

Third, the theories and explanations that a new movement will draw on will have an open character, rather than being passed off as a single and certain revolutionary science. . . .

Fourth, a new radical movement will abandon the notion that it is theoretically and practically focused on a single decisive area of human oppression [class] and a single social agent who can pull the lever to transform it [the proletariat]. . . .

Finally, if there is to be a movement, it will have to become one as a coalition of groups and forces each seeking their own changes. It will be based on a plurality of needs and demands, will have to focus on changing a plurality of structures and practices and attitudes, and its various component groups will have to learn how to interact collectively and with mutual respect. Its general appeal — its unity — if it is to exist, will have to be built group by group, block by block.

In short, if there is to be a new radical project, it will scarcely resemble what we children of Marx have come to expect. (pp. 179–180)

He also argues that morality should be at the center of this new, radical project.

Feuer, Lewis S., ed. *Marx and Engels: Basic Writings on Politics and Philosophy*. Garden City, NY: Anchor, Doubleday, 1959, HX276 .M27736. [Chap. 4]

The eighteen papers in this collection outline the basic philosophy of Karl Marx and Friedrich Engels, their criticism of capitalism, and their vision of a socialist transformation. This anthology includes *The Communist Manifesto* and excerpts from *Capital: A Critique of Political Economy*.

Harrington, Michael. *Socialism: Past and Future*. New York: Arcade/Little, Brown and Company, 1989, HX44 .H35 1989.

Harrington reviews the history of socialism and argues for democratic socialism.

## • ANARCHISM

Ehrlich, Howard J., ed. *Reinventing Anarchy, Again*. San Francisco: AK Press, 1996, HX833 .R43 1995. Revised edition of *Reinventing Anarchy*, 1978.

Anarchism, often maligned as promoting chaos, destruction, and bloodshed, actually promotes cooperation and personal responsibility. The thirty-four essays in this collection describe contemporary anarchist theory and practice, particularly anarchafeminism, worker self-management, liberatory culture, self-liberation, and the process of building an anarchist society.

Goldman, Emma. *Living my Life*. New York: Dover Publications, 1970, HX843 .G6A3 1970 [New York: Knopf, 1931].

In this autobiography, anarchist Goldman (1869–1940) describes how she fought for the poor and oppressed, and then how the United States deported her to the Soviet Union in 1919. There, she discovered the dark side of the Bolshevik Revolution and began speaking out against leftist oppression as well as capitalist oppression.

Krimerman, Leonard I., and Lewis Perry, eds. *Patterns of Anarchy: A Collection of Writings on the Anarchist Tradition*. Garden City, NY: Doubleday/Anchor, 1966, HX828 .K7.

The fifty-seven essays in this collection look at anarchism from a variety of perspectives. The collection includes articles by Peter Kropotkin, Michael Bakunin, Leo Tolstoy, Dorothy Day, Alexander Berkman, Emma Goldman, Max Stirner, George Woodcock, Bertrand Russell, Paul Goodman, Colin Ward, and many others.

Kropotkin, Peter. *Kropotkin's Revolutionary Pamphlets: A Collection of Writings by Peter Kropotkin*. Introduction, biographical sketch, and notes by Roger N. Baldwin, ed. New York: Dover Publications, 1970 [1927], HX915 .K89.

_____. *The Essential Kropotkin*. Emile Capouya and Keitha Tompkins, eds. New York: Liveright, 1975, HX828 .K73 1975.

At the time when capitalist ideas of unfettered competition were coming to dominate society, Kropotkin focused on developing a workable anarchist society — one based on mutual aid, reciprocity, and cooperation. This collection of his writings presents his practical ideas for reshaping all aspects of society.

Ward, Colin. *Anarchy in Action*. Fourth Printing. London: Freedom Press, 1982 [1973], HX833 .W37.

Ward explores the ways that people organize themselves when they are not restricted by government or other coercive structures.

### • OTHER VISIONS

Satin, Mark. *New Options for America: The Second American Experiment Has Begun*. Fresno: The Press at California State University, Fresno, 1991.

In these essays from his *New Options* magazine, Satin describes a variety of innovative ideas developed and promoted by various nonprofit organizations. Though some of the ideas seem naïve or misguided, many are fascinating.

Shuman, Michael H. *Going Local: Creating Self-Reliant Communities in a Global Age*. New York: The Free Press, Simon & Schuster, 1998, HC110 .E5S49 1998. [App. A]

Shuman proposes a new economics based primarily on the support of local communities. Specifically, he makes a convincing case for for-profit businesses whose shareholders are required to be local residents of a community. He argues these corporations would be more likely to be socially responsible than global corporations, perhaps even more than nonprofits, cooperatives, or public enterprises.

He provides an excellent critique of multinational corporations and global trade and offers a variety of sensible policy initiatives that would strengthen communities and make them more responsive to the people who live in them. These include:

• Investing in locally owned businesses like credit unions, municipally owned utilities, community land-trusts, community development corporations, cooperatives, small worker-owned companies, and especially local shareholder-owned companies.

• Developing local industries that can conserve or produce essential items such as food, energy, and natural resources that are typically imported instead of encouraging and enticing industries oriented towards export.

• Changing tax and trade laws that disempower communities or that subsidize irresponsibility.

## Critiques of Society

**Note**: There are thousands of excellent books offering progressive critiques of society. Listed here are a few that provide an overview, some that are particularly relevant to the thesis of this book, and a few with particularly interesting perspectives. Consult the catalogs of the progressive publishers listed at the end of this chapter for more comprehensive lists of recent books. Especially noteworthy, are the many works by Noam Chomsky and Michael Parenti.

### • GENERAL

Benewick, Robert, and Philip Green, eds. *The Routledge Dictionary of Twentieth-Century Political Thinkers*. 2nd ed. London and New York: Routledge, 1997, JA83 .R725 1997.

This dictionary provides a useful guide to political ideas in the twentieth century. Each of the 174 entries includes a short biography of the individual profiled, his or her main ideas, commentary on the ideas, and a short bibliography.

Miller, David, ed. *The Blackwell Encyclopedia of Political Thought*. Oxford, UK: Blackwell Publishers, 1987, JA61 .B57 1987. [Chap. 4]

This valuable reference has 350 entries covering both political philosophies and the people who conceived and promoted them. Each entry includes commentary and a short bibliography.

Outhwaite, William, and Tom Bottomore, eds. *The Blackwell Dictionary of Twentieth-Century Social Thought*. Oxford, UK, and Cambridge, MA: Blackwell Publishers, 1993, H41 .B53 1993.

This valuable reference focuses on recent social philosophies.

Ruggiero, Greg, and Stuart Sahulka, eds. *The New American Crisis: Radical Analyses of the Problems Facing America Today*. New York: New Press, 1995, E885 .N48 1996.

These 23 essays and interviews address many of the essential issues of our time and offer alternative solutions.

## • THE POWER ELITE

Barlett, Donald L., and James B. Steele. *America: What Went Wrong?*. Kansas City, MO: Andrews and McMeel, 1992, HC106.8 .B373 1992.

Based on their articles in the *Philadelphia Inquirer*, Barlett and Steele describe how elite interests in Washington and on Wall Street have changed the rules to benefit the privileged, the powerful, and the influential at the expense of everyone else.

Domhoff, G. William. *The Higher Circles: The Governing Class in America*. New York: Random House, 1970, HN58 .D575.

Domhoff explores various characteristics of the upper class. He also demonstrates a variety of research methods for analyzing this group, which is difficult to study using the usual methods.

_____. *The Powers that Be: Processes of Ruling Class Domination in America*. New York: Random House, Vintage, 1978, HN90 .E4D65 1979b. [Chap. 3]

Domhoff reveals how the owners and managers of large banks and corporations obtain special tax breaks, subsidies, and other economic favors from the government. He also examines the way they dominate government regulatory policy, foreign policy, economic development programs, and the candidate selection process.

_____. *Who Rules America Now?: How the "Power Elite" Dominates Business, Government, and Society*. New York: Simon & Schuster/Touchstone, 1986, HN90 .E4 D652 1986. [Chap. 3]

_____. *Who Rules America: Power and Politics in the Year 2000*. 3rd ed. Mountain View, CA: Mayfield Publishing, 1998, HN90 .E4 D654 1998. [Chap. 3]

Domhoff presents systematic, empirical evidence that elite interests dominate the American economy and government. In this most recent edition, he uses a variety of terms — "the power elite," "the power structure," "the corporate community," "the powers that be," "the higher circles," "the corporate rich," "the corporate-conservative coalition," and "the dominant class" — to describe the various elements and aspects of the elite.

Hightower, Jim. *There's Nothing in the Middle of the Road But Yellow Stripes and Dead Armadillos*. New York: HarperCollins, 1997, E885 .H56 1997.

In this funny and accessible book, populist Hightower details the class war being waged by the power elite and corporations against the rest of us.

Lapham, Lewis H. *Money and Class in America: Notes and Observations on our Civil Religion*. New York: Weidenfeld & Nicolson, 1988, HC110 .W4 L24 1988.

Mills, C. Wright. *The Power Elite*. New York: Oxford University Press, 1956, E169.1 .M64. [Chap. 3]

Mills describes the circle of rich people, politicians, corporation executives, celebrities, and admirals and generals who constitute the power elite.

Trounstein, Philip J., and Terry Christensen. *Movers and Shakers: The Study of Community Power*. New York: St. Martin's Press, 1982, JC330 .T86. [Chap. 3]

Trounstein and Christensen explain several theories about community power, then use the reputational method to identify the most powerful people in San Jose, California.

## • CORPORATIONS

Barnet, Richard J., and Ronald E. Mueller. *Global Reach: The Power of the Multinational Corporations*. New York: Touchstone/Simon and Schuster, 1974, HD69 .I7 .B32.

Estes, Ralph W. *Tyranny of the Bottom Line: Why Corporations Make Good People Do Bad Things*. San Francisco: Berrett-Koehler Publishers, 1996, HD60 .E784 1996.

Estes describes how corporations — largely unconstrained by captive regulatory agencies — have achieved a powerful dominance over society. This has resulted in poisoning of the environment, unsafe working conditions, unhealthy and dangerous products, massive layoffs, skyrocketing CEO salaries, and lavish financial bailouts. He offers a specific reform plan for creating more effective and humane companies by means of an evaluation system to tally the effects of a corporation's actions on all its stakeholders, not just its stockholders.

Kallen, Laurence. *Corporate Welfare: The Megabankruptcies of the 80s and 90s*. Secaucus, NJ: Carol Publishing. Group, 1991, KF1539 .K34 1990.

Korten, David C. *When Corporations Rule the World*. West Hartford, CT: Kumarian Press; San Francisco: Berrett-Koehler Publishers, 1995, HD2326 .K647 1995.

Korten, a former U.S. Agency for International Development official, describes the power of global corporations and the devastating consequences of economic globalization.

Greider, William. *Who Will Tell the People?: The Betrayal of American Democracy*. New York: Simon & Schuster/Touchstone, 1992, JK1764 .G74 1992.

Greider describes the reality of power in Washington, especially the hidden relationships that link politicians with corporations and the rich. He also shows how these power dynamics subvert the needs of ordinary citizens.

Waldman, Michael, and the staff of Public Citizen's Congress Watch. *Who Robbed America?: A Citizen's Guide to the S&L Scandal*. New York: Random House, 1990, HG2151 .W35 1990.

## • DISTRIBUTION OF WEALTH

Barlett, Donald L., and James B. Steele. ***America: Who Really Pays the Taxes?*** New York: Simon and Schuster, Touchstone, 1994, HJ2381 .B37 1994. [Ch. 3, App. A]

> Barlett and Steele show how tax policy targets the poor and the middle-class and benefits corporations and the rich.

Collins, Chuck, Betsy Leondar-Wright, and Holly Sklar. ***Shifting Fortunes: The Perils of the Growing American Wealth Gap***. Boston [37 Temple Place, 02111, (617) 423-2148 <http://www.stw.org>]: United for a Fair Economy, 1999.

> This small book provides an excellent overview of the gap in wealth between the rich and poor in the United States. It includes eighteen tables of recent data.

Phillips, Kevin. ***Boiling Point: Democrats, Republicans and the Decline of Middle-Class Prosperity***. New York: HarperCollins, 1994, HT690 .U6P48 1994. [App. A]

> Phillips, a Republican campaign strategist, describes the decline of the middle-class in the 1980s.

_____. ***The Politics of Rich and Poor: Wealth and the American Electorate in the Reagan Aftermath***. New York: Random House, 1990, HC110 .W4 P48 1990. [Chap. 3]

> Phillips shows how President Reagan's tax policies shifted money from the poor to the rich.

Pizzigati, Sam. ***The Maximum Wage: A Common-Sense Prescription for Revitalizing America by Taxing the Very Rich***. New York: Apex Press, 1992, HC110 .I5P59 1992. [Chap. 3, App. A]

> Pizzigati traces the history of U.S. tax policy and the many popular struggles to limit the incomes of the very wealthy. He argues for new federal income tax rates calibrated to the minimum wage that would tax away the excess income of the richest one percent and provide a hefty tax reduction for everyone else.

Zepezauer, Mark, and Arthur Naiman. ***Take the Rich Off Welfare***. Tucson: Odonian Press, 1996, HJ7537 .Z46 1996.

> In this short book, Zepezauer and Naiman enumerate the various subsidies, handouts, tax breaks, loopholes, and scams given to corporations and wealthy individuals that totaled at least $448 billion in 1996.

## • ECONOMICS

Albert, Michael, and Robin Hahnel. ***Looking Forward: Participatory Economics for the Twenty First Century***. Boston: South End Press, 1991. [Chap. 2]

> Albert and Hahnel propose a practical and humane economic system based on equitable consumption, participatory planning, and self-management organized efficiently and productively without hierarchical control.

Bowles, Samuel, and Richard Edwards. ***Understanding Capitalism: Competition, Command, and Change in the U.S. Economy***, 2nd ed. New York: Harper Collins College Publishers, 1993, HB171.5 .B6937 1993.

> Unlike most economics textbooks that promote neoclassical mythology, this one describes economic reality. It explores three kinds of economic relationships: (1) voluntary exchange and competition among relative equals in marketplaces — the ideal economy that most conventional economics texts cover, (2) unequal relationships in which one actor has the power to impose costs on another or to control the information that another receives — including monopolies, government regulation, manager/subordinate relationships, advertising-induced demand, and hostile takeovers, and (3) the changes that an economic system goes through over time. The book analyzes the efficiency of various economic systems and discusses how fair and democratic they are.

Folbre, Nancy, and the Center for Popular Economics. ***The New Field Guide to the U.S. Economy: A Compact and Irreverent Guide to Economic Life in America***. New York: The New Press, 1995, HC106.5 .F565 1995.

> Through stories, charts, graphs, short descriptions, and cartoons, this book presents a clear and accessible overview of the economy and how it affects a variety of people.

Henderson, Hazel. ***Building a Win-Win World: Life Beyond Global Economic Warfare***. San Francisco: Berrett-Koehler Publishers, 1996, HD75.6 .H458 1996.

> Economist Henderson argues that the global economy is based on shortsighted, narrow economic policies. She demonstrates that — because of its negative effects on employees, families, communities, and the ecosystem — it is unsustainable.

Kuttner, Robert. ***Everything for Sale: the Virtues and Limits of Markets***. A Century Foundation Book. Chicago: University of Chicago Press, 1996, HC106.82 .K87 1999.

> Kuttner shows how the implementation of free market ideology has retarded economic growth, increased income inequality, undermined democracy, and restricted access to health care and other important social provisions. He documents market failure in a variety of sectors including medicine, banking, securities, telecommunications, air travel, sports, and electric power. Kuttner explains that the call for "pure markets" — free of government regulation — is really a corporate plea to avoid responsibility for community and society well being.
>
> Kuttner calls for a mixed economy with strong government regulation of the private sector. He would also have the government administer basic social programs like health care and pension benefits. He argues that government should provide incentives to corporations that treat their employees in a socially responsible manner. Moreover, Kuttner advocates for a more progressive tax system that could redistribute economic and political power. To keep markets in their place, he believes Americans must actively participate in civic affairs and maintain a strong democracy.

Mander, Jerry, and Edward Goldsmith, eds. *The Case Against the Global Economy and for a Turn toward the Local*. San Francisco: Sierra Club Books, 1996, HD75.6 .C376 1996.

The 43 essays in this collection, by leading economic, environmental, agricultural, and cultural experts, charge that free trade and economic globalization are producing exactly the opposite results from what has been promised. They argue instead for an international system based on revitalized democracy, local self-sufficiency, and ecological health.

Morrison, Roy. *We Build the Road as We Travel*. Philadelphia: New Society Publishers, 1991, HD3218 .M66 M67 1991. [Chap. 2]

Morrison describes the forty-year history of the Mondragon cooperative network in Spain, which consists of 170 worker-owned-and-operated cooperatives serving over 100,000 people and providing over 21,000 secure and well-paid jobs.

Schumacher, E. F. *Small is Beautiful: Economics as if People Mattered*. New York: Perennial Library/Harper & Row, 1973, HD82 .S37892 1975.

Schumacher argues for a human-oriented and human-sized economic system with products designed to be understood, built, and repaired by regular people.

Sklar, Holly. *Chaos or Community?: Seeking Solutions, Not Scapegoats for Bad Economics*. Boston: South End Press, 1995, HC110 .I5 S57 1995. [App. A]

Sklar explains how and why Americans, working harder than ever these days, still cannot achieve their dreams.

---

## • THE ENVIRONMENT

Bookchin, Murray. *Remaking Society: Pathways to a Green Future*. Boston: South End Press, 1990, HN18 .B635 1989.

Bookchin argues that today's global ecological crisis stems from social hierarchy and domination. He calls for "an ecological society based on nonhierarchical relationships, decentralized democratic communities, and eco-technologies like solar power, organic agriculture, and humanly scaled industries."

Brown, Lester R., Christopher Flavin, and Hilary French. *State of the World*. Annual. New York: W. W. Norton and Worldwatch Institute, 2000, HC59 .S76 2000.

This annual survey offers a comprehensive analysis of negative environmental trends and a guide to emerging solutions.

Milbrath, Lester W. *Envisioning a Sustainable Society: Learning Our Way Out*. Albany, NY: State University of New York Press, 1989, GF41 .M53 1989. [Chap. 2]

Milbrath provides a detailed summary of the Green perspective. He argues that our current dominator culture is not sustainable and advocates a paradigm shift in thinking toward a learning society, one that (p. 95–112):

• Utilizes a wealth of information

• Finds good ways to disseminate and utilize information

• Emphasizes integrative (holistic) and probabilistic thinking

• Emphasizes values as much as facts (and examines its values)

• Is critical of new technology

• Combines theory with practice

• Is consciously anticipatory

• Believes that change is possible

• Examines outcomes to learn from them

• Develops institutions to foster systemic and futures thinking

• Institutionalizes a practice of analyzing future impacts

• Re-orients education toward social learning

• Supports research

• Maintains openness and encourages citizen participation

Szasz, Andrew. *EcoPopulism: Toxic Waste and the Movement for Environmental Justice*. Minneapolis: University of Minnesota Press, 1994, GE170 .S9 1994.

---

## • COMMUNICATION MEDIA

Ansolabehere, Stephen, and Shanto Iyengar. *Going Negative: How Political Advertisements Shrink and Polarize the Electorate*. New York: Free Press, 1996, JF2112 .A4 A57 1996.

Based on a six-year study, these two political scientists establish a link between negative political advertising and low voter turnout.

Bagdikian, Ben H. *The Media Monopoly*. 5th ed. Boston: Beacon Press, 1997, P96 .E252 U625 1997. [Chap. 3]

Bagdikian provides a detailed analysis of the growing concentration of the major communications media. In the original 1984 edition of this book, Bagdikian found that fifty corporations dominated control of daily newspapers, magazines, radio, television, books, and movies. With greater consolidation, he now finds that "in 1996 the number of media corporations with dominant power in society is closer to ten." These ten, with some of their most prominent holdings, are: Disney (ABC, America On-Line), Westinghouse (CBS), General Electric (NBC), Murdoch's News Corporation Limited (Fox, *TV Guide*), Time Warner (*Time*, *People*, *Sports Illustrated*, Warner Brothers, HBO, CNN, TNT), Viacom, Sony, Tele-Communications, Inc. (TCI), Seagram, and Gannett. Bagdikian also points out that the Telecommunications Act of 1996 has allowed these corporations to own a share of each other and develop strategic partnerships with each other, thus eliminating most competition.

Fallows, James. *Breaking the News: How the Media Undermine American Democracy*. New York: Pantheon Books, 1996, PN4888 .O25 F35 1996.

Fallows, Washington editor of the *Atlantic Monthly*, charges the U.S. media with arrogance, irresponsibility, and negativism. Instead of providing useful facts and engaging the public in debate about vital issues, he argues the media provide celebrity-based entertainment and endless scare-stories about a world out of control.

Herman, Edward S., and Noam Chomsky. *Manufacturing Consent: The Political Economy of the Mass Media.* New York: Pantheon Books, 1988, P95.82 .U6H47 1988. [Chap. 3]

In this meticulously documented book, Herman and Chomsky show how the marketplace and the economics of publishing — as well as an underlying elite consensus — shape the news. They reveal how issues are framed and topics chosen to manufacture public consent for elite policies.

Lee, Martin A., and Norman Soloman. *Unreliable Sources: A Guide to Detecting Bias in News Media.* New York: Carol Publishing Group/Lyle Stuart, 1990, PN4888 .O25 L44 1990. [Chap. 1]

McChesney, Robert W. *Corporate Media and the Threat to Democracy.* New York: Seven Stories Press, 1997, P96 .I5 M337 1997.

In this short book, media scholar McChesney persuasively argues that corporate control of the mass media undercuts democracy.

McChesney, Robert W. *Rich Media, Poor Democracy: Communication Politics in Dubious Times.* Urbana, IL: University of Illinois Press, 1999, P95.82 .U6M38.

McChesney describes the contradiction "between a for-profit, highly concentrated, advertising-saturated, corporate media system and the communication requirements of a democratic society." He calls for vigorous antitrust litigation against media conglomerates, robust regulation of corporate broadcasters, and government subsidies for nonprofit journalism.

Parry, Robert. *Fooling America: How Washington Insiders Twist the Truth and Manufacture the Conventional Wisdom.* New York: Morrow, 1992, HN90 .P8 P37 1992.

Parry, a former reporter for the Associated Press and *Newsweek* details the opinion-shaping process in the United States.

### • HUNGER

Lappé, Frances Moore, Joseph Collins, and Peter Rosset with Luis Esparza. *World Hunger: 12 Myths.* 1986. 2nd ed. fully rev. and updated. London: Earthscan Publications Ltd., 1998, HD9000.5 .L35 1998. [Chap. 1]

Lappé, Frances Moore, and Joseph Collins. *Food First: Beyond the Myth of Scarcity.* 1977. Rev. and updated. New York: Ballantine Books, 1979, HD9000.6 .L34 1979. [Chap. 1]

In these two books, researchers at the Institute for Food and Development Policy (Food First) show that hunger is caused by a lack of democracy (control over one's life), not a lack of food.

### • RACISM

Hale, Grace Elizabeth. *Making Whiteness: The Culture of Segregation in the South,* 1890-1940. New York: Pantheon Books, 1998, F215 .H18 1998.

Hale examines the social construction of whiteness and the "culture of segregation."

Jacobson, Matthew Frye. *Whiteness of a Different Color: European Immigrants and the Alchemy of Race.* Cambridge, MA: Harvard University Press, 1998, E184 .E95 J33 1998.

In the 19th century, "whiteness" was reserved for Anglo-Saxons. Slowly, the concept of whiteness evolved to include the Irish, Northern Europeans, and Scandinavians, then other white gentiles, then Jews. Jacobson investigates the reasons for this change.

Kivel, Paul. *Uprooting Racism: How White People Can Work for Racial Justice.* Philadelphia: New Society Publishers, 1995, E184 .A1K477 1995.

Kivel offers concrete examples of the day-to-day privileges provided to white people (European Americans) and shows that even well intentioned white people unknowingly act in ways that promote injustice. He offers suggestions for how white people can work toward equity and equality for everyone.

West, Cornel. *Race Matters.* Boston: Beacon Press, 1993, E185.615 .W43 1993.

In this collection of essays, West points out the limits of the intellectual frameworks used by whites, blacks, liberals, and conservatives in discussing race in the United States. He vigorously criticizes racism, but also challenges black conservatives, black anti-Semitism, and our market-driven culture that devastates those at the bottom.

Woodward, C. Vann. *The Strange Career of Jim Crow.* 3rd rev. ed. New York: Oxford University Press, 1974, E185.61 .W86 1974.

Woodward examines the Jim Crow segregation laws in the post-Civil War South. He discovers that the imposition of strict segregation did not immediately follow the War. He also finds that the adoption of Jim Crow laws was not due simply to racism — political factors played a major role.

Wright, Bruce. *Black Robes, White Justice.* Secaucus, NJ: Lyle Stuart, 1987, KF373 .W67 A33 1987.

New York Supreme Court Justice Wright charges that most judges — predominantly male, white, and upper middle-class — have little understanding of racism or its influence on their thinking and conduct.

### • PRISONS

Abu-Jamal, Mumia. *Live From Death Row.* Reading, MA: Addison-Wesley, 1995, HV8699 .U5 A65 1995.

Abu-Jamal, an award-winning radio reporter and prisoner awaiting the death penalty, excoriates the brutality of prisons and criticizes the racism and political bias in the American judicial system that, he argues, led to his own wrongful conviction.

## • SUPPRESSION OF ACTIVISTS

Center for Research on Criminal Justice. ***The Iron Fist and the Velvet Glove: An Analysis of the U.S. Police.*** Berkeley, CA: Center for Research on Criminal Justice, 1975, HV8138 .C46 1975.

This book looks at the history of police forces and their use in maintaining political control, finding that the police have always been used to thwart progressive change efforts.

Cowan, Paul, Nick Egleson, and Nat Hentoff. ***State Secrets: Police Surveillance in America.*** New York: Holt, Rinehart & Winston, 1974, JC599 .U5C67.

*It is dangerous to be right when the government is wrong.*
— Voltaire

Donner, Frank. ***The Age of Surveillance: The Aims and Methods of America's Political Intelligence System.*** New York: Knopf, Random House, 1980, JK468 .I6 .D65 1980.

Donner traces the emergence of the "intelligence" establishment from its modest origins to its present position as a massive, oppressive institution for enforcing social control.

Glick, Brian. ***War at Home: Covert Action Against U.S. Activists and What We Can Do About It.*** Boston: South End Press, 1989, HV8141 .G57 1988. [Chap. 3]

Glick summarizes the many ways in which the government's COINTELPRO program waged covert action against activists in the 1960s and how similar efforts were directed against activists working in the 1980s to end oppression in Central America.

Goldstein, Robert. ***Political Repression in Modern America: 1870 to the Present.*** Cambridge, MA: Schenkman Publishing, 1977, JC599 .U5G58. [Chap. 3]

In this comprehensive study of government attacks on dissenters in the past century, Goldstein shows that repression has been a consistent instrument of government policy, frequently altering the course of history.

Halperin, Morton H., Jerry J. Berman, Robert L. Borosage, and Christine M. Marwick. ***The Lawless State: The Crimes of U.S. Intelligence Agencies.*** New York: Penguin Books, 1976, JK468 .I6 .L38.

Drawing on the 1976 Senate Select Committee on Intelligence Activities report and many other official public sources, this book devastatingly and undeniably describes the vast scope of government surveillance and harassment of activists carried out by the CIA, FBI, National Security Agency (NSA), Internal Revenue Service (IRS), military intelligence agencies, and grand juries. It focuses particularly on the 1960s and early 1970s.

Helvarg, David. ***The War Against the Greens: The Wise Use Movement, the New Right, and Anti-Environmental Violence.*** San Francisco: Sierra Club Books, 1994, GE197 .H45 1994. [Chap. 3]

Helvarg describes current violence and terrorism directed at environmentalists.

Schultz, Bud, and Ruth Schultz. ***It Did Happen Here: Recollections of Political Repression in America.*** Berkeley: University of California Press, 1989, JC599 .U518 1989.

This book contains interviews with 34 U.S. activists who were attacked and repressed in the twentieth century. It includes an annotated bibliography of other books on repression.

## • COMPETITION

Axelrod, Robert M. "The Evolution of Cooperation." *Science* 211 (March 27, 1981): 1390–1396. [Chap. 1]

Axelrod, Robert M. ***The Evolution of Cooperation.*** New York: Basic Books, 1984, HM131 .A89 1984. [Chap. 1]

Social scientists have often employed the Prisoner's Dilemma game to study behavior. In the Prisoner's Dilemma, two players must decide — without conferring — to cooperate with each other or to defect. If they both decide to cooperate, they achieve a certain amount of benefit (say having a value of 3). If one tries to cooperate, but the other defects, then the cooperator gains nothing, but the defector achieves even more benefit (say of value 5). If they both defect, then they both gain only minimally (say of value 1). This game is fascinating because it explores the tension between cooperation and selfishness. If one player can defect while enticing the other to try to cooperate, then that player can win big. However, if both cooperate, they both do better than if they both defect.

Using a computer simulation, Axelrod shows that in an environment in which the game is played repeatedly, one of the most productive and stable strategies is the one known as "Tit for Tat." Tit for Tat is the policy of cooperating in the first round and then doing whatever the other player did in the last round. Tit for Tat cooperates well with other cooperative strategies, thus achieving a fairly large payoff. However, when confronted with an uncooperative strategy, it is not exploited. It is a "nice" strategy (always trying to cooperate at first), one that is provoked by a defection from the other player, and yet is very forgiving (it only retaliates once). It encourages other players to cooperate and never attempts to exploit another player.

Taking an ecological approach, Axelrod created an environment with many players that used a variety of strategies (as posed by other game theorists) and pitted them against each other. Then he calculated what would happen if each of the strategies were submitted to the next round in proportion to its success in the previous round. This process was repeated for many rounds and Tit For Tat ended up displacing all the other strategies: it was the most robust and stable strategy. By cooperating with other cooperative strategies, it was able to increase its strength enough to outpace the non-cooperative strategies.

Axelrod also points out that, even in an environment dominated by "mean" strategies (ones that always defect), a cluster of Tit For Tat players can cooperate enough with each other that they can eventually build themselves up and outdistance the others. This suggests a possibly promising approach for progressive change activists.

Kohn, Alfie. *No Contest: The Case Against Competition*, rev. ed. Boston: Houghton Mifflin Company, 1992, HM291 .K634 1992.

Kohn convincingly condemns the kind of competition that requires the failure of another for one's own success. Backing his arguments with extensive citations from social science research, he demolishes four myths:

- Competition is an inherent part of "human nature."
- Competition motivates us to do our best.
- Contests provide the best way to have a good time.
- Competition builds character and self-confidence.

Strip away all the assumptions about what competition is supposed to do, all the claims in its behalf that we accept and repeat reflexively. What you have left is the essence of the concept: mutually exclusive goal attainment (MEGA). One person succeeds only if another does not. From this uncluttered perspective, it seems clear right away that something is drastically wrong with such an arrangement. How can we do our best when we are spending our energies trying to make others lose — and fearing that they will make us lose? Can this sort of struggle really be the best way to have a good time? What happens to our self-esteem when it becomes dependent on how much better we do than the next person? Most striking of all is the impact of this arrangement on human relationship: a structural incentive to see other people lose cannot help but drive a wedge between us and invite hostility. . . .

All of these conclusions seem to flow from the very nature of competition. As it happens, they also are corroborated by the evidence — what we see around us and what scores of studies have been finding. . . .

I have become convinced that competition is an inherently undesirable arrangement, that the phrase *healthy competition* is actually a contradiction in terms. This is nothing short of heresy because only two positions on the question are normally recognized: enthusiastic support and qualified support. . . .

I believe that the case against competition is so compelling that parenthetical qualifications to the effect that competing can sometimes be constructive would be incongruous and unwarranted. (p. 9)

Taylor, Michael. *Anarchy and Cooperation*. New York: John Wiley and Sons, 1976, HX833 .T38 1976.

Taylor explores whether people would cooperate with each other without the intervention of government. He argues that Hobbes' *Leviathan* and Hume's *Treatise for Government* describe the human situation in a way that can be modeled by an iterated Prisoner's Dilemma game. He then shows that despite the precariousness of the mutual cooperation situation in this iterated game, it is still rational under some circumstances for the players to cooperate, even if they only pursue their own self-interest.

## • FEMINIST CRITIQUES

Brownmiller, Susan. *Against Our Will: Men, Women and Rape*. New York: Simon and Schuster, 1975, HV6558 .B76.

In this classic feminist analysis, Brownmiller systematically identifies and dispels the many myths about rape.

Ehrenreich, Barbara, and Deirdre English. *For Her Own Good: 150 Years of the Experts' Advice to Women*. Garden City, NY: Anchor Books/Doubleday, 1998, HQ1426 .E38.

Ehrenreich and English present a clear analysis of the ways in which "expert" professionals, especially doctors, have treated women.

Koedt, Anne, Ellen Levine, and Anita Rapone, eds. *Radical Feminism*. New York: Quadrangle Books, 1973, HQ1426 .K63.

This classic collection of essays presents the new ideas of the second wave of feminism developed in the 1960s and early 1970s.

## • CHILDREN

Edelman, Marian Wright. *Families in Peril: An Agenda for Social Change*. Cambridge, MA: Harvard University Press, 1987, HV699 .E34 1987.

## • CHILDREARING

Greven, Philip. *Spare the Child: The Religious Roots of Punishment and the Psychological Impact of Physical Abuse*. New York: Alfred A. Knopf, Random House, 1991, HQ770.4 .G74 1990.

This research study by historian Greven focuses on Christians' use of Biblical texts to justify corporal punishment. He analyzes the destructive effects this punishment has on our culture.

Karr-Morse, Robin, and Meredith S. Wiley. *Ghosts from the Nursery: Tracing the Roots of Violence*. New York: Atlantic Monthly Press, 1997, HQ784 .V55K37 1997.

Karr-Morse and Wiley present evidence that violent behavior is fundamentally linked to abuse and neglect in the first two years of life (from conception to 18 months of age). They describe recent research that shows how trust, empathy, conscience, and lifelong learning (or alternatively, a predisposition to violent behavior) are "hardwired" into the brain during pregnancy and infancy.

Lewis, Thomas, Fari Amini, and Richard Lannon. *A General Theory of Love*. New York: Random House, 2000, BF575 .L8 L49 2000.

These three doctors review the neurological literature and argue that affection, communication, and play are essential for the proper development of children. They call for more cuddling and for babies to sleep with their parents.

Miller, Alice. ***For Your Own Good: Hidden Cruelty in Child-Rearing and the Roots of Violence***. Hildegarde and Hunter Hannum, trans. New York: Farrar Straus Giroux, 1983, HQ769 .M531613 1983; originally published in German as ***Am Anfang war Erziehung***, 1980. [Chap. 3]

Through analyzing a variety of case studies, German psychotherapist Alice Miller contends that when children's vital needs for love, respect, and protection are frustrated and they are instead exploited, beaten, punished, manipulated, neglected, or deceived — without the intervention of any witness — then their psyches will be severely damaged. If, further, they are prevented from expressing their natural anger, pain, and fear, they will often completely suppress their feelings, repress their memories of the trauma, and sometimes even idealize those who abused them. Later, these intense, repressed feelings are likely to be directed towards others as criminal behavior or against themselves as drug addiction, alcoholism, prostitution, mental illness, or suicide. If these battered children grow up to become parents, they often direct their repressed anger towards their own children.

She explores the cultural and religious ideas used to justify beating, manipulating, or humiliating children that drives the willfulness and joy out of them. She shows how this "poisonous pedagogy" leads to adults who are docile, servile, and unfeeling and thus ripe for exploitation by dictators like Adolph Hitler.

Small, Meredith F. ***Our Babies, Ourselves: How Biology and Culture Shape the Way We Parent***. New York: Bantam Books, 1998, RJ61 .S6345 1998.

Anthropologist Meredith Small summarizes a variety of academic studies that examine parenting behavior. She discovers that numerous studies show babies cry less (are more content) when they are (1) attended to immediately when they cry, (2) fed as needed rather than on a schedule, and (3) spend most of their time being held or in body contact with their mothers or other caretakers.

She points out that throughout human history babies have spent most of their time being held in close contact by their mothers in slings and being breastfed whenever they want. Biologically that is what babies require and that is what they get in most of the world. However, babies in the western world spend a tremendous amount of time alone, isolated from their mothers' bodies in chairs, car seats, cribs, and walkers. Most western babies also sleep alone, typically isolated in their own rooms.

### • SCHOOLS

Holt, John. ***How Children Fail***. New York: Dell Publishing, 1964, LB1555 .H78.

In this classic book, Holt describes his experience as a young teacher in "above average" schools working with "bright" students. He describes the mind-crippling malaise induced by typical educational methods and offers positive alternatives.

_____. ***How Children Learn***. New York: Dell Publishing, 1967, LB1555 .H79.

Holt describes the way children are hurt and oppressed by the education system and the ways they actually learn in a supportive environment.

Illich, Ivan. ***Deschooling Society***. New York: Harper & Row, 1971, LA210 .I4 1971.

Kozol, Jonathan. ***Savage Inequalities: Children in America's Schools***. New York: HarperPerennial Library, 1992, LC4091 .K69 1992.

Kozol reveals the separate and unequal nature of the public school system in this country. He contrasts the old, crumbling, over-crowded, equipment-starved schools in poor black and Hispanic neighborhoods with the new, well-stocked schools in more affluent white and Asian neighborhoods nearby.

Neill, A. S. ***Summerhill: A Radical Approach to Child Rearing***. New York: Hart Publishing, 1960, P499 .N41.

Neill describes the transformation that boys made when they attended an alternative school he operated in England in the 1950s. They changed from being selfish, sullen, and angry to being responsible and cooperative.

Russell, Bertrand. ***Education and the Social Order***. New Ed. London: Allen and Unwin, 1967, LB775 .R83 1967.

### • OTHER DESTRUCTIVE CULTURAL NORMS

Eisler, Riane. ***The Chalice & The Blade: Our History, Our Future***. San Francisco: Harper & Row, 1987, HQ1075 .E57 1987. [Chap. 2, 4]

Reviewing the archaeology literature, Eisler argues provocatively that for many thousands of years in prehistoric times humans lived in societies that were not violent, hierarchic, or dominated by men. She suggests these gentle and cooperative societies were eventually conquered by violent outsiders. She argues that we could, once again, choose a gentle partnership model of society based on caring, compassion, and nonviolence instead of a dominator model based on competition and war.

Fromm, Erich. ***The Sane Society***. New York: Rinehart, 1955. Reprinted New York: Henry Holt, 1990, HM271 .F75 1990. [Chap. 3]

Psychoanalyst Fromm convincingly makes the case that we live in an insane society. He champions communitarian socialism as a healthy alternative.

Grossman, Dave. ***On Killing: The Psychological Cost of Learning to Kill in War and Society***. Boston: Little, Brown and Company/Back Bay Books, 1995, U22.3 .G76 1995.

Lieutenant Colonel Grossman describes how modern armies, using Pavlovian and operant conditioning, have developed ways to overcome humans' natural aversion to killing people. He argues this conditioning is responsible for the increase in post-traumatic stress syndrome. He further asserts that contemporary society, especially the media, has replicated the army's conditioning techniques, leading to a more violent society and rising murder rates.

Schaef, Anne Wilson. ***When Society Becomes an Addict.*** San Francisco: Harper & Row, 1987, BF575 .D34S33 1987. [Chap. 3]

Schaef argues that society acts like an addict, exhibiting and promoting such dysfunctional behavior as self-centeredness, repression, dishonesty, shame, greed, obsessions, confusion, denial, perfectionism, judgmentalism, forgetfulness, dependency, zero-sum orientation, negativism, cynicism, defensiveness, tunnel vision, blame, irresponsibility, arrogance, and fear.

Lakoff, George. ***Moral Politics: What Conservatives Know that Liberals Don't.*** Chicago: University of Chicago Press, 1996, HN90 .M6L35 1996.

Lakoff, a cognitive scientist, offers a groundbreaking analysis of the concepts of "conservative" and "liberal" in our society. He finds they correlate with two very different moral worldviews based on two distinct childrearing philosophies.

He argues that conservative thought is based on Strict Father morality and Authoritarian childrearing which assign high moral value to absolutist ideas, authority, strength, self-discipline, reward and punishment, and a moral hierarchy with God above men, men above women, adults above children, and humans above animals and the natural environment. In contrast, liberal thought is based on Nurturant Parent morality and Authoritative or Harmonious childrearing that assign high moral value to empathy, fairness, protection of those who need it, and nurturance.

In exploring these conflicting perspectives, Lakoff finds that Nurturant Parent morality reflects actual reality and is self-correcting. In contrast, Strict Father morality makes erroneous assumptions about how humans behave and so often produces faulty analyses and poor results.

Putnam, Robert D. ***Bowling Alone: The Collapse and Revival of American Community.*** New York: Simon & Schuster, 2000, HN65 .P878 2000.

Putnam explores the phenomenon of Americans' reduced engagement in civic and community life. He tracks the decline in participation in public clubs like the Elks and Shriners and social gatherings like family dinners and poker playing. He finds that many religious organizations now tend only to the needs of churchmembers and ignore the larger society. Using statistics and time diaries, he plots various indicators of civic engagement, and finds that it peaked in the early 1960s and then declined.

As civic engagement declines, people have fewer relationships with other people. This means they have fewer people they can rely on for help with simple chores or for more extensive support during hard times.

Putnam finds several causes of the decline in civic engagement: television, the entrance of women into the workforce, high levels of divorce, and urban sprawl.

This book has stimulated a controversy explored in the articles listed here: <http://www.epn.org/issues/civilsociety.html>

Sale, Kirkpatrick. ***Human Scale.*** New York: Coward, McCann & Geoghegan, 1980, HC106.7 .S24 1980. [Chap. 11]

Sale argues that our society operates at a level beyond the capacity of humans to understand or control and calls for institutions that are more human-sized.

### • GROUPTHINK AND CULTS

Janis, Irving. ***Groupthink: Psychological Studies of Policy Decisions and Fiascoes.*** 2nd ed. Boston: Houghton-Mifflin, 1982, E744 .J29 1982. [Chap. 3]

Janis discusses the tendency of insular groups self-righteously to assume their perspectives are correct, which leads them to make poor decisions. He outlines several means for preventing groupthink.

———. "Groupthink." ***Psychology Today*** (Nov. 1971): 43–46, 74–76. [Chap. 3]

Hassan, Steven. ***Combatting Cult Mind Control.*** Rochester, VT: Park Street Press, 1988, BP603 .H375 1988. <http://www.shassan.com> [Chap. 3]

Hassan, a former member of the Moonie cult, describes the methods of mind control used by cults.

## Social Change History

### • GENERAL

Bacon, Margaret Hope. ***The Quiet Rebels: The Story of the Quakers in America.*** New York: Basic Books, 1969, BX7635 .B3; Philadelphia: New Society Publishers, 1985.

Bacon recounts the story of the Society of Friends in the United States, showing that Quakers generally were honest and respectful in their dealings with native Americans, that they refused to participate in war, and they pioneered efforts for penal reform, racial justice, women's rights, and nonviolent action.

Cooney, Robert, and Helen Michalowski, eds. ***The Power of the People: Active Nonviolence in the United States.*** Rev. ed. Philadelphia: New Society Publishers, 1987, HN64 .P88 1987.

This pictorial encyclopedia of nonviolent action includes over 300 photographs and explanatory text. It covers peace churches and early secular peace organizations, the women's rights movement, the anti-slavery movement, the labor movement, conscientious objectors to war, nuclear pacifism, the Civil Rights movement, the anti-Vietnam war movement, the environmental movement, and women's peace encampments.

Diggins, John Patrick. ***The Rise and Fall of the American Left.*** New York: W.W. Norton & Company, 1992, HN90 .R3D556 1992. [Chap. 4]

Diggins describes the rise of four leftist movements in this century: the Lyrical Left of the First World War years, the Old Left during the Great Depression, the New Left of the 1960s, and the Academic Left of the 1990s.

Loewen, James W. *Lies My Teacher Told Me: Everything Your American History Textbook Got Wrong*. New York: New Press, 1995, E175.85 .L64 1995.

Loewen relates various fallacies found in U.S. history textbooks, showing how social issues are misreported and ideas are misrepresented.

Zinn, Howard. *A People's History of the United States: 1492 to the Present*. 20th anniversary ed. New York: Harpercollins, 1999 [1979], E178 .Z75 1999.

In this excellent alternative history book, Zinn looks at history from the perspective of those who have been exploited politically or economically.

### • THE POPULIST MOVEMENT (1870S–1890S)

Burns, Stewart. "The Populist Movement and the Cooperative Commonwealth: the Politics of Non-Reformist Reform." Ph.D. Dissertation, University of California, Santa Cruz, 1984.

In this doctoral dissertation, historian Burns investigates the rise and fall of the Populist Movement. He argues that to bring about true reform of society, social change movements in the United States should combine various aspects of grassroots democracy — especially direct action, political education, and the creation of new institutions and ideologies — with traditional forms of electoral-representative democracy.

Goodwyn, Lawrence. *The Populist Moment: A Short History of the Agrarian Revolt in America*. New York: Oxford University Press, 1978, E669 .G672 1978; abridged edition of *The Democratic Promise: The Populist Moment in America*. [Chap. 4, 5, 7]

Goodwyn provides the definitive history of the Populist movement.

### • EARLY TWENTIETH CENTURY EFFORTS

Weinstein, James. *The Decline of Socialism in America: 1912–1925*. New York: Monthly Review Press, 1967; New Brunswick, NJ: Rutgers University Press, 1984, HX83 .W4 1984.

Weinstein describes the history of the Socialist Party during a crucial time when it shrank drastically in size and power.

### • THE LABOR MOVEMENT

Brecher, Jeremy. *Strike!* Rev. ed. Boston: South End Press, 1997, HD5324 .B7 1997.

Brecher narrates the history of the U.S. labor movement from the point of view of rank-and-file workers.

Kornbluh, Joyce L., ed. *Rebel Voices: An IWW Anthology*. New and expanded ed. Chicago: Charles H. Kerr Publishing, 1998, HD8055 .I5 R43 1998.

Renshaw, Patrick. *The Wobblies: The Story of the IWW and Syndicalism in the United States*. Chicago: Ivan R. Dee, 1999, [1967], HD8055 .I4 R46 1999.

Renshaw tells the story of the Industrial Workers of the World (IWW), the revolutionary labor union founded in Chicago in 1905. The IWW sought to organize the American working class — and eventually workers all over the world — into one big labor union with a syndicalist philosophy.

### • EFFORTS IN THE 1950S

Isserman, Maurice. *If I Had a Hammer: The Death of the Old Left and the Birth of the New Left*. New York: Basic Books, 1987, HN90 .R3187 1987. [Chap. 6]

Isserman describes the period between World War II and the 1960s when the American Left was at a low point. He shows that — contrary to the common understanding — lessons learned by the Old Left were passed on to the New Left.

Tracy, James. *Direct Action: Radical Pacifism from the Union Eight to the Chicago Seven*. Chicago: University of Chicago Press, 1996, HM278 .T73 1996.

Tracy tells the story of a small group of radical pacifists who were incarcerated during World War II as conscientious objectors and then became major players in the Civil Rights, antiwar, and anti-nuclear movements in the 1950s and 1960s.

### • THE 1960S MOVEMENTS

Burns, Stewart. *Daybreak of Freedom: The Montgomery Bus Boycott*. Chapel Hill, NC: University of North Carolina Press, 1997, F334 .M79N39. [Chap. 5]

_____. *Social Movements of the 1960s: Searching for Democracy*. Boston: Twayne Publishers, 1990, HN59 .B86 1990.

Burns explores four main social movements of the 1960s — the black freedom movement, the anti-Vietnam War movement, the "counterculture," and the feminist movement — and describes lessons that can be learned for future efforts.

Carson, Clayborne. *In Struggle: SNCC and the Black Awakening of the 1960s*. Cambridge, MA: Harvard University Press, 1981, E185.92 .C37 1981.

Carson recounts the progression of the Student Non-Violent Coordinating Committee (SNCC) from its early days when it was focused on assimilation of Blacks into White society, through its militant period when its leaders demanded more radical change, through its separatist period when "Black Power" was the primary goal, and then back again into conventional politics.

Cluster, Dick, ed. *They Should Have Served that Cup of Coffee: Seven Radicals Remember the '60s*. Boston: South End Press, 1979, HN90 .R3 T47.

This is a very readable collection of essays by and interviews with activists involved in the civil rights, Black Power, women's, and anti-Vietnam War movements.

Dellinger, Dave. *More Power than We Know: The People's Movement toward Democracy*. Garden City, NY: Anchor Press/Doubleday, 1975, HN90 .R3 .D47.

Pacifist Dellinger describes his role in the anti-war movement of the 1960s and points out that the movement was much more powerful than its participants knew or its detractors would admit.

Gitlin, Todd. *The Sixties: Years of Hope, Days of Rage*. New York: Bantam Books, 1987, E841 .G57 1987.

Gitlin, an early president of Students for a Democratic Society (SDS), recounts the history of the social movements of the 1960s.

_____. *The Whole World is Watching: Mass Media in the Making and Unmaking of the New Left*. Berkeley, CA: University of California Press, 1980, P95.82 .U6 G57.

Gitlin describes how the mass media first ignored the anti-Vietnam War movement of the 1960s, then selected and emphasized aspects of the story in a way that distorted and destroyed it. He shows how the media turned movement leaders into celebrities and inflated revolutionary rhetoric and militancy. He argues that the media do not conspire to disparage social change movements, but editors and reporters assume the social order is legitimate and that demonstrations of political opposition are simply noisy complaints by disaffected whiners. So their reports rely on official interpretations of reality and treat political dissent as either a peculiar oddity or a crime.

Rexroth, Kenneth. *The Alternative Society: Essays from the Other World*. New York: Herder and Herder, 1970, PS3535 .E923 A16 1970.

Roszak, Theodore. *The Making of a Counter Culture: Reflections on the Technocratic Society and its Youthful Opposition*. Garden City, NY: Doubleday, 1969, HN17.5 .R6.

Roszak investigates the 1960s protest movements and argues that the rejection of the "technocracy" — the regime of corporate and technological experts that dominate industrial society — spawned both anti-war activism and the development of the counterculture.

Sale, Kirkpatrick. *SDS: Ten Years toward a Revolution*. New York: Random House, 1973, LB3602 .S8363 .S24.

Sale presents a comprehensive history of the national office of Students for a Democratic Society (SDS), the main New Left and anti-Vietnam War organization of the 1960s. [Chap. 9]

Zinn, Howard. *SNCC: The New Abolitionists*. Boston: Beacon Press, 1964, E185.61 .Z49.

### • MOVEMENTS IN THE 1970S, 1980S, AND 1990S

Adams, Tom. *Grass Roots: Ordinary People Changing America*. New York: Carol Publishing Group/Citadel Press, 1991, HN65 .A62 1991.

Driver, David E. *Defending the Left: An Individual's Guide to Fighting for Social Justice, Individual Rights and the Environment*. Chicago: The Noble Press, 1992, E881 .D75 1992.

Epstein, Barbara. *Political Protest and Cultural Revolution: Nonviolent Direct Action in the 1970s and 1980s*. Berkeley, CA: University of California Press, 1991, HN90 .R3E67 1991.

As both participant and observer, historian Epstein describes the nonviolent direct action anti-nuclear movement of the late 1970s and early 1980s: the Clamshell Alliance in New England and the Abalone Alliance and Livermore Action Group in California. She focuses particularly on these movements' intersection with religious beliefs — feminist spirituality, Wiccan magic, Quakerism, and radical Catholicism.

Folsom, Franklin, and Connie Fledderjohann. *The Great Peace March: An American Odyssey*. Santa Fe, NM: Ocean Tree Books, 1988, JX1974.7 .F65 1988.

In 1986, 1,200 people began to walk from Los Angeles across the United States to demand an end to the nuclear arms race. The march nearly ended two weeks later in the Mohave Desert with the financial collapse of its sponsoring organization. But the hardiest of the Marchers continued on, organizing themselves and financing the Great Peace March by direct outreach to people in the communities through which they passed.

Folsom and Fledderjohann describe the March, the participants, how they organized themselves, and what it was like to be part of this traveling alternative community.

Starhawk. *Dreaming the Dark: Magic, Sex & Politics*. Boston: Beacon Press, 1982, BF1572 .S4S7 1982.

Starhawk, a practitioner of Wiccan magic, describes working with the Abalone Alliance against nuclear power using nonviolent direct action, consensus decision-making, and magic.

Walls, David. *The Activist's Almanac: The Concerned Citizen's Guide to the Leading Advocacy Organizations in America*. New York: Fireside/ Simon & Shuster, 1993, HN55 .W35 1993.

Walls describes in detail more than one hundred groups working for change — most of them progressive.

## Methods of Changing Society

### • THEORY AND ANALYSIS
— *Also see the* Competition *section above.*

Altman, Dennis. *Rehearsals for Change: Politics and Culture in Australia*. Victoria Australia: Fontana/Collins, 1979, JQ4031 .A45. [Preface]

Analyzing the prospects for change in Australia, Altman argues that both grassroots cultural change (new social movements) and political change (working through the Australian Labor Party) are necessary to achieve a more humane, egalitarian, and free society.

Chong, Dennis. ***Collective Action and the Civil Rights Movement***. Chicago: University of Chicago Press, 1991, HB846.5 .C48 1991. [Chap. 9]

In this very accessible book, Chong uses the Civil Rights Movement to illustrate the dynamics of public-spirited collective action. Applying rational choice theory, Chong argues that collective action can best be viewed as an assurance game in which activists must coordinate their activity and convince enough people to take action simultaneously.

He emphasizes the crucial role that leaders play in assuring others that an action will take place and will be successful. He also points out that people often feel compelled to engage in public action to maintain their reputations as champions of positive values.

_____. "Coordinating Demands for Social Change." ***Annals of the American Academy of Political and Social Science*** 528 (July 1993): 126–141. [Chap. 9]

Cook, Terrence. ***The Great Alternatives of Social Thought: Aristocrat, Saint, Capitalist, Socialist***. Savage, MD: Rowland and Littlefield, 1991, HN17.5 .C66 1991.

Cook divides all political philosophers into four camps based on two criteria: whether they identify with the rich or the poor and whether they believe in limiting wants to fit within ecological limitations or they believe in trying to overcome scarcity through technological growth. The four resulting categories are: Capitalists (identify with the rich, expand limits), Socialists (identify with the poor, expand limits), Aristocrats (identify with the rich, fit within limits), and Saints (identify with the poor, fit within limits).

Evans, Sara M., and Harry C. Boyte. ***Free Spaces: The Sources of Democratic Change in America***. New York: Harper and Row, 1986, HN57 .E9 1986.

Based on their study of the anti-slavery struggle, the populist movement, the women's movement, the labor movement, and the civil rights movement, Evans and Boyte argue that democratic movements need "free spaces" — public places deeply rooted in the life and traditions of the community where individuals can gain self-confidence and develop a larger sense of the common good. Free spaces are settings between private lives and large-scale institutions where citizens can learn citizenship — a place where they can develop and practice democratic and communitarian skills, values, and aspirations. These spaces are typically voluntary forms of association like religious organizations, clubs, self-help and mutual aid societies, reform groups, neighborhood groups, civic organizations, ethnic groups, and other community associations.

Flacks, Richard. ***Making History: The American Left and the American Mind***. New York: Columbia University Press, 1988, JK1764 .F57 1988. [Chap. 3]

Flacks, a founder and early leader of Students for a Democratic Society (SDS) and now a sociologist, looks at the potential for revitalizing the left tradition of grassroots democracy in the United States. He points out that most Americans have a strong "commitment to everyday life" and their participation in politics is usually directed to preserving their rights and their opportu-

nity for self-determination. He hopes for a society in which daily life and making history are integrated.

Gorz, André. ***Socialism and Revolution***. Translated by Norman Denny. Garden City, NY: Anchor Press/Doubleday, 1973, HX44 .G613. [Chap. 5]

_____. ***Strategy for Labor: A Radical Proposal***. Translated by Martin A. Nicolaus and Victoria Ortiz. Boston: Beacon Press, 1967, HD8431 .G613. [Chap. 5, 7]

Gowan, Susanne, George Lakey, William Moyer, and Richard Taylor. ***Moving Toward a New Society***. Philadelphia: New Society Press, 1976, HN65 .M65. [Chap. 5]

Originally titled, ***Revolution: Quaker Prescription for a Sick Society***, this book uses a medical metaphor to describe the ills of society and how we might heal it through a nonviolent revolution. Written by members of the Philadelphia-based and Quaker-influenced Movement for a New Society (MNS), it critically examines U.S.-Third World relations, U.S. domestic policy, and the environmental crisis.

Schindler, Craig, and Gary Lapid. ***The Great Turning: Personal Peace, Global Victory***. Santa Fe, NM: Bear and Company, 1989, HM132 .S3518 1989.

Schindler and Lapid of Project Victory seek to create win/win dialogues for resolving world conflicts. They describe the changes we must go through individually and as a society to become skilled in the art of dialogue.

Tarrow, Sidney. ***Struggle, Politics, and Reform: Collective Action, Social Movements, and Cycles of Protest***, Occasional Paper No. 21. Ithaca, NY: Western Societies Program, Center for International Studies, Cornell University, 1989, HN90 .R3 .T35 1989.

Wasburn, Philo C. ***Political Sociology: Approaches, Concepts, Hypotheses***. Englewood Cliffs, NJ: Prentice-Hall, 1982, JA76 .W36.

Wood, James L., and Maurice Jackson. ***Social Movements: Development, Participation, and Dynamics***. Belmont, CA: Wadsworth Publishing, 1982, HM216 .W66 1982.

## • SIMPLE LIVING

Simple Living Collective, American Friends Service Committee. ***Taking Charge: Personal and Political Change Through Simple Living***. New York: Bantam Books, 1977.

The Simple Living Collective shares its practical suggestions for living simply and changing the world.

## • OVERCOMING DESTRUCTIVE CULTURAL NORMS

Allen, Robert F., with Charlotte Kraft and the staff of the Human Resources Institute. *Beat the System!: A Way to Create More Human Environments*. New York: McGraw-Hill, 1980, HM101 .A574. [Chap. 3, 4]

> This book is based on the premise that many of today's pressing societal and personal needs can be met by a systematic, humanistic, people-involving change process, one which focuses on the culture and makes use of the power of the culture to bring about improvement in the human condition. The key hypotheses we present are these:
>
> • The cultures in which we live have an immense impact on each of us as individuals and on our institutions, without our being fully aware of what is happening to us.
>
> • Our cultures are much more changeable, for better or worse, than most of us realize.
>
> • By using a planned, systematic, people-involved strategy for change, we can consciously transform our environments and in that way re-create ourselves. (p. vii)

Eisler, Riane, and David Loye. *The Partnership Way: New Tools for Living and Learning, Healing Our Families, Our Communities, and Our World*. San Francisco: HarperCollins, 1990, HQ1075 .E58 1990. <http://www.partnershipway.org> [Chap. 2]

> Eisler and Loye detail a program for shifting to "a partnership way" in which human relations are based on equality, nonviolence, and harmony with nature.

*It's never to late to have a happy childhood.*
— Bumpersticker

Holt, John. *Escape from Childhood*. New York, E. P. Dutton, 1974, HQ769 .H725.

> Holt argues that parents should treat children like real people, not as pets or slaves. In particular, he contends children should have all the rights and responsibilities specified in the U.S. Bill of Rights.

## • OVERCOMING DYSFUNCTIONAL EMOTIONAL CONDITIONING

Berne, Eric. *Games People Play: The Psychology of Human Relationships*. New York: Ballantine Books, 1964, HM291 .B394.

> Berne describes 33 dysfunctional games that people often play in what he calls Transactional Analysis and contrasts them with behavior that is free of game playing.

Bradshaw, John. *Creating Love: The Next Great Stage of Growth*. New York: Bantam, 1994.

> Bradshaw describes how past experiences create destructive patterns and how we can open ourselves to the soul-building work of real love.

_____. *Healing the Shame that Binds You*. Deerfield Beach, FL: Health Communications, 1988, RC455.4 .S53 B73 1988.

> Bradshaw describes how toxic shame, typically induced by abusive parents and teachers, produces feelings of deep inade-

quacy and can lead to a lifetime of compulsions, codependencies, addictions, and the drive to superachieve. He describes the signs of toxic shame and how to overcome it.

Gottman, John, with Joan DeClaire. *The Heart of Parenting: How to Raise an Emotionally Intelligent Child*. New York, NY: Fireside/Simon & Schuster, 1997, BF723 .E6G67 1997.

> We have studied parents and children in very detailed laboratory studies and followed the children as they developed. After a decade of research in my laboratory my research team encountered a group of parents who did five very simple things with their children when the children were emotional. We call these five things 'Emotion Coaching.' We discovered that the children who had Emotion-Coaching parents were on an entirely different developmental trajectory than the children of other parents.
>
> The Emotion-Coaching parents had children who later became what Daniel Goleman calls "emotionally intelligent" people. These coached children simply had more general abilities in the area of their own emotions than children who were not coached by their parents. (p. 16)
>
> The parents:
>
> 1. become aware of the child's emotion;
>
> 2. recognize the emotion as an opportunity for intimacy and teaching;
>
> 3. listen empathetically, validating the child's feelings;
>
> 4. help the child find words to label the emotion he is having; and
>
> 5. set limits while exploring strategies to solve the problem at hand. (p. 24)

Harris, Thomas A. *I'm OK, You're OK: A Practical Guide to Transactional Analysis*. New York: Harper & Row, 1969, RC480.5 .H32.

> Harris describes the consequences of a person thinking herself to be OK or not OK and thinking that others are OK or not OK.

Hendrix, Harville. *Getting the Love You Want: A Guide for Couples*. HarperCollins, 1988, HQ734 .H49 1988b.

> Hendrix presents a clear summary of the understanding of humans developed by psychologists over the past century. He also presents sixteen exercises that people can use to help themselves change so that their behavior is conscious and deliberate, rather than reactive and based on unconscious fears and suppressed needs from childhood. The exercises are designed for married couples, but could easily be adapted to any close relationship. They are simple and positive — designed to foster understanding of and love for oneself and one's partner.
>
> Ten Characteristics of a Conscious Marriage (from pp. 90–92):
>
> 1. You realize that your love relationship has a hidden purpose — the healing of childhood wounds.
>
> 2. You create a more accurate image of your partner.
>
> 3. You take responsibility for communicating your needs and desires to your partner.
>
> 4. You become more intentional in your interactions.
>
> 5. You learn to value your partner's needs and wishes as highly as you value your own.
>
> 6. You embrace the dark side of your personality.
>
> 7. You learn new techniques to satisfy your basic needs and desires.

8. You search within yourself for the strengths and abilities you are lacking.

9. You become more aware of your drive to be loving and whole and united with the universe.

10. You accept the difficulty of creating a good marriage.

---

*One of the deep secrets of life is that all that is really worth doing is what we do for others.* — Lewis Carroll

---

Jackins, Harvey. *The Human Side of Human Beings: The Theory of Re-evaluation Counseling*. Seattle, WA [PO Box 2081, Main Office Station, 98111]: Rational Island Publishers, 1965, BF637 .C6J3.

Jackins, founder and leader of Re-evaluation Counseling, Inc., argues that human beings are naturally smart, strong, loving, cooperative, and zestful, but when hurt, especially as children, they act out dysfunctional behavior. He argues that by providing a safe environment in which people can discharge emotions (by crying, shaking in fear, laughing, and so on), they can recover their full potential.

Gordon, Thomas. *Leader Effectiveness Training, LET: The No-Lose Way to Release the Productive Potential of People*. New York: Wyden Books, 1977, BF637 .L4 .G63.

Based on the ideas he first formulated with Parent Effectiveness Training (PET), Gordon describes positive methods for listening to people (active listening), saying things to change another person using "I-messages," and coming to a win-win solution using a 6-step problem solving method.

---

## • EDUCATION

Adams, Frank. *Unearthing Seeds of Fire: The Idea of Highlander*. Winston-Salem, NC: John F. Blair, 1975, LD7501 .M82 .A83.

Adams describes the history of the Highlander Folk School in Tennessee. Myles Horton founded it in 1932 to teach adults how to solve problems and conflicts by tapping their own experience and awareness.

Freire, Paulo. *Pedagogy of the Oppressed*. Translated by Myra Berman Ramos. New York: Continuum, 1986 [1970], LB880.F73 P4313 1986.

Freire argues that real education should be liberating and subversive — teaching people to think for themselves. He promotes educational methods that pose the question "Why?" about all aspects of students' lives and their society.

Holt, John. *Freedom and Beyond*. New York: Dell Publishing, 1972, LB885 .H6394 1972.

Holt calls for massive reform of the educational system to make it learner-directed, non-coercive, and focused on interest-inspired learning.

Horton, Myles, with Judith and Herbert Kohl. *The Long Haul: An Autobiography*. New York, Doubleday, 1990, LC5301 .M65H69 1990.

Horton's autobiography tells the history of the Highlander Folk School in Tennessee.

Leonard, George. *Education and Ecstasy*. New York: Delacorte Press, 1968, LA210 .L46.

Philadelphia Macro-Analysis Collective of the Movement for a New Society. *Organizing Macro-Analysis Seminars: Study and Action for a New Society*. Philadelphia: New Society Publishers, 1981. [Chap. 6]

This book describes how to set up and run a self-run study group. It includes a number of exercises useful for envisioning a good society and examining critical issues.

---

## • PERSUASION AND LOBBYING

Kawasaki, Guy. *Selling the Dream: How to Promote Your Product, Company, or Ideas — and Make a Difference — Using Everyday Evangelism*. New York: HarperCollins, 1991, HF5415 .K355 1991.

Based on what he learned as Apple Computer's original software evangelist for the Macintosh, Kawasaki describes how to convince people to believe passionately in a product or project by projecting one's fervor and zeal.

Snyder, Edward F., et al. *Witness in Washington: Fifty Years of Friendly Persuasion*. Richmond, IN: Friends United Press, 1994, BX7748 .C5W58 1996.

Snyder describes the honest and ethical lobbying carried out by the Quaker organization Friends Committee on National Legislation (FCNL) in Washington, DC.

Weimann, Gabriel. *The Influentials: People Who Influence People*. Albany, NY: State University of New York Press, 1994, HM261 .W42 1994.

Some people are influential in shaping the opinions of those around them. Weimann reviews 3,900 studies on these influential people and opinion leaders. He finds that opinion leaders generally are gregarious, socially connected, and knowledgeable.

---

## • BUILDING SOCIAL CHANGE MOVEMENTS

Boyte, Harry. *The Backyard Revolution: Understanding the New Citizen Movement*. Philadelphia: Temple University Press, 1980, HN69 .B69.

Friedland, William H., with Amy Barton, Bruce Dancis, Michael Rotkin, and Michael Spiro. *Revolutionary Theory*. Totowa, NJ: Allanheld, Osmun, 1982, JC491 .F73. [Chap. 5]

Hopper, Rex D. "The Revolutionary Process: A Frame of Reference for the Study of Revolutionary Movements." *Social Forces* 28:3 (March 1950), pp. 270–279. [Ch. 5]

Neuman, W. Russell. *The Paradox of Mass Politics: Knowledge and Opinion in the American Electorate.* Cambridge, MA: Harvard University Press, 1986, JK1967 .N48 1986. [Chap. 3, 6, App. C]

Olmosk, Kurt E. "Seven Pure Strategies of Change." *The 1972 Annual Handbook for Group Facilitators*: 163–172. [Fig. 7.4]

Oppenheimer, Martin. *The Urban Guerrilla.* Chicago, Quadrangle Books, 1969, JC491 .O6. [Fig. 7.5]

Rejai, Mostafa. *The Strategy of Political Revolution.* Garden City, NY: Doubleday, Anchor Press, 1973, JC491 .R381. [Fig. 5.3]

> Rejai provides an excellent summary of the scholarly literature on revolutionary strategy.

Rogers, Everett M. *Diffusion of Innovations*, 3rd ed. New York: The Free Press, Macmillan, 1983, HM101 .R57 1983. [Chap. 9]

> Rogers summarizes the results of over 3,000 studies that analyze the process of diffusing new ideas and practices throughout society. He describes what is necessary to communicate new ideas to people and various ways to encourage people to adopt them.

## • COMMUNITY ORGANIZING

Boyte, Harry. *CommonWealth: A Return to Citizen Politics.* New York: Free Press; London: Collier Macmillan, 1989, JK1764 .B694 1989.

Delgado, Gary. *Organizing the Movement: The Roots and Growth of ACORN.* Philadelphia: Temple University Press, 1986, HN85 .A3D45 1985.

Piven, Frances Fox, and Richard Cloward. *Poor People's Movements: Why They Succeed, How They Fail.* New York: Vintage, Random House, 1979, HD8076 .P55 1979.

> Piven and Cloward study four protest movements in the twentieth century carried out by poor people. They explore the successes and failures of mass defiance and disruption as compared with conventional electoral politics.

Stout, Linda. *Bridging the Class Divide and Other Lessons for Grassroots Organizing.* Boston: Beacon Press, 1996, HN65 .S75 1996. [Chap. 7]

> Based on her experience organizing the innovative and multi-racial Piedmont Peace Project in a poor, rural area of North Carolina, Stout offers several outstanding ideas about how to build powerful social change organizations. She argues against traditional hierarchical leadership dominated by a single top leader and argues in favor of a shared model in which everyone is encouraged to take leadership. She also promotes ongoing training in diversity and leadership. Furthermore, she urges groups to develop strategic plans, develop budgets and marketing plans, provide good benefits to group staffmembers, find effective ways to work with the news media, and communicate honestly with foundations about the true costs of good organizing.

## • ORGANIZING MANUALS AND HANDBOOKS

Alinsky, Saul D. *Rules for Radicals: A Practical Primer for Realistic Radicals.* New York: Vintage Books/Random House, 1971, HN65 .A675.

_____. *Reveille for Radicals.* New York: Vintage Books/ Random House, 1969 [1946], HM131 .A42 1969.

> In these two classic books, Alinsky describes some of the organizing techniques for which he is famous.

Bartlett, John W., ed. *The Future is Ours: A Handbook for Student Activists in the 21st Century.* New York: Henry Holt and Company, 1996, LB3610 .F88 1996.

> This organizing manual for students includes essays and many success stories.

Bobo, Kim, Jackie Kendall, and Steve Max. *Organizing for Social Change: A Manual for Activists in the 1990s.* Cabin John, MD: Seven Locks Press, 1991, JC328.3 .B63 1991.

> This excellent manual, oriented towards community organizing, is based on the curriculum of the Midwest Academy, a Chicago-based organizing school associated with Citizen Action.

Coover, Virginia, Ellen Deacon, Charles Esser, and Christopher Moore. *Resource Manual for a Living Revolution.* 2nd ed. Philadelphia: New Society Press, 1978, HN65 .R47 1978. [Chap. 6]

> This book is an excellent general resource guide for those seeking fundamental social change through nonviolence. It was written by members of Movement for a New Society (MNS) who helped create the nonviolent direct action anti-nuclear power movement of the 1970s. It includes sections on strategizing, group dynamics, meeting facilitation, decision-making, conflict resolution, training, and organizing.

Hedemann, Ed, ed. *War Resisters League Organizer's Manual.* New York: War Resisters League, 1981, HM136 .W34 1981.

> This valuable resource manual has four chapters describing different political perspectives (nonviolence, socialism, anarchism, and feminism), fourteen chapters explaining different organizing techniques, eight focusing on different constituencies, five on different methods of literature production, nine on various aspects of nonviolent direct action, and four on more conventional political work (lawsuits, elections, lobbying, and the media).

Isaac, Katherine. *Ralph Nader Presents Civics for Democracy: A Journey for Teachers and Students.* A Project of the Center for Study of Responsive Law and Essential Information. Washington, DC: Essential Books, 1992, JK1764 .I83 1992.

> Isaac presents short histories of five social change movements: the civil rights movement, the labor movement, the women's rights movement, the consumer movement, and the environmental movement. Then she describes how to use public

education, research, direct action, lobbying, and the courts to bring about positive change. She concludes with activities for students to get involved.

Kahn, Si. *Organizing: A Guide for Grassroots Leaders*. New York: McGraw-Hill, 1982, HM141 .K29.

Kahn covers all facets of community and union organizing.

MacEachern, Diane. *Enough is Enough: The Hellraiser's Guide to Community Activism (How to Organize a Successful Campaign for Change)*. New York: Avon Books, 1994, JS341 .M33.

MacEachern describes most aspects of community organizing, especially fundraising, communications, and lobbying. She provides examples of ordinary people organizing winning campaigns.

Shaw, Randy. *The Activist's Handbook: A Primer for the 1990s and Beyond*. Berkeley, CA: University of California Press, 1996, HN65 .S48 1996.

Shaw, a housing activist in San Francisco, describes various ways to strategize, challenge elected officials, work in coalitions, promote ballot initiatives, work with the media, work with lawyers, and engage in direct action.

Wollman, Neil, ed., *Working for Peace*. San Luis Obispo, CA: Impact Publishers, 1985, JX1963.W72 1985. [Chap. 6]

### • *Action Handbooks*

Abalone Alliance, *Diablo Canyon Blockade/Encampment Handbook*. 1980.

American Peace Test. *Nonviolence Trainers' Manual*. 2nd ed. Las Vegas, NV, January 1987.

Livermore Action Group. *International Day of Nuclear Disarmament Action Handbook*. Berkeley, CA, 1981.

Pledge of Resistance/Emergency Response Network. *Basta!: No Mandate for War*. San Francisco, CA, 1984.

South Africa Catalyst Project. *Organize*. Palo Alto, CA, 1978.

### • NONVIOLENT STRUGGLE

Ackerman, Peter, and Christopher Kruegler. *Strategic Nonviolent Conflict: The Dynamics of People Power in the Twentieth Century*. Westport, CT: Praeger, 1994, JC328.3 .A28 1994. [Chap. 5]

Ackerman and Kruegler analyze six twentieth-century nonviolent campaigns and delineate twelve strategic principles that enhance the prospects for success.

Bondurant, Joan V. *Conquest of Violence: The Gandhian Philosophy of Conflict*. Rev. ed. Berkeley, CA: University of California Press, 1965 [1958], HM278 .B6 1965.

Bondurant provides an excellent introduction to Gandhi's political thought and the operation of Satyagraha in specific campaigns.

Burrowes, Robert J. *The Strategy of Nonviolent Defense: A Gandhian Approach*. Albany, NY: State University of New York Press, 1996, HM278 .R85 1995.

Burrowes integrates the strategic theories of military battle developed by Carl von Clausewitz with those of nonviolent struggle developed by Mohandas Gandhi.

Cummings, Allan. *How Nonviolence Works*. Dunedin, New Zealand [20 Gillespie St.]: Nonviolent Action Network, 1985.

In this small book, Cummings explains the dynamics of a nonviolent campaign and how it can effectively bring about positive change.

Deming, Barbara. "On Revolution and Equilibrium." Published as a pamphlet by A.J. Muste Memorial Institute, 339 Lafayette St., New York, NY 10012, and included in Jane Myerding, ed., *We Are All Part of One Another: A Barbara Deming Reader*. Philadelphia: New Society Publishers, 1984, PS3554 .E475 W38 1984; reprinted from *Liberation Magazine* (February 1968): 179. [Chap. 5]

This short essay provides an excellent response to those who assume that powerful, radical struggle must necessarily be violent and maintain that nonviolence is meek, moralistic, or suicidal. Deming argues that nonviolent struggle can be as bold, powerful, and radical as armed struggle.

Irwin, Bob, and Gordon Faison. "Why Nonviolence? Nonviolence Theory and Strategy for the Anti-Nuclear Movement." Movement for a New Society, 4722 Baltimore Avenue, Philadelphia, PA 19143, 1978.

In this short pamphlet, Irwin and Gordon summarize the history, theory, and practice of nonviolent action.

King, Martin Luther, Jr. "Loving Your Enemies" [1957] and "Letter from a Birmingham Jail" [1963] published as a pamphlet by A.J. Muste Memorial Institute, 339 Lafayette Street, New York, NY 10012.

In these classic papers, King explains his philosophy of nonviolent action.

Lakey, George. *Powerful Peacemaking: A Strategy for a Living Revolution*. Philadelphia: New Society Publishers, 1987; revised edition of *Strategy for a Living Revolution*, New York: Grossman Publishers, 1973, HM278 .L32 1973. [Chap. 3, 5]

Lakey proposes a five-stage strategy for nonviolent revolution. His comprehensive approach focuses on social empowerment and grassroots organizations.

Moyer, Bill. *The Movement Action Plan: A Strategic Framework Describing the Eight Stages of Successful Social Movements*. San Francisco: Social Movement Empowerment Project [721 Shrader St., 94117, (415) 387-3361], Spring 1987. [Chap. 5, 9]

Bill Moyer (not to be confused with television journalist Bill Moyers) worked on the staff of the Southern Christian Leadership Conference's Poor People's Campaign and co-founded the Movement for a New Society and its Philadelphia Life Center.

He was involved with the movements working against the Vietnam War, against nuclear energy and weapons, for European nuclear disarmament, and against intervention in Central America.

In this pamphlet, Moyer describes the eight stages through which social change movements typically progress. For each stage, he describes the role of change activists, powerholders, and the public, then sketches appropriate goals for activists, and finally describes the pitfalls activists may encounter.

Moyer points out that successful nonviolent campaigns "aim to educate and win over an increasingly larger majority of the public, and to mobilize the majority public into an effective force that brings about social change." When the campaign grows large enough, it severely undercuts support for the powerholders. Without the tacit support of most people in society, powerholders are then forced to make changes or to turn over their authority to those who will.

_____. *The Practical Strategist*. Social Movement Empowerment Project, July 1990.

In this pamphlet, Moyer expands his analysis of the Movement Action Plan (MAP). He describes its strategic assumptions and discusses four particular roles of an activist: as a citizen, reformer, rebel, and change agent.

Sharp, Gene. *Gandhi as a Political Strategist*. Boston: Porter Sargent Publishers, 1979, DS481 .G3 .S4769.

Sharp explores the workings of Gandhi's social change efforts and their moral basis.

_____. *The Politics of Nonviolent Action*, 3 volumes. Boston: Porter Sargent Publishers, 1973, JC328.3 .S45.

In this classic treatise, Sharp describes a comprehensive theory of nonviolent action. Volume 1 argues that the general public can restrict or sever the power wielded by societal leaders by withdrawing its support of and cooperation with those leaders. Volume 2 describes 198 specific techniques of nonviolent struggle and illustrates each one with examples. Volume 3 examines the dynamics of nonviolent action used against a violent, repressive opponent.

## • BUILDING SOCIAL CHANGE ORGANIZATIONS

*Communities Directory: A Guide to Cooperative Living*. 1995 ed. Ann Langley, WA: Fellowship for Intentional Community, 1995, HX654 .D57.

This directory, published periodically, lists over 600 intentional communities with detailed cross-references. It also includes 31 articles on communitarian issues.

Downton, James, Jr., and Paul Wehr. *The Persistent Activist: How Peace Commitment Develops and Survives*. Boulder, CO: Westview Press/ HarperCollins, 1997, JX1953.3 .D65 1997.

Downton and Wehr interviewed thirty long-term activists in Colorado and identified the factors that led them to continue to work for peace even as others stopped their efforts.

Green, Tova, and Peter Woodrow with Fran Peavey. *Insight and Action: How to Discover and Support a Life of Integrity and Commitment to Change*. Philadelphia: New Society Publishers, 1994, HM133 .G7. [Chap. 6]

This valuable book offers three practical means to support friends and colleagues in making difficult decisions and sustaining their commitments. It describes how to provide ongoing, mutual sustenance through support groups, how to assist individuals to make wise decisions using clearness groups, and how to unearth a person's dreams and insight, even when buried beneath fear and helplessness, through the process of strategic questioning.

Lakey, Berit, George Lakey, Rod Napier, and Janice Robinson. *Grassroots and Nonprofit Leadership: A Guide for Organizations in Changing Times*. Philadelphia, PA: New Society Publishers, 1996, HD62.6 .G72 1995.

This book provides a practical toolkit for leaders to deal creatively and concretely with organizational issues including strategy, structure, diversity, meetings, morale, gossip, and conflict.

Shaffer, Carolyn R., and Kristin Annundsen. *Creating Community Anywhere: Finding Support and Connection in a Fragmented World*. Los Angeles: Jeremy P. Tarcher, 1993, HM131 .S437 1993.

Shaffer and Annundsen describe a variety of supportive groups: workplace teams, shared residences, social clubs, ritual groups, support groups, neighborhood associations, intellectual salons, spiritual communities, and electronic networks. They show how to set up these groups and how to make them work well.

Shields, Katrina. *In the Tiger's Mouth: An Empowerment Guide for Social Action*. Philadelphia: New Society Publishers, 1994, HN49 .V64S55 1994.

Shields provides a wide variety of practical methods for sustaining and enjoying social action.

## • COOPERATIVE DECISION-MAKING

### • Theory and Analysis

Barber, Benjamin. *Strong Democracy: Participatory Politics for a New Age*. Berkeley, CA: University of California Press, 1984, JC423 .B243 1984.

Barber argues for a strong, participatory democracy.

### • Consensus Decision-Making

Butler, C. T. Lawrence, and Amy Rothstein, *On Conflict and Consensus: A Handbook on Formal Consensus Decisionmaking*, Cambridge, MA [1430 Massachusetts Avenue, Room 306-35, 02138, (617) 864-8786]: Food Not Bombs Publishing, 1987.

Butler and Rothstein codify "Formal Consensus" — a highly structured procedure based on presenting a proposal and then modifying it in response to concerns. They seek to codify consensus decision-making the same way that Robert's Rules of Order codifies parliamentary procedure.

Center for Conflict Resolution. *Building United Judgment: A Handbook for Consensus Decision Making*. Philadelphia: New Society Publishers, 1981.

This book reviews a variety of practical methods for making consensus decision-making work.

_____. *A Manual for Group Facilitators*. Philadelphia: New Society Publishers, 1977.

This manual provides a variety of ideas about communication, planning, creative problem solving, conflict resolution, and moving groups toward their goals.

Doyle, Michael, and David Straus, *How to Make Meetings Work: The New Interaction Method*. New York: Wyden Books, 1976, HM131 .D68.

Doyle and Straus provide an excellent introduction to win/win decision-making including an adaptation of the consensus process for business groups with a manager who finally approves all decisions. They show how a facilitator, recorder, and a group memory (wall chart) help achieve good decisions, and they explain how to develop agendas, how to arrange meeting rooms, and how to deal with sixteen types of problem people.

Gastil, John. *Democracy in Small Groups: Participation, Decision Making, and Communication*. Philadelphia: New Society Publishers, 1993, HM133 .G28 1993.

Gastil describes the essential elements required for democracy in a small group and spells out when democratic methods should be used.

Institute for Nonviolence Education, Research and Training (INVERT). *Sharing Consensus: A Handbook for Consensus Workshops*. Monroe, ME [P.O. Box 776]: INVERT, 1978.

This handbook presents a non-directive approach to teaching consensus decision-making based on exercises that encourage self-initiation and responsibility. It emphasizes problem solving skills and working together.

### • Problem Solving

Adams, James L. *Conceptual Blockbusting: A Guide to Better Ideas*. 3rd ed. Reading, MA: Addison-Wesley, 1986, BF441 .A28 1986.

Adams discusses various impediments to solving problems and presents approaches for overcoming them.

de Bono, Edward. *New Think: The Use of Lateral Thinking in the Generation of New Ideas*. New York: Basic Books, 1968 [1967], BF455 .D38 1968

De Bono contrasts "vertical thinking" (careful, logical analysis and problem solving based on the available data) with "lateral thinking" in which one uses different viewpoints and unusual approaches to come up with fresh ideas. Other books by de Bono describe ways to encourage this creative lateral thinking.

### • Conflict Resolution

Beer, Jennifer E. with Eileen Stief. *The Mediator's Handbook*. 3rd ed. Developed by Friends Conflict Resolution Programs. Gabriola Island, BC: New Society Publishers, 1997, BF637 .N4 B447 1997.

This resource book provides a flexible methodology for conflict resolution. It describes each of the steps of an effective mediation.

Bramson, Robert M. *Coping with Difficult People*. New York: Dell, 1981, HF5548.8 .B683.

Bramson presents a six-step plan for effectively dealing with seven types of difficult people.

Filley, Alan C. *Interpersonal Conflict Resolution*. Glenview, IL: Scott, Foresman, 1975, HM132 .F54.

Filley discusses and integrates various studies on the handling of conflict.

Fisher, Roger, and William Ury. *Getting to Yes: Negotiating Agreement without Giving In*. 2nd ed. New York: Penguin Books, 1991 [1981], BF637 .N4F57 1991.

Fisher and Ury argue against positional bargaining of either the soft type (participants see themselves as friends trying to agree) or hard type (participants see themselves as adversaries trying to win a victory) and argue for a negotiation process in which the participants see themselves as mutual problem solvers. Their method of principled negotiation — negotiating in a fair manner based on the merits of each position — produces good results for both sides. It relies on four techniques: separating the people from the problem; focusing on interests, not positions; inventing options that provide mutual gain; and insisting on using objective criteria.

### • BUILDING ACTIVIST FINANCES

Dominguez, Joe, and Vicki Robin. *Your Money or Your Life: Transforming Your Relationship with Money and Achieving Financial Independence*. New York: Penguin Books, 1992, HG179 .D624 1992.

Dominguez and Robin offer a nine-step program for gaining financial independence by tracking and acknowledging how you spend money, reducing your expenditures for things that provide little satisfaction, increasing your income, and investing your savings in safe long-term, income-producing investments.

Everett, Melissa. *Making a Living While Making a Difference: A Guide to Creating Careers with a Conscience*. New York: Bantam Books, 1995, HF5381 .E853 1995.

Everett provides a ten-step program for finding or creating socially responsible work.

Mogil, Christopher, and Anne Slepian. *We Gave Away a Fortune: Stories of People Who Have Devoted Themselves and their Wealth to Peace, Justice, and a Healthy Environment*. Philadelphia: New Society Publishers, 1992, HV27 .M64 1992.

Mogil and Slepian relate the stories of sixteen wealthy people who have given away much of their material wealth to help create a more livable world. These provocative stories encourage us to reconsider the role of money in our lives, culture, and economy.

**OTHER**

Diamond, Sara. *Spiritual Warfare: The Politics of the Christian Right*. Boston: South End Press, 1989, BR1642 .U5D53 1989.

Diamond, Sara. *Not by Politics Alone: The Enduring Influence of the Christian Right*. New York: Guilford Press, 1998, BR1642 .U5D52 1998.

Sociologist Diamond investigated the Christian Right to determine how it has maintained its influence in the United States for more than two decades. She finds it relies on a web of cultural institutions, including evangelical talk radio programs, publishing companies, bookstores, law firms, and music studios, that meet the personal as well as ideological needs of its members.

*Books are the quietest and most constant of friends; they are the most accessible and wisest of counsellors, and the most patient of teachers.* — Charles W. Eliot, educator

## Other Cited Works

Albert, Michael. *Why Radicalism?* Lecture recorded at Z Media Institute, Summer 1998, Boston, MA, available from *Z Magazine*. [Chap. 7]

American Academy of Pediatrics. "Policy Statement: Breastfeeding and the Use of Human Milk (RE9729)." *Pediatrics* 100, no. 6 (December 1997): 1035-1039.
<http://www.aap.org/policy/re9729.html> [Chap. 2]

Anderson, Joseph M. *The Wealth of U.S. Families in 1995* (127 Hesketh Street, Chevy Chase, MD: Capital Research Associates, June 1, 1998).
<http://www.ml.com/woml/forum/wealth1.htm> [Chap. 3]

Associated Press. "Special Interests' Spending Disclosed." *San Francisco Chronicle* (23 Sept. 1996): A7. [Ch. 3]

Atlee, Tom. "How Nonviolent Social Change Movements Develop: An Interview with Bill Moyer." *ThinkPeace* (Oakland, CA), 6, no. 2 (March/April 1990): 3–6. [Chap. 7]

Bailey, Stephen K. *Congress Makes a Law*. New York: Columbia University Press, 1950. [Chap. 3]

"Beautiful Dreamer: Is Phil Gramm Right About 1950?" *Too Much* (Summer 1995): 2. Council on International and Public Affairs, Suite 3C, 777 United Nations Plaza, New York 10017. [Chap. 3]

Beitchman, Joseph H., Kenneth J. Zucker, Jane E. Hood, Granville A. daCosta, Donna Akman, and Erika Cassavia. "A Review of the Long-term Effects of Child Sexual Abuse." *Child Abuse & Neglect* 16 (1992): 101–118. [Chap. 3]

Benn, Stanley. "The Problematic Rationality of Political Participation." In Peter Laslett and James Fishkin, eds. *Philosophy, Politics and Society*. 5th series. New Haven: Yale University Press, 1979, JA71 .L27. [Chap. 7]

Bleifuss, Joel. "Sacred Cow, Or Bull? Questioning the Tenets of Political Organizing." *In These Times* 21, no. 25–26 (November 23, 1997): 16–17. [Chap. 6]

Bluestone, Barry, and Stephen Rose. "Overworked and Underemployed: Unraveling an Economic Enigma," *The American Prospect*, no. 31 (March-April 1997).
<http://www.prospect.org/archives/31/31bluefs.html> [Ch. 2]

Blum, William. "A Brief History of U.S. Interventions: 1945 to the Present." *Z Magazine* 12, no. 6 (June 1999): 25–30. [Chap. 3]

_____. *Killing Hope: US Military and CIA Interventions Since World War II*. Monroe, ME: Common Courage Press, 1995, JK468 .I6B59 1995.
<http://members.aol.com/bblum6/American_holocaust.htm> [Chap. 3]

Bonczar, Thomas P., and Allen J. Beck. "Lifetime Likelihood of Going to State or Federal Prison." U.S. Department of Justice, Bureau of Justice Statistics, Report Number NCJ-160092, March 1997.
<http://www.ojp.usdoj.gov:80/bjs/pub/pdf/llgsfp.pdf> [Ch. 2]

BP Amoco. *BP Amoco Statistical Review of World Energy, 1999*.
<http://www.bp.com/worldenergy/pdf/oil.pdf> [Chap. 2]

Bradsher, Keith. "Gap in Wealth in U.S. Called Widest in West." *New York Times* (17 April 1995): p. A1. [Chap. 3]

Browne, Angela, and David Finkelhor. "Impact of Child Sexual Abuse: A Review of the Research." *Psychological Bulletin* 99, no. 1 (1986), 66–77. [Chap. 3]

Burnstein, Paul, Rachel L. Einwohner, and Jocelyn A. Hollander. "The Success of Political Movements: A Bargaining Perspective." In J. Craig Jenkins and Bert Klandermans, eds. *The Politics of Social Protest: Comparative Perspectives on States and Social Movements*. Minneapolis: University of Minnesota Press, 1995, JA76 .P6235 1995. [Fig. 7.6]

Burt, Martha, Laudan Aron, Toby Douglas, Jesse Valente, Edgar Lee, Britta Iwen. *Homelessness: Programs and the People They Serve — Findings of the National Survey of Homeless Assistance Providers and Clients*. Urban Institute. Prepared for the Federal Interagency Council on the Homeless. 7 December 1999.
<http://www.urban.org/housing/homeless/homeless.html>
<http://www.urban.org/housing/homeless/homelessness.pdf> [Chap. 2]

Center for a New American Dream. "New Poll Shows Marketing to Kids Taking its Toll on Parents, Families," 6930 Carroll Ave., Suite 900, Takoma Park, MD 20912, July 1999.
<http://www.newdream.org/campaign/kids/press-release.html> [Chap. 2]

Center for Defense Information. "World Military Expenditures." Website accessed 14 October 2000.
<http://www.cdi.org/issues/wme/> [Chap. 2]

Center for Third World Organizing. "Training Centers & Organizing Networks." *Third Force*, Special Section published in conjunction with *The Neighborhood Works* 5, no. 1 (March/April 1997): 32. [Chap. 6]

Centers for Disease Control and Prevention. "Rates of Homicide, Suicide, and Firearm-Related Death Among Children — 26 Industrialized Countries." ***Morbidity and Mortality Weekly Report*** 46, no. 5 (7 February 1997): 101–105. [Chap. 2]

———. "Suicide in the United States." National Center for Injury Prevention and Control, Division of Violence Prevention. Web page revised January 28, 2000.
<http://www.cdc.gov/ncipc/factsheets/suifacts.htm> [Chap. 2]

Cohen, Jeff. "Propaganda from the Middle of the Road: The Centrist Ideology of the News Media." ***Extra!*** 2, no. 4 (October/ November 1989). [Chap. 3]

Cook, Philip J., and Jens Ludwig. ***Guns in America: Results of a Comprehensive National Survey on Firearms Ownership and Use***. Washington, DC: Police Foundation, 1997).
[Chap. 2]

Derber, Charles. ***The Wilding of America: How Greed and Violence Are Eroding Our Nation's Character***. New York: St. Martin's Press, 1996, HN90 .V5D47 1996. [Chap. 2]

Dugger, Ronnie. "Real Populists Please Stand Up: A Call to Citizens." ***The Nation*** (August 14/21, 1995): 159.
<http://www.thealliancefordemocracy.org/misc/dugger.htm>
[App. A]

Durning, Alan. "Asking How Much is Enough." ***State of the World, 1991: A Worldwatch Institute Report on Progress toward a Sustainable Society***. Lester R. Brown, Project Director. New York: Norton, 1991, HC59 .S733 1991. [Chap. 3]

Earle, Ralph B. ***Helping To Prevent Child Abuse — and Future Criminal Consequences: Hawai'i Healthy Start***. U.S. Department of Justice, Office of Justice Programs, National Institute of Justice, NCJ Report Number 156216, October 1995.
<http://www.ncjrs.org/txtfiles/hawaiihs.txt>
<http://www.ncjrs.org/pdffiles/hawaiihs.pdf> [App. A]

Easterbrook, Gregg. "Apocryphal Now: The Myth of the Hollow Military." ***The New Republic*** (11 September 2000).
<http://www.tnr.com/091100/easterbrook091100_print.html>
[Chap. 2]

Economic Policy Institute. "European Vacations." Economic Snapshots web page, May 10, 2000 (Washington, DC: Economic Policy Institute, 2000).
<http://www.epinet.org/webfeatures/snapshots/archive/2000/05 1000/snapshots051000.html> [Chap. 2]

Fellner, Kim. "Is Nothing Sacred?!" ***The Ark***. Newsletter of the National Organizers Alliance 10 (January 1998): 12–16.
[Chap. 6]

Flournoy, Craig, and Randy Lee Loftis. "Toxic Neighbors: Residents of Projects Find Common Problem: Pollution." ***Dallas Morning News*** (1 October 2000): 1A. [Chap. 2]

Friends Committee on National Legislation (FCNL). "A Glut of Military Spending." ***FCNL Washington Newsletter*** 641 (March 2000): 1. [Chap. 2]

Fullerton, Michael, ed. ***What Happened to the Berkeley Co-op?: A Collection of Opinions***. Davis, CA: Center for Cooperatives, University of California, 1992. [Chap. 4]

Gelles, Richard J., and John W. Harrop. "The Nature and Consequences of the Psychological Abuse of Children: Evidence from the Second National Family Violence Survey." Paper presented at the Eighth National Conference on Child Abuse and Neglect, Salt Lake City, Utah. October 24, 1989. [Chap. 3]

Geoghegan, Vincent. ***Utopianism and Marxism***. London: Methuen, 1987, HX806 .G46 1987. [Chap. 12]

Handgun Control, Inc. (HCI), Washington, DC.
<http://www.handguncontrol.org/research/progun/firefacts.asp>
[Chap. 2]

Hartung, William D. ***Welfare for Weapons Dealers: The Hidden Costs of the Arms Trade, 1996***. New York, NY: World Policy Institute, Arms Trade Resource Center.
<http://worldpolicy.org/projects/arms/reports/hcrep.html#uncle sam> [Chap. 2]

Hodgkinson, Virginia A., and Murray S. Weitzman. ***Giving and Volunteering in the United States***, ***1996***. Washington, DC [1200 Eighteenth Street, NW, Suite 200, 20036]: Independent Sector, 1996. <http://www.indepsec.org> [Chap. 1]

Holhut, Randolph T. "A Horrible Year for Journalism." Opinion column, ***San Francisco Bay Guardian*** (6 January 1999): 11. [Chap. 3]

Human Rights Watch. ***World Report 2001***. "USA Overview."
<http://www.hrw.org/wr2k1/usa/index.html> [Chap. 2]

Jackins, Harvey. ***The Enjoyment of Leadership***. Seattle: Rational Island Publishers, 1987. [Chap. 6]

Kay, Jane Holtz. ***Asphalt Nation: How the Automobile Took Over America and How We Can Take It Back***. Berkeley, CA: University of California Press, 1998, HE5623 .K36 1998. [Chap. 2]

Kilpatrick, Dean, and Benjamin Saunders. "The Prevalence and Consequences of Child Victimization." U.S. Department of Justice, Office of Justice Programs, National Institute of Justice, NIJ Research Preview, Report Number FS 000179, April 1997.
<http://www.ncjrs.org/pdffiles/fs000179.pdf> [Chap. 3]

Kirsch, Irwin S., Ann Jungeblut, Lynn Jenkins, and Andrew Kolstad. ***Adult Literacy in America: A First Look at the Findings of the National Adult Literacy Survey***. Washington, DC: National Center for Education Statistics, Office of Educational Research and Improvement, U.S. Dept. of Education, 1993, LC5251 .A6437 1993.
<http://nces.ed.gov/nadlits/naal92/> [Chap. 3]

Levitas, Ruth. ***The Concept of Utopia***. New York: np, 1990. [Chap. 12]

Margolis, Howard. ***Selfishness, Altruism and Rationality: A Theory of Social Choice***. New York: Cambridge University Press, 1982, HB846.8 .M37. [Chap. 7]

Maxfield, Michael G., and Cathy Spatz Widom. "The Cycle of Violence Revisited 6 Years Later." ***Archives of Pediatric and Adolescent Medicine*** 150 (April 1996): 390–395. [Chap. 3]

McGinn, Anne Platt. "Rocking the Boat: Conserving Fisheries and Protecting Jobs." ***WorldWatch Paper 142***. Washington, DC: WorldWatch Institute, 1995.
<http://www.worldwatch.org/pubs/paper/142.html> [Chap. 2]

Morris, David. "Why is Local Self Reliance Important? A Conversation with David Morris." Interview by Michael Closson, Center for Economic Conversion. *Positive Alternatives* 8, no. 3 (Spring 1998): 7-9. [App. A]

Morris, William. *Political Writings of William Morris*. A.L. Morton, ed. London: Lawrence and Wishart, 1984, HX246 .M72 1984. [Chap. 1]

Mumford, Lewis. *The Transformations of Man*. 1956; reprint New York: Harper & Row, Torchbooks, 1972, CB53 .M82 1956. [Chap. 3]

Muste, A. J. *The Essays of A. J. Muste*. Nat Hentoff, ed. Indianapolis: Bobbs-Merrill Co., 1967, JX1963 .M8455. [Chap. 6]

Nader, Ralph *The Concord Principles: An Agenda for a New Initiatory Democracy*. Pamphlet. 1 February 1992. <http://www.greenparties.org/articles/concord.html> [App. A]

National Opinion Research Center, The University of Chicago. *1997-1998 National Gun Policy Survey*. September 1998. [Chap. 2]

Nelson, Portia. "Autobiography in Five Short Chapters." In *There's a Hole in my Sidewalk: The Romance of Self-Discovery*. Hillsboro, OR: Beyond Words Publishing, 1993, BF637 .S4N45 1993. [Chap. 4]

Nussbaum, Martha, and Jonathan Glover, eds. *Women, Culture, and Development: A Study of Human Capabilities*. Cambridge: Clarendon Press, 1995, HQ1236 .W6377 1994. [Ch. 2]

This study, prepared for the World Institute for Development Economics Research (WIDER) of the United Nations University, looks at current approaches to development policy from a philosophical and economic perspective.

Oliver, Pamela E. "Formal Models of Collective Action." *Annual Review of Sociology* 19 (1993): 271-300. [Chap. 7]

Olson, Mancur. *The Logic of Collective Action: Public Goods and the Theory of Groups*. 1965; rev. ed. New York: Schocken Books, 1971, HM131 .O55 1971. [Chap. 7]

Olson explores the factors that encourage and prevent people from working together and describes the "free rider" problem in which non-contributors have little incentive to work collectively with others because they receive the same benefits from public works as do hard-working contributors.

Ornstein, Norman, Andrew Kohut, and Larry McCarthy. *The People, the Press, & Politics: The Times Mirror Study of the American Electorate, Conducted by The Gallup Organization*. Reading, MA: Addison-Wesley, Times Mirror, 1988, HN90 .P8076 1988. [App. C]

Based on an extensive in-person survey of 4,244 people in September 1987 that asked 348 questions, this study categorized the public into eleven distinct groups based on their voting inclinations, values, and attitudes.

Orum, Anthony M. *Introduction to Political Sociology: The Social Anatomy of the Body Politic*, 2nd ed. Englewood Cliffs, NJ: Prentice-Hall, 1983, JA76 .O78 1983. [Fig. 5.3]

Osborn, Barbara Bliss. "If It Bleeds, It Leads… If It Votes, It Don't: A Survey of L.A.'s Local 'News' Shows." *Extra* 7, no. 5 (Sept./Oct. 1994): 15. [Chap. 1]

PEN, the People's Education Network. <http://www.penpress.org> [Chap. 1, 2]

Rand, Michael. *Criminal Victimization 1997: Changes 1996-97 with Trends 1993-97*. National Crime Victimization Survey, Bureau of Justice Statistics, U.S. Department of Justice, Report NCJ 173385, December 1998, p. 3. <http://www.ojp.usdoj.gov/bjs/pub/pdf/cv97.pdf> [Chap. 3]

Reiss, Albert, Jr., and Jeffrey A. Roth, eds. *Understanding and Preventing Violence: Panel on the Understanding and Control of Violent Behavior*. Washington, DC: National Academy Press, 1993, HN90 .V5U53 1993. <http://books.nap.edu/books/0309054761/html/index.html> [App. A]

Renner, Michael. "Rethinking the Role of the Automobile." *Worldwatch Paper 84*. Washington, DC: Worldwatch Institute, June 1988, HE5611 .R46 1988. [Chap. 2]

Rogers, Joel. "Turning to the Cities: A Metropolitan Agenda." *In These Times* 22, no. 22 (Oct. 14, 1998): 14–17. [App. A]

Schor, Juliet. *The Overworked American: The Unexpected Decline in Leisure*. New York: Basic Books, 1991, HD4904.6 .S36 1991. [Chap. 2]

Schumaker, Paul D. "Policy Responsiveness to Protest-Group Demands." *Journal of Politics* 37 (May 1975): 494–495. [Fig. 7.6]

Scitovsky, Tibor. *The Joyless Economy: An Inquiry into Human Satisfaction and Consumer Dissatisfaction*. New York: Oxford University Press, 1976, HB801 .S35. [Chap. 7]

The Sentencing Project. "Facts about Prisons and Prisoners." April 2000. <http://www.sentencingproject.org/brief/facts-pp.pdf> [Chap. 2]

Sherman, Lawrence W., Denise C. Gottfredson, Doris L. MacKenzie, John Eck, Peter Reuter, and Shawn D. Bushway. *Preventing Crime: What Works, What Doesn't, What's Promising*. NIJ Research in Brief Series, U.S. Department of Justice, Office of Justice Programs, National Institute of Justice, Report Number 171676, July 1998. <http://www.ncjrs.org/txtfiles/171676.txt> <http://www.ncjrs.org/pdffiles/171676.pdf> [App. A]

Sklar, Holly. "Economics for Everyone." *Z Magazine* 8, no. 7/8 (July/August 1995): 44. [App. A]

Taylor, Michael. *Community, Anarchy, and Liberty*. New York: Cambridge University Press, 1982, HX833 .T39 1982. [Ch. 7]

_____, ed. *Rationality and Revolution*. New York: Cambridge University Press, 1988, HX550 .R48R37 1988. [Chap. 7]

Taylor, Michael, and Sara Singleton. "The Communal Resource: Transaction Costs and the Solution of Collective Action Problems." *Politics & Society* 21, no. 2 (June 1993): 195–214. [Chap. 7]

Tjaden, Patricia, and Nancy Thoennes. *Prevalence, Incidence, and Consequences of Violence Against Women: Findings From the National Violence Against Women Survey*, NIJ Research in Brief Series, U. S. Department of Justice, Office of Justice Programs, National Institute of Justice, Report Number 172837, November 1998. <http://ncjrs.org/pdffiles/172837.pdf> [Ch. 2, 3]

20/20 Vision. *1998-99 Biennial Report.* 1828 Jefferson Place, NW, Washington, DC: 2000. [Chap. 2]

United Nations Children's Fund (UNICEF), *The State of the World's Children, 1999.*
<http://www.unicef.org/sowc99/feature3.htm>
<http://www.unicef.org/sowc99/facts3.htm> [Chap. 2]

United Nations General Assembly. *Universal Declaration of Human Rights.* <http://www.un.org/Overview/rights.html>
<http://www.hrw.org/universal.html> [Chap. 2]

United Nations Development Programme. *Human Development Report 1994.* New York: Oxford University Press, 1994, HD72 .H85 1994. <http://www.undp.org/hdro> [Chap. 2]

_____. *Human Development Report 1998.* New York: Oxford University Press, 1998, HD72 .H852 1998.
<http://www.undp.org/hdro> [Chap. 1]

_____. *Human Development Report 1999.* New York: Oxford University Press, 1999, HD72 .H85 1999.
<http://www.undp.org/hdro> [Chap. 2, 3, App. A]

Urban Institute. "America's Homeless II: Populations and Services." Slideshow released 1 February 2000 based on work by researchers Martha Burt and Laudan Aron.
<http://www.urban.org/housing/homeless/numbers/sld002.htm> [Chap. 2]

U.S. Census Bureau. *Health Insurance Coverage: 1999 (P60-211).* March 2000 Current Population Surveys.
<http://www.census.gov/Press-Release/www/2000/cb00-160.html>, <http://www.census.gov/hhes/www/hlthin99.html> [Chap. 2]

_____. *Poverty in the United States: 1999 (P60-210).* March 2000 Current Population Surveys.
<http://www.census.gov/Press-Release/www/2000/cb00-158.html>,
<http://www.census.gov/hhes/www/povty99.html> [Chap. 2]

_____. *Statistical Abstract of the United States.*
<http://www.census.gov:80/statab/www/index.html>
[Chap. 1, 2, 3]

U.S. Department of Defense. *Annual Defense Report 2000.*
<http://www.dtic.mil/execsec/adr2000/adr2000.pdf> [Chap. 2]

_____. *Introduction to the United States Department of Defense.* Website updated 3 July 2000.
<http://www.defenselink.mil/pubs/dod101/busiest.html> [Chap. 2]

_____. Defense Security Cooperation Agency. International Military Education and Training (IMET) Program website.
<http://www.dsca.osd.mil/programs/imet/imet2.htm>
<http://129.48.104.198/introsa98/sld016.htm> [Chap. 2]

_____. Washington Headquarters Services. Directorate for Information Operations and Reports. *Active Duty Military Personnel Strengths by Regional Area and by Country (309A).* 31 March 2000.
<http://web1.whs.osd.mil/mmid/m05/hst0300.pdf> [Chap. 2]

_____. Washington Headquarters Services. Directorate for Information Operations and Reports. *Selected Manpower Statistics, Fiscal Year 1999.* 30 September 1999.
<http://web1.whs.osd.mil/mmid/m01/fy99/m01fy99.pdf> [Chap. 2]

U.S. Department of Health and Human Services. "A Nation's Shame: Fatal Child Abuse and Neglect in the United States — A Report of the U.S. Advisory Board on Child Abuse and Neglect." Administration for Children and Families. April 1995. HE23 .1002:AB 9. [Chap. 3]

U.S. Department of State. Bureau of Arms Control. *World Military Expenditures and Arms Transfers 1998.*
<http://www.state.gov/www/global/arms/bureau_vc/wmeat98vc.html>
<http://www.state.gov/www/global/arms/bureau_vc/wmeat98fs.html> [Chap. 2]

U.S. Environmental Protection Agency. Office of Water. *National Water Quality Inventory: 1998 Report to Congress* (EPA 841-R-00-001).
<http://www.epa.gov/305b/98report/98summary.html> [Ch. 2]

U.S. General Accounting Office. "Department Of Defense: Financial Audits Highlight Continuing Challenges to Correct Serious Financial Management Problems." Statement of Gene L. Dodaro, Assistant Comptroller General, Accounting and Information Management Division. GAO/T-AIMD/NSIAD-98-158. 16 April 1998. [Chap. 2]

U.S. National Science Foundation. Division of Science Resources Studies. *Science and Engineering Indicators 1998.*
<http://www.nsf.gov/sbe/srs/seind98> [Chap. 2]

Verba, Sidney, Kay Lehman Schlozman, and Henry E. Brady. *Voice and Equality: Civic Voluntarism in American Politics.* Cambridge, MA: Harvard University Press, 1995, JK1764 .V475 1995. [App. C]

Based on a telephone survey of 15,053 people and 2,517 long personal interviews, the authors analyze citizen participation in politics. They show that both the motivation and the capacity to take part in politics are rooted in the non-political institutions of their lives — family and school in the early years and then affiliations on the job, in non-political organizations, and in religious organizations. Their model of the participatory process — the Civic Voluntarism Model — shows how some of the factors that foster political activity (like money, education, and civic skills) are stockpiled over the course of a lifetime, frequently conferring additional advantage on those already privileged.

Their study reports on the factors that foster three kinds of political activity: voting, time-based activities (like working on a political campaign, lobbying public officials, serving on a community board, attending protest demonstrations, and working with an informal community group), and monetary contributions to political campaigns. They find that voting is most strongly fostered by people's strong interest in politics, high levels of knowledge about political ideas, strong support for a particular political party, and to a lesser extent, high levels of church attendance. The factors that foster time-based activities are a high level of civic skill and strong interest in politics. Factors that have some effect are high levels of education, large amounts of free time, strong interest in politics, and strong beliefs in the effectiveness of their efforts. The factor that fosters money contributions most strongly is a high family income. A strong interest in politics also has some effect.

Vissing, Yvonne M., Murray A. Straus, Richard J. Gelles, and John W. Harrop. "Verbal Aggression by Parents and Psychosocial Problems of Children." *Child Abuse & Neglect* 15, no. 3 (1991): 223–238. [Chap. 3]

Weeks, Robin, and Cathy Spatz Widom. *Early Childhood Victimization Among Incarcerated Adult Male Felons*. NIJ Research Preview, U.S. Department of Justice, Office of Justice Programs, National Institute of Justice, Report Number FS 000204, April 1998. <http://www.ncjrs.org/txtfiles/fs000204.txt> [Chap. 3]

_____. "Self-Reports of Early Childhood Victimization Among Incarcerated Adult Male Felons." *Journal of Interpersonal Violence* 13, no. 3 (June 1998): 346–361. [Chap. 3]

Whyte, William Hollingsworth. *The Organization Man*. New York: Simon and Schuster, 1956, BF697 .W47. [Chap. 9]

Widom, Cathy Spatz. "Does Violence Beget Violence?: A Critical Examination of the Literature." *Psychological Bulletin* 106, no. 1 (1989): 3–28. [Chap. 3]

_____. *Victims of Childhood Sexual Abuse — Later Criminal Consequences*. NIJ Research in Brief Series, U.S. Department of Justice, Office of Justice Programs, National Institute of Justice, Report Number NCJ 151525, March 1995. <http://www.ncjrs.org/pdffiles/abuse.pdf> [Chap. 3]

Washington Post Wire Service. "House Takes Up Lobbying Reform Bill." *San Francisco Chronicle* (25 November 1995). [Chap. 3]

_____. "Senate OKs Tighter Rules for Lobbyists." *San Jose Mercury News* (7 May 1993). [Chap. 3]

Wolff, Edward N. "Recent Trends in the Size Distribution of Household Wealth." *Journal of Economic Perspectives* 12, no. 3 (Summer 1998). [Chap. 3]

World Health Organization. "World Health Organization Assesses the World's Health Systems." Press release describing *The World Health Report 2000 — Health Systems: Improving Performance*. Geneva, Switzerland: WHO, June 2000. <http://www.who.int/whr/2000/en/press_release.htm> [Ch. 2]

Young, Iris. *Justice and Politics of Difference*. Princeton, NJ: Princeton University Press, 1990, JC578. Y68 1990. [Chap. 2]

Young, Michal Ann, M.D. "Press Statement on American Academy of Pediatrics Breastfeeding Recommendations." 17 December 1997. <http://www.aap.org/advocacy/washing/brfeed.htm> [Chap. 2]

Zero to Three: National Center for Infants, Toddlers and Families, "Year 2000 Parent & Public Survey," (734 15th St., NW, Suite 1000, Washington, D.C. 20005, 202-638-1144), October 2000. <http://www.zerotothree.org/2000poll-results.html> [Chap. 9]

## BOOK PUBLISHERS

The books and magazines produced by these progressive publishers provide up-to-date critiques of society as well as reports on the efforts to bring about progressive change.

*If there is a book you really want to read but it hasn't been written yet, then you must write it.*
— Toni Morrison

### SOUTH END PRESS
7 Brookline Street, Suite 1, Cambridge, MA 02139, (617) 547-4002, (800) 533-8478, southend@igc.org <http://www.lbbs.org/sep/sep.htm>

### COMMON COURAGE PRESS
Box 702, Monroe, Maine 04951, (800) 497-3207, comcour1@agate.net, <http://www.commoncouragepress.com>.

### SEVEN STORIES PRESS
140 Watts Street, New York, NY, 10013, infor@sevenstories.com, <http://www.sevenstories.com/>

### NEW SOCIETY PUBLISHERS
P. O Box 189, Gabriola Island, BC, Canada V0R 1X0, (250) 247-9737, (800) 567-6772, info@newsociety.com <http://www.newsociety.com/index.html>

### THE APEX PRESS/BOOTSTRAP PRESS
Council on International and Public Affairs, 777 United Nations Plaza, Suite 3C, New York, NY 10017 or P.O. Box 337, Croton-on-Hudson, NY 10520 (800) 316-2739, <http://www.cipa-apex.org/>

### VERSO PRESS
180 Varick Street, New York, NY 10014-4606, (212) 807-9680, Versoinc@aol.com, <http://www.versobooks.com/>

### MONTHLY REVIEW PRESS
112 West 27th St., New York, NY 10001, (800) 670-9499, mreview@igc.org., <http://www.monthlyreview.org/mrpress.htm>

### ZED PRESS
7 Cynthia Street, London N1 9JF, +44 (0)207 837 4014, <http://www.zedbooks.demon.co.uk/>

### BLACK ROSE BOOKS
<http://www.web.net/~blakrose/index.htm>

# MAGAZINES

Here are a few general interest magazines:

### THE NATION

72 Fifth Avenue New York, New York 10011, (212) 242-8400, <http://www.TheNation.com/>

Founded: 1865. Published: 47 times per year.

This is the oldest progressive magazine in the United States. It has articles, columns, investigatory articles, and book reviews.

### IN THESE TIMES

2040 N. Milwaukee Ave., Chicago, IL 60647, (773) 772-0100, itt@igc.org, <http://www.inthesetimes.com>

Founded: 1976. Published: 24 times per year.

"Independent News and Views." This magazine has regular columns on labor, African-Americans, media, and political campaigns as well as in-depth articles on general topics, investigatory articles, and book reviews.

### Z MAGAZINE

18 Millfield St., Woods Hole, MA 02543, (508) 548-9063, Lydia.Sargent@zmag.org, <http://www.zmag.org>

Founded: 1987. Published: 11 times per year.

This magazine covers political, cultural, social, and economic life in the U.S. and activist efforts to create a better future. It has regular articles by Noam Chomsky, Edward S. Herman, Brian Tokar, Lydia Sargent, and several others as well as articles on general topics and book reviews.

### THE PROGRESSIVE

409 E. Main St., Madison, WI 53703, (608) 257-4626, editorial@progressive.org or circ@progressive.org <http://www.progressive.org>

Founded: 1909. Published: 12 times per year.

This magazine has articles, interviews, columns, poems, art, and political humor about peace and social justice in America.

### MOTHER JONES

The Foundation for National Progress, 731 Market Street, Suite 600, San Francisco, CA 94103, (415) 665-6637, <http://www.motherjones.com>

Founded: 1976. Published: 6 times per year.

This colorful magazine includes general and investigatory articles on a variety of progressive issues.

### EXTRA!

Fairness and Accuracy in Reporting (FAIR), 130 West 25th Street, New York, NY 10001, (212) 633-6700, <http://www.fair.org>

Founded: 1986. Published: 6 times per year.

FAIR is a national media watch group that offers well-documented criticism of media bias and censorship.

### LABOR NOTES

Labor Notes, 7435 Michigan Ave., Detroit, MI 48210, (313) 842-6262, labornotes@labornotes.org, <http://www.labornotes.org/>

Founded: 1979. Published: 12 times per year.

This magazines offers the voices of union activists who want to "put the movement back in the labor movement" through rank and file democracy. It covers important labor news from a progressive perspective.

### DOLLARS AND SENSE: WHAT'S LEFT IN ECONOMICS

The Economic Affairs Bureau, Inc., 740 Cambridge Street, Cambridge, MA 02141-1401, (617) 876-2434, dollars@igc.org, <http://www.dollarsandsense.org>

Founded: 1974. Published: 6 times per year.

Published by a collective, this magazine provides "left perspectives on current economic affairs" with articles by journalists, activists, and scholars on a broad range of topics including the economy, housing, union reform, government regulation, unemployment, the environment, urban conflict and activism.

### THE NONVIOLENT ACTIVIST

War Resisters League (WRL), 339 Lafayette Ave., New York, New York 10012, (212) 228-0450, wrl@igc.org, <http://www.nonviolence.org/wrl/nva.htm>.

Founded: 1983. Published: 6 times per year.

Articles about the WRL and its national and local pacifist organizing as well as articles on nonviolent change and general topics.

### PEACEWORK

The New England Regional Office of the American Friends Service Committee (AFSC), 2161 Massachusetts Avenue, Cambridge, MA 02140, (617) 661-6130, pwork@igc.org, <http://www.afsc.org/peacewrk.htm>

Founded: 1972. Published: 11 times per year.

Serves the movements for nonviolent social change, particularly in the Northeast, by covering social justice and peace issues and linking grassroots work with national and international perspectives.

### YES! A JOURNAL OF POSITIVE FUTURES

Positive Futures Network, P. O. Box 10818, Bainbridge Island, WA 98110, (206) 842-0216, yes@futurenet.org, <http://www.futurenet.org>

Founded: 1996. Published: 4 times per year.

Combines analysis of important problems with news about actions people are taking in the United States and around the world to create a more positive future.

### EARTH ISLAND JOURNAL

Earth Island Institute, 300 Broadway, Suite 28, San Francisco, CA 94133, (415) 788-3666, <http://www.earthisland.org>

Founded: 1982. Published: 4 times per year.

Often on the cutting edge of the environmental movement.

### UTNE READER

LENS Publishing Co. Inc., 1624 Harmon Place, Minneapolis, MN 55403, (612) 338-5040, <http://www.utne.com/>

Founded: 1984. Published: 6 times per year.

Reprints selected articles from over 2,000 alternative media sources plus summarizes articles on emerging issues.

### WHOLE EARTH

Point Foundation, 1408 Mission Avenue, San Rafael, CA 94901, (415) 256-2800, info@wholeearthmag.com, <http://www.wholeearthmag.com>

Founded: 1974. Published: 4 times per year.

Has eclectic articles and book reviews on a variety of progressive and counter-culture issues.

## RADIO PROGRAMS

### DEMOCRACY NOW

This excellent one-hour show, broadcast every weekday, is hosted by Amy Goodman and Juan Gonzalez and is carried by about 65 stations.

<http://www.democracynow.org>
<http://www.pacifica.org>

### MAKING CONTACT

The International Radio Project — whose motto is "Radio that activates!" — produces this half-hour show that is heard on over 150 stations each week. "Making Contact" airs voices not usually heard on the radio.

<http://www.radioproject.org>

### ALTERNATIVE RADIO

David Barsamian produces this one-hour show that is heard on over 100 stations each week.

<http://www.alternativeradio.org>

### RADIONATION

Marc Cooper interviews authors of recent articles in *The Nation* magazine each week in two half-hour shows broadcast on over 100 stations.

<http://www.radionation.org>

## WEB SITES

### COMMON DREAMS NEWSCENTER

"News & Views for the Progressive Community" <http://www.commondreams.org/>

### INSTITUTE FOR GLOBAL COMMUNICATIONS (IGC)

PeaceNet, LaborNet, ConflictNet, WomensNet, and EcoNet. <http://www.igc.org/igc/>

### ZNET

"A community of people concerned about social change" (associated with *Z Magazine*). <http://www.lbbs.org>

### INDEPENDENT MEDIA CENTER

A collective of independent media organizations and hundreds of journalists offering grassroots, non-corporate coverage — a democratic media outlet for the creation of radical, accurate, and passionate tellings of truth. <http://www.indymedia.org/>

### WORKING FOR CHANGE

News, opinion columns, and action sponsored by Working Assets. <http://www.workingforchange.com/>

### CO-OP AMERICA

Social change information and action for consumers and investors. <http://www.coopamerica.org/>

### THE NONVIOLENT WEB

<http://www.nonviolence.org>

### THE VERNAL PROJECT

This site includes information about this book and the Vernal Project, the papers used in the workshops that I facilitate on nonviolent direct action and cooperative decision-making, and links to a large number of progressive organizations. <http://www.vernalproject.org>

## NOTES FOR CHAPTER 12

[1] Ronald Aronson, **After Marxism** (New York: Guilford Press, 1995, HX44.5 .A78 1994), p. 267. For discussions of the function of utopia Aronson points to Ruth Levitas, **The Concept of Utopia** (New York: np, 1990) and Vincent Geoghegan, **Utopianism and Marxism** (London: Methuen, 1987, HX806 .G46 1987).

# *A*

# *Appendix A: Some Positive Near-Term Policy Changes*

---

## STEPS TOWARD A GOOD SOCIETY

The society described in Chapter 2 is quite different from our current society. To get from here to there will require many intermediary steps.

*If you have built castles in the air, your work need not be lost; that is where they should be. Now put the foundations under them.*
— Henry David Thoreau

Below are listed some examples of specific policy changes that I believe would begin the shift toward a good society.[1] Though they would be significant steps forward, these policy changes would not alter the basic nature of current institutions, nor would they require large changes in our culture or the U.S. Constitution. Most could be enacted now by federal, state, or local governments. I believe these measures would serve well as near-term, achievable objectives of progressive change movements.

Note that these are only *my* ideas about near-term progressive goals. Other progressive activists may seek to move in other directions.

## Elections

• Eliminate barriers to voter registration.

• Establish a national Voting Day holiday to encourage maximum voter turnout and participation.

• Send a pamphlet containing detailed information about each initiative and candidate on the ballot to every registered voter several weeks before each election. This pamphlet should include the candidates' positions on at least ten important issues.

• Provide free media (TV, radio, and newspapers) for in-depth debate among candidates for office.

• Heavily tax all other political advertising (at perhaps a rate of 25%) to discourage blatant propagandizing.

• Prohibit any media coverage of candidates or advertising by the candidates for the last few days before an election and on the day of the election.

• Cut the power of special interests by limiting campaign contributions to $100 from each person who is a permanent resident of the candidate's district. Alternatively, ban *all* private financing of political campaigns.

• Prohibit contributions and other political activity by businesses to ensure we have a government by *citizens*, not interests.

---

*The business of politics consists of a series of unsentimental transactions between those who need votes and those who have money... a world where every quid has its quo.*
— Don Tyson, Chair of the Board, Tyson Foods[2]

• Ban all gifts to office-holders and candidates. Prohibit office-holders from accepting any honoraria.

• Reduce the salaries of all office-holders to no more than five or ten times the minimum wage.

• Establish binding initiative, referendum, and recall votes in every state so that concerned citizens can pass and rescind laws directly and remove wayward representatives. Establish a national referendum procedure.

• In some arenas, replace winner-take-all elections with proportional representation or preference voting. For example, an enlarged U.S. Senate (with 200 or 300 members) might be filled by members of each party in proportion to the number of citizens voting nationwide for their party. The Senate might then choose the president from among its ranks. To avoid too great a concentration of power, a panel of three independent "Judicial Appointers," with only the power to appoint judges to the Supreme Court and other federal posts, might be elected by nationwide majority vote. Members of the House of Representatives might continue to be elected by majority vote in local districts.

## Citizen Access to Information

• Rewrite laws in easy-to-understand language.

• Require all government data (except personal information about individuals) to be freely and easily accessible via the Internet.

• Protect government and corporate whistle-blowers from intimidation and job loss.

• Require all users and generators of toxic chemicals to provide full information about the chemicals to workers and the community.

## Employment and Poverty

• Set a minimum income that meets basic human needs. Raise the minimum wage so that it provides this income (a "livable wage" of perhaps $10–15/ hour) and index it so that it automatically rises with the cost of living.

*The child was diseased at birth, stricken with a hereditary ill that only the most vital men are able to shake off. I mean poverty — the most deadly and prevalent of all diseases.* — Eugene O'Neill, playwright

• Provide a job for everyone who can work. If the private sector cannot generate enough jobs, then the federal government should establish a Job Corps that can hire people to fix bridges, build housing, restore the environment, provide childcare, provide nursing care, or perform other socially beneficial work.

• For those who are sick or disabled, establish a refundable tax credit to bring their income up to the minimum.

• Shorten the standard workweek to 32 hours. This would mean businesses would hire more workers, reducing unemployment. It would also provide people with more time for childcare, leisure, and civic activities.

• Prohibit mandatory overtime. Prohibit more than 150 hours of overtime per year.

• Mandate six weeks of paid vacation annually.

• Mandate six months of paid maternity and paternity leave. Mandate leave for parents to take care of their sick children.

• Mandate periodic paid sabbaticals — perhaps a six-month sabbatical every eight years.

• Provide identical Social Security benefits to everyone regardless of individual work history.

## Personal Income Taxes

• Raise the amount of the combined standard deduction and personal exemption to a level equal to the poverty level so those living in poverty pay no income taxes and no one is taxed on the income necessary for basic living expenses.

• Increase the range and number of personal income tax rates. Lower the bottom rates and raise the top rates to make the rates more progressive. For example, lower the bottom personal income tax rate from 15% to 5%, add a 50% tax bracket for families with income over $200,000/year, add a 75% tax bracket for income over $500,000/year, and add a 90% tax bracket for all income received over $1 million. Index these rates to compensate for inflation.

Alternatively, add a 100% rate for all income higher than ten times the minimum wage (the Ten Times rule).[3]

• Tax capital gains at the same progressively graduated rates as normal income.

• Eliminate all itemized tax exemptions including mortgage interest and retirement funds to prevent tax dodges and subsidies to the wealthy.

• Reduce or end the tax exemption for municipal bonds (which are held primarily by the rich). To compensate state and city governments, allow them to tax U.S. Treasury securities.

*We can have democracy in this country or we can have great wealth concentrated in the hands of a few, but we can't have both.*
— Supreme Court Justice Louis D. Brandeis

• Alternatively, restrict use of funds raised from tax-free municipal bonds to socially responsible contractors.

• Re-introduce income averaging so that a windfall in one year is not subject to an overly high tax rate.

• Impose income taxes on the capital gains of all holdings at death (capital gains are now exempted).

• Raise inheritance and gift taxes — perhaps to a rate of 50% of the value of estates and gifts over $500,000 and 90% of the value of estates and gifts over $1 million. This would reduce the amount of unearned wealth passed down through elite families and would help to create a "level playing field" among young people.

• Institute a wealth tax on all personal assets over $2 million — perhaps at a rate of 10%/year — to help redistribute wealth from the rich to the poor.

## Corporate Taxes and Subsidies

• Base corporation taxes on gross receipts in addition to net income to reduce tax avoidance schemes. For multinational corporations, use a formula based on the percent of the firm's property, payroll, and sales within the United States compared to its global property, payroll, and sales, to prevent transfer pricing scams.

• Eliminate all subsidies and tax breaks to corporations including oil depletion allowances, road building in national forests, subsidized foreign sales, exemptions for pension funds, and so on.

*We may congratulate ourselves that this cruel war is nearing its end. It has cost a vast amount of treasure and blood. It has indeed been a trying hour for the Republic; but I see in the near future a crisis approaching that unnerves me and causes me to tremble for the safety of my country. As a result of the war, corporations have been enthroned and an era of corruption in high places will follow, and the money power of the country will endeavor to prolong its reign by working upon the prejudices of the people until all wealth is aggregated in a few hands and the Republic is destroyed. I feel at this moment more anxiety for the safety of my country than ever before, even in the midst of war. God grant that my suspicions may prove groundless.*

— U.S. President Abraham Lincoln, letter to Col. William F. Elkins, 21 November 1864

## Other Taxes

• Lower the Social Security tax rate and remove the cap on taxable income. Exempt the first $15,000 of income from the Social Security tax. If this depletes the Social Security fund, refill it with income tax revenue.

• Replace the standard property tax system with a split-level tax system as advocated by Henry George with high property taxes on the value from area-wide property appreciation and low taxes on the value derived from improvements to the particular property.

• Standardize the rate of sales, property, and state income taxes across the country to eliminate the downward spiral of competition for business.

• Scrap local and state property taxes and replace them with an income tax.

• Institute a tax on the sale of stocks, bonds, options, derivatives, and other financial entities at a rate of perhaps 1%. This would raise significant revenue from one of the few commodities whose sale is not now taxed. It would also discourage rampant speculation.

*Here are three Constitutional changes that would forever change the scale of politics and economics in America. Three four-word amendments that could change the shape of our future. "Corporations are not people." "Money is not speech." "Waste is not commerce." If the Supreme Court had interpreted the Constitution as they should have, and if they had adhered to the will of the people, these amendments would not be necessary. But it didn't and they are.* — David Morris, Institute for Local Self-Reliance[4]

• Institute a tax on advertising at a rate of perhaps 10%. This would raise significant revenue from another untaxed commodity and would discourage propagandizing and the inducement of unnecessary desires.

• Institute a tax on the broadcast of commercial programming as a way to pay for public-interest programming.

• Raise taxes on resources extracted from the environment (oil, natural gas, minerals, and timber), but not on recycled or re-used resources.

• Sharply raise gasoline taxes (until gasoline costs perhaps $4/gallon) to discourage urban sprawl, long commutes, and pollution. Use the income to subsidize public transit.

• Increase the tax on cigarettes by $0.50/pack every year until no one smokes anymore.

• Increase the tax on alcohol by $0.50/drink and use the revenue to discourage alcoholism and irresponsible behavior after drinking.

• Institute a tax on guns and ammunition as a way to discourage killing and encourage nonviolence.

## Defense

• Cut the military budget sharply — perhaps from its current level of about $300 billion/year (in 2000) to about $25 billion/year.

• Shift to a "non-offensive defense" strategy with the goal of eventually employing a strictly defensive civilian-based nonviolent defense.

*It is the habit of every aggressor nation to claim that it is acting on the defensive.*
— Jawaharlal Nehru

• Close U.S. military bases abroad.

• Restrict U.S. intervention into other countries strictly to nonviolent efforts conducted under the auspices of the United Nations. Stop all covert action.

• Support non-governmental groups that train volunteers to nonviolently witness and intervene in military conflicts.

• Dismantle all currently stockpiled nuclear, biological, and chemical weapons and prohibit their manufacture.

• Develop and promote international treaties that abolish nuclear, biological, and chemical weapons.

• Stop the sale of all military equipment to repressive countries.

• Eventually, prohibit the sale of all weapons to other countries and strongly push other countries to do the same.

• Eliminate military alliances like NATO and work through the United Nations instead.

## Conflict Resolution

• Make nonviolent conflict resolution part of the core school curriculum at every grade.

• Support community programs dedicated to peaceful conflict resolution.

• Strengthen international mediation and legal bodies like the International Court of Justice (World Court).

## Corporate Accountability

• Abolish laws that make corporations legally "persons."

• Require corporations to re-apply for corporate status every five years. Revoke the charters of corporations that engage in repeated wrongdoing (illegal activities, unfair labor practices, massive polluting, and production of unsafe products). This would dissolve these corporations.

• Re-establish strict personal civil and criminal liability for corporate officers and agents.

*So the question is, do corporate executives, provided they stay within the law, have responsibilities in their business activities other than to make as much money for their stockholders as possible? And my answer to that is, no they do not.*
— Milton Friedman

• Rewrite corporate law to require democratically chosen worker representation on corporate boards of directors.

• Establish publicly owned "yardstick" companies to serve as positive role-models and compete with privately owned corporations in important industries: utilities, communications, banking, and perhaps insurance, automobiles, chemicals, oil, air travel, and computers.

• Provide easy means for citizens to join consumer action groups that can watchdog corporations and advocate for the public interest.

## International Agreements

• Establish international standards for minimum wages, labor practices, consumer safety, and environmental regulation. These should be set to the highest level currently in effect in any country — not "harmonized" to the lowest common denominator in the name of "free trade." Prohibit imports from any country that does not adhere to these standards. This would force countries to either raise their wages and standards or stop exporting.

• Prohibit the export of toxic and hazardous substances that are banned in the United States. Pressure other countries to establish similar rules.

• Prohibit trade with countries that allow banks and corporations to keep their accounting books closed or secret (such as "secret Swiss bank accounts").

• Adjust international aid programs to encourage renewable energy, appropriate technology, organic farming, and food production for local needs (not export).

*Goods produced under conditions which do not meet a rudimentary standard of decency should be regarded as contraband and ought not to be able to pollute the channels of interstate commerce.* — President Roosevelt in a message to Congress on the 1937 Fair Labor Standards Act

• Track down the funds stolen by dictators and use these funds to pay off debts.

• Write off Third World debt to First World countries and corporations — consider the debt more than paid by colonialism, neocolonialism, and usurious interest rates.

## Unions

• Repeal laws requiring a majority vote to form a bargaining unit — permit minority unions.

• Repeal the anti-labor provisions of the Taft-Hartley Act.

• Strengthen the Labor Relations Board and require equal representation from business and labor.

## Banking

• Change the Federal Reserve System so that it is publicly controlled.

• Regulate banks and insurance companies more closely to eliminate redlining and other discriminatory practices.

## Housing

• Use public monies to provide low/no-interest loans for homes.

• Build enough good housing for everyone to have a decent place to live. If the private sector cannot build enough living units, the federal government should build or upgrade housing.

## News Media

• Subsidize community-controlled and -supported TV, radio, and newspapers.

*Every man has the right to be heard; but no man has the right to strangle democracy with a single set of vocal chords.*
— Adlai E. Stevenson

• Reinstate the Fairness Doctrine that required every TV and radio station to provide equal time for opposing viewpoints and free time for public interest announcements. Extend this practice to any daily newspaper that has a monopoly in its area.

• Bar any individual or corporation from owning more than one newspaper, magazine, radio station, television station, or publishing house.

## Childrearing Assistance

• Provide programs like Head Start and Hawai'i's Healthy Start to every poor child and to those at-risk of family neglect or violence.[5]

## Childcare

• Create after-school programs at every school.

• Provide quality childcare close to the parents' places of work for every parent who needs it. If the private sector cannot provide enough childcare at reasonable cost, federal, state, or local government should provide it.

## Education

• Fund schools using state or national income taxes instead of local property taxes to help ensure equal funding of schools.

• Ensure equal opportunity — good schools for everyone — from preschool to adult education.

• Through high schools or community colleges, provide free or inexpensive training in socially beneficial areas: basic life skills (cooking, health, birth control, time management), childrearing, critical thinking, citizen involvement and responsibility, participatory democracy, mediation, peer counseling, facilitation of cooperative meetings, overcoming racism, sexism, ageism, and so on.

• Provide job training to everyone who wants it.

• Publicly fund college expenses so that no one must forgo a college education for economic reasons.

## Health Care

• Establish a single-payer national health insurance program with universal coverage, as in Canada.

• Establish a community-owned, community-controlled public nursing home system.

• Produce informative health shows for television and radio and air them regularly on public stations.

• Greatly increase funding for mental health agencies, social services, and other support agencies so everyone can get help during their difficult times.

• Subsidize the cost of birth control of all types.

• Require all health plans to cover the cost of birth control.

*It was once said that the moral test of government is how that government treats those who are in the dawn of life, the children; those who are in the twilight of life, the elderly; and those who are in the shadows of life — the sick, the needy and the handicapped.*
— Hubert H. Humphrey

## Environment

• Increase the sale price of timber, oil, gas, and other minerals on public lands.

• Fund research for environmentally benign substitutes for wood pulp, timber, oil, and minerals.

• Institute taxes on dangerous chemicals — like pesticides — to reduce their use.

• Require cradle-to-grave management of all dangerous materials so that no toxic wastes are dumped in an unsafe manner.

• Tax every consumable item at a high enough rate to provide money for its safe disposal.

• Require government to use recycled materials whenever possible.

• Strengthen laws that protect endangered species and the environment.

## Discrimination

• Pass and strictly enforce laws that ban discrimination on the basis of race, gender, national origin, ethnicity, age, religion, wealth, disability, marital status, sexual orientation, immigration status, and political beliefs.

• Bolster affirmative action programs until every segment of society truly has equal opportunity.

## Community Development

• Institute regional planning that encompasses whole urban areas. Restrict development outside of the current developed area and support infill development.

• Allocate government spending on transportation infrastructure (roads, bridges, mass transit) according to population — more to urban areas and less to rural and suburban areas.

• Eliminate broad-based incentives that subsidize companies but only provide meager job development.

• Provide incentives and support for nonprofit and democratically controlled enterprises such as cooperatives, employee-owned firms, community land trusts, community development banks, community loan funds, credit unions, democratic unions, and so on.

• Increase subsidies for volunteer services, libraries, cooperative enterprises, and nonprofit organizations.

• Subsidize forums for public discourse.

• Require pension funds to be invested in socially responsible enterprises and require that they be controlled by community boards.

• Repeal federal laws that ban or restrict stronger health, safety, or environmental laws at the state or local level.

• Encourage parents to have fewer children and to be responsible parents.

## Domestic Violence

• Outlaw corporal punishment (spanking).

• Revamp laws to protect everyone from domestic violence and to convict and rehabilitate abusers.

• Greatly increase funding for crisis lines and shelters for victims of spouse abuse, child abuse, incest, and rape.

• Greatly increase funding for victim and abuser counseling, for victim housing and job counseling, and for an improved foster home system.

*It is the duty of the government to make it difficult for people to do wrong, easy to do right.*
— William E. Gladstone

• Allow children to choose to move to a foster home or shelter if they feel oppressed or abused in their family. This could greatly reduce the number of runaways and suicides.

• Greatly increase enforcement of alimony and child support settlements.

## Gun Control

• Outlaw assault weapons and cheap handguns.

• Greatly restrict the sale of guns to limit access for criminals and gangsters.

## Conversion

• Establish planning agencies that can ensure a smooth conversion from military production, tobacco farming, and other socially undesirable production to beneficial alternatives.

---

## Some Recommended Programs to Prevent Violence

The National Academy of Sciences established a Panel on the Understanding and Control of Violent Behavior, to review the status of research on violence. It found that "While sentencing for violent crimes grew substantially harsher between 1975 and 1989, the number of violent crimes failed to decrease. This happened apparently because the violence prevented by longer and more common prison sentences was offset by increases due to other factors and suggests a need for greater emphasis on preventing violent events before they occur." It therefore recommended the following long-range preventative measures.[6]

### Child Development Programs

• Implement programs and materials to encourage and teach parents to be nonviolent role models, provide consistent discipline, and limit children's exposure to violent entertainment.

• Provide regular postpartum home visits by public health nurses who make available health information, teach parenting skills, and give well-baby care, while taking the opportunity to detect signs of possible child abuse.

• Implement programs such as Head Start preschool enrichment and early-grade tutoring to reduce the risk of early-grade school failure, a well-known precursor of violent behavior.

• Provide social learning programs for parents, teachers, and children that teach social skills for avoiding violence, nonviolent means to express anger and meet other needs, and ways to view television critically.

• Provide school-based anti-bullying programs.

### Biomedical Strategies

• Implement programs to reduce maternal substance abuse during pregnancy, children's exposure to lead in the environment, and head injuries.

• Provide intensive alcohol abuse treatment and counseling programs for those in their early adolescent years whose behavior patterns include both conduct disorder and alcohol abuse, especially if alcohol dependence runs in their families.

• Develop pharmacological therapies to reduce craving for non-opiate illegal drugs, much as methadone reduces demand for heroin.

• Complete the development of medicines that reduce potentials for violent behavior during withdrawal from opiate addiction.

## Drug Policy

• Establish a national addiction-treatment system that can provide adequate help for everyone who needs it.

• Classify cigarettes and alcohol as dangerous drugs.

• Decriminalize the possession of all drugs.

• Forbid sales of all currently illegal drugs except by nonprofit entities to eliminate the profit motive for sales. Tax all of these drugs to discourage their use.

## Law Enforcement and Prisons

• Greatly increase enforcement of all laws. Devote special attention to ending violent acts (including political terrorism and domestic violence), corporate crime, and high-level corruption.

*Distrust all men in whom the impulse to punish is powerful.* — Friedrich Nietzsche

• For those accused of a crime and unable to afford counsel, pay court-appointed lawyers at a rate comparable to the going rate.

• Institute civilian review boards to oversee every police force including state police, marshals, sheriffs, highway patrol, prison guards, the Secret Service, and the FBI. These boards must have the power to suspend corrupt or out-of-control officers.

• Change the orientation of jails and prisons from punishment to rehabilitation and protection of the public. Change sentences to emphasize restitution, reconciliation, counseling of offenders, and as a last resort, separation of offenders from society.

---

## Programs Shown to Prevent Crime

Very few crime prevention programs have been evaluated using scientifically rigorous standards and methodologies. After evaluating 500 prevention program evaluations, researchers found only 15 programs with enough evidence to show that they work (listed below).[7] All other programs have either not yet been evaluated sufficiently to determine their value or been shown not to work. This includes drug prevention classes focused on fear and other emotional appeals, neighborhood watch programs, storefront police offices, and correctional boot camps using military basic training. The programs that do work include:

• **For infants**: Frequent home visits by nurses and other professionals.

• **For preschoolers**: Classes with weekly home visits by preschool teachers.

• **For delinquent and at-risk preadolescents**: Family therapy and parent training.

• **For schools**:
  • Organizational development for innovation.
  • Communication and reinforcement of clear, consistent norms.
  • Teaching social competency skills.
  • Coaching high-risk youth in "thinking skills."

• **For older male ex-offenders**: Vocational training.

• **For rental housing with drug dealing**: Nuisance abatement action on landlords.

• **For high-crime hot spots**: Extra police patrols.

• **For high-risk repeat offenders**:
  • Monitoring by specialized police units.
  • Incarceration.

• **For domestic abusers who are employed**: On-scene arrests.

• **For convicted offenders**: Rehabilitation programs with risk-focused treatments.

• **For drug-using offenders in prison**: Therapeutic community treatment programs.

# NOTES FOR APPENDIX A

[1] Many of these ideas are suggested and further described in these references:

Holly Sklar, "Economics for Everyone," *Z Magazine* 8, no. 7/8 (July/August 1995): 44, which is adapted from Holly Sklar, *Chaos or Community? Seeking Solutions, Not Scapegoats for Bad Economics* (Boston: South End Press, 1995, HC110 .I5 S57 1995).

Ronnie Dugger, "Real Populists Please Stand Up: A Call to Citizens," *The Nation* (August 14/21, 1995): 159. <http://www.thealliancefordemocracy.org/misc/dugger.htm>

Donald L. Barlett and James B. Steele, *America: Who Really Pays the Taxes?* (New York: Simon and Schuster, 1994, HJ2381 .B37 1994).

Kevin Phillips, *Boiling Point: Democrats, Republicans and the Decline of Middle-Class Prosperity* (New York: Harper-Collins, 1994, HT690 .U6P48 1994).

Ralph Nader, *The Concord Principles: An Agenda for a New Initiatory Democracy*, pamphlet, 1 February 1992. <http://www.greenparties.org/articles/concord.html>

Joel Rogers, "Turning to the Cities: A Metropolitan Agenda," *In These Times* 22, no. 22 (Oct. 14, 1998): 14–17.

Michael H. Shuman, *Going Local: Creating Self-Reliant Communities in a Global Age* (New York: The Free Press, Simon & Schuster, 1998, HC110 .E5S49 1998).

United Nations Development Programme, *Human Development Report*, annual (New York: Oxford University Press, 1998, HD72 .H852). <http://www.undp.org/hdro>

An overview of the UNDP recommendations for the first ten years is here: <http://www.undp.org/hdro/10year.html>

[2] Don Tyson, Senior Chair of the Board, Tyson Foods, Inc. quoted in *National Review*, February 20, 1995.

[3] For more on the Ten Times rule see Sam Pizzigati, *The Maximum Wage: A Common-Sense Prescription for Revitalizing America — by Taxing the Very Rich* (New York: Apex Press, 1992, HC110 .I5P59 1992).

[4] David Morris, "Why is Local Self Reliance Important? A Conversation with David Morris," interview by Michael Closson, Center for Economic Conversion, *Positive Alternatives* 8, no. 3 (Spring 1998): 7-9.

[5] The Hawai'i Healthy Start program, first begun in 1985, uses paid paraprofessional home visitors from the community to provide services to at-risk families. Its goals are to reduce family stress and improve family functioning, improve parenting skills, enhance child health and development, and prevent abuse and neglect. Workers visit the family from the birth of a child (or before) until age 5. They visit weekly for the first 6 to 12 months. They offer a range of services and arrange support from other social service agencies.

A preliminary evaluation found that the program cut abuse and neglect by a factor of more than 2.6 and improved the health and development of the children. Ralph B. Earle, *Helping To Prevent Child Abuse — and Future Criminal Consequences: Hawai'i Healthy Start*, U.S. Department of Justice, Office of Justice Programs, National Institute of Justice, NCJ Report Number 156216, October 1995. <http://www.ncjrs.org/txtfiles/hawaiihs.txt> <http://www.ncjrs.org/pdffiles/hawaiihs.pdf>

[6] Albert J. Reiss, Jr. and Jeffrey A. Roth, eds., *Understanding and Preventing Violence: Panel on the Understanding and Control of Violent Behavior* (Washington, DC: National Academy Press, 1993, HN90 .V5U53 1993). <http://books.nap.edu/books/0309054761/html/index.html>

The study also recommended three situational approaches and further research into social and community-level interventions.

[7] Lawrence W. Sherman, Denise C. Gottfredson, Doris L. MacKenzie, John Eck, Peter Reuter, and Shawn D. Bushway, *Preventing Crime: What Works, What Doesn't, What's Promising*, NIJ Research in Brief Series, U.S. Department of Justice, Office of Justice Programs, National Institute of Justice, Report Number 171676, July 1998. <http://www.ncjrs.org/txtfiles/171676.txt> <http://www.ncjrs.org/pdffiles/171676.pdf>

The full text of the 1997 report and annual updates are here: <http://www.preventingcrime.org>

# B

# Appendix B: Additional Figures

This appendix contains additional figures that show in greater detail the form that the Vernal Project might take as it evolved. Let me emphasize that these figures describe just one possible proposal for its development. Even if the Vernal Project proceeded the way I wished, the actual scenario that unfolded would likely be very different than presented here. I present this one possibility in detail simply to show there is at least one realistic configuration and to provide a preliminary plan.

## VERNAL WORKSHOPS

As I envision it, each Vernal session would include four ten-day workshops and a five-day orientation workshop held at a retreat center. All thirty students in the session would attend these workshops together. Figure B.1 shows a possible structure for these workshops.

## Figure B.1: Possible Arrangements of Classes in Vernal Workshops

### Five-Day Orientation Workshop

|  | Mon. | Tues. | Wed. | Thur. | Fri. |
|---|---|---|---|---|---|
| **Morning** |  | Class | — | *Work* | Class |
| **Afternoon** | *Intro* | Class | Class | Class | *Cleanup* |
| **Evening** | Class | Class | Class | *Party* |  |

Total Number of Classes = 8

### Ten-Day Standard Workshop

|  | Tues. | Wed. | Thur. | Fri. | Sat. |
|---|---|---|---|---|---|
| **Morning** |  | Class | — | Class | Class |
| **Afternoon** | *Intro* | Class | Class | Class | Class |
| **Evening** | *Discuss* | Class | Class | — | Class |

|  | Sun. | Mon. | Tues. | Wed. | Thur. |
|---|---|---|---|---|---|
| **Morning** | — | Class | *Work* | Class | Class |
| **Afternoon** | Class | *Work* | Class | Class | *Cleanup* |
| **Evening** | Class | — | Class | *Party* |  |

Total Number of Classes = 18

**Intro** = Arrival, check in, move in, and introductions
**Discuss** = Structured discussion and evaluation of study groups, internships, social change work, and so on
**—** = Free time, informal discussion, time to read, study, use computer tutorials, read the newspaper, meet informally with Vernal staffmembers, and so on
**Work** = Work for retreat center to offset some of the cost
**Party** = Partytime!
**Clean up** = Clean up of the retreat center and departure

As I envision it, the five-day orientation workshop would begin on Monday afternoon and continue through Friday afternoon, thus avoiding the generally more expensive weekend period. Students would travel to the retreat center Monday morning and arrive in the early afternoon. They would register, move into their rooms, and orient themselves to the retreat center. Then, in the late afternoon, students would assemble to meet each other and the Vernal staffmembers. That evening they would have their first regular class. The next day they would have three more regular classes. By Wednesday they would probably be tired and overflowing with new knowledge, so they would have a break in the morning instead of a class. Classes would continue Wednesday afternoon and evening.

On Thursday morning they would perform some work duty for the retreat center in exchange for reduced rental fees.* This work would also help strengthen bonds between the students and teach cooperation skills. That evening they would have a party instead of a class. Friday morning they would have the last class, and then in the afternoon they would clean up the retreat center, pack up their belongings, and say good-bye to the other students. Over this week, they would have attended eight regular classes, each one 2 1/2 hours long.

Each of the four ten-day workshops would begin on Tuesday and continue through Thursday of the following week (thereby spanning only a single weekend). These workshops would follow a similar schedule of classes, breaks, work for the retreat center, and a party on the last evening. Over the ten days, students would attend eighteen classes and work for the retreat center during two class periods. There would also be one class period devoted to discussion and evaluation of students' internships, study groups, support groups, and social change work. This discussion period would provide an opportunity for students to critically evaluate the session and for Vernal staffmembers to learn what changes they must make to ensure that the rest of the session was successful.

As shown in Figure B.2, a typical workshop day might have three separate classes, each one 2 1/2 hours long. Classes would start at 9:00 A.M., 2:00 P.M., and 7:30 P.M. Two staffmembers would co-facilitate each class. Each class would have a mix of short lectures, demonstrations, small- and large-group discussion, participatory exercises, and simulation games.

As I envision it, each student at the workshop would have a support buddy — another student she had paired up with for the duration of the workshop. For a half hour after lunch (right before the afternoon class), each student would check to see how her support buddy was feeling and give that person loving attention and hugs. This structured time would ensure that each student received some personal

## Figure B.2: Possible Daily Schedule at Vernal Session Workshops

| | All | Kitchen Crew |
|---|---|---|
| | 2 Facilitators | 1 Cook plus students (# of students in parens.) |
| 7:00 A.M. | | Breakfast Prep (1) |
| 8:00 | Breakfast | |
| | | Breakfast Cleanup (2) |
| 9:00 | | |
| 10:00 | Morning Class | |
| 11:00 | | |
| | | Lunch Prep (2) |
| Noon | | |
| | Lunch | |
| 1:00 | | Lunch Cleanup & Dinner Prep (2) |
| | Support Buddies | |
| 2:00 | | |
| 3:00 | Afternoon Class | |
| 4:00 | | |
| | | Dinner Prep (4) |
| 5:00 | | |
| 6:00 | Dinner | |
| | | Dinner Cleanup (4) |
| 7:00 | | |
| 8:00 | Evening Class | |
| 9:00 | | |
| 10:00 | | |
| | Singing, games, etc. | |
| 11:00 | | |

attention each day and had a chance to express fears or vent frustrations. It also would provide an opportunity for students to get to know at least one other student on a more personal and emotional level. The half-hour period after the last class, at 10:00 P.M. would also be a special structured time set aside for students to sing together, play games, or give each other massages.

---

* If there were no work available for students to do, then this period could be used for another class, left as a free time period, or devoted to some other activity (like a group hike).

During the free times of the day, students would have a chance to individually read, study, or work through computer tutorials related to their classes. They could also walk, hike, meditate, exercise, swim, ski, bake bread, sing, converse with other students, play games, discuss politics, exchange massages, nap, and take care of their personal hygiene needs. At certain times, they might choose to make a short presentation on a topic of interest to other students or hold special interest meetings with a few other students (such as those working on a particular project). They might also meet individually or in small groups with a Vernal staffmember to discuss problems with their internships or to informally discuss social change ideas.

At certain times of the day, a few students would help the retreat center's cook prepare meals, serve them, and clean up afterwards. As indicated in this figure, half of the students (fifteen) would help each day with one of these tasks — one helping with breakfast preparation, two helping with breakfast cleanup, and so on.

## VERNAL PROGRAM TIME ALLOCATION

Figures B.3, B.4, and B.5 show the amount of time students might devote to each of the Vernal Program components for each of the 52 weeks of the session. As outlined here, the five-day orientation workshop at the retreat center would take place in the first week. Then the four ten-day workshops (labeled A, B, C, and D) would occur in Weeks 10/11, 20/21, 31/32, and 41/42. In these weeks, students would attend classes and study in preparation for those classes. In the weeks they were not attending a workshop or on vacation, students would attend study group meetings and work for their internship organizations. They would also read books and magazine articles to prepare for their study groups and perform social change work and social service work. In every week of the session, students would attend support group meetings and read progressive magazines and newspapers. Together, these activities would generally take about fifty hours each week as shown in the last column of Figure B.3. Students would have a weeklong vacation at the end of every quarter (Weeks 13, 26, 39, and 52) in which they would do no Vernal activity. At the end of Week 51, students would attend a one-day graduation ceremony with their family and friends.

Overall, as shown at the bottom of Figure B.3, students would attend 80 classes (200 hours) during 45 days of workshops. They would attend 116 study group meetings (348 hours). Their internships would require 360 hours, and they would do 174 hours of social change work.

Over the year, students would spend 2,296 hours on Vernal activities. Almost one-third of this time would be spent reading and studying in preparation for study group meetings. About 15 percent of the time would be spent attending study groups and another 15 percent would be spent in internships. About 12 percent of the time would be spent attending workshop classes and reading materials in preparation for these classes.

*[Text continues on page 253]*

# Figure B.3: Typical Time Students Might Devote to the Vernal Program by Week

| Qtr | Mon | Week | Work-shop Name | Num of Days in Wrkshp | Num of Classes at Wrkshp | Hours Per Week | | | | | | | | | Total Hours/ Week |
|---|---|---|---|---|---|---|---|---|---|---|---|---|---|---|---|
| | | | | | | Wkshp Classes | Outside Study for Wrkshp | Study Group | Study for Study Group | Add'l Study News | Intern-ship | Social Chnge Work | Social Servc Work | Supprt Group/ Therapy | |
| 1Q | 1 | 1 | Orient. | 5 | 8 | 20 | 8 | | | 6 | | | | 2 | 36 |
| | | 2 | | | | | | 12 | 24 | 6 | | | | 2 | 44 |
| | | 3 | | | | | | 12 | 24 | 6 | | 3 | 3 | 2 | 50 |
| | 2 | 4 | | | | | | 12 | 24 | 6 | | 3 | 3 | 2 | 50 |
| | | 5 | | | | | | 12 | 24 | 6 | | 3 | 3 | 2 | 50 |
| | | 6 | | | | | | 12 | 24 | 6 | | 3 | 3 | 2 | 50 |
| | | 7 | | | | | | 12 | 24 | 6 | | 3 | 3 | 2 | 50 |
| | | 8 | | | | | | 12 | 24 | 6 | | 3 | 3 | 2 | 50 |
| | 3 | 9 | | | | | | 12 | 24 | 6 | | 3 | 3 | 2 | 50 |
| | | 10 | A | 5 | 10 | 25 | 10 | | | 6 | | | | 2 | 43 |
| | | 11 | A | 5 | 8 | 20 | 8 | | | 6 | | | | 2 | 36 |
| | | 12 | | | | | | 12 | 24 | 6 | | 3 | 3 | 2 | 50 |
| | | 13 | | | | Vacation | | | | | | | | | 0 |
| 2Q | 4 | 14 | | | | | | 9 | 18 | 6 | 12 | 3 | | 2 | 50 |
| | | 15 | | | | | | 9 | 18 | 6 | 12 | 3 | | 2 | 50 |
| | | 16 | | | | | | 9 | 18 | 6 | 12 | 3 | | 2 | 50 |
| | | 17 | | | | | | 9 | 18 | 6 | 12 | 3 | | 2 | 50 |
| | 5 | 18 | | | | | | 9 | 18 | 6 | 12 | 3 | | 2 | 50 |
| | | 19 | | | | | | 9 | 18 | 6 | 12 | 3 | | 2 | 50 |
| | | 20 | B | 5 | 10 | 25 | 10 | | | 6 | | | | 2 | 43 |
| | | 21 | B | 5 | 8 | 20 | 8 | | | 6 | | | | 2 | 36 |
| | 6 | 22 | | | | | | 9 | 18 | 6 | 12 | 3 | | 2 | 50 |
| | | 23 | | | | | | 9 | 18 | 6 | 12 | 3 | | 2 | 50 |
| | | 24 | | | | | | 9 | 18 | 6 | 12 | 3 | | 2 | 50 |
| | | 25 | | | | | | 9 | 18 | 6 | 12 | 3 | | 2 | 50 |
| | | 26 | | | | Vacation | | | | | | | | | 0 |
| 3Q | 7 | 27 | | | | | | 9 | 18 | 6 | 12 | 3 | | 2 | 50 |
| | | 28 | | | | | | 9 | 18 | 6 | 12 | 3 | | 2 | 50 |
| | | 29 | | | | | | 9 | 18 | 6 | 12 | 3 | | 2 | 50 |
| | | 30 | | | | | | 9 | 18 | 6 | 12 | 3 | | 2 | 50 |
| | 8 | 31 | C | 5 | 10 | 25 | 10 | | | 6 | | | | 2 | 43 |
| | | 32 | C | 5 | 8 | 20 | 8 | | | 6 | | | | 2 | 36 |
| | | 33 | | | | | | 9 | 18 | 6 | 12 | 3 | | 2 | 50 |
| | | 34 | | | | | | 9 | 18 | 6 | 12 | 3 | | 2 | 50 |
| | 9 | 35 | | | | | | 9 | 18 | 6 | 12 | 3 | | 2 | 50 |
| | | 36 | | | | | | 9 | 18 | 6 | 12 | 3 | | 2 | 50 |
| | | 37 | | | | | | 9 | 18 | 6 | 12 | 3 | | 2 | 50 |
| | | 38 | | | | | | 9 | 18 | 6 | 12 | 3 | | 2 | 50 |
| | | 39 | | | | Vacation | | | | | | | | | 0 |
| 4Q | 10 | 40 | | | | | | 6 | 15 | 6 | 12 | 9 | | 2 | 50 |
| | | 41 | D | 5 | 10 | 25 | 10 | | | 6 | | | | 2 | 43 |
| | | 42 | D | 5 | 8 | 20 | 8 | | | 6 | | | | 2 | 36 |
| | | 43 | | | | | | 6 | 15 | 6 | 12 | 9 | | 2 | 50 |
| | 11 | 44 | | | | | | 6 | 15 | 6 | 12 | 9 | | 2 | 50 |
| | | 45 | | | | | | 6 | 15 | 6 | 12 | 9 | | 2 | 50 |
| | | 46 | | | | | | 6 | 15 | 6 | 12 | 9 | | 2 | 50 |
| | | 47 | | | | | | 6 | 15 | 6 | 12 | 9 | | 2 | 50 |
| | 12 | 48 | | | | | | 6 | 15 | 6 | 12 | 9 | | 2 | 50 |
| | | 49 | | | | | | 6 | 15 | 6 | 12 | 9 | | 2 | 50 |
| | | 50 | | | | | | 6 | 15 | 6 | 12 | 9 | | 2 | 50 |
| | | 51 | Grad. | 1 | 0 | 0 | | 6 | 15 | 6 | 12 | 9 | | 2 | 50 |
| | | 52 | | | | Vacation | | | | | | | | | 0 |
| Total | | | | 46 | 80 | 200 | 80 | 348 | 726 | 288 | 360 | 174 | 24 | 96 | 2,296 |
| Percent of Total | | | | | | 8.7% | 3.5% | 15.2% | 31.6% | 12.5% | 15.7% | 7.6% | 1.0% | 4.2% | 100.0% |

# Figure B.4: Typical Time Students Might Devote to the Vernal Program by Week

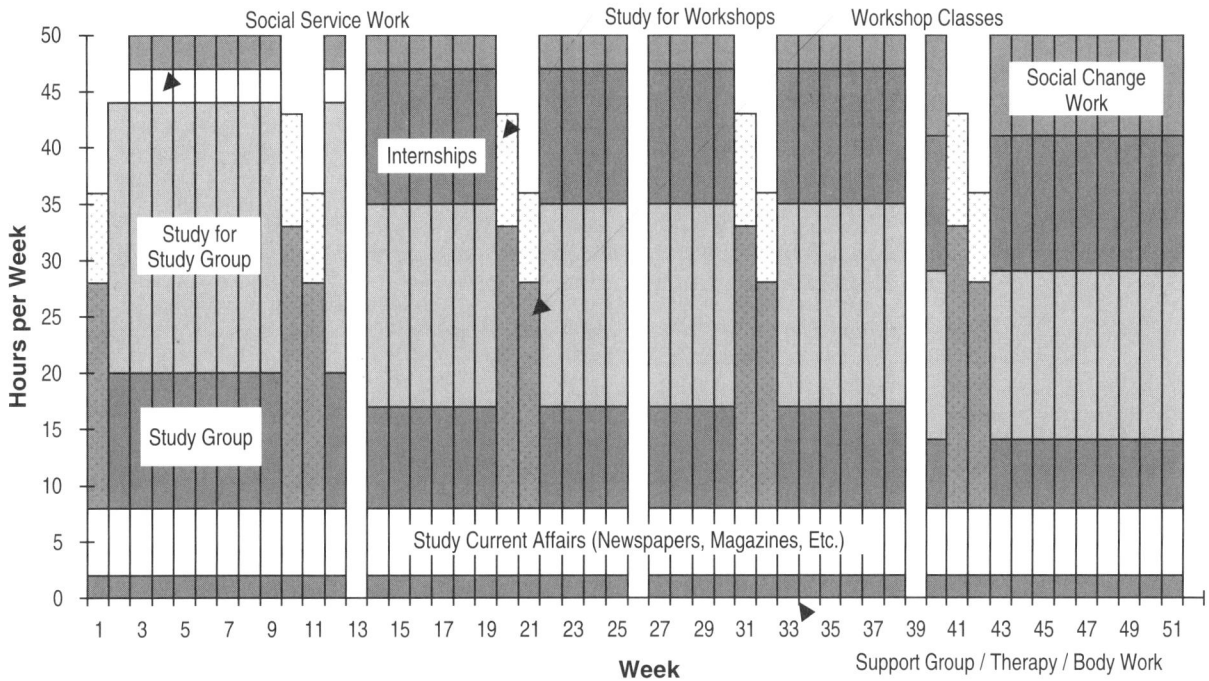

# Figure B.5: Typical Percent of Total Time Students Might Devote to Different Parts of the Vernal Program

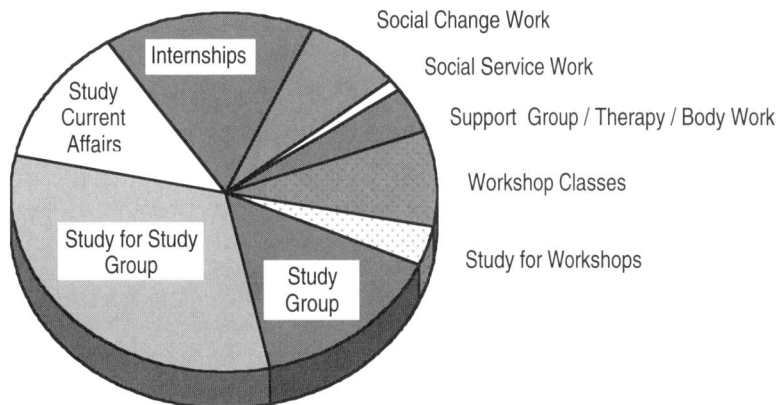

# Figure B.6: Typical Vernal Team Calendar

| | Sun | Mon | Tue | Wed | Thu | Fri | Sat | Week | |
|---|---|---|---|---|---|---|---|---|---|
| | 2 | 3 | 4 | 5 | 6 | 7 | 8 | 1 | **Orientation for Session 47** |
| January | 9 | 10 | 11 | 12 | 13 | 14 | 15 | 2 | Workshop D for Session 44 |
| | 16 | 17 | 18 | 19 | 20 | 21 | 22 | 3 | |
| | 23 | 24 | 25 | 26 | 27 | 28 | 29 | 4 | |
| | 30 | 31 | 1 | 2 | 3 | 4 | 5 | 5 | Workshop C for Session 45 |
| | 6 | 7 | 8 | 9 | 10 | 11 | 12 | 6 | |
| February | 13 | 14 | 15 | 16 | 17 | 18 | 19 | 7 | Workshop B for Session 46 |
| | 20 | 21 | 22 | 23 | 24 | 25 | 26 | 8 | |
| | 27 | 28 | 1 | 2 | 3 | 4 | 5 | 9 | |
| | 6 | 7 | 8 | 9 | 10 | 11 | 12 | 10 | **Workshop A for Session 47** |
| March | 13 | 14 | 15 | 16 | 17 | 18 | 19 | 11 | |
| | 20 | 21 | 22 | 23 | 24 | 25 | 26 | 12 | Graduation for Session 44 |
| | 27 | 28 | 29 | 30 | 31 | 1 | 2 | 13 | |
| | 3 | 4 | 5 | 6 | 7 | 8 | 9 | 14 | Orientation for Session 48 |
| April | 10 | 11 | 12 | 13 | 14 | 15 | 16 | 15 | Workshop D for Session 45 |
| | 17 | 18 | 19 | 20 | 21 | 22 | 23 | 16 | |
| | 24 | 25 | 26 | 27 | 28 | 29 | 30 | 17 | |
| | 1 | 2 | 3 | 4 | 5 | 6 | 7 | 18 | Workshop C for Session 46 |
| May | 8 | 9 | 10 | 11 | 12 | 13 | 14 | 19 | |
| | 15 | 16 | 17 | 18 | 19 | 20 | 21 | 20 | **Workshop B for Session 47** |
| | 22 | 23 | 24 | 25 | 26 | 27 | 28 | 21 | |
| | 29 | 30 | 31 | 1 | 2 | 3 | 4 | 22 | |
| | 5 | 6 | 7 | 8 | 9 | 10 | 11 | 23 | Workshop A for Session 48 |
| June | 12 | 13 | 14 | 15 | 16 | 17 | 18 | 24 | |
| | 19 | 20 | 21 | 22 | 23 | 24 | 25 | 25 | Graduation for Session 45 |
| | 26 | 27 | 28 | 29 | 30 | 1 | 2 | 26 | |
| | 3 | 4 | 5 | 6 | 7 | 8 | 9 | 27 | Orientation for Session 49 |
| July | 10 | 11 | 12 | 13 | 14 | 15 | 16 | 28 | Workshop D for Session 46 |
| | 17 | 18 | 19 | 20 | 21 | 22 | 23 | 29 | |
| | 24 | 25 | 26 | 27 | 28 | 29 | 30 | 30 | |
| | 31 | 1 | 2 | 3 | 4 | 5 | 6 | 31 | **Workshop C for Session 47** |
| | 7 | 8 | 9 | 10 | 11 | 12 | 13 | 32 | |
| August | 14 | 15 | 16 | 17 | 18 | 19 | 20 | 33 | Workshop B for Session 48 |
| | 21 | 22 | 23 | 24 | 25 | 26 | 27 | 34 | |
| | 28 | 29 | 30 | 31 | 1 | 2 | 3 | 35 | |
| | 4 | 5 | 6 | 7 | 8 | 9 | 10 | 36 | Workshop A for Session 49 |
| September | 11 | 12 | 13 | 14 | 15 | 16 | 17 | 37 | |
| | 18 | 19 | 20 | 21 | 22 | 23 | 24 | 38 | Graduation for Session 46 |
| | 25 | 26 | 27 | 28 | 29 | 30 | 1 | 39 | |
| | 2 | 3 | 4 | 5 | 6 | 7 | 8 | 40 | Orientation for Session 50 |
| October | 9 | 10 | 11 | 12 | 13 | 14 | 15 | 41 | **Workshop D for Session 47** |
| | 16 | 17 | 18 | 19 | 20 | 21 | 22 | 42 | |
| | 23 | 24 | 25 | 26 | 27 | 28 | 29 | 43 | |
| | 30 | 31 | 1 | 2 | 3 | 4 | 5 | 44 | Workshop C for Session 48 |
| | 6 | 7 | 8 | 9 | 10 | 11 | 12 | 45 | |
| November | 13 | 14 | 15 | 16 | 17 | 18 | 19 | 46 | Workshop B for Session 49 |
| | 20 | 21 | 22 | 23 | 24 | 25 | 26 | 47 | |
| | 27 | 28 | 29 | 30 | 1 | 2 | 3 | 48 | |
| | 4 | 5 | 6 | 7 | 8 | 9 | 10 | 49 | Workshop A for Session 50 |
| December | 11 | 12 | 13 | 14 | 15 | 16 | 17 | 50 | |
| | 18 | 19 | 20 | 21 | 22 | 23 | 24 | 51 | **Graduation for Session 47** |
| | 25 | 26 | 27 | 28 | 29 | 30 | 31 | 52 | |

# Figure B.7: Possible Staffing for Two Contiguous Ten-Day Workshops

|— Workshop C for Session 45 —|          |— Workshop B for Session 46 —|

| Tue | Wed | Thu | Fri | Sat | Sun | Mon | Tue | Wed | Thu | Fri | Sat | Sun | Mon | Tue | Wed | Thu | Fri | Sat | Sun | Mon | Tue | Wed | Thu |
|-----|-----|-----|-----|-----|-----|-----|-----|-----|-----|-----|-----|-----|-----|-----|-----|-----|-----|-----|-----|-----|-----|-----|-----|
| W | W | W | W | W |   |   |   |   |   |   |   |   |   | W | W | W | W | W |   |   |   |   |   |
|   |   |   | X | X | X | X | X |   |   |   |   |   |   |   |   |   | X | X | X | X | X |   |   |
|   |   |   |   |   | Y | Y | Y | Y | Y |   |   |   |   | Y | Y | Y |   |   |   |   |   | Y | Y |
| Z | Z | Z |   |   |   |   |   | Z | Z |   |   |   |   |   |   |   |   |   | Z | Z | Z | Z | Z |

**Assumptions:**

There are four staffmembers in each Vernal team (designated here as W, X, Y, and Z).

Only two staffmembers are needed to facilitate all the classes and other activities in a day.

## VERNAL STAFFMEMBER TIME ALLOCATION

Facilitating workshops would be a large part of the work of Vernal staffmembers. Figures B.6 and B.7 show that it would be possible for a Vernal team to facilitate four separate sessions at the same time without being stretched too thin.

Figure B.6 shows a typical center schedule in which a new session starts at the beginning of each quarter. Structured this way, none of the workshops overlap and there are many weeks with no workshops at all. To make it easier to understand this figure, I have shaded the workshops associated with one particular session (Session 47). From Orientation in Week 1 to Graduation in Week 51, the workshops for Session 47 are intertwined with the workshops associated with the preceding sessions (44, 45, and 46) and the succeeding ones (48, 49, and 50).

Figure B.7 shows how a Vernal team with four full-time staffmembers could facilitate two of these ten-day workshops when they occurred on four contiguous weeks. In this arrangement, each staffmember would work no more than five days in a row, and there would be at least four days between their facilitation stints. This arrangement also

# Figure B.8: Examples of Tuition Distributions that Produce Average Income of $3,600 from Each Student

|  |  |  | Percent of Students | | | |
|---|---|---|---|---|---|---|
| **Situation** | **Annual Tuition Paid** | **Stipend Received** | **A** | **B** | **C** | **D** |
| Full Tuition | $5,000 |  | 40% | 50% | 35% | 35% |
| Partial Scholarship | $3,500 |  | 35% | 20% | 25% | 30% |
| Half Scholarship | $2,500 |  | 15% | 20% | 40% | 30% |
| Large Scholarship | $1,000 |  |  |  |  | 5% |
| Large Scholarship | $500 |  |  |  |  |  |
| Full Scholarship | $0 |  | 10% |  |  |  |
| Full Scholarship + Stipend | $0 | $1,000 |  | 10% |  |  |
| Full Scholarship + Stipend | $0 | $3,000 |  |  |  |  |
|  |  |  | 100% | 100% | 100% | 100% |
| **Avg. Income Collected from Each Student =** |  |  | **$3,600** | **$3,600** | **$3,600** | **$3,600** |

**Note:** All figures are in 1995 dollars.

# Figure B.9: Examples of Tuition Distributions that Produce Average Income of $2,400 from Each Student

| Situation | Annual Tuition Paid | Stipend Received | Percent of Students | | | | | |
|---|---|---|---|---|---|---|---|---|
| | | | A | B | C | D | E | F |
| Full Tuition | $5,000 | | 25% | 30% | 15% | 10% | 20% | 20% |
| Partial Scholarship | $3,500 | | 25% | 20% | 5% | | 15% | 20% |
| Half Scholarship | $2,500 | | 15% | 15% | 60% | 80% | 45% | 40% |
| Large Scholarship | $1,000 | | | | | | 5% | |
| Large Scholarship | $500 | | 10% | 5% | 5% | | | |
| Full Scholarship | $0 | | 10% | 10% | 10% | | 5% | 10% |
| Full Scholarship + Stipend | $0 | $1,000 | 15% | 20% | 5% | 10% | | |
| Full Scholarship + Stipend | $0 | $3,000 | | | | | 10% | 10% |
| | | | 100% | 100% | 100% | 100% | 100% | 100% |
| **Avg. Income Collected from Each Student =** | | | **$2,400** | **$2,400** | **$2,400** | **$2,400** | **$2,400** | **$2,400** |

**Note:** All figures are in 1995 dollars.

allocates the same amount of work to each staffmember, pairs each of the staffmembers with each other about the same amount of time, and minimizes the number of trips staffmembers must make to and from the retreat center. Of course, real life would hardly ever be this orderly, and it would seldom be possible to satisfy all these criteria. This arrangement would require that every staffmember know how to facilitate every class and be able to facilitate with any other staffmember. Still, even given the chaos of normal life and the additional scheduling constraints required by real people, staffmembers could probably work out an arrangement that prevented them from working too much.

## VERNAL PROGRAM TUITION

Figures 6.11 and 6.12 showed some typical tuition distributions that would produce an average of $3,600 and $2,400 from each student (in 1995 dollars). Figure B.8 shows four additional examples of tuition payments that produce an average income of $3,600. Figure B.9 shows six more examples that produce an average income of $2,400. In one of these examples, 50 percent of the students pay full tuition of $5,000; in other examples, as few as 10 percent do. In one example, 30 percent of students receive a full scholarship; in another one, no student does. Clearly, there are a variety of reasonable ways to achieve these levels of average income depending on the composition of the students in a session.

*[Text continues on next page]*

## VERNAL REGIONS AND CENTERS

For the Vernal Project to transform all of society, there must be fundamental progressive social change in every part of the country to ensure most people can be directly influenced. To show this is possible, I divided the United States into ten Vernal regions and picked forty-five large and dispersed cities for the fifty Vernal centers. Because their metro areas have such large populations, Los Angeles and New York City would each have three centers and Chicago would have two. As much as possible, I chose each region so that it contains contiguous states that have some cultural kinship. I also tried to choose regions so they would all have approximately the same population — though this was impossible and the largest has three times the population of the smallest. I chose the fifty Vernal center sites so that they would span the country and each would encompass a population of more than 1.5 million people.

Figure B.10 is a map of the United States showing the ten regions and the fifty Vernal centers. I have drawn a circle with a radius of 75 miles around each center to indicate the approximate area that is within a reasonable frequent driving distance of each center.

Figure B.11 shows the population associated with each Vernal region and center.* The figure lists the fifty Vernal centers (in bold type) and indicates which Census Bureau Metropolitan Statistical Areas (MSAs) and Primary Metropolitan Statistical Areas (PMSAs) are within 75 miles of each one. Also listed is the population of each metropolitan area and its percentage of the total U.S. population. For each Vernal region, I have indicated how much of the total population is near a Vernal center. At the bottom of each region is a sum of the population in the other MSAs in that region that are not within 75 miles of a Vernal center and the rural population that is outside of MSAs. These values are shaded to indicate they are not near a Vernal center.

In some cases, where there is relatively little population near a Vernal center, I have allocated to it an MSA that is farther away than 75 miles (indicated in italic type). Figure B.12 lists these MSAs and how far they are from their associated Vernal center. Ten of these fourteen MSAs are within 130 miles of their associated center.

I assume the Vernal team at these centers would devote special effort to include students from the distant areas. In some cases, this would require that the staffmembers drive or fly hundreds of miles. To minimize trips, staffmembers would need to carefully arrange their visits to study groups and internship sites.

Overall, if these were the locations of the fifty Vernal centers, they would, on average, address a population of about three million people. Austin, Texas would address the smallest population of 1,620,436 and Philadelphia the largest population of 7,499,618. Overall, about two-thirds of the U.S. population would be within the realm of these fifty Vernal centers.

I have assumed that the one-third of the population that is outside of the listed MSAs would not be a part of the Vernal Project. I do not make this assumption because I want to exclude anyone from the Project or because I think the people in smaller cities or rural areas are unimportant. I make this assumption only because it is so difficult to design a Project that could cover all of this immense country and yet would consume few resources.

Still, even though the Vernal Project does not focus on these areas directly, it might still reach the people in the unserved areas through a number of processes:

(1) Since people in this country often move from place to place, some Vernal graduates would likely migrate to areas that do not have a Vernal center during the time they were actively working for change.

(2) As part of their efforts to expand their campaigns for change, Vernal graduates might deliberately travel to those areas that do not have a Vernal center and offer weekend workshops or consulting help to local activists.

(3) I assume that the reading lists and notes prepared by Vernal staffmembers for use in the Vernal Program would be put on the web for anyone to download and use. People in the unserved areas might create their own local educational programs using these materials.

(4) I assume the ideas and practices of Vernal graduates would spread through normal activist channels to activists working in every area of the country. Activists in areas not directly served would pick up these ideas and pass them on to others through their normal change work.†

*[Text continues on page 261]*

---

* In this figure, states and cities are listed roughly in geographic order sweeping from west to east.

† Remember that the Vernal Project is merely a supplement to other activist work, not a replacement of it. I assume that most progressive activists would never attend a Vernal Education Program and many activists would never have any direct contact with a Vernal graduate.

# Figure B.10: Map of Possible

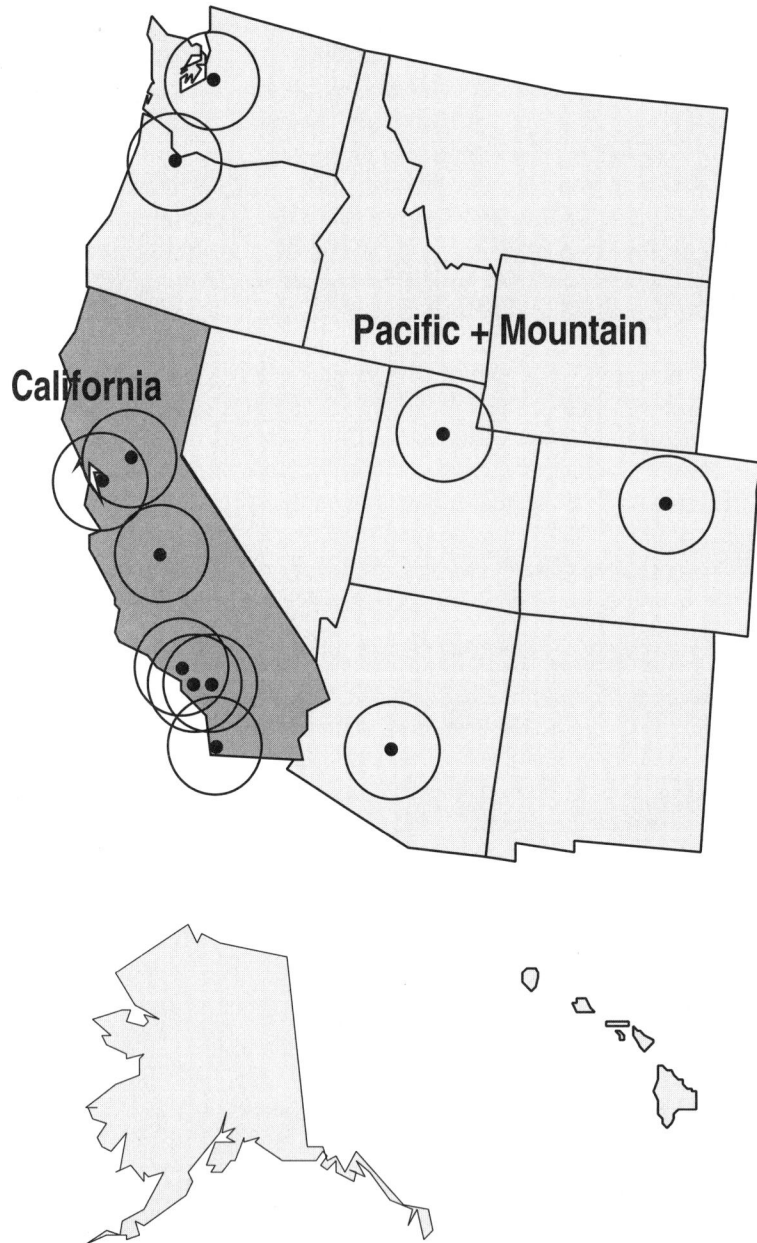

# Vernal Regions and Centers

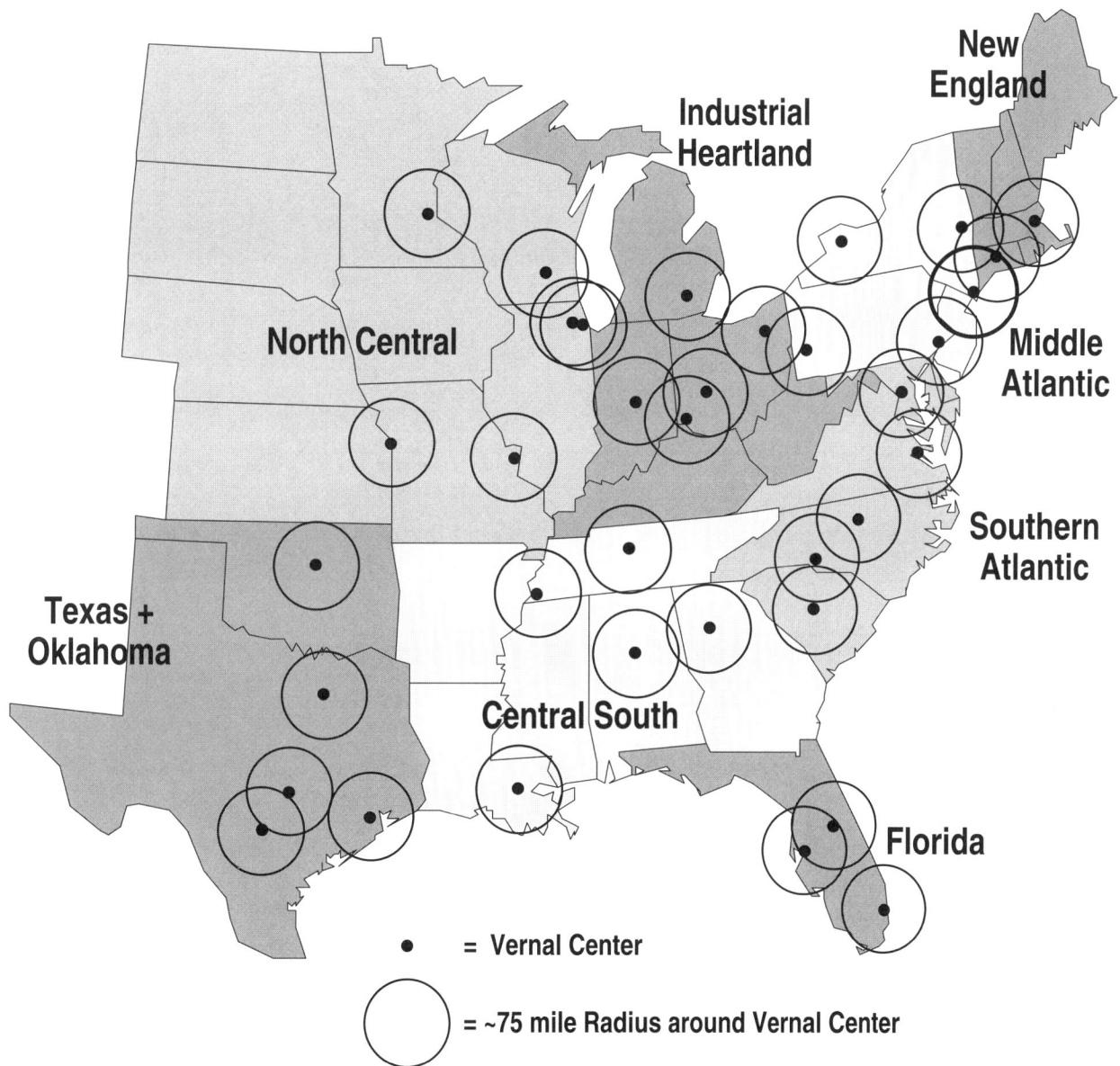

New England

Industrial Heartland

North Central

Middle Atlantic

Texas + Oklahoma

Southern Atlantic

Central South

Florida

• = Vernal Center

◯ = ~75 mile Radius around Vernal Center

# Figure B.11: Possible Vernal Regions, Vernal Centers, and their Associated Population

| Region / Vernal Center / Metropolitan Statistical Area | Estimated Population in July 1995 | Near Vern % | % Total 1995 Pop. |
|---|---|---|---|
| California | 28,851,864 | 91.4 | 11.0 |
| Oakland, CA | 6,302,933 | | 2.4 |
| Oakland, CA PMSA | 2,195,411 | | 0.8 |
| San Francisco, CA PMSA | 1,645,815 | | 0.6 |
| San Jose, CA PMSA | 1,565,253 | | 0.6 |
| Santa Rosa, CA PMSA | 414,569 | | 0.2 |
| Vallejo-Fairfield-Napa, CA PMSA | 481,885 | | 0.2 |
| Sacramento, CA | 2,539,563 | | 1.0 |
| Sacramento, CA PMSA | 1,456,955 | | 0.6 |
| Yolo, CA PMSA | 147,769 | | 0.1 |
| Stockton-Lodi, CA MSA | 523,969 | | 0.2 |
| Modesto, CA MSA | 410,870 | | 0.2 |
| Fresno, CA | 2,003,071 | | 0.8 |
| Fresno, CA MSA | 844,293 | | 0.3 |
| Merced, CA MSA | 194,407 | | 0.1 |
| Visalia-Tulare-Porterville, CA MSA | 346,843 | | 0.1 |
| *Bakersfield, CA MSA (112 miles)* | 617,528 | | 0.2 |
| Los Angeles Area, CA | 15,362,165 | | 5.8 |
| Los Angeles-Long Beach, CA PMSA | 9,138,789 | | 3.5 |
| Orange County, CA PMSA | 2,563,971 | | 1.0 |
| Riverside-San Bernardino, CA PMSA | 2,949,387 | | 1.1 |
| Ventura, CA PMSA | 710,018 | | 0.3 |
| San Diego, CA | 2,644,132 | | 1.0 |
| San Diego, CA MSA | 2,644,132 | | 1.0 |
| Rest of Region | 2,713,616 | | 1.0 |
| Pacific + Mountain | 13,403,760 | 51.3 | 5.1 |
| Seattle, WA | 3,265,139 | | 1.2 |
| Seattle-Bellevue-Everett, WA PMSA | 2,197,451 | | 0.8 |
| Tacoma, WA PMSA | 648,994 | | 0.2 |
| Bremerton, WA PMSA | 226,720 | | 0.1 |
| Olympia, WA PMSA | 191,974 | | 0.1 |
| Portland, OR | 2,021,982 | | 0.8 |
| Portland-Vancouver, OR-WA PMSA | 1,710,260 | | 0.7 |
| Salem, OR PMSA | 311,722 | | 0.1 |
| Salt Lake City, UT | 2,636,870 | | 1.0 |
| Salt Lake City-Ogden, UT MSA | 1,199,323 | | 0.5 |
| Provo-Orem, UT MSA | 298,789 | | 0.1 |
| *Las Vegas, NV-AZ MSA (419 miles)* | 1,138,758 | | 0.4 |
| Denver, CO | 2,916,187 | | 1.1 |
| Denver, CO PMSA | 1,831,308 | | 0.7 |
| Boulder-Longmont, CO PMSA | 253,850 | | 0.1 |
| Greeley, CO PMSA | 148,014 | | 0.1 |
| Colorado Springs, CO MSA | 465,800 | | 0.2 |
| Fort Collins-Loveland, CO MSA | 217,215 | | 0.1 |
| Phoenix, AZ | 2,563,582 | | 1.0 |
| Phoenix-Mesa, AZ MSA | 2,563,582 | | 1.0 |
| Rest of Region | 12,724,429 | | 4.8 |

| Region / Vernal Center / Metropolitan Statistical Area | Estimated Population in July 1995 | Near Vern % | % Total 1995 Pop. |
|---|---|---|---|
| Texas + Oklahoma | 14,580,005 | 66.0 | 5.5 |
| Stillwater, OK | 2,327,228 | | 0.9 |
| Oklahoma City, OK MSA | 1,015,174 | | 0.4 |
| Tulsa, OK MSA | 746,500 | | 0.3 |
| Enid, OK MSA | 57,330 | | 0.0 |
| *Wichita, KS MSA (127 miles)* | 508,224 | | 0.2 |
| Arlington, TX | 4,548,211 | | 1.7 |
| Dallas, TX PMSA | 2,957,910 | | 1.1 |
| Fort Worth-Arlington, TX PMSA | 1,491,965 | | 0.6 |
| Sherman-Denison, TX MSA | 98,336 | | 0.0 |
| Austin, TX | 1,620,436 | | 0.6 |
| Austin-San Marcos, TX MSA | 999,936 | | 0.4 |
| Killeen-Temple, TX MSA | 289,903 | | 0.1 |
| *Waco, TX MSA (100 miles)* | 200,111 | | 0.1 |
| *Bryan-College Station, TX MSA (105 miles)* | 130,486 | | 0.0 |
| San Antonio, TX | 1,919,737 | | 0.7 |
| San Antonio, TX MSA | 1,460,809 | | 0.6 |
| *Victoria, TX MSA (116 miles)* | 79,992 | | 0.0 |
| *Corpus Christi, TX MSA (153 miles)* | 378,936 | | 0.1 |
| Houston, TX | 4,164,393 | | 1.6 |
| Houston, TX PMSA | 3,710,844 | | 1.4 |
| Galveston-Texas City, TX PMSA | 237,533 | | 0.1 |
| Brazoria, TX PMSA | 216,016 | | 0.1 |
| Rest of Region | 7,496,245 | | 2.9 |
| Central South | 11,730,553 | 44.7 | 4.5 |
| Baton Rouge, LA | 2,433,902 | | 0.9 |
| Baton Rouge, LA MSA | 563,994 | | 0.2 |
| New Orleans, LA MSA | 1,315,294 | | 0.5 |
| Lafayette, LA MSA | 365,857 | | 0.1 |
| Houma, LA MSA | 188,757 | | 0.1 |
| Memphis, TN | 2,112,471 | | 0.8 |
| Memphis, TN-AR-MS MSA | 1,068,891 | | 0.4 |
| Jackson, TN MSA | 83,715 | | 0.0 |
| *Little Rock-North Little Rock, AR MSA (137 r* | 543,568 | | 0.2 |
| *Jackson, MS MSA (213 miles)* | 416,297 | | 0.2 |
| Nashville, TN | 1,726,373 | | 0.7 |
| Nashville, TN MSA | 1,093,836 | | 0.4 |
| Clarksville-Hopkinsville, TN-KY MSA | 189,477 | | 0.1 |
| *Chattanooga, TN-GA MSA (129 miles)* | 443,060 | | 0.2 |
| Birmingham, AL | 1,891,031 | | 0.7 |
| Birmingham, AL MSA | 881,761 | | 0.3 |
| Tuscaloosa, AL MSA | 158,732 | | 0.1 |
| Gadsden, AL MSA | 100,259 | | 0.0 |
| Anniston, AL MSA | 117,263 | | 0.0 |
| *Huntsville, AL MSA (95 miles)* | 317,684 | | 0.1 |
| *Montgomery, AL MSA (91 miles)* | 315,332 | | 0.1 |
| Atlanta, GA | 3,566,776 | | 1.4 |
| Atlanta, GA MSA | 3,431,983 | | 1.3 |
| Athens, GA MSA | 134,793 | | 0.1 |
| Rest of Region | 14,490,067 | | 5.5 |

**Note**: Though relatively small, college town Stillwater, Oklahoma, is centrally located between three Oklahoma cities — Oklahoma City, Tulsa, and Enid — and Wichita, Kansas. Arlington, Texas, is about halfway between Dallas and Fort Worth. Baton Rouge, Louisiana is centrally located between New Orleans and Lafayette.

# Figure B.11 (continued)

| Region / Vernal Center / Metropolitan Statistical Area | Estimated Population in July 1995 | Near Vern % | % Total 1995 Pop. |
|---|---|---|---|
| **Southern Atlantic** | **16,166,089** | **70.0** | **6.1** |
| **Columbia, SC** | **1,670,939** | | **0.6** |
| Columbia, SC MSA | 481,718 | | 0.2 |
| Florence, SC MSA | 122,769 | | 0.0 |
| Augusta-Aiken, GA-SC MSA | 453,209 | | 0.2 |
| Sumter, SC MSA | 106,823 | | 0.0 |
| *Charleston-North Charleston, SC MSA (113* | 506,420 | | 0.2 |
| **Spartanburg, SC** | **2,691,167** | | **1.0** |
| Greenville-Spartanburg-Anderson, SC MSA | 884,306 | | 0.3 |
| Charlotte-Gastonia-Rock Hill, NC-SC MSA | 1,289,177 | | 0.5 |
| Hickory-Morganton-Lenoir, NC MSA | 310,236 | | 0.1 |
| Asheville, NC MSA | 207,448 | | 0.1 |
| **Burlington, NC** | **2,228,986** | | **0.8** |
| Greensboro--Winston-Salem--High Point, N( | 1,123,840 | | 0.4 |
| Raleigh-Durham-Chapel Hill, NC MSA | 995,256 | | 0.4 |
| Danville, VA MSA | 109,890 | | 0.0 |
| **Williamsburg, VA** | **2,467,881** | | **0.9** |
| Norfolk-Virginia Beach-Newport News, VA-N | 1,540,446 | | 0.6 |
| Richmond-Petersburg, VA MSA | 927,435 | | 0.4 |
| **Washington, DC** | **7,107,116** | | **2.7** |
| Washington, DC-MD-VA-WV PMSA | 4,509,932 | | 1.7 |
| Baltimore, MD PMSA | 2,469,985 | | 0.9 |
| Hagerstown, MD PMSA | 127,199 | | 0.0 |
| **Rest of Region** | **6,911,920** | | **2.6** |
| **North Central** | **18,437,359** | **52.3** | **7.0** |
| **Kansas City, KS** | **2,014,400** | | **0.8** |
| Kansas City, MO-KS MSA | 1,663,453 | | 0.6 |
| Topeka, KS MSA | 165,062 | | 0.1 |
| Lawrence, KS MSA | 88,206 | | 0.0 |
| St. Joseph, MO MSA | 97,679 | | 0.0 |
| **St. Louis, MO** | **2,547,686** | | **1.0** |
| St. Louis, MO-IL MSA | 2,547,686 | | 1.0 |
| **Minneapolis, MN** | **2,994,558** | | **1.1** |
| Minneapolis-St. Paul, MN-WI MSA | 2,723,137 | | 1.0 |
| St. Cloud, MN MSA | 158,802 | | 0.1 |
| Rochester, MN MSA | 112,619 | | 0.0 |
| **Milwaukee, WI** | **2,430,740** | | **0.9** |
| Milwaukee-Waukesha, WI PMSA | 1,457,939 | | 0.6 |
| Racine, WI PMSA | 182,892 | | 0.1 |
| Kenosha, WI PMSA | 139,938 | | 0.1 |
| Sheboygan, WI MSA | 108,326 | | 0.0 |
| Madison, WI MSA | 393,296 | | 0.1 |
| Janesville-Beloit, WI MSA | 148,349 | | 0.1 |
| **Chicago, IL** | **8,449,975** | | **3.2** |
| Chicago, IL PMSA | 7,724,770 | | 2.9 |
| Kankakee, IL PMSA | 102,046 | | 0.0 |
| Gary, IN PMSA | 623,159 | | 0.2 |
| **Rest of Region** | **16,825,979** | | **6.4** |

| Region / Vernal Center / Metropolitan Statistical Area | Estimated Population in July 1995 | Near Vern % | % Total 1995 Pop. |
|---|---|---|---|
| **Industrial Heartland** | **17,558,082** | **54.6** | **6.7** |
| **Ann Arbor, MI** | **6,483,941** | | **2.5** |
| Ann Arbor, MI PMSA | 522,916 | | 0.2 |
| Detroit, MI PMSA | 4,320,203 | | 1.6 |
| Flint, MI PMSA | 436,381 | | 0.2 |
| Lansing-East Lansing, MI MSA | 437,633 | | 0.2 |
| Jackson, MI MSA | 154,010 | | 0.1 |
| Toledo, OH MSA | 612,798 | | 0.2 |
| **Indianapolis, IN** | **2,128,524** | | **0.8** |
| Indianapolis, IN MSA | 1,476,865 | | 0.6 |
| Lafayette, IN MSA | 167,879 | | 0.1 |
| Kokomo, IN MSA | 100,226 | | 0.0 |
| Muncie, IN MSA | 118,577 | | 0.0 |
| Terre Haute, IN MSA | 149,769 | | 0.1 |
| Bloomington, IN MSA | 115,208 | | 0.0 |
| **Columbus, OH** | **2,570,078** | | **1.0** |
| Columbus, OH MSA | 1,437,512 | | 0.5 |
| Mansfield, OH MSA | 176,154 | | 0.1 |
| Dayton-Springfield, OH MSA | 956,412 | | 0.4 |
| **Akron, OH** | **4,032,365** | | **1.5** |
| Akron, OH PMSA | 678,834 | | 0.3 |
| Cleveland-Lorain-Elyria, OH PMSA | 2,224,974 | | 0.8 |
| Canton-Massillon, OH MSA | 403,695 | | 0.2 |
| Youngstown-Warren, OH MSA | 602,608 | | 0.2 |
| Sharon, PA MSA | 122,254 | | 0.0 |
| **Cincinnati, OH** | **2,343,174** | | **0.9** |
| Cincinnati, OH-KY-IN PMSA | 1,591,837 | | 0.6 |
| Hamilton-Middletown, OH PMSA | 315,601 | | 0.1 |
| Lexington, KY MSA | 435,736 | | 0.2 |
| **Rest of Region** | **14,592,979** | | **5.6** |

**Note**: Ann Arbor, Michigan, is centrally located between four Michigan cities — Detroit, Flint, Lansing, and Jackson — and Toledo, Ohio. Akron, Ohio, is centrally located between Cleveland, Youngstown, and Canton.

**Note**: Columbia, South Carolina, is centrally located between two South Carolina cities — Charleston and Florence — and Augusta, Georgia. Though relatively small, Spartanburg, South Carolina, is centrally located between Greenville, South Carolina, and Charlotte, North Carolina. Also relatively small Burlington, North Carolina, is centrally located between Winston-Salem, Greensboro, Chapel Hill, Durham, and Raleigh. And tiny Williamsburg, Virginia is about halfway between Norfolk and Richmond.

# Figure B.11 (continued)

| Region / Vernal Center / Metropolitan Statistical Area | Estimated Population in July 1995 | Near Vern % | % Total 1995 Pop. |
|---|---|---|---|
| **Middle Atlantic** | **32,112,341** | **82.5** | **12.2** |
| **Pittsburg, PA** | **2,792,695** | | **1.1** |
| Pittsburgh, PA MSA | 2,394,702 | | 0.9 |
| Wheeling, WV-OH MSA | 157,349 | | 0.1 |
| Johnstown, PA MSA | 240,644 | | 0.1 |
| **Philadelphia, PA** | **7,499,618** | | **2.9** |
| Philadelphia, PA-NJ PMSA | 4,950,866 | | 1.9 |
| Vineland-Millville-Bridgeton, NJ PMSA | 138,058 | | 0.1 |
| Atlantic-Cape May, NJ PMSA | 332,336 | | 0.1 |
| Wilmington-Newark, DE-MD PMSA | 546,063 | | 0.2 |
| Allentown-Bethlehem-Easton, PA MSA | 613,466 | | 0.2 |
| Reading, PA MSA | 349,583 | | 0.1 |
| Lancaster, PA MSA | 447,521 | | 0.2 |
| Dover, DE MSA | 121,725 | | 0.0 |
| **New York, NY** | **17,845,173** | | **6.8** |
| New York, NY PMSA | 8,570,212 | | 3.3 |
| Nassau-Suffolk, NY PMSA | 2,659,476 | | 1.0 |
| Newburgh, NY-PA PMSA | 359,744 | | 0.1 |
| Newark, NJ PMSA | 1,936,096 | | 0.7 |
| Jersey City, NJ PMSA | 550,183 | | 0.2 |
| Bergen-Passaic, NJ PMSA | 1,308,655 | | 0.5 |
| Middlesex-Somerset-Hunterdon, NJ PMSA | 1,080,450 | | 0.4 |
| Trenton, NJ PMSA | 330,305 | | 0.1 |
| Monmouth-Ocean, NJ PMSA | 1,050,052 | | 0.4 |
| **Rochester, NY** | **2,272,568** | | **0.9** |
| Rochester, NY MSA | 1,088,516 | | 0.4 |
| Buffalo-Niagara Falls, NY MSA | 1,184,052 | | 0.5 |
| **Albany, NY** | **1,702,287** | | **0.6** |
| Albany-Schenectady-Troy, NY MSA | 873,361 | | 0.3 |
| Glens Falls, NY MSA | 122,559 | | 0.0 |
| Dutchess County, NY PMSA | 262,062 | | 0.1 |
| Pittsfield, MA NECMA | 135,743 | | 0.1 |
| *Utica-Rome, NY MSA (93 miles)* | 308,562 | | 0.1 |
| **Rest of Region** | **6,805,080** | | **2.6** |
| **New England** | **10,460,300** | **78.6** | **4.0** |
| **Hartford, CT** | **4,491,528** | | **1.7** |
| Hartford, CT NECMA | 1,115,223 | | 0.4 |
| New Haven-Bridgeport-Stamford-Waterbury- | 1,625,513 | | 0.6 |
| New London-Norwich, CT NECMA | 250,404 | | 0.1 |
| Providence-Warwick-Pawtucket, RI NECMA | 907,801 | | 0.3 |
| Springfield, MA NECMA | 592,587 | | 0.2 |
| **Boston, MA** | **5,968,772** | | **2.3** |
| Boston-Worcester-Lawrence-Lowell-Brockton | 5,768,968 | | 2.2 |
| Barnstable-Yarmouth, MA NECMA | 199,804 | | 0.1 |
| **Rest of Region** | **2,844,811** | | **1.1** |

| Region / Vernal Center / Metropolitan Statistical Area | Estimated Population in July 1995 | Near Vern % | % Total 1995 Pop. |
|---|---|---|---|
| **Florida** | **10,204,768** | **71.9** | **3.9** |
| **Orlando, FL** | **2,516,802** | | **1.0** |
| Orlando, FL MSA | 1,390,574 | | 0.5 |
| Ocala, FL MSA | 226,678 | | 0.1 |
| Daytona Beach, FL MSA | 448,904 | | 0.2 |
| Melbourne-Titusville-Palm Bay, FL MSA | 450,646 | | 0.2 |
| **Tampa, FL** | **3,272,372** | | **1.2** |
| Tampa-St. Petersburg-Clearwater, FL MSA | 2,180,484 | | 0.8 |
| Sarasota-Bradenton, FL MSA | 525,806 | | 0.2 |
| Punta Gorda, FL MSA | 129,381 | | 0.0 |
| Lakeland-Winter Haven, FL MSA | 436,701 | | 0.2 |
| **Fort Lauderdale, FL** | **4,415,594** | | **1.7** |
| Fort Lauderdale, FL PMSA | 1,412,165 | | 0.5 |
| Miami, FL PMSA | 2,031,336 | | 0.8 |
| West Palm Beach-Boca Raton, FL MSA | 972,093 | | 0.4 |
| **Rest of Region** | **3,979,387** | | **1.5** |
| | | | |
| **Population Near Vernal Centers** | **173,505,121** | | **66.0** |
| | | | |
| **Total Population in All MSAs** | **209,595,501** | | **79.7** |
| | | | |
| **Total Vernal Centers** | **50** | | |
| Minimum Population near a Vernal Center | 1,620,436 | 0.6 | |
| Maximum Population | 7,499,618 | 2.9 | |
| Median Population | 2,667,650 | 1.0 | |
| Mean Population | 3,470,102 | 1.3 | |
| Standard Deviation | 1,601,359 | 0.6 | |
| Harmonic Mean Population | 2,884,822 | 1.1 | |

**Note**: Fort Lauderdale, Florida, is centrally located between Miami and West Palm Beach.

**Source**: Population estimates for July 1, 1995 are from the Census Bureau as reported on December 30, 1986.

**Note**: A more detailed version of this figure is available at <http://www.vernalproject.org>.

It is also possible that ten or twenty years into Vernal Phase 3 (Vernal Year 30 or 40), when the Vernal centers were strong and operating well, that the staffmembers could occasionally travel farther than 75 miles to recruit students, arrange internships, support study groups, and facilitate workshops. This might enable the Vernal Project to reach many excluded cities and more people who live in rural areas. If every Vernal center could periodically reach out 200 miles in every direction (instead of just 75 miles), then the fifty centers could reach almost all of the country. Only the states of Hawaii and Alaska and rural areas in northern Maine, the western plains, and the Rocky Mountains would be missed. If this were possible, the Vernal Project could then directly reach perhaps 90 – 95 percent of the total population.

## Figure B.12: Distant MSAs Associated with Vernal Centers

| Vernal Center | Distant MSA | Distance (Miles) |
|---|---|---|
| Fresno, CA | Bakersfield, CA MSA | 112 |
| Salt Lake City, UT | Las Vegas, NV-AZ MSA | 419 |
| Stillwater, OK | Wichita, KS MSA | 127 |
| Austin, TX | Waco, TX MSA | 100 |
| | Bryan-College Station, TX MSA | 105 |
| San Antonio, TX | Victoria, TX MSA | 116 |
| | Corpus Christi, TX MSA | 153 |
| Memphis, TN | Little Rock-North Little Rock, AR MSA | 137 |
| | Jackson, MS MSA | 213 |
| Nashville, TN | Chattanooga, TN-GA MSA | 129 |
| Birmingham, AL | Huntsville, AL MSA | 95 |
| | Montgomery, AL MSA | 91 |
| Columbia, SC | Charleston-North Charleston, SC MSA | 113 |
| Albany, NY | Utica-Rome, NY MSA | 93 |

nal region* — generally in the most progressive regions first. These lead centers then establish centers in the rest of the region.†

I have assumed that the first center would be in Oakland, California to cover the San Francisco Bay Area. This would be the only center in Phase 1 of the project (Vernal Years 1 to 5). In each of the first two years, it would facilitate just a single session. The center would grow slowly over the next few years, facilitating only two sessions in Year 3 and three in Year 4. This would provide adequate time for the staffmembers to arrange retreat center rentals, establish relationships with internship organizations, attract students, and learn to work together as a team.

In the first three years, the team would comprise only three full-time equivalent (FTE) staffmembers, but in Year 4 it would have a full staff of four FTE. By the fourth year, I assume the Oakland staffmembers would feel comfortable working together and their work procedures would be well established. Moreover, by that time the center should have established a good reputation in its area, making it relatively easy to attract new students.

In Year 5, the Oakland center would reach its full capacity of four sessions. In this year, it would also initiate the process of replicating the Vernal Program to other regions. As the first center, the Oakland center would have the special responsibility of seeding all the other regions. In Year 5, the Oakland center would hire the first new staff preparer who would then hire and prepare staffmembers for a new center in Philadelphia. Oakland staffmembers would also travel to Philadelphia at the end of this year to investigate possible internship organizations and retreat centers and to transmit their experiences to the new Philadelphia staffmembers.‡

*[Text continues on page 264]*

## VERNAL CENTER REPLICATION

For the Vernal Project to be successful, it must rapidly establish fifty Vernal centers all across the country so that a critical mass of graduates are all working together and can see they are not alone in their efforts. Figures B.13 and B.14 show one possible way to propagate Vernal centers across the country. In this model, Vernal centers are first established in the largest and most progressive cities in each Ver-

---

\* Note that some Vernal centers are located in relatively small cities that are located between large cities.

† In choosing the order and pace of replication, I had to balance the requirement that the Vernal Project expand rapidly against the imperative to minimize costs. I painstakingly adjusted the values in Figures B.13, B.14, B.15, B.16, B.17, B.18, and 6.12 to ensure they were reasonable, self-consistent, and resulted in the lowest overall cost.

‡ One of the Oakland staffmembers might become the first new staff preparer. The Oakland center would then hire a new staffmember to replace this person. Also, some of the Oakland staffmembers might decide to move to Philadelphia and become the first staffmembers there.

# Figure B.13: Possible Number of Vernal Sessions Beginning Each Year by Region and Center

| Pha | Vern Proj Year | California (Oak) | MidAtlantic (Philadel) | NCentral (Chicago) | IndHeart (AnnArbor) | PacMnt (Seattle) | TexOkl (Houston) | SAtlantic (Washington) | CenSouth (Atlanta) | NEng (Boston) | Florida (Ft. Lauderdale) | Tot. Per Year |
|---|---|---|---|---|---|---|---|---|---|---|---|---|
| 1 | 1 | 1 | | | | | | | | | | 1 |
|   | 2 | 1 | | | | | | | | | | 1 |
|   | 3 | 2 | | | | | | | | | | 2 |
|   | 4 | 3 | | | | | | | | | | 3 |
|   | 5 | 4 | | | | | | | | | | 4 |
| 2 | 6 | 4 | 1 | | | | | | | | | 5 |
|   | 7 | 4 | 1 | 1 | | | | | | | | 6 |
|   | 8 | 4 | 2 | 1 | 1 | | | | | | | 8 |
|   | 9 | 4 2 | 3 | 2 | 1 | 1 | | | | | | 13 |
|   | 10 | 4 4 2 | 4 | 3 | 2 | 1 | 1 | | | | | 21 |
|   | 11 | 4 4 4 2 | 4 | 4 | 3 | 2 | 1 | 1 | | | | 29 |
|   | 12 | 4 4 4 4 2 | 4 | 4 | 4 | 3 | 2 | 1 | 1 | | | 37 |
|   | 13 | 4 4 4 4 4 2 | 4 2 | 4 | 4 | 4 | 3 | 2 | 2 | 1 | 1 | 48 |
|   | 14 | 4 4 4 4 4 4 2 | 4 2 | 4 2 | 4 2 | 4 | 4 | 3 | 3 | 2 | 1 | 65 |
|   | 15 | 4 4 4 4 4 4 4 | 4 4 2 | 4 4 2 | 4 4 2 | 4 2 | 4 | 4 | 4 | 3 | 2 | 85 |
|   | 16 | 4 4 4 4 4 4 4 | 4 4 4 2 | 4 4 4 2 | 4 4 4 2 | 4 4 2 | 4 2 | 4 | 4 | 4 | 3 | 105 |
|   | 17 | 4 4 4 4 4 4 4 | 4 4 4 4 2 | 4 4 4 4 2 | 4 4 4 4 2 | 4 4 4 | 4 4 2 | 4 2 | 4 2 | 4 | 4 | 128 |
|   | 18 | 4 4 4 4 4 4 4 | 4 4 4 4 4 2 | 4 4 4 4 4 2 | 4 4 4 4 4 | 4 4 4 2 | 4 4 4 2 | 4 4 2 | 4 4 2 | 4 2 | 4 | 154 |
|   | 19 | 4 4 4 4 4 4 4 | 4 4 4 4 4 4 | 4 4 4 4 4 4 | 4 4 4 4 4 | 4 4 4 4 | 4 4 4 4 2 | 4 4 4 2 | 4 4 2 | 4 4 | 4 2 | 178 |
|   | 20 | 4 4 4 4 4 4 4 | 4 4 4 4 4 4 | 4 4 4 4 4 4 | 4 4 4 4 4 | 4 4 4 4 | 4 4 4 4 | 4 4 4 4 | 4 4 4 2 | 4 4 2 | 4 4 2 | 194 |
| 3 | 21 | 4 4 4 4 4 4 4 | 4 4 4 4 4 4 | 4 4 4 4 4 4 | 4 4 4 4 4 | 4 4 4 4 | 4 4 4 4 | 4 4 4 4 | 4 4 4 4 | 4 4 | 4 4 4 | 200 |
|   | 22 | 4 4 4 4 4 4 4 | 4 4 4 4 4 4 | 4 4 4 4 4 4 | 4 4 4 4 4 | 4 4 4 4 | 4 4 4 4 | 4 4 4 4 | 4 4 4 4 | 4 4 | 4 4 4 | 200 |
|   | 23 | 4 4 4 4 4 4 4 | 4 4 4 4 4 4 | 4 4 4 4 4 4 | 4 4 4 4 4 | 4 4 4 4 | 4 4 4 4 | 4 4 4 4 | 4 4 4 4 | 4 4 | 4 4 4 | 200 |
|   | 24 | 4 4 4 4 4 4 4 | 4 4 4 4 4 4 | 4 4 4 4 4 4 | 4 4 4 4 4 | 4 4 4 4 | 4 4 4 4 | 4 4 4 4 | 4 4 4 4 | 4 4 | 4 4 4 | 200 |
|   | 25 | 4 4 4 4 4 4 4 | 4 4 4 4 4 4 | 4 4 4 4 4 4 | 4 4 4 4 4 | 4 4 4 4 | 4 4 4 4 | 4 4 4 4 | 4 4 4 4 | 4 4 | 4 4 4 | 200 |
|   | 26 | 4 4 4 4 4 4 4 | 4 4 4 4 4 4 | 4 4 4 4 4 4 | 4 4 4 4 4 | 4 4 4 4 | 4 4 4 4 | 4 4 4 4 | 4 4 4 4 | 4 4 | 4 4 4 | 200 |
|   | 27 | 4 4 4 4 4 4 4 | 4 4 4 4 4 4 | 4 4 4 4 4 4 | 4 4 4 4 4 | 4 4 4 4 | 4 4 4 4 | 4 4 4 4 | 4 4 4 4 | 4 4 | 4 4 4 | 200 |
|   | 28 | 4 4 4 4 4 4 4 | 4 4 4 4 4 4 | 4 4 4 4 4 4 | 4 4 4 4 4 | 4 4 4 4 | 4 4 4 4 | 4 4 4 4 | 4 4 4 4 | 4 4 | 4 4 4 | 200 |
|   | 29 | 4 4 4 4 4 4 4 | 4 4 4 4 4 4 | 4 4 4 4 4 4 | 4 4 4 4 4 | 4 4 4 4 | 4 4 4 4 | 4 4 4 4 | 4 4 4 4 | 4 4 | 4 4 4 | 200 |
|   | 30 | 4 4 4 4 4 4 4 | 4 4 4 4 4 4 | 4 4 4 4 4 4 | 4 4 4 4 4 | 4 4 4 4 | 4 4 4 4 | 4 4 4 4 | 4 4 4 4 | 4 4 | 4 4 4 | 200 |
| **Total for first 30 years** | | | | | | | | | | | | **3087** |

# Figure B.14: Possible Replication of Vernal Centers

| Yr | Calif | MAtlan | NCentral | IndHeart | PacMnt | TexOkl | SAtlan | CSouth | NEngld | Florida |
|----|-------|--------|----------|----------|--------|--------|--------|--------|--------|---------|
| | | | | Vernal Region | | | | | | |
| 1 | **Oakland** | | | | | | | | | |
| 2 | | | | | | | | | | |
| 3 | | | | | | | | | | |
| 4 | | | | | | | | | | |
| 5 | | | | | | | | | | |
| 6 | **Oakland** | -> Philadelphia | | | | | | | | |
| 7 | **Oakland** | | ------------ > **Chicago A** | | | | | | | |
| 8 | **Oakland** | | | ---------------------------- > **Ann Arbor** | | | | | | |
| 9 | **Oakland** | | | | --------------------------------------------- > **Seattle** | | | | | |
| | **Oakland** | --> Sacramento | | | | | | | | |
| 10 | **Oakland** | | | | | --------------------------------------------------------------> **Houston** | | | | |
| | **Oakland** | --> Los Angeles A | | | | | | | | |
| 11 | **Oakland** | | | | | | --------------------------------------------------------------------------> **Washington** | | | |
| | **Oakland** | --> Los Angeles B | | | | | | | | |
| 12 | **Oakland** | | | | | | | ------------------------------------------------------------------------------------> **Atlanta** | | |
| | **Oakland** | --> Los Angeles C | | | | | | | | |
| 13 | **Oakland** | | | | | | | | ---------------------------------------------------------------------------------------- > **Boston** | |
| | **Oakland** | --> San Diego | | | | | | | | |
| | | **Philadelphia** --> New York A | | | | | | | | |
| 14 | **Oakland** | | | | | | | | | ---------------------------------------------------------------------------------------------------------- > **Ft. Lauderdale** |
| | **Oakland** | --> Fresno | | | | | | | | |
| | | **Philadelphia** --> New York B | | | | | | | | |
| | | | **Chicago A** --> Chicago B | | | | | | | |
| | | | | **Ann Arbor** --> Akron | | | | | | |
| 15 | | **Philadelphia** --> New York C | | | | | | | | |
| | | | **Chicago A** --> Minneapolis | | | | | | | |
| | | | | **Ann Arbor** --> Columbus | | | | | | |
| | | | | | **Seattle** --> Denver | | | | | |
| 16 | | **Philadelphia** --> Pittsburgh | | | | | | | | |
| | | | **Chicago A** --> St. Louis | | | | | | | |
| | | | | **Ann Arbor** --> Cincinnati | | | | | | |
| | | | | | **Seattle** --> Phoenix | | | | | |
| | | | | | | **Houston** --> Arlington | | | | |
| 17 | | **Philadelphia** --> Rochester | | | | | | | | |
| | | | **Chicago A** --> Milwaukee | | | | | | | |
| | | | | **Ann Arbor** --> Indianapolis | | | | | | |
| | | | | | | **Houston** --> San Antonio | | | | |
| | | | | | | | **Washington** --> Williamsburg | | | |
| | | | | | | | | **Atlanta** --> Baton Rouge | | |
| 18 | | **Philadelphia** --> Albany | | | | | | | | |
| | | | **Chicago A** --> Kansas City | | | | | | | |
| | | | | | **Seattle** --> Portland | | | | | |
| | | | | | | **Houston** --> Austin | | | | |
| | | | | | | | **Washington** --> Burlington | | | |
| | | | | | | | | **Atlanta** --> Memphis | | |
| | | | | | | | | | **Boston** --> Hartford | |
| 19 | | | | | **Seattle** --> Salt Lake City | | | | | |
| | | | | | | **Houston** --> Stillwater | | | | |
| | | | | | | | **Washington** --> Spartanburg | | | |
| | | | | | | | | **Atlanta** --> Nashville | | |
| | | | | | | | | | | **Ft. Lauderdale** --> Tampa |
| 20 | | | | | | | **Washington** --> Columbia | | | |
| | | | | | | | | **Atlanta** --> Birmingham | | |
| | | | | | | | | | | **Ft. Lauderdale** -> Orlando |

**Note**: The lead center in each region is shown in **bold type**.

In Year 6 (the beginning of Phase 2), the Oakland center would continue to facilitate a regular workload of four sessions and the new center in Philadelphia would facilitate a single session. In this year, the Oakland center and the new staff preparer would also establish a new Vernal center in Chicago. In Year 7, the Oakland center and the new staff preparer would establish a new Vernal center in Ann Arbor, Michigan. The Philadelphia and Chicago centers would each facilitate a single session, and the Oakland center would continue to facilitate four sessions.

In Year 8, the new Ann Arbor center and the Chicago center would each facilitate one session, and the Philadelphia center would facilitate two sessions. The Oakland center would continue to facilitate four sessions. By this time, the process of establishing new centers should be more routine and much easier. So in this year, the Oakland center and the new staff preparer would establish new centers in two cities: Seattle and Sacramento.

Since Sacramento is close to Oakland, and since the program in Oakland would be several years old by then and have developed a good reputation, it should be easier to arrange internships in Sacramento, find a good retreat center, and attract students. The Sacramento center would be the second center in the California region, so with its establishment, it would also be time to hire a regional administrator.

With support from the Oakland center and the regional administrator, the Sacramento center should have a big head start in getting established. So I assume it would be able to facilitate two sessions in its first year (Year 9) and four in its second year. In Year 9 there would also be a second new staff preparer to help hire, prepare, and support all the new staffmembers.

As shown in Figures B.13 and B.14, this procedure would continue until all fifty centers were established and each was facilitating a full load of sessions. The Oakland center would continue through Year 14 to establish centers in new regions (Houston, Washington, Atlanta, Boston, and Ft. Lauderdale) as well as new centers in the California region.

Each newly formed center in a region would facilitate just one session in its early years and slowly work up to full capacity. Once the first center in a region had reached full capacity, it would then help establish new centers in that region every year. For example, in Year 13, the Philadelphia center (which would then be eight years old) would help establish a new center in New York City. In Year 14, the Philadelphia center would establish a second center in New York City, the Chicago center would establish a second center in Chicago, and the Ann Arbor center would establish a new center in Akron, Ohio. In Year 15, the Philadelphia center would help establish a third new center in New York City, the Chicago center would establish a center in Minneapolis, Minnesota, the Ann Arbor center would establish a center in Columbus, Ohio, and the Seattle center would establish a center in Denver, Colorado.

As soon as there were two centers in a region, a regional administrator would be hired to provide accounting and payroll services and to coordinate cooperation between all the centers. Another 0.5 FTE administrator would be hired for each additional new center until there were twenty-five FTE in all. As the total number of Vernal staff grew, there would also be additional new staff preparers to help hire, prepare, and support the new employees. After the initial start-up period, there would be four new staff preparers. I assume that, with support from the regional administrators and new staff preparers, the second and subsequent centers in each region should be able to facilitate two sessions in their first year of operation and then jump to full capacity in their second year.

By following this rapid growth trajectory, the replication process could be fully completed in Vernal Year 21, the first year of Phase 3. The total number of sessions held each year would grow from just five in Year 6 to two hundred in Year 21. The total number of students entering each year would grow from 150 to 6,000.

Figure B.15 summarizes the number of sessions that would start in each region for the first thirty years.

## NUMBER OF VERNAL STAFFMEMBERS

Figures B.16 and B.17 show the number of Vernal staffmembers and regional administrators required during the first thirty years of the Vernal Project in each region. Figure B.18 totals these values and indicates how many new staffmembers must be hired each year, assuming that an average staffmember leaves after six years (plus or minus two years). It also shows how many of these slots might be filled with Vernal graduates assuming that one graduate from each session would be available four years after that session had ended (plus or minus one year). With these assumptions, there would be more graduates available to become Vernal staffmembers than would be needed in every year after Year 14.

Figure B.18 also shows the number of staffmembers needed in the development phases. In the last year of Development Phase 1 and all three years of Development Phase 2, I assume there would be at least three people working together to promote the Vernal Project, develop the curriculum and workshop agendas, arrange internships, and facilitate the test sessions. However, I assume much of their effort would be volunteered. This figure only shows the number of paid staffmembers: one half-time person in the last year of Vernal Development Phase 1, one person in Year Prep-1, two people in Year Prep-2, and two and one-half people in Year Prep-3.

# Figure B.15: Possible Number of Vernal Sessions Beginning Each Year by Vernal Region

| Phase | Vernal Project Year | Number of Vernal Sessions Each Year by Region | | | | | | | | | | Total Per Year | Notes |
|---|---|---|---|---|---|---|---|---|---|---|---|---|---|
| | | Cal | MAtl | NCen | IndH | PMnt | TxO | SAtl | CSou | NEng | Flor | | |
| *D1* | | | | | | | | | | | | | *Test workshops:1 day long* |
| *D2* | *Prep-1* | | | | | | | | | | | | *Test workshop:10 days long* |
| | *Prep-2* | | | | | | | | | | | | *Test workshop:10 days long* |
| | *Prep-3* | 0.5 | | | | | | | | | | 0.5 | *Pilot Session: 6 mon. long* |
| 1 | 1 | 1 | | | | | | | | | | 1 | First full session begins |
| | 2 | 1 | | | | | | | | | | 1 | |
| | 3 | 2 | | | | | | | | | | 2 | |
| | 4 | 3 | | | | | | | | | | 3 | |
| | 5 | 4 | | | | | | | | | | 4 | |
| 2 | 6 | 4 | 1 | | | | | | | | | 5 | Expand to other regions |
| | 7 | 4 | 1 | 1 | | | | | | | | 6 | |
| | 8 | 4 | 2 | 1 | 1 | | | | | | | 8 | |
| | 9 | 6 | 3 | 2 | 1 | 1 | | | | | | 13 | |
| | 10 | 10 | 4 | 3 | 2 | 1 | 1 | | | | | 21 | |
| | 11 | 14 | 4 | 4 | 3 | 2 | 1 | 1 | | | | 29 | |
| | 12 | 18 | 4 | 4 | 4 | 3 | 2 | 1 | 1 | | | 37 | |
| | 13 | 22 | 6 | 4 | 4 | 4 | 3 | 2 | 2 | 1 | | 48 | |
| | 14 | 26 | 10 | 6 | 6 | 4 | 4 | 3 | 3 | 2 | 1 | 65 | |
| | 15 | 28 | 14 | 10 | 10 | 6 | 4 | 4 | 4 | 3 | 2 | 85 | |
| | 16 | 28 | 18 | 14 | 14 | 10 | 6 | 4 | 4 | 4 | 3 | 105 | |
| | 17 | 28 | 22 | 18 | 18 | 12 | 10 | 6 | 6 | 4 | 4 | 128 | |
| | 18 | 28 | 26 | 22 | 20 | 14 | 14 | 10 | 10 | 6 | 4 | 154 | |
| | 19 | 28 | 28 | 24 | 20 | 18 | 18 | 14 | 14 | 8 | 6 | 178 | |
| | 20 | 28 | 28 | 24 | 20 | 20 | 20 | 18 | 18 | 8 | 10 | 194 | |
| 3 | 21 | 28 | 28 | 24 | 20 | 20 | 20 | 20 | 20 | 8 | 12 | 200 | Project at full size |
| | 22 | 28 | 28 | 24 | 20 | 20 | 20 | 20 | 20 | 8 | 12 | 200 | |
| | 23 | 28 | 28 | 24 | 20 | 20 | 20 | 20 | 20 | 8 | 12 | 200 | |
| | 24 | 28 | 28 | 24 | 20 | 20 | 20 | 20 | 20 | 8 | 12 | 200 | |
| | 25 | 28 | 28 | 24 | 20 | 20 | 20 | 20 | 20 | 8 | 12 | 200 | |
| | 26 | 28 | 28 | 24 | 20 | 20 | 20 | 20 | 20 | 8 | 12 | 200 | |
| | 27 | 28 | 28 | 24 | 20 | 20 | 20 | 20 | 20 | 8 | 12 | 200 | |
| | 28 | 28 | 28 | 24 | 20 | 20 | 20 | 20 | 20 | 8 | 12 | 200 | |
| | 29 | 28 | 28 | 24 | 20 | 20 | 20 | 20 | 20 | 8 | 12 | 200 | |
| | 30 | 28 | 28 | 24 | 20 | 20 | 20 | 20 | 20 | 8 | 12 | 200 | |
| **Total for first 30 years** | | 567 | 451 | 377 | 323 | 295 | 283 | 263 | 262 | 116 | 150 | **3,087** | Note that Phase 3 continues until Project Year 60 |

**Note**: The last year of Phase D1 and all 3 years of Phase D2 are shown here, but are not included in the totals.

# Figure B.16: Possible Number of Vernal Team Staffmembers Needed Each Year in Each Vernal Region

| Phase | Vernal Project Year | Number of Team Staffmembers Needed Each Year (Full-Time Equivalent) Region | | | | | | | | | | Total Team Staff Needed | Add'l This Year |
|---|---|---|---|---|---|---|---|---|---|---|---|---|---|
| | | Cal | MAtl | NCen | IndH | PMnt | TxO | SAtl | South | NEng | Flor | | |
| D1 | | | | | | | | | | | | | |
| D2 | Prep-1 | | | | | | | | | | | | |
| | Prep-2 | | | | | | | | | | | | |
| | Prep-3 | | | | | | | | | | | | |
| 1 | 1 | 3.0 | | | | | | | | | | 3.0 | |
| | 2 | 3.0 | | | | | | | | | | 3.0 | 0.0 |
| | 3 | 3.0 | | | | | | | | | | 3.0 | 0.0 |
| | 4 | 4.0 | | | | | | | | | | 4.0 | 1.0 |
| | 5 | 4.0 | | | | | | | | | | 4.0 | 0.0 |
| 2 | 6 | 4.0 | 3.0 | | | | | | | | | 7.0 | 3.0 |
| | 7 | 4.0 | 3.0 | 3.0 | | | | | | | | 10.0 | 3.0 |
| | 8 | 4.0 | 3.0 | 3.0 | 3.0 | | | | | | | 13.0 | 3.0 |
| | 9 | 8.0 | 4.0 | 3.0 | 3.0 | 3.0 | | | | | | 21.0 | 8.0 |
| | 10 | 12.0 | 4.0 | 4.0 | 3.0 | 3.0 | 3.0 | | | | | 29.0 | 8.0 |
| | 11 | 16.0 | 4.0 | 4.0 | 4.0 | 3.0 | 3.0 | 3.0 | | | | 37.0 | 8.0 |
| | 12 | 20.0 | 4.0 | 4.0 | 4.0 | 4.0 | 3.0 | 3.0 | 3.0 | | | 45.0 | 8.0 |
| | 13 | 24.0 | 8.0 | 4.0 | 4.0 | 4.0 | 4.0 | 3.0 | 3.0 | 3.0 | | 57.0 | 12.0 |
| | 14 | 28.0 | 12.0 | 8.0 | 8.0 | 4.0 | 4.0 | 4.0 | 4.0 | 3.0 | 3.0 | 78.0 | 21.0 |
| | 15 | 28.0 | 16.0 | 12.0 | 12.0 | 8.0 | 4.0 | 4.0 | 4.0 | 4.0 | 3.0 | 95.0 | 17.0 |
| | 16 | 28.0 | 20.0 | 16.0 | 16.0 | 12.0 | 8.0 | 4.0 | 4.0 | 4.0 | 4.0 | 116.0 | 21.0 |
| | 17 | 28.0 | 24.0 | 20.0 | 20.0 | 12.0 | 12.0 | 8.0 | 8.0 | 4.0 | 4.0 | 140.0 | 24.0 |
| | 18 | 28.0 | 28.0 | 24.0 | 20.0 | 16.0 | 16.0 | 12.0 | 12.0 | 8.0 | 4.0 | 168.0 | 28.0 |
| | 19 | 28.0 | 28.0 | 24.0 | 20.0 | 20.0 | 20.0 | 16.0 | 16.0 | 8.0 | 8.0 | 188.0 | 20.0 |
| | 20 | 28.0 | 28.0 | 24.0 | 20.0 | 20.0 | 20.0 | 20.0 | 20.0 | 8.0 | 12.0 | 200.0 | 12.0 |
| 3 | 21 | 28.0 | 28.0 | 24.0 | 20.0 | 20.0 | 20.0 | 20.0 | 20.0 | 8.0 | 12.0 | 200.0 | 0.0 |
| | 22 | 28.0 | 28.0 | 24.0 | 20.0 | 20.0 | 20.0 | 20.0 | 20.0 | 8.0 | 12.0 | 200.0 | 0.0 |
| | 23 | 28.0 | 28.0 | 24.0 | 20.0 | 20.0 | 20.0 | 20.0 | 20.0 | 8.0 | 12.0 | 200.0 | 0.0 |
| | 24 | 28.0 | 28.0 | 24.0 | 20.0 | 20.0 | 20.0 | 20.0 | 20.0 | 8.0 | 12.0 | 200.0 | 0.0 |
| | 25 | 28.0 | 28.0 | 24.0 | 20.0 | 20.0 | 20.0 | 20.0 | 20.0 | 8.0 | 12.0 | 200.0 | 0.0 |
| | 26 | 28.0 | 28.0 | 24.0 | 20.0 | 20.0 | 20.0 | 20.0 | 20.0 | 8.0 | 12.0 | 200.0 | 0.0 |
| | 27 | 28.0 | 28.0 | 24.0 | 20.0 | 20.0 | 20.0 | 20.0 | 20.0 | 8.0 | 12.0 | 200.0 | 0.0 |
| | 28 | 28.0 | 28.0 | 24.0 | 20.0 | 20.0 | 20.0 | 20.0 | 20.0 | 8.0 | 12.0 | 200.0 | 0.0 |
| | 29 | 28.0 | 28.0 | 24.0 | 20.0 | 20.0 | 20.0 | 20.0 | 20.0 | 8.0 | 12.0 | 200.0 | 0.0 |
| | 30 | 28.0 | 28.0 | 24.0 | 20.0 | 20.0 | 20.0 | 20.0 | 20.0 | 8.0 | 12.0 | 200.0 | 0.0 |

**Assumptions**

Assume a team of four staffmembers (full-time equivalent) can facilitate four sessions and also attract new students, arrange internships, counsel and support students, research and prepare class materials, help prepare new staffmembers, and provide all necessary administration.

Assume that a team of three staffmembers can handle the workload for the first few years of each new center when it facilitates just one or two sessions.

# Figure B.17: Possible Number of Regional Administrators Needed Each Year in Each Vernal Region

| Phase | Vernal Project Year | Number of Regional Administrators Needed Each Year (Full-Time Equivalent) Region | | | | | | | | | | Total Region Admins Needed |
| | | Cal | MAtl | NCen | IndH | PMnt | TxO | SAtl | South | NEng | Flor | |
|---|---|---|---|---|---|---|---|---|---|---|---|---|
| D1 | | | | | | | | | | | | |
| D2 | Prep-1 | | | | | | | | | | | |
| | Prep-2 | | | | | | | | | | | |
| | Prep-3 | | | | | | | | | | | |
| 1 | 1 | | | | | | | | | | | 0.0 |
| | 2 | | | | | | | | | | | 0.0 |
| | 3 | | | | | | | | | | | 0.0 |
| | 4 | | | | | | | | | | | 0.0 |
| | 5 | | | | | | | | | | | 0.0 |
| 2 | 6 | | | | | | | | | | | 0.0 |
| | 7 | | | | | | | | | | | 0.0 |
| | 8 | | | | | | | | | | | 0.0 |
| | 9 | 1.0 | | | | | | | | | | 1.0 |
| | 10 | 1.5 | | | | | | | | | | 1.5 |
| | 11 | 2.0 | | | | | | | | | | 2.0 |
| | 12 | 2.5 | | | | | | | | | | 2.5 |
| | 13 | 3.0 | 1.0 | | | | | | | | | 4.0 |
| | 14 | 3.5 | 1.5 | 1.0 | 1.0 | | | | | | | 7.0 |
| | 15 | 3.5 | 2.0 | 1.5 | 1.5 | 1.0 | | | | | | 9.5 |
| | 16 | 3.5 | 2.5 | 2.0 | 2.0 | 1.5 | 1.0 | | | | | 12.5 |
| | 17 | 3.5 | 3.0 | 2.5 | 2.5 | 1.5 | 1.5 | 1.0 | 1.0 | | | 16.5 |
| | 18 | 3.5 | 3.5 | 3.0 | 2.5 | 2.0 | 2.0 | 1.5 | 1.5 | 1.0 | | 20.5 |
| | 19 | 3.5 | 3.5 | 3.0 | 2.5 | 2.5 | 2.5 | 2.0 | 2.0 | 1.0 | 1.0 | 23.5 |
| | 20 | 3.5 | 3.5 | 3.0 | 2.5 | 2.5 | 2.5 | 2.5 | 2.5 | 1.0 | 1.5 | 25.0 |
| 3 | 21 | 3.5 | 3.5 | 3.0 | 2.5 | 2.5 | 2.5 | 2.5 | 2.5 | 1.0 | 1.5 | 25.0 |
| | 22 | 3.5 | 3.5 | 3.0 | 2.5 | 2.5 | 2.5 | 2.5 | 2.5 | 1.0 | 1.5 | 25.0 |
| | 23 | 3.5 | 3.5 | 3.0 | 2.5 | 2.5 | 2.5 | 2.5 | 2.5 | 1.0 | 1.5 | 25.0 |
| | 24 | 3.5 | 3.5 | 3.0 | 2.5 | 2.5 | 2.5 | 2.5 | 2.5 | 1.0 | 1.5 | 25.0 |
| | 25 | 3.5 | 3.5 | 3.0 | 2.5 | 2.5 | 2.5 | 2.5 | 2.5 | 1.0 | 1.5 | 25.0 |
| | 26 | 3.5 | 3.5 | 3.0 | 2.5 | 2.5 | 2.5 | 2.5 | 2.5 | 1.0 | 1.5 | 25.0 |
| | 27 | 3.5 | 3.5 | 3.0 | 2.5 | 2.5 | 2.5 | 2.5 | 2.5 | 1.0 | 1.5 | 25.0 |
| | 28 | 3.5 | 3.5 | 3.0 | 2.5 | 2.5 | 2.5 | 2.5 | 2.5 | 1.0 | 1.5 | 25.0 |
| | 29 | 3.5 | 3.5 | 3.0 | 2.5 | 2.5 | 2.5 | 2.5 | 2.5 | 1.0 | 1.5 | 25.0 |
| | 30 | 3.5 | 3.5 | 3.0 | 2.5 | 2.5 | 2.5 | 2.5 | 2.5 | 1.0 | 1.5 | 25.0 |

**Assumptions**

Assume each region needs an additional 0.5 FTE administrator for every Vernal center in that region when there are two or more centers in a region. Administrators would provide accounting and payroll services and coordinate cooperation between the centers.

# Figure B.18: Possible Total Number of Vernal Staffmembers Needed Each Year

| Phase | Year | Num. of Students Enrolled | Total Sessions | Operational Vernal Centers | Staffmembers - Number of Full-Time Equivalent Required (Facilitate, Administrate, Hire/Prepare New Staff) | | | | | | |
|---|---|---|---|---|---|---|---|---|---|---|---|
| | | | | | Team Staff | Region Admin. | New Staff Preparers | Total Paid Staff | New Staff Needed | Avail. Vernal Grads | Required from Outside |
| D1 | | | | | 0.5 | | | 0.5 | 0.5 | | 0.5 |
| D2 | P-1 | 30 | 0.2 | | 1.0 | | | 1.0 | 0.5 | | 0.5 |
| | P-2 | 30 | 0.2 | | 2.0 | | | 2.0 | 1.0 | | 1.0 |
| | P-3 | 30 | 0.5 | | 2.5 | | | 2.5 | 0.5 | | 0.5 |
| 1 | 1 | 30 | 1 | 1 | 3.0 | | | 3.0 | 0.5 | | 0.5 |
| | 2 | 30 | 1 | 1 | 3.0 | | | 3.0 | 0.0 | | 0.0 |
| | 3 | 60 | 2 | 1 | 3.0 | | | 3.0 | 0.0 | | 0.0 |
| | 4 | 90 | 3 | 1 | 4.0 | | | 4.0 | 1.0 | | 1.0 |
| | 5 | 120 | 4 | 1 | 4.0 | | 1.0 | 5.0 | 2.0 | 1.0 | 1.0 |
| 2 | 6 | 150 | 5 | 2 | 7.0 | | 1.0 | 8.0 | 3.5 | 1.0 | 2.5 |
| | 7 | 180 | 6 | 3 | 10.0 | | 1.0 | 11.0 | 3.5 | 2.0 | 1.5 |
| | 8 | 240 | 8 | 4 | 13.0 | | 1.0 | 14.0 | 3.5 | 3.0 | 0.5 |
| | 9 | 390 | 13 | 6 | 21.0 | 1.0 | 2.0 | 24.0 | 10.5 | 4.0 | 6.5 |
| | 10 | 630 | 21 | 8 | 29.0 | 1.5 | 2.0 | 32.5 | 10.0 | 5.0 | 5.0 |
| | 11 | 870 | 29 | 10 | 37.0 | 2.0 | 2.0 | 41.0 | 10.5 | 6.0 | 4.5 |
| | 12 | 1,110 | 37 | 12 | 45.0 | 2.5 | 2.0 | 49.5 | 11.0 | 9.0 | 2.0 |
| | 13 | 1,440 | 48 | 15 | 57.0 | 4.0 | 3.0 | 64.0 | 19.0 | 14.0 | 5.0 |
| | 14 | 1,950 | 65 | 20 | 78.0 | 7.0 | 3.0 | 88.0 | 30.0 | 21.0 | 9.0 |
| | 15 | 2,550 | 85 | 24 | 95.0 | 9.5 | 3.0 | 107.5 | 27.0 | 29.0 | — |
| | 16 | 3,150 | 105 | 29 | 116.0 | 12.5 | 4.0 | 132.5 | 34.0 | 38.0 | — |
| | 17 | 3,840 | 128 | 35 | 140.0 | 16.5 | 5.0 | 161.5 | 41.0 | 50.0 | — |
| | 18 | 4,620 | 154 | 42 | 168.0 | 20.5 | 5.0 | 193.5 | 48.0 | 66.0 | — |
| | 19 | 5,340 | 178 | 47 | 188.0 | 23.5 | 5.0 | 216.5 | 42.5 | 85.0 | — |
| | 20 | 5,820 | 194 | 50 | 200.0 | 25.0 | 4.0 | 229.0 | 36.5 | 106.0 | — |
| 3 | 21 | 6,000 | 200 | 50 | 200.0 | 25.0 | 4.0 | 229.0 | 30.0 | 129.0 | — |
| | 22 | 6,000 | 200 | 50 | 200.0 | 25.0 | 4.0 | 229.0 | 36.0 | 153.0 | — |
| | 23 | 6,000 | 200 | 50 | 200.0 | 25.0 | 4.0 | 229.0 | 38.5 | 175.0 | — |
| | 24 | 6,000 | 200 | 50 | 200.0 | 25.0 | 4.0 | 229.0 | 40.5 | 190.0 | — |
| | 25 | 6,000 | 200 | 50 | 200.0 | 25.0 | 4.0 | 229.0 | 39.5 | 198.0 | — |
| | 26 | 6,000 | 200 | 50 | 200.0 | 25.0 | 4.0 | 229.0 | 38.5 | 200.0 | — |
| | 27 | 6,000 | 200 | 50 | 200.0 | 25.0 | 4.0 | 229.0 | 36.5 | 200.0 | — |
| | 28 | 6,000 | 200 | 50 | 200.0 | 25.0 | 4.0 | 229.0 | 36.5 | 200.0 | — |
| | 29 | 6,000 | 200 | 50 | 200.0 | 25.0 | 4.0 | 229.0 | 37.0 | 200.0 | — |
| | 30 | 6,000 | 200 | 50 | 200.0 | 25.0 | 4.0 | 229.0 | 38.5 | 200.0 | — |
| Total for first 30 years | | 92,610 | 3,087 | | | | | | 705.5 | 2,285.0 | 39.0 |

**Note**: The last year of Phase D1 and all 3 years of Phase D2 are shown here, but are not included in the totals.

**Assumptions**

Assume that for every 10 (or so) new staffmembers hired in a year, there is a new staff preparer to help hire, prepare, and support them.

Assume that staffmembers work for 6 years (±2 years) and then retire or move on to other work.

Assume that 4±1 years after each session, one graduate from that session is available to become a staffmember.

**Assumptions about the Development Phases**

Even though there would be only a single ten-day workshop in Years Prep-1 and Prep-2 and a six-month pilot session in Year Prep-3, assume that preparing for these workshops and for the rest of the project requires staffing at the levels shown.

# C

# Appendix C: Even More Figures

This Appendix contains additional figures that show in greater detail how the Vernal Project might contribute to societal transformation. These figures mostly relate to items discussed in Chapters 7 and 9.

how many of the graduates from this year would still be very active in the year indicated at the left.

Moving down a column, the total number of very active graduates of Vernal sessions held in that year decreases until every graduate becomes less active. The sum across each row is then the total number of Vernal graduates from all sessions who would be very active in that year. This total is shown at the right side of the Figure.

Figure C.2 calculates the same numbers for the optimistic scenario.

Figure C.3 summarizes these counts for all sixty years of the Vernal Project and the ten years after it ends. This figure shows the number of Vernal students, very active graduates, and less active graduates for both the baseline and optimistic scenarios.[*]

*(Text continues on page 274)*

## THE NUMBER OF VERNAL GRADUATES

Figure C.1 calculates the number of Vernal graduates who would be very active each year for the first thirty years of the Vernal Project. It uses the baseline assumptions about the rate that graduates would become less active from Figure 7.2 and the number of total sessions that would be facilitated each year from Figure B.13.

Each column tracks the Vernal students who would enroll in all the Vernal sessions that would begin in the year shown at the top of the column. The total number of students enrolled in that year is shown in italics as the first entry in each column. The entries in each row below shows

---

[*] Note that the number of less active graduates shown in Figure C.3 is somewhat smaller than the values shown in Figures C.1 and C.2. In Figure C.3, I have assumed that Vernal graduates eventually either drift away from fundamental progressive change or grow old and die. To model this process, I have used a stepped schedule that roughly follows a Normal curve with a mean of twenty-five years and a standard deviation of seven years. One year after graduating, I assume that 0.1% of the graduates would no longer be doing any kind of work for fundamental progressive change. Seven years after graduating, I assume that another 1.5% would stop, thirteen years after graduating, I assume another 8.3% would stop, nineteen years after graduating, I assume another 23.5% would stop, and so on according to the schedule shown at the bottom of the figure. According to this schedule, forty-nine years after graduating from a Vernal session, all of the graduates would have drifted away or died.

# Figure C.1: Very Active Graduates in Each

Year that Session Begins

| Vern Year | 1 | 2 | 3 | 4 | 5 | 6 | 7 | 8 | 9 | 10 | 11 | 12 | 13 | 14 | 15 | 16 | 17 | 18 | 19 | 20 |
|---|---|---|---|---|---|---|---|---|---|---|---|---|---|---|---|---|---|---|---|---|
| **Number of Vernal Sessions Beginning in this Year** | 1 | 1 | 2 | 3 | 4 | 5 | 6 | 8 | 13 | 21 | 29 | 37 | 48 | 65 | 85 | 105 | 128 | 154 | 178 | 194 |
| 1 | *30* | | | | | | | | | | | | | | | | | | | |
| 2 | 26 | *30* | | | | | | | | | | | | | | | | | | |
| 3 | 22 | 26 | *60* | | | | | | | | | | | | | | | | | |
| 4 | 19 | 22 | 52 | *90* | | | | | | | | | | | | | | | | |
| 5 | 16 | 19 | 44 | 78 | *120* | | | | | | | | | | | | | | | |
| 6 | 13 | 16 | 38 | 66 | 104 | *150* | | | | | | | | | | | | | | |
| 7 | 11 | 13 | 32 | 57 | 88 | 130 | *180* | | | | | | | | | | | | | |
| 8 | 9 | 11 | 26 | 48 | 76 | 110 | 156 | *240* | | | | | | | | | | | | |
| 9 | 7 | 9 | 22 | 39 | 64 | 95 | 132 | 208 | *390* | | | | | | | | | | | |
| 10 | 2 | 7 | 18 | 33 | 52 | 80 | 114 | 176 | 338 | *630* | | | | | | | | | | |
| 11 | 0 | 2 | 14 | 27 | 44 | 65 | 96 | 152 | 286 | 546 | *870* | | | | | | | | | |
| 12 | 0 | 0 | 4 | 21 | 36 | 55 | 78 | 128 | 247 | 462 | 754 | *1,110* | | | | | | | | |
| 13 | 0 | 0 | 0 | 6 | 28 | 45 | 66 | 104 | 208 | 399 | 638 | 962 | *1,440* | | | | | | | |
| 14 | 0 | 0 | 0 | 0 | 8 | 35 | 54 | 88 | 169 | 336 | 551 | 814 | 1,248 | *1,950* | | | | | | |
| 15 | 0 | 0 | 0 | 0 | 0 | 10 | 42 | 72 | 143 | 273 | 464 | 703 | 1,056 | 1,690 | *2,550* | | | | | |
| 16 | | 0 | 0 | 0 | 0 | 0 | 12 | 56 | 117 | 231 | 377 | 592 | 912 | 1,430 | 2,210 | *3,150* | | | | |
| 17 | | | 0 | 0 | 0 | 0 | 0 | 16 | 91 | 189 | 319 | 481 | 768 | 1,235 | 1,870 | 2,730 | *3,840* | | | |
| 18 | | | | 0 | 0 | 0 | 0 | 0 | 26 | 147 | 261 | 407 | 624 | 1,040 | 1,615 | 2,310 | 3,328 | *4,620* | | |
| 19 | | | | | 0 | 0 | 0 | 0 | 0 | 42 | 203 | 333 | 528 | 845 | 1,360 | 1,995 | 2,816 | 4,004 | *5,340* | |
| 20 | | | | | | 0 | 0 | 0 | 0 | 0 | 58 | 259 | 432 | 715 | 1,105 | 1,680 | 2,432 | 3,388 | 4,628 | *5,820* |
| 21 | | | | | | | 0 | 0 | 0 | 0 | 0 | 74 | 336 | 585 | 935 | 1,365 | 2,048 | 2,926 | 3,916 | 5,044 |
| 22 | | | | | | | | 0 | 0 | 0 | 0 | 0 | 96 | 455 | 765 | 1,155 | 1,664 | 2,464 | 3,382 | 4,268 |
| 23 | | | | | | | | | 0 | 0 | 0 | 0 | 0 | 130 | 595 | 945 | 1,408 | 2,002 | 2,848 | 3,686 |
| 24 | | | | | | | | | | 0 | 0 | 0 | 0 | 0 | 170 | 735 | 1,152 | 1,694 | 2,314 | 3,104 |
| 25 | | | | | | | | | | | 0 | 0 | 0 | 0 | 0 | 210 | 896 | 1,386 | 1,958 | 2,522 |
| 26 | | | | | | | | | | | | 0 | 0 | 0 | 0 | 0 | 256 | 1,078 | 1,602 | 2,134 |
| 27 | | | | | | | | | | | | | 0 | 0 | 0 | 0 | 0 | 308 | 1,246 | 1,746 |
| 28 | | | | | | | | | | | | | | 0 | 0 | 0 | 0 | 0 | 356 | 1,358 |
| 29 | | | | | | | | | | | | | | | 0 | 0 | 0 | 0 | 0 | 388 |
| 30 | | | | | | | | | | | | | | | | 0 | 0 | 0 | 0 | 0 |
| 31 | | | | | | | | | | | | | | | | | 0 | 0 | 0 | 0 |

**Notes**:

    Numbers in each column represent the number of Vernal graduates who would attend a Vernal session in the year shown in the top row who would continue to remain very active in the year shown in the column to the left.

    Each row represents the number of Vernal graduates from all years who would be very active in the year shown in the first column.

    The number of enrolled Vernal students is shown in italics.

# Figure C.2: Very Active Graduates in Each

**Note**: To conserve space, this figure is not printed here. It can be found at <http://www.vernalproject.org>.

# Year, All Regions — Baseline Scenario

| 21 | 22 | 23 | 24 | 25 | 26 | 27 | 28 | 29 | 30 | 31 | Number of Students | Num. of Very Act Grads | Num. of Less Act Grads | Total | Sessions Begun to Date |
|---|---|---|---|---|---|---|---|---|---|---|---|---|---|---|---|
| 200 | 200 | 200 | 200 | 200 | 200 | 200 | 200 | 200 | 200 | 200 | | | | | |
| | | | | | | | | | | | 30 | 0 | 0 | **30** | 1 |
| | | | | | | | | | | | 30 | 26 | 4 | **60** | 2 |
| | | | | | | | | | | | 60 | 48 | 12 | **120** | 4 |
| | | | | | | | | | | | 90 | 93 | 27 | **210** | 7 |
| | | | | | | | | | | | 120 | 157 | 53 | **330** | 11 |
| | | | | | | | | | | | 150 | 237 | 93 | **480** | 16 |
| | | | | | | | | | | | 180 | 331 | 149 | **660** | 22 |
| | | | | | | | | | | | 240 | 436 | 224 | **900** | 30 |
| | | | | | | | | | | | 390 | 576 | 324 | **1,290** | 43 |
| | | | | | | | | | | | 630 | 820 | 470 | **1,920** | 64 |
| | | | | | | | | | | | 870 | 1,232 | 688 | **2,790** | 93 |
| | | | | | | | | | | | 1,110 | 1,785 | 1,005 | **3,900** | 130 |
| | | | | | | | | | | | 1,440 | 2,456 | 1,444 | **5,340** | 178 |
| | | | | | | | | | | | 1,950 | 3,303 | 2,037 | **7,290** | 243 |
| | | | | | | | | | | | 2,550 | 4,453 | 2,837 | **9,840** | 328 |
| | | | | | | | | | | | 3,150 | 5,937 | 3,903 | **12,990** | 433 |
| | | | | | | | | | | | 3,840 | 7,699 | 5,291 | **16,830** | 561 |
| | | | | | | | | | | | 4,620 | 9,758 | 7,072 | **21,450** | 715 |
| | | | | | | | | | | | 5,340 | 12,126 | 9,324 | **26,790** | 893 |
| | | | | | | | | | | | 5,820 | 14,697 | 12,093 | **32,610** | 1,087 |
| 6,000 | | | | | | | | | | | 6,000 | 17,229 | 15,381 | **38,610** | 1,287 |
| 5,200 | 6,000 | | | | | | | | | | 6,000 | 19,449 | 19,161 | **44,610** | 1,487 |
| 4,400 | 5,200 | 6,000 | | | | | | | | | 6,000 | 21,214 | 23,396 | **50,610** | 1,687 |
| 3,800 | 4,400 | 5,200 | 6,000 | | | | | | | | 6,000 | 22,569 | 28,041 | **56,610** | 1,887 |
| 3,200 | 3,800 | 4,400 | 5,200 | 6,000 | | | | | | | 6,000 | 23,572 | 33,038 | **62,610** | 2,087 |
| 2,600 | 3,200 | 3,800 | 4,400 | 5,200 | 6,000 | | | | | | 6,000 | 24,270 | 38,340 | **68,610** | 2,287 |
| 2,200 | 2,600 | 3,200 | 3,800 | 4,400 | 5,200 | 6,000 | | | | | 6,000 | 24,700 | 43,910 | **74,610** | 2,487 |
| 1,800 | 2,200 | 2,600 | 3,200 | 3,800 | 4,400 | 5,200 | 6,000 | | | | 6,000 | 24,914 | 49,696 | **80,610** | 2,687 |
| 1,400 | 1,800 | 2,200 | 2,600 | 3,200 | 3,800 | 4,400 | 5,200 | 6,000 | | | 6,000 | 24,988 | 55,622 | **86,610** | 2,887 |
| 400 | 1,400 | 1,800 | 2,200 | 2,600 | 3,200 | 3,800 | 4,400 | 5,200 | 6,000 | | 6,000 | 25,000 | 61,610 | **92,610** | 3,087 |
| 0 | 400 | 1,400 | 1,800 | 2,200 | 2,600 | 3,200 | 3,800 | 4,400 | 5,200 | 6,000 | 6,000 | 25,000 | 67,580 | **98,580** | 3,287 |

# Year, All Regions — Optimistic Scenario

# Figure C.3: Summary of the Number of Vernal Activists

| Phase | Vernal Year | Total Students and Graduates | Baseline Scenario | | | Optimistic Scenario | | |
|---|---|---|---|---|---|---|---|---|
| | | | Number of Students | Number of Very Active Graduates | Number of Less Active Graduates | Number of Students | Number of Very Active Graduates | Number of Less Active Graduates |
| 1 | 1 | 30 | 30 | 0 | 0 | 30 | 0 | 0 |
| | 2 | 60 | 30 | 26 | 4 | 30 | 28 | 2 |
| | 3 | 120 | 60 | 48 | 12 | 60 | 55 | 5 |
| | 4 | 210 | 90 | 93 | 27 | 90 | 109 | 11 |
| | 5 | 330 | 120 | 157 | 53 | 120 | 189 | 21 |
| 2 | 6 | 480 | 150 | 237 | 93 | 150 | 293 | 37 |
| | 7 | 660 | 180 | 331 | 149 | 180 | 421 | 59 |
| | 8 | 900 | 240 | 436 | 224 | 240 | 571 | 89 |
| | 9 | 1,289 | 390 | 576 | 323 | 390 | 770 | 129 |
| | 10 | 1,918 | 630 | 820 | 468 | 630 | 1,091 | 197 |
| | 11 | 2,787 | 870 | 1,232 | 685 | 870 | 1,621 | 296 |
| | 12 | 3,895 | 1,110 | 1,785 | 1,000 | 1,110 | 2,343 | 442 |
| | 13 | 5,332 | 1,440 | 2,456 | 1,436 | 1,440 | 3,247 | 645 |
| | 14 | 7,279 | 1,950 | 3,303 | 2,026 | 1,950 | 4,406 | 923 |
| | 15 | 9,822 | 2,550 | 4,453 | 2,819 | 2,550 | 5,973 | 1,299 |
| | 16 | 12,964 | 3,150 | 5,937 | 3,877 | 3,150 | 8,014 | 1,800 |
| | 17 | 16,791 | 3,840 | 7,699 | 5,252 | 3,840 | 10,502 | 2,449 |
| | 18 | 21,391 | 4,620 | 9,758 | 7,013 | 4,620 | 13,469 | 3,302 |
| | 19 | 26,704 | 5,340 | 12,126 | 9,238 | 5,340 | 16,940 | 4,424 |
| | 20 | 32,490 | 5,820 | 14,697 | 11,973 | 5,820 | 20,824 | 5,846 |
| 3 | 21 | 38,441 | 6,000 | 17,229 | 15,212 | 6,000 | 24,868 | 7,573 |
| | 22 | 44,379 | 6,000 | 19,449 | 18,930 | 6,000 | 28,744 | 9,635 |
| | 23 | 50,289 | 6,000 | 21,214 | 23,075 | 6,000 | 32,218 | 12,071 |
| | 24 | 56,162 | 6,000 | 22,569 | 27,593 | 6,000 | 35,255 | 14,907 |
| | 25 | 61,998 | 6,000 | 23,572 | 32,426 | 6,000 | 37,853 | 18,145 |
| | 26 | 67,795 | 6,000 | 24,270 | 37,525 | 6,000 | 39,994 | 21,801 |
| | 27 | 73,537 | 6,000 | 24,700 | 42,837 | 6,000 | 41,659 | 25,878 |
| | 28 | 79,216 | 6,000 | 24,914 | 48,302 | 6,000 | 42,865 | 30,351 |
| | 29 | 84,797 | 6,000 | 24,988 | 53,809 | 6,000 | 43,685 | 35,112 |
| | 30 | 90,261 | 6,000 | 25,000 | 59,261 | 6,000 | 44,230 | 40,031 |
| | 31 | 95,602 | 6,000 | 25,000 | 64,602 | 6,000 | 44,594 | 45,008 |
| | 32 | 100,812 | 6,000 | 25,000 | 69,812 | 6,000 | 44,818 | 49,994 |
| | 33 | 105,868 | 6,000 | 25,000 | 74,868 | 6,000 | 44,938 | 54,930 |
| | 34 | 110,744 | 6,000 | 25,000 | 79,744 | 6,000 | 44,988 | 59,756 |
| | 35 | 115,407 | 6,000 | 25,000 | 84,407 | 6,000 | 45,000 | 64,407 |
| | 36 | 119,842 | 6,000 | 25,000 | 88,842 | 6,000 | 45,000 | 68,842 |
| | 37 | 124,029 | 6,000 | 25,000 | 93,029 | 6,000 | 45,000 | 73,029 |
| | 38 | 127,945 | 6,000 | 25,000 | 96,945 | 6,000 | 45,000 | 76,945 |
| | 39 | 131,573 | 6,000 | 25,000 | 100,573 | 6,000 | 45,000 | 80,573 |
| | 40 | 134,905 | 6,000 | 25,000 | 103,905 | 6,000 | 45,000 | 83,905 |
| | 41 | 137,958 | 6,000 | 25,000 | 106,958 | 6,000 | 45,000 | 86,958 |
| | 42 | 140,753 | 6,000 | 25,000 | 109,753 | 6,000 | 45,000 | 89,753 |
| | 43 | 143,260 | 6,000 | 25,000 | 112,260 | 6,000 | 45,000 | 92,260 |
| | 44 | 145,449 | 6,000 | 25,000 | 114,449 | 6,000 | 45,000 | 94,449 |
| | 45 | 147,318 | 6,000 | 25,000 | 116,318 | 6,000 | 45,000 | 96,318 |
| | 46 | 148,903 | 6,000 | 25,000 | 117,903 | 6,000 | 45,000 | 97,903 |
| | 47 | 150,274 | 6,000 | 25,000 | 119,274 | 6,000 | 45,000 | 99,274 |
| | 48 | 151,485 | 6,000 | 25,000 | 120,485 | 6,000 | 45,000 | 100,485 |
| | 49 | 152,512 | 6,000 | 25,000 | 121,512 | 6,000 | 45,000 | 101,512 |
| | 50 | 153,336 | 6,000 | 25,000 | 122,336 | 6,000 | 45,000 | 102,336 |

*(continued on next page)*

# Figure C.3 (continued)

| Phase | Vernal Year | Total Students and Graduates | Baseline Scenario | | | Optimistic Scenario | | |
|---|---|---|---|---|---|---|---|---|
| | | | Number of Students | Number of Very Active Graduates | Number of Less Active Graduates | Number of Students | Number of Very Active Graduates | Number of Less Active Graduates |
| 3 (cont.) | 51 | 153,963 | 6,000 | 25,000 | 122,963 | 6,000 | 45,000 | 102,963 |
| | 52 | 154,434 | 6,000 | 25,000 | 123,434 | 6,000 | 45,000 | 103,434 |
| | 53 | 154,810 | 6,000 | 25,000 | 123,810 | 6,000 | 45,000 | 103,810 |
| | 54 | 155,133 | 6,000 | 25,000 | 124,133 | 6,000 | 45,000 | 104,133 |
| | 55 | 155,395 | 6,000 | 25,000 | 124,395 | 6,000 | 45,000 | 104,395 |
| | 56 | 155,589 | 6,000 | 25,000 | 124,589 | 6,000 | 45,000 | 104,589 |
| | 57 | 155,718 | 6,000 | 25,000 | 124,718 | 6,000 | 45,000 | 104,718 |
| | 58 | 155,800 | 6,000 | 25,000 | 124,800 | 6,000 | 45,000 | 104,800 |
| | 59 | 155,857 | 6,000 | 25,000 | 124,857 | 6,000 | 45,000 | 104,857 |
| | 60 | 155,905 | 6,000 | 25,000 | 124,905 | 6,000 | 45,000 | 104,905 |
| End | 61 | 149,943 | 0 | 25,000 | 124,943 | 0 | 45,000 | 104,943 |
| | 62 | 143,968 | 0 | 19,800 | 124,168 | 0 | 39,400 | 104,568 |
| | 63 | 137,989 | 0 | 15,400 | 122,589 | 0 | 34,000 | 103,989 |
| | 64 | 132,001 | 0 | 11,600 | 120,401 | 0 | 28,800 | 103,201 |
| | 65 | 126,011 | 0 | 8,400 | 117,611 | 0 | 23,800 | 102,211 |
| | 66 | 120,020 | 0 | 5,800 | 114,220 | 0 | 19,200 | 100,820 |
| | 67 | 114,028 | 0 | 3,600 | 110,428 | 0 | 14,800 | 99,228 |
| | 68 | 108,035 | 0 | 1,800 | 106,235 | 0 | 10,600 | 97,435 |
| | 69 | 102,132 | 0 | 400 | 101,732 | 0 | 6,600 | 95,532 |
| | 70 | 96,228 | 0 | 0 | 96,228 | 0 | 4,600 | 91,628 |
| **Total in** | | | | | | | | |
| Phase 1 (Year 1 - 5) | | | 330 | | | 330 | | |
| Phase 2 (Year 6 - 20) | | | 32,280 | | | 32,280 | | |
| Phase 3 (Year 21 - 60) | | | 240,000 | | | 240,000 | | |
| Whole Project (1 - 60) | | | 272,610 | | | 272,610 | | |
| Main Struggle (31 - 60) | | | 180,000 | | | 180,000 | | |
| **Average in** | | | | | | | | |
| Phase 1 (Year 1 - 5) | | | 66 | 65 | 19 | 66 | 76 | 8 |
| Phase 2 (Year 6 - 20) | | | 2,152 | 4,390 | 3,105 | 2,152 | 6,032 | 1,462 |
| Phase 3 (Year 21 - 60) | | | 6,000 | 24,448 | 90,489 | 6,000 | 43,018 | 71,919 |
| Whole Project (1 - 60) | | | 4,544 | 17,401 | 61,104 | 4,544 | 30,193 | 48,312 |
| Main Struggle (31 - 60) | | | 6,000 | 25,000 | 108,686 | 6,000 | 44,978 | 88,708 |

**Assumptions**:

Assume all Vernal graduates die or drift away from fundamental progressive social change (and are therefore no longer included in any of these categories) according to the stepped schedule below. This schedule roughly corresponds to a Normal curve with a mean of twenty-five years and a standard deviation of seven years.

| Years After Graduating | Percent Who Die or Drift Away |
|---|---|
| 1 | 0.1 % |
| 7 | 1.5 % |
| 13 | 8.3 % |
| 19 | 23.5 % |
| 25 | 33.2 % |
| 31 | 23.5 % |
| 37 | 8.3 % |
| 43 | 1.5 % |
| 49 | 0.1 % |
| | 100.0 % |

In the baseline scenario, the number of very active graduates would rise to 25,000 by Vernal Year 30 and would remain at that same level until the Project ended. In the optimistic scenario, the number of very active graduates would rise to 45,000 in Vernal Year 35 and would remain constant until the end of the Project.

In the baseline scenario, during Phase 3 of the Vernal Project (Years 21 to 60), there would be an average of 6,000 Vernal students, 24,448 very active graduates, and 90,489 less active graduates. In the optimistic scenario, more of the graduates would be very active (43,018) and fewer would be less active (71,919).

## AMOUNT OF EFFORT DIRECTED TOWARD FUNDAMENTAL PROGRESSIVE CHANGE

*How many people now work for progressive change and how much work do they do? How much of their effort moves society towards fundamental transformation? How much additional work might Vernal activists contribute to fundamental progressive change?*

Estimating these quantities is extremely difficult. There is no way to define specifically what constitutes fundamental progressive change work, and there is no way to determine how many people now spend time doing this work. Speculating how these values would change in the future is even more difficult.

However, to ensure that the Vernal Project would be worthwhile, I have done my best to define some categories and to make some rough estimates of total change effort. First, I estimate how many people are really progressive social change activists. Then I estimate how many of these activists are working for fundamental progressive change.[1]

### Current Efforts

Most people in our society are goodhearted and compassionately help their neighbors and friends. Their civility and kindness lifts society up and makes life bearable. But typically their efforts are narrowly restricted to their family and close personal friends. Their generosity does not extend to strangers or even to acquaintances.

Only a portion of the population is concerned about the world as a whole and desires a better life for everyone. I estimate that only about one-fourth of the U.S. population (perhaps fifty million adults) consider themselves progressive in this way. Moreover, many of these people, though well intentioned, actually do little work to create a better society. They may identify with progressive ideals and sympathize with progressive causes, but they do not make any effort to bring about change.

Those who actually do the bulk of the work of making the world a better place include enlightened parents, progressive childcare workers, progressive teachers, social work-

ers, benevolent clergypeople, employees of progressive non-profit agencies, benevolent doctors and nurses, progressive labor unionists, enlightened businesspeople, and liberal legislators. But much of their socially oriented effort typically fits in the category of social *service* work: teaching skills, repairing damage to the natural environment, and assisting those who need help — children, uneducated adults, the aged, poor people, disabled people, and those afflicted with illness or emotional problems.

Social service work is, of course, absolutely essential in a good society. It helps the recipients of the aid to have better lives, encourages the givers of aid to be more open to living and working with other people, and generally makes society more civil. However, social service work typically does not address situations in which our current societal structures injure, stymie, or retard people. This work does not challenge the power structure or alter oppressive institutions. It does not demand democracy or justice. It does not embolden people to resist oppression or defy the elite. It helps people only as much as the current political, economic, cultural, and social structures allow. So typically, only a small portion of the benevolent work these concerned people perform really brings about progressive *change*.

And unfortunately, of the actual progressive change work people do perform, a significant portion is typically channeled into shallow reform measures or into measures that help one oppressed group at the expense of another. For example, activists advocating on behalf of the poor, when confronted by obstinate legislators, may accept a deal in which funds that were previously earmarked for children's programs would instead be steered to job training. Because of this shift of funds, one oppressed

*Sorry, we are too busy mopping the floor to turn off the faucet.*
— Office Graffiti

group (poor people) would benefit, but another oppressed group (children) would suffer. The political system that imposed this ugly tradeoff would remain untouched. Considering that these kinds of deals are quite common, only a small percentage of change work really gets to the roots of problems and *fundamentally* restructures basic political, economic, social, or cultural institutions.

Even social change organizations dedicated to fundamental progressive change spend a great deal of their time convincing and cajoling their supporters to donate money to their organization rather than actually working for change. This effort is absolutely essential to ensure the continued existence of these important organizations, but it is not social change work.

Furthermore, many people who do some progressive work also support anti-progressive measures out of ignorance or necessity. For example, when war fever is rampant, many progressive activists accept — and sometimes actively support — military intervention. Also, when faced with a choice between furthering the common good and increasing their own personal gain, many activists opt for their own

# Figure C.4: Estimate of the Number of Activists Working for Fundamental Progressive Change, Now and in Vernal Phase 3

| | Hours of Work per Week | | Now | | | Vernal Project Phase 3 (Vernal Project Year 40) | | | Ratio Phase 3 / Now | |
|---|---|---|---|---|---|---|---|---|---|---|
| | Range | Avg. | Number of People | Total Hours Per Week of Work | % of Hrs Contribtd by this Group | Number of People | Total Hours Per Week Of Work | % of Hrs Contribtd by this Group | Num. | Hrs |
| **Very Active Vernal Grads** | 36 – 45 | 40 | | | | 5,000 | 200,000 | 5.2 % | | |
| | 25 – 35 | 30 | | | | 5,000 | 150,000 | 3.9 % | | |
| | 20 – 24 | 22 | | | | 15,000 | 330,000 | 8.5 % | | |
| **Total** | | | | | | 25,000 | 680,000 | 17.6 % | ∞ | ∞ |
| **Other Steadfast Activists*** | 36 – 60 | 45 | 5,000 | 225,000 | 21.2 % | 15,000 | 675,000 | 17.5 % | 3.0 | 3.0 |
| | 15 – 35 | 25 | 8,000 | 200,000 | 18.9 % | 24,000 | 600,000 | 15.5 % | 3.0 | 3.0 |
| | 8 – 14 | 10 | 10,000 | 100,000 | 9.4 % | 30,000 | 300,000 | 7.8 % | 3.0 | 3.0 |
| | 3 – 7 | 5 | 27,000 | 135,000 | 12.7 % | 81,000 | 405,000 | 10.5 % | 3.0 | 3.0 |
| **Total** | | | 50,000 | 660,000 | 62.3 % | 150,000 | 1,980,000 | 51.3 % | 3.0 | 3.0 |
| **Progressive Advocates*** | 1.5 – 2.9 | 2 | 100,000 | 200,000 | 18.9 % | 300,000 | 600,000 | 15.5 % | 3.0 | 3.0 |
| | 0.2 – 1.4 | 1 | 200,000 | 200,000 | 18.9 % | 600,000 | 600,000 | 15.5 % | 3.0 | 3.0 |
| **Total** | | | 300,000 | 400,000 | 37.7 % | 900,000 | 1,200,000 | 31.1 % | 3.0 | 3.0 |
| **Grand Total** | | | 350,000 | 1,060,000 | 100.0 % | 1,075,000 | 3,860,000 | 100.0 % | 3.1 | 3.6 |

**Notes**:

(1) Activists working for fundamental progressive change include social workers, clergypeople, labor activists, and others.

(2) The part-time figures include the time that full-time activists spend working for fundamental progressive change. Few full-time activists can work full-time for fundamental progressive change — even those who mostly adhere to progressive ideals usually spend some of their time doing fundraising or working on moderate reforms.

(3) By the middle of Vernal Phase 3 (Vernal Year 40), I assume there would be enough additional money available to pay 15,000 more activists to work full-time for fundamental change. Here, I assume that 5,000 of these full-time activists would be very active Vernal graduates and 10,000 would be other steadfast activists

* Note: Many of the steadfast activists and progressive advocates would likely be Vernal students or less active graduates.

benefit. And just to live their lives, progressive activists must engage in some anti-progressive behavior.*

Overall, based on my experience and research, I estimate that only about 350,000 people (about one-sixth of one percent of adults in the United States) do a substantial amount of work (more than a few hours each year) for fundamental progressive change. This represents an average of

about 800 people in each Congressional District.† Of this number, I estimate only 50,000 steadfast activists work three or more hours each week for fundamental progressive transformation — an average of 115 per Congressional District.

The left-hand side of Figure C.4 shows my specific estimates of the number of activists who now work a particular number of hours each week for fundamental change. For example, the fifth row in the table specifies that 5,000 activists (an average of eleven in each Congressional District) now work between 36 and 60 hours each week. Assuming

---

* All of us who work for fundamental progressive change inadvertently support the status quo in various ways. We buy products from obnoxious companies, we pay rent to reactionary landlords, we pollute the environment with our cars, we vote for moderate politicians who have a chance of winning instead of more progressive candidates who cannot, and so on. Our progressive efforts are therefore offset to some extent by our anti-progressive efforts.

† Right now, of course, some CDs exceed the average and have many times this number of people working for fundamental progressive change while others have only a small fraction of this number.

they average 45 hours per week, I estimate these 5,000 activists currently perform about 225,000 hours of fundamental progressive change work each week. Altogether, I assume that the 350,000 activists working for progressive change perform about one million hours of work each week directed toward fundamental progressive transformation.

## Supplemental Gain Provided by Vernal Activists

If implemented as described in this book, the Vernal Project should increase this number severalfold. As shown in the right-hand side of Figure C.4, I assume that by the middle of Vernal Project Phase 3 (Vernal Year 40), there would be 25,000 very active Vernal graduates working at least twenty hours per week for progressive change. I assume 15,000 would work 20 to 24 hours per week for fundamental change and 10,000 would work significantly more than that — some as many as 45 hours per week.* At these levels of effort, very active Vernal graduates would contribute an additional 680,000 hours per week toward fundamental social change.

With the strong support of these very active Vernal graduates and the general upsurge of various progressive social change movements they would help generate, I assume that more people would feel comfortable joining progressive change organizations. Vernal graduates would probably be able to convince their activist colleagues to spend more of their change effort working for truly fundamental transformation of society. Also, more people would likely contribute money to progressive change organizations, enabling more activists to be hired to work for change (see the next section). With all this support and encouragement, and supplemented with 6,000 Vernal students and around 100,000 less active graduates, I assume that the number of steadfast activists working three or more hours each week for fundamental change would triple from 50,000 to 150,000 and the number of progressive advocates working a few hours per week would triple from 300,000 to 900,000.†

In all, I estimate there would be about 3.1 times as many activists working for fundamental change in Vernal Year 40 as now (more than a million altogether), and they would work about 3.8 million hours each week — about 3.6 times as many as now. Since Vernal graduates would be quite knowledgeable, skilled, and experienced and they would do their best to pass their expertise on to those with whom they worked, I expect activists in this year would be significantly more effective than progressive activists today. I estimate the overall effort to bring about fundamental progressive trans-

## Figure C.5: Estimate of Monetary Contributions Made by Additional Progressive Advocates in Vernal Year 40

| Average Donation Amount/Year ($) | Number of Additional Progressive Advocates | Total Donation Amount/Year ($ million) |
|---|---|---|
| 2,500 | 50,000 | 125 |
| 1,000 | 250,000 | 250 |
| 500 | 200,000 | 100 |
| 100 | 100,000 | 10 |
| **Total** | **600,000** | **485** |

Number of full-time activists this could support at $32,000/year (for salary + benefits) =

|  |  |
|---|---|
| Nationwide | 15,156 |
| Per Congressional District (CD) | 34 |

**Note:** All figures are in 1995 dollars.

formation of society would be three or four times more powerful than it is now.‡

## MONETARY CONTRIBUTIONS OF ADDITIONAL PROGRESSIVE ADVOCATES

If my estimates are accurate, in Vernal Year 40 there would be 600,000 more progressive advocates than there are now. I assume most of these additional advocates would be very supportive of fundamental progressive change work. They would probably want to work more for change than they do but would be restricted to just a few hours each week by their jobs or their childrearing responsibilities. However, since many of these advocates would have conventional jobs or would be married to someone with a conventional job, they would probably be wealthy enough to contribute a few hundred or even a few thousand dollars each year towards support of fundamental progressive change work.§

---

* I assume, to avoid burnout, Vernal graduates would work no more than 45 hours per week for change.

† As shown in Figure C.3, I estimate there would be 6,000 Vernal students and about 104,000 less active graduates in Vernal Year 40 (a total of 110,000). So I assume in this year that about 15% of the estimated 150,000 steadfast activists (22,500) and 10% of the 900,000 progressive advocates (90,000) would be Vernal students or less active graduates.

‡ All the factors contributing to this estimate are highly uncertain. Therefore, this estimate is necessarily also extremely rough. I can imagine that even if the Vernal Project proceeded exactly as described here, the effort to bring about fundamental progressive change in Vernal Year 40 might be only twice as powerful as now or it might be as much as ten times as powerful.

§ The 100,000 additional steadfast activists in Vernal Year 40 might also contribute additional money towards fundamental change. But here, to be conservative, I have assumed that they are all relatively poor and devote all their resources to supporting themselves.

In Figure C.5, I have made estimates of the amount of money that these additional advocates might contribute. I assume that 50,000 of them would be wealthy enough to contribute an average of $2,500 each year (in 1995 dollars). I assume the rest would contribute a smaller amount. Together, I assume they would contribute about $485 million each year. This would be enough to support more than 15,000 additional full-time activists — the same number of additional full-time activists I assumed in Figure C.4 (5,000 more full-time very active Vernal graduates and 10,000 more full-time steadfast activists).

## HOW POPULATION TURNOVER CAN ACCELERATE CHANGE

Progressive social change movements that continue at a high level for decades can bring about much more change than movements that arise and then fade after just a few years. Not only are more people eventually exposed to progressive ideas, but people are also more likely to be immersed steadily in progressive values over a long period and to consistently interact with progressive institutions. This makes them much more likely to change their perspective and their activities. Once people have adopted progressive values and are living in a stable, on-going positive environment, they seldom voluntarily return to their previous hurtful ideas or switch back to oppressive conventional institutions. Furthermore, once convinced of the value of progressive alternatives, they are usually strong and consistent promoters of fundamental progressive change. So a powerful effort for fundamental progressive change, if sustained long enough, will eventually transform all of society. The natural course of population turnover can greatly accelerate this transformation process.

Over a hundred year period, the population of society turns over completely: all those alive at the beginning of the period die sometime within one hundred years, and they are supplanted by their children, grandchildren, and great-grandchildren. A completely new set of people then constitutes society. If the new generation decides to adopt entirely different norms or institutions, no one from the previous era is still around to stop them. Clearly, societal traditions and institutions endure for centuries only because young people accept and adopt the same ones as their elders.

This situation changes in a period of social upheaval and change. During the forty years of Vernal Project Phase 3, when more than a million progressive activists would be vigorously working for social change, about half of the U.S. population would die and would be replaced by the next generation. If, during this period, progressive social change movements were effective in widely raising issues and offering progressive alternatives, many young people would be exposed to and adopt alternative ideas and practices as part of their normal childhood rearing. There would be no need

to erase hurtful ideas like racism, sexism, homophobia, or self-hatred from their minds since they would never have had these ideas inculcated into them in the first place. There would be no need to persuade them of the value of progressive alternatives since they would see the advantages as they used these institutions in their everyday lives.

Today, children accept as normal such things as jet aircraft, television, computers, credit cards, fast food outlets, the military, massive corporations, mind-altering drugs, gangs, competition, and widespread poverty. In the same way, children raised in a transforming society would likely embrace honesty, cooperative businesses, co-housing, consensus decision-making, and nonviolent struggle, and prejudice, child abuse, extortion, and all other forms of oppression would repel them. Young people would easily adopt progressive alternatives without any explicit encouragement from progressive activists.

### Population Turnover

Figure C.6 shows a typical distribution of the relative number of people in the United States in each ten-year age cohort. Since people die from accidents and disease as they grow older, each age group has a smaller number of people than the previous one. The number of children under age 10 (about 13.2 percent of the population) is more than three times as large as those in their 80s (about 4.1 percent of the population). Those in their 90s constitute less than 1 percent of the population and only a handful of people are older than 100. To simplify the analysis below, I have assumed that this age distribution remains the same over the next century.

## Figure C.6: Typical Population in Each Ten-Year Age Cohort

| Age Cohort | Percent of Population |
|---|---|
| 00s | 13.2 % |
| 10s | 13.2 |
| 20s | 13.0 |
| 30s | 12.9 |
| 40s | 12.5 |
| 50s | 11.9 |
| 60s | 10.5 |
| 70s | 7.8 |
| 80s | 4.1 |
| 90s | 0.9 |
| **Total** | **100.0** |

## General Effect of Progressive Movements

When Vernal-supported progressive social movements first begin to grow in size and strength, probably only the activists' closest familymembers and friends would be exposed to the new ideas. And only a subset of those people — those who were most open to progressive ideas — would change their perspectives very much. Over time, though, more people would be exposed to progressive ideas and more would change their perspectives. As an ever-larger number of people were surrounded by other people who held progressive perspectives and who treated them with love and compassion, change would accelerate.

Children are particularly open to change. Since humans are born ignorant of the world, they must learn almost everything. So children learn constantly as they grow up. They learn from their environment, from their elders, from their peers, and from their teachers in school. As a result, children are more likely to hear new ideas than older people, and they are usually more open to adopting new ideas.

Consequently, they are more likely to be affected by massive progressive change movements.

When the children who were exposed to progressive ideas in the early years of the Vernal Project grew up and started families, many would try to relate to their own children in ways consistent with progressive ideals. They would treat their children with love and support, they would protect them from abuse, they would teach them positive ideas, and they would expose them to progressive institutions. As the number of progressive young adults rose over time, the proportion of children raised in loving, supportive families would go up, and the proportion subjected to abuse and mind-numbing oppression would go down. As these children then grew up, there would be even more adults able to think clearly and they would be even more likely to treat other people well. Fewer would be dysfunctional, anti-social, or filled with rage.

Over time, dysfunctional adults and those with rigid, conservative ideas would retire and die, while capable young people with positive perspectives would gain in number and influence. As progressives assumed greater control of soci-

## Figure C.7: Three Categories of People Based on the Amount that They are Affected by Progressive Social Change Movements

| | **Hardly Affected** | **Moderately Affected** | **Strongly Affected** |
|---|---|---|---|
| **Understanding of how society affects people** | Little or no understanding of how society shapes perspectives, how emotional and cultural conditioning constricts behavior, and how societal institutions steer lives | Some understanding or society's influence | Deep and clear understanding of society's influence |
| **Awareness and acceptance of progressive change groups, activities, and ideas** | Unaware; or aware, but feel unconnected and view progressives with disinterest, suspicion, or hostility; or aware, mildly interested, and somewhat accepting | Connected to progressive ideas and activity; aware of many progressive perspectives and find them mostly persuasive | Deeply connected to progressive ideas and activity; aware of progressive perspectives and find them very persuasive; understand and support nonviolent social change methods |
| **Desire for progressive change** | Little or no desire for progressive change | Some desire | Strong desire |
| **Efforts for progressive change** | Generally, little or no effort (though usually some effort to act ethically); firmly entrenched in conventional institutions and cultural norms | Moderate efforts to act ethically, teach children progressive ideas, vote for liberal or progressive candidates for political office, contribute small amounts of money to progressive causes, and patronize alternative institutions | Strong, active, and consistent efforts to overcome dysfunctional conditioning and emotional blocks, to live according to progressive ideals, to teach children progressive ideas, to vote for progressive politicians, to support alternative institutions, to boycott destructive enterprises, and to contribute to progressive change organizations; also some effort to campaign for progressive politicians, lobby legislators, speak out, circulate petitions, attend hearings, attend rallies, and so on * |
| **Self-label** | Conservative, moderate, or liberal | Liberal or progressive | Strong progressive |

\* Note: I assume that even at the peak of activity at the end of Phase 3 of the Vernal Project, only about a million people (0.5 percent of the adult population) would be devoting a substantial amount of effort (one hour per week or more) toward fundamental progressive change.

ety's institutions, even more people would be exposed to alternative ideas and there would be less resistance to progressive change. Change would then accelerate even more. Every year, more of the people who were born before this period of widespread progressive movements would retire and die. By Vernal Year 100, almost all of them would have died.

## Specific Numbers

Figure C.8 is an attempt to quantify this general understanding and analyze the extent to which population turnover might actually assist Vernal-supported progressive movements. For the purpose of this analysis, I have grouped people into three categories according to how much they would be affected by progressive change movements: strongly, moderately, and hardly at all. Figure C.7 describes these three categories.

In the time before Vernal Project Year 1, I assume that most people would be in the hardly-affected category. Though progressive movements have strongly affected many people over the last hundred years, poverty, war, institutional indoctrination, domestic violence, and conservative counter-movements have also strongly affected people and neutralized or undone much of the effect. As I write this, progressive movements are quite small and have limited influence. In this analysis, I assume that all progressive movements in the time before Vernal Year 1 have strongly affected only about 1 percent of the population and moderately affected about 5 percent. I assume most people (94 percent) are in the hardly-affected category. I further assume that all age cohorts have been affected to about the same degree.

For the first dozen years of the Vernal Project, I assume the Project would have minimal impact and progressive movements would have about the same limited influence they do now. However, by Vernal Project Year 15, large numbers of Vernal graduates would be actively working to support progressive movements. With this support, progressive movements would begin to grow rapidly and become highly visible and powerful. By the beginning of Vernal Phase 3 in Year 20, these movements would begin to significantly affect society. By Year 40, with twenty years of powerful and sustained effort, I assume progressive movements would have a profound effect on society, probably having at least as much impact as the progressive movements of the 1960s and 1970s. By the end of the Vernal Project in Year 60, after an unprecedented period of forty continuous years of powerful, sustained effort, I assume that progressive movements would have deeply affected all aspects of society.

## Influence on Various Age Cohorts

Those people who were oldest in Vernal Project Year 1 would likely be most set in their ways and therefore least

likely to be influenced by these progressive movements. Moreover, many of them would die before they ever talked with a progressive activist or had time to change in any way. Most people in this age group would therefore remain in the hardly-affected category for their entire lives.

Teenagers and small children in Vernal Year 1 would be more likely to be influenced since they would grow up during the first part of this period of change and would be affected throughout their lives. They would have time to absorb the ideas, change their perspectives, work through their emotional and cultural conditioning, and change their behavior. Those who were not born until Vernal Year 20 or later would be affected even more, especially since their parents might have already been influenced before they were born — some might be strongly affected by their parents beginning when they are toddlers. Even more of these later generations would be affected as they moved into their teen years and were exposed to ideas in school and from the news media. Consequently, a much larger proportion of young people would be affected than of older people. As time passed, those born later, and influenced more, would constitute an ever larger proportion of society.

I have quantified these tendencies in columns 11 to 22 of Figure C.8 using specific values that seem reasonable.* For example, consider those who would be 20 to 29 years old in Vernal Project Year 1 (the lower of the two shaded rows in the figure). I have assumed that by Vernal Year 21 when they were in their forties and constituted 12.5 percent of the total population, only 1 percent would be strongly affected by progressive movements, 5 percent would be moderately affected, and 94 percent would be hardly affected — the same values as if the Vernal Project did not exist.

Only later, after twenty years of powerful progressive change movement activity supported by Vernal activists, would they be affected to any degree, and they would still be only minimally affected. In Vernal Year 41 when they were in their sixties and constituted 10.5 percent of the total population, I assume just 12 percent of them would be strongly affected. I assume 32 percent would be moderately affected, and 56 percent would be hardly affected. By Vernal Year 61 when they were in their eighties and constituted only 4.1 percent of the total population, I assume that 25 percent would be strongly affected, 51 percent moderately affected, and 24 percent would still be hardly affected. By Vernal Year 81, virtually all of these people would have died — those few still alive would be more than 100 years old.

*(Text continues on page 284)*

---

* I have tried to choose values which might reasonably be induced by progressive social change movements of the size I believe Vernal activists could foster and support. Though based on my experience and my best thinking, these figures are, of course, complete conjecture.

# Figure C.8: The Assumed Influence over Time

| Age Cohrt in Yr 1 | Age Cohrt in Yr 21 | Age Cohrt in Yr 41 | Age Cohrt in Yr 61 | Age Cohrt in Yr 81 | Prcnt of Pop Yr 1 | Prcnt of Pop Yr 21 | Prcnt of Pop Yr 41 | Prcnt of Pop Yr 61 | Prcnt of Pop Yr 81 | (Assumed) Percent of Each Age Cohort Influenced by Vernal Year 21 (%) | | | (Assumed) Percent of Each Age Cohort Influenced by Vernal Year 41 (%) | | |
|---|---|---|---|---|---|---|---|---|---|---|---|---|---|---|---|
| | | | | | | | | | | Strong | Mod | Hardly | Strong | Mod | Hardly |
| — | — | — | — | 00s | — | — | — | — | 13.2 | — | — | — | — | — | — |
| — | — | — | — | 10s | — | — | — | — | 13.2 | — | — | — | — | — | — |
| — | — | — | 00s | 20s | — | — | — | 13.2 | 13.0 | — | — | — | — | — | — |
| — | — | — | 10s | 30s | — | — | — | 13.2 | 12.9 | — | — | — | — | — | — |
| — | — | 00s | 20s | 40s | — | — | 13.2 | 13.0 | 12.5 | — | — | — | 15.0 | 41.0 | 44.0 |
| — | — | 10s | 30s | 50s | — | — | 13.2 | 12.9 | 11.9 | — | — | — | 16.0 | 44.0 | 40.0 |
| — | 00s | 20s | 40s | 60s | — | 13.2 | 13.0 | 12.5 | 10.5 | 1.0 | 5.0 | 94.0 | 16.0 | 44.0 | 40.0 |
| — | 10s | 30s | 50s | 70s | — | 13.2 | 12.9 | 11.9 | 7.8 | 1.0 | 5.0 | 94.0 | 15.0 | 41.0 | 44.0 |
| 00s | 20s | 40s | 60s | 80s | 13.2 | 13.0 | 12.5 | 10.5 | 4.1 | 1.0 | 5.0 | 94.0 | 14.0 | 38.0 | 48.0 |
| 10s | 30s | 50s | 70s | 90s | 13.2 | 12.9 | 11.9 | 7.8 | 0.9 | 1.0 | 5.0 | 94.0 | 13.0 | 35.0 | 52.0 |
| 20s | 40s | 60s | 80s | — | 13.0 | 12.5 | 10.5 | 4.1 | — | 1.0 | 5.0 | 94.0 | 12.0 | 32.0 | 56.0 |
| 30s | 50s | 70s | 90s | — | 12.9 | 11.9 | 7.8 | 0.9 | — | 1.0 | 5.0 | 94.0 | 10.0 | 30.0 | 60.0 |
| 40s | 60s | 80s | — | — | 12.5 | 10.5 | 4.1 | — | — | 1.0 | 5.0 | 94.0 | 7.0 | 27.0 | 66.0 |
| 50s | 70s | 90s | — | — | 11.9 | 7.8 | 0.9 | — | — | 1.0 | 5.0 | 94.0 | 3.0 | 23.0 | 74.0 |
| 60s | 80s | — | — | — | 10.5 | 4.1 | — | — | — | 1.0 | 5.0 | 94.0 | — | — | — |
| 70s | 90s | — | — | — | 7.8 | 0.9 | — | — | — | 1.0 | 5.0 | 94.0 | — | — | — |
| | | | | Total | 100.0 | 100.0 | 100.0 | 100.0 | | | | | | | |

# Figure C.9: Assumed Percent of Those Strongly Affected by Social Change Movements over Time by Age Cohort

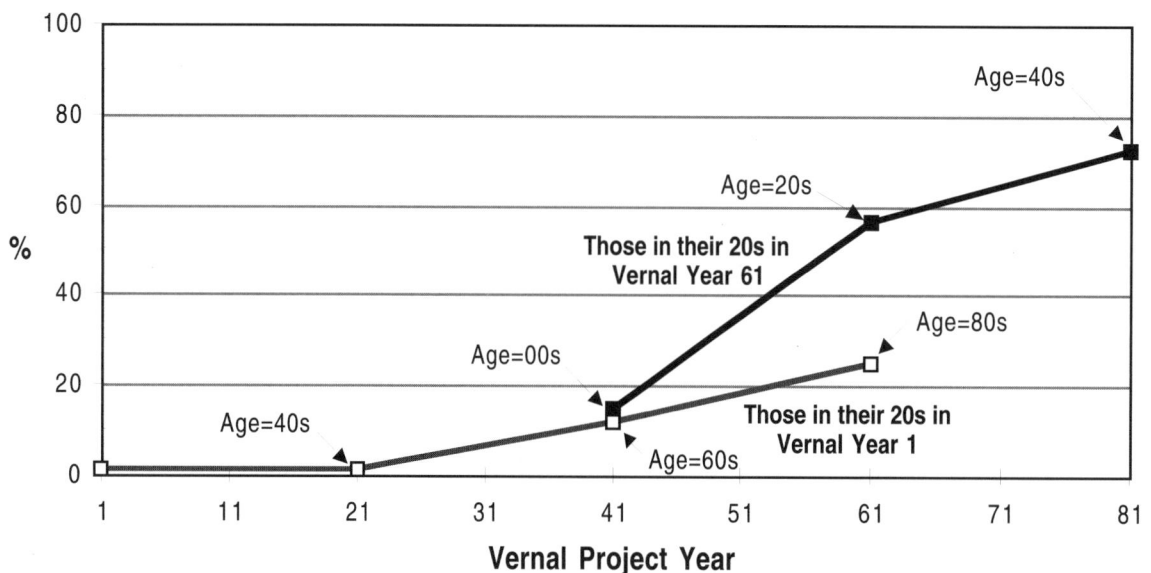

# of Progressive Social Change Movements by Age Cohorts

| (Assumed) | | | (Assumed) | | | (Calculated) | | | (Calculated) | | | (Calculated) | | | (Calculated) | | |
|---|---|---|---|---|---|---|---|---|---|---|---|---|---|---|---|---|---|
| Percent of Each Age Cohort Influenced by Vernal Year 61 (%) | | | Percent of Each Age Cohort Influenced by Vernal Year 81 (%) | | | Percent of Total Pop. Influenced in Year 21 (%) | | | Percent of Total Pop. Influenced in Year 41 (%) | | | Percent of Total Pop. Influenced in Year 61 (%) | | | Percent of Total Pop. Influenced in Year 81 (%) | | |
| Strong | Mod | Hardly | Strong | Mod | Hardly | Strng | Mod | Hrdly | Strng | Mod | Hrdly | Strng | Mod | Hrdly | Strng | Mod | Hrdly |
| — | — | — | 76.0 | 23.0 | 1.0 | — | — | — | — | — | — | — | — | — | 10.0 | 3.0 | 0.1 |
| — | — | — | 80.0 | 19.0 | 1.0 | — | — | — | — | — | — | — | — | — | 10.6 | 2.5 | 0.1 |
| 52.0 | 38.0 | 10.0 | 80.0 | 19.0 | 1.0 | — | — | — | — | — | — | 6.9 | 5.0 | 1.3 | 10.4 | 2.5 | 0.1 |
| 56.0 | 36.0 | 8.0 | 76.0 | 23.0 | 1.0 | — | — | — | — | — | — | 7.4 | 4.8 | 1.1 | 9.8 | 3.0 | 0.1 |
| 56.0 | 36.0 | 8.0 | 72.0 | 26.0 | 2.0 | — | — | — | 2.0 | 5.4 | 5.8 | 7.3 | 4.7 | 1.0 | 9.0 | 3.3 | 0.3 |
| 52.0 | 38.0 | 10.0 | 68.0 | 29.0 | 3.0 | — | — | — | 2.1 | 5.8 | 5.3 | 6.7 | 4.9 | 1.3 | 8.1 | 3.5 | 0.4 |
| 48.0 | 40.0 | 12.0 | 64.0 | 32.0 | 4.0 | 0.1 | 0.7 | 12.4 | 2.1 | 5.7 | 5.2 | 6.0 | 5.0 | 1.5 | 6.7 | 3.4 | 0.4 |
| 44.0 | 42.0 | 14.0 | 60.0 | 34.0 | 6.0 | 0.1 | 0.7 | 12.4 | 1.9 | 5.3 | 5.7 | 5.2 | 5.0 | 1.7 | 4.7 | 2.7 | 0.5 |
| 38.0 | 45.0 | 17.0 | 54.0 | 36.0 | 10.0 | 0.1 | 0.7 | 12.2 | 1.8 | 4.8 | 6.0 | 4.0 | 4.7 | 1.8 | 2.2 | 1.5 | 0.4 |
| 32.0 | 48.0 | 20.0 | 46.0 | 38.0 | 16.0 | 0.1 | 0.6 | 12.1 | 1.5 | 4.2 | 6.2 | 2.5 | 3.7 | 1.6 | 0.4 | 0.3 | 0.1 |
| 25.0 | 51.0 | 24.0 | — | — | — | 0.1 | 0.6 | 11.8 | 1.3 | 3.4 | 5.9 | 1.0 | 2.1 | 1.0 | — | — | — |
| 16.0 | 54.0 | 30.0 | — | — | — | 0.1 | 0.6 | 11.2 | 0.8 | 2.3 | 4.7 | 0.1 | 0.5 | 0.3 | — | — | — |
| — | — | — | — | — | — | 0.1 | 0.5 | 9.9 | 0.3 | 1.1 | 2.7 | — | — | — | — | — | — |
| — | — | — | — | — | — | 0.1 | 0.4 | 7.3 | 0.0 | 0.2 | 0.7 | — | — | — | — | — | — |
| — | — | — | — | — | — | 0.0 | 0.2 | 3.9 | — | — | — | — | — | — | — | — | — |
| — | — | — | — | — | — | 0.0 | 0.0 | 0.8 | — | — | — | — | — | — | — | — | — |

## Average Amount of Influence (%)

| | Vernal Year 21 | | | Vernal Year 41 | | | Vernal Year 61 | | | Vernal Year 81 | | |
|---|---|---|---|---|---|---|---|---|---|---|---|---|
| | Strng | Mod | Hrdly | Strng | Mod | Hrdly | Strng | Mod | Hrdly | Strng | Mod | Hrdly |
| Influence on total population: | 1 | 5 | 94 | 14 | 38 | 48 | 47 | 40 | 12 | 72 | 26 | 3 |
| Influence on adults: | 1 | 5 | 94 | 13 | 37 | 50 | 45 | 42 | 14 | 70 | 27 | 3 |

**Assumptions**:
Assume the overall population distribution would remain about the same as now.
Before progressive social change movements become prominent, assume that about 1% of the public is strongly influenced by existing movements for progressive change, 5% are moderately influenced, and the rest are hardly affected.

## Figure C.10: Assumed Percent of the Public Affected by Progressive Social Change Movements by Year 21

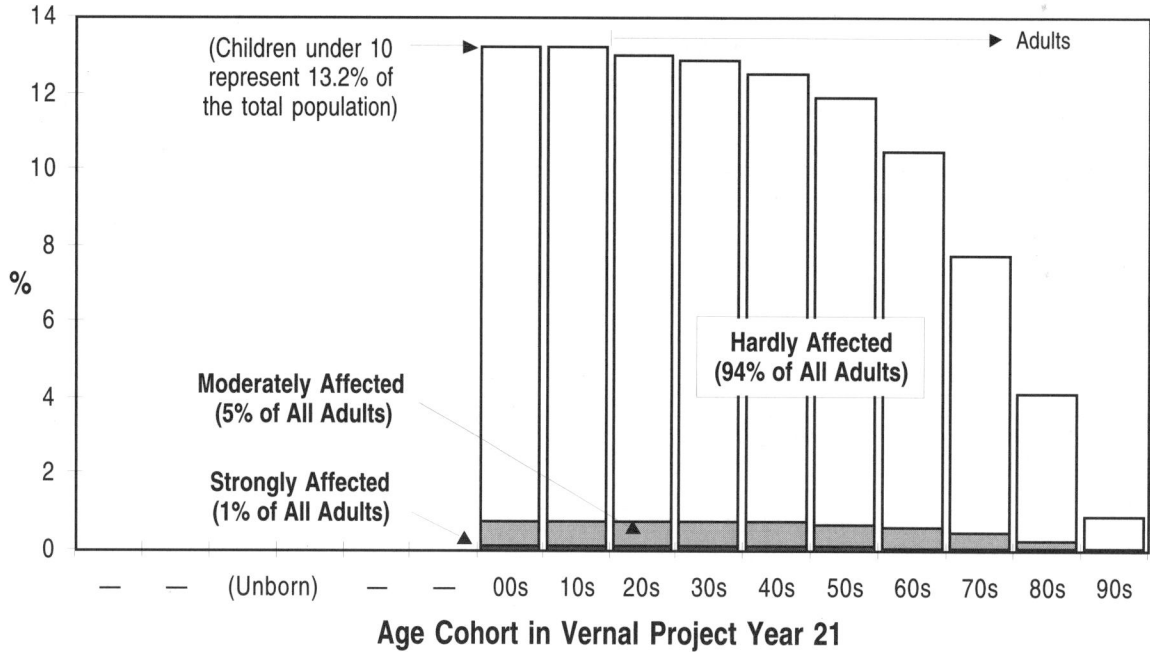

(Children under 10 represent 13.2% of the total population)

► Adults

Moderately Affected (5% of All Adults)

Strongly Affected (1% of All Adults)

Hardly Affected (94% of All Adults)

%

14
12
10
8
6
4
2
0

— — (Unborn) — — 00s 10s 20s 30s 40s 50s 60s 70s 80s 90s

**Age Cohort in Vernal Project Year 21**

## Figure C.11: Assumed Percent of the Public Affected by Progressive Social Change Movements by Year 41

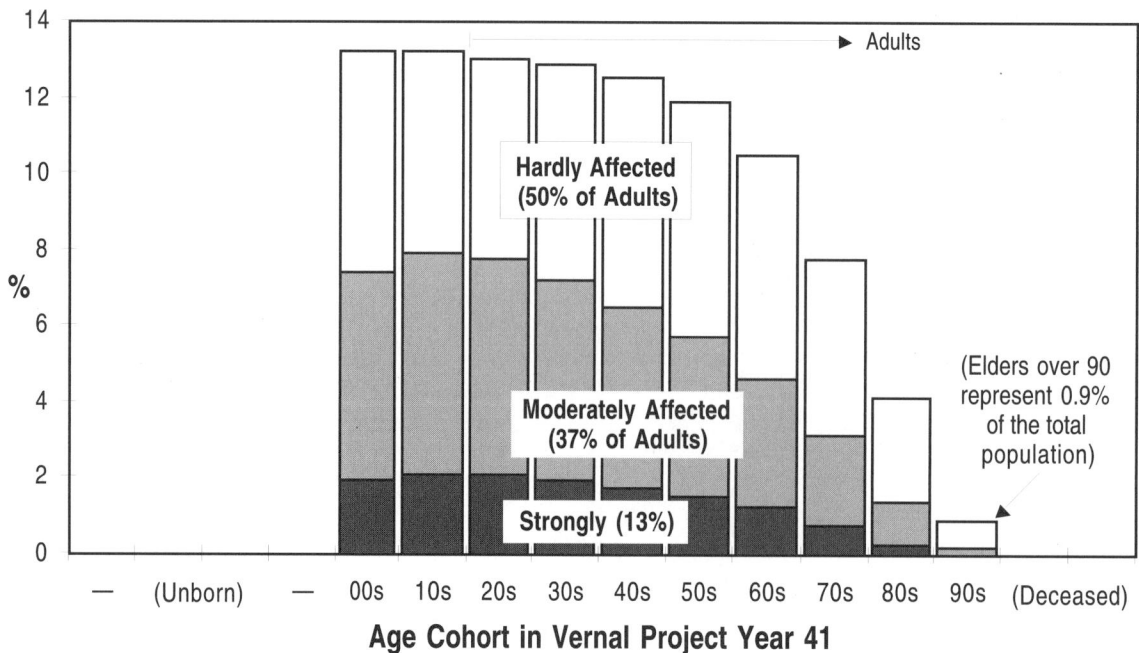

► Adults

Hardly Affected (50% of Adults)

Moderately Affected (37% of Adults)

Strongly (13%)

(Elders over 90 represent 0.9% of the total population)

%

14
12
10
8
6
4
2
0

— (Unborn) — 00s 10s 20s 30s 40s 50s 60s 70s 80s 90s (Deceased)

**Age Cohort in Vernal Project Year 41**

## Figure C.12: Assumed Percent of the Public Affected by Progressive Social Change Movements by Year 61

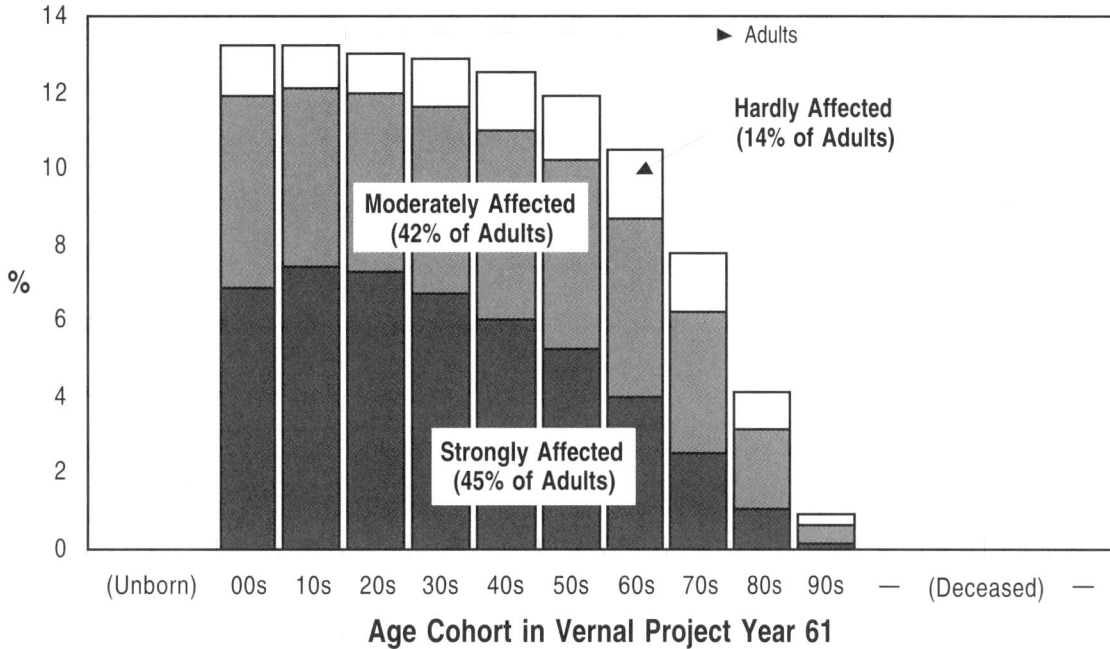

**Age Cohort in Vernal Project Year 61**

## Figure C.13: Assumed Percent of the Public Affected by Progressive Social Change Movements by Year 81

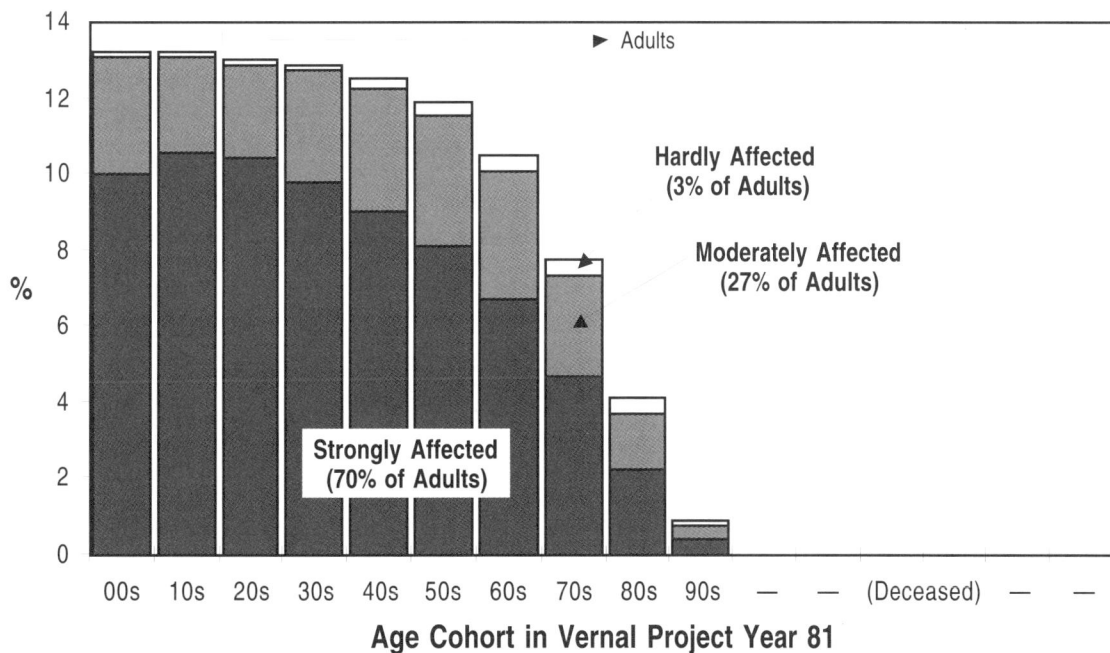

**Age Cohort in Vernal Project Year 81**

In contrast, those people who were born sixty years later in Vernal Years 41 to 50, and hence would be in their twenties in Year 61 (shown as the upper shaded row in the figure), would be affected much more strongly by Vernal-supported progressive movements. Growing up and coming of age in the middle of a period of intense progressive activity, they would be quite aware of progressive ideas. In Year 41, when they were infants, toddlers, and young children, I assume 15 percent of them would be strongly affected and 41 percent would be moderately affected (about the same percent as their parents). I assume 44 percent would be hardly affected.

After another twenty years of intense progressive activity surrounding them, they would be influenced even more. In Year 61 when they were in their twenties and constituted 13.0 percent of the total population, I assume 56 percent of them would be strongly affected, 36 percent would be moderately affected, and only 8 percent would be hardly affected. In Year 81 when they were in their forties and had been surrounded by intense progressive activity for their entire lives, I assume 72 percent would be strongly affected and 26 percent would be moderately affected. By this year, I assume only 2 percent would be hardly affected.

Figure C.9 compares the percentage of those who would be strongly affected in these two age cohorts. In Year 61, only a quarter of those in their 80s would be strongly affected by progressive movements. Of those in their 20s in Year 61, 56 percent would be strongly affected.

The rightmost twelve columns of Figure C.8 calculate the combined impact of population turnover and progressive movement influence to indicate the percent of the total population who would be affected. At the bottom of these columns, I sum these columns to show the total percentage of the population and the total percentage of the adults (those twenty years old or older in this analysis) who would be affected in Years 21, 41, 61, and 81.

In Year 21, Vernal-supported progressive movements would only strongly affect about 1 percent of all adults and moderately affect about 5 percent, just as if the Vernal Project did not exist. But by Year 41, Vernal-supported progressive movements would affect half of the adult population — strongly affecting 13 percent of the adults and moderately affecting another 37 percent. By Year 61, Vernal-supported progressive movements would strongly affect 45 percent of the adults and moderately affect 42 percent more.

In Year 81, only 5 percent of those who were alive at the beginning of the Vernal Project would still be around. Those who were born after Vernal Year 20 — when Vernal-supported progressive movements first became prominent — would constitute 76.7 percent of the total population. By this year, 70 percent of the adults and 72 percent of the total population would be strongly affected by progressive movements. Only 3 percent would still be hardly affected.

Figures C.10, C.11, C.12, and C.13 graphically display these changes. In Figure C.10, which shows the situation in Vernal Year 21, only about 1 percent of each of the ten-year age cohorts would be strongly affected by progressive movements, just as if the Vernal Project did not exist. Figure C.11 shows that twenty years later each cohort would be more progressive than before. A large percentage of the youngest cohorts would be moderately or strongly affected, but most of the members of the oldest cohorts would still be hardly affected. Just as important, though, the oldest cohorts would have shrunk in size and two new relatively large and progressive cohorts would have been born.

Figures C.12 and C.13 show the situation twenty and forty years later. Each cohort would continue to get more progressive over time, and the older cohorts — those least affected by progressive movements — would continue to shrink in size. New generations, affected much more strongly than their elders, would be born and make up a larger percentage of society.

In these figures, I assume that the Vernal Project — over the full course of its sixty-year existence — would have little influence on more than two-thirds of those who were older than 40 years of age in Vernal Year 1. The Project would strongly affect less than one-quarter of all those who were alive in this first year. Still, by ensuring there was a high level of progressive change activity over this long period, the Vernal Project could have a powerful impact on society. If the Project had the influence assumed here, it would strongly affect 70 percent and moderately affect another 27 percent of all those adults still living in Vernal Year 81. Only 3 percent of the population would remain unaffected. Clearly, aging and population turnover could greatly magnify the impact of the Vernal Project.

# NOTES FOR APPENDIX C

[1] To help me make these estimates, I analyzed the results of several studies of the U.S. population.

Sidney Verba and Norman Nie, ***Participation in America: Political Democracy and Social Equality*** (New York: Harper & Row, 1972, JK2274 .A3V4) describes a study of citizens' political activity in 1967. Based on a large survey, they placed the population in seven distinct categories based on their primary participation mode:

**Percent**    **Primary Participation Mode**

22%    **Inactive**: those who take almost no part in political life, even voting

21%    **Voting Specialists**: those who only engage in voting

4%    **Parochial Participants**: those who contact state or local officials on personal concerns only

20%    **Communalists**: those who work primarily with others on local problems and issues — as well as voting

15%    **Campaigners**: those who work primarily on political campaigns — as well as voting

11%    **Complete Activists**: those who engage in all forms of political activity

7%    **Unclassifiable**

W. Russell Neuman, ***The Paradox of Mass Politics: Knowledge and Opinion in the American Electorate*** (Cambridge, MA: Harvard University Press, 1986, JK1967 .N48 1986) summarizes several studies of participation in electoral activity. Neuman concludes that about 20 percent of people are completely apolitical, 75 percent are marginally attentive to politics (they vote fairly regularly, but are aroused to further action only when society appears to be in a crisis), and only 5 percent are political activists.

Norman Ornstein, Andrew Kohut, and Larry McCarthy, ***The People, the Press, & Politics: The Times Mirror Study of the American Electorate*** (Reading, MA: Addison-Wesley, Times Mirror, 1988, HN90 .P8076 1988) describes an in-person survey of 4,244 people. At the time of the survey in September 1987, 47 percent of the respondents strongly supported the civil rights movement, 46 percent strongly supported the peace movement, 39 percent strongly identified as environmentalists, 29 percent strongly supported the women's movement, and 8 percent strongly supported the gay rights movement. Of the respondents, 27 percent were strong supporters of unions and 28 percent were strong supporters of business interests. Also, 27 percent of the respondents strongly identified as conservatives, and 19 percent strongly identified as liberals. Respondents reported that in the previous four years they had engaged in these activities:

**Percent**    **Reported this Activity**

55%    Signed a petition

30%    Wrote a letter, telephoned, or sent a telegram to an editor, public official, or company

17%    Were members of an organization that supported a particular cause

14%    Boycotted a company

6%    Spoke at a public hearing or forum

Sidney Verba, Kay Lehman Schlozman, Henry E. Brady, ***Voice and Equality: Civic Voluntarism in American Politics*** (Cambridge, MA: Harvard University Press, 1995, JK1764 .V475 1995) describes an extensive survey in 1989 and 1990. Based on telephone interviews with 15,053 people and 2,517 long personal interviews, respondents reported the following levels of political participation in the previous year or two (pp. 50-52):

**Percent**    **Reported this Activity**

71%    Voted in the 1988 presidential election (though records show only about 50% of the public voted)

24%    Contributed money to a political campaign effort

8%    Worked as a volunteer on an electoral campaign

34%    Initiated contact with a public official (letter, phone, personal contact)

6%    Engaged in a protest, march, or demonstration on a local or national issue

17%    Worked informally with others in the community to deal with a community issue or problem

14%    Attended a local board or council meeting

3%    Were members of a local board or council

48%    Were affiliated with an organization that takes political stands

29%    Attended meetings of a political organization

Looking in more depth at electoral activity, they report:

Considering the public as a whole, we find that the average American gave about 36 minutes a week and about $58 to campaign activity during the 1988 campaign season. Only 4 or 5 percent of the public made what might be considered substantial contributions — more than five hours a week or more than $250. The picture changes somewhat when we consider the amount given by the activists, especially with respect to time. Although only a small share of the public works in political campaigns, those who do take part give substantial time during the campaign: half dedicate more than five hours a week to campaign activity; and not insignificant proportions give more than ten, or even twenty, hours per week during the campaign. On average, those who work in a campaign devote seven and a half hours per week to it. Among financial donors, the volume given is also not unsubstantial. About one in five of the donors gives over $250, and the average contribution is $247. (53-54)

There is also variation in how often citizens engage in such acts as contacting and protesting. Those who get in touch with government officials tend to do so relatively often. In the initial screener survey, only 19 percent of those who indicated having gotten in touch with a public official within the past twelve months made only one contact, and 39 percent indicated having done so four or more times. In contrast, those who report protesting are likely to do so only once. Over half, 53 percent, of the protesters had done so only once, and only 16 percent had done so as many as four times — even though the period covered by our question was two years rather than just one. (54, fn. 4)

These studies seem to establish that, at most, perhaps ten percent of the population is heavily engaged in political work. Of those people who are politically engaged, many probably work against progressive change, many take moderate positions, and many support only mild progressive change. Hence, it is likely that only a small fraction of the population works heavily for fundamental progressive change.

Though informed by these studies, my estimates rely mostly on my own knowledge and experience of social change efforts in the United States.

# *Index*

# ORDER FORM

Order additional copies of **Inciting Democracy** directly from SpringForward Press and get a discount!

**Web**: connect to <http://www.vernalproject.org>, pay by credit card.

**Mail** a check to:
> SpringForward Press
> P.O. Box 608867
> Cleveland, OH  44108

Price: $23.95 — Orders for one or two books are discounted 20% — just $19.16 per book plus $5 shipping for the first book and $2 for each additional book.

Three or more books are discounted 40% — just $14.37 per book plus $5 shipping for the first book and $2 for each additional book.

Name: _____

Address: _____

City: _____ State: _____ Zip: _____

Telephone: _____

E-mail address: _____

Please indicate the desired number of copies of **Inciting Democracy**:

| Number | Discounted Price per book | Shipping | Total Cost |
|--------|---------------------------|----------|------------|
| 1 | $19.16 | $5 | $24.16 |
| 2 | $19.16 | $5+2 | $45.32 |
| 3 | $14.37 | $5+2+2 | $52.11 |
| _____ | $14.37 | _____ | _____ |

Please include sales tax for books shipped to Ohio addresses.
Shipping prices for addresses outside the U.S. and Canada are $10 for the first book and $4 for each additional book.